ACHI 2024

The Seventeenth International Conference on Advances in Computer-Human Interactions

May 26 - 30, 2024

Barcelona, Spain

ACHI 2024 Editors

Susanne Stigberg, Østfold University College, Halden, Norway

Joakim Karlsen, Østfold University College, Halden, Norway

Nicholas H. Müller, Technical University of applied Sciences Würzburg-Schweinfurt, Germany

Printed from e-media with permission by:

Curran Associates, Inc.
57 Morehouse Lane
Red Hook, NY 12571

Some format issues inherent in the e-media version may also appear in this print version.

International Academy, Research, and Industry Association (IARIA)
412 Derby Way
Wilmington, DE 19810

Phone: (408) 893-6407
Fax: (408) 527-6351

petre@iaria.org

Additional copies of this publication are available from:

Curran Associates, Inc.
57 Morehouse Lane
Red Hook, NY 12571 USA
Phone: 845-758-0400
Fax: 845-758-2633
Email: curran@proceedings.com
Web: www.proceedings.com

Table of Contents

ACHI 2024

Forward

The Seventeenth International Conference on Advances in Computer-Human Interactions (ACHI 2024), held between May 26th and May 30th, 2024, in Barcelona, Spain, was a result of a paradigm shift in the most recent achievements and future trends in human interactions with increasingly complex systems. Adaptive and knowledge-based user interfaces, universal accessibility, human-robot interaction, agent-driven human computer interaction, and sharable mobile devices are a few of these trends. ACHI 2024 also brought a suite of specific domain applications, such as gaming, social, medicine, education, and engineering.

The event was very competitive in its selection process and very well perceived by the international scientific and industrial communities. As such, it is attracting excellent contributions and active participation from all over the world. We were very pleased to receive a large number of top-quality contributions. The accepted papers covered a wide range of human-computer interaction related topics such as graphical user interfaces, input methods, training, recognition, and applications. We believe that the ACHI 2024 contributions offered a large panel of solutions to key problems in all areas of human-computer interaction.

We take here the opportunity to warmly thank all the members of the ACHI 2024 technical program committee, as well as all the reviewers. The creation of such a high-quality conference program would not have been possible without their involvement. We also kindly thank all the authors who dedicated much of their time and effort to contribute to ACHI 2024. We truly believe that, thanks to all these efforts, the final conference program consisted of top-quality contributions. We also thank the members of the ACHI 2024 organizing committee for their help in handling the logistics of this event.

We hope that ACHI 2024 was a successful international forum for the exchange of ideas and results between academia and industry and for the promotion of progress in the field of human-computer interactions.

ACHI 2024 Chairs

ACHI 2024 Steering Committee
Sibylle Kunz, IU Internationale Hochschule, Germany
Lasse Berntzen, University of South-Eastern Norway, Norway
Weizhi Meng, Technical University of Denmark, Denmark
Flaminia Luccio, University of Venice, Italy

ACHI 2024 Publicity Chairs
Sandra Viciano Tudela, Universitat Politecnica de Valencia, Spain
Laura Garcia, Universidad Politécnica de Cartagena, Spain

ACHI 2024
Committee

ACHI 2024 Steering Committee

Sibylle Kunz, IU Internationale Hochschule, Germany
Lasse Berntzen, University of South-Eastern Norway, Norway
Weizhi Meng, Technical University of Denmark, Denmark
Flaminia Luccio, University of Venice, Italy

ACHI 2024 Publicity Chairs

Sandra Viciano Tudela, Universitat Politecnica de Valencia, Spain
Laura Garcia, Universidad Politécnica de Cartagena, Spain

ACHI 2024 Technical Program Committee

Mark Abdollahian, Claremont Graduate University, USA
Mostafa Alani, Tuskegee University, USA
Marran Aldossari, University of North Carolina at Charlotte, USA
Obead Alhadreti, Umm Al-Qura University, Al-Qunfudah, Saudi Arabia
Asam Almohamed, University of Kerbala, Iraq
Mehdi Ammi, Univ. Paris 8, France
Anmol Anubhai, Amazon, USA
Prima Oky Dicky Ardiansyah, Iwate Prefectural University, Japan
Charles Averill, University of Texas at Dallas, USA
Snježana Babić, Juraj Dobrila University, Croatia
Matthias Baldauf, OST - Eastern Switzerland University of Applied Sciences, Switzerland
Giulio Barbero, Leiden University (Leiden Institute of Advanced Computer Science), The Netherlands
Catalin-Mihai Barbu, University of Duisburg-Essen, Germany
Yacine Bellik, IUT d'Orsay | Université Paris-Saclay, France
Lasse Berntzen, University of South-Eastern Norway, Norway
Ganesh D. Bhutkar, Vishwakarma Institute of Technology (VIT), Pune, India
Cezary Biele, National Information Processing Institute, Poland
Christos J. Bouras, University of Patras, Greece
Christian Bourret, UPEM - Université Paris-Est Marne-la-Vallée, France
Sabrina Bouzidi-Hassini, Ecole nationale Supérieure d'Informatique (ESI), Algeria
James Braman, The Community College of Baltimore County, USA
Justin Brooks, University of Maryland Baltimore County / D-Prime LLC, USA
Pradeep Buddharaju, University of Houston - Clear Lake, USA
Paolo Burelli, IT University of Copenhagen, Denmark
Idoko John Bush, Near East University, Cyprus
Minghao Cai, University of Alberta, Canada
Lindsey D. Cameron, Wharton School | University of Pennsylvania, USA
Klaudia Carcani, Østfold University College, Norway
Alicia Carrion-Plaza, Sheffield Hallam University, UK
Stefano Caselli, Institute of Digital Games | University of Malta, Malta

Meghan Chandarana, NASA Ames Research Center, USA
Ramon Chaves, Federal University of Rio de Janeiro, Brazil
Chen Chen, University of California San Diego, USA
Bhavya Chopra, Indraprastha Institute of Information Technology, Delhi, India
António Correia, University of Jyväskylä, Finland
Lara Jessica da Silva Pontes, University of Debrecen, Hungary
Andre Constantino da Silva, Federal Institute of São Paulo - IFSP, Brazil
Vesna Djokic, ILLC - University of Amsterdam, The Netherlands / Goldsmiths University, UK
Krzysztof Dobosz, Silesian University of Technology - Institute of Informatics, Poland
Margaret Drouhard, University of Washington, USA
Robert Ek, Luleå University of Technology, Sweden
Ahmed Elkaseer, Karlsruhe Institute of Technology, Germany
Pardis Emami-Naeini, Carnegie Mellon University, USA
Marina Everri, University College Dublin, Ireland
Ben Falchuk, Peraton Labs, USA
Matthias Fassl, CISPA Helmholtz Center for Information Security, Germany
Stefano Federici, University of Perugia, Italy
Kenneth Feinstein, Sunway University, Malaysia
Peter Fröhlich, AIT - Austrian Institute of Technology, Austria
Jicheng Fu, University of Central Oklahoma, USA
Somchart Fugkeaw, Mahidol University - Nakhonpathom, Thailand
Pablo Gallego, Independent Researcher, Spain
Dirlukshi Gamage, Berkman Klein Centre, Internet Society at Harvard University, USA
Nermen Ghoniem, Jabra / Hello Ada, Denmark
Dagmawi Lemma Gobena, Addis Ababa University, Ethiopia
Benedikt Gollan, Research Studios Austria FG mbH, Austria
Miguel González Mendoza, Escuela de Ingeniería y Ciencias | Tecnológico de Monterrey, Mexico
Denis Gracanin, Virginia Tech, USA
Andrina Granic, University of Split, Croatia
Lea Gröber, CISPA Helmholtz Center for Information Security, Saarbrücken, Germany
Celmar Guimarães da Silva, University of Campinas, Brazil
Ibrahim A. Hameed, Norwegian University of Science and Technology (NTNU), Norway
Ragnhild Halvorsrud, SINTEF Digital, Norway
Richard Harper, Lancaster University, UK
Carlo Harvey, Birmingham City University, UK
Mengjie Huang, Xi'an Jiaotong - Liverpool University, China
Gerhard Hube, University of Applied Sciences in Würzburg, Germany
Haikun Huang, University of Massachusetts, Boston, USA
Yue Huang, CSIRO's Data61, Australia
Maria Hwang, Fashion Institute of Technology (FIT), New York City, USA
Gökhan İnce, Istanbul Technical University, Turkey
Francisco Iniesto, Universidad Nacional de Educación a Distancia, Spain
Jamshed Iqbal, University of Hull, UK
Janio Jadan Guerrero, Universidad Indoamérica, Ecuador
Angel Jaramillo-Alcázar, Universidad de Las Américas, Ecuador
Amit Jena, ITER - Siksha 'O' Anusandhan University / IITB - Monash Research Academy, India
Sofia Kaloterakis, Utrecht University, Netherland
Yasushi Kambayashi, Sanyo-Onoda City University, Japan

Ahmed Kamel, Concordia College, USA
Suzanne Kieffer, Université catholique de Louvain, Belgium
Si Jung "SJ" Kim, University of Nevada, Las Vegas (UNLV), USA
Elisa Klose, Universität Kassel, Germany
Susanne Koch Stigberg, Østfold University College, Norway
Josef Krems, Chemnitz University of Technology, Germany
Sibylle Kunz, IU Internationale Hochschule, Germany
Wen-Hsing Lai, National Kaohsiung University of Science and Technology, Taiwan
Monica Landoni, Università della Svizzera italiana, Switzerland
Chien-Sing Lee, Sunway University, Malaysia
Blair Lehman, Educational Testing Service, USA
Maria Teresa Llano Rodriguez, Monash University, Melbourne, Australia
Tsai-Yen Li, National Chengchi University, Taiwan
Wenjuan Li, The Hong Kong Polytechnic University, Hong Kong
Xiaomeng Li, Centre for Accident Research and Road Safety-Queensland (CARRS-Q) | Queensland University of Technology (QUT), Australia
Fotis Liarokapis, Cyprus University of Technology, Cyprus
Richen Liu, Nanjing Normal University, China
Sunny Xun Liu, Stanford University, USA
Jun-Li Lu, University of Tsukuba, Japan
Zhicong Lu, University of Toronto, Canada
Flaminia Luccio, University of Venice, Italy
Sergio Luján-Mora, University of Alicante, Spain
Yan Luximon, The Hong Kong Polytechnic University, Hong Kong
Damian Lyons, Fordham University, USA
Ishaani M., Amazon, USA
Yaoli Ma, Autodesk Inc., USA
Galina Madjaroff, University of Maryland Baltimore County, USA
Sebastian Maneth, University of Bremen, Germany
Guido Maiello, Justus Liebig University Giessen, Germany
Sanna Malinen, University of Turku, Finland
Matthew Louis Mauriello, University of Delaware, USA
Laura Maye, School of Computer Science and Information Technology - University College Cork, Ireland
Horia Mărgărit, Stanford University, USA
Weizhi Meng, Technical University of Denmark, Denmark
Xiaojun Meng, Noah's Ark Lab | Huawei Technologies, Shenzhen, China
Daniel R. Mestre, CNRS Institute of Movement Sciences - Mediterranean Virtual Reality Center, Marseilles, France
Mariofanna Milanova, University of Arkansas at Little Rock, USA
Harald Milchrahm, Institute for Software technology - Technical University Graz, Austria
Leslie Miller, Iowa State University - Ames, USA
Alexander Mirnig, Center for Human-Computer Interaction | University of Salzburg, Austria
Arturo Moquillaza, Pontificia Universidad Católica del Perú, Peru
Nicholas H. Müller, University of Applied Sciences Würzburg-Schweinfurt, Germany
Sachith Muthukumarana, Auckland Bioengineering Institute | The University of Auckland, New Zealand
Yoko Nishihara, College of Information Science and Engineering - Ritsumeikan University, Japan
Milda Norkute, Thomson Reuters, Switzerland
Renata Ntelia, University of Lincoln, UK

Yoshimasa Ohmoto, Shizuoka University, Japan
Cláudia Pedro Ortet, University of Aveiro, Portugal
George Palamas, Malmö University, Sweden
Aditeya Pandey, Northeastern University, Boston, USA
Athina Papadopoulou, Massachusetts Institute of Technology (MIT), USA
Evangelos Papadopoulos, National Technical University of Athens, Greece
Vida Pashaei, University of Arizona, USA
Dennis Paulino, INESC TEC / University of Trás-os-Montes e Alto Douro, Portugal
Freddy Alberto Paz Espinoza, Pontificia Universidad Católica del Perú, Peru
Gerald Penn, University of Toronto, Canada
Jorge Henrique Piazentin Ono, New York University - Tandon School of Engineering, USA
Ana C. Pires, Universidade de Lisboa, Portugal
Jorge Luis Pérez Medina, Universidad de Las Américas, Ecuador
Brian Pickering, IT Innovation Centre - University of Southampton, UK
Thomas M. Prinz, Friedrich Schiller University Jena, Germany
Annu Sible Prabhakar, University of Cincinnati, USA
Mike Preuss, Leiden University, Netherlands
Namrata Primlani, Northumbria University, UK
Marina Puyuelo Cazorla, Universitat Politècnica de València, Spain
Yuanyuan (Heather) Qian, Carleton University in Ottawa, Canada
Claudia Quaresma, Universidade NOVA de Lisboa, Portugal
Aiswarya R., Tata Consultancy Services, India
Neha Rani, University of Florida, USA
Mariusz Rawski, Warsaw University of Technology, Poland
Carsten Röcker, inIT - Institute Industrial IT / TH OWL University of Applied Sciences and Arts, Germany
Joni Salminen, Qatar Computing Research Institute, Qatar
Sandra Sanchez-Gordon, Escuela Politécnica Nacional, Ecuador
Antonio-José Sánchez-Salmerón, Instituto de Automática e Informática Industrial - Universidad Politécnica de Valencia, Spain
Paulus Insap Santosa, Universitas Gadjah Mada - Yogyakarta, Indonezia
Markus Santoso, University of Florida, USA
Diana Saplacan, University of Oslo, Norway
Hélène Sauzéon, Centre Inria Bordeaux, France
Daniel Schneider, Federal University of Rio de Janeiro, Brazil
Trenton Schulz, Norwegian Computing Center, Norway
Kamran Sedig, Western University, Ontario, Canada
Sylvain Senecal, HEC Montreal, Canada
Fereshteh Shahmiri, Georgia Tech, USA
Yuhki Shiraishi, Tsukuba University of Technology, Japan
Zdzisław Sroczyński, Silesian University of Technology, Gliwice, Poland
Ben Steichen, California State Polytechnic University, Pomona, USA
Han Su, RA - MIT, USA
Federico Tajariol, University Bourgogne Franche-Comté, France
Sheng Tan, Trinity University, Texas, USA
Cagri Tanriover, Intel Corporation (Intel Labs), USA
Ranjeet Tayi, User Experience - Informatica, San Francisco, USA
Masashi Toda, Kumamoto University, Japan
Milka Trajkova, Indiana University, Indianapolis, USA

David Unbehaun, University of Siegen, Germany
Simona Vasilache, University of Tsukuba, Japan
Katia Vega, University of California, Davis, USA
Vignesh Velmurugan, University of Hertfordshire, UK
Nishant Vishwamitra, University at Buffalo, USA
Konstantinos Votis, Information Technologies Institute | Centre for Research and Technology Hellas, Greece
Lin Wang, U.S. Census Bureau, USA
Pinhao Wang, Zhejiang University - College of Computer Science and Technology, Hangzhou, China
Gloria Washington, Howard University, USA
Andreas Wendemuth, Otto-von-Guericke University, Germany
Zhanwei Wu, Shanghai Jiao Tong University, China
Shuping Xiong, KAIST, South Korea
Tong Xue, Beijing Film Academy, China
Bo Yang, The University of Tokyo, Japan
Rui Yang, Xi'an Jiaotong-Liverpool University, China
Ye Zhu, Cleveland State University, USA

Copyright Information

Evaluating Digital Avatars in VR - A Systematic Approach to Quantify the Uncanny Valley Effect

Hakan Arda
Faculty of Computer Science and Business Information Systems
Technical University of Applied Sciences Würzburg-Schweinfurt
Würzburg, Germany
e-mail: hakan.arda@thws.de

Andreas Henneberger
Faculty of Computer Science and Business Information Systems
Technical University of Applied Sciences Würzburg-Schweinfurt
Würzburg, Germany
e-mail: andreas.henneberger@study.thws.de

***Abstract*—Virtual reality has undergone drastic developments in recent years. At the forefront are almost perfectly rendered real-life objects that can hardly be distinguished from the original. However, while the improvements in the realism of the environment significantly increase the user's immersion in the world, the increase in the realism of human-like avatars seems to have the opposite effect. Extremely realistic depictions of people in computer games, films, or other immersive applications often evoke negative feelings and can thus lead to a break in immersion. This emotional break is illustrated by looking at the uncanny valley curve. In this work, we have tried to develop a way to evaluate human-like avatars according to the uncanny valley curve and thus to determine more precisely where the discomfort comes from. To do this, we created a database of over 200 images of avatars and used studies to determine various precise characteristics that make these avatars like humans. In addition, we were able to evaluate the approach of this work with a pilot study and thus offer a possibility for evaluations of avatars according to the uncanny valley for future research.**

Keywords—Uncanny valley; avatars; human-likeness; database; virtual reality.

I. Introduction

The Uncanny Valley effect is a psychological phenomenon that describes the unease or discomfort people experience when encountering human-like entities that are almost, but not quite, convincingly realistic. This emotional break is illustrated by looking at the uncanny valley curve. In Figure 1, you can see a slight increase until the graph reaches around the 50 percent mark and then drops rapidly. This drop is known as the uncanny valley. The term “Uncanny Valley” was coined by robotics professor Masahiro Mori in 1970 [1]. The concept suggests that as the appearance or behavior of humanoid entities becomes increasingly close to human-like, there is a point at which they elicit a strong negative emotional response before eventually becoming indistinguishable from real humans.

There have already been many far-reaching attempts to investigate the effects of the human likeness of robots on people's emotional reaction [2–8]. One example of this is the work of Kim et al. [6], who used the open-source Anthropomorphic RoBOT (ABOT) database to analyze the human similarity of 251 robots. They asked a group of 150 participants to rate images of robots from the ABOT database according to their human likeness and uncanny valley factor. With the results of this survey, they have found evidence of Mori's uncanny valley [1]. This valley was evident in participants' perceived uncanniness of 251 robots that varied widely in terms of the range and characteristics of human likeness. They also found evidence of another, second valley of uncanniness in robots that showed a moderately weak resemblance to humans.

The developers of the ABOT [3] database took a similar approach in their study, providing a basis for research in this area. The researchers found that the human-like appearance of robots can be divided into three dimensions of human-like appearance: the robots' surface features (e.g., skin, hair, clothing), the main components of the robots' body manipulators (e.g., torso, arms, legs) and the robots' facial features (e.g., eyes, mouth, face) [6]. These results suggest that the overall perception of the physical human-likeness of robots and its relationship to emotional reactions to the robots can be explained by different constellations of the three human-like appearance dimensions. If the hypothesized uncanny valley phenomenon could be understood at the level of specific human-like appearances, this could also lead to the improvement of virtual avatars.

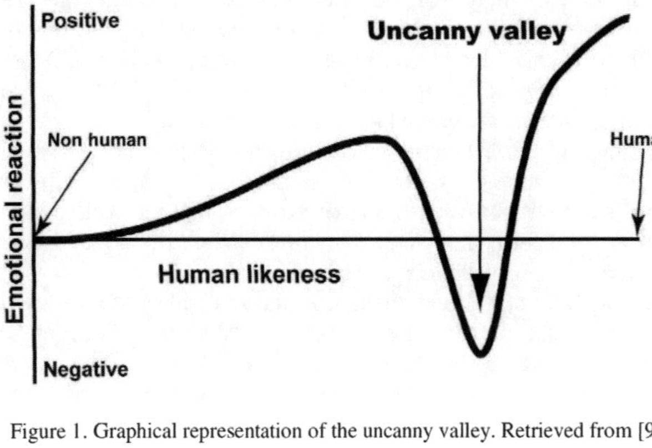

Figure 1. Graphical representation of the uncanny valley. Retrieved from [9].

This approach of using a large database, such as ABOT, to evaluate different human-like robots for their uncanny valley factors does not exist in relation to digital avatars currently. One reason for this could be the absence of such a database and the associated basis for the resulting research. Another reason is that there is currently no systematic, evidence-based approach for categorizing avatars into a continuum of perceived human-likeness. Consequently, researchers and designers are usually forced to rely on heuristics and intuitions when it comes to selecting human-like avatars for studies or developing human-like features in avatar design. This approach faces several problems. Firstly, there is currently no quantitative system to describe the degree of human likeness in different avatars, which makes it difficult to compare research results between different studies. Therefore, a precise scale is needed to compare different avatars on a common scale and allow researchers to replicate their results with their avatars.

Secondly, even when researchers manage to quantitatively assess the impression people have of an avatar's appearance, they usually treat the concept of "human likeness" as one-dimensional. However, human likeness can be expressed in different ways. For example, through gestures and facial expressions or, more generally, through the mere presence of arms and legs. Humanity has many different characteristics and therefore also different features that need to be considered.

Thirdly, the effects of the appearance of avatars on different types of avatars must be considered in the investigations. While it may be of practical advantage to limit yourself to a certain type of avatar, such as simplified human likenesses like the ones Meta uses in her Horizon. However, these constraints can mean that certain minor differences between avatars are lost. Consequently, the psychological insights from such work may not generalize to a diverse range of avatars.

In addition, previous studies have extensively explored methods to overcome the uncanny valley in character design. For example, the work by Schwind et al. examined how atypical features (strong deviations from the human norm) for high levels of realism cause negative sensations in humans and animals [10] [11]. The negative effects of atypical features, such as unnaturally large eyes or human emotions in realistic animals, are stronger for more realistic characters, than for characters with reduced realism. Consistently, rendered realism can reduce the negative effects of atypicality and increase affinity, as shown by the first peak in the uncanny valley. Therefore, it is important to avoid combining realistic renderings and detailed textures of skin or eyes with non-human-like features. At high levels of realism, atypical features can cause the uncanny valley. Another possibility is to avoid so-called "dead eyes". A virtual character's eyes are crucial in determining its realism. The work of Schwind et al., which used eye tracking, found that users first fixate on the eyes before assessing other features. This is consistent with previous research showing that the realism and inconsistencies of human characters are primarily judged based on the realism of their eyes [12]. This also explains why skin makeup does not affect animacy, unlike atypical eyes or the eyes of a deceased person. The symptom of "dead eyes" can make artificial characters feel eerie and strange. The eyes communicate intentions, behavior, and well-being, which are essential for assessing and creating affinity for the depiction. It is important to clarify this and many other problems regarding the appearance of the avatars beforehand in order to increase user acceptance. Uncanniness could distract the user from the actual idea and thus reduce acceptance [11].

To solve these problems and to offer a way to conduct more systematic, general, and repeatable research on virtual human-like avatars, we developed a database for avatars based on the findings of Phillips et al. and thus continues the research of the uncanny valley. This paper begins by highlighting the problems that arise when there is no fixed way to evaluate the concept of the uncanny valley. Section 2 presents the methodologies employed to construct the database of avatars, the instructions for the human-likeness and uncanny valley questions, and the specific details of the survey. Section 3 presents the results of the survey and Section 4 interprets the results accordingly. Finally, Section 5 summarizes the results of the collected work.

II. METHOD

A. The Avatar Database

Similar to the ABOT database by Phillips et al., the avatar database pursues three goals. Firstly, it offers an overview of the broad landscape of different human-like avatars. Secondly, the avatar database provides standardized images of human-like avatars and a growing dataset of people's perceptions of these avatars, both of which will be made public for further research in the future. Thirdly, the Avatar Database can help us better understand what makes an avatar appear human. To begin, we will discuss the development of the database. Then, two empirical studies will identify various dimensions of avatar appearance and determine which of these dimensions contribute to the perception of overall human-likeness of avatars. Subsequently, a further empirical study on the validation of the database is presented and a possibility for future research is introduced.

B. The Development of the Avatar Database

To create a comprehensive database of human-like avatar images, we searched for as many avatars as possible with the required human-like appearance characteristics. The avatars were identified from various sources, such as game characters, technology-oriented media, companies and university websites, online communities and discussion forums, and general Google searches. To identify avatars that had not yet received significant media attention, we also created our own avatars based on real humans and fictional characters, using various modular systems and scanning tools. Between January 2024 and April 2024, we created an initial collection of over 200 images of human-like avatars, each with one or more different characteristics.

Next, we reviewed the collection of avatars and removed those that were already represented in the same or similar enough form, for example avatars that only differed in clothing but not in body. In addition, avatars that are too similar to animals have also been removed because this study explicitly looks at human avatars. Each image also had to fulfil a certain standard to be included in the collection: No obstacles, no motion blur, no groups pictures, in color, and the entire body (With feet, hands, and head). In addition, all pictures were taken one more time in a close-up of the face. This allowed the participants to examine the entire body and then explicitly the face for the individual features. Any image that did not fulfil this standard was either not included in the collection or removed accordingly. For characters that were important for the collection, such as avatars that reflect a well-known personality, we created a suitable avatar ourselves. We also included avatars based on images created by artificial intelligence (Midjourney) and labelled them for later investigation. Based on this approach, we have created a collection of 200 avatars, with the corresponding source for downloading the avatars.

It was important to us that we cover as many different types as possible with the large number of avatars, such as cartoonish, stylized, realistic or minimalist. In addition, it should be possible to find an avatar that is reduced to the desired characteristics with the help of filters. This is a similar concept to searching for robots in the ABOT database. With the difference that here the avatars can be downloaded with the help of the source and used for further purposes. Some of the characters were also tested with the help of the unity engine and put to the test for suitable images. This was especially the case with avatars that we developed ourselves for this collection.

The images in the database were sorted and edited to ensure uniform recognition. This was done to ensure consistency in the images. Avatars were photographed in a frontal and neutral position with a neutral facial expression whenever possible. For avatars where this was not possible, and the model was available for free download we rendered them again in the unity engine and photographed accordingly. Finally, the images were cropped to just the avatars with a white background using photoshop and tagged with different tags for better analysis. Here, for example, attention was paid to the recognizable gender, potential age, art style and source. In Figure 2 you can see all the avatars used for this study.

C. Measuring the human-likeness

To accurately determine the degree of humanity in avatars, the individual avatars must be evaluated according to clearly defined characteristics. Because we are dealing here with human-like avatars and not anthropomorphic robots, we are unfortunately unable to use the results of the work by Phillip et al. [3] But, we can use a similar approach to determine the characteristics that we will use later. We rely on a bottom-up, feature-based approach and base our expectations on the results of the work of Phillip et al. Our goal with this approach was to define the individual features that constituted humanity in avatars and then bundle them together.

To determine the appearance characteristics of our avatars, we have created a collection of possible characteristics based on the work of Phillip et al. [3]. We then checked all the images for the respective characteristics and deleted any that did not fit. This included features that were rare, repeated, or confusing. As a result, we defined 16 characteristics that we used for our further procedure. In addition, like Phillip et al., we decided to contribute definitions for the features. We started with relevant definitions from the Oxford English dictionary [13] and adapted them according to our application. For example, we were able to retain the biological functions for features such as "mouth" because our test objects are not robots but human-like avatars. This resulted in a table of features and their definitions. These definitions served as a way for our participants to focus on certain characteristics when evaluating the avatars. Since they are human-like avatars and not robots, all characteristics are always present in some form. They only differ in their design. For example, each avatar has a "skin" that can be black, white, brown, et cetera. However, there are also avatars that do not have smooth white skin and are instead green with lots of dots. Therefore, the question here is not whether the respective characteristic is present, but rather to what degree it stands out. With the help of these characteristics, we were able to provide clear points of reference for the participants to evaluate the avatars.

TABLE 1. COLLECTION OF APPEARANCE FEATURES AND ASSOCIATED DEFINITIONS

Feature	***Definition***
Arm	The upper limb of the human body, or the part of the upper limb between the shoulder and the wrist.
Eye	The organ of sight. Either of the paired globular organs of sight in the head of humans.
Eyebrow	The (usually arched) line of short fine hair along the upper edge of each of a person's eye sockets.
Eyelashes	The line of hairs fringing each edge of an eyelid, serving to help keep the eye free of dust or other extraneous matter.
Face	The front part of the head, from the forehead to the chin, and containing the eyes, nose, and mouth.
Finger	Each of the five slender jointed parts attached to either hand.
Genderedness	Features of appearance that can indicate biological sex, or the social categories of being male or female.
Hand	The terminal part of an arm, typically connected to the arm by a wrist. A hand is normally used for grasping, manipulating, or gesturing.
Head	The uppermost part of a body, typically connected to the torso by a neck. The head may contain facial features such as the mouth, eyes, or nose.
Head hair	A collection of threadlike filaments on the head.
Leg	The lower limb of the human body, or the part of the lower limb between the hip and the ankle.
Mouth	The orifice in the head of a human or other vertebrate through which food is ingested and vocal sounds emitted.
Nose	The part of the head or face in humans which lies above the mouth and contains the nostrils.
Skin	The layer of tissue forming the external covering of the body.

D. Measuring the uncanniness

For the question of how uncanny the avatars are, we used the study by Kim et al. [6] as a guide. They also conducted a large-scale study with the help of the ABOT database and, based on the results of Phillip et al. [3], conducted a follow-up study in

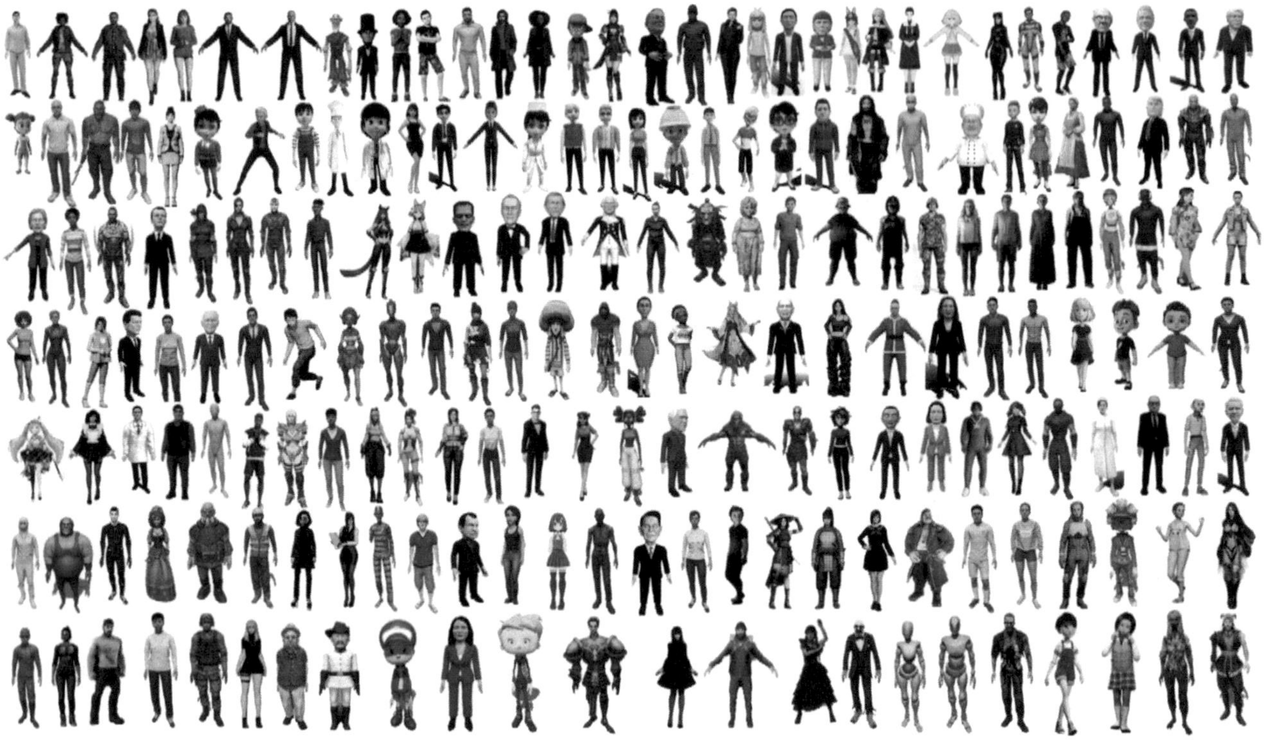

Figure 2. All 200 human-like VR avatars in the database.

which they compared the robots in terms of human-likeness and uncanniness. We also used the same definition of uncanniness to encourage participants to apply a standardized criterion in the evaluation. The participants were given the following definition, uncanniness is: "The characteristic of seeming mysterious, weird, uncomfortably strange or unfamiliar." This definition was derived from the Oxford English dictionary's definition of uncanniness.

E. Participants

For the study, we recruited a total of 160 participants via Prolific crowdsourcing website. Data collected via crowdsourcing, websites such as Prolific is currently very much in vogue. This is mainly due to the fact that the data can be collected very easily and quickly and there are already studies showing that the data collected here can keep up with traditional methods in terms of quality [14]. Nevertheless, the data should also be checked for quality [15]. We have therefore decided to incorporate various quality checks into the data collection process. Firstly, all data sets with incorrect answers to six or more "catch trials" are removed. Secondly, we considered a lack of variation in ratings between participants as an indicator of inattention. Therefore, we removed data from participants whose ratings had a standard deviation of less than 10 ($SD < 10$) on a scale of 0 - 100. Finally, we compared each participant's ratings with the average of the remaining judgements in their group (between participants) by calculating the correlation between the individual judgements and the remaining judgements in their group. If this correlation between the individual participant's ratings and the group mean was less than 30, the participant's data were discarded as these individuals may have been performing a different assessment task to the group. After this quality check, the total number of participants was 143 (M Age = 20, SD Age = 10, 104 Male, 41 Female, 2 No Responses). This means that each avatar had a rating of 15 - 20 participants.

F. Design and procedure

The 200 avatars were divided random into four groups of 50 avatars each. Each group was also provided with 10 catch trials. This meant that each group had 60 avatars, which were rated by 20 participants. Because two different questions were asked in this study, one asking, "how human-like is the avatar?" and the other "how uncanny is the avatar?", we asked each group twice. This gave us a total of 4 groups of 60 avatars per question.

The participant begins the survey with a brief introduction to the topic and a short briefing on how to complete the survey. This was followed by an example task on how the participant should rate the avatars. The same example avatar was used for each block. The participant sees two pictures of an avatar on their screen. On the left the entire body and on the right the profile picture with the face in focus. Below the pictures is the definition of the respective question. For the question about human likeness, the participant sees the various characteristics that make an avatar like humans and a slider from 0 to 100. Above the slider is the question "How similar to humans do you think this avatar is?" (0 - not at all like humans and 100 - very similar to humans). We used a similar method for the question of how uncanny you think the avatars are. You can see the same pictures and again a slider from 0 to 100 but this time with the definition about uncanniness and the question "How uncanny do you think this avatar is?" (0 - not uncanny at all and 100 - very uncanny). The participants are randomized into one of the respective groups and are only allowed to answer one question

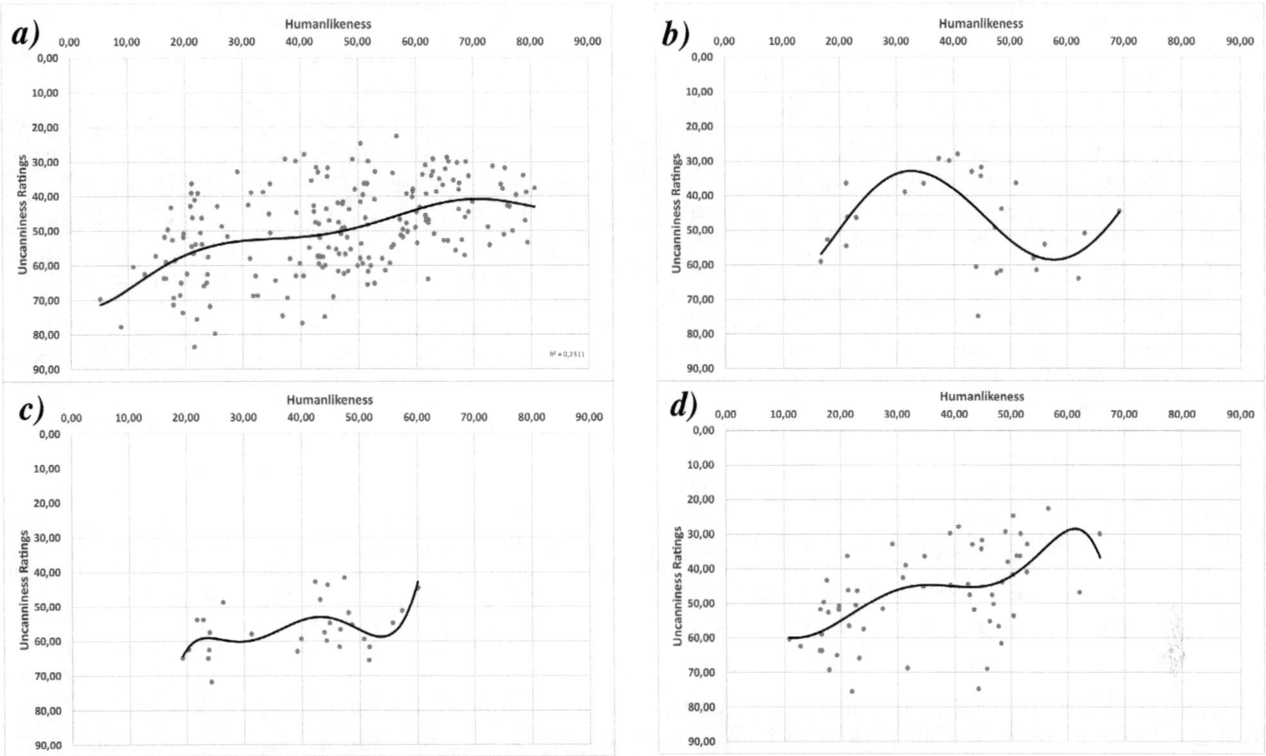

Figure 3. Four scatterplots a) Total scope of all avatars b) Only avatars representing children c) Avatars caricaturing a real-life person d) Avatars representing a cartoonized style. This Y axis has been inverted to represent the uncanny valley.

type. This is to prevent the questions from influencing each other. The catch trials are pictures of real people or objects that have also been randomized into the respective groups.

After half of the questions, the participants were given a 10-second break during which their attention was drawn to the definition and characteristics again. After judging all the images, participants were asked to complete a demographic questionnaire in which they were asked to indicate their age, gender, native language, level of education, previous knowledge of robotics and experience with virtual avatars. The entire study took approximately 5 minutes to complete, and participants received $1 as compensation for their participation.

III. Results

For the data analysis, all the results of the individual surveys were added together and an average for human likeness and uncanniness was calculated for each avatar. We then inserted these results into Microsoft Excel to generate various graphs. Looking at the first graph (Figure 3 a), no uncanny valley can be recognized. Instead, there is a linear gradient between the two factors uncanniness and human likeness, with uncanniness decreasing as human likeness increases. However, if one does not look at the entire amount of data and instead only at certain categories, such as only avatars that represent children, an uncanny valley is clearly recognizable. Just as in Mori's uncanny valley hypothesis [1], a large valley can be recognized between the moderately realistic and realistic avatars. When looking at other avatar categories, a slight uncanny valley can also be recognized. The other avatar categories, such as avatars that are based on a real person and represent them as a caricature, also have a slightly uncanny valley. The same applies to avatars that are not based on a real person but are depicted as a cartoon. based on a real person and represent them as a caricature, also have a slightly uncanny valley. The same applies to avatars that are not based on a real person but are depicted as a cartoon. To further investigate these results, we performed a polynomial mixed fit for the three different categories of. We determined the different coefficients of determination = r^2 for different polynomial mixed effects 3rd, 4th, and 5th models. In addition, based on the results of Kim et. al. [6] we also assumed that if there are one or more valleys here, then these are recognized in the 4th or 5th polynomial model.

IV. Discussion

Using a database of 200 different VR avatars, we were able to find evidence for the uncanny valley phenomenon of Mori et al. [1]. Contrary to expectations, however, this was not the case for the entire sample, but only when we looked more closely at different sub-categories of avatars. This means that when many different avatar categories, such as different age classes or different styles, are analyzed together, the individual graphs overlap and thus close the uncanny valley. The valley can only be created if the data is sorted precisely.

Particularly noticeable here were avatars representing children. We found that when trying to make this type of avatar more realistic, some avatars were perceived much more negatively than avatars that did not try. Avatars that received a lower human-likeness score of under 40 out of 100 points for uncanniness were significantly better than those with a higher humanlike score and over 60 out of 100 points for uncanniness.

This phenomenon cannot be replicated in the other age groups. We assume this is due to the proportions of the avatars. Because the unrealistic avatars in particular have a significantly larger head than the realistic avatars, which have normal proportions here. We were able to make this observation with the caricatures of real personalities such as former presidents of the USA. An uncanny valley can also be recognized here and, like the avatars representing children, these are mainly avatars with unusual proportions. This could be since an attempt was made here to depict real people and by increasing the similarity the avatars fall into uncanny again. However, categorization has also significantly reduced the number of data sets, which means that the coefficients of determination are very low and therefore not highly representative. This in turn can lead to the fact that certain types of avatars could not be evaluated to their full extent and an even larger database with many more avatars is needed. For example, a minimum number of avatar types could be predefined to ensure representativeness and thus fill the database more evenly. Furthermore, as a pilot study, the work focused on the development of the database and the study itself. As a result, the chapters Results, Discussion and Conclusion are somewhat shorter. The focus on the results and thus the length of the respective chapters will change in the subsequent papers.

V. CONCLUSION

With the drastic development of virtual reality and the constantly growing environment and possibilities it offers us, human-like avatars are also becoming an important topic that will affect us in the coming years. Even now, avatars from different areas are being rated according to their appearance and the term uncanny valley is being used more and more frequently. Based on the results of this study, we were able to find out that the uncanny valley is not an all-encompassing phenomenon in relation to VR avatars. Instead, the uncanny valley can only be found when taking a closer look at the individual subcategories of avatars. For example, if you take all the avatars in this database, there is an increasingly linear development between human-likeness and uncanniness, with the uncanny factor decreasing as human-likeness increases. However, if you look at certain subcategories, you can see a valley. This observation can also be observed in other categories, which leads us to assume that an overlap between the individual categories means that the uncanny valley is closed and thus balanced out by different avatars. In order to confirm this assumption, further and possibly even larger-scale studies than this one are needed. And by continuing to develop this database, we want to make this possible for everyone.

ACKNOWLEDGMENT

This work was supported by the Würzburg-Schweinfurt University of Applied Sciences. We would like to acknowledge the work of Kim et al. and the developers of the ABOT database. Their work can be found in [3] and [6].

REFERENCES

[1] M. Mori, K. MacDorman, and N. Kageki, "The Uncanny Valley [From the Field]," IEEE Robot. Automat. Mag., vol. 19, no. 2, pp. 98–100, 2012, doi: 10.1109/MRA.2012.2192811.

[2] B. Verplank, A. Sutcliffe, W. Mackay, J. Amowitz, and W. Gaver, Eds., Proceedings of the 4th conference on Designing interactive systems: processes, practices, methods, and techniques. New York, NY, USA: ACM, 2002.

[3] E. Phillips, X. Zhao, D. Ullman, and B. F. Malle, "What is Human-like?," in Proceedings of the 2018 ACM/IEEE International Conference on Human-Robot Interaction, Chicago IL USA, 2018, pp. 105–113.

[4] M. B. Mathur and D. B. Reichling, "Navigating a social world with robot partners: A quantitative cartography of the Uncanny Valley," Cognition, vol. 146, pp. 22–32, 2016, doi: 10.1016/j.cognition.2015.09.008.

[5] K. F. MacDorman and H. Ishiguro, "The uncanny advantage of using androids in cognitive and social science research," IS, vol. 7, no. 3, pp. 297–337, 2006, doi: 10.1075/is.7.3.03mac.

[6] B. Kim, M. Bruce, L. Brown, E. de Visser, and E. Phillips, "A Comprehensive Approach to Validating the Uncanny Valley using the Anthropomorphic RoBOT (ABOT) Database," in 2020 Systems and Information Engineering Design Symposium (SIEDS), Charlottesville, VA, USA, 2020, pp. 1–6.

[7] C. F. DiSalvo, F. Gemperle, J. Forlizzi, and S. Kiesler, "All robots are not created equal," in Proceedings of the 4th conference on Designing interactive systems: processes, practices, methods, and techniques, London England, 2002, pp. 321–326.

[8] C. Bartneck, T. Kanda, H. Ishiguro, and N. Hagita, "Is The Uncanny Valley An Uncanny Cliff?," in RO-MAN 2007 - The 16th IEEE International Symposium on Robot and Human Interactive Communication, Jeju, South Korea, 2007, pp. 368–373.

[9] K. Sasaki, K. Ihaya, and Y. Yamada, "Avoidance of Novelty Contributes to the Uncanny Valley," Frontiers in psychology, vol. 8, p. 1792, 2017, doi: 10.3389/fpsyg.2017.01792.

[10] D. Chattopadhyay and K. F. MacDorman, "Familiar faces rendered strange: Why inconsistent realism drives characters into the uncanny valley," Journal of vision, vol. 16, no. 11, p. 7, 2016, doi: 10.1167/16.11.7.

[11] V. Schwind, K. Wolf, and N. Henze, "Avoiding the uncanny valley in virtual character design," interactions, vol. 25, no. 5, pp. 45–49, 2018, doi: 10.1145/3236673.

[12] R. K. Moore, "A Bayesian explanation of the 'Uncanny Valley' effect and related psychological phenomena," Scientific reports, vol. 2, p. 864, 2012, doi: 10.1038/srep00864.

[13] Oxford English Dictionary. [Online]. Available: https://www.oed.com/ (accessed: Apr. 7 2024).

[14] K. Mortensen and T. L. Hughes, "Comparing Amazon's Mechanical Turk Platform to Conventional Data Collection Methods in the Health and Medical Research Literature," Journal of general internal medicine, vol. 33, no. 4, pp. 533–538, 2018, doi: 10.1007/s11606-017-4246-0.

[15] D. J. Ahler, C. E. Roush, and G. Sood, "The micro-task market for lemons: data quality on Amazon's Mechanical Turk," PSRM, pp. 1–20, 2021, doi: 10.1017/psrm.2021.57.

Further Comparison of 2D Virtual Learning Environments with Classic Video Conferencing Systems for Tertiary Education

Gerhard Hube, Nicholas H. Müller
THWS Business School and
Faculty of Computer Science and Business Information Systems
Technical University of Applied Sciences Würzburg-Schweinfurt
Würzburg, Germany
e-mail: gerhard.hube@thws.de
e-mail: nicholas.mueller@thws.de

Abstract— **This work is a follow up to our previous studies "2D Virtual Learning Environments for Tertiary Education" carried out in 2022 and "Comparison of 2D Virtual Learning Environments with Classic Video Conferencing Systems for Tertiary Education" carried out in 2023. The main focus was to analyse the suitability of a 2D Virtual Learning Environment (VLE) for tertiary education using the desktop-based 2D immersive environment 'gather.town' and to compare it with classic video conferencing systems. In these two studies, the results suggest that the immersive 2D environment is holistically suitable as a learning environment in the tertiary sector and, including exam grades, it was found that students perform better with virtual 2D learning environments than with classic video conferencing systems. In this short paper, we conclude the study of the Master`s courses with the video conferencing system in the series of seminars and look forward to the next round of examination with the virtual 3D learning environment.**

Keywords-Virtual Learning Environments; Online Teaching; Tertiary Education; 2D Environments; Desktop Virtual Reality; Zoom; gather.town; 3D Environment.

I. INTRODUCTION

This paper is based on the first studies published in 2022 in the International Journal on Advances in Systems and Measurements, vol. 15, no. 3 & 4 with the title "2D Virtual Learning Environments for Tertiary Education" [1] and the related to that "Comparison of 2D Virtual Learning Environments with Classic Video Conferencing Systems for Tertiary Education" published in 2023 [2] [3]. To complete the comparison, the two seminars were conducted and examined, as shown in Figure 1. Contrary to the original planning in [2], a 3D desktop environment was not used, but Zoom as a classic videoconferencing system. The use of 3D desktop is now planned for the winter term 24/25. Several studies have been published on online learning, especially with Learning Management Systems (LMS) such as Moodle and video conferencing systems, especially Zoom [4] [5] [6], accompanied by papers on the phenomenon of "Zoom fatigue" [7] [8] [9]. This highlights the need for alternative online learning environments with less immersive desktop environments such as gather.town [10]. Lo and Song [11] con-

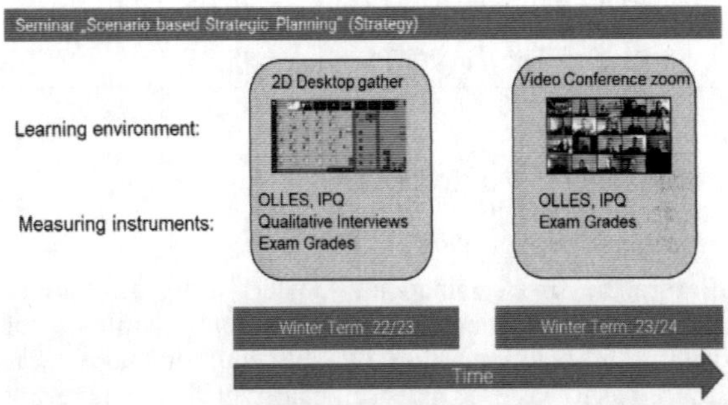

Figure 1. Timeline, seminars, learning environments and measuring instruments for this study.

ducted a review of the empirical studies in gather.town and found that there is still a lack of studies outside of computer science courses that examine students behaviour and learning outcomes. The authors also found that most of the studies were of short duration and suggested studies of longer duration. In conclusion, the suitability of 2D Virtual Learning Environments for tertiary education has been analysed descriptively and tested statistically through a first comparison between 2D Virtual Learning Environments and classic video conferencing systems. This comparison will now be completed with the inclusion of the second seminar strategy. The aim of this and the following research is to analyse the differences between the learning environments in order to improve online education in tertiary education. As the learning environments gather.town and Zoom have been described in our previous paper [2], as well as the measurement tools used, the Online Learning Environment Survey (OLLES) [12], the Igroup Presence Questionnaire (IPQ) [13] and qualitative interviews we only give the experimental procedure and the sample in Section 2. Section 3 summarises the results, which are then discussed with some limitations in Section 4. Section 5 concludes the paper with the main conclusions and future research.

TABLE I. MANN-WHITNEY U TEST WITH RESULTS OLLES FOR STRATEGY

Dimension	*Median gather.town*	*Median Zoom*	*exact p*	*z-Value*	*Effect size r*
Student Collaboration (SC)	3.30	3.80	0.169	-1.401	-0.275
Computer Competence (CC)	5.00	4.90	0.858	-0.201	-0.039
Active Learning (AL)	3.10	3.20	0.521	-0.667	-0.131
Tutor Support (TS)	3.80	3.60	0.159	-1.432	-0.281
Information Design and Appeal (IDA)	3.40	3.60	0.765	-0.318	-0.062
Material Environment (ME)	4.05	4.00	0.907	-0.133	-0.026
Reflective Thinking (RT)	2.85	3.00	0.688	-0.422	-0.083

II. METHOD

A. *Experimental procedure*

Before the first seminar, all subjects were familiarised with the Zoom environment, which was quite common for students. In addition, the OLLES questionnaire was introduced as it was used in its original English language, but the subjects were not native English speakers. Both seminars were held over 4-5 days, with each session starting in the early afternoon and lasting 5-6 hours. Both seminars were held exclusively in Gather and Zoom, respectively, with a total of one measurement point after the last seminar. Both questionnaires were completed online immediately after the seminar. Assuming similar results for the qualitative interviews at the point of Zoom as in the previous round [2], they were not condurcted for the Zoom seminar in this round.

B. *Sample*

All data were collected at the Technical University of Applied Sciences Würzburg-Schweinfurt during the seminar "Scenario-based Strategic Planning" (hereafter just "Strategy") of the master programme "Integrated Innovation Management". The seminar "Strategy" was held in Zoom, as shown in Figure 1. As could be shown in the previous studies, it seems to be sufficient to have only one measuring point. This was proved by using the Wilcoxon test, which showed that there was no difference between time point 1 and time point 2 regarding the OLLES questionnaire. The same was done for the IPQ. There were differences on one scale, which can be explained, and the difference was not confirmed in the second seminar Trend [2]. A total of 12 subjects participated in the Strategy seminar. However, only 10 subjects completed the questionnaires. This leaves n = 10 valid subjects for the final analysis. The average age of the subjects is 24.3 years, with a minimum of 22 years and a maximum of 26 years. Of the n = 10 subjects, 6 are female (60.0%) and 4 are male (40.0%).

III. RESULTS

In this first round of data analysis, the results of the OLLES questionnaire were compared to check for differences between the two different online learning environments. This was done by checking whether the central means and medians of the two surveys were significantly different. This is done by calculating whether the mean or median of the "Strategy Zoom" survey differs from the mean or median of the "Strategy gather.town" survey. The t-test for independent samples (two-sample t-test) is used to calculate the differences between the means. This requires that the indices are normally distributed. This is not the case for the CC_Mean and TS_Mean indices. Therefore, the analyses are recalculated using the U-test for independent samples (Mann-Whitney U-test). This calculates whether the two medians are significantly different. As shown in Table I,the medians of the two surveys, gather.town and Zoom, are not significantly different.

IV. DISCUSSION

In contrast to the results of the second round in winter term 22/23, the results show no significant differences between the virtual learning worlds gather.town and Zoom. In the second round, significant differences were found in the variables Active Learning (AL) and Information Design and Appeal (IDA) [3]. Although it was a different seminar, the didactic and structural elements are very similar and therefore do not explain the difference. Probably the small number of subjects makes it difficult to interpret the results. A further analysis of the not yet evaluated data could possibly help. Therefore, in the next step, also the results of questionnaire IPQ and the exam grades of the Strategy and Trend seminar will also be examined. Furthermore, it might be interesting to look at the different results of the two seminars in Zoom, once in Strategy and once in Trend (Figure 2).

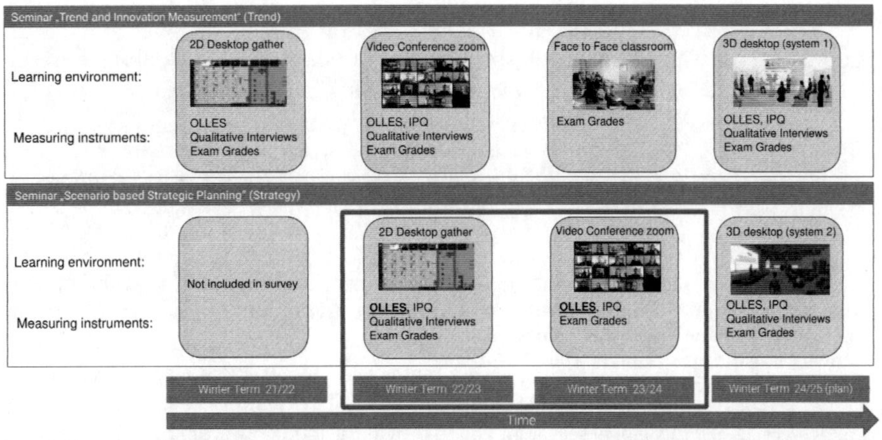

Figure 2. Overview of seminars, learning environments and measuring instruments for finished and planned studies.

V. Conclusion And Future Work

This study, with the partial results of the third round of the long-term study on virtual learning environments, confirms the previous rather small differences between the virtual learning environments gather.town and Zoom. At least for the results of the OLLES questionnaire that has been analysed so far in the third round. The differences in the OLLES variables Active Learning (AL) and Information Design and Appeal (IDA) could not be confirmed in this round; in fact, there were no statistically significant differences. The results of the IPQ questionnaire have yet to be analysed. In addition, another round is planned for WS 24/25, in which the same seminars will be held in a virtual 3D desktop environment (Figure 2). As discussed in previous publications, the small number of subjects is a limiting factor in interpreting the results, but at the same time the research design allows for comparative analysis over a long period of time. Nevertheless, it will be explored how the number of subjects could be increased and also to what extent ethical aspects could be addressed by the use of VLE in education [14] [15].

References

[1] G. Hube, K. Pfeffel, and N. H. Müller, "2D Virtual Learning Environments for Tertiary Education" International Journal on Advances in Systems and Measurements, ISSN 1942-261x, vol. 15, no. 3 & 4, pp. 81-92, 2022.

[2] G. Hube, K. Pfeffel, and N. H. Müller, "Comparison of 2D Virtual Learning Environments with Classic Video Conferencing Systems for Tertiary Education", IARIA Congress 2023 International Conference on Technical Advances and Human Consequences, ISBN: 978-1-68558-089-6, pp 48-57, 2023.

[3] G. Hube, K. Pfeffel, and N. H. Müller, "Comparison of 2D Virtual Learning Environments with Classic Video Conferencing Systems for Tertiary Education", IARIA Congress 2023 presentation available at https://www.iaria.org/conferences2023/filesIARIACongress23/iariacongress_50108.pdf, 2024.04.26

[4] G. Q. Hu, "Qualitative Analysis of Students' Online Learning Experiences after the University Reopening," Journal of Education, Humanities and Social Sciences, vol. 7, pp. 115–134, Jan. 2023, doi: 10.54097/ehss.v7i.4074.

[5] I. Assaly and U. Atamna, "Who Needs Zoom? Female Arab Students' Perceptions of Face-to-Face Learning and Learning on Zoom," Sustainability, vol. 15, no. 10, 8195, 2023.

[6] N. Kocyigit and F. Yilmaz, "Effects of Zoom Fatigues on Life Satisfaction: A Research on Teachers," [Online]. https://www.researchgate.net/publication/371970282_EFFECTS_OF_ZOOM_FATIGUE%27S_ON_LIFE_SATISFACTION_A_RESEARCH_ON_TEACHERS 2024.05.05

[7] A. Carțiș, ""Zoom Fatigue" In Higher Education: Videoconferencing Impact On Students' Fatigue," Education Facing Contemporary World Issues - EDU WORLD 2022, vol. 5, pp. 1355-1364, 2023, doi: 10.15405/epes.23045.138.

[8] L. Knox, S. Berzenski, and S. Drew, "Measuring Zoom Fatigue in College Students: Development and Validation of the Meeting Fatigue Scale for Videoconferencing (MFS-V) and the Meeting Fatigue Scale for In-Person (MFS-I)," Media Psychology, Advance online publication, 2023, doi: 10.1080/15213269.2023.2204529

[9] A. Ngien and B. Hogan, "The relationship between Zoom use with the camera on and Zoom fatigue: considering self-monitoring and social interaction anxiety," Information Communication & Society, vol. 26, no. 10, pp. 2052-2070, 2023, doi: 10.1080/1369118X.2022.2065214.

[10] Gather Presence, Inc. gather.town. [Online]. https://www.gather.town 2024.05.05.

[11] C. K. Lo and Y. Song, "A Scoping Review of Empirical Studies in Gather.town," 11th International Conference on Information and Education Technology (ICIET), 2023, pp. 1-5, Electronic ISBN: 978-1-6654-6548-9 doi: 10.1109/ ICIET56899.2023.10111430.

[12] J. Clayton, "Development and Validation of an Instrument for Assessing Online Learning Environments in Tertiary Education: The Online Learning Environment Survey (OLLES)," [Online]. https://espace.curtin.edu.au/handle/20.500.11937/550 2024.05.05.

[13] T. Schubert, F. Friedmann, and H. Regenbrecht, "The experience of presence: Factor analytic insights," Presence, vol. 10, no. 3, pp. 266–281, 2001, doi: 10.1162/105474601300343603.

[14] S. Kaddoura and F. Al Husseiny, "The rising trend of Metaverse in education: Challenges, opportunities, and ethical considerations". PeerJ Computer Science, 9, e1252, 2023.

[15] M. J. Sá and S. Serpa, "Metaverse as a learning environment: Some considerations." Sustainability 15.3 2186, 2023.

A Collaborative Digital Platform for Charity Thrift Store Workers

Fathima Jubina Pathari, Eshita Kabir, Boishakhi Ghosh Mukta, Joakim Karlsen
Department of Computer Science and Communication
Østfold University College
Halden, Norway
email:{fathima.j.pathari, eshita.kabir, boishakhi.g.mukta, joakim.karlsen}@hiof.no

***Abstract*—This paper introduces a digital platform concept derived from a comprehensive study of a clothing charity thrift store and its operational model, aimed at enhancing communication and coordination among a diverse workforce. The platform was created using Participatory Design (PD) and Computer Supported Cooperative Work (CSCW) principles. Insights into the thrift store's operations were gained through observation and interviews, informing subsequent co-design workshops where the final artifact was collaboratively developed. The resulting platform prioritizes accessibility and usability, featuring a dashboard display with a stylus and a mobile application that promotes collaboration and communication via mixed-reality technology and shared space. It emphasizes the ability of collaborative digital platforms to improve communication, organization, and productivity among charity thrift store employees.**

Keywords-participatory design; PD; computer supported cooperative work; CSCW; thrift store.

I. Introduction

Fast Fashion (FF) is a retail technique whereby businesses use marketing strategies to keep up with the newest fashion trends by regularly updating products with quick renewal cycles and quickly turning the inventory [1]. The Spanish corporation Zara introduced the concept of FF to the United States in the 1980s, which quickly gained popularity. Over the past two decades, there has been significant growth in the FF market share. In fact, the consumption of apparel is predicted to increase by 63% by the year 2030 [2]. Though clothing poverty is a topic that sheds light on the uneven development of our society, revealing a hidden world of fashion that many are not aware of emphasizing the social and environmental consequences associated with the FF industry [3]. For many people who are living in poverty, buying clothes is a luxury that they simply cannot afford. This issue has led to a growing movement of charitable organizations that focus on providing clothing to those in need. Not only is this work beneficial for those who lack the means to buy new clothes, but it can also be environmentally friendly.

Non-Profit Organizations (NPOs) with philanthropic and social goals are known as charities [4]. Charity thrift stores play an important role in assisting those in need by providing low-cost or free clothing and other items. It has a significant positive impact on the economy, society, and the environment [2]. However, volunteers frequently face difficulties collaborating with one another while organizing donations and maintaining inventory [5]. Compared to for-profit organizations, NPOs tend to be more decentralized [4]. This study focuses on creating a collaborative digital platform for charity thrift store employees to enhance communication and task coordination, ultimately improving the efficiency and effectiveness of the store's operations. This platform aims to address these challenges and provide a more rewarding work experience for charity thrift store employees while better serving their communities by leveraging the principles of PD and CSCW.

Our study is based on a Clothing Center, which has provided free clothing to more than 1,600 people since May of 2022. According to the clothing center, a significant number of people in this area are experiencing financial difficulties, with low-income households relying on social benefits, disability allowances, unemployment benefits, and other forms of assistance. The clothing center exemplifies how charitable organizations can have a significant impact on the community, and our proposed digital platform will help similar organizations by streamlining the donation and inventory management processes by improving communication and coordination among employees.

The purpose of this study is to investigate the creation of a collaborative digital platform specifically designed for charity thrift store employees. Our primary goal is to answer the following research question: " How can a collaborative digital platform improve the efficiency and effectiveness of communication and task coordination among workers in a charity thrift store?".

The paper is structured as follows. Section 2 provides an overview of existing literature, while Section 3 presents the framework used in this study. Section 4 outlines the methodology utilized, and Section 5 presents the study's findings. Finally, Section 6 engages in a discussion, while Section 7 concludes the study.

II. Literature Review

Few researchers have looked into the possibility of PD and CSCW collaboration in a variety of settings. Paras et al., investigated the current clothing reuse industry in order to develop a charity-driven model for the reuse-based clothing value chain in their study [5]. David and his co-authors proposed a new online collaboration platform for the exchange of goods between various organizations in order to improve communication, foster collaboration, and more efficiently and effectively fulfill each organization's mission while also increasing community involvement [6].

Vyas & Dillahunt, emphasize how people who are financially struggling demonstrate resilience in the face of adversity, which may assist them in understanding how technologies can support their current efforts [7]. Then, they offer empirical insights into their participants' situated resilience and articulate how design can support their existing social and collaborative practices. In a study conducted by Bysani et al., they proposed an Remote Sharing Network (RSN) solution for the workplace that promotes collaboration [8]. The system enables people to work both independently and collaboratively, spawning a new category of professionals known as e-professionals, who can collaborate online regardless of their physical location [8]. Michelini et al., aimed to shed light on how new digital technology is reshaping alternative distribution networks and what kind of value is added by the many developing models in their paper [9].

However, few or no studies have focused on enhancing collaboration and communication within NPOs such as charity thrift stores using the PD method and CSCW. Therefore, this study aims to fill this research gap by exploring how PD and CSCW principles can be tailored to the context of NPOs, specifically charity thrift stores, to enhance collaboration and communication among volunteers and staff members.

III. Framework

Effective collaboration demands diverse participation and clear communication, integrating varied perspectives for success [10]. Cultural backgrounds shape communication styles [11]. Shared-space technologies enhance coordination in cooperative work environments [12]. Mixed reality expands collaboration possibilities, reshaping how we understand and model collaborative efforts [13]. Our project leverages mixed reality in a dashboard display and mobile application. Cooperative work relies on communication to determine task significance. Activity theory informs our understanding of human-computer interaction [14].

CSCW is a field of study that looks into individual collaboration and the impact of technology on teamwork. Understanding team member roles, assessing the effects of technology on collaboration, and promoting effective communication are all necessary design principles and guidelines for encouraging authentic teamwork. The location or context of CSCW design is not fixed or predetermined [15] [16] [17].

PD is a collaborative design approach where designers involve end-users in the design process to prioritize their needs and promote empowerment and ownership over technology. PD has been globally implemented and demonstrated its effectiveness in meeting users' requirements [18] [19]. PD considers users as domain experts, ensuring their crucial role in the design process and producing computer systems that address real-world practical challenges [20]. Designers choose PD for practical or political reasons, recognizing users' right to have a say in the technology they use [21].

IV. Methodology

Our research aimed to develop a collaborative digital platform for charity thrift staff members to enhance their communication, organization, and productivity. The methodology included observation, interviews, and workshops with the staff members. The following sections describe each step in detail.

A. Contextual Background of the Thrift Store

The charity thrift store, which serves as the focus of our project, operates as a small organization reliant on the efforts of approximately 30 individuals. Among these workers are individuals of varying ages, with most facing disabilities or illnesses. Operating for four days each week with two shifts, the store undertakes diverse tasks. Initially, workers interact with customers and collect clothing donations, meticulously documenting each item received to ensure equitable distribution. Subsequently, workers transition to the warehouse phase, where tasks include sorting, cleaning, and organizing items. Communication and task management are facilitated through platforms like Facebook, aiding in information dissemination and task coordination. Additionally, workers handle diverse items such as children's toys, accessories, sports equipment, shoes, and ornaments. Periodic events necessitate enhanced communication and collaboration among staff members. Considering the diverse backgrounds and abilities of volunteers, the development of an accessible and user-friendly collaborative digital platform is deemed imperative for the organization's productivity and success. Such a platform has the potential to optimize communication, task organization, and overall workplace efficiency.

B. Initial Discussion

Before engaging in formal data collection, an initial discussion session was conducted to establish rapport and gain an overview of the thrift store's history, mission, and operational dynamics. A sense of trust and collaboration was hoped to be established with the staff members by authors, through establishing a relationship with them, which was believed to help facilitate the research process.

C. Observations

Two observation sessions were conducted to gain insights into the thrift store's operations. The first session, held after an initial discussion, aimed to validate and contextualize information obtained during discussions. This timing allowed for observations of day-to-day activities, collaboration patterns, and interactions among staff members and with customers.

The second session, conducted after interviews, included a visit to their warehouse to observe activities, collaboration, and cooperation inside the warehouse and between the store and warehouse, and the overall setup of both the warehouse and the store. Activities, communication patterns, and interactions during both sessions, noting any notable behaviors or practices was observed by the authors. During the warehouse visit, it was observed that staff members are using a manual dashboard, including a blackboard and pen to manage their work

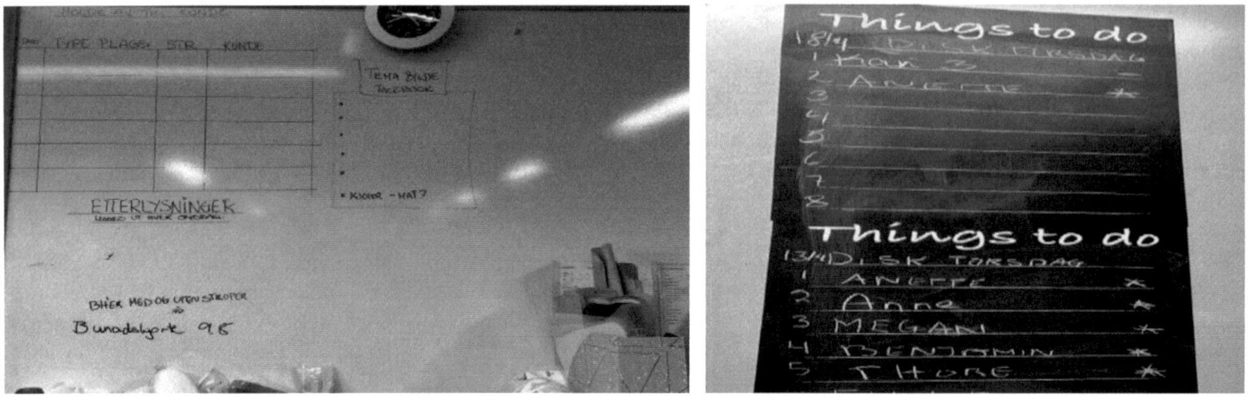

(a) Whiteboard (b) Whiteboard

Figure 1. Manual dashboard inside the warehouse.

schedules and a whiteboard to write their to-do lists. The to-do list included different themed Facebook posts that needed to be posted and a goods holding list for customers. The customer holding list included the date, the type of goods the customer needed, its size, and customer details. Refer to the manual dashboard, as illustrated in Figure 1, observed during the warehouse visit. This observation provided additional insights into the daily operations of the charity thrift store, supplementing the data obtained through interviews. These observations were structured to provide a holistic view of the thrift store's functioning and complement insights gained from discussions and interviews.

D. Interview

The interview was conducted after the initial observation session to gain a deeper understanding of the thrift store's daily work processes and communication patterns among staff members. To accomplish this, a semi-structured interview was conducted with the founder of the thrift store. The reason for interviewing the founder is the founder's extensive experience since the store's inception and their role as both leader and worker.

Pre-prepared open-ended questions facilitated discussions on topics including tasks, workloads, and communication systems used within the store. This approach aimed to uncover challenges, identify opportunities for improvement, and explore potential technological interventions.

The interview was scheduled during a working day at the thrift store and took place in a private room within the store. Throughout the interview, detailed notes were taken, and audio recordings were made to ensure the accuracy and completeness of the data. The interview session lasted approximately 30 minutes.

E. Workshop for Co-Design

The workshop was conducted on two different days, with each day featuring different sessions. The first session focused on ideating the artifact, while the second session centered on implementing the ideas generated in the first session. Five staff members from various roles within the charity thrift store, all above 18 years old, participated in the workshop. This diverse representation aimed to capture unique insights and experiences to enrich the design process. While the selected participants may not fully encompass all roles within charity thrift stores, they were chosen to reflect common responsibilities. An introduction to the research and the goals of the PD workshops was provided to the participants. More details about the workshop are provided below.

1) Ideation: After conducting observations and interviews, a workshop was held with the staff members of the charity thrift store, involving five participants. The workshop included the founder of the thrift store and various staff members involved in different activities from different sections of the store. Customers were not included as participants, as the collaborative platform was initially aimed at serving the needs of the store's staff exclusively.

The main objective of the ideation session was to utilize the information and challenges that the participants shared through interviews and observations to create a possible solution for the thrift store employees, making their work easier and more efficient. Participants and authors engaged in detailed discussions about potential features and technologies. Pen and paper were provided to facilitate the drawing and explanation of ideas and features. Additionally, different types of application examples were shown to the participants to provide insight into possible technologies and stimulate brainstorming.

Through their involvement in the ideation process, participants developed a collective understanding of the platform's essential features. While they initially expressed uncertainty about their exact needs, they ultimately concluded that an application and digital dashboard would be beneficial for the staff.

2) Design Implementation: After the conclusion of the first session, it was collectively decided that what kind of digital tools they will have. Subsequently, a second session was conducted to design these digital tools in collaboration with the staff.

Figure 2. Photos during the workshop activities.

During this phase, a hands-on approach was adopted, using paper and colors to create an interactive environment. Mobile interface-sized paper pieces were provided in green, reflecting the staff's preference as indicated in the previous ideation session and aligning with the store's logo color. Additionally, small pieces of paper containing function names suggested by the staff were distributed to aid in the design process. Furthermore, additional A4-sized papers, mobile screen-sized photos, paper pieces to add new features, crayons, colored pencils, markers, pen, pencil, scissors, and a scale were provided to empower staff members to introduce new features or elements to the application. Refer to Figure 2 for photos from the workshop. Though most of the implementation was for the mobile application, for the dashboard, they preferred it the same as the manual dashboard that they were using and only added some other functionalities as they could access the dashboard using their mobile application. This participatory approach aimed to facilitate flexibility in design, allowing for customization according to the staff's preferences and operational needs.

F. Ethical Considerations

Participants were provided with informed consent forms before observations, interviews, and workshops, ensuring transparency and respect for privacy. The consent form outlined the scope of discussions, confidentiality measures, and data handling procedures. These measures upheld participants' rights and privacy throughout the research process.

V. RESULTS

After the ideation session, the team agreed on implementing a dashboard display with a stylus and a mobile application for the charity thrift store. The application offers essential functionalities for collaboration and communication. Particularly, the dashboard with a stylus aims to replace traditional whiteboards and blackboards in the warehouse. The mobile app enables staff to access and manipulate the dashboard, along with other features. Instead of using manual whiteboards and blackboards to keep track of tasks and schedules, workers can write on the dashboard just like they would with a pen

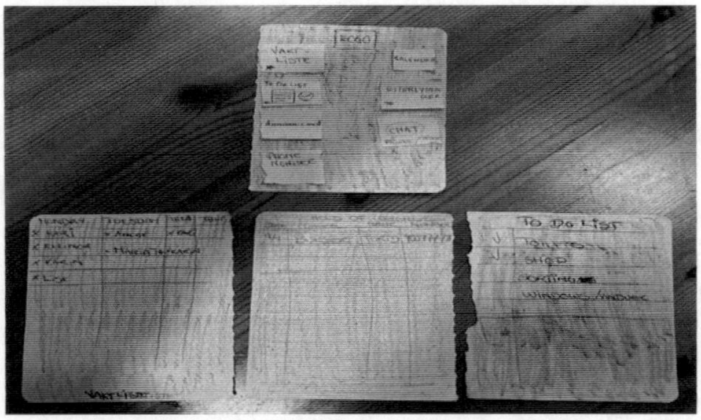

Figure 3. Designed application interface.

and paper. They can easily update tasks, mark off what's been done, and see what needs attention, all in one place. With the help of mobile app, workers can access the warehouse dashboard from anywhere. Even if they're not in the warehouse, they can still see what's going on and add notes or tasks as needed. The team opted for a green color to align with the store logo and specified desired application features.

During the design implementation phase, the team collaborated to design the mobile application interfaces based on staff preferences for color, features, and aesthetics. Figure 3 illustrates the designed mobile application interface. The home page (Figure 4a) showcases various features divided into left and right sections. The left side includes the Work schedule, To-do-list, Announcement, and contact information for staff and officials. The right side contains the Schedule calendar, Etterlysninger, and a chat option. Features marked with a star indicate newly designed interfaces. The Work schedule allows staff members to choose their schedules, similar to Doodles (refer to Figure 4c). The To-do list (refer to Figure 4b) outlines daily tasks. The Announcement feature facilitates event announcements, while including staff phone numbers enable easy communication.

The Schedule Calendar resembles the Outlook calendar for scheduling appointments and tasks. The Etterlysninger feature lists customer requests (refer to Figure 4d), including the date,

(a) Home page (b) To-do list (c) Work schedule (d) Hold items

Figure 4. The application interface designed during the workshop.

type of goods, name, and number. The chat option supports both group and individual chats.

Regarding the display with the stylus, staff preferred functionalities similar to their current manual system in the warehouse (refer to Figure 1). Staff can input information using the stylus on the display or through the mobile application, allowing access to information from anywhere without the need for multiple applications or being physically present in the store.

VI. Discussion

The principles of PD and CSCW as key concepts throughout our study. PD principles guided our approach to engaging charity thrift store staff in the different methods, ensuring that the end-users voices and perspectives were central to the design of the collaborative digital platform. Our goal was to empower and instill a sense of ownership over technology among staff members by actively involving them in the design process. This approach aimed to cultivate a feeling of investment and commitment to the project.

The sequential approach of our observation sessions and interviews provided valuable insights into the activities of the thrift store. The first observation session yielded valuable insights into collaboration patterns and interactions among staff members, customers, and donors. Meanwhile, the second observation session, which occurred after conducting the interview, helped us to learn more about the warehouse operations and the store itself. This sequential approach allowed us to deepen our insights into how the store and warehouse work together.

The initial observation phase laid the base for our interviews with the founder. In the interview, the founder shared the foundation of the store, experiences, store's functioning, daily work processes, work culture, and the challenges they've encountered. Their reflections enhanced our understanding and provided valuable context for the observations made earlier, as well as for the second observation.

In the second observation, it is observed that the staff members use a manual dashboard in the warehouse. Although this aspect wasn't explicitly mentioned by during the interview, it highlights the practical tools and methods integrated into their daily work routines. This observation emphasizes the significance of triangulating data from multiple sources to attain a comprehensive understanding of the event [22].

By combining insights from both observation sessions and interviews, we were able to gain a thorough understanding of the thrift store's operations and procedures. This approach enabled us to capture the nuances of how the store operates on a day-to-day basis, as well as the broader context in which it functions.

After the workshop, collaboratively proposed a solution to enhance collaborative systems within a charity thrift store. That was a mobile application and a digital display dashboard with a stylus. Workers can access and manipulate information using both the mobile application and the digital dashboard, with the latter containing essential features such as a to-do list.

One significant advantage of this solution is its accessibility to workers of varying technological familiarity, as the digital dashboard offers a user-friendly interface, particularly beneficial for older workers. Moreover, the platform grants employees the capability to access the dashboard from any location, harnessing the power of mixed reality technology to facilitate more efficient collaboration and communication. This means that workers can seamlessly interact with the digital dashboard and engage in tasks regardless of their physical proximity to the workplace. By leveraging mixed reality technology, the platform transcends traditional boundaries, enabling employees to collaborate effectively whether they are in the store, at home, or on the go.

Indeed, shared space demonstrates the potential benefits of creating a common information space that promotes collaboration and improves communication among workers. By establishing a shared space and common information, employees can easily access and contribute to a centralized repository of information, facilitating collaboration and ensuring everyone is aware of tasks and progress. This fosters a sense of unity and shared purpose among team members, ultimately enhancing efficiency and productivity within the workplace.

During the PD work, participants expressed enjoyment and effectiveness in being engaged throughout the process, especially during workshops where they had the opportunity to design their own technology and prioritize their needs and preferences. One member even found it effortless to explain design concepts. This positive feedback from staff members regarding the PD approach underscores the importance of actively involving end-users in the design process of technological solutions. Ultimately, this user-centered solution is poised to enhance their work experience, fostering easier, happier, and more effective work for employees overall.

As the next step, we will conduct separate evaluations for the application and the digital dashboard. First, a high-fidelity prototype of the mobile application will be created and distributed to staff members for a week-long evaluation. During this period, we will provide them with notes to capture any comments or thoughts about the application. Following this evaluation, we will gather feedback, including insights from the provided notes, to iteratively improve the application's performance and user interface. Secondly, we will evaluate the digital dashboard. Staff members will interact with the mobile application, and we will simulate the interaction between the digital dashboard and the mobile application to ensure seamless communication and functionality between the two platforms. Throughout these evaluations, we will focus on assessing various efficiency metrics, such as the time taken by users to perform tasks, user satisfaction levels, and the effort required by users. These metrics will be compared between the existing methods and the proposed platform in charity thrift stores, providing valuable insights into the effectiveness of the digital solutions.

VII. Conclusion

In conclusion, this research paper aimed to develop a collaborative digital platform for charity thrift staff members to enhance their communication, collaboration, organization, and productivity. The research methodology involved several steps, as described in Section 4. The study revealed valuable insights into the daily work processes, communication patterns, and needs of the staff members, which allowed for the identification of potential opportunities for technological intervention. The workshops were designed to involve the staff members in the design process of the digital platform, which resulted in two promising solutions, a dashboard display with a stylus and a mobile application. Overall, this paper highlights the importance of PD in developing technological solutions that meet the needs of users and contribute to their productivity and success.

References

[1] S. Gupta and J. W. Gentry, "Evaluating fast fashion: Examining its micro and the macro perspective," in Eco-Friendly and Fair, Routledge, 2018.

[2] R. Zanjirani Farahani, N. Asgari, and L. N. Van Wassenhove, "Fast Fashion, Charities, and the Circular Economy: Challenges for Operations Management," Prod. Oper. Manag., vol. 31, no. 3, pp. 1089–1114, Mar. 2022, doi: 10.1111/poms.13596.

[3] A. Brooks, Clothing Poverty: The Hidden World of Fast Fashion and Second-Hand Clothes. Bloomsbury Publishing, 2019.

[4] G. Berenguer and Z.-J. (Max) Shen, "OM Forum—Challenges and Strategies in Managing Nonprofit Operations: An Operations Management Perspective," Manuf. Serv. Oper. Manag., vol. 22, no. 5, pp. 888–905, Sep. 2020, doi: 10.1287/msom.2018.0758.

[5] M. Paras et al., "An Exploratory Study of Swedish Charities to Develop a Model for the Reuse-Based Clothing Value Chain," Sustainability, vol. 10, no. 4, p. 1176, Apr. 2018, doi: 10.3390/su10041176.

[6] S. David, M. E. De Abreu, and A. Trigo, "CharX: a proposal for a collaborative information system for the eXchange of goods between charities," in Proceedings of the International Conference on Information Systems and Design of Communication, Lisbon Portugal: ACM, May 2014, pp. 1–7. doi: 10.1145/2618168.2618169.

[7] D. Vyas and T. Dillahunt, "Everyday Resilience: Supporting Resilient Strategies among Low Socioeconomic Status Communities," Proc. ACM Hum.-Comput. Interact., vol. 1, no. CSCW, pp. 1–21, Dec. 2017, doi: 10.1145/3134740.

[8] R. N. Bysani, S. K N, and U. V, "Remote Sharing Network (RSN): A Collaborative Platform," Int. J. Comput. Appl., vol. 117, no. 11, pp. 15–19, May 2015, doi: 10.5120/20598-3167.

[9] L. Michelini, L. Principato, and G. Iasevoli, "Understanding Food Sharing Models to Tackle Sustainability Challenges," Ecol. Econ., vol. 145, pp. 205–217, Mar. 2018, doi: 10.1016/j.ecolecon.2017.09.009.

[10] H. Persson, H. Åhman, A. A. Yngling, and J. Gulliksen, "Universal design, inclusive design, accessible design, design for all: different concepts—one goal? On the concept of accessibility—historical, methodological and philosophical aspects," Univers. Access Inf. Soc., vol. 14, no. 4, pp. 505–526, Nov. 2015, doi: 10.1007/s10209-014-0358-z.

[11] J. Collins, "From the Classroom an Introduction to Ethical Theory," J. Leg. Stud. Educ., vol. 13, no. 1, pp. 163–171, 1995, doi: 10.1111/j.1744-1722.1995.tb00120.x.

[12] S. Benford, C. Brown, G. Reynard, and C. Greenhalgh, "Shared spaces: transportation, artificiality, and spatiality," in Proceedings of the 1996 ACM conference on Computer supported cooperative work - CSCW '96, Boston, Massachusetts, United States: ACM Press, 1996, pp. 77–86. doi: 10.1145/240080.240196.

[13] B. Ens et al., "Revisiting collaboration through mixed reality: The evolution of groupware," Int. J. Hum.-Comput. Stud., vol. 131, pp. 81–98, Nov. 2019, doi: 10.1016/j.ijhcs.2019.05.011.

[14] V. Kaptelinin and B. Nardi, "Activity Theory as a Framework for Human-Technology Interaction Research," Mind Cult. Act., vol. 25, no. 1, pp. 3–5, Jan. 2018, doi: 10.1080/10749039.2017.1393089.

[15] P. Bjørn and N. Boulus-Rødje, "The multiple intersecting sites of design in CSCW research," Comput. Support. Coop. Work, vol. 24, no. 4, pp. 319–351, 2015, doi: 10.1007/s10606-015-9227-4.

[16] W. Pratt, M. C. Reddy, D. W. McDonald, P. Tarczy-Hornoch, and J. H. Gennari, "Incorporating ideas from computer-supported cooperative work," J. Biomed. Inform., vol. 37, no. 2, pp. 128–137, Apr. 2004, doi: 10.1016/j.jbi.2004.04.001.

[17] M. Fjeld et al., "Physical and Virtual Tools: Activity Theory Applied to the Design of Groupware," Comput. Support. Coop. Work CSCW, vol. 11, no. 1, pp. 153–180, Mar. 2002, doi: 10.1023/A:1015269228596.

[18] J. Simonsen and T. Robertson, "Routledge International Handbook of Participatory Design," Routledge & CRC Press. Accessed: May 04, 2024. [Online]. Available: https://www.routledge.com/Routledge-International-Handbook-of-Participatory-Design/Simonsen-Robertson/p/book/9780415720212

[19] D. Simmonds and L. Reynolds, "Designing with Colour," in Computer Presentation of Data in Science: a do-it-yourself guide, based on the Apple Macintosh, for authors and illustrators in the Sciences, D. Simmonds and L. Reynolds, Eds., Dordrecht: Springer Netherlands, 1989, pp. 107–119. doi: 10.1007/978-94-015-7844-8_9.

[20] C. Spinuzzi, "The Methodology of Participatory Design," Tech. Commun., vol. 52, pp. 163–174, May 2005.

[21] T. Bratteteig and I. Wagner, "Unpacking the Notion of Participation in Participatory Design," Comput Support. Coop Work, vol. 25, no. 6, pp. 425–475, Dec. 2016, doi: 10.1007/s10606-016-9259-4.

[22] N. Carter, "The Use of Triangulation in Qualitative Research," Number 5 Sept. 2014, vol. 41, no. 5, pp. 545–547, Aug. 2014, doi: 10.1188/14.ONF.545-547.

Exploring Technology Probes in Co-Creation

Understanding Stakeholders' Familiarity with Emerging Technologies for Socio-Technical Innovation

Fahd Bin Malek Newaz
Department of Informatics
University of Oslo
Oslo, Norway
fbnewaz@uio.no
Faculty of Computer Science, Engineering and Economics
Østfold University College
fahd.b.newaz@hiof.no

Abstract— **Designers facilitating processes of co-creation to innovate socio-technical solutions often have the need to better understand stakeholders' familiarity with the technologies being addressed. This article investigates the utility of technology probes to elicit such insights from participants concerning emerging technologies, such as Augmented Reality (AR) and Virtual Reality (VR). Focusing on an early phase workshop in a multi-stage co-creation project, this study scrutinizes the utilization of a custom-built application as a technology probe. Findings from the workshop shed light on how the technology probe elicited the participants' varying levels of familiarity and perceptions regarding the technologies in question. These insights enabled the designers to customize how technologies were mobilized and used in creating the representational tools needed in facilitating for further co-creation activities.**

Keywords-co-creation; co-design; technology probes; participatory design; mixed reality; cultural heritage; education.

I. Introduction

In recent years, technology probes have gained prominence as valuable tools in the pre-design stage of co-design frameworks, facilitating exploration and understanding of emerging technologies within specific contexts [1]. As described by Newaz, Karlsen, and Herstad [2] "the pARTiciPED project, jointly financed by the Norwegian Research Council and the Østfold University College, aims to undertake research on how cross-sectorial collaboration can lead to better ways of learning for future generations. The overall goal of the project is to develop concepts and principles to explain how Cross-Sectoral Collaborations (CSC) should be organized and implemented to secure transformative mutuality. Further, the goal is to explore and provide empirical evidence on how to organize and implement CSC in teacher education, to empower teacher students as confident, interested and engaged autonomous actors in these projects. This may improve and enhance the student teacher's pedagogical toolbox and strengthen the research-based foundation for educating new teachers." Throughout the project, the student teachers (from Østfold University College) collaborated with museum educators (from Moss town and industrial museum), teacher educators (from Østfold University College) and us (as designers), in order to co-create a technology-assisted teaching activity, as opposed to traditional lectures with limited scope for engagement and interactivity. The aim of the activity would be to help middle school students actively learn about their cultural heritage, more specifically the industrial history of Moss town. Within this framework of co-design, understanding the role of technology probes becomes imperative, particularly in gauging participants' familiarity and perceptions of emerging technologies. This may include technologies, such as Augmented Reality (AR) and Virtual Reality (VR), which may enable a greater engagement among students within educational settings. Reflecting on our pre-design workshop, we discuss the role of technology probes in understanding the participants' familiarity with technology, and how the process itself may contribute to building familiarity. In the following sections, we discuss existing literature with regards to co-design and technology probes (Section II), present our methodology (Section III), discuss our findings (Section IV) and finally present our conclusion and plans for future work (Section V).

II. Related Work

Theoretical underpinnings of co-design frameworks emphasize the importance of active participation and engagement of stakeholders throughout the design process [3]. Technology probes serve as lightweight interventions or artifacts that elicit responses and insights from users, thereby informing the design process [1]. In the context of the pARTiciPED project, probes were chosen as a means to understand the student teachers' attitudes towards technology in general, as well as a specific technological solution prepared specifically in the context of the project.

Hutchison et al. [1] describe technology probes to be a specific type of probe that can serve multiple goals: social - they gather information about technology use and users in real-world settings, engineering - field-test the technology, and design - inspire users and designers to envision new technological solutions. A well-designed technology probe must strike a balance between these different disciplinary influences. From a social science perspective, technology probes depart from the notion of collecting 'unbiased' ethnographic data. Rather, they acknowledge that the introduction of probes may alter user behavior. In the first workshop of the pARTiciPED project, which we consider as part of the pre-design stage of the co-design process [4], the focus was on the social goal, observing changes in the student teachers' attitude towards and their understanding of the technologies presented. However, as the project progressed to its generative stage, the focus shifted towards the design goals, exploring the possible implementation of these technologies as part of a future solution.

From the perspective of design research, technology probes draw parallels to cultural probes, such as those introduced by Gaver, Dunni, and Pacenti [5], which aim to stimulate reflection through materials like disposable cameras and diaries. The term 'cultural' denotes the particular technique employed, which can be adapted to other approaches, such as empathy or technology [6]. Cultural probes, however, often are tied to a single activity conducted at a specific time and may be a representation of the relevant technologies rather than the actual technology itself. Unlike cultural probes, technology probes involve the use of actual technology in real-world contexts to observe its use and gather insights to inform future technology design [7][8].

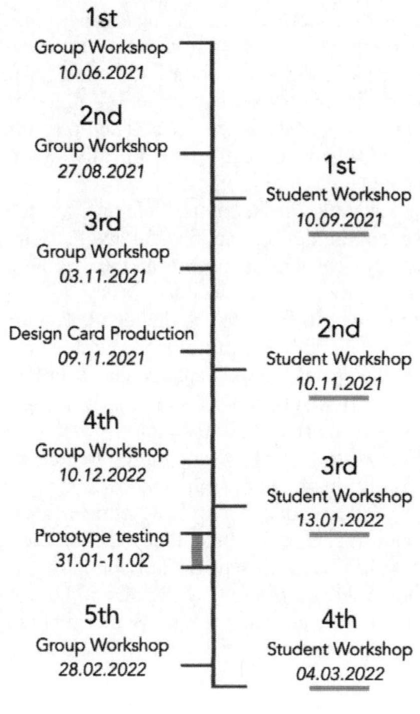

Figure 1. Project Timeline

A successful technology probe is characterized by simplicity and flexibility, serving as a tool to identify promising avenues for future technology design rather than a fully-fledged prototype. Moreover, it is open-ended and co-adaptive, allowing users to both adapt to the technology and creatively shape its use for their own purposes [1][9]. Previous research has highlighted the effectiveness of technology probes in stimulating creativity, imagination, and collaboration among participants in various domains, including education [10][11]. This was also the case in our project, where we observed creativity both in the content that was created during the use of the probe, and in the suggestions of how different technologies could be used to enhance cultural heritage teaching.

III. METHODOLOGY

The research methodology employed in the pARTiciPED project draws upon Participatory Design (PD) principles, emphasizing active involvement and collaboration among stakeholders. Figure 1. Project Timeline presents the timeline of major activities of the project. Over the course of nine months, a series of 9 workshops were conducted (Figure 1), guided by PD principles, such as 'having a say' and 'mutual learning' [12]. In this article, we discuss the first student workshop. This workshop was held on June 10, 2021, serving as a foundational exploration of various emerging technologies, such as AR, VR and geolocation in the context of educational innovation.

A. *Pre-Design Workshop*

The main participants for this workshop were 51 pre-service students (university students studying to become teachers) who were currently in the 4th year of their teaching studies. The workshop commenced with an introduction to the industrial history of Moss, Norway, facilitated by a museum educator from Østfold Museums (Figure 2). They were then given time to discuss the different themes that emerged in the presentation and visualize their ideas in the form of mind maps. This contextualization provided participants with insights into the historical significance of the town, setting the stage for the exploration of AR and VR technologies.

Figure 2. Museum educator presenting historical context

Following the history lesson, the participants were asked to fill out an online survey so we, the designers, could gain an understanding of their familiarity with technology. As presented in the first image in Figure 3. From left to right, Screen shot of 1st survey, 2nd survey, and geolocated content creation app the survey included questions regarding the participants' previous experiences with technology. We subsequently introduced the participants to several technologies, such as AR, VR, 360 imagery, and projection mapping. The presentation included images and videos of how these technologies are, and could be, used to share knowledge, especially in the context of cultural heritage and museums.

Figure 3. From left to right, Screen shot of 1st survey, 2nd survey, and geolocated content creation app

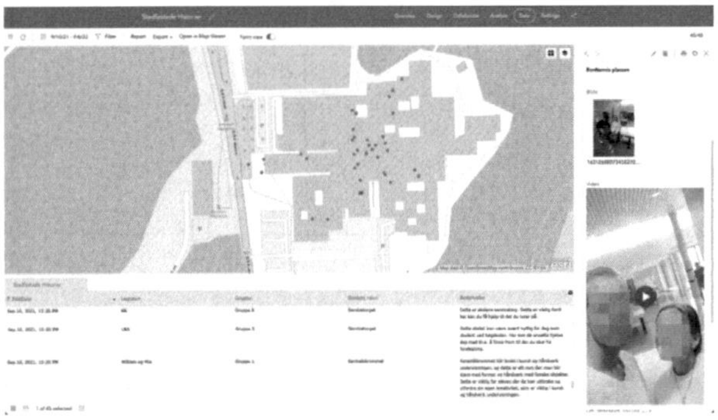

Figure 4. Screenshot of results of all the submitted geolocated content that was presented in front of all the participants

After a lunch break, we conducted a 45-minute session that focused on our technology probe which also introduced the students to geolocation technology. The students were given a custom-made mobile application, to create a 'virtual museum' of the university campus. They did this by taking pictures, recording videos, and adding text descriptions about different parts of the campus, while positioning the media on a map (this could be done automatically using their device's GPS, or by selecting the location manually). The 3rd image in Figure 3 shows the interface of the mobile application that was used by the participants. All the content created by the participant groups were automatically accumulated into one 'virtual museum'.

The content was visible as markers on a map, and upon clicking the markers, it was possible to see the images and videos, and read the text. The interface where all the submitted content was aggregated and could be accessed, is presented in Figure 4. The map is the most prominent feature, with text content below it. Images and videos are visible on the right side of the interface.

We spent another 30 minutes together with all participants, looking through some of the content that was created, and ended the session with another survey (second image in Figure 3) about the activity they had just completed. The survey consisted of questions about their experience with the mobile application, any challenges they faced, as well as possible applications of such technology in the context of this project.

The final session of the workshop lasted for 30 minutes. During this session, the participants were asked to identify 3 important takeaways from the day's activities, reflecting on the history of Moss town, the impact the industry had on its society, the technological possibilities, as well as the educational component of engaging middle school students to learn about these topics. We ended the day with a 15-minute session to wrap up and discuss what we would be doing going forward. The data from this workshop formed the basis for the subsequent workshops in the pARTiciPED, and also informed the tools and techniques that would be used going forward.

B. *Scientific Method*

As briefly described by Newaz, Karlsen, and Herstad [2], a combination of observation, and surveys was employed to gather comprehensive data during the workshop. Each method was selected to provide a nuanced understanding of the collaborative process and the participants' interaction with the technology probe, their surroundings, and each other. We also wanted to learn about the participants' familiarity with various technologies, as well as their creativity during the workshop.

Observation, as a research method, offers insights into phenomena within "naturally occurring settings" [13][14]. By immersing ourselves in the participants' environment, we gained invaluable insights into their interactions, experiences, and reactions. Through direct observation and retrospective examination via notes, photographs, and audio recordings, we uncovered unspoken cues and authentically observed how participants engaged in the activities.

Survey responses from all participants formed another crucial aspect of our data collection strategy. Participants were given 2 surveys to complete. One at the beginning of the technology session, and a second survey after they had completed the activities related to the technology probe. The surveys were designed to capture both tangible and nuanced aspects of the participants' engagement throughout the workshop. The first survey was aimed at learning about the participants' familiarity with technology and consisted of questions related to the use of technology in their daily lives, as well as questions related to their knowledge of emerging technologies. The second survey was more reflective about the workshop. The questions focused on the different technologies that were presented, the technology probe that was used, and relevant future applications of the technologies presented in an educational context. Combining survey data with qualitative observations fostered a holistic understanding of the role of the technology probe.

Given the exploratory nature of our study, we opted for an inductive approach to data analysis, building codes from the ground up [15]. Initially, each question was assigned a distinct code category for analysis. We conducted an initial round of in vivo coding, meticulously examining responses to the selected questions. Subsequently, a second round of coding was performed through thematic analysis, grouping responses into cohesive themes [16]. Our analysis encompassed a detailed examination of the responses from both surveys provided by the 43 student teachers that participated in this workshop.

By analyzing the gathered data, we were able to reflect upon the influence of the technology probe on the participants' familiarity with the technologies.

IV. Findings and Discussion

A. Technology probe

During the probing activity, as the students were going around the university campus in their groups, we observed a high level of engagement, and energy. The participants were actively creating photo and video content and uploading it to the 'virtual museum' application. It was apparent that they were enjoying the activity, as many of the participants were laughing as they were creating content and reviewing it before submitting it to the system.

Several of the participants approached us during the activity as they were not able to upload their videos. We realized that the system would not be able to accept files larger than 10 megabytes. This was one of the major challenges that many of the participants faced. We categorized this as a technical challenge. Interestingly, most of the participants were able to troubleshoot the problem themselves. They understood the file size limit, and subsequently created and uploaded shorter videos. However, some of the participants were not able to identify the reason for the upload error by themselves (despite the error message as shown in Figure 5), and therefore were not able to troubleshoot the error either. They of course received help from us to circumvent the error.

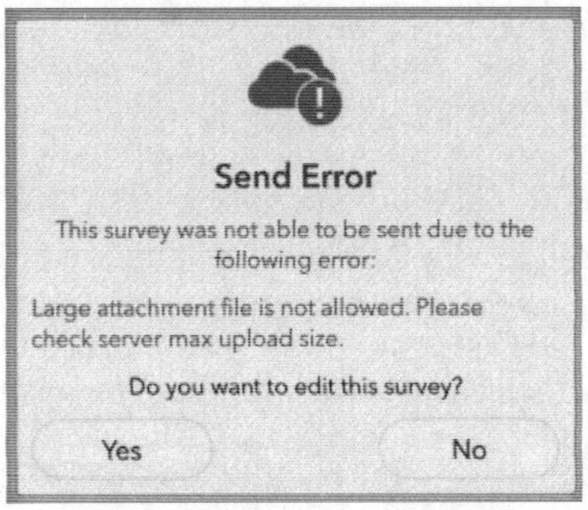

Figure 5. Error notification about file size that popped up for many of the participants

More than half of the participants did not feel this technical issue was a major challenge (Figure 6). Rather they expressed frustration with the following: the fact that it was hard to be creative when choosing the location and creating relevant content for that location; practical things, such as background noise and people moving in the background when filming. 25% of the participants did not feel they faced any significant challenges during the activity.

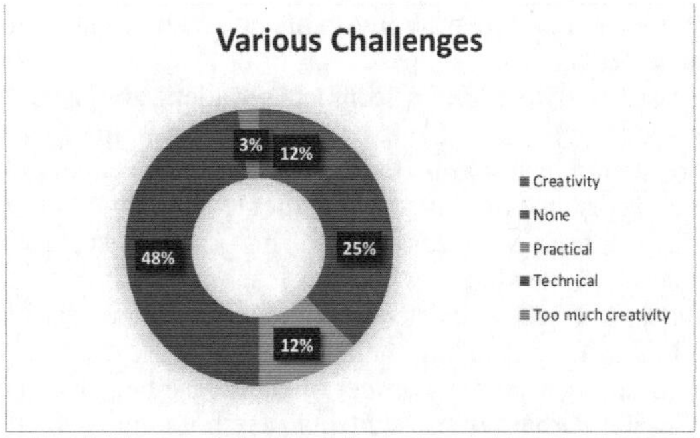

Figure 6. Various challenges reported by the participants

In terms of interest and aptitude, the participants displayed a strong inclination for the technology in use. The hands-on experience provided valuable insights into their comprehension of the available technologies and its potential benefits within an educational environment. The participants recognized the ability of this technology to improve student engagement and learning experiences. This was evident when all agreed on the relevance of geolocated content-creation application for teaching middle school students about their cultural heritage, with many highlighting its pedagogical value. Some recommended the use of VR and AR to enhance the students' experience, while others suggested using tools that the middle school students are already familiar with. One student said, "most of our students these days use TikTok, so we could use something like that, to let the students share their knowledge with others".

B. Familiarity

The idea of using tools that are familiar, is also relevant in the context of our workshop. Analysis of participants' interactions with the technology probe, coupled with survey responses before and after the activity, provided valuable insights into their familiarity and comfort levels with the technologies we presented, such as Augmented Reality (AR) and Virtual Reality (VR) and geolocation. Initially, less than 14% of participants were acquainted with AR, while over 90% demonstrated awareness of VR technology. Those familiar with AR cited examples, such as 'snapchat filters' and 'Pokémon Go', showcasing their understanding of the concept in relation to systems they were familiar with. Interestingly, all participants were familiar with GPS technology, although only 23% could fully articulate its definition.

Drawing from Herstad and Holone's [17] insights on familiarity as a subjective phenomenon, we understand that familiarity encompasses individuals' understanding of themselves, their surroundings, and the activities they engage in. It manifests through signs, such as easiness, confidence, success, and performance [18]. In the context of our project, familiarity with the presented technologies is crucial for participants' readiness to incorporate these tools into their teaching practices. Heidegger's [19] concepts of involvement, understanding, and the unity of self and world further explain the nuanced relationship between individuals and technology. Participants' interactions with the technology probe during the workshop provided tangible evidence of their engagement with the tools and their ability to adapt to new technological environments.

Despite encountering technical challenges during the activity, such as file size limitations, participants demonstrated problem-solving skills and adaptability, reflecting their familiarity with the technology and their willingness to overcome obstacles. This proactive approach to troubleshooting aligns with Heidegger's [19] notion of readiness to respond and act appropriately in each situation.

On the other hand, the challenge of being creative, though only raised by a smaller number of could also be attributed to familiarity. Perhaps, those students were not familiar with the process of creating digital content? Our data shows otherwise, as only 2 of the 43 students had never edited a video before. Perhaps they were not creating content online? Or perhaps, despite regularly creating content to share with friends and family, these participants were not comfortable doing the same when the content would be available publicly, or at least to a group that extended beyond a certain threshold. While we did not collect any data in this regard, it could be valuable to explore these questions from the perspective of familiarity.

The workshop not only provided insights into participants' familiarity with various technologies but helped us create scaffolds that contributed to their increased understanding and enthusiasm for utilizing these tools in educational contexts. Sanders [20] suggests that that designers should understand the aspirations of ordinary individuals and create scaffolds to help them realize these aspirations. These scaffolds, according to Sanders and Stappers [3], are frameworks for experiential engagement that can facilitate collaborative innovation and creative expression among stakeholders. In our project, we see parallels with Sanders' notion of scaffolds. In our case, we employed technology probes as tools to elicit insights, foster collaboration, and inspire creative expression among participants. Sanders [21] further elaborates on the concept of scaffolds, defining them as tools that foster everyday creativity and collective creativity. This conceptualization aligns closely with our approach to Technology Probes, where we aim to provide participants with tangible experiences and opportunities to explore emerging technologies, such as Augmented Reality (AR) and Virtual Reality (VR) in the context of education.

C. *Outcomes*

Based on the final feedback session of the workshop, the top 3 insights we could extract from the workshop include: 1) as a result of all the activities throughout the day, the participants were able to establish some common goals for the project at large, 2) the participants were able to achieve collaborative creativity while working with each other, not only in the context of the thematic discussions, but also in the context of creating content for the 'virtual museum' application, and suggesting future developments, and finally 3) the participants gained a heightened awareness of technological possibilities.

The participants displayed varied levels of understanding and familiarity regarding the technology introduced. Initially hesitant about the unfamiliar technology, their understanding improved as the workshop proceeded, eventually transforming skepticism into inspiration. Their recognition of the pedagogical value of technology, particularly in teaching middle school students about cultural heritage, underscores the potential of technology probes in fostering co-creation and collaborative innovation in education. When asked whether they could see this kind of technology could be relevant to teach cultural heritage to middle schoolers, an overwhelming majority responded positively, as evident from the following selection of responses:

> *"Yes, it can. Then you don't have to travel to places to visit them - which can be nice in a pandemic."*
> *"Yes; absolutely, you can go around and explore different places and at the same time document it for others"*
> *"Yes absolutely! One can use it to make informative videos about cultural history"*
> *"Yes, you can use technology to convey so that you can see what you want and see at any time. Not just when there is a lecture."*

The hands-on experience with the technology probe also helped create a scaffold and enabled participants to imagine its potential applications. This served as a springboard for structuring subsequent generative workshops. As the participants became more familiar with the technology and its applications, they also gained a deeper understanding of history from the museum educator. To further the design process, we realized we needed to devise tools and techniques that could build on this newly gained familiarity and understanding of both the historical theme and the technology's potential. The ultimate goal was to allow the student teachers to conceive of an engaging teaching activity using the technology, effectively familiarizing middle school children with their cultural heritage in a fun and easy way. Consequently, we decided to create design cards, and use them in the next co-design workshop to represent the historical themes, technological landscape, and educational requirements for such a teaching activity.

V. CONCLUSION AND FUTURE WORK

The utilization of technology probes in the pre-design stage of the co-design process proved instrumental in eliciting responses and insights from participants. The hands-on workshop allowed us to gauge the participants' familiarity with emerging technologies like AR and VR and laid the groundwork for a collaborative design process that can facilitate collaborative innovation among the stakeholders, thereby informing the design and implementation of certain tools and techniques in the subsequent stages of the co-creation process. Moving forward, further research in this area holds the potential to enrich our understanding of the role of technology probes in educational innovation and participatory design processes, ultimately contributing to the enhancement of learning experiences for students.

ACKNOWLEDGMENT

We would like to thank all the wonderful participants in schools, museums, and universities.

REFERENCES

[1] H. Hutchinson et al., 'Technology probes: inspiring design for and with families', in Proceedings of the SIGCHI Conference on Human Factors in Computing Systems, Ft. Lauderdale Florida USA: ACM, Apr. 2003, pp. 17–24. doi: 10.1145/642611.642616.

[2] F. B. M. Newaz, J. Karlsen, and J. Herstad, 'Making Technology Matter for Processes of Co-Creation and Innovation in Cross-Sectorial Collaborations', ACHI 2023, The Sixteenth International Conference on Advances in Computer-Human Interactions, Apr. 2023.

[3] E. B.-N. Sanders and P. J. Stappers, "Co-creation and the new landscapes of design," CoDesign, vol. 4, no. 1, pp. 5–18, Mar. 2008, doi: 10.1080/15710880701875068.

[4] A. Liem and E. B.-N. Sanders, "The Impact of Human-Centred Design Workshops in Strategic Design Projects," in Human Centered Design, vol. 6776, M. Kurosu, Ed., in Lecture Notes in Computer Science, vol. 6776. , Berlin, Heidelberg: Springer Berlin Heidelberg, 2011, pp. 110–119. doi: 10.1007/978-3-642-21753-1_13.

[5] B. Gaver, T. Dunne, and E. Pacenti, "Design: Cultural probes," interactions, vol. 6, no. 1, pp. 21–29, Jan. 1999, doi: 10.1145/291224.291235.

[6] K. Boehner, J. Vertesi, P. Sengers, and P. Dourish, "How HCI interprets the probes," in Proceedings of the SIGCHI Conference on Human Factors in Computing Systems, San Jose California USA: ACM, Apr. 2007, pp. 1077–1086. doi: 10.1145/1240624.1240789.

[7] T. Hemmings, K. Clarke, M. Rouncefield, A. Crabtree, and T. Rodden, "Probing the probes," in PDC, 2002, pp. 42–50.

[8] A. Voida and E. D. Mynatt, 'Conveying user values between families and designers', in CHI '05 Extended Abstracts on Human Factors in Computing Systems, Portland OR USA: ACM, Apr. 2005, pp. 2013–2016. doi: 10.1145/1056808.1057080.

[9] P. Knierim, P. W. Woźniak, Y. Abdelrahman, and A. Schmidt, "Exploring the Potential of Augmented Reality in Domestic Environments," in Proceedings of the 21st International Conference on Human-Computer Interaction with Mobile Devices and Services, Taipei Taiwan: ACM, Oct. 2019, pp. 1–12. doi: 10.1145/3338286.3340142.

[10] C. DiSalvo, P. Sengers, and H. Brynjarsdóttir, "Mapping the landscape of sustainable HCI," in Proceedings of the SIGCHI Conference on Human Factors in Computing Systems, Atlanta Georgia USA: ACM, Apr. 2010, pp. 1975–1984. doi: 10.1145/1753326.1753625.

[11] F. Kensing and J. Blomberg, "Participatory Design: Issues and Concerns," Computer Supported Cooperative Work (CSCW), vol. 7, no. 3–4, pp. 167–185, Sep. 1998, doi: 10.1023/A:1008689307411.

[12] J. Simonsen and T. Robertson, Eds., "Tools and techniques: ways to engage telling, making and enacting," in Routledge International Handbook of Participatory Design, 0 ed., Routledge, 2012, pp. 165–201. doi: 10.4324/9780203108543-14.

[13] M. Crang and I. Cook, Doing ethnographies. Los Angeles: SAGE, 2007.

[14] J. Lazar, J. H. Feng, and H. Hochheiser, Research methods in human-computer interaction, Second edition. Cambridge, MA: Elsevier, Morgan Kaufmann Publishers, 2017.

[15] J. Fereday and E. Muir-Cochrane, "Demonstrating Rigor Using Thematic Analysis: A Hybrid Approach of Inductive and Deductive Coding and Theme Development," International Journal of Qualitative Methods, vol. 5, no. 1, pp. 80–92, Mar. 2006, doi: 10.1177/160940690600500107.

[16] V. Clarke and V. Braun, "Thematic Analysis," in Encyclopedia of Critical Psychology, T. Teo, Ed., New York, NY: Springer New York, 2014, pp. 1947–1952. doi: 10.1007/978-1-4614-5583-7_311.

[17] J. Herstad and H. Holone, "Making sense of co-creative tangibles through the concept of familiarity," in Proceedings of the 7th Nordic Conference on Human-Computer Interaction: Making Sense Through Design, Copenhagen Denmark: ACM, Oct. 2012, pp. 89–98. doi: 10.1145/2399016.2399031.

[18] P. Turner and G. V. D. Walle, "Familiarity as a basis for universal design," Gerontechnology, vol. 5, no. 3, pp. 150–159, Jul. 2006, doi: 10.4017/gt.2006.05.03.004.00.

[19] M. Heidegger, Being and Time. in Library of philosophy and theology. Basil Blackwell, 1962. [Online]. Available: https://books.google.no/books?id=qLvvEAAAQBAJ,et [retrieved: May, 2024]

[20] E. B.-N. Sanders, "Scaffolds for Experiencing in the New Design Space," 2002. [Online]. Available: https://api.semanticscholar.org/CorpusID:111744729, [retrieved: May, 2024]

[21] E. B.-N. Sanders, "Scaffolds for building everyday creativity," Design for effective communications: Creating Contexts for Clarity and Meaning, pp. 65–77, 2006.

Facilitating Labs for Innovating Cross-sectorial Collaborations in Teacher Education

Kristine Høeg Karlsen
Faculty of Teacher Education and Languages
Østfold University College
Halden, Norway
kristine.h.karlsen@hiof.no

Joakim Karlsen
Faculty of Computer Science Engineering and Economics
Østfold University College
Halden, Norway
joakim.karlsen@hiof.no

Lisbet Skregelid
Faculty of Fine Arts
University of Agder
Kristiansand, Norway
lisbet.skregelid@uia.no

***Abstract*—Teacher education programs should equip future teachers with the knowledge and experience needed to engage in cross-sectorial collaborations with external partners. Within our teacher education programs, we have strategically planned and organized multiple labs to explore how such learning activities should be designed. In this article, we present and discuss the implementation and impact of the three labs from the perspective of the project leaders. By using the design choice framework for co-creation, we shed light on the decision-making process undertaken by project management to facilitate these labs as third spaces.**

Keywords: co-creation; cross-sectorial collaboration; teacher education; third space.

I. INTRODUCTION

External partners increasingly seek and gain access to Norwegian schools to provide learning activities. Examples of initiatives organized as Cross-Sectorial Collaborations (CSCs) include The Technological Schoolbag, Young Entrepreneurship, and The Cultural Schoolbag (TCS). To ensure value for both the external partner and the school, both parties need to take active roles in organizing teaching activities. The skills needed to actively participate in such collaborations need to be considered in teacher education. This increases the likelihood that student teachers will be able to create value from these partnerships as future professionals to a greater extent.

In the current article, we elucidate the findings of our research project, *pARTiciPED*, led by Østfold University College (ØUC) and funded by the Research Council of Norway. As part of this project, we have carefully planned and organized multiple interventions for student teachers to acquire new skills, perform new roles, and become confident in cooperation with external partners. The work undertaken by project leaders (management) has focused on orchestrating "co-creation processes" that emphasize active participation and mutual learning, situated in dynamic and democratic frameworks, or "third spaces" [1, s. 205]. To understand the many design choices that we have made to support the learning activities undertaken in this project, we present and discuss them according to Lee et al.'s [2] *design framework for co-creation*. The framework, with its roots in participatory design [3] and action research [4], supports the democratic values pursued in the pARTiciPED project and systematizes the main aspects that have been considered by the research team.

In the following, we examine the design and implementation of three labs where stakeholders from multiple sectors have come together to co-create courses in teacher education, with the objective of empowering student teachers in CSCs as future professionals. The following research questions guided the analysis:

What are the merits of the design choices made when implementing labs to understand and innovate CSC within teacher education?

The present article follows a six-section structure, as follows: Section II describes our empirical context—TCS—an example of CSC in teacher education. In Section III, we delve into the details of the three laboratories. The labs aimed to engage participants in dialog and co-creation. In Section IV, we gain insights into the various decisions made by project leaders to facilitate "third spaces" using the design choice framework for co-creation. Finally, Section V discusses the implications of the innovating labs for both practice and the field of research, culminating in the final remarks in Section VI.

II. THE CULTURAL SCHOOLBAG AS THE EMPIRICAL CONTEXT OF THE STUDY

In the three labs, TCS is utilized as an example of a CSC, representing the most extensive third-party collaboration with Norwegian schools. Since 2001, the program has been part of the government's culture policy, offering arts and culture to every primary and secondary school in Norway, which encompasses literature, music, visual arts, performing arts, film, and cultural heritage. Internationally, there are similar arts-in-school programs that provide arenas for pupils to experience professional arts and culture, such as the *Skapande skola* (Creative School) in Sweden, the *Lincoln Center Institute* in New York City, and *Listaleypurin* on the Faroe Islands [5][6][7]. According to Breivik and

Christophersen [6, s. 27, authors translation], these "programmes, and others in for example, Denmark, the United Kingdom, and Australia, are however less comprehensive and reach out to fewer pupils." Due to its widespread coverage, TCS stands as "one of the largest programmes in the world that aims to bring professional arts and culture to children" [8, s. 33].

Nevertheless, research indicates that teachers often perceive themselves as having limited influence on TCS activities they participate in [9], that they lack a clear understanding of their role [10], and that there is an asymmetric power relationship between schools and cultural institutions in TCS [11][12][13][14]. The tensions that may arise in connection with TCS school visits could be rooted in different perceptions of the status quo [15]. These challenges may hinder the fulfillment of the government's requirement for TCS, which clearly assigns teachers the responsibility of "enabling students to have enriching art and cultural experiences, while also deriving academic benefits from DKS visits." [40]. As a result, it is crucial to prepare future teachers to take active roles when collaborating with artists and cultural workers, thereby creating value for their pupils.

Recently, there has been a notable increase in the number of studies offering valuable insights into TCS within the context of teacher education, addressing various aspects, such as codesign [16][17], educational design [18], educational dissensus [19][20][21], and evaluations of course design [22][23][24]. However, few studies have attempted to develop concepts and principles that not only describe but also elucidate how CSCs can be facilitated in teacher education. This underscores the need for further research to advance this field.

III. THREE LABS FOR STRENGTHENING THE RESEARCH-BASED FOUNDATION FOR TEACHER EDUCATION

The three laboratories led by the three authors of this article all aimed to strengthen the research-based foundation for TCS/CSC in teacher education and thus promote change, pursuing a research strategy summarized by Lars Mathiassen as "engaged research" [25]. The three laboratories were involved in two different types of teacher education in Norway from 2021–2022.

Laboratory 1: Performing Arts (Lab Art) invited participants from teacher education, art education, and primary schools to co-create a mandatory course unit in teacher education. The unit provided fourth-year student teachers, studying to become educators for grades 1–7, with the opportunity to team up with professional art students to develop and implement a TCS-performing art project as part of their placement practice in primary schools. The first phase focused on sharing practices and finding common ground; subsequent sessions utilized a multimodal choreography-informed method to design the first parts of the course units; and the final stage centered on implementing and evaluating the course module as a whole.

Laboratory 2: Cultural heritage (Lab Museum) included an interprofessional design team with participants from teacher education, museum education, technology design education, and primary education to co-create and implement a course unit for fourth-year student teachers to becoming educators for grades 5 through 10. In the co-creation of the course unit, most of the time, they were accustomed to finding common ground and negotiating roles and making contributions to the plan and the course materials. In the course itself, the student teachers first obtained insights into the museum's collections, topics, goals, and aspirations to consider how these resources could fit with the requirements for their teaching. In the next activity, they used a design game, here using bespoke design cards, to co-create learning experiences requiring museum/school partnerships and collaboration in schools. Finally, the students tried some of these ideas in secondary schools in the county as part of their placement practice. Both the Lab Art and Lab Museum were constructed at a university college in southeastern Norway.

Laboratory 3: Visual art (Lab Dissensus)**,** which included a range of partners in a forum, was initiated in an earlier phase prior to pARTiciPED. The Forum consisted of representatives from teacher education at a university in southern Norway, a teacher, an artist, and researchers who collaborate on and discuss on a local level how the inclusion of TCS in teacher education can lead to a better integration of art in general and TCS in particular in schools. In the first phase, the students participated in a TCS visual art project. The experiences were reflected on and discussed in the Forum and influenced how the next TCS project was organized for the student teachers. Here, master's students in arts and crafts responded to and discussed observations with pupils taking part in the project. Based on that, they brought these responses to the Forum, which was used to inform further realization of the project for student teachers.

The three laboratories were organized and implemented with the aim of establishing "third spaces" where participants learned from each other through dialog and co-creation. The staging of such a *third space* aimed to invite researchers and practitioners to "come together to rehearse 'the possible'" [1, s. 205]. The notion of the third space is found in a range of writings [26][27]. In the literature on education, for example, it is used to describe the gap between the knowledge that is disseminated at school and the knowledge that students bring with them themselves [28]. Recently, the concept has been adopted in art educational contexts [21][29] to provide fresh ground for exploring the space between art and pedagogy and between artists and teachers [30][31][32].

TABLE I. THE DESIGN CHOICES FRAMEWORK FOR CO-CREATION [2]

Group	*Design choice*	*Brief explanation*
Project preconditions	Openness of the brief	Decides the degree of flexibility available for interpretation and innovation within the requirements of the design project.
	Purpose of change	Decides how the co-creation activities seek to achieve change.
	Scope of design	Scope of design decides what is to be designed in the co-creation workshops.

Group	*Design choice*	*Brief explanation*
Participants	Diversity in knowledge	Assemble participants who, collectively, encompass all the necessary knowledge and practice-based expertise relevant to the practices impacted by the co-creation.
	Differences in interests	Accommodate for differing interests between the participants.
	Distribution of power	Equalizing power asymmetries between the participants.
Co-creation events	Types of activities	Deciding types of activities.
	Setting for co-creation	Selecting the appropriate setting.
Project results	Outputs of the project	Immediate deliverables.
	Outcomes of the project	Long-term impact.

IV. FACILITATING THE LABS

To gain insights into the various decisions made by project leaders to facilitate the use of labs as third spaces, we use the *design choice framework for co-creation* developed by Lee et al. [2]. The framework comprises 10 design choices categorized into four groups (Table 1).

A. Navigating design choices for project preconditions

The design choices pertaining to project preconditions, as outlined by Lee et al. [2], is openness to the brief, purpose of the change and the scope of design. In all three labs, the project team started with a predefined brief with the clear aim of strengthening student teachers in future collaborations with the art and cultural sector. The mode of inquiry and the level of flexibility afforded were, in accordance with Lee et al. [2], limited, because there was little openness to thinking outside the box regarding the objectives and problems the laboratories were meant to address. The main reason for this was that the laboratories originated from pARTiciPED, an externally funded project, and the project leaders had received support specifically to address challenges in teacher education regarding CSC.

According to Lee et al. [2, s. 21], instigating change through co-creation activities can be directed at diverse levels (from individuals to organizations) or extend across multiple organizations. The overarching goal across all three laboratories was to make contributions to innovation processes and instigate transformative practices spanning the various sectors in the domains of art, culture, and education. In all three cases, the main purpose of change was to strengthen student teachers' ability to take new roles in TCS. Although the Lab Art and Lab Museum sought to challenge traditional roles in which artists create art and teachers handle the preparations and follow-up of TCS workshops, the Lab Dissensus chose to innovate in other novel ways and did not seek to contest these role understandings.

According to Lee et al. [2, s. 21–22], the scope of design varies from tangible components, such as service touchpoints, to more abstract and comprehensive elements, such as cross-organizational collaboration models. Across the three laboratories, we provided the materials, structure, and content for TCS learning activities where student teachers could explore multiple collaborative modes in TCS.

B. Design decisions shaping how participants were engaged

Design choices related to participants, as proposed by Lee et al. [2], encompass critical decisions regarding making room for diversity of knowledge and interests and the distribution of power in co-creation activities. In all three laboratories, essential stakeholders with expertise in their respective fields and domains actively participated. In line with Lee et al. [2, s. 22], these participants collectively possessed comprehensive knowledge about the processes they were developing, along with extensive understanding of the practices affected by their co-creations, spanning performing arts (Lab Art), cultural heritage learning (Lab Museum), and visual art (Lab Dissensus). Labs 1 and 3 included student teachers, teacher educators, teachers, and professional artists. The Lab Museum included museum educators and design researchers, in addition to student teachers, teacher educators, and teachers.

In a co-creation project, participants will "have different degrees of power because of their different knowledge levels, interests, roles, societal, and organizational backgrounds, and so on" [2, s. 23]. It is imperative for Lab leaders to thoroughly assess how various participants are engaged and accommodated in sharing their perspectives, thoughts, and reflections, irrespective of their knowledge levels, backgrounds, or roles. In the establishment of the Forum in Lab Dissensus, all involved stakeholders gained a voice in the discussion regarding how the inclusion of TCS in teacher education can enhance the integration of art, both in general and specifically within TCS. Student teachers were also provided with the opportunity to share their perspectives on the Forum, ensuring that their opinions were voiced.

Reflecting on the Lab Museum, several of the student teachers would have benefited from additional preparatory tasks and lessons in history. This would have enabled them to engage with the historical topics and material with more confidence and to motivate them to try a more equal role in relation to the museum educators. This is, of course, a well-known issue in the participatory design (PD) literature—the importance of providing training to less-knowledgeable parties in the design process to equalize power relations when they are unbalanced.

In Lab Art, all participants were afforded the opportunity to present their approaches to learning and teaching and/or to the learning and teaching of art, aiming to establish a foundation for co-creation. However, challenges arose early in the project because the participants' opportunities to influence workshop plans were not clearly articulated from the outset. When disagreements about workshop activities surfaced, the group found itself lacking the necessary tools to resolve them.

C. Facilitating effective co-creation events

The three laboratories strategically framed a range of co-creation activities to ensure that the project goals could be achieved. In the Lab Art and Lab Museum, tools and techniques from PD were chosen, while a forum was established in Lab Dissensus. Across the three laboratories, the teacher education campuses served as the main venues, but also included excursions to art institutions and museums. The Lab Art and Lab Museum utilized schools in the region as venues for experimenting with and implementing new collaborative modes for TCS production.

Exploring Lab Art, the process started with a future workshop and subsequently advanced through two full-day dialog-based workshops. During these workshops, various stakeholders shared their perspectives, theories, and methodologies. Choreopattern [16], a PD method, was then developed by the PhD candidate, together with the other teacher educators, aimed at co-creating the course unit. However, disagreements arose regarding this method, which ultimately led to its abandonment after two iterations. Subsequently, the design team convened regular meetings to develop the final days of the course. In this course, student teachers collaborated with art students to develop and implement a performing art TCS project in primary schools within the county. This involved 45 student teachers and art students, seven schoolteachers, and approximately 175 pupils. During placement practice, the design team closely followed the projects in the schools. The course concluded with a collaborative evaluation on campus, in which both art students and student teachers were invited to reflect on the completed curriculum. Subsequent iterations of the course in the following years integrated additional art forms, such as literature and film, involving new cohorts of student teachers, artists, educators, and pupils.

In the Lab Museum, the design team organized four preparatory workshops before the course, with the goal of exploring the participants' competencies and knowledge. As part of the course, the student teachers participated in three full-day workshops to plan and prepare their placement practices. The first day focused on exploring the materials provided by the museum educator, the school curriculum, and relevant AR/VR technologies for use in cultural learning designs. On the second day, they designed concepts for AR/VR learning activities using crafted design cards [17]. On the third day, they explored a prototype for engaging with historical images, together with *reacting to the past* historical role-playing framework [33]. They used all the outputs from the full-day workshops in planning and implementing multimodal cultural learning activities in their classrooms during their placement practice. Overall, approximately 70 student teachers, 15 schoolteachers, and 376 pupils were involved in this process. Similar to Lab Art, this lab persisted over the subsequent years, incorporating new art forms, students, and pupils.

In Lab 3, a forum similar to a local advisory board was established, holding regular meetings throughout the project duration. The members of Forum who were directly involved in the two TCS productions of this lab planned, realized, and discussed the initiatives and brought these discussions to the Forum meetings. During these meetings, the stakeholders had the opportunity to comment on what was shared and to contribute ideas about upcoming events. The student teachers participated in two types of TCS productions focusing on visual art [21]. This was carried out very similarly to what was done for the children in school. The responses from students taking part in the workshop contributed to how these productions were realized for the student teachers in the following years. Members of Forum and students from master's in arts and crafts who observed when carried out for pupils thought the workshop should be altered. In line with principles in action research, preliminary results from the first intervention led to an action and change in the second intervention. Approximately 300 student teachers participated in the workshops over the two years.

D. *Design choices related to project outputs*

The immediate outputs from the three labs are multifaceted. Across all three laboratories, a significant achievement was in the development of course designs that center on art and culture framed by TCS. The course designs emerged through collaborative efforts within the design teams and were subsequently integrated into the respective teacher education programs. All courses reflect knowledge, outcomes, and activities stemming from the diverse domains of the interprofessional design team. This integration was pivotal for empowering student teachers to take part in the design and implementation of TCS projects in schools together with art students (Lab Art) and museum educators and designers (Lab Museum). The present study provides valuable insights into the use of TCSs as CSCs in schools (all three laboratories).

V. DISCUSSION

In the following section, we will discuss the merit of the design choices made in facilitating three labs for strengthening future teachers in CSCs. Because the context of this contribution is a research project, we frame this according to Matthiassen's [25] framework for engaged scholarship.

A. *Contribution to practice*

A key objective of the laboratories, here aligned with Mathiassen [25, s. 19], was to ground the research in a real-world problem, specifically addressing the challenge faced by teachers who occasionally perceive a lack of influence and involvement during the TCS visits. This situation can lead them to disengage from their assigned responsibilities and encounter challenges in helping them create meaningful experiences for their pupils. In the three laboratories within the pARTiciPED project, we have strived to engage student teachers in various ways. First, on an emotional level, they are allowed to experience art and culture (Labs 1–3). Second, we provide firsthand exposure to how TCS projects can be developed through collaboration with professional artists and museum educators (Labs 1–2). The subsequent discussion will outline this in more depth.

As project leaders of the three laboratories, our initial step was to explore and identify new ways of *working* together in teacher education based on principles, methods, tools, and techniques from PD. The project thereby chose an antiauthoritarian and multivocal approach to innovation and problem solving to ensure that the experts, in our case, the teacher educators, were not the sole makers of the curriculum. Finding common ground is not always straightforward, however, and disagreements and conflicts arose because of the diverse knowledge, interests, and power dynamics among the participants in the labs.

Another essential component of our work was the establishment of TCS courses in teacher education programs as part of the three labs. In the Lab Art and Lab Museum, these courses are mandatory. Since 2021, student teachers in their fourth year (of their five-year program) have taken a one-year unit, including a placement practice, where they are required to contribute to the implementation of a real TCS project that tours schools. The course is given in collaboration with the local TCS in the municipality and involves a wide range of professional artists from various fields. In 2023/2024, students, for example, had the valuable opportunity to collaborate with the film director Carl Javér on the implementation of the documentary film "Reconstructing Utøya," [41] as well as interact with Madam Pysj, the theater troupe behind the playful production "Star Wårs (med å)" [42].

At Lab Dissensus, all student teachers in year three participate in TCS workshops on campus, which are carried out in the same way as for pupils in school. As part of the course, the student teachers were invited to reflect on and discuss their participation in TCS workshops. Examples of production include "Tapeorama" (orig. Tapeorama) workshops in 2021 (21) and "To build new buildings" (orig. "Å bygge nye bygg") in 2022. It is worth mentioning that the course is part of an interdisciplinary holistic framework that covers various subjects to ensure that teachers gain relevant knowledge beyond their specific subjects.

The courses that have been developed as part of Lab 1-3 have both gained national recognition [34] and have raised awareness among other teacher educators [35][36]. Furthermore, the activities undertaken across the three laboratories have contributed to several articles, sparking fresh insights into our understanding of CSC within the context of teacher education [16][17][21][24][36]-[39].

B. Contribution to the field of research

When we conceptualized the pARTiciPED project, our intention was for the laboratories to contribute knowledge that extends beyond the immediate context of the co-creation activities (the local workshops conducted during Labs 1–3). Thus, these laboratories can be viewed as a scientific inquiry approach, generating new knowledge and contributions to a broader *area of concern* [25, s. 19]. As proposed by Mathiassen [25, s. 25], this area should align with the context of the problem, allowing for a two-way knowledge contribution from the area to the problem and from data collected in the setting to the area. The three laboratories in pARTiciPED have significantly deepened our understanding of three key areas: i) cross-sector collaboration, ii) interprofessional practice, and iii) the role of art within schools. Following this, we elaborate further on the particular contributions made by these labs, which can serve as a foundational basis for enhancing teacher education.

First, our laboratory provides a clear contribution to understanding how *CSC* can be understood in the context of teacher education. The labs provided knowledge about the organizational context, including frameworks, opportunities, and challenges for new collaborative models to emerge in TCS. The active forward oriented facilitation of co-creation activities supported new modes of collaboration that articulated how such modes could and should be supported.

Second, our labs contribute to how we perceive *interprofessional practice* in teacher education. The labs provide insights into the goals, values, and skills of all stakeholders (i.e., student teachers, artists, arts educators, cultural workers, and teacher educators) and how these matter in developing new interprofessional practices in teacher education. Furthermore, we have learned about co-creation as a process and collaborative model, explored resources and conditions (opposition and collaboration forces), communication, and, importantly, role understanding in interprofessional collaboration.

Third, our labs contribute to understanding the role of art in schools. The labs have provided insight into how TCS program can enrich *art education* and inform the implementation of aesthetic approaches to teaching, highlighting opportunities and challenges within teacher education. Lab Dissensus, for example, contributes to what could be referred to as the pedagogy of dissensus, an arts-based pedagogy informed by the dissensual and what can be referred to as the disturbing characteristics of art [29]. At Lab Dissensus, discussions about what art can offer education are initiated. The student´s experiences often center around how art, with its processual and open-ended character, has the possibility to challenge existing norms and habits and contributes to new ways of seeing oneself, others, and one's surroundings. Placing art at the center and enabling dissensus in education can contribute to a contrast to the dominating policy led by economic ambition and competition.

VI. CONCLUSION AND FUTURE WORK

In pARTiciPED, we explored core concepts and principles to elucidate how CSCs can be effectively organized and implemented to empower student teachers to be confident, interested in, and actively engaged in such collaborations. In this article, drawing upon Lee et al.'s [2] design choice framework, we explored how CSCs in teacher education, particularly centered on TCS as the main platform, can be organized and planned within interprofessional teams comprising stakeholders from the education and cultural sectors to provide student teachers with the knowledge and experience needed to take more active roles in TCS. Across all three labs, various TCS productions have either been developed or refined to align with the context of teacher education. Through this work, we have developed a critical understanding of how co-creation activities, facilitated as "third spaces" [1, s. 205], can strengthen the research-based foundations for teaching CSC in teacher education.

Future research can take two distinct directions. First, future research can contribute by providing concrete tools and techniques that project leaders can employ in the case of conflicts. Such contributions would be valuable additions to Lee's [2] design choice framework. Second, research can enhance our understanding of laboratories as a research methodology; this involves delving into the fundamental essence—the ontological and epistemological foundations—of utilizing co-creation labs as a research approach. Only by doing so can laboratories become dynamic spaces where future teachers forge the knowledge and experience necessary to actively participate in CSC to the advantage of students in school.

ACKNOWLEDGMENTS

We express our gratitude to the Norwegian Research Council and our own institutions for funding the pARTiciPED project (no. 301594).

REFERENCES

[1] E. Brandt, T. Binder, and E. B.-N. Sanders, "Tools and Techniques: Ways to engage telling, making and enacting", in *Routledge international handbook of participatory design*, J. Simonsen and T. Robertson, Red., London: Routledge, 2013, p. 145–181.

[2] J.-J. Lee, M. Jaatinen, A. Salmi, T. Mattelmäki, R. Smeds, and M. Holopainen, "Design choices framework for co-creation projects", *Int. J. Des.*, bd. 12, no. 2, 2018.

[3] F. Kensing and J. Greenbaum, "Heritage:having a say", in *Routledge international handbook of participatory design*, J. Simonsen and T. Robertson, Eds., London: Routledge, 2013, p. 21–37.

[4] P. Reason and H. Bradbury, "Introduction", in *The Sage Handbook of Action Research. Participative Inquiry and Practice*, P. Reason and H. Bradbury, Red., London: Sage Publications, 2008, p. 1–10.

[5] J.-K. Breivik and C. Christophersen, "The Cultural Schoolbag - an exploratory note" [orig. "Den kulturelle skolesekken - et utredningsnotat"], Stein Rokkan Centre for Social Studies, Working paper, oct. 2012. https://norceresearch.brage.unit.no/norceresearch-xmlui/handle/1956/7825. Retreived May 1th 2024. Retreived April 13rd 2024

[6] J.-K. Breivik, "The Battle for Art: Artists' Experiences" [orig. "Kampen om kunsten: kunstneres erfaringer"[. In J.-*K*. Breivik and C. Christophersen (Eds), *The Cultural Schoolbag* [orig. *Den Kulturelle skolesekken*], p. 154–178, 2013. Oslo, Bergen: Kulturrådet Fagbokforlaget

[7] L. Rykkja and A. Homme, "Passionate and Enthusiastic: The Cultural Schoolbag's Cheerleading Team" [orig. "Heftig og begeistret: Den kulturelle skolesekkens heiagjeng"]. In J.-*K*. Breivik and C. Christophersen (Eds), *The Cultural Schoolbag* [orig. *Den Kulturelle skolesekken*], p. 85–105, 2013. Oslo, Bergen: Kulturrådet Fagbokforlaget.

[8] A. Bamford, "Arts and cultural education in Norway", Norwegian Centre for Arts and Culture in Education [Nasjonalt senter for kunst og kultur i opplæringen]. Bodø, 2012.

[9] I. Digranes, "The Cultural Schoolbag: narratives and myths of educational practice in DKS projects within the subject art and crafts" [orig. "Den kulturelle skulesekken : narratives and myths of educational practice in DKS projects within the subject art and crafts", PhD, AHO, Oslo, 2009. https://aho.brage.unit.no/aho-xmlui/handle/11250/93038. Retreived December 8th 2020.

[10] K. Holdhus and M. Espeland, "School and Concert - from Dissemination to Dialogue (DiSko): Production Report" [orig. "Skole og konsert - frå formidling til dialog (DiSko): Produksjosrapport", Center for Creativities, Arts and Science in Education (CASE), CASE 2018/1, 2018. https://hvlopen.brage.unit.no/hvlopen-xmlui/handle/11250/2651977. Retreived December 8th 2020.

[11] E. Aslaksen, J. S. Borgen, and A. T. Kjørholt, "The Cultural Schoolbag – Research, Development, and Evaluation" [orig. "Den kulturelle skolesekken – forskning, utvikling og evaluering"], aug. 2003. https://nifu.brage.unit.no/nifu-xmlui/handle/11250/280512. Retreived April 13th 2024.

[12] J. S. Borgen and S. S. Brandt, "Extraordinary or Ordinary? Evaluation of The Cultural Schoolbag in Schools" [orig. "Ekstraordinært eller selvfølgelig? Evaluering av Den kulturelle skolesekken i grunnskolen"], NIFU STEP, NIFU STEP-rapport 5–2006, sep. 2006. https://nifu.brage.unit.no/nifu-xmlui/handle/11250/275575. Retreived March 30 2020.

[13] C. Christophersen, J.-K. Breivik, A. D. Homme, and L. H. Rykkja, "The cultural rucksack. A national programme for arts and culture in Norwegian schools". Bergen: Fagbokforlaget, 2015.

[14] E. S. Hauge, V. S. Knutsen, and M. R. Ervik, "Closeness, Autonomy, and Democratization: Evaluation of the Direct Municipality Scheme in The Cultural Schoolbag" [orig. "Nærhet, autonomi og demokratisering: Evaluering av direktekommuneordningen i Den Kulturelle Skolesekken"], Oxford Research, Oslo, 2017. https://oxfordresearch.no/publications/naerhet-autonomi-og-demokratisering/ Retreived December 8th 2020.

[15] Oxford Research, "Investigation of DKS and Arts for Young Audiences Norway" [orig. "Utredning av DKS og Kulturtanken"], Kultu- og likestillingsdepartementet, Report, mar. 2023. https://www.regjeringen.no/no/dokumenter/utredning-av-dks-og-kulturtanken/id2970673/. Retreived April 13 2024.

[16] F. Devonas Hoffmann and K. H. Karlsen, "Choreographic Infrastructuring for Design Things: A New Method for Participatory Design in Teacher Education", in *Proceedings of the Participatory Design Conference 2022 - Volume 1*, i PDC '22. New York, NY, USA: Association for Computing Machinery, aug. 2022, p. 230–240. doi: 10.1145/3536169.3537796.

[17] F. B. M. Newaz, J. Karlsen, and J. Herstad, "Making Technology Matter for Processes of Co-Creation and Innovation in Cross-Sectorial Collaborations", *ACHI 2023: The Sixteenth International Conference on Advances in Computer-Human Interactions* (ACHI). International Academy, Research and Industry Association (IARIA), p. 9–16, 2023.

[18] T. P. Østern, A.-L. Bakken, A. Lund, A. G. Sørum, C. Myhre, and C. W. Nesse, "Arts, crafts, and dance - developing aesthetic learning processes in arts and crafts through a general teacher education and higher dance education collaboration", *Dance Articulated*, bd. 9, nr. 1, Art. nr. 1, Dec.. 2023, doi: 10.5324/da.v9i1.5061.

[19] L. Skregelid, "Tensed possibilities: The Cultural Schoolbag as dissensus in teacher education", *Några Nord. Nedslag*, p. 47, 2020.

[20] L. Skregelid, "Encounters with the World through Cultural Schoolbag Workshops for Teacher Students", *Nord. J. Art Res.*, bd. 10, no. 2, Art. no. 2, may 2021, doi: 10.7577/information.4449.

[21] L. Skregelid, "The Cultural Schoolbag as Dissent and the Significance of Art in Teacher Education" [orig. "Den kulturelle skolesekken som dissens og kunstens betydning i lærerutdanningen"], *FormAkademisk*, bd. 16, nr. 2, Art. no. 2, Jan.. 2023, doi: 10.7577/formakademisk.4806.

[22] K. H. Karlsen and G. B. Bjørnstad, "Artistic Pedagogical Encounters in Teacher Education: A Study of Teacher Students' Perceptions of the Dance Art Project KROM Across Primary School Teacher Education" [orig. "Kunstpedagogiske møter i lærerutdanningen:–en studie av lærerstudenters oppfatning av dansekunstprosjektet KROM på tvers i grunnskolelærerutdanningen"], i *Skaperglede, engasjement og utforskertrang. Nye perspektiver på estetiske-& tverrfaglige undervisningsmetoder i pedagogisk virksomhet.* Oslo: Universitetsforlaget, 2019.

[23] K. H. Karlsen, G. B. Bjørnstad, and H. R. Høeg, "Magic in Movements! The art of teaching creative dance through the cultural schoolbag". In C.S. Nielsen & S. Burridge (Eds.) *Dancing Across Borders Perspectives on Dance, Young People and Change*, p. 179–182. Oxon / New York: Routledge.

[24] G. B. Bjørnstad and K. H. Karlsen, "An artful encounter with dance – empowering future teachers in cross-sectoral collaborations with the

Cultural Schoolbag as an example", *Dance Articulated*, bd. 9, no. 1, Art. nr. 1, Dec. 2023, doi: 10.5324/da.v9i1.5068.

[25] L. Mathiassen, "Designing Engaged Scholarship: From Real-World Problems to Research Publications", *Engaged Manag. Rev.*, bd. 1, nr. 1, jun. 2017, doi: 10.28953/2375-8643.1000.

[26] H. Bhabha og J. Rutherford, "Interview with Homi Bhabha: the third space", *Identity Community Cult. Differ.*, p. 207–221, 1990.

[27] E. W. Soja, "Thirdspace: Journeys to Los Angeles and other Real-and-Imagined Places", *Cap. Cl.*, bd. 22, no. 1, p. 137–139, mar. 1998, doi: 10.1177/030981689806400112.

[28] L. K. Maniotes, "The transformative power of literary third space", PhD, University of Colorado at Boulder, 2005. https://search.proquest.com/openview/d9a6e1ed86b63d6ea9ed7c8320 28c4f1/1?pq-origsite=gscholar&cbl=18750&diss=y. Retreived April 13 2024.

[29] L. Skregelid, "Dissens and Sensibility: Why Art Matters in Education". Intellect Discover, 2024. https://intellectdiscover.com/content/books/9781789389838. Retreived April 13 2024

[30] K. D. Gutiérrez, "Developing a Sociocritical Literacy in the Third Space", *Read. Res. Q.*, bd. 43, no. 2, p. 148–164, 2008, doi: 10.1598/RRQ.43.2.3.

[31] E. J. Klein, M. Taylor, C. Onore, K. Strom, and L. Abrams, "Exploring Inquiry in the Third Space: Case Studies of a Year in an Urban Teacher-Residency Program", *New Educ.*, bd. 12, no. 3, p. 243–268, jul. 2016, doi: 10.1080/1547688X.2016.1187980.

[32] K. Zeichner, "Rethinking the Connections Between Campus Courses and Field Ezperiences in College- and University-Based Teacher Education", *J. Teach. Educ.*, bd. 61, no. 1–2, p. 89–99, Jan. 2010, doi: 10.1177/0022487109347671.

[33] E. C. Watson and T. C. Hagood, Red., "Playing to Learn with Reacting to the Past". Palgrave Macmillan, 2018. https://link.springer.com/book/10.1007/978-3-319-61747-3. Retreived April 14 2024.

[34] M. Glanville, M. "The Cultural Schoolbag into Teacher Education" [orig. "Den kulturelle skolesekken inn i lærerutdanningen". Kulturtanken, June 7th. 2022. https://www.kulturtanken.no/aktuelt/2022/den-kulturelle-skolesekken-inn-i-laererutdanningen/. Retreived April 15th 2024.

[35] L. Skregelid, L. and I. Willbergh, "The Significance of Coercion and Freedom in Teacher Students' Encounters with The Cultural Schoolbag" [orig. "Betydningen av tvang og frihet i lærerstudenters møter med Den kulturelle skolesekken"]. Fagseminar: Løsninger? Den kulturelle skolesekken på lærerutdanningene. Kulturtanken, Oct. 19th 2023. Oslo. https://www.kulturtanken.no/kalender/2023/losninger-den-kulturelle-skolesekken-pa-laererutdanningene/ Retreived April 15th 2024.

[36] G. B. Bjørnstad, K. H. Karlsen, and A. M. Andersen. Vi er alltid der som støtte: Lærerstudenters erfaringer med kunstmøter i utdanningen. Fagseminar: Løsninger? Fagseminar: Løsninger? Den kulturelle skolesekken på lærerutdanningene. Kulturtanken, Oct. 19th 2023. Oslo. https://www.kulturtanken.no/kalender/2023/losninger-den-kulturelle-skolesekken-pa-laererutdanningene/ Retreived April 15th 2024.

[37] K. H. Karlsen, J. Karlsen, and S. K. Stigberg. "Transprofessional course design in teacher education". ACHI-COCREATE: Design Practices for Co-Creation and Learning. May 26, 2024 to May 30, 2024 - Barcelona, Spain. The Seventeenth International Conference on Advances in Computer-Human Interactions.

[38] G. C. Motzfeldt and K. H. Karlsen. « Educating Student Teachers for Interprofessional Collaboration through the Codesign of Cultural Heritage with the Use of Augmented Reality (AR) Technology". ACHI-COCREATE: Design Practices for Co-Creation and Learning. May 26, 2024 to May 30, 2024 - Barcelona, Spain. The Seventeenth International Conference on Advances in Computer-Human Interactions.

[39] F. Devonas Hoffmann. Learning to navigate in the unknown: attuning to affordances in artist visits in schools. 2024. *Pedagogy, Culture & Society*, 1-18. https://www.tandfonline.com/doi/epdf/10.1080/14681366.2024.2338 810?needAccess=true. Retreived May 10th 2024.

[40] Authors translation of the schools and teachers mandate in TCS at "The Norwegian Directorate for Education and Training" (UDIR): https://www.udir.no/laring-og-trivsel/lareplanverket/stotte/den-kulturelle-skolesekken/ Retreived May 9th 2024.

[41] C. Javér, (2018). "Rekonstruksjon Utøya". FilmCamp. https://www.filmcamp.no/produksjoner/rekonstruksjon-utoya.

[42] Madam Pysj: https://www.madampysj.no/reportoire/star-wars.

User-Centric Mobile Application for Long-Term Data Collection: Design and Strategy

Ann-Charlott Beatrice Amundsen Karlsen
Faculty of Computer Science, Engineering and Economics
Østfold University College
1757 Halden, Norway
e-mail: ann.c.karlsen@hiof.no

Abstract— **This paper presents a work in progress on the design and development of a user-centered mobile application intended for data collection in Randomized Controlled Trials (RCTs) and longitudinal studies. Focusing on the future implementation of gamification and other engagement strategies, this project aims to mitigate survey fatigue—a significant challenge in sustained data collection efforts. The proposed application will incorporate user involvement throughout its design and development to ensure features that promote consistent and reliable data submission, thereby aiming to reduce the necessity for data imputation and minimize attrition bias. The paper outlines anticipated elements critical to the success of the application, including questionnaire design, strategic incentive usage, and adaptation of surveys to align with user preferences and technological interfaces. Through a planned iterative design and testing process, involving A/B testing and focus group evaluations, the study will seek to determine effective methods for user involvement and develop a mobile tool that closely meets the needs of both researchers and participants.**

Keywords-Survey Fatigue; Gamification; Data Collection; Mobile Application Design and Development; User-Centered Design

I. INTRODUCTION

This paper explores theory and concepts to consider into the planning stages of the development of a mobile application centered around user involvement, aimed at enhancing the quality and consistency of data collection for research purposes, particularly where standardized questionnaires are used to collect quantitative data over a longer period. The essence of our approach lies in the hypothesis that incorporating user feedback and involvement throughout the development process will significantly boost the frequency and reliability of data submission from study participants. By doing so, we anticipate a reduction in the need for data imputation, a decrease in attrition bias, and the maintenance of statistical power, thereby preserving the integrity and longitudinal insight of the study.

Randomized Controlled Trials (RCTs) and longitudinal studies rely on participants to complete and return questionnaires over extended periods. This fundamental requirement remains unchanged whether the data collection is via traditional pen-and-paper methods or through digital forms. Inadequate compliance and incomplete surveys lead to several challenges, including missing data, necessitated data imputation, attrition bias, diminished statistical power, and potentially, an increase in project costs and resource utilization [1][2].

There are numerous web and mobile application solutions available for data collection, catering to various user groups including domain experts and general users, such as healthcare apps. The purpose of these solutions varies based on the technology employed and the involvement of stakeholders. For instance, health apps are commonly utilized for self-assessment. Enabling users to monitor diverse health metrics like heart rate, stress levels, sleep patterns, activity levels, and food and water consumption [3]. Much of this data is seamlessly collected through wearables such as smartwatches, activity trackers, and the latest addition, activity rings [4]. Meaning that collecting data through wearables eliminates the need for manual input from the user. However, the potential of wearables as a data collection tool in research can be restricted by privacy regulations like General Data Protection Regulation GDPR [5], and the high costs associated with providing participants with devices like smartwatches.

This paper aims to explore different methodologies for designing a user-centric mobile application tailored for data collection in research settings. We aim to investigate different strategies for involving users in the development process and how to motivate and encourage to regularly and timely submit data, which is crucial for the success of longitudinal studies and RCTs.

This paper is structured as follows: Section II delves into the theoretical framework, focusing on gamification and questionnaire design, and explores how these elements can enhance user engagement and reduce survey fatigue. Section III discusses practical strategies for involving users in the research process and addresses the challenges encountered in survey design to engage users effectively. Finally, Section IV provides an overview of future work, detailing further research on questionnaire design and the use of gamification to improve response rates and data integrity.

II. THEORY

This section explores the theoretical foundations focusing on gamification and questionnaire design, which are central to the development of our mobile application for data collection in controlled studies. This insight aims to deepen our understanding of how gamification can enhance user engagement and how effectively designed questionnaires can mitigate survey fatigue, thereby improving data quality and participant retention in RCTs and longitudinal studies. By analyzing existing literature and outcomes from previous research, we seek to identify and integrate the most effective practices and innovative approaches from these areas. Emphasizing gamification, we will examine how game-like elements can motivate and maintain participant interest over time. In terms of questionnaire design, we will consider various strategies to ensure clarity, reduce bias, and enhance the overall user experience, thereby ensuring high-quality data collection tailored to our research needs.

A. Gamification

Gamification is a method that has become popular across various domains, including education at both primary and tertiary levels [6][7], as well as in self-assessment and health applications [8]. Additionally, gamification elements have even been integrated into various gaming platforms to motivate and encourage users to engage in gameplay. Examples of this is awarding players with trophies for different playing styles or for in-game achievements [9].

Gamification is frequently employed in subjects that demand logical thinking and problem-solving skills, particularly within STEM disciplines, such as mathematics and programming [10][11]. This approach has been shown to motivate students by presenting challenging and abstract concepts through mediums they are more familiar with, such as games [12] [13]. The incorporation of game-like elements, including rewards, points, trophies and badges, leverages the concept of "positive reinforcement," thereby enhancing student motivation. This strategy capitalizes on the inherent human response to rewards, as detailed in psychological research on positive reinforcement [14]. By rewarding students for their achievements, gamification in educational contexts encourages engagement and persistence in learning, making difficult subjects more accessible and enjoyable.

Gamification elements have increasingly been integrated into health and self-assessment mobile applications [15], creating engaging and motivational aspects found in different game elements. Acknowledging the inherent challenges of maintaining a healthy lifestyle and engaging in regular exercise these apps utilize gamification strategies to make the process more appealing and rewarding. Through challenges and reward systems, like being awarded stars and badges for completing specific tasks or reaching goals, users find it more motivating to reach their health objectives [16]. Leveling systems which reward users with various benefits as they progress to higher levels are also a familiar element in health apps, ranging from step counters to water consumption trackers.

Level and bonus systems isn't limited to health applications but also extends to other sectors, including booking platforms and numerous other service-oriented applications, demonstrating the broad applicability of gamification strategies. Furthermore, these apps often employ mechanisms of loss aversion, a psychological principle suggesting that the fear of losing is more compelling than the prospect of gaining [17]. By "punishing" users through the removal of benefits, level down-grade or the breaking of "streaks," apps tap into this aversion to loss, compelling users to stick to the app's requirements to maintain or enhance their status, levels, points, or other forms of rewards [18][19]. Indicating that the use of both positive reinforcement and negative reinforcement creates a powerful motivator for users to engage regularly with the apps.

B. Questionnaire design

Crafting a questionnaire or survey that yields reliable and unbiased responses is a nuanced psychological science [20]. The formulation, presentation, context, and language of questions can significantly influence how participants respond [21]. How questions are phrased and their placement within the survey can also impact how participants respond to other previous or later questions, called "order-effect bias" [22]. Research on survey methodology shows that small changes in question formulation can lead to significantly different answers [21].

UserGuiding identifies five types of survey fatigue: 1) Questionnaire fatigue, 2) Frequency fatigue, 3) Repetition fatigue, 4) Design fatigue, and 5) Incentive fatigue. These factors, including lengthy and complex questionnaires, survey frequency, repetitive questions, poor design, and incentive-driven responses, can overwhelm users and affect the quality of survey responses, potentially leading to biased results [23].

Bias can be introduced into surveys through various means, including participant recruitment, questionnaire design, and the way questions are posed. Similar to how survey fatigue affects participants, different types of biases can impact data collection, such as sampling bias, non-response bias, acquiescence bias, social desirability bias, question order bias, and interview bias [24]. Effective measures to mitigate these biases include avoiding leading questions, using interview guides, maintaining respondent anonymity, and providing the option to skip questions. Being able to skip questions has been shown to prevent users from quitting mid-process.

Additionally, it's crucial to ensure that surveys are compatible with various browsers and systems to prevent non-response bias and facilitate comprehensive data collection. Inaccessible or unreadable surveys can lead to significant data loss. Therefore, conducting a test round where surveys are sent to different emails and opened in various apps and browsers can help identify and prevent potential issues before the actual dispatch.

III. Discussion

In this section of the paper, we will discuss and ideate around how users can be involved in the project, identifying specific stages where their input is crucial. The research indicates that survey fatigue could be a primary reason for reduced participant motivation. Therefore, it's essential to strategically involve users where feasible. However, there are constraints, such as the formulation of questions, where user input is limited due to the standardized nature of the questionnaires planned for the study. The challenges associated with question frequency and repetition are significant, especially since the study aims to measure changes over an extended period, requiring participants to complete the same survey weekly. While the structure and frequency of the surveys are fixed to meet the study's objectives, this setup presents an excellent opportunity for user involvement in designing app features that could help mitigate typical survey fatigue issues. This involvement can enhance user engagement and potentially improve the quality and consistency of the data collected.

The list below presents some of the key elements and focus points we must consider and further research continuing the project before development:

- Question bias.
- Survey fatigue.
- Design layout and instructions.
- False participants, only there for gifts.

Working with the hypotheses that incorporating user feedback into the design and functionality of the tool is essential for enhancing participant engagement and mitigating survey fatigue. One effective strategy to keep participants motivated throughout the study is the integration of game-like elements. Previous research has demonstrated that gamification can significantly enhance motivation and engagement. In determining the specific game-like elements to incorporate the involvement of potential participants is key. Actively engaging them in this process allows for a design that is more effectively tailored to their preferences and needs, which in turn boosts their overall engagement with the mobile application [25]. Techniques such as loss aversion and positive reinforcements including leveling, rewards, and bonuses have been shown to be effective. Exploring the incorporation of these elements in the way incentives are given or achieved could be a valuable strategy to enhance participant interaction and satisfaction.

However, careful consideration should be given to the use of incentives, ensuring they are appropriate for the target group to avoid attracting participants who are not genuinely interested in the study or rushing participants to "just answer something". Sharing insights with participants about how their responses are used can also reinforce the value of their contributions, enhancing their engagement and willingness to participate [23].

Effective survey design is also essential. Surveys should have clear instructions, easy navigation, and a user-friendly layout. Conducting A/B testing on different survey designs can help identify the most effective elements that enhance user experience and response rates. Deciding when, how often, and where surveys are administered is another critical factor. Utilizing focus groups can provide insights into the preferences and aversions of potential participants, helping to plan survey delivery that minimizes disturbance and annoyance. This strategic involvement of users at various stages not only helps in tailoring the survey experience to their needs but also ensures that the tool developed is user-centered and effective.

IV. Conclusion and Future Work

This paper explores the preliminary planning for the design and development process for a mobile application aimed at enhancing data collection in controlled studies, specifically RCTs and longitudinal trials. The primary objective is to reduce data loss caused by participant dropout or response failure. By gathering insight into various theories and concepts, such as gamification we explored how we can better motivate participants to stay engaged and consistently report data. It is evident the theoretical frameworks that studies involving data collection through surveys are susceptible to survey fatigue. This paper examines the factors contributing to survey fatigue and discusses strategies for involving users in the design process to mitigate these risks.

Several key features and design elements require additional research before proceeding with development. Future plans involve further investigation and usability testing focused on questionnaire design, particularly how different biases can be minimized through strategic layout and question presentation. Preliminary research suggests that allowing participants to skip questions could prevent them from abandoning the survey midway. We intend to explore this aspect through A/B split testing and interviews to assess the potential impacts on data integrity when participants have the option to skip and return to questions.

Additionally, gamification has shown promise in enhancing user engagement across various platforms. Moving forward, we will investigate how to integrate gamification effectively into the research data collection application to encourage frequent and consistent participant responses. Another area of interest is the integration of incentives into reward and leveling systems, ensuring they do not inadvertently prompt participants to rush through responses, thereby compromising data quality.

References

[1] P. Cummings, 'Missing Data and Multiple Imputation', *JAMA Pediatr*, vol. 167, no. 7, p. 656, Jul. 2013, doi: 10.1001/jamapediatrics.2013.1329.

[2] J. Engels, 'Imputation of missing longitudinal data: a comparison of methods', *Journal of Clinical Epidemiology*, vol. 56, no. 10, pp. 968–976, Oct. 2003, doi: 10.1016/S0895-4356(03)00170-7.

[3] J. Liang *et al.*, 'Usability Study of Mainstream Wearable Fitness Devices: Feature Analysis and System Usability Scale Evaluation', *JMIR Mhealth Uhealth*, vol. 6, no. 11, p. e11066, Nov. 2018, doi: 10.2196/11066.

[4] M. Asgari Mehrabadi *et al.*, 'Sleep Tracking of a Commercially Available Smart Ring and Smartwatch Against Medical-Grade Actigraphy in Everyday Settings: Instrument Validation Study', *JMIR Mhealth Uhealth*, vol. 8, no. 10, p. e20465, Nov. 2020, doi: 10.2196/20465.

[5] V. Vijayan, J. P. Connolly, J. Condell, N. McKelvey, and P. Gardiner, 'Review of Wearable Devices and Data Collection Considerations for Connected Health', *Sensors*, vol. 21, no. 16, p. 5589, Aug. 2021, doi: 10.3390/s21165589.

[6] S. D. Prykhodchenko, O. Yu. Prykhodchenko, O. S. Shevtsova, and S. Yu. Semenov, 'Gamification of Learning Scratch in Elementary School', p. 11 pages, 637204 bytes, 2020, doi: 10.4230/OASICS.ICPEC.2020.20.

[7] Z. Zhan, L. He, Y. Tong, X. Liang, S. Guo, and X. Lan, 'The effectiveness of gamification in programming education: Evidence from a meta-analysis', *Computers and Education: Artificial Intelligence*, vol. 3, p. 100096, 2022, doi: 10.1016/j.caeai.2022.100096.

[8] H.-M. Kim, I. Cho, and M. Kim, 'Gamification Aspects of Fitness Apps: Implications of mHealth for Physical Activities', *International Journal of Human–Computer Interaction*, vol. 39, no. 10, pp. 2076–2089, Jun. 2023, doi: 10.1080/10447318.2022.2073322.

[9] G. Richter, D. R. Raban, and S. Rafaeli, Studying gamification: The effect of rewards and incentives on motivation. Springer, 2015.

[10] P. Andrade, E. L.-C. Law, J. C. Farah, and D. Gillet, 'Evaluating the Effects of Introducing Three Gamification Elements in STEM Educational Software for Secondary Schools', in *32nd Australian Conference on Human-Computer Interaction*, Sydney NSW Australia: ACM, Dec. 2020, pp. 220–232. doi: 10.1145/3441000.3441073.

[11] E. Elmawati, B. A. P. Martadiputra, and C. M. Samosir, 'Gamification Research Focus in Learning Mathematics', in *2023 The 5th World Symposium on Software Engineering (WSSE)*, Tokyo Japan: ACM, Sep. 2023, pp. 142–149. doi: 10.1145/3631991.3632012.

[12] R. Kasahara, K. Sakamoto, H. Washizaki, and Y. Fukazawa, 'Applying Gamification to Motivate Students to Write High-Quality Code in Programming Assignments', in *Proceedings of the 2019 ACM Conference on Innovation and Technology in Computer Science Education*, Aberdeen Scotland Uk: ACM, Jul. 2019, pp. 92–98. doi: 10.1145/3304221.3319792.

[13] H. Ying, 'The Application of Game Teaching Method in the Course of "Web Design and Production" in the Teaching Project', in *2021 2nd International Conference on Education Development and Studies*, Hilo HI USA: ACM, Mar. 2021, pp. 55–62. doi: 10.1145/3459043.3459054.

[14] S. A. Macdonald and S. Brewster, 'Gamification of a To-Do List with Emotional Reinforcement', in *Extended Abstracts of the 2019 CHI Conference on Human Factors in Computing Systems*, Glasgow Scotland Uk: ACM, May 2019, pp. 1–6. doi: 10.1145/3290607.3313060.

[15] L. Sardi, A. Idri, and J. L. Fernández-Alemán, 'A systematic review of gamification in e-Health', *Journal of Biomedical Informatics*, vol. 71, pp. 31–48, Jul. 2017, doi: 10.1016/j.jbi.2017.05.011.

[16] S. Al-Rayes *et al.*, 'Gaming elements, applications, and challenges of gamification in healthcare', *Informatics in Medicine Unlocked*, vol. 31, p. 100974, 2022, doi: 10.1016/j.imu.2022.100974.

[17] 'Loss aversion', The Decision Lab. Accessed: Apr. 15, 2024. [Online]. Available: https://thedecisionlab.com/biases/loss-aversion

[18] N. Bandeira Romão Tomé, M. Klarkowski, C. Gutwin, C. Phillips, R. L. Mandryk, and A. Cockburn, 'Risking Treasure: Testing Loss Aversion in an Adventure Game', in *Proceedings of the Annual Symposium on Computer-Human Interaction in Play*, Virtual Event Canada: ACM, Nov. 2020, pp. 306–320. doi: 10.1145/3410404.3414250.

[19] Y. Lin, J. Wang, Z. Luo, S. Li, Y. Zhang, and B. C. Wünsche, 'Dragon Hunter: Loss Aversion for Increasing Physical Activity in AR Exergames', in *2023 Australasian Computer Science Week*, Melbourne VIC Australia: ACM, Jan. 2023, pp. 212–221. doi: 10.1145/3579375.3579403.

[20] J. A. Krosnick, 'Questionnaire Design', in *The Palgrave Handbook of Survey Research*, D. L. Vannette and J. A. Krosnick, Eds., Cham: Springer International Publishing, 2018, pp. 439–455. doi: 10.1007/978-3-319-54395-6_53.

[21] 1615 L. St NW, S. 800 Washington, and D. 20036 U.-419-4300 | M.-857-8562 | F.-419-4372 | M. Inquiries, 'Writing Survey Questions', Pew Research Center. Accessed: Apr. 15, 2024. [Online]. Available: https://www.pewresearch.org/our-methods/u-s-surveys/writing-survey-questions/

[22] W. D. Perreault, 'Controlling Order-Effect Bias', *The Public Opinion Quarterly*, vol. 39, no. 4, pp. 544–551, 1975.

[23] H. Çökeli, 'Fighting Survey Fatigue: Types, Examples & Best Practices', UserGuiding. Accessed: Apr. 15, 2024. [Online]. Available: https://userguiding.com/blog/survey-fatigue/

[24] quantilope, '6 Types of Survey Biases and How To Avoid Them'. Accessed: Apr. 15, 2024. [Online]. Available: https://www.quantilope.com/resources/glossary-six-types-of-survey-biases-and-how-to-avoid

[25] 'What is User Centered Design (UCD)?', The Interaction Design Foundation. Accessed: Mar. 11, 2024. [Online]. Available: https://www.interaction-design.org/literature/topics/user-centered-design

Rules of Play to Balance Ideation and Decision Making in Co-design Games

Tina Helene Bunæs, Michelle Husebye, Joakim Karlsen
Department of Computer Science and Communication,
Faculty of Computer Science, Engineering and Economics,
Østfold University College,
1757 Halden, Norway
Tina.h.bunas@hiof.no, Michelle.husebye@hiof.no, Joakim.karlsen@hiof.no

Abstract—**Virtual simulations for medical training and learning should be designed together with expert users to ensure that the digital learning environment reflects the complexity of their practice. Practitioners and educators are often brought into the design process only to validate prototypes, which can leave the final application unfitting to the practice it is intended to support. In this paper, we explore how a generative design game can support medical educators to make meaningful decisions about design. The design game was developed to mitigate the practitioner's unfamiliarity with the technical and domain specific languages of designing virtual simulations. Reporting from the design process of creating the design game and a collaborative workshop with medical educators and students, we reflect on how a design game using design cards and specific rules can structure design activities, enable non-designers to explore design ideas together, and create concepts for feasible solutions for virtual medical simulations.**

Keywords-design game; design cards; generative tool; virtual simulation; co-design.

I. INTRODUCTION

The tools we use in design can be both influential and critical to successful design outcomes [1]. Design tools provide a range of benefits in a design process as they are "useful for catalysing interactions, building relationships, and enabling diverse communities to creatively take action and innovate" [1, p. 3]. Sanders and Stappers [2] explain how users can take part in the design process and become a part of the design team as experts of their experiences. By contributing directly to the design process, the users can become co-designers. Bringing users into the process, allowing them to be a part of the design of a solution, needs careful structuring and facilitation. Non-designers can however make feasible design decisions when given the right tool for expressing themselves. Sanders and Stappers [3] explain how methods and tools for making enable both designers and non-designers to "make 'things' that describe future objects, concerns and opportunities" [3, p. 2]. Such frameworks and generative tools are often specific to their purpose and reveal a new language of both verbal and visual components that can be combined in various meaningful ways to enable both designers and non-designers to express ideas, thoughts and feelings. Sanders [4] found that generative tools are useful for collaborative thinking, mapping, dreaming, storytelling and visioning. One type of generative tool is design games. As described by Brandt [5], design games are a form of play where we use props and specific rules to structure and organize design with users, where the "aim is to take advantage of the various skills and expertise's represented and jointly explore various design possibilities within a game setting" [5, p. 2]. With a growing number of tailored design games available, design tools like analogue design cards are reported being used in the early stages of collaborative design processes [1]. Many design cards (also referred to as 'ideation cards') have been made and deployed in various research settings, like the IDEO's Method Cards, Tiles and PLEX [1][6][7]. Design cards can be used to address specific domains, like exertion games [8], internet of things [7] and mixed reality games [9]. In the fields of domain-specific human-centered design, design cards are used in systematic design methods and procedures [10].

In this paper, we reflect on how a design game using cards and a specific ruleset in a co-design workshop with medical educators support the claim that design cards enable non-designers to make meaningful decisions about the design of information and communication technological (ICT) solutions. The design game we created focuses on virtual simulation technologies and serious games created to support training and learning on medical procedures and routines. Using virtual simulations in the training of medical practitioners are today being explored, and several commercial companies specialize in creating these types of training applications (see for example InSimu [11] and Virtual Medical Simulation [12]). There is, however, a dearth of research into how these should be designed to support everyday collaborative medical practice [13][14]. Multiple studies do recommend involving end-users in the design and development process [15][16] [17].

Collaborating with a medical training and education center at Østfold University College in Norway, we investigate how these virtual simulations should be designed as an educational learning platform with the goal of ensuring a high use value and adequate learning possibilities for medical students. To explore this, we created the MixED design game – a toolkit consisting of 47 design cards and ruleset – and used it in a co-design workshop with educators, students, and research-designers. The main rationale for creating the design game was to mitigate the practitioner's unfamiliarity with the technical and domain specific languages of design so as to enable them in expressing feasible and fitting solutions to their educational needs.

In this paper, we will present our reflections on the lessons learned when creating and using the design game in the workshop, and we ask: how did the design game support non-designers to make meaningful design decisions?

The paper is structured as follows: in Section II, we present related research, before presenting the MixED design game in Section III. Here, we describe the design process, the cards and the rules that constitute the game. In Section IV, we retell the collaborative workshop held with stakeholders and participants. In Section V, we present the study's methodology, before summarizing the findings in Section VI. In Section VII, we discuss the lessons learned and provide insights to the design community. Section VIII summarize the study with implications for future work.

II. Related Work

Organizing participatory and co-design events often involves including people with different backgrounds, expertise, interests and professional languages [5]. These differences need to be accommodated for by the designers with the aim of allowing every participant to explore, negotiate multiple views and make decisions about design. Design is all about making decisions based on inquiries and explorations of possibilities and the process is not straight forward. Löwgren and Stolterman [18] shed light on two approaches in design thinking, namely convergent and divergent design. Where divergence is about designers expanding their thinking, and exploring possibilities and alternatives to design, convergence is about "focusing on a specific solution or a synthesis of several ideas" [18, p. 29]. The design process often ends in a convergence phase, but the early design phase is mostly driven by divergent activities where designers develop and explore several ideas instead of a singular one. This divergent thinking keeps designers from "falling in love" with one initial idea, by working with several ideas in parallel [18, p. 30].

In these early phases in design processes, non-designers are dependent on appropriate tools to help them think like designers without having extensive knowledge in the field of design. Non-designers need to be allowed to be experts in their own fields and be given tools that can help them express their expertise in an easy way. This is especially important in interdisciplinary teams where domains may collide (e.g., in the design of new ICT solutions in healthcare). With the right tools, non-designers can explore feelings, past experiences, and/or assess their understandings and insights. Using the right tool for the job is important as different tools can yield different insights in different contexts [4].

Design games are one such tool designers can create and utilize to help non-designers express themselves. Brandt [5] describes four types of exploratory design games, namely 1) games to conceptualize design, 2) the "exchange perspective"-design game, 3) the negotiation and work-flow oriented design game, and 4) the scenario-oriented design game. Common for these is that they provide a structure that is flexible and provide people with game materials (tangible game pieces and rules) that they can relate to and make meaning from. The design game helps people to explore aspects of the project and context together and to generate new insights and a common ground for "where the future design work should be headed" [5, p. 9]. Design games to trigger a creative ideation process can take many forms, including future workshops, tabletop games with game pieces and boards, and design cards.

Design cards can support designers across all stages in a design process but are most often used early on for ideation [19]. According to Tahir and Wang [20], design cards "offer an approachable way to introduce information as part of the collaborative design process, and their abstraction level has enabled researchers to successfully use them in a wide variety of fields" [20, p. 2]. Domains include emergency medical services technology [21] and mixed reality games [9]. In a recent study, Hsieh et al. [19] analyzed 161 decks of design cards and identified seven types of design knowledge supported by the decks: creative inspiration, human insight, material and domain, methods and tooling, problem definition, team building, and value in practice.

Design researchers have found various characteristics of cards that make them valuable to design practice [20]. Li et al. [22] explain how designers can leverage the modularity of the cards to address complex design problems across disciplines by letting the cards represent different categories, like domain cards and technology cards [22]. Wetzel et al. [9] reports that ideation cards are a 'viable design method utilized by professional designers' [9:4] and give examples of cards used for ideation; IDEO method cards, PLEX cards [6] and Verbs, Nouns and Adjective cards [23]. Li et al. [22] also points out how design cards can be used to support both designers and non-designers, like with their Flexi Card game. Kwaitkowska et al. [24] report how design cards or game-like cards can support ideation in co-design and participatory design processes. Wetzel et al. [9] describes how they used their ideation cards to synthesize design knowledge about mixed reality games, and how their cards "enable collaborative design in a playful manner" [9, p. 2]. They report the cards being a helpful tool for rapid idea generation and for in-depth idea development for designers of mixed reality games. In their work, they identified six properties the design decks should elicit. Design cards should 1) encapsulate domain-specific knowledge, 2) foster collaboration between teams of designers, and they should 3) avoid overwhelming designers. Further, the cards should 4) avoid making designers feel restricted, 5) support initial and rapid generation of ideas, and they should 6) support a more in-depth development of ideas.

III. MixED Design Game

In this section, we will present the MixED design game. First, we will describe the process of designing the cards, the categories and layout, before explaining the rules of the design game.

A. *Designing the Cards*

The cards were the result of an iterative design process involving four meetings and workshops with stakeholders, including three educators from the medical center. These interactions supported the gradual emergence of a common language and a shared understanding of the domains. These meetings, along with observations, e-mails, informal conversations, and discussions, informed the selection of content and categories.

The research-designers conducted six design workshops (total of 54 hours), with a focus on integrating the categories and content into the card's layout. Inspiration was also drawn from established decks like PLEX, Tiles and Ideation decks [6][7][25]. As can be seen in Table 1, this resulted in a deck of 47 cards in five categories: scenario, medium, interaction, learning outcomes, and challenges.

As illustrated in Fig. 1, the layout was kept simple. Each category was color-coded and displayed a background-image

TABLE I. THE CATEGORIES AND KEYWORDS IN THE DESIGN GAME

Category	Keywords
1 Scenario	Traffic accident, drowning accident, fire accident, home nursing, psychiatry, accident site, prison, falling accident, inside the body, overdose, heart attack.
2 Medium	2D images (slideshow), 2D video, 3D video, 360 video, augmented reality, virtual reality, mixed reality.
3 Interaction	Speech, button, gesticulation, holding objects, movement, looking, feeling.
4 Learning outcome	Empathy, time management, stress management, collaboration, multitasking, communication, confidence, physical skills, technical skills, focus, problem-solving, critical thinking, adaptivity, leadership.
5 Challenges	How is this performed individually? How is this performed in a group? How does the educator fit in? How does collaboration work? How does the marker fit in? Too little time. Too small or big space.

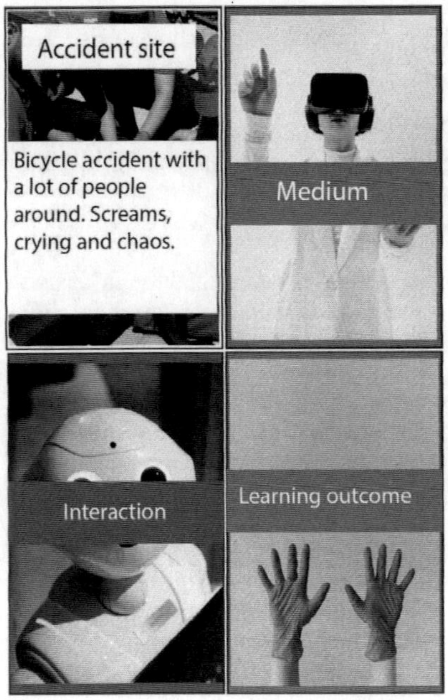

Figure 1. Layout of the cards.

representing the card's content and a keyword or single line of text. These keywords were chosen based on the labels listed in Table 1. The images were sourced from royalty-free services, like Unsplash.

B. *Rules of Play*

The workshop was divided into four phases, each with a specific time limit. We have summarized the phases in Table 2, as well as giving a longer description in Section IV. Each phase builds on the previous one, leading the non-designers through the design process. We also created a rule sheet intended for the participants during the workshop, explaining the rules and phases. Here, the colors of the text corresponded to the cards they would be drawing (i.e., green for Medium cards, blue for Learning outcome).

IV. CONCEPTS GENERATION IN A CO-DESIGN WORKSHOP

The two-hour workshop was held in a classroom at the medical center on April 1st, 2022. In total, nine participants divided into teams of three partook in the workshop. The participants were four educators and facilitators from the center, three bachelor students in production design and one design-researcher. The classroom was big enough so that the teams were able to be placed far enough from each other so that there would be no distractions or collaboration between the different teams. In addition, the workshop had two facilitators, one who led the workshop and one who observed and took notes. The nine participants were intentionally placed in mixed teams of three by the facilitators to encourage interprofessional discussions and avoid reestablishing old ideas and thinking between colleagues. Before starting the workshop, the lead facilitator gave a short presentation on the day's agenda, the cards and the rules.

TABLE II. PHASES AND TASKS IN THE DESIGN GAME

Phase	Task
Individual assignment (15 minutes)	1. Random draw: participants choose one card from category one to four. 2. Create a scenario using the selected cards and take notes. 3. Repeat this process three times using 5 minutes for each round.
Team assignment (20 minutes)	1. Participants present their individual ideas and scenarios. 2. The team decides on one scenario to work with, either from an individual segment or by combining aspects from multiple scenarios.
Team assignment with challenge cards (10 minutes)	1. The team is introduced to the challenge cards, and applies two random drawn cards from this deck to the chosen scenario from the previous phase. 2. Discuss how the challenge card impacts the scenario and make any necessary changes. 3. Repeat this process twice for 5 minutes each round.
Team assignment and presentation (50 minutes)	1. The teams finalize their scenarios and prepare presentations with freedom in how the scenario is to be expressed (e.g., roleplay, video, PowerPoint). 2. Each team have 5 minutes to present their scenario, with opening for questions from other teams. 3. All teams participate in a discussion and use a dot voting system where the participants vote on their favorite idea/scenario with stickers.

As illustrated in Fig. 2, the participants were also given a worksheet with the tasks and times as referenced during the workshop. They were also provided with materials like papers, post-it notes and pencils to document and illustrate their ideas.

In phase one, the participants picked three random cards from each category except the challenge-cards and were asked to create three scenarios. The ideas where then shared with the rest of the team members in phase two. After sharing their ideas, the participants discussed all the ideas from phase one with the goal of creating one shared scenario they would work one and develop further into a concept. They were allowed to mix and match individual ideas to create this scenario. When the second round was done and all the teams had one scenario to work with further, the challenge cards were introduced. In this third phase, the participants picked two challenge cards and were asked to improve their scenario to accommodate for these. The challenge cards sparked interesting discussions in the teams as some of their scenarios had to be completely re-designed based on the new cards. The teams finally presented their final scenario (illustrated in Fig. 3) to the rest of the participants leading to creative and open discussions regarding the feasibility of the three scenarios.

Figure 2. Participants using MixED when designing scenarios in the workshop.

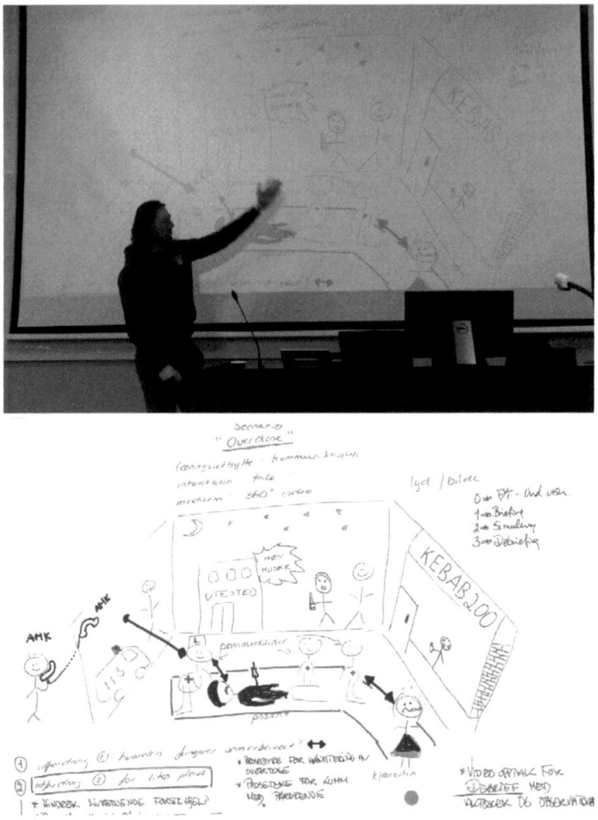

Figure 3. Participant presenting the scenario and the design outcome.

In this section, we have looked closer at the use of the design game in a co-design workshop. We will now report on the study's research method and analysis.

V. METHODOLOGY

We will here give an overview of the methods used for collecting and analyzing data both prior and during the co-design workshop.

A. Research Method

This study employs research through design (RtD) as a qualitative method to gain new insights. RtD, a method rooted in practical inquiry, involves creating and evaluating novel artifacts or systems to generate knowledge that can be applied across contexts [26]. These artifacts not only have the potential to reshape our world toward desired outcomes but also serve as benchmarks, facilitating the seamless transfer of research insights to the Human-Computer Interaction (HCI) community.

As Gaver [26] suggests, integrating design practices into specific HCI research allows researchers to discern both challenges and opportunities. Through RtD, we can delve into novel ideas, theories, or concepts, while also exploring the practical applications of newly designed artifacts within the field.

B. Data Collection

Prior to the workshop, information was gathered in the form of notes and memos from formal project meetings and an online workshop with three educators at the medical center. We also performed direct observation of physical simulation training during class at the medical center. The goal was to gain insight on how student learning is organized and facilitated for at the center. We also observed a large-scale simulation which included students and educators, medical emergency responders from the local hospital and the municipality's fire department. The data was collected through notes and images and was analyzed and used as a basis for the design cards.

We also held an initial pilot workshop with one design-researcher and four master students in applied computer science at Østfold University College, testing the preliminary version of the design game. Data gathered during the pilot were audio recordings, photos, notes, and the design output created by each team. The data lead to a revision of some of the keywords and accompanying illustrations. During the co-design workshop, data was gathered via audio recordings, photographs, note-taking, subsequent discussions with participants, and the tangible design results produced by each team, including Post-it notes and paper sketches.

C. Analysis

The data was individually analyzed by two of the design-researchers using the method thematic analysis. Thematic analysis involves organizing data and identifying recurring themes and aims to enhance comprehension of the data gathered from workshops, meetings, and observations [27]. The researchers were here able to have an open mind during the analysis, find themes and discuss their findings with each other. The audio recordings from the workshops were transcribed and analyzed iteratively in a step-by-step process. The steps included 1) line-by-line color-coding, 2) narrowing the data down, 3) creating descriptive categories, and 4) generating the themes presented in Table 3 by finding data that correlated with each other, e.g., participant's statements from different teams [27].

The study adhered to ethical guidelines set forth by Østfold University College and the Norwegian Center for Research Data (NSD). Data management and consent forms utilized in the study received approval from NSD (NSD number 788872). Participants gave written consent to the gathering and use of data from the workshop and other research activities related to the collaboration.

TABLE III. THEMES FROM THE DATA FOUND BY THE TWO RESEARCHERS.

Researcher	Themes
1	Breaking or changing the rules, management and organization, difficulties, content creation, clarification/collaboration/negotiation, engagement/motivation, technical skills and practical skills, decision making
2	Creative collaboration, own experience, stakeholder experience, technology knowledge, health knowledge, the use of terms, understanding the rules, feedback.

VI. FINDINGS

Before using the design game, the three design-researchers and three of the educators at the medical center spent a lot of time trying to agree on how we were going to proceed with design and development of a medical educational platform for the center. There was little consensus, and a lot of ideas were being exchanged back and forth with little structure to the conversation. The educators suggested solutions with a lack of regard to how a virtual simulation could be implemented at the center, or how the simulations would work in practice. In this phase, it became evident that we struggled to find common ground and bridge our respective fields [28].

Introducing the design game to the process provided structure to the conversations and opened for a more constructive negotiation of ideas and concepts. It enabled the educators to think like designers by giving them a tool that enabled reflection on not only what type of technology should be used, but how it should be used in the context of the practice of providing medical training. The different teams in the workshop grounded their ideas, they set realistic expectations regarding suitable technologies and discussed how the simulations could be implemented as an educational component in the training of many students.

From analyzing the data, the teams (referred to as G1, G2 and G3) worked very differently in the four phases of the design game. They all, however, created three feasible scenarios regarding the choice of technology, facilitation and learning outcomes. Several themes emerged from analyzing this process.

Firstly, the teams demonstrated the ability to express ideas beyond the cards. For example, G1 discussed how they could implement difficulty levels and variations in the scenarios, adding elements outside normal procedure and represent the complexity of patient treatment. They also discussed adding multiple-choice and branching scenarios, where events evolve over time based on the choices of the students.

Secondly, they demonstrated joint decision making and an ability to conceptualize scenarios together. For example, when finishing working on their presentation, G1.1 said "this is the type of things we can make. We can create videos of emergency situations, and then students can play the roles [of patient or bystanders]". When summarizing their idea into one concept, G3 quickly went through everything they had discussed up until that point, including facilitation and collaboration during training sessions, the roles of everybody involved, and technical requirements of visualizing sequences of events, exclaiming that "this is absolutely doable" #G3.3. They expressed engagement, as G3.1 says "I think this is really exiting, if we can make this happen. [...] There is a lot of students that can experience enjoyment from this."

Lastly, they displayed an ability to make realistic decisions about the use of technologies by tempering their expectations. They discussed pitfalls with the different technologies and considered the utility and cost of choosing between them. When one member in G3 suggested an advanced multimedia representation of escalating events, another said "You know… this is fun, but it will be difficult to make" #G3.1.

VII. Discussion

As part of our discussion for this paper, we will first reflect on the three findings from our analysis, and why and how the design game supported the participants in creating ideas and feasible concepts. We will then discuss how divergent and convergent design thinking is equally important to facilitate for when using generative design tools.

A. The Rules of the Game

The participants demonstrated an ability to use the cards to create and express ideas beyond what was stipulated in the cards. Reflecting on this, we believe that the card's expressiveness (the categories, the keywords in each category, and the images) fostered creativity. Not only that, but the cards represented the two fields (design of ICT solution and healthcare) with just the right amount of ambiguity for non-designers to make meaning from them. It is our understanding that the groundwork we did prior to designing and using the cards contributed to the card's usefulness in the design game. The project meetings we held with the stakeholders, the simulations we observed at the center, and the e-mails and conversations we had gave us insights into the everyday work of the educators and their field. When designing the cards, this deepened understanding helped us make better choices regarding categories and keywords. It shall be said that not all the cards captured the field of medical practice well. Participants were confused about some of the cards, like the medium card 'MR'. MR is the Norwegian term for MRI and while the design-researchers intended this card to stand for 'mixed reality' it was interpreted by participants with medical backgrounds as a medical device similar to an X-ray. As design-researchers, it should fall to us to help cross boundaries and create something that makes sense across disciplines. We therefore recommend other designers and researchers working in the intersection of disciplines to use extensive time with the stakeholders to gain a good understanding of the domain the deck of cards are expected to express and represent.

During the workshop we also saw how the participants were able to create good ideas together through joint decision making. We believe this is due to the rules of the design game and how we structured the activities in the different phases. Where we previously held several unstructured meetings discussing the design choices, the rules in the design game structured collaboration in a constructive way. Rapid, individual ideation in phase one broadened their view of what this ICT solution could be, and each participant brought their unique ideas into the next phase. In phase two, they spent a lot of time negotiating and coming to an agreement on which ideas to pursue further, evaluating design decision and making design moves together.

In initial project meetings between the design-researchers and stakeholders, there seemed to be little consensus on what to design. Stakeholders often discussed unrealistic ideas about what this ICT solution should be, with little regard for how the technology would work. For example, when discussing what technology to implement, one stakeholder voiced a need for creating educational training modules using virtual reality as medium. This would require a specific setup in the room intended for the virtual simulation, and it would be difficult for 60+ students to use these efficiently. What we saw during the workshop was that the participants could use the cards to generate ideas and then evaluate those ideas in a constructive way, for example to make realistic choices regarding the choice of technologies. Phase three urged them to reflect on the limitations that space (physical room), cost and organization of the simulation would require. The cards helped them to concretize, understand and evaluate the components of the technical solution. This enabled the participants to make meaningful decisions about the creation of complex ICT systems – something which is well outside their domain of expertise.

B. Convergent Design Games

Reflecting on what took place in the design game, we seem to have found a balance between openness and preciseness in the rules of using the cards. The ideation activities in phase one and the start of phase two gave room for exploration of the categories and components of a virtual simulation for learning. By dividing the workshop into sequential phases where design activities built upon each other drove the design process forward in a natural way. This gave the workshop a constructive pace: the facilitator controlled the workshop's activities and guided the participants to the next phase. During the activities, participants were given room to openly explore ideas and be creative all the while moving forward to a more concrete and realistic design outcome.

We believe that this is a good example of the divergent and convergent design thinking processes described by Löwgren and Stolterman [18]. Where divergent design thinking is about creating choices, convergent design thinking is about which choices to pursue further. By analyzing the structure of our workshop, we see that phases one and two are clear examples of divergent design activities. Further, we see a mixture of divergent and convergent activities in phase three. Introducing the challenge cards helped narrow and focus the scenarios by putting contextual constraints on their solutions. In phase four they demonstrated their ability to discuss, negotiate and make decisions by converging their ideas into one final concept.

Brandt [5] explains how exploratory design games can 1) stage participation (organize collaboration) and 2) help open up for multiple ideas. In the literature, the terms "ideation cards" and "design cards" are used interchangeably. Ideation is the process of opening up and producing many ideas, but for anything meaningful to coming from a design process, designers and participants also need to close in and make decisions regarding the design. Therefore, it is important to balance divergent and convergent activities when creating and facilitating design games. Design cards are usually used in the fuzzy front end of design, which by nature is messy [2]. The same can be said of interdisciplinary collaboration; before common ground is found, cooperation across disciplines can be challenging. Therefore, at the start of a design project, where people from different disciplines come together to create a product, an artefact or a solution, ideas are bounced back and forth based on each participants' expertise and experiences. In turn, this can result in nonstop divergence, with new ideas and concepts being generated but where no move is made towards the making of meaningful decisions. Using a design game with cards and a specific set of rules to support participants in understanding the problem space and giving them 'things-to-think-with' is most certainly useful. However, designers also need to provide non-designers with tools and a framework that helps them make design moves and choices when creating design concepts that have a real chance of being built. Rules that stop the generation of new ideas, help them discuss these ideas, and move from ideation to conceptualization. To facilitate for decision making through both divergent and convergent design activities.

VIII. CONCLUSION AND FUTURE WORK

In this paper, we have reported on the creation of a generative design game for medical virtual simulations, as well as findings from a co-design workshop with medical educators. In so doing, we have shed light on the need for collaborative design approaches in the design of virtual simulations for medical training and learning. The conventional practice of involving expert users solely for prototype validation often results in digital learning environments that inadequately capture the intricacies of medical practice.

Through a collaborative workshop involving medical educators and students, we demonstrated how the design game facilitated for meaningful decision making about medical virtual simulation. Utilizing design cards and structured rules provided a framework that enabled non-designers to engage in design activities. By bridging the gap between practitioners' expertise in medical education and design of virtual simulations as learning environment, the design game empowered participants to explore innovative design ideas, and critically reflect on possibilities and limitations with ICT-solutions.

Drawing on Löwgren and Stoltermans [18] notion on divergent and convergent design thinking, this study also shed light on the importance of finding a balance between ideation and making design moves. For future work, it would be interesting to see more research on how designers and researchers can structure design activities after the principles of divergent and convergent design, and in so doing facilitate for both ideation and decision making during co-design activities.

REFERENCES

[1] D. Peters, L. Loke, and N. Ahmadpour, "Toolkits, cards and games – a review of analogue tools for collaborative ideation," CoDesign, vol. 17, no. 4, pp. 410–434, Oct. 2021, Accessed: Apr. 30, 2024. doi: 10.1080/15710882.2020.1715444.

[2] E. B.-N. Sanders and P. J. Stappers, "Co-creation and the new landscapes of design," CoDesign, vol. 4, no. 1, pp. 5–18, Mar. 2008, Accessed: Apr. 28, 2024. doi: 10.1080/15710880701875068.

[3] E. B.-N. Sanders and P. J. Stappers, "Probes, toolkits and prototypes: three approaches to making in codesigning," CoDesign, vol. 10, no. 1, pp. 5–14, Jan. 2014, Accessed: Apr. 21, 2024. doi: 10.1080/15710882.2014.888183.

[4] E. B.-N. Sanders, "Generative Tools for Co-designing," in Collaborative Design, S. A. R. Scrivener, L. J. Ball, and A. Woodcock, Eds., London: Springer London, 2000, pp. 3–12. Accessed: Apr. 12, 2024. doi: 10.1007/978-1-4471-0779-8_1.

[5] E. Brandt, Designing Exploratory Design Games: A Framework for Participation in Participatory Design?, vol. 2006. 2006, p. 66. Accessed: Apr. 12, 2024. doi: 10.1145/1147261.1147271.

[6] A. Lucero and J. Arrasvuori, "PLEX Cards: a source of inspiration when designing for playfulness," in Proceedings of the 3rd International Conference on Fun and Games - Fun and Games '10, Leuven, Belgium: ACM Press, 2010, pp. 28–37. Accessed: Apr. 25, 2024. doi: 10.1145/1823818.1823821.

[7] S. Mora, F. Gianni, and M. Divitini, "Tiles: A Card-based Ideation Toolkit for the Internet of Things," in Proceedings of the 2017 Conference on Designing Interactive Systems, Edinburgh United Kingdom: ACM, Jun. 2017, pp. 587–598. Accessed: Jan. 15, 2024. doi: 10.1145/3064663.3064699.

[8] F. Mueller, M. R. Gibbs, F. Vetere, and D. Edge, "Supporting the creative game design process with exertion cards," in Proceedings of the SIGCHI Conference on Human Factors in Computing Systems, Toronto Ontario Canada: ACM, Apr. 2014, pp. 2211–2220. Accessed: Apr. 06, 2024. doi: 10.1145/2556288.2557272.

[9] R. Wetzel, T. Rodden, and S. Benford, "Developing Ideation Cards for Mixed Reality Game Design," Transactions of the Digital Games Research Association, vol. 3, no. 2, Art. no. 2, 2017, Accessed: Feb. 08, 2022. [Online]. Available: http://todigra.org/index.php/todigra/article/view/73

[10] R. Roy and J. P. Warren, "Card-based design tools: a review and analysis of 155 card decks for designers and designing," Design Studies, vol. 63, pp. 125–154, Jul. 2019, Accessed: Mar. 16, 2024. doi: 10.1016/j.destud.2019.04.002.

[11] "The Virtual Patient Simulator for Clinical Training and Assessment | InSimu." Accessed: Apr. 15, 2024. [Online]. Available: https://insimu.com/

[12] "Virtual Medical Simulation - Virtual Patient - Practical Training," Virtual Medical Simulation. Accessed: Apr. 15, 2024. [Online]. Available: https://virtualmedicalsimulation.com/

[13] J. M. Padilha, P. P. Machado, A. L. Ribeiro, and J. L. Ramos, "Clinical Virtual Simulation in Nursing Education," Clinical Simulation in Nursing, vol. 15, pp. 13–18, Feb. 2018, Accessed: Mar. 20, 2024. doi: 10.1016/j.ecns.2017.09.005.

[14] T. Bunæs and J. Karlsen, Using Single Player Virtual Simulations for Training on Collaborative Medical Practice. Oct. 2019. In *Proceedings of the european conference on games-based learning* (pp. 119-126).

[15] F. E. Garcia and V. P. de Almeida Neris, "A framework for tailorable games: toward inclusive end-user development of inclusive games," Univ Access Inf Soc, Nov. 2020, Accessed: Apr. 12, 2024. doi: 10.1007/s10209-020-00779-8.

[16] A. Ahmad, E. L.-C. Law, and A. Moseley, "Integrating Instructional Design Principles in Serious Games Authoring Tools: Insights from Systematic Literature Review," in Proceedings of the 11th Nordic Conference on Human-Computer Interaction: Shaping Experiences, Shaping Society,

Tallinn Estonia: ACM, Oct. 2020, pp. 1–12. Accessed: Jan. 21, 2024. doi: 10.1145/3419249.3420133.

[17] A. Slootmaker, H. Hummel, and R. Koper, "Evaluating the Usability of Authoring Environments for Serious Games," Simulation & Gaming, vol. 48, no. 4, pp. 553–578, Aug. 2017, Accessed: Apr. 06, 2024. doi: 10.1177/1046878117705249.

[18] J. Lowgren and E. Stolterman, Thoughtful Interaction Design: A Design Perspective on Information Technology. Cambridge, UNITED STATES: MIT Press, 2004. Accessed: Feb. 09, 2024. [Online]. Available: http://ebookcentral.proquest.com/lib/hiof-ebooks/detail.action?docID=3339158

[19] G. Hsieh, B. A. Halperin, E. Schmitz, Y. N. Chew, and Y.-C. Tseng, "What is in the Cards: Exploring Uses, Patterns, and Trends in Design Cards," in Proceedings of the 2023 CHI Conference on Human Factors in Computing Systems, Hamburg Germany: ACM, Apr. 2023, pp. 1–18. Accessed: Mar. 14, 2024. doi: 10.1145/3544548.3580712.

[20] R. Tahir and A. I. Wang, "Transforming a Theoretical Framework to Design Cards: LEAGUE Ideation Toolkit for Game-Based Learning Design," Sustainability, vol. 12, no. 20, Art. no. 20, Jan. 2020, Accessed: Feb. 02, 2024. doi: 10.3390/su12208487.

[21] P. Schlosser and B. Matthews, "Designing for Inaccessible Emergency Medical Service Contexts: Development and Evaluation of the Contextual Secondary Video Toolkit," in CHI Conference on Human Factors in Computing Systems, New Orleans LA USA: ACM, Apr. 2022, pp. 1–17. Accessed: Apr. 30, 2024. doi: 10.1145/3491102.3517538.

[22] H. Li, A. H. Khan, K. M. Hurtig, P. Jarusriboonchai, and J. Häkkilä, "Flexi Card Game: A Design Toolkit for Unconventional Communication Systems for Long-Distance Relationships," in Proceedings of the Fifteenth International Conference on Tangible, Embedded, and Embodied Interaction, Salzburg Austria: ACM, Feb. 2021, pp. 1–16. Accessed: Apr. 30, 2024. doi: 10.1145/3430524.3440650.

[23] A. Kultima, J. Niemelä, J. Paavilainen, and H. Saarenpää, "Designing game idea generation games," in Proceedings of the 2008 Conference on Future Play: Research, Play, Share, Toronto Ontario Canada: ACM, Nov. 2008, pp. 137–144. Accessed: Apr. 29, 2024. doi: 10.1145/1496984.1497007.

[24] J. Kwiatkowska, A. Szóstek, and D. Lamas, "(Un)structured sources of inspiration: comparing the effects of game-like cards and design cards on creativity in co-design process," in Proceedings of the 13th Participatory Design Conference on Research Papers - PDC '14, Windhoek, Namibia: ACM Press, 2014, pp. 31–39. Accessed: Apr. 30, 2024. doi: 10.1145/2661435.2661442.

[25] M. Golembewski and M. Selby, "Ideation decks: a card-based design ideation tool," in Proceedings of the 8th ACM Conference on Designing Interactive Systems, Aarhus Denmark: ACM, Aug. 2010, pp. 89–92. Accessed: Apr. 30, 2024. doi: 10.1145/1858171.1858189.

[26] W. Gaver, "What should we expect from research through design?," in Proceedings of the SIGCHI Conference on Human Factors in Computing Systems, Austin Texas USA: ACM, May 2012, pp. 937–946. Accessed: Apr. 28, 2024. doi: 10.1145/2207676.2208538.

[27] V. Braun and V. Clarke, "Using thematic analysis in psychology," Qualitative Research in Psychology, vol. 3, no. 2, pp. 77–101, Jan. 2006, Accessed: Apr. 28, 2024. doi: 10.1191/1478088706qp063oa.

[28] T. Bunæs, M. Husebye, and J. Karlsen, Finding Common Ground: Design Cards Supporting Mutual Learning in Co-design. 2023. In Stigberg, Susanne Koch & Karlsen, Joakim (Red.), *ACHI 2023: The Sixteenth International Conference on Advances in Computer-Human Interactions*. International Academy, Research and Industry Association (IARIA). Accessed: Apr. 30, 2024. ISSN 978-1-68558-078-0. s. 34–44.

Researching X-professional Collaborations through Co-design and Co-creation

Mapping An Emerging Field

Joakim Karlsen, Michelle Husebye
Department of Computer Science and Communication
Faculty of Computer Science, Engineering and Economics
Østfold University College
1757 Halden, Norway
{joakim.karlsen, michelle.husebye}@hiof.no

Kristine Høeg Karlsen
Department of Pedagogy, ICT and Learning
Faculty of Education
Østfold University College
1757 Halden, Norway
Kristine.h.karlsen@hiof.no

***Abstract*-This article reviews and maps the literature on how co-creation and co-design have been used in relation to research on interprofessional collaborations in education and in practice. Through a review of the 105 research articles, we find that both co-creation and co-design have mattered more recently, both as methodological approaches and to describe aspects of interprofessional collaboration. Researchers attuned to working directly with practitioners to solve pressing societal issues increasingly use co-design and co-creation for this purpose.**

Keywords-co-creation; co-design; interprofessional collaboration; mapping literature review.

I. INTRODUCTION

Interprofessional collaborations are needed to develop solutions for many current problems in society. Often problems that can be characterized as being "wicked" [1]-[3] requiring ongoing collaboration between disciplines and professions to provide sustainable solutions.

> Wicked problems, including conflict and sustainability, that transcend the resources for any single disciplinary or even traditional interdisciplinary approach for solution have become primary sources of material for contemporary transdisciplinary work. [3, p. 9]

Methods, tools, and techniques to address wicked problems have been developed in the design fields, popularized by the spread and use of "design thinking" [1][4] One such flavor of design thinking is co-design, a practice focusing on involving various stakeholders in envisioning and creating solutions that address complex problems. While co-design practices are often object oriented, aiming to provide products, services and systems, the more general practice of co-creation can have broader aims, focusing for instance on collaboration, and to innovate and transform future practices.

In our case, we aim to shed light on the conditions for cross-sectorial collaborations between schools and cultural institutions in Norway. We undertake a research project aiming to bridge existing contradictions within the cultural schoolbag—an ongoing program designed to grant students access to cultural expressions within educational settings. Specifically, we explore how student teachers can transform into agents of change by facilitating connections between schools and the cultural sector as part of their teacher training. The backdrop for our investigation lies in the asymmetric power relations between schools and cultural institutions within the cultural schoolbag [5]-[8] where teachers view themselves as having limited influence in TCS activities they facilitate for [5][9] and lack a clear understanding of their role [10]. Our project seeks to empower these educators through co-design and co-creation activities, equipping them with the knowledge and tools to navigate this complex landscape. In organizing the co-creation activities, we have sought to provide support and scaffolding for new collaborative practices to emerge – to be able to understand the socio-material conditions for such practices to be made more likely and durable. We have been guided by the ideal captured by the concept of "transformative mutuality" which Eyal & Yarm [11, p. 680] describe as collaborations,

> ...characterized by both parties taking an active approach, engaging willingly and enthusiastically in shared educational deliberation, and devising and implementing educational activities that have a synergistic effect, contributing to the growth of both parties on an individual and organizational level, as well as to the students. [11, p. 680]

To support an investigation of the potential of co-design and co-creation activities to shed light on the conditions for establishing sustainable transprofessional practices in cross-sectorial collaborations, we have performed a mapping literature review to ground further studies. Before describing the methods followed in Section III, the mapping in Section IV and its implications for our research in Sections V and VI, we will provide definitions of the key concepts used in our search, co-design, co-creation and cross-, multi-, inter-, and trans-professionality in Section II.

II. CONCEPTS

A. cross-, multi-, inter-, and trans-professionality

The distinctions between cross-, multi-, inter-, and trans-professionality closely follow the distinctions between cross-, multi-, inter-, and trans-disciplinarity. According to Mahler et al. [12] the difference between a discipline and profession is that a discipline seeks to develop theory to understand the world, while a profession is a practically applied discipline. For both disciplines and professions, the prescripts cross, multi, inter and trans denote the degree of collaboration in a x-disciplinary or x-professional team as categorized in Table I.

TABLE I. DEGREE OF COLLABORATION IN X-DISCIPLINARY TEAMS.

Prescript	Collaboration
Intra	Mono
Multi	Alongside
Cross	Alongside and informing each other
Inter	Partially overlapping
Trans	Almost fully overlapping

The knowledge about the nature and utility of x-professional collaboration so far relies heavily on the mostly programmatic research on x-disciplinarity. The origins, development and current issues of transdisciplinarity have been presented by Bernstein [3]. In the following, we therefore ground our search concepts on Choi and Pak's [13] thorough review of the differences in the definitions of multidisciplinarity, interdisciplinarity and transdisciplinarity in the literature from 1982 to 2006. They distinguish between multi-, inter-, and transdisciplinarity this way:

> Multidisciplinary, being the most basic level of involvement, refers to different (hence "multi") disciplines that are working on a problem in parallel or sequentially, and without challenging their disciplinary boundaries. Interdisciplinary brings about the reciprocal interaction between (hence "inter") disciplines, necessitating a blurring of disciplinary boundaries, in order to generate new common methodologies, perspectives, knowledge, or even new disciplines. Transdisciplinary involves scientists from different disciplines as well as nonscientists and other stakeholders and, through role release and role expansion, transcends (hence "trans") the disciplinary boundaries to look at the dynamics of whole systems in a holistic way.[13, p. 359].

In summary, they define multidisciplinarity as additive (2+2=4), interdisciplinarity as interactive (2+2=5) and transdisciplinarity as holistic (2+2=yellow). They denote the output of transdisciplinarity as yellow to signify that transdisciplinary collaborations have to potential to make contributions that can't be traced directly to the individual contributions made by disciplines being involved. Figure 1 depicts a common graphic to explain the differences between the x-disciplinarities.

B. *Co-design and co-creation*

Sanders and Stappers [14] provide much cited definitions for co-creation and co-design. According to their perspective, co-creation encompasses "any act of collective creativity, i.e., creativity that is shared by two or more people." [14, p. 6] They further relate co-design to co-creation, asserting that co-design is a specific instance of co-creation. In essence, Sanders and Stappers [14] co-design represents a subset of the broader concept of co-creation. Mattelmäki and Visser [15] offer an alternative perspective. They view co-creation as a "creative moment" or "method" within the co-design process. We believe these problems with mapping the relationship between co-creation and co-design signifies that the phenomena the concepts seek to describe are on the same level – it is equally sensible to write that co-creation activities relies on co-design or that co-design activities rely on co-creation. We have recently clarified this by understanding co-design and co-creation as related but different practices, involving many of the same practitioners, but with differing goals and rationales – co-design being mostly object oriented and co-creation being mostly process oriented.

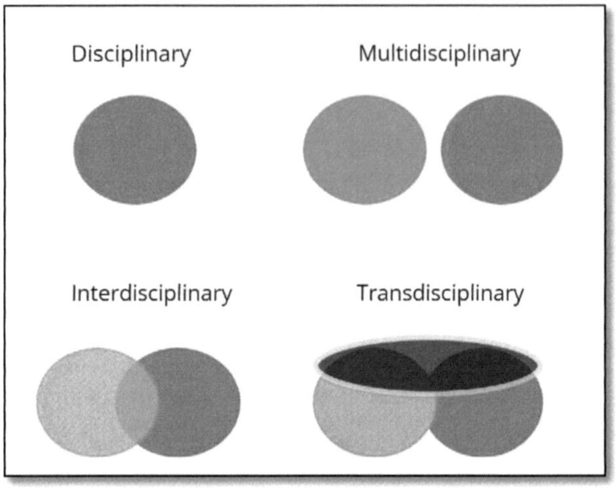

Figure 1: Based on graphic from Holistic Education Network (no longer available online).

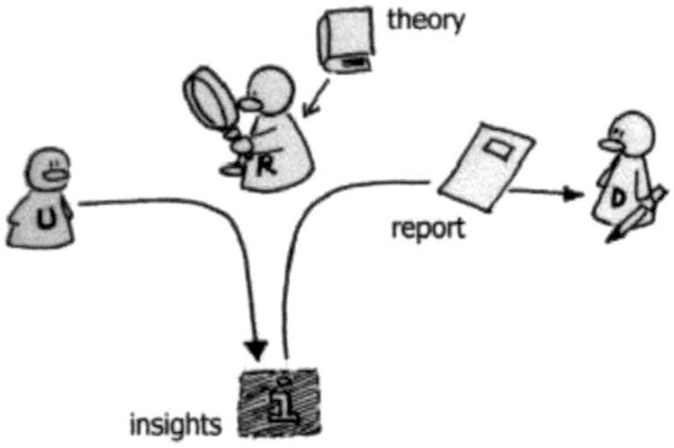

Figure 2. Pre-planned and designer/researcher-led activities to study users for insights informing the design of something. Image from Sanders and Stappers [14, p.11].

For our purposes here, we follow Sanders and Stappers [14] in that co-creation emphasize the importance of participation and creativity in co-design processes. How co-creation signifies how all stakeholders should be involved in design, and where the designers need to take on new roles to facilitate for this.

Figure 3. Designers, researchers and stakeholders co-creating insights together using fitting representational tools. Image from Sanders and Stappers [14, p.11].

Co-creation inspires a move from pre-planned and designer-led activities where design researchers study users for insights informing the design of something, to a model where the designers and stakeholders co-create insights together using fitting representational tools. Figures 2 and 3 show how the two collaborative models are depicted in Sanders and Stappers [14]

III. METHODOLOGY

The targeted scope [16] of the mapping literature review was research using co-design or co-creation to enhance x-professional collaborations in problem solving. In addition, we used English and scientific peer-reviewed articles published in electronic databases without a year limit, as inclusion criteria (cf. [17]). Table I summarizes the five criteria of inclusion used for this mapping. An important clarification is that for inclusion, articles must employ or investigate co-design or co-creation as a means, i.e., as an action or intervention, not solely as, for example, "co-creation of knowledge", where the output stems from any kind of dialogue or activity. Furthermore, the study must aim to describe and develop an understanding of what supports x-professional collaborations (or cross-, multi-, trans-), where it is not merely one finding among several.

TABLE II. CRITERIA OF INCLUSION

No.	Criterion type	Description
1	Topic	Research using co-design or co-creation to enhance interprofessional collaborations in problem solving.
2	Date	No limit
3	Language	English
4	Type of paper	Scientific peer-reviewed articles
5	Source	Electronic databases

Four searches were conducted in discipline-specific bibliographic databases: Web of Science, Scopus, Eric (Education Resources Information Center), and ACM Digital Library in March 2024. ACM is the largest collection of literature in computer science, information technology, and telecommunications. We made this decision to include studies emphasizing interprofessional collaboration drawing upon methodologies from the design fields, which we considered relevant to our research aims. Each search undertaken, utilized either the term co-creation or co-design, along with one of the four terms cross-, multi-, inter-, trans-professional, to identify relevant studies. In the searches we used Boolean operator "OR" to combine the terms within each concept, and "AND" to combine the different concepts (cf. [17, p. 109] as follows:

co-creation
OR
co-design

AND

cross-professional
OR
multi-professional
OR
inter-professional
OR
trans-professional

Based on the search, a total of 148 references were considered potentially relevant and consequently listed in a spreadsheet. The articles were then independently coded by the two first authors using the codes co-x (covering the terms co-design and co-creation) and x-professional (for the terms cross-, multi-, inter-, trans-professional). To identify whether the study uses, for instance, co-x as a method or if the researcher(s) addresses co-x as a phenomenon, each axis was further divided into two aspects, resulting in four codes: co-x method, co-x phenomenon, x-prof method, and x-prof phenomenon. The first author coded the articles based on the abstract, while the second author reviewed the full articles.

The outcome of the coding was that 29 studies were immediately excluded because they were coded only on either the co-x axis or the x-prof axis by both coders. Out of the remaining articles (119), the first and second authors coded differently on one or more of the four codes in 35 of the studies. After a brief screening, we found that nine of these could be excluded because, despite different coding, they were not coded along both axes of co-x and x-professional. Subsequently, we were left with 26 studies that the first and second authors reviewed and coded together, ultimately agreeing upon a final coding. As a result of this process, an additional five articles were excluded because they were not coded along both axes. In summary, out of the 148 studies, we were left with 105 articles that met all inclusion criteria.

The final step in the coding involved identifying the sector addressed in the studies—whether it pertained to health, education, or other domains—and categorizing the research into vocational research and educational research.

IV. FINDINGS

A. The relationship between co-x and x-professional

The first group of articles in Table III (Group 1) [18]-[49] uses variants of both co-x and x-professionality only as descriptive, analytical concepts – as is common in the social sciences. Four groups (Groups 2, 3, 4 and 6) all use co-x as methodological approach, and in addition engaging x-professionals in this. The difference between these groups is whether they also use the terms as analytical concepts:

- only to describe x-professionality (Group 2) [50]-[72]
- to describe both co-x and x-professionality (Group 3) [73]-[93]
- neither to describe co-x nor x-professionality (Group 4) [94]-[113]
- only to describe co-x (Group 6) [114][115]

Two small groups of articles (Groups 5 and 8), [116]-[119] use co-x as methodological approach but combined with x-professionality only as an analytical concept. A few articles (Groups 7 and 9) use x-professionality methodologically but combined co-x only as an analytical concept [120]-[122].

Overall, the main finding is that the studies reviewed in this article either use both concepts as a methodological approach (66) or purely analytically (32).

TABLE III. MAIN MAPPING.

	Group				Art#
	co-x		*x-professionality*		
	Meth.	Phen.	Meth.	Phen.	
1	n	y	n	y	32
2	y	n	y	y	23
3	y	y	y	y	21
4	y	n	y	n	20
5	y	n	n	y	3
6	y	y	y	n	2
7	n	y	y	y	2
8	y	y	n	y	1
9	n	y	y	n	1
				SUM	105

B. *Field and type of research*

In the coding of the 105 studies, it became evident that among the articles identified in this review, the majority are situated within the health sector (92 studies) (see Table IV).

TABLE IV. EDUCATION OR PROFESSIONAL PRACTICE.

Type	Sectors		
	Health	Edu.	Other
Vocational research	78	5	6
Educational research	14	1	1
Summary	92	6	7
In total			105

Looking at the type of research conducted within these studies, vocational research predominates, represented in 78 of the 92. These are studies that explore professional practices and how practitioners acquire knowledge and skills within health and care services, both in the private and public sectors. Out of the health studies, 14 constitute educational research, focusing on how higher education institutions prepare students for the workforce.

In the field of education, 6 in total, 5 are vocational research, while only one focuses on higher education. Additionally, 7 studies were identified in other sectors (cf. enterprise, management) of which 6 are vocational research.

Given these findings, it is evident that there is a dearth of research on x-professional collaborations through co-creation in the educational sector both in the health and educational sector (and others, in the review). Specifically, how higher education institutions equip students for such collaborative efforts in their professional lives as educators. Bridging this research gap could lead to future studies aimed at enhancing pedagogical practice in higher education institutions, which in turn demand innovative approaches to curriculum design and development.

V. DISCUSSION

Most of the studies identified and mapped in this review use the term interprofessional (Table V). According to the distinctions between degrees of collaboration in x-disciplinary teams made by Choi and Pak [13] this signifies a high degree of collaboration between the professionals being studied, where the professionals actively engage with one another to provide better solutions (2+2=5). Very few studies use the term transprofessional, however.

TABLE V. THE USE OF INTER-, MULTI-, CROSS- AND TRANSPROFESSIONAL IN THE MAPPED STUDIES.

Search engine	Term	Occurrences
Web of Science	Inter	66
	Multi	13
	Cross	2
	Trans	0
Scopus	Inter	79
	Multi	19
	Cross	1
	Trans	1
Eric	Inter	9
	Multi	0
	Cross	0
	Trans	0
ACM	Inter	54
	Multi	6
	Cross	4
	Trans	1

There could be several reasons for little use of the term transprofessional in this literature. Many researchers will probably use transdisciplinary instead, or maybe it is because the precise meaning of transprofessional collaboration remains elusive, or maybe we don't need a category denoting an even higher degree of collaboration than interprofessional [13]. Regardless, the answer to these questions, our mapping indicates the need for more theory building and research to clearly delineate transprofessional- from other types x-professional collaborations – and further, into how such collaborations can inform research on what conditions sustainable practices involving multiple sectors, disciplines and / or professions.

VI. CONCLUSION AND FUTURE WORK

The literature mapping clearly indicates that more research is needed to provide more certainty in what transprofessional practice is. Providing such clarity will meet the increased demand to better understand and accommodate for inter-agency working often requested in public policies [123]. Hulme et al. [123] clarify the notion of transprofessionalism as an "expanded professionalism" relying on common language and shared understandings with the potential to overcome professional and disciplinary boundaries. They seek “new forms of collaborative working and a commitment to the co-construction of knowledge” [123, p. 539] and work with operationalizing “collaborative practitioner enquiry” to “open up spaces that allow new transprofessional dialogues to develop.” [123, p. 542] While Hulme et al. [123] frame practitioner inquiry as facilitating for third spaces, we look to co-design and participatory design to achieve the same goals. In participatory design there is a well-established discourse on how to facilitate for the emergence of a third space [124] more specifically and in line with Hulme et al. [123] of how to facilitate spaces for reciprocity and mutual learning [125]. Exploring such an agenda is in our valuable, and something we will pursue in our ongoing and future research projects.

VII. References

[1] R. Buchanan, "Wicked Problems in Design Thinking", Design Issues, vol. 8, no. 2, pp. 5–21, Apr. 1992.

[2] H. W. J. Rittel and M. M. Webber, "Dilemmas in a general theory of planning", Policy Sci, vol. 4, no. 2, pp. 155–169, Jun. 1973.

[3] J. Bernstein, "Transdisciplinarity: A Review of Its Origins, Development, and Current Issues", Publications and Research, Jul. 2015. [Online]. Available: https://academicworks.cuny.edu/kb_pubs/37

[4] N. Cross, "From a Design Science to a Design Discipline: Understanding Designerly Ways of Knowing and Thinking", in Design Research Now, R. Michel, Ed., in Board of International Research in Design. , Birkhäuser Basel, 2007, pp. 41–54. Accessed: Oct. 24, 2014. [Online]. Available: http://link.springer.com/chapter/10.1007/978-3-7643-8472-2_3

[5] J.-K. Breivik and C. Christophersen, Den Kulturelle skolesekken. Oslo, Bergen: Kulturrådet Fagbokforlaget, 2013, p. 207. Accessed: Apr. 22, 2020. [Online]. Available: http://kulturradet.no/vis-publikasjon/-/asset_publisher/N4dG/content/publikasjon-den-kulturelle-skolesekken

[6] C. Cristophersen, J.-K. Breivik, A. D. Homme, and L. H. Rykkja, "The cultural rucksack; a national programme for arts and culture in Norwegian schools", Kulturrådet, Fagbokforlaget, Oslo, Bergen, 2015. Accessed: Dec. 08, 2020. [Online]. Available: https://www.norskeserier.no/_the-cultural-rucksack-9788270811687

[7] I. Digranes, "Den kulturelle skulesekken – Kvalitetsskule eller kulturarroganse?", FormAkademisk, vol. 8, no. 2, Art. no. 2, Oct. 2015.

[8] E. S. Hauge, V. S. Knutsen, and M. R. Ervik, "Nærhet, autonomi og demokratisering: Evaluering av direktekommuneordningen i Den Kulturelle Skolesekken", Oxford Research, Oslo, 2017. Accessed: Dec. 08, 2020. [Online]. Available: https://oxfordresearch.no/publications/naerhet-autonomi-og-demokratisering/

[9] I. Digranes, "Den kulturelle skulesekken : narratives and myths of educational practice in DKS projects within the subject art and crafts", PhD, AHO, Oslo, 2009. Accessed: Dec. 08, 2020. [Online]. Available: https://aho.brage.unit.no/aho-xmlui/handle/11250/93038

[10] K. Holdhus and M. Espeland, "Skole og konsert - frå formidling til dialog (DiSko): Produksjosrapport", Center for Creativities, Arts and Science in Education (CASE), CASE 2018/1, 2018. Accessed: Dec. 08, 2020. [Online]. Available: https://hvlopen.brage.unit.no/hvlopen-xmlui/handle/11250/2651977

[11] O. Eyal and M. Yarm, "Schools in Cross-Sector Alliances: What Do Schools Seek in Partnerships?", Educational Administration Quarterly, vol. 54, no. 4, pp. 648–688, Oct. 2018.

[12] C. Mahler, T. Gutmann, S. Karstens, and S. Joos, "Terminology for interprofessional collaboration: Definition and current practice", GMS Z Med Ausbild, vol. 31, no. 4, p. Doc40, Nov. 2014.

[13] B. C. K. Choi and A. W. P. Pak, "Multidisciplinarity, interdisciplinarity and transdisciplinarity in health research, services, education and policy: 1. Definitions, objectives, and evidence of effectiveness", Clinical and Investigative Medicine, vol. 29, no. 6, pp. 351–64, Dec. 2006.

[14] E. B.-N. Sanders and P. J. Stappers, "Co-creation and the new landscapes of design", CoDesign, vol. 4, no. 1, pp. 5–18, 2008.

[15] T. Mattelmäki and F. S. Visser, "Lost in CO-X - Interpretations of Co-Design and Co-Creation", Proceedings of IASDR"11, 4th World Conference on Design Research, Delft University, 2011. Accessed: Jan. 09, 2023. [Online]. Available: https://research.aalto.fi/en/publications/lost-in-co-x-interpretations-of-co-design-and-co-creation

[16] D. Gough, S. Oliver, and J. Thomas, An Introduction to Systematic Reviews. SAGE, 2017.

[17] G. Brunton, C. Stansfield, and J. Thomas, "Finding relevant studies", in An introduction to systematic reviews, J. Thomas, D. Gough, and S. Oliver, Eds., SAGE Publications, 2012, pp. 107–134.

[18] D. Cadilhac et al., "A Stepped-Wedge Cluster-Randomized Trial to Improve Adherence to Evidence-Based Practices for Acute Stroke Management", Joint Commission Journal on Quality and Patient Safety, vol. 48, no. 12, pp. 653–664, Dec. 2022.

[19] E. Holmboe, T. Foster, and G. Ogrinc, "Co-Creating Quality in Health Care Through Learning and Dissemination", Journal of Continuing Education in the Health Professions, vol. 36, pp. S16–S18, SUM 2016.

[20] S. Hyde et al., "Co-designing community-focused rural placements for collaborative practice", Australian Journal of Rural Health, vol. 29, no. 2, pp. 284–290, 2021.

[21] L. Jeffs et al., "Collaborative Care Transitions Symposium: Insights from Participants", Nursing leadership (Toronto, Ont.), vol. 30, no. 2, pp. 39–56, 2017.

[22] A. van Gils, L. Tak, H. Sattel, and J. Rosmalen, "Development and User Experiences of a Biopsychosocial Interprofessional Online Course on Persistent Somatic Symptoms", Frontiers in Psychiatry, vol. 12, p. 725546, Nov. 2021.

[23] G. Goderis et al., "Evaluating Large-Scale Integrated Care Projects: The Development of a Protocol for a Mixed Methods Realist Evaluation Study in Belgium", International Journal of Integrated Care, vol. 20, no. 3, Jul. 2020.

[24] I. Liu, B. Rabin, M. Manivannan, E. Laney, and R. Philipsborn, "Evaluating strengths and opportunities for a co-created climate change curriculum: Medical student perspectives", Frontiers in Public Health, vol. 10, p. 1021125, Oct. 2022.

[25] L. Kinnaer, I. Kenis, V. Foulon, and A. Van Hecke, "Evaluation of interprofessional care processes for patients treated with oral anticancer drugs", Journal of Interprofessional Care, vol. 36, no. 4, pp. 509–519, Jul. 2022.

[26] K. Courtney, "Exploring Virtual Opportunities to Enhance and Promote an Emergent Community of Practice", Electronic Journal of e-Learning, vol. 5, no. 4, pp. 261–270, 2007.

[27] L. Sudbury-Riley and P. Hunter-Jones, "Facilitating inter-professional integration in palliative care: A service ecosystem perspective", Social Science & Medicine, vol. 277, p. 113912, May 2021.

[28] A. Ryan and D. Tilbury, "Flexible Pedagogies: New Pedagogical Ideas. Flexible Pedagogies: Preparing for the Future Series", Higher Education Academy, 2014.

[29] A. Wiehl, "From documentary networks to documentary worknets: Strategies of participation and co-creation in emerging practices of factual storytelling", New Cinemas, vol. 17, no. 1, pp. 3–19, 2020.

[30] H. Khalili et al., "Global leadership in IPECP research; an intro to co-creation of best practice guidelines", Journal of Interprofessional Education and Practice, vol. 24, p. 100445, 2021.

[31] L. Zhou and M. B. Nunes, "Identifying Knowledge Sharing Barriers in the Collaboration of Traditional and Western Medicine Professionals in Chinese Hospitals: A Case Study", Journal of Librarianship and Information Science, vol. 44, no. 4, pp. 238–248, Dec. 2012.

[32] D. Herchline, R. Tenney-Soiero, and J. Mehta, "Impact of hospitalists' social identities on perceptions of teamwork", Journal of Interprofessional Care, pp. 1–8, Nov. 2021.

[33] B. Jensen and R. L. Iannone, "Innovative approaches to continuous professional development (CPD) in early childhood education and care (ECEC) in Europe: Findings from a comparative review", European Journal of Education, vol. 53, no. 1, pp. 23–33, 2018.

[34] A. Boisselle and M. Simmonds, "Interdisciplinary partnerships between rehabilitation therapists and computer scientists: a proposed model", in Proceedings of the 7th International Conference on PErvasive Technologies Related to Assistive Environments, in PETRA "14. New York, NY, USA: Association for Computing Machinery, 2014, pp. 1–4.

[35] K. Saia, K. Toros, and D. DiNitto, "Interprofessional collaboration in social rehabilitation services for dually-involved Estonian youth: Perceptions of youth, parents, and professionals", Children and Youth Services Review, vol. 113, p. 104945, Jun. 2020.

[36] A. R. Suorsa, "Knowledge creation and play: A phenomenological study within a multi-professional and multi-organizational community", Journal of Documentation, vol. 73, no. 6, pp. 1167–1191, 2017.

[37] A. Kitson et al., "Knowledge translation within a population health study: How do you do it?", Implementation Science, vol. 8, no. 1, pp. 1–9, 2013.

[38] P. Clark, "Narrative in interprofessional education and practice: implications for professional identity, provider-patient communication and teamwork", Journal of Interprofessional Care, vol. 28, no. 1, pp. 34–39, Jan. 2014.

[39] A. Da Ros et al., "Physiotherapy as part of primary health care, Italy", Bulletin of the World Health Organization, vol. 100, no. 11, pp. 669–675, Nov. 2022.

[40] N. Andersen, "Potentialization: loosening up relations between public organizations and societal function systems", Management & Organizational History, vol. 15, no. 1, pp. 65–89, 2020.

[41] C. Øye, V. Wilson, and K. Manley, "Practice Development – Towards Co-Creation, Innovation and Systems Transformation to Foster Person-Centred Care", in International Practice Development in Health and Social Care, Second Edition, 2021, pp. 251–264.

[42] J. F. Giddens et al., "Re-envisioning clinical education for nurse practitioner programs: Themes from a national leaders" dialogue", Journal of Professional Nursing, vol. 30, no. 3, pp. 273–278, 2014.

[43] C. Dindler and O. S. Iversen, "Relational expertise in participatory design", in Proceedings of the 13th Participatory Design Conference: Research Papers - Volume 1, in PDC "14. New York, NY, USA: Association for Computing Machinery, 2014, pp. 41–50.

[44] I. Dufour et al., "Research protocol of the Laval-ROSA Transilab: a living lab on transitions for people living with dementia", BMC Health Services Research, vol. 23, no. 1, p. 1255, Nov. 2023.

[45] S. Barile and M. Saviano, "Resource integration and value co-creation in cultural heritage management", in Handbook of Research on Management of Cultural Products: E-Relationship Marketing and Accessibility Perspectives, 2014, pp. 58–82.

[46] K. Hays et al., "Smooth Transitions: Enhancing Interprofessional Collaboration when Planned Community Births Transfer to Hospital Care", Journal of Midwifery & Womens Health, vol. 67, no. 6, pp. 701–706, Nov. 2022.

[47] S. S. Van Der Kruk and Z. Tiantian, "Studying the evolution of the interorganizational information infrastructure (ioii) in finnish health care from a practice theoretical perspective", presented at the ECIS 2013 - Proceedings of the 21st European Conference on Information Systems, 2013, p. 11. [Online]. Available: https://www.scopus.com/inward/record.uri?eid=2-s2.0-84905845368&partnerID=40&md5=44e638f20eed52550157cea9b3ab6cf4

[48] J. Nie et al., "The Perceived Ease of Use and Perceived Usefulness of a Web-Based Interprofessional Communication and Collaboration Platform in the Hospital Setting: Interview Study With Health Care Providers", JMIR Human Factors, vol. 10, p. e39051, 2023.

[49] P. Moss, P. Nixon, S. Baggio, and D. Newcomb, "Turning Strategy into Action-Using the ECHO Model to Empower the Australian Workforce to Integrate Care", International Journal of Integrated Care, vol. 23, no. 2, Apr. 2023.

[50] S. Singh et al., "A road-map for addressing antimicrobial resistance in low- and middle-income countries: lessons learnt from the public private participation and co-designed antimicrobial stewardship programme in the State of Kerala, India", Antimicrobial Resistance and Infection Control, vol. 10, no. 1, pp. 1–9, Feb. 2021.

[51] M. Paterson et al., "Action Research as a Qualitative Research Approach in Inter-Professional Education: The QUIPPED Approach", Qualitative Report, vol. 12, no. 2, pp. 332–344, Jun. 2007.

[52] C. Gray et al., "Building a Digital Bridge to Support Patient-Centered Care Transitions From Hospital to Home for Older Adults With Complex Care Needs: Protocol for a Co-Design, Implementation, and Evaluation Study", JMIR Research Protocols, vol. 9, no. 11, p. e20220, Nov. 2020.

[53] J. Busari, H. Yaldiz, R. Gans, and A. Duits, "Clinical Leadership as an Agent for Change: A Health System Improvement Intervention in Curacao", Journal of Multidisciplinary Healthcare, vol. 13, pp. 787–798, 2020.

[54] T. Tang, M. Lim, E. Mansfield, A. McLachlan, and S. Quan, "Clinician user involvement in the real world: Designing an electronic tool to improve interprofessional communication and collaboration in a hospital setting", International Journal of Medical Informatics, vol. 110, pp. 90–97, Feb. 2018.

[55] N. E. M. France, S. Kaye, and M. Smith, "Co-Creating Caring Science-Based Interprofessional Simulation Through the Living Experience", International Journal for Human Caring, vol. 26, no. 1, pp. 31–39, 2022.

[56] M. Poitras et al., "Co-design, implementation, and evaluation of an expanded train-the-trainer strategy to support the sustainability of evidence-based practice guides for registered nurses and social workers in primary care clinics: a developmental evaluation protocol", BMC Primary Care, vol. 23, no. 1, p. 84, Apr. 2022.

[57] T. Rendell, J. Barnett, and D. Wright, "Co-designing a community pharmacy pharmacogenomics testing service in the UK", Bmc Health Services Research, vol. 22, no. 1, p. 378, Mar. 2022.

[58] A. Taylor, H. R. Lee, A. Kubota, and L. D. Riek, "Coordinating Clinical Teams: Using Robots to Empower Nurses to Stop the Line", Proc. ACM Hum.-Comput. Interact., vol. 3, no. CSCW, pp. 1–30, Nov. 2019.

[59] S. Ahn and S. Edelbring, "Designing a virtual patient as an interprofessional enactment: lessons learnt from the process", Int. J. Learn. Technol., vol. 15, no. 3, pp. 204–218, Jan. 2020.

[60] T. Rendell, J. Barnett, S. Scott, and D. Wright, "Designing an evidence based community pharmacy service specification for a pharmacogenomic testing service", International Journal of Clinical Pharmacy, vol. 44, no. 6, pp. 1406–1416, Dec. 2022.

[61] S. G. Anjara et al., "Embedding collective leadership to foster collaborative inter-professional working in the care of older people (ECLECTIC): Study protocol", HRB Open Research, vol. 3, 2020.

[62] A. L. Gallagher, C. Murphy, P. F. Conway, and A. Perry, "Engaging multiple stakeholders to improve speech and language therapy services in schools: An appreciative inquiry-based study", BMC Health Services Research, vol. 19, no. 1, pp. 1–17, 2019.

[63] L. Garvey et al., "Enhancing Cultural Capabilities Amongst Health Professions Students: A Pilot Study of Interprofessional Tag Team Simulation", Clinical Simulation in Nursing, vol. 62, pp. 83–91, Jan. 2022.

[64] D. O"Brien et al., "Exploring the current and future osteoarthritis health service delivery needs in Aotearoa New Zealand", New Zealand Medical Journal, vol. 136, no. 1573, pp. 55–66, Apr. 2023.

[65] R. Valaitis et al., "Health TAPESTRY: Co-designing interprofessional primary care programs for older adults using the persona-scenario method", BMC Family Practice, vol. 20, no. 1, pp. 1–11, 2019.

[66] C. Paltved, A. Morcke, and P. Musaeus, "Insider action research and the microsystem of a Danish surgical ward", Action Research, vol. 14, no. 2, pp. 184–200, Jun. 2016.

[67] L. Seppänen et al., "Interplay of coordination, co-creation and community building: examining interprofessional collaboration in workplace development efforts in health care", Journal of Workplace Learning, vol. 34, no. 5, pp. 455–465, May 2022.

[68] A. Andersson et al., "Iterative co-creation for improved hand hygiene and aseptic techniques in the operating room: experiences from the safe hands study", BMC Health Services Research, vol. 18, pp. 1–12, Jan. 2018.

[69] J. Molenaar, I. Korstjens, M. Hendrix, R. de Vries, and M. Nieuwenhuijze, "Needs of parents and professionals to improve shared decision-making in interprofessional maternity care practice: A qualitative study", Birth-Issues in Perinatal Care, vol. 45, no. 3, pp. 245–254, Sep. 2018.

[70] T. Marufu, N. Taylor, S. Fox, R. Boardman, and J. Manning, "Paediatric family activation rapid response (FARR) in tertiary healthcare organisations: Protocol for an online, multi-lingual, application (app) intervention development study", BMC Pediatrics, vol. 23, no. 1, p. 297, Jun. 2023.

[71] N. Muinga et al., "Using a human-centred design approach to develop a comprehensive newborn monitoring chart for inpatient care in Kenya", BMC Health Services Research, vol. 21, no. 1, pp. 1–14, Sep. 2021.

[72] E. Paraskevopoulos et al., "Utilizing Co-Creative Principles to Develop an E-Learning Platform for Interprofessional Training on Tinnitus: The Erasmus plus Project Tin-TRAC", International Journal of Environmental Research and Public Health, vol. 19, no. 14, p. 8323, Jul. 2022.

[73] A. Jelen, R. Goldfarb, J. Rosart, L. Graham, and B. Rubin, "A qualitative co-design-based approach to identify sources of workplace-related distress and develop well-being strategies for cardiovascular nurses, allied health professionals, and physicians", BMC Health Services Research, vol. 24, no. 1, pp. 1–12, Feb. 2024.

[74] L. Kinnaer et al., "A qualitative evaluation of the process of creating and implementing an interprofessional care pathway for patients treated with oral anticancer drugs", European Journal of Oncology Nursing, vol. 61, p. 102218, Dec. 2022.

[75] E. Quillerou and S. Boulnois, "Analysing human activity development through (work)spaces in a human-centered design project for commercial airline pilots", Journal of Workplace Learning, vol. 33, no. 1, pp. 62–80, Mar. 2021.

[76] S. Williams et al., "Building effective engagement for implementation with i-PARIHS: a collaborative enquiry into paediatric pain care in the emergency department", BMC Health Services Research, vol. 22, no. 1, p. 330, Mar. 2022.

[77] J. Baayd et al., "Catalyzing Collaboration Among Interprofessional Birth Transfer Teams Through Simulation", Journal of Midwifery & Womens Health, pp. 458–465, Apr. 2023.

[78] J. Murray et al., "Co-creation of five key research priorities across law enforcement and public health: A methodological example and outcomes", Journal of Psychiatric and Mental Health Nursing, vol. 28, no. 1, pp. 3–15, Feb. 2021.

[79] S. Belko, M. Hutchinson, G. Hayden, and R. Pugliese, "Co-designing Diabetes Care With Patients", Journal of Diabetes Science and Technology, vol. 18, no. 1, pp. 53–58, 2024.

[80] C. Wong, K. Kumpulainen, and A. Kajamaa, "Collaborative creativity among education professionals in a co-design workshop: A multidimensional analysis", Thinking Skills and Creativity, vol. 42, p. 100971, Dec. 2021.

[81] A. Salmi, O. Ahonen, and P. Pöyry-Lassila, "Crossing Asymmetries in Multistakeholder Service Design in Integrated Care", in Service Design Practices for Healthcare Innovation:Paradigms, Principles, Prospects, 2022, pp. 133–156.

[82] D. O"Donnell, G. O"Donoghue, É. Shé, M. O"Shea, and S. Donnelly, "Developing competence in interprofessional collaboration within integrated care teams for older people in the Republic of Ireland: A starter kit", Journal of Interprofessional Care, vol. 37, no. 3, pp. 480–490, May 2023.

[83] M. Sirimsi et al., "Development of a toolkit to improve interprofessional collaboration and integration in primary care using qualitative interviews and co-design workshops", Frontiers in Public Health, vol. 11, p. 1140987, Apr. 2023.

[84] Y. Slaghmuylder, P. Pype, A. Van Hecke, and E. Lauwerier, "Development of an intervention aimed at the prevention and treatment of chronic pain in breast cancer survivors: An intervention mapping approach", Patient Education and Counseling, vol. 108, p. 107618, Mar. 2023.

[85] N. Reid et al., "Enhancing interprofessional practice through the co-design of a holistic culturally and developmentally informed First Nations child health assessment", Australian Journal of Primary Health, vol. 29, no. 1, pp. 30–37, 2023.

[86] R. Brown et al., "Insights from an inaugural eight-month interprofessional collaborative co-design educational experience between occupational therapy and industrial design", Journal of Accessibility and Design for All, vol. 11, no. 1, pp. 148–177, 2021.

[87] J. Young et al., "Interprofessional learning about medication safety", Clinical Teacher, vol. 18, no. 6, pp. 656–661, Dec. 2021.

[88] J. Walter et al., "Intervention Codesign in the Pediatric Cardiac Intensive Care Unit to Improve Family Meetings", Journal of Pain and Symptom Management, vol. 64, no. 1, pp. 8–16, Jul. 2022.

[89] K. Rygh and A. Morrison, "Negotiating Care Through Tangible Tools and Tangible Service Designing in Emergent Public Health Service Ecosystems", in Service Design Practices for Healthcare Innovation:Paradigms, Principles, Prospects, 2022, pp. 77–114.

[90] L. Ogden and R. Williams, "Supporting Patrons in Crisis through a Social Work-Public Library Collaboration", Journal of Library Administration, vol. 62, no. 5, pp. 656–672, Jul. 2022.

[91] N. Cresswell, S. Walker, C. Harrison, and F. Kent, "Teaching digital interprofessional collaboration", Clinical Teacher, p. e13651, Sep. 2023.

[92] P. Ross et al., "The Australian and New Zealand Clinician Educator Network (ANZCEN) Unconference: What"s an unconference and how can it develop communities of practice?", Journal of Interprofessional Care, vol. 35, no. 2, pp. 310–315, Mar. 2021.

[93] G. Brand et al., ""You don"t see what I see": Co-designing simulation to uncover and address cognitive bias in healthcare", Medical Teacher, pp. 1–4, Feb. 2024.

[94] D. Sabater-Hernández et al., "A stakeholder co-design approach for developing a community pharmacy service to enhance screening and management of atrial fibrillation", Bmc Health Services Research, vol. 18, pp. 1–10, Feb. 2018.

[95] F. Bracco et al., "Adaptation of non-technical skills behavioural markers for delivery room simulation", BMC Pregnancy and Childbirth, vol. 17, pp. 1–7, Mar. 2017.

[96] L. Gahan, E. Gaffy, B. Dow, and B. Brijnath, "Advancing methodologies to increase end-user engagement with complex interventions: The case of co-designing the Australian elder abuse screening instrument (AuSI)", Journal of Elder Abuse & Neglect, vol. 31, no. 4–5, pp. 325–339, 2019.

[97] M. L. Ciccarelli and C.-J. C. Harris, "Children"s computer interaction in schools: a case study for promoting healthy computer use", in CHI "13 Extended Abstracts on Human Factors in Computing Systems, in CHI EA "13. New York, NY, USA: Association for Computing Machinery, 2013, pp. 673–678.

[98] S. Lightfoot et al., "Co-creating a suite of patient decision aids for parents of an infant or young child with differences of sex development: A methods roadmap", Frontiers in Urology, vol. 2, p. 1020152, 2022.

[99] L. Rose et al., "Co-designed and consensus based development of a quality improvement checklist of patient and family-centered actionable processes of care for adults with persistent critical illness", Journal of Critical Care, vol. 72, p. 154153, Dec. 2022.

[100] A. Freudenthal, T. Stüdeli, P. Lamata, and E. Samset, "Collaborative co-design of emerging multi-technologies for surgery", Journal of Biomedical Informatics, vol. 44, no. 2, pp. 198–215, 2011.

[101] E. Angelini, A. Wolf, H. Wijk, H. Brisby, and A. Baranto, "Evaluating a targeted person-centred pain management intervention programme in lumbar spine surgery - a controlled segment-specific before-and-after interventional design", BMC Health Services Research, vol. 24, no. 1, p. 315, 2024.

[102] A. Dwyer et al., "Evaluating co-created patient-facing materials to increase understanding of genetic test results", Journal of Genetic Counseling, vol. 30, no. 2, pp. 598–605, Apr. 2021.

[103] A. S. Macdonald, G. Teal, C. Bamford, and P. J. Moynihan, "Hospitalfoodie: An interprofessional case study of the redesign of the nutritional management and monitoring system for vulnerable older hospital patients", Quality in Primary Care, vol. 20, no. 3, pp. 169–177, 2012.

[104] R. Rostetter, B. Jenni, S. Eggmann, J. T. Meyer, and K.-U. Schmitt, "Implementing an interprofessional user-centered design approach to develop a bedside leg exercise device", Technol. Health Care, vol. 30, no. 4, pp. 981–992, Jan. 2022.

[105] N. Daniëls, L. Hochstenbach, M. van Bokhoven, A. Beurskens, and P. Delespaul, "Implementing Experience Sampling Technology for Functional Analysis in Family Medicine - A Design Thinking Approach", Frontiers in Psychology, vol. 10, p. 2782, Dec. 2019.

[106] M. Frödin et al., "Interactive Interventions Can Improve Hand Hygiene and Aseptic Techniques During Perioperative Care-Experience From the ?Safe Hands? Project", Journal of Perianesthesia Nursing, vol. 38, no. 2, pp. 284–290, Apr. 2023.

[107] M. Malek et al., "Interprofessional Needs Analysis and User-Centred Prototype Evaluation as a Foundation for Building Individualized Digital Education in Dementia Healthcare Supported by Artificial Intelligence: A Study Protocol", Healthcare (Switzerland), vol. 11, no. 10, p. 1508, 2023.

[108] F. Bugeaud and E. Soulier, "OntoStoria 2: A shared representation and a web-based tool for the collaboration of services providers", Web Intelligence and Agent Systems, vol. 10, no. 2, pp. 247–260, 2012.

[109] K. Pateman et al., "Partnering with consumers to co-design a person-centred coding framework for qualitative patient experience data", PATIENT EDUCATION AND COUNSELING, vol. 116, Nov. 2023.

[110] A. Salonen, S. Kärkkäinen, and T. Keinonen, "Teachers Co-Designing and Implementing Career-Related Instruction", Education Sciences, vol. 9, no. 4, p. 255, Dec. 2019.

[111] E. Angelini, A. Wolf, H. Wijk, H. Brisby, and A. Baranto, "The impact of implementing a person-centred pain management intervention on resistance to change and organizational culture", BMC Health Services Research, vol. 21, no. 1, pp. 1–11, Dec. 2021.

[112] J. Youm and W. Wiechmann, "The Med AppJam: A Model for an Interprofessional Student-Centered mHealth App Competition", J. Med. Syst., vol. 39, no. 3, pp. 1–6, Mar. 2015.

[113] A. Paterson et al., "The Smarter Sleep educational interventions: an initiative to reduce hypnotic prescribing in in-patient psychiatric care", Bjpsych Bulletin, vol. 46, no. 4, pp. 242–250, Aug. 2022.

[114] A. Poberznik et al., "A modifiable virtual reality game for neurological physiotherapy - Multiprofessional development and pilot testing", presented at the SeGAH 2022 - 2022 IEEE 10th International Conference on Serious Games and Applications for Health, 2022, pp. 1–6.

[115] D. Kingsmore et al., "A national co-design workshop of a mobile-based application for vascular access as a patient decision aid", Journal of Vascular Access, vol. 25, no. 1, pp. 187–192, Jan. 2024.

[116] B. McCormack, L. Peelo-Kilroe, M. Codd, and D. Baldie, "A strategically engaged programme of person-centred culture development in health services: The courage of the Irish!", in Innovative Staff Development in Healthcare, 2021, pp. 101–114.

[117] E. Renehan, D. Goeman, and S. Koch, "Development of an optimised key worker framework for people with dementia, their family and caring unit living in the community", BMC Health Services Research, vol. 17, no. 1, pp. 1–16, 2017.

[118] R. Harrison et al., "Evaluating clinician experience in value-based health care: the development and validation of the Clinician Experience Measure (CEM)", Bmc Health Services Research, vol. 22, no. 1, p. 1484, Dec. 2022.

[119] A. Martin et al., "Co-constructive Patient Simulation A Learner-Centered Method to Enhance Communication and Reflection Skills"", Simulation in Healthcare-Journal of the Society for Simulation in Healthcare, vol. 16, no. 6, pp. E129–E135, Dec. 2021.

[120] S. Collins et al., "Next generation terminology infrastructure to support interprofessional care planning", J. of Biomedical Informatics, vol. 75, no. C, pp. 22–34, Nov. 2017.

[121] S. Jean et al., "Serious games as a catalyst for boundary crossing, collaboration and knowledge co-creation in a watershed governance context", Journal of Environmental Management, vol. 223, pp. 1010–1022, Oct. 2018.

[122] K. Darcel et al., "Implementing artificial intelligence in Canadian primary care: Barriers and strategies identified through a national deliberative dialogue", Plos One, vol. 18, no. 2, p. e0281733, Feb. 2023.

[123] R. Hulme, D. Cracknell, and A. Owens, "Learning in third spaces: developing trans-professional understanding through practitioner enquiry", Educational Action Research, vol. 17, no. 4, pp. 537–550, Dec. 2009.

[124] M. Muller and A. Druin, "Participatory Design: The Third Space in HCI", Handbook of HCI, Jan. 2002.

[125] J. Gregory, "Scandinavian approaches to participatory design", International Journal of Engineering Education, vol. 19, no. 1, pp. 62–74, 2003.

Transprofessional Course Design in Teacher Education

Facilitating Spaces for Negotiating Roles and Finding Common Ground

Kristine Høeg Karlsen
Faculty of Teacher Education and Languages
Østfold University College
Halden, Norway
kristine.h.karlsen@hiof.no

Joakim Karlsen
Faculty of Computer Science, Engineering and Economics
Østfold University College
Halden, Norway
joakim.karlsen@hiof.no

Susanne Koch Stigberg
Faculty of Computer Science, Engineering and Economics
Østfold University College
Halden, Norway
susanne.k.stigberg@hiof.no

Abstract **- In today's rapidly changing world, educators stand at the crossroads. Tomorrow's teachers are responsible for equipping their pupils with essential 21st-century skills, a task that transcends mere professional boundaries. As the educational landscape evolves, teacher education programs grapple with the mandate to adapt curricula to this new societal complexity. Our study delves into uncharted territory: the intersection where arts, culture, technology design and pedagogy converge. Collaborations between stakeholders from these diverse domains yield a wealth of insights. Through co-design, we negotiate roles, seeking common ground - a reflective practice that may give rise to a "third space". Drawing from our analyses, we propose essential aspects for facilitators of such processes to consider. These insights could contribute to the goal of nurturing safe, innovative "third" spaces where educators assume new roles and shape the future of interdisciplinary course design in teacher education.**

Keywords - curriculum design; co-design; professional collaboration; teacher education; role release; role expansion.

I. Introduction

To prepare teachers who can adeptly respond to the rapidly changing future demands in both society and the workforce, teacher education must align with 21st-century skills [1][2]. This imperative extends to the curriculum, which serves as a pivotal policy document across educational levels [3]. While primary school curricula have received significant attention in curriculum research, there has been a noticeable gap within higher education according to Karseth [3]. In this study, we delve into the dynamics that unfold when stakeholders from diverse disciplines collaborate to co-design a course in Teacher Education (TE) with the purpose of empowering future teachers through *cross-sectoral collaboration*. Through this effort, the aim is to enhance student teachers' ability to navigate the complexities of education, that extends beyond professional boundaries.

Internationally, Cross-Sectoral Collaboration (CSC) in school is common [4]-[7]. In Norway, increasingly, school time is allocated to external partners such as The Technological Schoolbag, Young Entrepreneurship, and The Cultural Schoolbag (TCS). While these partners play a role in realizing the curriculum, their primary purpose is to enrich students' experiences, knowledge, and skills. However, this development can pose challenges for teachers who must balance achieving educational goals with limited time for CSC. Therefore, it is crucial to empower future teachers to maximize the benefits of working with external actors and effectively integrate these experiences into the school day.

The study originates from the extensive project, pARTiciPED, which receives funding from The Research Council of Norway (2020-2024). The aim of pARTiciPED has been to foster CSCs between the cultural and educational sectors. Specifically, it seeks to address the contradictions within TCS program, which aims to provide students with access to cultural expressions during their education. The project investigates how student teachers can be empowered to act as agents of change in bridging the gap between schools and the cultural sector. Notably, this initiative arises from the asymmetric power relations that exist between schools and cultural institutions within the cultural schoolbag [8]-[11], where some teachers view themselves as having limited influence in TCS activities they facilitate for [8][12] and lack a clear *understanding of their roles* [13].

In the pARTiciPED project, we have aimed to facilitate for the emergence of novel collaborative practices and to understand the socio-material factors supporting the likelihood and longevity of such practices. In this, we have been steered by the aspirational concept of 'transformative mutuality' [14]. This concept encapsulates a reciprocal and transformative relationship, where participants engage in mutual learning, growth, and change. It transcends mere cooperation and delves into a deeper synergy—one that reshapes perspectives, empowers individuals, and enriches collective actions characterized by Eyal and Yarm as:

> …both parties taking an active approach, engaging willingly and enthusiastically in shared educational deliberation, and devising and implementing educational activities that have a synergistic effect, contributing to the growth of both parties on an individual and organizational level, as well as to the students. [14, p. 680]

We remained committed to nurturing 'third spaces' where transformative mutuality can develop, fostering connections that transcends disciplinary and professional boundaries, to facilitate dialogue among stakeholders in teacher education institutions (both students and teachers), partner schools, and TCS. According to Gutiérrez [15] a third space is "a transformative space where the potential for an expanded form of learning and the development of new knowledge are heightened" [15, p. 152], where staff are engaged "in substantive dialogue about educational values, goals, and methods, leading to pedagogical innovation" [14, p. 651]. Third spaces thus aim at becoming "a place of invention and transformational encounters" [16, p. 244]. The third space is intended to operationalize the role of the (future) teacher, in line with Mølstad and Prøitz's [17, p. 4] understanding of the teachers' autonomy, defined as "the freedom and responsibility given to the teaching profession to plan teaching based on professional decisions and justification" (p. 4). A prerequisite when facilitating such third spaces is to develop an acute awareness and understanding of the importance of negotiating roles across the intersecting disciplines and professions. The negotiating of roles is critical to foster *interprofessionality* or even *transprofessionality*.

In this paper, we investigate the negotiation of roles when stakeholders from diverse disciplines collaborate to co-design a course in TE with the purpose of empowering future teachers through CSC in the pARTiciPED project. In Section 2, we present an elaborated background on roles in transprofessional collaborations, followed by the introduction of the two labs in the pARTiciPED project in Section 3. Our methodology is described in Section 4, while Section 5 presents our findings from unpacking the role negotiation concept in our labs. Lastly, in Section 6, we propose three central aspects for negotiating roles and fostering mutual understanding within professional co-design teams.

II. BACKGROUND

A. Roles in transprofessional collaborations

To understand types of professionalism we need to distinguish between a discipline and a profession. A discipline involves developing theories to comprehend the world. It encompasses the systematic study of a specific subject or field. A profession is essentially a practically applied discipline [18]. Disciplines can be separate and distinct from one another, each focusing on its unique area of inquiry. The degree of collaboration between disciplines can vary, leading to different levels of interaction:

- **Intra:** Disciplines exist in isolation (monodisciplinary).
- **Multi:** Disciplines coexist alongside each other.
- **Cross:** Disciplines interact and inform each other.
- **Inter:** Disciplines partially overlap.
- **Trans:** Disciplines almost fully overlap, fostering mutual learning and reciprocity.

Bernard C.K. Choi and Anita W.P. Pak [19] thoroughly review the differences in the definitions of multidisciplinary, interdisciplinarity and transdisciplinarity in the literature (1982-2006). They conclude by giving the following distinctions.

- At its most fundamental level, multidisciplinary collaboration is *additive* and involves various disciplines working independently or in sequence on a problem, maintaining their distinct boundaries.
- Interdisciplinary, on the other hand, fosters reciprocal *interaction* between disciplines, leading to the merging of boundaries and the creation of new shared methods, perspectives, and knowledge.
- Finally, transdisciplinary extends beyond academic disciplines, including non-scientists and other stakeholders, to examine whole systems *holistically*.

They emphasize how transdisciplinarity requires both *role release and role expansion. Role release* refers to the intentional relinquishing of specific responsibilities or tasks by team members. It involves allowing others to take over certain functions that were previously within an individual's domain. *Role expansion* involves broadening the scope of a team member's responsibilities. It encourages individuals to take on additional tasks or explore new areas.

The types of disciplinarity and how they depend on the (re)negotiation of roles in teams apply to transprofessional teams as well. It is important to note however, that in the same team the same individual can negotiate disciplinarity and professionality differently, depending on context.

B. Curriculum planning in transprofessional teams

In our context, a collaborative effort unites team members from diverse backgrounds, including cultural work, technology design, and education. Together, they co-design a TE course with the aim of fostering CSCs between the cultural and educational domains.

Curriculum planning, according to Goodlad [20], is an ongoing, hands-on process that aims to design educational programs to enhance learners' knowledge, skills, and attitudes. It is driven by the desire to close the gap between current state and future goals, with educational institutions bearing the responsibility to achieve these objectives [20]. Curriculum development requires decision-making at various level. Despite its importance across all educational levels, research on higher education curricula is relatively sparse [3]. This study contributes to this area by analyzing transprofessionalism in TE course design.

In Norway, TE is regulated by Framework Plan for Primary and Lower Secondary Teacher Education for Years 1-7 and 5–10. These plans outline the goals, structure, content, and desired educational outcomes for teaching at these levels [32][33]. This article zeroes in on curriculum for a course in TE focusing on CSC in Norwegian schools (from here referred to as the "CSC-course"), developed during the pARTiciPED project. The main aim of the course is to deepen student teachers understanding of interprofessional collaboration in schools and to elucidate their role in such cooperative undertakings.

Goodlad et al. [21] present five curricular perspectives, with this article focusing on the perceived level—how the formal curriculum is interpreted into *local* lesson plans. Støren [22] suggests that local curriculum efforts can be seen in three dimensions: as a recipe to be understood, as a framework to be filled, and as a framework to be developed further. She posits with reference to Tronsmo [23] that at the third dimension, teachers in their professional community creatively engage with the curriculum to evolve their practice and understanding of it.

C. Operationalizing spaces for negotiating roles and finding common ground

In pARTiciPED, we have aimed to democratize not only the way student teachers are empowered to become change agents as future teachers, but also how the course has *been designed*. In this, we have developed a methodological approach indebted to the core principles of co-design [24] adapted to our purposes as securing:

- *alternative visions* of 1) how new knowledge is created and shared and 2) how new skills and competences create conditions, opportunities and challenges related to what to learn and how in CSCs.
- *mutual learning* by finding common ground and ways of working that emphasize engagement, expressiveness, negotiation, and problem solving and that take place in actual settings in teacher education.
- *democratic practices* where power relations are equalized by giving everyone a voice and where all stakeholders act both in their own interest and in the interest of the common good.

In line with how Muller and Druin [25] see co-design as operationalizing third spaces in design, where the third space represents an in-between region where participants in the design process can engage in collaborative activities that transcend traditional boundaries, an intermediary zone where diverse knowledge and insights converge to inform the needs of organizations, institutions, products, and services. The experience is characterized by the 1) questioning of assumptions, possibly leading to fresh perspectives, 2) reciprocal learning where participants learn from one another, fostering mutual understanding, 3) the creation of new ideas by negotiating and co-creation of identities, working languages, and relationships and 4) polyvocal discussions where diverse voices contribute to rich discussions across differences [25].

III. TWO CASES – ONE CURRICULUM

The pARTiciPED project has established various TCS labs, bringing together participants from diverse educational and creative backgrounds such as student teachers, teacher educators, artists, art educators, cultural workers, designers, and intermediaries. These labs host co-design workshops that employ a variety of methods and tools, promoting mutual learning and transformative partnerships. As part of this effort, the CSC-course in TE, was co-designed (in TE). A summary of two pivotal labs analyzed in this study is presented below.

A. Lab Performing Arts

The first TCS lab, hereafter referred to as Lab Art, fostered a collaboration between teacher education and an art institution, involving both educators and students, along with local partner schoolteachers, to solidify a practical application of co-design. Among the participants, some had a shared history of collaboration from previous projects, while others joined in the pARTiciPED project. The aim was to co-design and implement the CSC-course in TE tailored for aspiring primary school teachers. The process involved five workshops: the initial three focused on establishing a mutual understanding and mapping competencies and roles within the design team, allowing stakeholders to share perspectives on curriculum development. Choreopattern, a novel choreography-based design approach, merging station-based tasks with movement section, was employed in the two latter workshops to jointly co-design the content of the course [31]. A crucial aspect of this work was to develop relations between professional practice of education and art, as outlined in [32]. The intriguing aspect of role dynamics lies in the challenges encountered by the participants in the design team, which will have the primary focus in the discussion.

B. Lab Museum

The second TCS lab focused on engaging student teachers in designing Cultural Heritage Learning Experiences (CHLE) in collaboration with museum educators for four whole-day seminars. Student teachers were challenged to collaborate with museum educators and to include gaming technologies in their CHLE designs. To facilitate these student seminars, we had four co-design workshops involving teacher educators, technology experts, teachers, and museum educators. Between these workshops, weekly digital collaboration meetings were held to address practical issues. The initial co-design workshop served as an icebreaker, fostering mutual understanding, exchanging expectations, and providing an overview of the project and the applied co-design methodology. The second workshop inquired into TCS focusing on the challenges and opportunities in schools. The third workshop entailed a museum visit fostering a mutual understanding of the museum educator's perspective. Lastly, during the fourth workshop, we developed design cards to be utilized by students in the seminar to enable them to design a CHLE. An account of the seminars has been reported by [30]. Here, we focus on the collaboration of experts to co-design the student seminars.

IV. METHODOLOGY

In this paper, we revisit our experiences from co-designing the CSC-course in TE to discuss how we negotiated roles and found a common ground as reflective practice. Reflective practice is 'learning through and from experience towards gaining new insights of self and practice' [26]. John Dewey [27] was among the first to identify reflection as a specialized form of thinking. He considered reflection to stem from doubt, hesitation, or perplexity related to a directly experienced situation and stresses how we learn from 'doing', i.e., practice. Donald Schön [28] defines reflection as a method to move from one design cycle to another until one reaches a final product. He proposes two types of reflection that contribute to the advancement of design work: reflection-in-action referring to the act of thinking and doing while in action, and reflection-on-action referring to the analysis of a design move after the process has happened. We have applied Schön's notion of reflection-on-action to reflect on negotiating roles and finding common ground in two labs in the pARTiciPED project, where we have been leading researchers and have collaborated with other stakeholders to maintain a co-design methodology to enable transprofessional collaboration in the course design.

We did our reflective analysis in two steps. The initial step commenced with a meeting among us researchers, where we shared our experiences from the two labs. We reviewed archived materials including meeting minutes, workshop plans, and prior publications detailing the lab activities. Through this process, we identified and categorized the evolving roles of participants and analyzed how these roles were manifested during workshops. We applied the concepts of *role release* and *role expansion* in another cycle of analysis in each of the two labs to explore the different facets of negotiating roles and finding common ground. We have chosen a storytelling approach to share our findings by exemplifying findings with vignettes from our labs. We were inspired by the concept of method stories [29], where Lee calls on the design field to "reflect and re-specify its research direction for design methods, especially for empathic design methods, that is, not by developing new tools or pinning-down practices into recipes, but rather towards empowering designers to be more sensitive and comfortable with the design-led, local approaches that are essential to empathic design methods".

V. UNPACKING ROLES

In the following, we aim to highlight three intriguing aspects that illustrate the complexity of negotiating roles and finding common ground in transprofessional course design in teacher education: the challenge of balancing many roles simultaneously, overlapping competence, and perceived ownership.

TABLE I. FORMAL ROLES IN LAB ART

	Teacher educators			Art educators	Student teachers	In-service teachers
Participants no.	1	1	1	3	1	2
Project/Lab leader	X					
PhD-candidate			X			
PhD supervisor	X					
Scientific researcher	X	X	X			
Artistic researcher		X		X		
Educator	X	X	X	X		
Student					X	
School teachers						X
Art teachers			X	X		
Professional artists			X	X		
Principals				X		
Workshop leader	X	X	X	X		
Manager of the co-created course in TE		X				

A. Balancing roles in course design

During Lab Art, educators from teacher education and professional art institutions assumed multiple roles that were not sufficiently articulated or negotiated throughout the series of workshops. Rather, the roles were fluid, with educators transitioning between them as they deemed necessary. Table I illustrates some of the formal roles that became apparent as participants engaged with the lab.

Notably, the table indicates that educators from teacher education and art education face a particularly demanding challenge in managing multiple roles, ranging from at least four to six each. They must make strategic decisions about which roles to adopt as the project unfolds. For example, within a single session, the project leader (first author) must balance PhD supervision, manage the pARTiciPED project, and lead and facilitate the workshop. Meanwhile, art educators are balancing their responsibilities as principals of their art university college, their roles as professional artists, and their participation in co-design workshops. The potential for 'role release' adds another layer of complexity to managing these roles on an individual level. To illustrate, consider the first workshop in the Lab Art: Teacher educators had organized a session employing scenario-based drama to simulate a typical visit by TCS to a school. The participants were cast in acting roles, which some of them found uncomfortable and ineffective. Consequently, the activity fell short of its potential.

In Lab Museum, roles were assigned based on participants' backgrounds. A workshop facilitator orchestrated the workshop activities, informed by participant input, and worked closely with the project leader. Each participant had a specific role: a project leader, a PhD candidate, a teacher educator, a museum educator, a student teacher, and two in-service teachers (see Table II). Participants' roles intersected mainly in the role as scientific researcher, emphasizing a shared commitment to research objectives and the collection and analysis of workshop data.

TABLE II. FORMAL ROLES IN LAB MUSEUM

	Technology Designers			Teacher educator	Museum communicator	Student teacher	In-service teachers
Participants no.	1	1	1	1	1	1	2
Project/Lab leader	X						
PhD-candidate			X				
PhD supervisor	X						
Scientific researcher	X	X	X	X			
Teacher educator				X			
Student						X	
School teachers							X
Museum educator					X		
Workshop leader		X					
Manager of the co-created course in TE				X			

B. Overlapping competence

From Table 1, it is evident that the design team in Lab Art have overlapping roles. Although at different educational levels, all participants are educators in some form, except for the two students. One of the teacher educators, who is also a PhD candidate, has formal education in art and art pedagogy, expertise that aligns with that of the art educators. Moreover, several participants have informal background in art, such as theater, dance, and music, indicating a level of disciplinary expertise. The art educators, having been associated with various TE programs in Norway for years, possess knowledge of that context. They also share a research interest with one of the teacher educators who engages in artistic research. Additional role overlaps also exist. However, what is particularly intriguing are situations when participants in the workshop bring to the table expertise usually confined to other's domain, necessitating a release of roles to allow others to take over certain functions, a transition that can be challenging.

An example that stands out is the instance where the PhD candidate utilized her art expertise to co-develop Choreopattern with the other teacher educators, drawing upon choreographic elements. This joint effort led the teacher educators to venture into the realm of the art educators, which introduced challenges in the design team [31]. These challenges demanded immediate attention to propel curriculum development forward. During this period of change, art educators stepped into principal roles, while teacher educators shouldered the responsibilities of project leaders and PhD supervisors. Notably, the shift in roles among some team members precipitated new roles for others. If not handled judiciously, such role shifts can swiftly lead to counterproductive interactions.

In Lab Museum, participants assumed roles as experts in their respective fields, with minimal overlap in competence. During the second workshop, the in-service teachers took center stage, discussing challenges and opportunities in facilitating for TCS activities in schools. The expertise of the teachers in framing TCS within school practices was acknowledged by the other participants. Likewise, during the third workshop, the museum educator took the lead, guiding the group through the museum and offering an enriching learning experience for the design group.

C. Perceived ownership

In Lab Art, stakes were high for both teacher- and art educators, each demonstrating significant perceived ownership. Teacher educators were invested, motivated by the course's alignment with their student teachers' needs and the overarching goals of the pARTiciPED project, of which they were owners. Similarly, the art educators, who also served as principals of their college, were committed to supervising their students in their artistic work. This shared perceived ownership of the outputs of a co-design process have numerous advantages: collective sense of responsibility, the imperative of a successful outcome, and intrinsic motivation for the tasks.

In contrast, not all participants perceived a high degree of ownership of the process and outputs in Lab Museum. The student teacher tended to adopt a polite and somewhat guest-like position in most workshops, perhaps due to feeling junior in comparison to other participants. While the in-service teachers contributed to discussions in the second workshop, they had few responsibilities throughout the seminars and workshops. The teacher educator and the project leader (who also had roles as PhD supervisor and researcher) felt the greatest sense of ownership for the co-design activities, the teacher educator being responsible for the implementation of the course being co-designed and the project leader being responsible for overall goals for the lab. The low perceived stakes made it less challenging to facilitate for safe interactions in Lab Museum, and we believe a higher degree of perceived ownership would have benefited the outputs and outcomes of the lab.

VI. Finding Common Ground

There are certain considerations project leaders must take when aiming to provide safe "third" spaces [25] for sharing and assuming new roles. We highlight three aspects worth considering when seeking to negotiate roles and establish common ground in professional co-design teams: the facilitators level of investment, the need for renegotiating roles and the degree of association between the professions.

A. The facilitators level of investment

In Lab Art and Lab Museum the facilitators assumed markedly different roles in organizing and leading the workshops. In Lab Museum, an external and experienced facilitator from the design field (third author) led the workshops. Her relatively low level of investment in the co-design outcomes allowed her to concentrate on optimizing the process. In Lab Art, teacher educators with limited participatory design experience at the time, led most workshops, including the first author. They had a high level of investment in the process however, as they were not only facilitators, but also directly responsible for the course to be co-designed. This required them to balance their facilitator role as securing participation from all parties with making active contributions in the design of the curriculum.

Based on these insights, we acknowledge that experienced facilitators, with relatively low level of investment in the outcomes of the process, have more flexibility to strategically position themselves to optimize the workshops by adapting the process to unforeseen situations. They can more effectively maintain focus on the processes and other participants are potentially less inclined to suspect the facilitator of pursuing his or her own interests. Therefore, it is essential to consider the level of investment that facilitators have in the co-design outcomes to ensure mutual learning, growth, and change within professional co-design teams

B. (Re)negotiating roles

In professional teams doing co-design workshops, the roles of participants need to be continuously negotiated. This collaborative process extends throughout the project, allowing participants to renegotiate their roles based on the specific design needs in different phases of the work. In Lab Art, where prior collaboration existed among several participants, role negotiation was informed by shared work history, and primarily served to integrate new team members rather than redefining roles held by existing team members. Conversely, in Lab Museum, where participants were initially unfamiliar with each other, role negotiation commenced from the project's inception to establish common ground.

This highlights the substantial influence of participants' shared work history on role negotiation. When team members are already working together, proactive negotiation or even reevaluation of roles becomes critical before delving into co-design activities, such as curriculum design. This deliberate step must facilitate for both role release and role expansion, to secure transprofessionality in the co-design activities. Upon reflection, Lab Art could have benefited from one or more pre-workshops where participants established a new common ground and explicitly defined new roles and expectations. Such clarity would have allowed for thorough discussions about each participant's responsibilities and contributions in the new project, ultimately enhancing dialogue among stakeholders.

Explicitly agreeing on roles, as well as re-negotiating and redefining them, emerges as a central topic when professional teams collaborate in co-design, becoming transprofessional.

C. *Association between the professions*

In the two labs, participants engaged in collaborative efforts, each contributing from their unique professional vantage point. The degree of collaboration between the professions varied, resulting in distinct negotiation dynamics among stakeholders.

When analyzing the interplay between teacher education and external partners in the pARTiciPED project, we observe a more solid association between the professions represented in Lab Museum compared to Lab Art. History dissemination as a practically applied discipline in museums is relevant for teacher education and teacher educators with history as subject. Both professional groups have compatible skills, knowledge, and educational aims. Conveying history is not exclusively reserved for museum educators. Teachers, social scientists, guides, and others can effectively communicate historical narratives across various contexts. In contrast, art occupy privileged positions in society. Creating art remains the domain of professional artists and artists participating in Lab Art can more readily leverage this position to assume power in the collaborative process.

Facilitators must possess the skills to detect and balance these emergent power dynamics. This necessitates a willingness among all involved participants to adapt their perspectives in alignment with the activities and project's overarching goals. Such adaptability can prove challenging for everyone, also artists, who naturally hold a strong sense of ownership over their artwork and their artistic processes.

VII. CONCLUSION

Facilitating safe "third" spaces for negotiating roles and finding common ground across professions remains a challenge. In this paper, we have highlighted and discussed some aspects of this work, using the ongoing research project pARTiciPED as case. When facilitating for negotiating roles it is important to 1) map the roles in play (one participant can have many), 2) map the participants' overlapping and not overlapping competence, and 3) map the participants' ownership of the outcomes of the process. The three maps will be helpful in the facilitation of co-design activities. We believe that to achieve high degree of collaboration (and engagement) between the professionals in design teams, articulating roles, goals, and competence is what should come first.

When facilitating for finding common ground we find it is important 1) to make sure that the facilitator has not conflicting roles and is not to invested in particular outcomes, 2) to provide participants with a shared work history the opportunity to renegotiate and reset their roles before going to deep into the design work and 3) to identify and handle power dynamics that become barriers to role release and role expansion – for instance if the participants insist on holding on to professional roles that traditionally have had a privileged position in society (i.e., artists, doctors and professors).

In conclusion, achieving high degree of collaboration in professional collaborations is not a straightforward process and demands deliberate and thoughtful facilitation. Sometimes a transprofessional outcome remains elusive, however. We believe that if there is little potential for both role release and role expansion in the team being mobilized, a facilitator needs to handle this head on. If the initial co-design workshop phase fails to facilitate for articulation and re-negotiation of roles, it is better to reassemble the group rather than re-articulating entrenched disciplinary and professional barriers to collaboration.

ACKNOWLEDGMENT

The pARTiciPED project receives funding from The Research Council of Norway (2020-2024), Project no. 301594. We extend our gratitude to the Norwegian Research Council and our affiliated institutions for funding the pARTiciPED project.

REFERENCES

[1] L. Darling-Hammond and A. Lieberman, Teacher education around the world. Routledge, 2013.

[2] A. Gümüs, "Twenty-first-century teacher competencies and trends in teacher training", *Educational theory in the 21st century: Science, technology, society and education*, pp. 243–267, 2022.

[3] B. Karseth, "Norwegian teacher education – everyone wants to have a say", *Läroplansteori i och om lärarutbildning*, pp. 35–50, 2020.

[4] G. Duffy and T. Gallagher, "Sustaining school partnerships: the context of cross-sectoral collaboration between schools in a separate education system in Northern Ireland", *Review of Education*, vol. 2, no. 2, pp. 189–210, 2014.

[5] B. Kisida, L. Goodwin, and D. H. Bowen, "Teaching history through theater: The effects of arts integration on students' knowledge and attitudes", *AERA Open*, vol. 6, no. 1, 2020.

[6] M. C. Mannathoko, "School-stakeholder-partnership enhancement strategies in the implementation of arts in Botswana basic education", *International Journal of Education Through Art*, vol. 15, no. 2, pp. 149–164, 2019.

[7] C. S. Nielsen, T. P. Østern, K. H. Karlsen, E. Anttila, and R. K. Martin, "Troubling arts education from a Nordic policy

perspective: A field with an interdisciplinary and cross-sectoral potential", *Dance Articulated*, vol. 9, no. 1, pp. 11-30, 2023.

[8] J.-K. Breivik and C. Christophersen, *The Cultural Schoolbag*. Oslo, Bergen: Kulturrådet Fagbokforlaget, 2013, p. 207. [Online]. Available: http://kulturradet.no/vis-publikasjon/-/asset_publisher/N4dG/content/publikasjon-den-kulturelle-skolesekken [retrieved: 04, 2024]

[9] C. Cristophersen, J.-K. Breivik, A. D. Homme, and L. H. Rykkja, "The cultural rucksack; a national programme for arts and culture in Norwegian schools", Kulturrådet, Fagbokforlaget, Oslo, Bergen, 2015. [Online]. Available: https://www.kulturdirektoratet.no/documents/10157/a746404 7-2cb6-4988-9948-ffd834508a5d [retrieved: 04, 2024]

[10] I. Digranes, "The cultural schoolbag – Quality at school or cultural arrogance?", *FormAkademisk*, vol. 8, no. 2, Art. no. 2, Oct. 2015

[11] E. S. Hauge, V. S. Knutsen, and M. R. Ervik, "Proximity, autonomy, and democratization: Evaluation of the direct municipality scheme in the cultural schoolbag.", Oxford Research, Oslo, 2017. [Online]. Available: https://oxfordresearch.no/publications/naerhet-autonomi-og-demokratisering/ [retrieved: 04, 2024]

[12] I. Digranes, "The Cultural Schoolbag: Narratives and Myths of Educational Practice in DKS Projects within the Subject of Art and Crafts. ", PhD, AHO, Oslo, 2009. [Online]. Available: https://aho.brage.unit.no/aho-xmlui/handle/11250/93038 [retrieved: 04, 2024]

[13] K. Holdhus and M. Espeland, "School and Concert - From Presentation to Dialogue (DiSko): Production Report", Center for Creativities, Arts and Science in Education (CASE), CASE 2018/1, 2018. [Online]. Available: https://hvlopen.brage.unit.no/hvlopen-xmlui/handle/11250/2651977 [retrieved: 04, 2024]

[14] O. Eyal and M. Yarm, "Schools in Cross-Sector Alliances: What Do Schools Seek in Partnerships?", *Educational Administration Quarterly*, vol. 54, no. 4, pp. 648–688, Oct. 2018, doi: 10.1177/0013161X18765268.

[15] K. D. Gutiérrez, "Developing a Sociocritical Literacy in the Third Space", *Reading Research Quarterly*, vol. 43, no. 2, pp. 148–164, 2008, doi: 10.1598/RRQ.43.2.3.

[16] E. J. Klein, M. Taylor, C. Onore, K. Strom, and L. Abrams, "Exploring Inquiry in the Third Space: Case Studies of a Year in an Urban Teacher-Residency Program", *The New Educator*, vol. 12, no. 3, pp. 243–268, Jul. 2016, doi: 10.1080/1547688X.2016.1187980.

[17] C. E. Mølstad and T. S. Prøitz, "Teacher-chameleons: the glue in the alignment of teacher practices and learning in policy", *Journal of Curriculum Studies*, vol. 51, no. 3, pp. 403–419, May 2019, doi: 10.1080/00220272.2018.1504120.

[18] C. Mahler, T. Gutmann, S. Karstens, and S. Joos, "Terminology for interprofessional collaboration: Definition and current practice", *GMS Z Med Ausbild*, vol. 31, no. 4, Nov. 2014, doi: 10.3205/zma000932.

[19] B. C. K. Choi and A. W. P. Pak, "Multidisciplinarity, interdisciplinarity and transdisciplinarity in health research, services, education and policy: 1. Definitions, objectives, and evidence of effectiveness", *Clinical and Investigative Medicine*, vol. 29, no. 6, pp. 351–64, Dec. 2006.

[20] J. I. Goodlad, Curriculum Decisions: A Conceptual Framework, 1973.

[21] J. I. Goodlad, Curriculum Inquiry : The Study of Curriculum Practice, McGraw-Hill, 1979.

[22] K. Støren, "Local curriculum development with subject renewal", *Nordisk tidsskrift for utdanning og praksis*, vol. 16, no. 1, pp. 40–58, 2022.

[23] E. Tronsmo, "Local curriculum development as knowledge work: A study of collaborative epistemic practices in the teaching profession (Publication Number 1564-3991)", *University of Oslo*, 2019.

[24] F. Kensing and J. Greenbaum, "Heritage: Having a say", *Routledge International Handbook of Participatory Design*, Routledge, 2013, pp. 21–36.

[25] M. Muller and A. Druin, "Participatory Design: The Third Space in HCI", *Handbook of HCI*, Jan. 2002.

[26] L. Finlay, "Reflecting on 'reflective practice'. Practice-based professional learning paper 52", *The Open University*, pp. 0–27, 2008.

[27] J. Dewey, *How we think: A restatement of the relation of reflective thinking to the educative process*. Houghton Mifflin, 1933.

[28] D. A. Schön, *The reflective practitioner: How professionals think in action*. Routledge, 2017.

[29] J.-J. Lee, "The true benefits of designing design methods", *Artifact: Journal of Design Practice*, vol. 3, no. 2, pp. 5–1, 2014.

[30] F. B. M. Newaz, J. Karlsen, and J. Herstad, "Making Technology Matter for Processes of Co-Creation and Innovation in Cross-Sectorial Collaborations", *The Sixteenth International Conference on Advances in Computer-Human Interactions (ACHI 2023)*, IARIA, pp. 9–16, 2023

[31] F. D. Hoffmann and K. H. Karlsen, "Choreographic Infrastructuring for Design Things: A New Method for Participatory Design in Teacher Education", *Embracing Cosmologies: Expanding Worlds of Participatory Design, Proceedings of the 17th Participatory Design Conference*, ACM, pp. 230–240, 2022

[32] F. D. Hoffmann, "Learning to navigate in the unknown: attuning to affordances in artist visits in schools", Pedagogy, Culture & Society, 2024

[33] "Regulation on the framework plan for primary school teacher education for grades 1-7 - Lovdata." [Online]. Available: https://lovdata.no/dokument/SF/forskrift/2016-06-07-860 [retrieved: 05, 2024]

[34] "Regulation on the framework plan for primary school teacher education for grades 5-10 - Lovdata." [Online]. Available: https://lovdata.no/dokument/SF/forskrift/2016-06-07-861 [retrieved: 05, 2024]

Educating Student Teachers for InterProfessional Collaboration through the Codesign of Cultural Heritage with the Use of Augmented Reality (AR) Technology

Gitte Cecilie Motzfeldt
Faculty of Teacher Education and Languages
Østfold University College
Halden, Norway
Gitte.c.motzfeldt@hiof.no

Kristine Høeg Karlsen
Faculty of Teacher Education and Languages
Østfold University College
Halden, Norway
Kristine.h.karlsen@hiof.no

Abstract—**In the current study, we focus on student teachers' perceptions of their involvement in InterProfessional Collaboration (IPC) as part of a mandatory course centered around The Cultural Schoolbag (TCS). The course emerged through collaborative efforts, drawing participants from the fields of education, design, and culture, guided by core principles of participatory design. Our article explores how student teachers perceive their participation, their roles, and responsibilities in promoting democracy, as well as their experiences in facilitating learning processes within their educational context. To analyze student teachers' active participation in the TCS, we employ an analytical framework that differentiates between three types of democratic participation: "about," "for," and "through." We find that by enhancing student teacher's ability to contribute to the design of the TCS through the course, they gained firsthand experiences democratic participation. Hence, their autonomy as educators increases, allowing them to voice concerns and foster active learning during their placement.**

Keywords- democratic participation; codesign; interProfessional collaboration; cultural heritage; AR technology.

I. INTRODUCTION

In a global context, external programs are gaining greater entry into schools. Norway serves as an example, with initiatives such as The Technological Schoolbag, Young Entrepreneurship, and TCS actively engaging with educational institutions. While these programs provide valuable opportunities, they may also vie for precious classroom time, alongside teachers' current curricula. To address this challenge, integrating InterProfessional Collaboration (IPC) within Teacher Education (TE) has emerged as a promising approach. By incorporating IPC, student teachers gain a deeper understanding of their roles and responsibilities, which empowers them to assert their voices when utilizing activities provided by external associates. Ultimately, this integration ensures that the learning experiences seamlessly align with the school's curriculum.

The pARTiciPED project [1], led by Østfold University College (ØUC), centers around a groundbreaking cross-sectorial partnership with schools in Norway. At its heart lies The Cultural Schoolbag (TCS) [2], which secured substantial NOK 330 million in government funding in 2023 (28 386 600 euro). Since 2001, TCS has been an integral part of Norway's cultural policy, enriching pupils' lives through high-quality art and cultural experiences. These cultural experiences span a diverse spectrum of forms, including literature, music, film, performing arts, visual arts, and cultural heritage (as outlined in White Paper 18 [3, p. 141]). However, despite its value, TCS faces challenges rooted in inherent power imbalances between schools and cultural institutions. Researchers, such as Christophersen et al. [4], Digranes [5], and Hauge et al. [6], have identified these complexities, emphasizing the need for more research to fully realize the artistic potential within this dynamic partnership.

In the present study, student teachers assume a distinctive role, empowering them to convey a cultural heritage TCS projects using AR, during their placement. This empowerment is facilitated through a collaborative design effort involving stakeholders from the cultural, design, and education sectors. Guided by core principles of participatory design outlined by Kensing and Greenbaum [7, pp. 33–34], these principles were tailored to achieve several objectives, with a key focus on establishing democratic practices. By doing so, the team aimed to equalize power dynamics, ensuring that every participant had a voice. All stakeholders were encouraged to act in both their individual interests and the collective good [7, p. 33]. The primary focus of the current article is to assess the level of participation and action competence acquired by student teachers as they prepare for and carry out the TCS project during their placement. To explore this issue, we formulated the following research question: "What perspectives do student teachers hold regarding their involvement in the TCS project targeting cultural heritage?"

The theoretical framework of this article draws from two key sources in participatory design: John Dewey's understanding of democracy [10] and Paulo Freire's insights into adult literacy [11]. These foundational perspectives inform our exploration of democratic participation within the context of our study. Additionally, we employ the analytical framework outlined by Stray and Sætra [9]. This framework categorizes democratic participation into three dimensions: "about," "for," and "through." These distinctions guide our examination of how democratic processes unfold. In Section II, the theoretical grounding and the analytical framework of the analyses are accounted for. Section III we provide an outline of the empirical case, followed by a description of the research design and analysis. In Section IV, we analyze and discuss the empirical evidence considering the theoretical and analytical framework. Finally, in Section V, we draw conclusions and recommendations for future work.

II. Participation in Societal Intercultural Collaboration

In the context of participatory design, democratic participation does not occur spontaneously. Instead, it requires deliberate effort. One influential thinker in this realm is John Dewey [10]. His ideas emphasize educating and engaging individuals to act in their own interests while also considering the common good (as discussed by [7], p. 33). Schools hold a crucial position as societal institutions with a democratic educational mandate. Education is essential not only for individual growth, but also for maintaining and actively participating in society. An education system that aims to foster democratic practices must be built on certain foundational principles. According to Dewey [10], equal communication plays a pivotal role. This principle ensures that individuals have a voice and can actively shape both their personal interests and collective well-being within society.

The current article explores the relationships among the pedagogy of the oppressed [11] and participatory design to understand how power dynamics can be aligned by providing student teachers with voice and action competence in the TCS as part of TE. In the twentieth century, the liberation educator Paulo Freire [11] was among those who laid a foundation for understanding power relations, humanity, and dialog for social change, aiming at a better future society. Born in Brazil in the 1960s, he developed an adult literacy methodology that has become one of the most respected pedagogical references in the world [12]. Freire created his liberating pedagogy based on how all people should become equal participants in communities and develop their identities by taking charge of their own environment [11, p. 11]. According to Freire [11], self-determination and codetermination are fundamental to people's quality of life. Unequal democratic practices and power relations make it necessary to transform the context of oppression-oppressors. Equalizing power relations includes finding ways to give a voice to those oppressed by structural conditions and social differences.

In school, Freire [11] points out that students become patient listening objects, while teachers are narrative subjects "filling the students' heads" with their understanding and reality, which might be completely foreign to the students' existential experience (p. 54). In this way, education becomes knowledge from those who "understand it" to those whom they consider completely ignorant. If one regards others as ignorant, this is a characteristic feature of the ideology of oppression. According to Freire, literacy is not only the ability to read and write, but also a transformative medium where individuals, through awareness, authentic experiences, and critical consciousness, might be given the ability to "understand the world". Allowing individuals to critically understand, problematize, and communicate their reality enables the transformation of the oppressed through "dialogical action" [11 p.71]. Dialog and action meet when there is a common desire to express views and transform the world (p. 72).

A goal of democracy education in Norwegian schools is to motivate and prepare students to act. The development of action competence is also linked to studies of power relations in which identifying and assessing alternative actions are important [13]. Mogensen and Schanck [14] discuss action competence as an ideal for education; they state that "action should be addressed to solutions of the problem and should not just be the activities as a counterweight to academic tuition" [14, p. 61]. This is because action competence and action-oriented teaching and learning have important learning potential. Being conscious and purposive might challenge the criteria on which today's education is based. This perspective on the notion of action means that action competence is necessary to change the circumstances that create and sustain challenges in the school system [14]. Hence, action competence can be viewed as a specific activity that potentially leads to increased consciousness and transformation.

A. *Analytic framework*

Working with democratic principles, such as equal participation, in the education system means having a conscious relationship with what democratic participation may entail. The analytical framework used in the current study is the three dimensions of teaching democratic participation, outlined by Stray and Sætra [9] and further elaborated by Stray [15], about, for, and through democratic participation. In addition, we emphasize the importance of developing action competence through practical experiences to be able to reflect on and transform current practices.

The starting point is that both democratic participation and actions can be learned [13]. We can differentiate between different dimensions of democratic participation. According to Stray [15], education about democracy means knowledge, that is, about the history of democracy, organizations, and political processes. This is important knowledge for understanding the functions of the society in which we live and become informed citizens. The purpose of education for democracy is for students to develop competence in critical thinking and communication skills [15]. Values and attitudes are explored and developed in the school's learning environment. In the last dimension, education through democratic participation, students acquire experiences of active participation in democratic processes. This implies that the teacher is a decisive participant, supervisor, and facilitator for active participation and for understanding democratic processes in the classroom [9]. We depart from this framework to examine and understand how student teachers, here through participatory approaches, were given a voice to communicate changes in asymmetric power relations when working with TCS and cultural heritage projects in TE and in their placement.

III. Cultural Schoolbags as Participatory Design Interventions

The following section provides an outline of the empirical case, followed by a description of the research design and analysis.

A. *Making use of AR technology in cocreating TCS art projects*

The pARTiciPED project aimed to provide empirical insights into organizing and implementing TCS within TEs. The goal was to empower student teachers as they transition into their roles as future educators. The project established three laboratories, each dedicated to different domains: performing arts, visual art, and cultural heritage. These laboratories served as spaces for exploring the educational practices related to TCS. In the Cultural Heritage Laboratory (CH lab), a design team of four coresearchers planned and organized five workshops together with one museum educator, two teachers, and one student teacher at ØUC. A primary objective was to employ participatory design with the use of serious games to facilitate the collaboration of museum educators, teachers, and students in creating cultural heritage TCS projects.

Furthermore, as part of the HC lab, the design team cocreated and conducted a course design tailored for fourth-year student teachers in TE (ØUC, 2023). The course comprised a total of four seminars. In the course, the student teachers were provided with tools and techniques from participatory design, such as the design card methodology [16]. Additionally, they were introduced to hybrid museum experiences centered around industrial history provided by the local museum, Moss town and industrial museum. Based on this foundation and working closely with the design team, the student teachers were assigned to cocreate a new learning experience (in alignment with [17]). This involved utilizing AR technology via a mobile application to grant pupils access to historical material and opportunities for self-expression within it. This project was integrated into an IPC during the student teacher's placement.

Through this work, we examine the reflective notes created by student teachers after their active participation in co-creating and implementing the project, allowed them to adapt and shape the content of TCS to align with their specific subjects, classes, and interests.

B. *Empirical data and analysis*

The pARTiciPED project has collected extensive data to explore various aspects of IPC within the context of TCS. These contributions include new and innovative methods for TCS in TE [18][19], insights into collaboration between artists and student teachers, highlighting the integration of TCS within everyday learning in schools (see, e.g., [20][21][22]) and negotiating roles [23], and building capacities for artist visits beyond generic knowledge and skills [24].

In the current article, our primary data source consists of reports written by the students upon completion of the course and placement. These reports span a total of 199 pages. The report was divided into two sections: collective and individual. In the collective part, the student teachers collaboratively reflected on their group efforts during the placement. This section provides insights into their joint experiences and observations. In the individual part, each student participated independently. We were particularly interested in their thoughts regarding their own involvement in the projects. Each report included 14 questions addressing these aspects.

In our data analysis, we followed a three-phase qualitative coding approach inspired by the method proposed by Saldaña [25]. In phase 1, we thoroughly reviewed all the material (199 pages). Our goal was to gain an overview of potential codes and interpretations related to student teachers' involvement and their own thoughts on the process (in accordance with [25], p. 19). We rapidly selected relevant codes, marking text passages within the material (p. 105). Examples of these codes included terms such as "collaboration and mutual support in implementation" and "multiple levels of engagement and action competence." This initial phase was conducted collaboratively, and an interesting observation emerged: Student teachers strongly believed that teachers should play a more significant role in planning and implementing TCS projects. In phase 2, we delved into the textual passages that we had coded in the initial review. Our aim was to organize these passages into a "smaller number of categories" [25, p. 236]. This step helped us prepare for the final phase. In the third and final phase, we realized that the analytical framework proposed by Stray and Sætra [9] could be used to effectively synthesize the material. By applying this framework, we identified emerging patterns and themes related to student teachers' experiences and perspectives.

Upon analyzing the data, a clear pattern emerged. Student teachers, when given the chance to cocreate their own TCS design using participatory design principles, not only encountered a markedly different approach to TCS, but also observed an intentional effort within the CH lab to balance power relationships—a departure from the typical dynamics associated with TCS projects in schools. Power relations are interconnected and complex. It is important to be aware that this analysis simplifies the complexity. Nevertheless, our goal is to shed light on an area that, as far as we know, has received limited research attention. This exploration may contribute with intriguing insights into new ways of understanding TCS and the collaboration between cultural, design and educational domains. In the subsequent sections, we present the results of the analysis and discuss these findings, which are firmly anchored in the research question.

IV. Participation through the Codesign of Cultural Heritage

The TCS aims to democratize access to art and culture for pupils in schools. It operates as a decolonized initiative, ensuring that all students can engage with various professional arts and cultures during their years in school. Teachers play a crucial role in integrating art and culture into the curriculum. Their mission is to make these visits accessible to all pupils, regardless of their backgrounds or abilities [3, p. 136]. However, achieving this goal involves navigating several challenges, especially when considering the democratic values of participation. In most cases, TCSs follow a "top-down" approach, where teachers are informed "about" when and what the TCS project entails by the school management or a coordinator. One of the student teachers reflected on past experiences with TCS: "I have gotten the impression that teachers experience many TCS projects are just something they need to undertake, without knowing much about them."

In this framework, teachers are actors who, once informed, can align their actions in accordance with the goals set for TCS. However, there is a risk, as per Freire's [11] perspective, that the teacher is cast in the role of "uninformed" (cf. [23]); they find themselves in a position where they must accommodate a TCS project that may or may not align with ongoing school activities. However, by enhancing action competence through participatory design workshops, student teachers increase their competence and critically reflect on the learning potential of TCS activities. This process bridges the gap between cultural experiences and the specific situations faced by student teachers in schools. This shift occurs when the focus moves from learning "about" democratic participation, as defined by Stray and Sætra [9], to learning "for" and "through" democratic participation.

When student teachers actively participate in democratic processes, they can critically adjust the TCS project in accordance with their knowledge of the pupils and their learning situations. One of the student teachers commented, "I envision that if teachers at the schools actively involve themes and teaching methods, it may encourage more pupils to drive TCS projects." Another student teacher put it this way: "I feel this has been a good exercise in making creative plans for the pupils. We have been pushed to think outside the box." The students' reflections imply that bridging the gap between cultural expertise and pedagogical knowledge will be advantageous for the TCS project.

Achieving this without expecting (student) teachers to become artists and artists to become teachers but rather allowing them to pursue their own professions (cf. [26]) presents a challenge, but it is essential for meaningful educational experiences for pupils in school. The participatory design process of TCS projects has given student teachers the ability to reflect on their own pedagogical practices. They have gained autonomy in implementing TCS projects related to cultural heritage, which has enhanced their action competence. Additionally, this has enabled them to think creatively and find new ways to engage pupils as active "subjects" in their own learning process. As one student stated, "I strongly believe that the pupils get more out of it and learn more by being a participant yourself." Another student affirmed, "The own-design TCS project was engaging and dealt with several activities where the pupils could try out something new, discuss, reflect, and try your hand at role-playing."

According to Freire's [11] perspective, involvement in work leads to a critical understanding of current practices. Through dialog and action, the student teachers have increased their voices and critical thoughts on TCS projects in school. This process allows them to address structural conditions that prompt democratic values and principles. The pupils do not enter school with empty heads. They are knowledgeable citizens who need to engage themselves in learning processes that not only make them informed citizens but also see different perspectives and critically assess their surroundings through exploratory teaching. This might contribute to developing pupils' understanding of how to learn and engage in activities in a wider community context. As one student teacher expressed, "being able to let go of control is an important learning, which gave a new aspect to the learning outcome for us students teachers." Dewey [10] emphasizes that learning and education are necessary both for individual development and for being active and independent citizens in a democratic society.

The significance of addressing solutions to handle challenges related to activities that counterbalance formal education is underlined by Mogensen and Schanck [14]. We argue that enhancing student teachers' action competence can be achieved by integrating it into TE programs. Thus, TE can serve as a catalyst for change. One of the student teachers highlighted that "what worked well with the TCS project we developed was that we had collaborated well [among us students] during the preparations, which allowed us to work seamlessly during the TCS project implementation in school." In the CH lab, these students were tasked with taking part in TCS on their own terms, and we observed an attempt to "level out" power dynamics.

In pARTiciPED, student teachers assumed new roles that allowed them to experience and work through democratic participation. Consequently, this experience may empower them to influence the educational system as they transition into school as future professionals. One student teacher expressed this as follows: ".... teachers can submit requests for which goals they want the students to achieve and themes that can be used. This will contribute to teachers seeing TCS as something meaningful for the school and not just a 'happening.'"

Based on this discussion, we have tailored Stray and Sætra's [9] three types of democratic participation "about," "for," and "through" to the context of TE when educating student teachers for IPC with artists and cultural workers as future professionals (see Table 1). We have incorporated strategies that succinctly describe the activities encountered by teacher students during their TE. Furthermore, we have revised and clarified the goals and explanations, drawing on relevant excerpts in our data corpus.

TABLE I. THREE MODES OF DEMOCRATIC PARTICIPATION DURING SCHOOL VISITS

Dimensions	Strategies	Goals	Excerpts
Teaching *about* TCS project Knowledge-based competence of the TCS projects and their subject-related content	Student teachers are "handed over" TCS project on campus to take part in, or to be implement as part of their placement.	Students' teachers acquire knowledge about TCS either during their classes on campus or as part of placement. This knowledge equips them to act in accordance with the instructions provided for TCS in schools.	"I have got the impression that teachers experience many TCS project as just something they need to undertake, without knowing much about them."
Teaching *for* democratic participation Value and attitude competence	Student teachers engage in exploratory teaching. Here, they develop competence in critical thinking and	Student teachers actively cultivate attitudes and values essential for democratic preparedness. Their understanding of the teacher's role	".... teachers can submit requests for which goals they want the students to achieve, and themes that can be used. This

	communication skills through active communication, sharing their own views, and actively listening to others.	undergoes transformation.	will contribute to teachers seeing TCS as something meaningful for the school, and not just a 'happening.'"
Teaching *through* democratic participation – action competence	The student teachers are given opportunities to act as an agent of change, striving to equalize participation and communication of TCS project.	Student teachers develop action competence through experiencing and exploring varied TCS project either on campus or in placement. The experience must create opportunities for the students to participate in democratic processes based on democratic principles when, for example, taking part in or co-designing and implementing TCS projects in schools.	"This was both new for me and for the pupils. It was, therefore, a bit scary to venture out on such a project. Having said that, being able to let go of control is an important learning, which gave a new aspect to the learning outcome for us student teachers."

V. CONCLUSION AND FUTURE WORK

Teachers play a crucial role in integrating art and culture into the curriculum. The mission of TCS is to make these visits accessible to all pupils, regardless of their backgrounds, interests, or abilities. However, achieving this goal involves navigating several challenges, especially when considering the democratic values of participation. In the future, enhancing the action competence of student teachers can increasingly enable them to reflect on TCS activities, communicate with them, and further develop TCS learning potential. This process bridges the gap between cultural experiences and the specific situations faced by student teachers in school, shifting the focus from learning "about" democratic participation to learning "for" and "through" democratic participation. This perspective aligns with Freire's [11] concept of adult literacy, which suggests that effective communication with others involves a range of skills beyond reading and writing.

What is intriguing about the participatory design process utilized in the CH lab in the TE is that our students' teachers gained a significantly different approach to TCS through active involvement. Moreover, based on their participation and input, the student teachers cocreated a digital museum experience for their pupils that they were able to test during their placement. What occurred in the CH lab was an attempt to "level out" the asymmetrical power imbalance to meet the criticism of the TCS, where teachers learn about the TCS project and often feel that they lack the necessary competence to collaborate in equal terms in the TCS project in schools. By collaborating with the design team and peers, the student teachers gained insight into an alternative approach to TCS, where they experienced significant autonomy, an important aspect of being professional teachers. We argue that when teachers embrace TCSs as future educators, they should not relinquish their autonomy; rather, they should assert it. The following question then arises: How can teachers engage as professional educators in TCS projects in schools without sacrificing their autonomy? We believe that by being "subjects" in their own teaching context and exercising their own action competence through IPC, the potential of TCS can be realized, aligning well with the mandate of professional teachers.

Teachers know their students well and can develop their action competence and critical thinking skills if they are allowed to participate actively in the development of TCS projects, not only by learning about them, but also by instructing them. This had a significant spill-off effect on the involvement of pupils in their own learning process, hence motivating both student teachers and pupils to work with TCS projects on cultural heritage. In this IPC undertaken in TE, student teachers had the opportunity to cocreate their own TCS design based on principles from participatory design, meaning that they were not provided with a preexisting TCS project that they learned about, and were instructed to implement. They worked with participatory principles from which they generated ideas for TCS projects to be further developed for practical use during their placement.

We posit that enhancing teachers' dialogical actions through IPC not only grants them increased autonomy but also empowers them to assume novel roles as conveyors of art and culture. However, we do not advocate for this approach to replace or supplant traditional modes of museum experiences (or art visits) facilitated by professional cultural workers. Instead, it can serve as a complementary supplement that directly engages teachers and offers a potential avenue for an actual collaboration between culture, and education. Further research on creating "dialogical space" could explore possibilities for articulating such possibilities within the framework of TCS. This might further contribute to transforming the teaching and learning processes of TCS from the more instruction "about" cultural heritage to active participation "for" and "through" their experiences as professions working with TCS projects.

ACKNOWLEDGMENTS

We extend our gratitude to the Norwegian Research Council and Østfold University College for funding the pARTiciPED project, which enabled us to conduct this research.

REFERENCES

[1] Grant No. 301594 at the Research Council of Norway. Retrieved: May 5th. 2024: https://prosjektbanken.forskningsradet.no/project/FORISS/301594.

[2] https://www.denkulturelleskolesekken.no/english-information/this-is-the-cultural-schoolbag/. Retrieved: May 5th. 2024.

[3] White paper 18 (2020–2021). «Experience, Create, Share - art and culture for, with, and by children and young people» [Originally: "Oppleve, skape, dele–kunst og kultur for, med og av barn og unge"]. Ministry of Culture, 2021 2020. https://www.regjeringen.no/contentassets/57f98cf5845f4d3093b84a5f47cef629/nn-no/pdfs/stm202020210018000dddpdfs.pdf. Retrieved: May 5th. 2024.

[4] C. Christophersen, J.-K. Breivik, A. D. Homme, and L. H. Rykkja, "The cultural rucksack. A national programme for arts and culture in Norwegian schools." Bergen: Fagbokforlaget, 2015.

[5] I. Digranes, «The Cultural Schoolbag – Quality School or Cultural Arrogance?" [Originally: "Den kulturelle skulesekken – Kvalitetsskule eller kulturarroganse?]," *FormAkademisk*, vol. 8, no. 2, Art. no. 2, Oct. 2015, doi: 10.7577/formakademisk.714.

[6] E. S. Hauge, V. S. Knutsen, and M. R. Ervik, «Evaluation of the direct municipality scheme in The Cultural Schoolbag» [Originally: "Evaluering av direktekommuneordningen i Den kulturelle skolesekken"], *Oslo: Oxford Research*, 2017, [Online]. Available: https://oxfordresearch.no/wp-content/uploads/2019/02/Evaluering-av-100-kommuner-%E2%80%93-Kulturtanken.pdf. Retrieved: May 5th. 2024.

[7] F. Kensing and J. Greenbaum, "Heritage: Having a say," in *Routledge international handbook of participatory design*, Routledge, 2012, pp. 21–36. https://api.taylorfrancis.com/content/chapters/edit/download?identifierName=doi&identifierValue=10.4324/9780203108543-3&type=chapterpdf. Retrieved: April 15th. 2024.

[8] Bødker, S., Dindler, C., Iversen, O. S., and Smith, R. C., *Participatory Design*. Springer International Publishing, 2022.

[9] J. H. Stray and E. Sætra, "Democratic Education in Schools" [Originally: "Demokratisk undervisning i skolen,"] *Dembra*, 2016, https://gammel.dembra.no/no/wp-content/uploads/sites/2/2020/11/Dembrahefte_1_2016.pdf#page=14. Retrieved: April 15th. 2024.

[10] Dewey, J, "*Democracy and Education: an introduction to the philosophy of education*." Createspace Independent Publishing Platform, 1916/2016.

[11] P. Freire, "*The Pedagogy of the Oppressed*" [Originally: "De undertryktes pedagogikk,"]. Ad Notam Gyldendal, 1999.

[12] B. Serpa, I. Portela, M. Costard, and S. Batista, "Political-pedagogical contributions to participatory design from Paulo Freire," in *Proceedings of the 16th Participatory Design Conference 2020 - Participation(s) Otherwise - Volume 2*, Manizales Colombia: ACM, Jun. 2020, pp. 170–174. doi: 10.1145/3384772.3385149.

[13] S. Eie and G. Motzfeldt, "To Understand the World Through Geography" [Originally: "Å forstå verden gjennom geografi". In R. Mikkelsen and P. J Sætre (Eds.), *Geography Didactics for the Classroom*, vol. 4, pp. 13–53, Cappelen Damm Akademisk, 2022.

[14] F. Mogensen and K. Schnack, "The action competence approach and the 'new' discourses of education for sustainable development, competence and quality criteria," in *Environmental and Sustainability Education Policy*, Routledge, 2010, pp. 59–74. https://www.taylorfrancis.com/chapters/edit/10.4324/9780203732359-12/action-competence-approach-new-discourses-education-sustainable-development-competence-quality-criteria-finn-mogensen-karsten-schnack. Retrieved: April 15th. 2024.

[15] J. H. Stray, "Democracy on the Timetable" [Originally: Demokrati på timeplanen"]. Fagbokforlaget, 2018.

[16] E. Brandt, T. Binder, and E. B.-N. Sanders, "Tools and techniques: Ways to engage telling, making and enacting," in *Routledge international handbook of participatory design*, Routledge, 2012, pp. 145–181. https://api.taylorfrancis.com/content/chapters/edit/download?identifierName=doi&identifierValue=10.4324/9780203108543-8&type=chapterpdf. Retrieved: April 15th. 2024.

[17] J.-J. Lee, M. Jaatinen, A. Salmi, T. Mattelmäki, R. Smeds, and M. Holopainen, "Design choices framework for co-creation projects," *International Journal of Design*, vol. 12, no. 2, 2018.

[18] F. Devonas Hoffmann and K. H. Karlsen, "Choreographic infrastructuring for design things: A new method for participatory design in teacher education," in *Participatory Design Conference 2022: Volume 1*, Newcastle upon Tyne United Kingdom: ACM, Aug. 2022, pp. 230–240. doi: 10.1145/3536169.3537796.

[19] F. B. M. Newaz, J. Karlsen, and J. Herstad, "Making technology matter for processes of co-creation and innovation in cross-sectorial collaborations," *ACHI 2023. The Sixteenth International Conference on Advances in Computer-Human Interactions.* https://www.researchgate.net/profile/Joakim-Karlsen/publication/371539637_Making_Technology_Matter_for_Processes_of_Co-Creation_and_Innovation_in_Cross-Sectorial_Collaborations/links/648974159bc5e436682e9235/Making-Technology-Matter-for-Processes-of-Co-Creation-and-Innovation-in-Cross-Sectorial-Collaborations.pdf Retreived April 15th, 2024.

[20] G. B. Bjørnstad and K. H. Karlsen, "An artful encounter with dance–empowering future teachers in cross-sectoral collaborations with the Cultural Schoolbag as an example," *Dance Articulated*, vol. 9, no. 1, 2023, https://www.ntnu.no/ojs/index.php/ps/article/view/5068. Retrieved: April 15th. 2024.

[21] G. B. Bjørnstad and K. H. Karlsen, "We had slightly different understandings of time - Negotiation and collaboration on the development of an art event in dance for students in school" [Originally: "Vi hadde litt ulik forståelse av tid – Forhandling og samarbeid om utviklingen av en kunsthendelse i dans for elever i skolen,"] *Nordic Journal of Dance*, in press.

[22] L. Skregelid, "The Cultural Schoolbag s dissensus and the importance of art in teacher education" [Orginially: "Den kulturelle skolesekken som dissens og kunstens betydning i lærerutdanningen,"] *Form Akademisk*, vol. 16, no. 2, 2023. https://journals.oslomet.no/index.php/formakademisk/article/view/4806. Retrieved: April 15th. 2024.

[23] S. K. Stigberg, K. H. Karlsen, and J. Karlsen, "Transprofessionalism course design in teacher education," *ACHI 2024, 2024. The Seventeenth International Conference on Advances in Computer-Human Interactions, ACHI-COCREATE: Design Practices for Co-Creation and Learning*, 2024.

[24] F. Devonas Hoffmann, "Learning to navigate in the unknown: attuning to affordances in artist visits in schools," *Pedagogy, Culture & Society*, pp. 1–18, Apr. 2024, doi: 10.1080/14681366.2024.2338810.

[25] J. Saldaña, "The coding manual for qualitative researchers". Sage, 2016.

[26] F. Devonas Hoffmann, "Designing for a shared setting: preparing student teachers for teacher-artist collaborations in teacher education," *Teaching and Teacher Education: An International Journal of Research and Studies*, Submitted.

Are Algorithms Enough?
Analyzing Fake News Solutions Designed by Students

Milica Milenkovic
University Union – Nikola Tesla
Belgrade, Serbia
e-mail: micagmekic@gmail.com

Essi Häyhänen
University of Vaasa, School of Marketing and Communication
Vaasa, Finland
e-mail: essi.hayhanen@gmail.com

Joni Salminen
University of Vaasa, School of Marketing and Communication
Vaasa, Finland
e-mail: jonisalm@uwasa.fi

Bernard J. Jansen
Qatar Computing Research Institute
Hamad Bin Khalifa University
Doha, Qatar
e-mail: bjansen@hbku.edu.qa

***Abstract*— We examine the fake news problem, emphasizing user-led solutions. Students were assigned a task to design a technology-based solution to combat online misinformation defined as fake news. Eighteen teams participated, a total of 89 students. Analysis reveals that 38.9% of teams devised algorithm-focused solutions, 27.8% proposed human-focused solutions, while 33.3% designed solutions that incorporated both algorithmic and human-centered approaches to addressing the misinformation problem. We identified a fundamental assumption regarding the effectiveness of Artificial Intelligence and algorithms, highlighting technological sophistication. These findings contribute to the ongoing discourse on combating fake news and provide directions for future research and development of effective technological interventions by considering human factors.**

Keywords- fake news; solutions; human factors; design.

I. INTRODUCTION

Fake news is fabricated and untruthful information spread deliberately to deceive a readership or viewers. It often resembles real news stories but contains false information and may mix real and fake sources, quotes, and information. While the Internet has enabled people to stay informed about global events, it has also become a breeding ground for spreading false and malicious news [1]. Consequently, fake news has become a global issue that affects people in various aspects of life, such as healthcare, transportation, education, and business.

Researchers have explored many techniques for detecting fake news [2]. These detection approaches often focus on social media, as fake news is frequently distributed on social media, also known as social media platforms or social network sites. While the consumption of news through social media is increasing due to its speed, accessibility, and affordability, social media also provides a platform for the widespread dissemination of fake news, which intentionally contains false information for political purposes, trolling, or other nefarious objectives [3]. The popularity of social media has led to a shift in how people access news, with traditional sources of journalism being replaced by online social media sources. In particular, the rapid rotation of news on social media can make it difficult to determine its reliability [4].

The creation and dissemination of fake news can potentially deceive users and influence their opinions, leading to undesirable consequences for society [5]. Online social networks like Twitter have increased the spread of false information and fake news. This misinformation can lead to harmful consequences for individuals who believe in inaccurate claims and articles. Therefore, the prevalence of false information and deceitful content in the form of articles, posts, videos, and URLs on popular social media platforms has raised concerns among journalists and editors, among other stakeholder groups, emphasizing the need for tools and processes to aid in content verification [6].

Detecting fake news is essential to prevent panic and confusion [7]. To tackle the issue of fake news, researchers tend to develop algorithms, models, and systems that aim to distinguish between real and fake news and help scientists and the public access accurate information [8]. However, the computing research community has not thus far been successful at delivering definitive solutions to the fake news problem. Despite impressive results in laboratory settings, these results are rarely implemented in real systems, and when they are, they are unable to address the full scope of issues relating to users' behaviors, psychology, and sociology, i.e., factors that cannot easily be affected using algorithms alone. So, there is a need to better understand the full scope of the fake news problem.

The current research approaches the problem through *co-creation with students* [9]. In our study, university undergraduate students who are experts in neither Machine Learning (ML) or fake news research (apart from general knowledge as users of online media) propose solutions to the fake news problem – the naïveté of these solutions can reveal novel angles about the problem, as business students are not "pre-programmed" by the current paradigms and models of approaching the problem, thereby potentially observing aspects that *might* be hidden or left with little attention in the computational research on fake news.

We analyze students' proposed solutions through six Research Questions (RQs), justified as follows:

RQ1: How many student teams designed algorithm-focused and how many human-focused solutions? This question is relevant as computational literature tends to focus on algorithms rather than human factors, potentially limiting the scope of solutions. We examine the division of the proposed solutions into these two broad categories.

RQ2: What themes can be observed in the students' fake news solutions? We conduct an open coding [10] of the material submitted by the student teams in order to inductively identify central themes in the solutions. This inquiry is of a qualitative nature.

RQ3: What are the central assumptions that the student solutions rely on? By analyzing the assumptions underlying the solution, i.e., what factors are required for the solutions to work, we aim to shed light into the conditions, especially those extending beyond the technological realm, of practically workable fake news solutions. The literature does not often discuss such conditions (see Section 2).

RQ4: What are the central risks that the student solutions involve? We asked the students to identify key risks in their solutions; here, we analyze the types of risks they identified.

RQ5: How realistic are the student solutions? What are the more realistic aspects? What are the less realistic aspects? With this RQ, we aim to dissect the parts in the student solutions that have a degree of possibility of succeeding and, symmetrically, the parts that are likely to fail (according to our assessment). For this, we conduct a critical inquiry into the content of the solutions.

RQ6: What metrics do students propose to measure if fake news solutions work? Finally, we address the question of how the students would suggest measuring the success of fake news solutions. Prior research has focused on technical metrics (e.g., F1 score, accuracy, precision, recall) to evaluate research contributions–however, these metrics focus on the internal performance of the models while ignoring their ecological validity, i.e., how well the models would contribute to the solution of the fake news problem when implemented. Naturally, this question is beyond the computational paradigm based on ML, but we precisely argue here that fresh ideas on evaluating fake news solutions can be fruitful and interesting for the research community. So, we analyze the metrics proposed by the students.

Our analysis is based on a qualitative interpretation of the student-based solutions. We do not attempt to present definitive facts about solving the fake news problem, as we believe doing so is extremely complex. What we aim to do instead is to shed light on the more rarely discussed aspects of the fake news problem – those not directly associated to the creation of better systems, models, and tools but instead indirectly affecting the implementation in actual user environments. While most research in this field is of technical nature, focused on factors like algorithm selection, hyperparameter optimization, training and test splits, and so on [11], we believe that the current study complements these technical views by offering a perspective closer to the *everyday user* of social media platforms. As such, we believe this inquiry has value for the research community.

Section 2 reviews prior research on this topic. Section 3 outlines the methodology for data collection and analysis. Section 4 presents the results, followed by a discussion of findings and future work in Section 5.

II. LITERATURE REVIEW

As discussed above, the fast spread of fake news is a significant concern. This has motivated researchers to introduce solutions for automatically classifying news items [12]. Much research has focused on Artificial Intelligence (AI). Previous research has concentrated on classifying online reviews and publicly accessible social media-based posts [13]. Automated fake news identification technologies, such as ML models, are essential in the current body of research [14]. Current techniques primarily rely on Natural Language Processing (NLP) and ML models [15]. While traditional ML methods have been used to detect fake news, genetic algorithms are potential due to converging to near optima with low computational complexity [15].

Many news agencies publish news on their websites, but not all are trustworthy. Therefore, before quoting any news from a website, it is necessary to evaluate the reputation of the news resource using a trusted website classifier. Mughaid et al. [2] proposed using the world rank of news websites as the main factor for news accuracy, along with a secondary factor that compares the current news with fake news to determine its accuracy [2]. Thus, the source of the news is considered a crucial factor in determining fake news.

According to Shu et al. [3], existing detection algorithms focus on clues within news content (e.g., text, semantics, images), which may not always be effective as fake news is often intentionally written to mimic true news; e.g., by making it sound professional and convincing. Therefore, it is necessary to explore auxiliary information to improve detection [3]. For example, sophisticated techniques are used to deliberately modify text or images to create fake news. Giachanou et al. [5] proposed a multimodal system that combined textual, visual, and semantic information to detect fake news. They utilized Bidirectional Encoder Representations from Transformers (BERT) to capture the underlying meaning of text. For a visual representation, they extracted image tags using the Visual Geometry Group-16 (VGG-16) model. The semantic representation was calculated using cosine similarity between the title and image tags embeddings [5].

Nikam and Dalvi [16] proposed a method for classifying fake news on Twitter using a web-based Graphical User Interface (GUI). They developed an ML model that compared tweets to genuine sources to identify fake news, using the Naïve Bayes (NB) and Passive Aggressive (PA) algorithms with Term Frequency-Inverse Document Frequency (TF-IDF) feature extraction [16].

Sheikhi [12] presented a system for detecting fake news articles based on content-based features and the Whale Optimization Algorithm-Extreme Gradient Boosting Tree

(WOA-xgbTree) algorithm. The proposed system can be applied in different scenarios to classify news articles. The approach consisted of two main stages: first, the useful features were extracted and analyzed, and then an xgbTree algorithm optimized by the WOA was used to classify news articles using the extracted features [12].

Huang and Chen [17] presented a deep learning-based fake news detection system. The proposed system preprocessed news articles and analyzed them using various training models [17]. To detect fake news, Huang and Chen [17] introduced an ensemble learning model called the Embedding Long Short-Term Memory (LSTM), Depth LSTM, Linguistic Inquiry and Word Count (LIWC) Convolutional Neural Network (CNN), and N-gram CNN. Moreover, they optimized the weights of the ensemble model using the Self-Adaptive Harmony Search (SAHS) algorithm [17].

Singhal et al. [18] argued that detecting fake news requires a multimodal approach. As most multimodal fake news detection systems rely heavily on subtasks such as event discrimination and correlation analysis, they proposed SpotFake, a multimodal framework for fake news detection that does not require any additional subtasks. Their approach leveraged both textual and visual features of an article, using BERT to extract text features, and VGG-19 to extract image features [18]. Gundapu and Mamidi [7] used an ensemble of three transformer models (BERT, ALBERT, and XLNET) for evaluating the reliability of information related to the COVID-19 pandemic shared on social media [7].

As in most NLP tasks, transformers represent the state-of-the-art in fake news detection (note that our review does not include Generative AI or Generative Pre-trained Transformer (GPT) models, as these were not broadly available at the time of the review). The accuracy achieved by these models is impressive, which is one reason why the research community should expand its scope of examination – it is unlikely that the algorithm will get much better from this point. Instead, we expect decreasing marginal returns, which is why it is logical to pursue other aspects of the problem, including the *implementation* and *application* aspects.

Overall, the predictive results are impressive. It is not evident how the researchers can continue improving them over time, as it appears we are already at the >90% performance. Thus, the domain requires new, fresh ideas to explore. Some of these ideas can originate from externality, outside the computing research community, for example, from students. To this end, we move forward to the empirical part of this study, addressing our research questions. Before that, we briefly summarize our methodology.

III. Methodology

A. Data Collection

Students were given an assignment to design a technology-based solution to fake news, which was defined as online misinformation. The students carried out the task in teams, and there were 18 teams (in total, the course had 89 students, so each team had 4.9 students on average). Each team submitted their solution in a slideshow presentation. The content of these slideshow presentations was coded into a spreadsheet and then analyzed to address the research questions. Students were informed that their contributions could be used as a part of ongoing research on fake news.

B. Data Analysis

For the analysis, first, we evaluated students' presentations. Each solution was assigned a unique ID (S01-18), and we analyzed the solutions individually. This procedure was as follows:

Step 1: Determine whether a solution is:

Algorithm-focused (i.e., the solution relies mainly on the technical aspect of the algorithm and technology to deal with the problem of misinformation).

Human-focused (i.e., the solution relies mainly on humans doing the activities of finding, filtering, and decision-making about misinformation)

Mixed-focused (i.e., the solution combines aspects of both algorithms and humans)

Step 2: Evaluate the level of realism (1-7) of the solution, 1 being not realistic at all, and 7 being very realistic. If a solution involved many different stakeholders aligning in their thinking, too much technical sophistication, too many aspects of misinformation covered in the solution, that would make the solution unrealistic, with a mark of 1 or 2. A specific solution focused on a specific form of misinformation, a specific platform, or a development of a new platform for a specific niche need, and has a clear view about its functioning. Such a solution was marked with 6 and 7; the difference between the two is the number of stakeholders involved in the solution being built and implemented or the likely amount of work needed to develop the solution. For example, S01 has a realism of 6, meanwhile, S09 has 7. This is because S09 is a feature integration with already existing social media platform(s), meanwhile, S01 proposes a standalone platform that gets information to and from different individuals and organizations and is more difficult to implement, as opposed to working directly with an already existing platform to improve this segment of misinformation handling.

Step 3: Evaluate the level of clarity (unknowns) of the solution, one, meaning there are a lot of unknowns, and 7, there are little unknowns about the solution presented. Too many unanswered questions on how the solution will be built, who the stakeholders are, and how it will be implemented, with what technology leads to marks 1 and 2. Opposing, having the most clarity and the least number of unanswered questions leads to marks 6 and 7. For example, S19 is a highly specific, niche solution for removing AI-generated misinformation, giving information on methods and technology that will be used, the implementation route, and the precise limitations of the solution.

Step 4: Extract assumptions, risks, and metrics from the students' presentations.

Step 5: Assign themes/taxonomy to each solution. Answering the questions: "What is common to the solutions – algorithm-focused or human-focused?", "How will the solution be implemented?", "What kind of app/solution will be developed?", "What misinformation aspects is the solution tackling?" Through qualitatively analyzing the solutions, we developed the themes presented in this paper.

Steps 1-5 were carried out by the lead author and verified by a senior research team member. After finishing the evaluation, we could unify the assumptions, risks, and metrics. Looking at similar occurrences with different wording, we were able to craft common assumptions. For example, we first separated all the Risks, and Metrics per presentation. Then, we started comparing them to each other, which then helped us quantify the results. For example, the most common metrics for success of the solution is Engagement rate, mentioned in 12 out of 18 solutions.

After finishing the evaluation and analysis of the results, we addressed the research questions. For RQ1, we have the exact number for each type of solution. For descriptions of the solutions, we specified the most realistic and clear solution in each type and the ones on the opposite side of that scale. For RQ2, we enlisted and described all the themes (whose development we explained above) and elaborated the main taxonomies that they belong to. We also mentioned their share of occurrence in the solutions. For RQ3, we grouped the central assumptions that the solutions relied on (as indicated by the students). For RQ4, we grouped the central risks that the solutions involved (as indicated by the students). For RQ5, referencing the previous step, evaluation, we were able to assess realism. Based on that and the decision-making behind the evaluations, we outlined the most and least realistic solutions. For RQ6, we identified and grouped the metrics that the students proposed.

IV. RESULTS

A. *RQ1: How many teams designed algorithm-focused and how many human-focused solutions?*

Inspecting the results, we observe that seven teams (38.9%) designed Algorithm-Focused Solutions (**AFS**), five (27.8%) Human-Focused Solutions (**HFS**), and six (33.3%) of them designed a Combined-Focus Solution (**CFS**) that contained both algorithm and human-focused approaches to solving the misinformation problem. Solutions in algorithm-focused approaches were the following (quotes indicate direct quotation from the student team's presentation):

AFS01: "The platform evaluates the news post's veracity before it can be published. The [...] algorithms will check from all over the Internet the accuracy of the news that they want to publish. If the AI cannot find a solution fast enough, people moderators will then look it up and decide."

AFS02: An application that integrates with social media, that has "better algorithms & filters that are ranking fake news visibility down and/or leading the reader via link to a confirmed site that has the right information."

AFS03: An application that integrates with social media consists of an "algorithm that scores the publications and identifies topics, phenomena, words, punctuation, vocabulary, abbreviations, and the presence of references. If the score is below the credibility limit, the publication will be investigated further."

AFS04: An application that integrates with Instagram, has an "algorithm using ML to detect the misinformation posts, stop the spread of them, and eliminate fake news content from Instagram. Methods used are an AI-based algorithm that detects the fastest spreading/biggest fake news on the platform based on e.g., the shares, (negative) comments, and reports by users on a certain post."

AFS05: A standalone social media platform that has an "algorithm that uses website crawlers. It crawls through different website sources. It recognizes keywords and this way connects related articles. It is designed to be connected to each user's posts and shows related articles according to what the user has posted. This way, other users can compare different sources to find the most reliable information and make decisions based on them."

AFS06: A standalone news platform "to help ensure that you are always using credible sources for research. The platform consists of peer-reviewed, reliable, and trustworthy articles that have been fact-checked."

AFS07: An application that integrates with social media to remove AI-generated misinformation.

In turn, solutions in human-focused approaches were:

HFS01: An integration that consists of an extensive user verification process (social security number and verifying the account with a video holding the ID) to eliminate fake accounts. The users would be encouraged to report suspicious activity, so the moderators could check and act.

HFS02: A standalone platform based on combatting misinformation with a user rating system, including informing users about the news considered misinformation, so that they would react by providing the real information.

HFS03: An educational platform that teaches users how to recognize misinformation. The platform would give different examples from different platforms on the Internet. This is not a news-sharing platform or integration with social media platforms, this is a training platform.

HFS04: A platform called Truth Seekers. Gamification of fact-checking. Users are presented with stories and articles that circulate on social media platforms. Users earn points by reporting stories with suspected misinformation with the help of an AI-powered fact-checking tool.

HFS05: An educational platform that allows users to practice and develop media literacy skills by answering problems that volunteering "creators" upload. The idea is to offer users the possibility to learn and educate themselves and simultaneously attract creators to the platform by offering a small profit every time they create hard enough questions that other users rate as helpful.

Finally, two solutions were mixed-focused approaches:

CFS01: A standalone AI-based fact-checking platform would enable users to upload content for verification against trusted sources. It would connect users with educational and research institutions to counter misinformation.

CFS02: A Social Media Integration tool with a Trust Factor, assigned to each account and posted on a scale of 1 to 100. The Trust Factor is based on user ratings and other factors, like its use in online games. This solution is highly realistic and effective.

B. *RQ2: What themes can be observed?*

While building themes, we focused on commonalities between solutions and their differentiating factors. The themes that we outlined are shown in Table 1.

TABLE I. FAKE NEWS SOLUTION THEMES

Description	Subthemes
Themes about the basic functionality of the solution (applicable to 61% - 11 solutions)	➢ User Verification (27%) ➢ User Rating System and/or Reporting System (44%) ➢ User Education (27%)
Themes about the type of the solution (applicable to all 18 solutions)	➢ SM Integration (39%) - Non-Specified SM Integration 28% - Specific SM Integration (Meta, Instagram) 11% ➢ Standalone Platforms (61%) - Non-Specified Standalone Platform (22%) - Standalone SM Platform (22%) - Standalone Educational Platform (11%) - Standalone News Platform (6%)
Themes about how the misinformation is viewed	➢ A multidimensional view of misinformation (72% - 13 solutions) ➢ Single-dimensional view of misinformation (28% - 5 solutions)
Themes about additional features/functionalities of the solution	➢ Online Game (S16) ➢ Collaboration with Law Enforcement (S15)

Having assumptions, risks, and metrics as the RQs prevented a possibility of a large pool of themes.

We will start elaborating on a taxonomy group that applies to all 18 solutions - **The type of the Solution.** This thematic categorization has two major themes in it: *Social Media Integration* and *Standalone Platforms*. Of these solutions, 61% were categorized as Standalone Platforms, while 39% were Social Media Integration applications. These are implemented leveraging existing platforms' infrastructure. This approach is less challenging in terms of business development. Standalone platforms offer more freedom but require a multi-dimensional approach, making them more difficult to build. Despite the complexity, most student solutions (approximately 2/3) fell into the standalone platform category. The other taxonomy group - **The basic functionality of a Solution** applies to 61% of the solutions (11 out of 18). This one focuses on how the solution works, and what the basic prerequisites are whether the solutions tackle multiple dimensions of misinformation, or whether they specialize and focus only on conspiracy theories, fake accounts, and bots, or catching clickbait content. The last and optional (additional) taxonomy group, closer to a simple tag or category, contains non-essential features, that are unique to the solution. **Additional features/functionalities of the solution**. These themes can be used as descriptors for the solutions. *Online Games* and *Collaboration with Law Enforcement*. Both solutions were rated 5 for realism and clarity.

C. *RQ3: What are the central assumptions?*

The assumptions, limitations/risks were presented together in students' solutions (see Table 2) because the assumption that something will work directly implies the risk to the solution. For example, assuming that the solution will have enough users (and then a growing base of users) is what is needed for the solution to work implies that not having enough users is a risk to the solution working.

TABLE II. THE MOST COMMON ASSUMPTIONS

Assumption	Occurrences	%
AI and algorithms working well - technological sophistication	7	39%
User participation & engagement	4	22%
Having enough trustworthy sources for the algorithm to use	4	22%
Good UI & UX	3	17%
Users willing to learn	3	17%
Having access to external platforms	2	11%
Transparency and credibility	2	11%

To elaborate further on the major assumption, we start with *AI and algorithms working well.* All algorithm-focused solutions have this assumption. This assumes, firstly, that the AI and the algorithm will do what they are built to do: detect various forms of misinformation. Secondly, a proper infrastructure is in place for the solution to be operational and efficient. As the idea of algorithms is to be able to connect to different sources of information, it is of utmost importance that the sources have a *high score of trustworthiness and reliability*. Three out of four solutions that highlighted these assumptions are standalone platforms. In turn, having *enough users, participation, and engagement* will ensure that the standalone application stays 'alive'.

Good User Interface (UI) & User Experience (UX) focus on standalone platforms, where users being able to find their way around the information-sharing or fact-checking platform is of great importance. Even though one would think that *user willingness to learn* would be tied to the Standalone Education Platform, this is not the case. Both occurrences are assumptions where the solution is not an education platform, but depends on users to rate, and/or follow true/real information. For that to happen, users need to be willing to find out the truth, even when it is not convenient. Also, for some solutions to work (as integrations with other Social Media (SM) platforms), they need to be *compatible for integration* (both technologically and business-wise). To build trust with users, *transparency and credibility* are necessary for the solution/integration to have enough users in the first place. We can identify relations between the assumptions. Here are some unique assumptions tied to the most realistic and clear solutions:

Currently, it is difficult to detect misinformation or verify; therefore, solution S09, which is an algorithm-focused solution, also assumes *that algorithms and AI are more objective than humans* regarding this issue.

By defining a niche focus, S10 provides more certainty in combatting misinformation. The goal is to use rapidly scaling news in terms of engagement and check whether it is fake news or not. *The assumption here is that negative news gets more comments and engagement, and that there is more misinformation among negative news.*

S19 has a basic assumption that one team (developers of the solution) will do better than the developers of solutions that spread fake content and misinformation.

D. RQ4: What are the central risks?

The common risks are presented in Table 3.

TABLE III. SELF-IDENTIFIED RISKS IN FAKE NEWS SOLUTIONS

Risk	Occurrences	%
Having enough users to participate	6	33%
Technology is a risk factor on its own	4	22%
The ability of the algorithm to be able to predict topics that are constantly changing	3	17%
The ability of the algorithm to determine the tone of the text	3	17%
Bias	3	17%
UI & UX	2	11%
Technology compatibility	2	11%
People are not following the links to the sources to find reliable information	2	11%
People not believing the information no matter how trustworthy	2	11%
Many people have multiple accounts	2	11%
Profitability	2	11%

Not having enough users is the most common risk to both standalone and integration solutions (in terms of people using the features of flagging the information).

Another major concern is *technology on its own* and AI development must be constant and consistent. The worry that technology can generate significantly more misinformation than users in any time frame is overwhelming. That is why it is a positive sign that one of the solutions is strictly directed at combating the misinformation generated by AI (S19).

The risks to implementing are AI-generated content and users already being on the platforms, therefore flagging the new ones would not delete the old bot accounts and old content that has been circulating, and the resources for the race against AI fake news generation may be scarce. For the algorithm-focused solutions, which are integrations with other platforms, this is not a concern, but rather the technical abilities of the algorithm to properly detect misinformation, adjust to the changing landscape, and develop ML capacity.

Another concern is *bias*. In human-based solutions, it is the bias of either moderators or users themselves. For algorithm-based solutions, it is the bias of the users whose content is used to train ML models, and the individuals building the ML capability. However, bias is not perceived as a large risk factor, as only three solutions outlined it as a risk factor.

In addition to the five most common risks, it is vital not to overlook whether the solutions are compatible and can be integrated with other platforms, considering that people tend to have multiple accounts. Winning over trust is difficult, as well as sparking curiosity which is important for fact-checking. Also, the solution, whether integration or standalone, must be commercially viable.

E. RQ5: How realistic are the student solutions?

Overall, the students' solutions were deemed more realistic than not. The decisions on whether a solution is realistic or not and to what extent was made taking into consideration the assumptions, risks, metrics, manpower needed, technological sophistication needed, number and scale of stakeholders involved, and the level of input from the users of the solution. In the more realistic aspects of the solutions, we identified the following:

4 realistic solutions (S09, S10, S17, and S19) proposed integrations with existing social media platforms. These solutions involved the development of algorithms to detect potential misinformation, the introduction of a "trust factor" for information sources, and the mitigation of AI-generated misinformation. These solutions were considered highly realistic due to their technological focus, as they specifically addressed the misinformation problem within platforms that were already engaged in combating misinformation.

3 realistic solutions (S01, S11, and S13) involved creating their own platforms: news, educational, and fact-checking. These solutions utilized AI and ML models, along with human input for reliability. Manual fact-checking was necessary due to language nuances and human social nature. Building an educational platform for spotting misinformation was considered realistic.

Most of these solutions have a theme of a *Multidimensional view of misinformation* (6 out of 7), meaning they focus on multiple aspects of misinformation (fake news, sensationalism, propaganda, click-bait, conspiracy theories, etc.). One solution has a user rating system (as users are sources of information), introducing a 'trust factor', which will be based on an algorithm.

In the unrealistic solutions, two findings emerged:

Two solutions had a score of 2. One solution proposed an extensive user verification process using multiple personal documents, including a social security number, which was deemed unrealistic (S02).

The other had an unrealistic expectation of integrating social media apps and their features (S14). Too many features, too many requests from users, and too many stakeholders were seen as unrealistic.

Of all unrealistic and less realistic solutions (scales 2, 3, 4), 30% were human-based solutions, 30% were technology-based, and 40% were mixed-based.

F. RQ6: What metrics do students propose?

Table 4 presents the most common measures, followed by a discussion on both quantitative and qualitative metrics.

The most common metric is *engagement rate*, regardless of whether the solution is a standalone platform or an integration with existing ones. Engagement rate has various meanings. For some solutions it is the number of likes and shares, or if a solution is commenting on the information and providing real information, in that case, comments on their own are a metric. This metric is quantitative, and the metrics such as the *number of reported misinformation instances* (fake news, clickbait, misleading, etc.), and the *number of users* or verified users are the most common quantitative metrics found in students' solutions.

TABLE IV. FAKE NEWS SOLUTION METRICS

Metric	N	%
Engagement rate	12	67%
Feedback from users	11	61%
Number of reported misinformation instances	6	33%
The ability of users to identify misinformation	3	17%
Number of users	3	17%
Reliability and accuracy of the information shared	3	17%
User satisfaction	3	17%
Independent analysis and verification	3	17%
Number of new verified accounts	2	11%
Reliability score of users	2	11%
3rd party reviews	2	11%
User behavior tracking	2	11%
Manual reviews of sample content	2	11%
Click through rate	2	11%
Bounce rate	2	11%
Conduct experiments to test the effectiveness	2	11%

Other **Quantitative Metrics** that were present in the realistic solutions, with the least number of unknowns, are:

Several texts downloaded from the platform: the solution involves a standalone platform where a user can upload a piece of text and get it checked through different reliable sources (scientific journals, papers, etc.) and obtain a reference that they can download.

Decrease in engagement: people react to fake news more than to actual news, which means that, if the algorithm does the job well, the platforms will have less misinformation, and, therefore, less engagement.

An appropriate user engagement metric, which was not observed in other solutions, is *Time spent on the platform*. Building on the above metric (even though these two metrics were not presented in the same students' solution) is deeply connected to this one. As engagement drops, an assumption would be that people spend less time, but a direct indicator that the algorithms work, and that people are not prone to get into any arguments over misinformation is the opposite curve on the graph for time spent on the platform.

Relevance, authority, and accuracy as metrics of the sources of information. This one is part of the solution which is a separate standalone news platform. Having these scores assigned to different sources would help the assessment of whether a news article from a particular source about a topic should be posted on this standalone news platform.

Moving onto **Qualitative Metrics**, from our list, 61% of solutions had *Feedback from users* as a necessary metric. The feedback from users would consist of any form of feedback provision through forms or surveys. There are also metrics for *third-party reviews & independent analysis and verification* including feedback from outsider bodies and organizations on the platform, algorithm, and the system implemented. Next, we have *user satisfaction* with the platform, feature (integration), and outcome. The outcome, in this sense, means the circulation of news and decreased proportion of misleading information.

The ability of users to identify fake news, as a metric, needs to track users' success in identifying different types of indicators that help determine if the news is fake.

Consumer education as a metric stems from solutions that have a training/education aspect to the platform or a feature. Users can learn on the spot through current news and examples of current news categorized as fake.

To summarize, the metrics are engagement rate, feedback from users, number of reported misinformation instances, the ability of users to identify misinformation, number of users, reliability and accuracy of the information, user satisfaction, and independent analysis and verification.

V. DISCUSSION AND CONCLUSION

This paper has examined user-led solutions to the problem of fake news. Our findings highlight a reliance on AI effectiveness and underscore the need for technological sophistication. These insights contribute to the ongoing discourse on combating fake news and suggest future research should integrate human factors in developing technological interventions.

A. Theoretical Implications

The findings involve several theoretical implications. First, identifying algorithm-focused, human-focused, and combined-focus solutions provides theoretical implications for combating fake news [19]. This underscores the importance of a balanced approach that combines technological advancements and human judgment.

Second, categorizing solutions as social media integration or standalone platforms emphasizes the need to adapt interventions to different technological contexts when addressing fake news [20]. This allows customization based on the specific misinformation problem and target audience.

Third, the assumption that AI and algorithms effectively combat fake news highlights technological sophistication. Because limited user engagement challenges the importance of user adoption and participation in successful interventions, this implies the need for user-friendly and accessible technological solutions. The prevalent use of engagement rate as an evaluation metric for both standalone platforms and Social Media Integration implies that interventions should prioritize metrics capturing user participation.

Fake news researchers should start approaching the problem more holistically, engaging in cross-disciplinary research collaboration. The goal is for users to be more information literate and critical, which requires not only a technical environment, but users also need to be incentivized about the need to be information literate.

B. Limitations and Future Research

The limitations include the lack of actual verbal presentations from the students, which may contain additional information. This could impact the ratings of realism and clarity. Another limitation is the absence of user opinions and concerns from different platforms regarding misinformation. It would be interesting to know how a fact-checking feature or platform would work and whether the users would use it in the first place. How will it be connected to the organizations and institutions that do research or other trusted sources and which ML models and algorithms will be used? Also, we would love to see the results of a test on spotting the misinformation with users and their reasoning about what and why something is some type of misinformation. That way, we can make a bridge between the current level of ability of users to spot misinformation, and what is needed to improve that. Human factors in fake news detection merit much more research.

REFERENCES

[1] R. R. Mandical, N. Mamatha, N. Shivakumar, R. Monica, and A. N. Krishna, 'Identification of Fake News Using Machine Learning', in *2020 IEEE International Conference on Electronics, Computing and Communication Technologies (CONECCT)*, Jul. 2020, pp. 1–6. doi: 10.1109/CONECCT50063.2020.9198610.

[2] A. Mughaid *et al.*, 'An intelligent cybersecurity system for detecting fake news in social media websites', *Soft. Comput.*, vol. 26, no. 12, pp. 5577–5591, Jun. 2022, doi: 10.1007/s00500-022-07080-1.

[3] K. Shu, S. Wang, and H. Liu, 'Beyond News Contents: The Role of Social Context for Fake News Detection', in *Proceedings of the Twelfth ACM International Conference on Web Search and Data Mining*, in WSDM '19. New York, NY, USA: Association for Computing Machinery, Jan. 2019, pp. 312–320. doi: 10.1145/3289600.3290994.

[4] R. Natarajan *et al.*, 'Intelligent gravitational search random forest algorithm for fake news detection', *Int. J. Mod. Phys. C*, vol. 33, no. 06, p. 2250084, Jun. 2022, doi: 10.1142/S012918312250084X.

[5] A. Giachanou, G. Zhang, and P. Rosso, 'Multimodal Multi-image Fake News Detection', in *2020 IEEE 7th International Conference on Data Science and Advanced Analytics (DSAA)*, Oct. 2020, pp. 647–654. doi: 10.1109/DSAA49011.2020.00091.

[6] S. Kaur, P. Kumar, and P. Kumaraguru, 'Automating fake news detection system using multi-level voting model', *Soft. Comput.*, vol. 24, no. 12, pp. 9049–9069, Jun. 2020, doi: 10.1007/s00500-019-04436-y.

[7] S. Gundapu and R. Mamidi, 'Transformer based Automatic COVID-19 Fake News Detection System'. arXiv, Jan. 21, 2021. doi: 10.48550/arXiv.2101.00180.

[8] M. Zivkovic, C. Stoean, A. Petrovic, N. Bacanin, I. Strumberger, and T. Zivkovic, 'A Novel Method for COVID-19 Pandemic Information Fake News Detection Based on the Arithmetic Optimization Algorithm', in *2021 23rd International Symposium on Symbolic and Numeric Algorithms for Scientific Computing (SYNASC)*, Dec. 2021, pp. 259–266. doi: 10.1109/SYNASC54541.2021.00051.

[9] N. Zarandi, A. Soares, and H. Alves, 'Strategies, benefits and barriers–a systematic literature review of student co-creation in higher education', *Journal of Marketing for Higher Education*, pp. 1–25, 2022.

[10] J. M. Corbin and A. Strauss, 'Grounded theory research: Procedures, canons, and evaluative criteria', *Qualitative sociology*, vol. 13, no. 1, pp. 3–21, 1990.

[11] A. A. A. Ahmed, A. Aljabouh, P. K. Donepudi, and M. S. Choi, 'Detecting fake news using machine learning: A systematic literature review', *arXiv preprint arXiv:2102.04458*, 2021.

[12] S. Sheikhi, 'An effective fake news detection method using WOA-xgbTree algorithm and content-based features', *Applied Soft Computing*, vol. 109, p. 107559, Sep. 2021, doi: 10.1016/j.asoc.2021.107559.

[13] R. K. Kaliyar, A. Goswami, P. Narang, and S. Sinha, 'FNDNet – A deep convolutional neural network for fake news detection', *Cognitive Systems Research*, vol. 61, pp. 32–44, Jun. 2020, doi: 10.1016/j.cogsys.2019.12.005.

[14] S. Vinothkumar, S. Varadhaganapathy, M. Ramalingam, D. Ramkishore, S. Rithik, and K. P. Tharanies, 'Fake News Detection Using SVM Algorithm in Machine Learning', in *2022 International Conference on Computer Communication and Informatics (ICCCI)*, Jan. 2022, pp. 1–7. doi: 10.1109/ICCCI54379.2022.9740886.

[15] D. Choudhury and T. Acharjee, 'A novel approach to fake news detection in social networks using genetic algorithm applying machine learning classifiers', *Multimed Tools Appl*, vol. 82, no. 6, pp. 9029–9045, Mar. 2023, doi: 10.1007/s11042-022-12788-1.

[16] S. S. Nikam and R. Dalvi, 'Machine Learning Algorithm based model for classification of fake news on Twitter', in *2020 Fourth International Conference on I-SMAC (IoT in Social, Mobile, Analytics and Cloud) (I-SMAC)*, Oct. 2020, pp. 1–4. doi: 10.1109/I-SMAC49090.2020.9243385.

[17] Y.-F. Huang and P.-H. Chen, 'Fake news detection using an ensemble learning model based on Self-Adaptive Harmony Search algorithms', *Expert Systems with Applications*, vol. 159, p. 113584, Nov. 2020, doi: 10.1016/j.eswa.2020.113584.

[18] S. Singhal, R. R. Shah, T. Chakraborty, P. Kumaraguru, and S. Satoh, 'SpotFake: A Multi-modal Framework for Fake News Detection', in *2019 IEEE Fifth International Conference on Multimedia Big Data (BigMM)*, Sep. 2019, pp. 39–47. doi: 10.1109/BigMM.2019.00-44.

[19] K. Somandepalli, T. Guha, V. R. Martinez, N. Kumar, H. Adam, and S. Narayanan, 'Computational media intelligence: human-centered machine analysis of media', *Proceedings of the IEEE*, vol. 109, no. 5, pp. 891–910, 2021.

[20] C. Vaccari and A. Chadwick, 'Deepfakes and disinformation: Exploring the impact of synthetic political video on deception, uncertainty, and trust in news', *Social Media+ Society*, vol. 6, no. 1, p. 2056305120903408, 2020.

Designing and Testing a Connected System for Heating Delivered Food for Elderly People

Introducing the AAL project PREPARIO

Sandra Draxler, Wolfgang Weiss
Institute for Digital Technologies
JOANNEUM RESEARCH Forschungsgesellschaft mbH
Graz, Austria
e-mail: sandra.draxler@joanneum.at
e-mail: wolfgang.weiss@joanneum.at

Manuela Ferreira
Município de Vila Nova de Cerveira
Gabinete de Projetos Internacionais
Vila Nova de Cerveira, Portugal
e-mail: investimento.adl@cm-vncerveira.pt

Henrik Schneider
SENSERNA A/S
Greve, Denmark
e-mail: henrik@senserna.com

Adriana Atunes
Santa Casa da Misericórdia de Lisboa
Lisbon, Portugal
e-mail: adriana.antunes@scml.pt

Celine Sommer
Exthex GmbH
Graz, Austria
e-mail: sommer.celine7@gmail.com

***Abstract*— Existing meal preparation solutions are inadequate for many elderly people who struggle to reheat their delivered meals. It is common for meals to be over- or under-heated, which can ruin the meal itself as well as the eating experience. In some cases, this leads to malnutrition and serious illness, and in other cases, caregivers are required to assist with food preparation on a daily basis, time that could be better spent with the client and a major financial burden to society. In addition, stakeholders, such as caregivers, have limited means of obtaining feedback from older people about potential problems with meal preparation, which prevents critical and efficient support. The Active and Assisted Living Joint Project (AAL JP) PREPARIO aims to develop a solution that enables seniors to prepare their meals safely and independently at home, with external digital monitoring to enable efficient care. The solution consists of an innovative microwave oven with wireless temperature control that enables fully automated heating of delivered meals to the optimal serving temperature. The entire heating process is supported by a digital voice assistance platform - "Emma" - and a Smart Living Data Space that collects all data relevant to the food preparation process and provides structured reports for caregivers and service providers for closer monitoring and support.**

Keywords: Smart Home; Food Preparation; User centered Service Design.

I. INTRODUCTION

The AAL project PREPARIO [1] aims to develop a connected and automated food preparation platform that integrates a microwave oven, a temperature probe, and a voice assistant, and connects these devices to a smart home environment that collects and visualizes data on usage, errors, and questionnaire results.

Despite the widespread adoption of the microwave oven since its invention over 70 years ago, its capabilities have remained largely unchanged and far from innovative compared to other household appliances. Most functions rely heavily on manual process control and prior user knowledge/experience due to the lack of temperature sensing capabilities. Now, more sophisticated solutions are emerging, with features that make meal preparation easier, such as the ability to scan package barcodes (GE Appliances' Scan-To-Cook technology [2]), use voice-activated commands (Whirlpool's Smart Over-the-Range Microwave [3]), and built-in sensors (Breville's Breville Quick Touch with Sensor iQ™ [4]) to tell you how to cook meals and when they are done. However, although these are interesting and innovative products, they are not suitable or tailored to the senior population. They often require a high level of technological knowledge and special connections to other devices that are simply not attractive or user-friendly for older adults. They are also considered premium devices and are often priced well above the average market price, making them unaffordable for most people. Importantly, they use non-ideal sensors (e.g., humidity or infrared sensors) to estimate when the meal is "ready" and require extensive user input, such as the type of food to be heated and the weight of the food. Such solutions are state of the art, but due to the lack of reliable temperature sensing, the heating result can vary widely and may not directly correspond to a "ready to eat" meal, as it may be too hot and far from the appropriate serving temperature. Therefore, in our opinion, even the emerging more sophisticated microwaves are not suitable for integration into current food delivery services and cannot offer an improvement to existing systems for older adults.

The PREPARIO system is designed to allow independent end-users to heat their pre-prepared and home-delivered meals to an appropriate and safe temperature for consumption in a fully automated manner. The interface of the microwave oven has been modified to be as easy to use as possible, i.e. only one button for "start", thus reducing the barriers to use. In addition, the heating process uses a developed and validated algorithm aimed at ensuring that the food is at the right temperature throughout (and not just on the surface or in the core). Users can continue with their activities and are notified by a voice interaction device when their meal is ready. A survey linked to the system can be answered via an easy-to-use interface on a tablet. The results are stored in a central database along with the data sent by the microwave. This provides a dashboard view of the microwave's usage and the user's well-being. For example, caregivers or family members can monitor whether hot meals have been prepared as expected.

The project was initiated by Senserna A/S - the company that invented the world's first temperature probe for microwave ovens - to further improve the idea and evaluate the prototype with partners from the technology, science and care sectors.

At a very early stage, a number of activities were carried out to gather requirements for the concept. The first action was a stakeholder questionnaire addressed to 81 social institutions with the aim of deepening the knowledge of the targeted primary end-users, their needs and expectations. This was followed by a user-centered design process for the applications to be implemented. Three co-creation workshops provided feedback on the prototype, its possible barriers, limitations and opportunities. The desire was expressed to further promote integration with solutions available on the market and to expand the user group to include people with cognitive or physiological disabilities.

The solution is being tested in a testbed environment with caregivers and elderly people in care centers in two trial phases. One trial has been completed and the other is ongoing. It turns out that most people are able to use the microwave to heat their meals and are almost always satisfied with the temperature of the food. The data from the questionnaires and the system parameters provide important technical information about the state and use of the solution. These results and the general feedback help to further improve the idea and its implementation.

This paper gives an insight into the methods used and the results obtained from the involved end-users and stakeholders, with an outlook on how the final product could become an integral part of care and independent living. The rest of the paper is structured as follows. Section 2 describes the methods used to develop the solution, which is evaluated in the project with trial runs, co-creation workshops and stakeholder questionnaires, as outlined in Section 3. The paper ends with a conclusion and outlook in Section 4.

II. METHODS

The project uses a user-centered approach to identify barriers, usability issues, and related problems (such as time efficiency for social workers) in order to develop a solution that addresses these shortcomings in the process of heating home-delivered meals. From there, user involvement will continue throughout all phases of the project to ensure optimal acceptance. The resulting prototypes will be presented to and tested by the target user groups and all feedback will be considered in the following phases. The general steps for this process are listed below:

1. Interviews with end users and subject-matter experts in person and through written surveys.
2. Hands-on experience: Heating a meal, eating and tasting the meal, evaluating the experience.
3. Identify and list problems.
4. Brainstorm technical solutions.
5. Define technical solutions to develop and test.
6. Define tests to evaluate solutions.
7. Evaluate and share results.

A. *What problem our solution is trying to solve*

Preparing food is one of the most important Instrumental Activities of Daily Living (IADLs) and helps people maintain a sense of self-worth and self-efficacy [5][6]. When cooking and obtaining the materials for this task becomes more difficult due to circumstances and changes in mobility, delivered meals are often a solution.

The microwave oven is a popular choice for heating pre-prepared meals. One of the major advantages is that a meal can be heated directly in the meal packaging, reducing the need for cleaning. Another advantage is the heating speed of only 4-6 minutes for a cold meal from the refrigerator that would normally take 25-30 minutes to heat in a conventional oven.

However, the microwave oven also has some drawbacks:

1. Complicated user interface - A microwave oven can have many different functions and automatic heating programs. Some interfaces have more than 20 buttons and only a simple 7-segment Light Emitting Diode (LED) display. Users are often unaware of the wealth of features and/or do not use them [7].
2. Lack of temperature control - The microwave oven can be viewed as a black box where the temperature cannot be measured and controlled during meal preparation. Therefore, the heating result is based on a trial and error approach, where the user guesses the heating time for a certain power setting, often resulting in suboptimal heating results.
3. Uneven heating - The heating efficiency of microwaves vary with the size, consistency and type of food that is heated. This, combined with the microwave's hot and cold spots, can result in large temperature differences in the heated food. In other words, a meal that appears searing hot on the outside may be cold or even frozen in the center.
4. Zero Connectivity - Home appliances have benefited from the tremendous technological developments of the past few decades. However, the vast majority of microwave

manufacturers have not embraced new technology and do not offer any form of connectivity. This is a current area of research and several studies are looking at making the kitchen smarter for older adults [8].

Figure 1. The adapted microwave and a meal with the probe inserted (Solution 1).

Figure 2. The innovative tray with built in sensors (Solution 2).

B. Description of the system and its functions

Senserna A/S has developed a revolutionary temperature sensor technology for microwave ovens that has the potential to mitigate the above mentioned disadvantages. With this new possibility in mind, two interesting solutions have been developed to improve the preparation of home delivered meals.

Solution 1 is a special microwave oven designed to automatically heat delivered meals to a pre-defined target temperature of 75°C using a novel probe-based temperature sensing and control mechanism. A Bluetooth module is built into the microwave for wireless transmission of measurable system parameters related to the heating process. The probe contains five temperature sensors and sends the average of the sensors to the microwave and via Bluetooth to devices beyond. The connected system can then display and respond to the current temperature. Errors can also be relayed and dealt with in this way. Figure 1 shows the system as it was used in the first test phase.

Solution 2 is a probe-less temperature sensing solution (see Figure 2), consisting of a dedicated meal tray with seamlessly integrated temperature sensors. This would be the most user friendly solution imaginable. The only thing a user would have to do to heat a meal is to take a meal from the refrigerator and place it in a special tray before placing it in the microwave. From there, the microwave would sense the meal and automatically heat it without any further user interaction.

This smart microwave system allows for connections to other devices, and for this project, the personal smart voice assistant "Emma" was used. The voice assistant receives the status of the meal and the heating process from the microwave via Bluetooth, and can, for example, issue a reminder when the food is ready to be picked up. This extends the scope of the "Emma" product, which functions as a connected voice assistant for the smart home, performing various tasks such as setting scenes, starting music, reminding people to take their medication and so on. "Emma" connects to the user's wireless network and transmits all information from the microwave to an intelligent digital database, which then allows remote access and visualization of the collected data. Unfortunately, this product has been discontinued while the project was ongoing (April 2024).

III. TRIALS, CO-CREATION AND FINDINGS

The goal of the first trial was to have 30 primary end users and 5 secondary end users (caregivers) test the solution with the connected microwave and temperature probe and provide feedback via a questionnaire and written observations of user behavior. The information collected during the trial was completely anonymous, and there was no way to link the responses and observations to a specific end-user.

The procedure of trial 1 was as follows:

1. Welcome the end-user and move to the trial location.
2. Introduce the user to the trial.
3. Introduce the user to the assessment app.
4. Begin the trial by answering questions via the assessment app.
5. Let the user select a meal.
6. Introduce the user to the microwave oven with automatic heating functionality.
7. Let the user warm a meal using microwave oven.
8. Let the user taste/eat the meal.
9. End the trial by answering more questions via the assessment app.
10. End of trial.

The trial was performed with one end-user at a time and a trial instructor present through the entire trial for support and taking notes.

The second trial will take place in July 2024 and will follow the same procedure as described above and have the same test users (if available). The trial will test the improved system with the connected audio system together with the tablet for the pre- and post-meal questionnaires.

A. Co-Creation Workshops

At the beginning of the project, two different questionnaires were carried out by the Municipality of Vila Nova de Cerveira to answer the questions posed by the project team: an online questionnaire addressed to 76 social institutions in the district of Viana do Castelo with the aim of deepening the methods used to deliver meals at home.

The second questionnaire, addressed to social institutions in the municipality of Vila Nova de Cerveira, aimed to deepen the knowledge about the end users, namely the characterization of the users (how many, age, average pension, mental and physical illnesses, situation of social and geographical isolation) and their needs and expectations.

As the project progressed, stakeholders and representatives of the target groups were invited to workshops to learn more about the current situation of elderly care and food delivery.

An online workshop was offered to Austrian stakeholders and two face-to-face workshops were held in Portugal. In addition, an international workshop with representatives from all participating countries will take place at the end of April 2024.

1) Online Workshop Austria

In Austria, a stakeholder workshop was held as an online videoconference with a total of 9 participants. Four of them were not involved in the project and represented the stakeholders. Two of them work in the management of a care organization, one in the management of a medical aid organization in the field of home care for the elderly, and one person comes from academia in the field of care research. The participating stakeholders are in close contact with the target primary user group. They know their needs, their living conditions and their daily structures.

The workshop started with an introduction of the participants followed by a presentation of the project. A video of the prototype solution was used to demonstrate how it works in a real-life scenario. The video was recorded by the partner in Portugal and showed one of their clients using the microwave to heat a meal. Another video demonstrated the use and capabilities of the EMMA smart home system. The presentation was followed by a moderated discussion with questions on (i) usage and benefits, (ii) functionality, and (iii) markets, business opportunities and revenue streams.

Statements about **usage and usefulness**:

- New microwaves are often no more user-friendly than old ones because they have so many buttons it becomes too complicated for people to use.
- The system should be a complete service, possibly with instructions to prepare a complete meal from the ingredients.
- Not sure how useful the data about the smart home system is. The dashboard data shows only a small excerpt from a whole day of a person. Other data will be completely missing, e.g., when a person eats somewhere else.

Statements about **functionality**:

- Integration with existing smart home solutions, e.g., Amazon Alexa is desired as some households already have those systems in use.
- Clients living in a care organization have a fixed daily routine; a system that reminds them would be helpful, for example when to start preparing meals.
- One care organization already uses a similar product for easy cooking (Thermomix®). It works well for their clients in assisted living. It gives people independence and self-efficacy. In addition, virtual voice assistants (e.g., Amazon Alexa) are in use and it works well for cognitive impaired people.
- A smart home system should speak in the voice of a familiar person; this would make things much easier.

Statements about **markets, business opportunities and revenue streams**:

- It is a niche product, but demand is possible.
- For many people a product like this is not top priority, they have other more fundamental problems to solve every day, e.g., mobility (wheel chair, stair lift, etc.). It can be seen as a luxury item.
- Possible new target groups: cognitive impaired or disabled persons.
- Possible business models: rent or buy.
- Target groups for selling this service could be:
    - Private customers who buy the microwave oven or the service.
    - Care organization who buy the microwave oven or the service and then rent it to their clients.
    - A subscription from a food delivery service, with the microwave oven included for free (or for a reduced price).

More co-creation workshops were held as face-to-face meetings by the two partners in Portugal. 17 people attended the workshop in Vila Nova de Cerveira (November 23rd, 2023) and 17 people attended the workshop in Lisbon (November 16th, 2023) - a total of 34 people took part in the discussions. Each workshop was attended by three people linked to the project who facilitated the session.

2) Workshop at Vila Nova de Cerveira (Portugal)

In view of the territorial context and the system of providing meals to the elderly through the Home Care Service in the Alto Minho region and in Lisbon, representative bodies of the most diverse sectors directly or indirectly involved in this service, on the one hand, and companies and organizations from the most diverse sectors of society, on the other hand, were invited to these workshops.

Thus, political representatives from local authorities, public social services, public health services, social institutions and private companies providing care for the elderly, companies in the food sector and new technologies for the elderly, and a company in the plastics processing sector were invited to participate in this workshop.

Specifically, the workshop in Cerveira was attended by a diverse group, including three participants as political representatives of local authorities, one from a public social service, two from public health services, two from social institutions, four people from private companies providing care for the elderly, one person from a company in the food sector, two from companies developing new technologies for the elderly, and one person from a company in the plastics processing sector.

At the beginning, the participants received an explanation of the workshop and the topics to be covered. The PREPARIO project was presented with its service model and technical components. A microwave prototype with a sensor probe was used to demonstrate the heating process.

During the workshop the following topics were discussed and the answers of the participants were recorded:

- In response to the home meal distribution service currently provided, please identify: 1 POSITIVE factor & 1 NEGATIVE factor.
- From the PREPARIO solution presented - Identify the most relevant function.
- From the PREPARIO solution presented: - Identify the biggest problem.
- General opinion on PREPARIO solution that we present to you.
- How much would you pay for the PREPARIO solution.
- How do you imagine the PREPARIO solution will be able to reach customers (from home delivery of meals to heating).

In conclusion, the provision of basic meals is a very important factor in giving people equal access to fresh, healthy and balanced meals and in facilitating their daily lives. The problems identified were congruent with those identified at the outset of the project: lack of control over the heating process, difficulties in handling food containers and uneven temperatures, and lack of feedback.

What the PREPARIO project offers was seen as valuable because it is simpler, with only one button, with acoustic reminders to take out the food, and with the possibility of giving feedback directly by voice or through a large touch interface. Issues identified were: reluctance to use a new device, the training that might be required, the cost of the system, the possibility of losing the probe as it is not connected to the microwave, and the hygiene of the probe. Stakeholder input also led to the conclusion that delivering cold meals would simplify the logistics of meal delivery and would require fewer delivery trips throughout the week compared to delivering hot meals.

3) Workshop in Lisbon (Portugal)

This workshop was also attended by 17 people invited to discuss aspects of the daily life and food preparation of adults aged 65+. The participants came from a variety of relevant backgrounds, namely: different departments of Santa Casa da Misericórdia de Lisboa, including the Department of Health, the Department of Studies and Strategic Planning, the Department of Intervention with Vulnerable Public, the Department of Technical Management and Monitoring, the Mission Unit - Lisbon, City of All Ages Program and the Department of Entrepreneurship and Social Economy. Also present were private institutions of social solidarity, representatives of the local council and of a food service company.

After the presentation of the project and its partners, the participants were invited to ask questions, to ask for clarifications and, last but not least, to give their feedback. This was divided into sections:

Current response to home-delivered meals for heating: participants were asked to identify one positive and one negative factor in the current system/service, followed by a debate among all participants on the current response to home-delivered meals.

PREPARIO solution: Everyone was asked to identify the most relevant function and the biggest problem in the PREPARIO solution, followed by a debate among all participants about the equipment under development.

Business Plan for the PREPARIO solution: Each of the participants was asked to identify how much they would pay for the PREPARIO solution, in an assigned value logic, followed by a debate among all the participants on what possible business model would make the equipment available to users/clients

Overall, the current situation was described with the positive points of guaranteed meals of good quality and dietary value, the facilitation of autonomous food intake; negative points were the failure points with autonomous heating leading to over or undercooked meals, the limited variety and environmental issues with packaging, among others.

The PREPARIO solution was seen as simple and fail-safe, with the additional data for monitoring as an advantage in care contexts, but the cost of the adapted microwave, the possibility of misplacing the probe and the uncertain acceptance of new technology were seen as risks. It was also mentioned that the target group is quite specific in that the person using it must be physiologically able to do so, it is not an enhanced asset for blind, bedridden or cognitively impaired people.

The question about pricing and business models was answered that prices would have to be kept quite low, and in the best case the microwave would be offered by a care organization, a municipality or the food supplier, and the costs would be covered by the general fees for services.

B. Findings

The overall findings from the co-creation efforts and the feedback from the observed heating processes and the tailored questionnaires were that the technology has great potential and that the heating process was, in most cases, very satisfying. The combination of questions about the quality of the food and the experience of heating it was helpful and not intrusive. The concerns raised, particularly about losing the probe and its hygiene, are being addressed in the second prototype with a specially designed food container with built-in temperature sensors. This will be tested in the second trial in July.

IV. Conclusion

The availability of food delivery services is considered important, especially in the aftermath of the COVID-19 pandemic, when people were even more homebound than before. However, food safety, food preparation safety and food quality remain issues in this context [9][10]. The PREPARIO system offers elderly people living independently a solution for heating delivered meals in an easy and safe way. Trials with the target groups showed promising results and very good acceptance. The additional functionality of monitoring the use of the system, and thus the data on suspected food intake, is considered valuable by caregivers and related parties, as determined during the co-creation workshops with stakeholders and care organizations, as well as during the trials with caregivers. Further trials with the sensorized food tray will provide additional insights and help improve the system for market readiness. By removing the burden of assisting with food preparation, caregivers or informal caregivers such as family members can focus on other tasks and use their time more efficiently.

We believe the end product could become an integral part of caregiving and independent living.

Acknowledgment

The authors would like to thank the participants in the user trials and the health care assistants who made the tests possible, as well as the attendees in the co-creation and stakeholder workshops for their open and valuable opinions. The project PREPARIO (AAL-2021-8-158-CP) has received funding from AAL JP, co-funded by the European Commission and National Funding Authorities of Austria, Denmark and Portugal.

References

[1] https://www.aal-europe.eu/projects/prepario/ [retrieved May 2024].

[2] https://geappliancesco.com/blog/ge-appliances-smart-wall-ovens-and-ranges-offer-a-new-way-for-consumers-to-discover-new-recipes-cook-and-shop/ [retrieved May 2024].

[3] https://producthelp.whirlpool.com/Connected_Appliances/Product_Info/Connected_Support/Scan_to_Cook_Feature_-_How_Does_it_Work%3F [retrieved May 2024].

[4] https://www.breville.com/us/en/products/microwaves/bmo850.html [retrieved May 2024]

[5] C. H. Hestevik, M. Molin, J. Debesay, A. Bergland, and A. Bye, "Older patients' and their family caregivers' perceptions of food, meals and nutritional care in the transition between hospital and home care: a qualitative study", BMC nutrition vol. 6 11. 18 Mar. 2020, doi:10.1186/s40795-020-00335-w.

[6] J. A. Jackson, A. Branscum, A. Tang, and E. Smit, "Food insecurity and physical functioning limitations among older U.S. adults", Preventive Medicine Reports, vol. 14, 100829, ISSN 2211-3355, 2019, https://doi.org/10.1016/j.pmedr.2019.100829.

[7] M. Zallio, P. Kelly, M. Jakuska, H. Rifai, and D. Berry, "Design of a community-supported CapAble microwave system for people with intellectual and physical disabilities", In: Cavallo, F., Marletta, V., Monteriù, A., Siciliano, P. (eds) Ambient Assisted Living. ForItAAL 2016. Lecture Notes in Electrical Engineering, vol 426. Springer, Cham., 2017, https://doi.org/10.1007/978-3-319-54283-6_5.

[8] M. Zallio, P. Kelly, B. Cryan, and D. Berry, "A co-Design approach to develop a smart cooking appliance. Applying a Domain Specific Language for a community supported appliance", arXiv preprint arXiv:2101.08886v3 [cs.HC], 2021, https://doi.org/10.48550/arXiv.2101.08886.

[9] A. Dickinson and W. Wills, "Meals on wheels services and the food security of older people", Health & Social Care in the Community, 30, pp. e6699–e6707, 2022, https://doi.org/10.1111/hsc.14092.

[10] C. Rudolph and S. Francis, "Making home-delivered meal programs relevant for today's aging adult.", J Public Health (Berl.) 30, pp. 141–150, 2022, https://doi.org/10.1007/s10389-020-01286-z.

Simulating Boyd's OODA Loop: Towards an ABM of Human Agency and Sensemaking in Dynamic, Competitive Environments

Mark Abdollahian & Chasen Jeffries
School of Social Science, Policy & Evaluation
Claremont Graduate University
Claremont, United States of America
Mark.abdollahian@cgu.edu, Chasen.Jeffries@cgu.edu

Abstract-**Increasingly complex global scenarios require advanced simulations of human decision-making. Existing models often neglect the nuanced cognitive processes essential in dynamic environments, leading to oversimplified analyses. Leveraging John Boyd's conceptualization of the Observe, Orient, Decide, Act (OODA) loop, we propose a novel, agent-based simulation exploring human agency and sensemaking within evolving competitive landscapes. By endowing agents with diverse cognitive capabilities across the OODA spectrum, we dissect the nuanced impacts of heterogeneous information processing and cognitive strategies on agent fitness and survival. While Boyd emphasized the strategic advantages of swiftly navigating the OODA loop or infiltrating an opponent's loop, we also explore the effects of diverse information processing and cognitive abilities on agent fitness. Central to our initial findings is the critical significance of the Orient and sensemaking phase, which emerges as a decisive factor in surpassing the mere possession of information, collection of data or swift and efficient execution of decisions and actions. We present several scenarios—ranging in complexity and resource availability— that underscore the superiority of deep sensemaking over other cognitive capabilities. Although only an initial step, we believe such approaches can expand both OODA loop's theoretical underpinnings and its practical relevance in enhancing strategic decision-making processes for human, behavioral, social, and cultural phenomena.**

Keywords-Agent-Based Modeling (ABM); OODA Loop; Complex Adaptive System; Co-Evolution.

I. INTRODUCTION

The concept of the Observe, Orient, Decide, Act (OODA) loop [2], introduced by Colonel John Boyd in the military context, has transcended its original domain and found applications in various fields, including human decision-making. The theoretical underpinnings of OODA loops in human decision-making stem from Boyd's original framework, which emphasizes the iterative and dynamic nature of decision-making. According to Boyd, individuals continuously cycle through the phases of observation, orientation, decision, and action, with each iteration informing subsequent cycles. This dynamic process enables individuals to adapt to changing circumstances and outmaneuver opponents effectively. Our research seeks to understand how variations in cognitive capabilities within the OODA loop affect strategic decision-making, and to explore the implications of these variations for achieving strategic advantage and survival in competitive environments.

Empirical research supports the efficacy of OODA loops in enhancing human decision making across various domains. For instance, in a study by González et al. [11], participants engaged in a simulated decision-making task involving time pressure and uncertainty. The results revealed that individuals who followed the OODA loop sequence exhibited faster response times and higher decision accuracy compared to those who adopted linear decision-making strategies. Similarly, in a neuroscientific investigation, Voss et al. [22] used functional Magnetic Resonance Imaging (fMRI) to examine the neural correlates of the OODA loop phases during decision-making. They found distinct patterns of brain activity associated with each phase, suggesting that the OODA loop framework corresponds to underlying cognitive processes in the brain. Furthermore, organizations can leverage OODA loops to enhance their decision-making processes and gain a competitive edge. By fostering a culture of rapid feedback and learning, organizations can adapt more quickly to market changes and exploit opportunities faster than their competitors [21].

In this paper, we agentize Boyd's OODA loop across each step of the process to simulate human agency and sensemaking under dynamic, competitive environments. We do this by varying agents' cognitive abilities in each step of the process. For Observe, we allow for different discrete levels of sensing their environments, ranging from local to global information. For the Orient step, we create two interactive vectors of cognitive abilities, one embracing determinism to stochasticity while the other focuses on the increasing complexity of mental models, to create a typology of twelve different mental models to make sense of competitive environments. For the Decide step, we instantiate three different levels of increasingly complex decision trees to capture various levels of agency. For the Act step, we then allow agents to execute their decision tree calculus with varying costs and time horizons. We then setup both single and double loop learning to occur, given agent OODA loop execution fitness scores. This enables us to explore agents' cognitive abilities both across and within each step of the OODA process.

The application of OODA loops in real-world decision-making contexts offers several practical benefits. One such benefit is improved decision agility, as individuals can rapidly cycle through the OODA loop to respond effectively to evolving situations. This capability is particularly valuable in dynamic and uncertain environments, such as emergency response operations [9]. Furthermore, organizations can leverage OODA loops to enhance their decision-making processes and gain a competitive edge. By fostering a culture of rapid feedback and learning, organizations can adapt more quickly to market changes and exploit opportunities faster than their competitors [2].

However, speed of OODA loop execution alone is only one small element: we focus on varying information and cognitive capabilities within each step of the loop to explore their respective implications for learning, competition, and efficiencies in dynamic environments. Below we outline our simulation approach, architecture and begin exploring its capabilities through running several scenarios across different dynamic resource landscapes as well as Simple, Moderate and Smart cognitive agents. While we only offer some initial findings, we believe that empirically calibrating and extending agentized OODA approaches such as this can provide significant insights into human agency and sensemaking in dynamic, competitive environments.

The rest of the paper is structured as follows. In Section II, we present the related works. In Section III, we present the model design. In Section IV, we present the model results. Finally, we conclude our work in Section V.

II. Related Works

A. *OODA*

In 1987, John Boyd originally developed the OODA loop as a decision-making model that could be applied in any competitive environment, be it military or business. This model encompasses four pivotal stages—Observe, Orient, Decide, Act—through which individuals continuously cycle, allowing each cycle to build upon the insights of the previous ones. This dynamic process enables individuals with environmental sensemaking and agency to adapt to changing circumstances and outmaneuver opponents effectively. Figure 1 outlines Boyd's steps, with feedback loops for single "input-output" learning and double loop learning where outcomes can also foster change to specific OODA steps' cognitive abilities given success or failures.

First, observe the environment to gain new information. This includes collecting immediate sensory information as well as more abstract data, such as changes in the competitive landscape or shifts in social dynamics. The objective of this step is to create a comprehensive snapshot of the current situation to inform subsequent decisions and actions [7]. Observation can be achieved through various means, including direct sensory perception, the use of technological tools (e.g., radar, surveillance systems), the collection of big data, open-source information, intelligence espionage, etc. [6]. In the military domain, Boyd emphasized the importance of rapid and accurate observation capabilities to gain a strategic advantage over adversaries [17].

Second, combine this new information with previous experiences, culture, and mental models to "Orient" and get an understanding of the current situation [4][5]. Orientation is the most complex and critical part of the OODA loop because it sets the context for decisions and actions. It involves filtering and processing the observed information through a framework of existing knowledge, experiences, and expectations [13] [15]. This step determines how individuals and organizations interpret their environment, assess threats and opportunities, and consider potential actions. In their study, Klein et al. [16] extended Boyd's framework by highlighting the role of mental models in the orientation phase. They proposed that individuals' decision-making processes are shaped by their mental representations of the environment, tasks, and goals. These mental models influence how individuals perceive, interpret, and respond to information, thereby affecting the effectiveness of their decisions. Orientation methodologies encompass cognitive processes, including situational awareness, mental simulation, schema activation, and decision-making under uncertainty. These processes are influenced by a myriad of factors, including training, cultural background, personal experiences, and the specific nature of the information received.

Third, review the options to determine the best course of action. The "Decide" step is a critical phase in John Boyd's OODA loop framework, acting as the bridge between understanding the situation (Orient) and taking action (Act). This step involves making a decision based on the analysis and synthesis of information collected during the Observe and Orient phases, under both risk and uncertainty [14]. The decision-making process is where strategies, tactics, or plans are formulated before being implemented in the Act phase. The "Decide" step is where choices are made about which course of action to take. This step is crucial for effective execution, as it determines the direction that actions will take. The quality of the decision-making process directly influences the outcome of the OODA loop, making it a pivotal point in the cycle. Decision-making methodologies in the context of the OODA loop can include analytical models, intuition-based approaches, decision theory, game theory, and scenario planning, among others depending on levels of uncertainty and risk. The chosen methodology often depends on the complexity of the situation, the amount of information available, and the time constraints faced by the decision-maker.

Finally, upon deciding, the chosen action is implemented. In the OODA loop, the "Act" step is where theory and planning confront reality. It's the execution phase where strategies and decisions are translated into concrete actions with the aim to achieve a desired outcome. This step is critical for the loop to be effective, as it is the point at which the individual or organization interacts directly with the environment to effect change. The methodologies for action can vary widely depending on the context, ranging from military operations, where it could involve maneuvering forces or engaging targets, to business strategies, where it might involve launching a new product or adjusting marketing tactics. The key is to act in a manner that is both timely and relevant to the information and orientation developed in the earlier steps of the OODA loop.

Although referred to as the OODA loop, in reality, it functions not as a circular process with independent steps but as a continuous operation [17], across multiple interconnected and coupled steps to produce outcomes. Since its introduction, it has become a popular framework for decision-making, especially under uncertainty [18]. Boyd identified several keys to success, including getting inside your opponent's OODA loop or running through your OODA loop more efficiently [3].

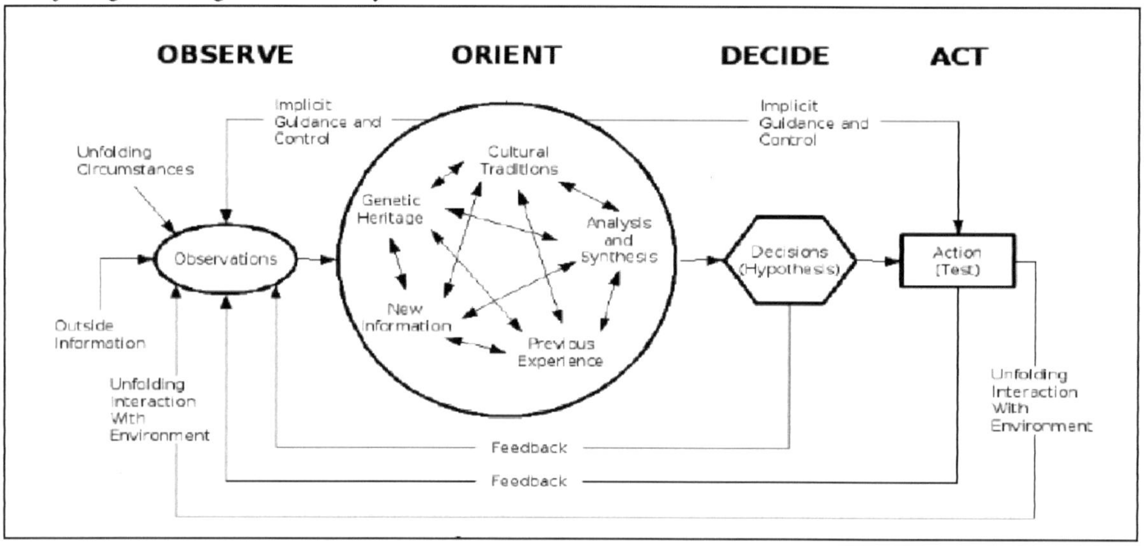

Figure 1. Boyd's OODA Loop [10].

B. An Agentized OODA Model

With the massive improvements in computational power and the popularization of agent-based modeling given complexity theory, the past several decades have seen many forays into simulating decision-making within complex adaptive systems [2][8][12][19]. These models employ a mix of game theory, rationality, and learning to simulate decision-making in dynamic complex systems under uncertainty [23]. Even relatively simple games, such as the El Farol problem, can yield intriguing results, unveil new strategies, and dynamic equilibria with slight increases in complexity [2][20]. Single-Loop and Double-Loop learning add a crucial dimension to these models, enabling actors to adapt to changing environments and optimize their fitness functions [24].

Complex adaptive systems are pervasive throughout the world, in domains such as business and military, and inherently operate under significant uncertainty and time constraints. Heterogeneous agents, by optimizing their fitness functions, create meso-level competitive social dynamics. These dynamics, in turn, shape macro-outcomes that influence decisions at all levels, both present and future [1]. Observing these interactions within a dynamic landscape, alongside agents' single and double-loop learning processes, offers opportunities to identify emergent, non-linear behaviors and potentially, resulting novel strategies. It also highlights the critical impact of varying agent capabilities across outcomes.

III. MODEL DESIGN

Figure 2 provides an overview of our agentized system. Individuals possess varying cognitive capability values on each one of the OODA vectors that influence their overall decision-making processes. These instantiate into local competitions on varying environmental landscapes, directly influencing outcomes and thereby increasing or decreasing agent wealth. The magnitude of these gains or losses triggers positive or negative feedback loops, prompting agents to update their capabilities given learning and expectations. This adaptation is crucial for their survival in dynamically evolving landscapes.

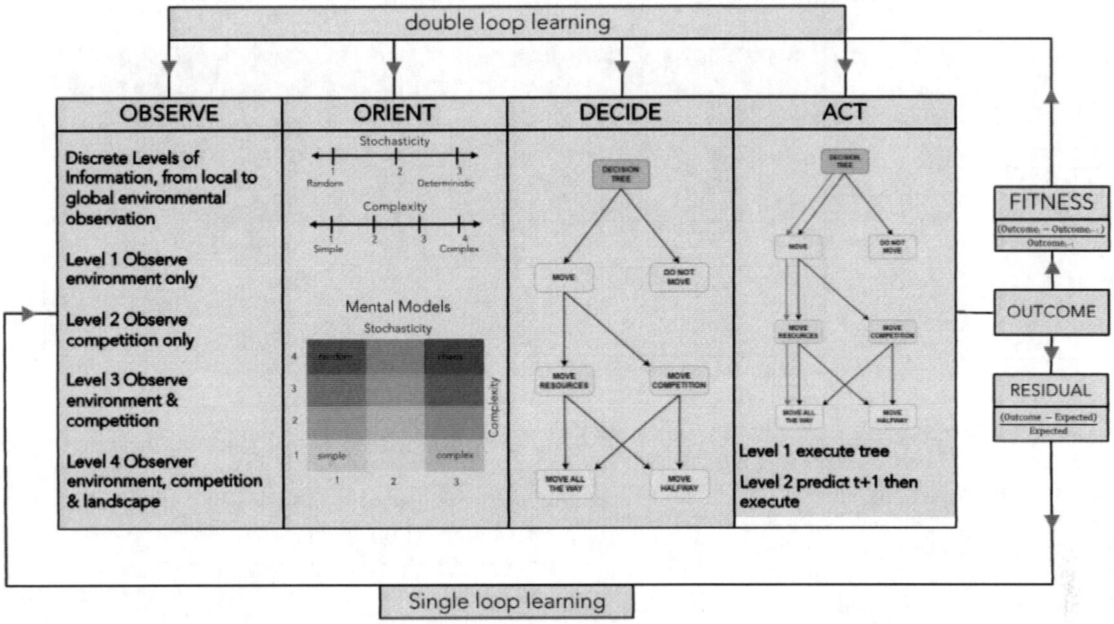

Figure 2. Agentized OODA Loop Architecture.

The Observe phase is a critical conduit for information gathering, enabling agents to perceive their local environment, competitors, and landscape. At the most basic levels, agents can either identify the resources available in each area or the positions of other agents within the local environment. Consequently, agents have three critical pieces of information to consider in the Orient step, encompassing resources, agent positions, and local landscape that influences their strategic planning. This provides four different discrete Observation levels for agents in Figure 3.

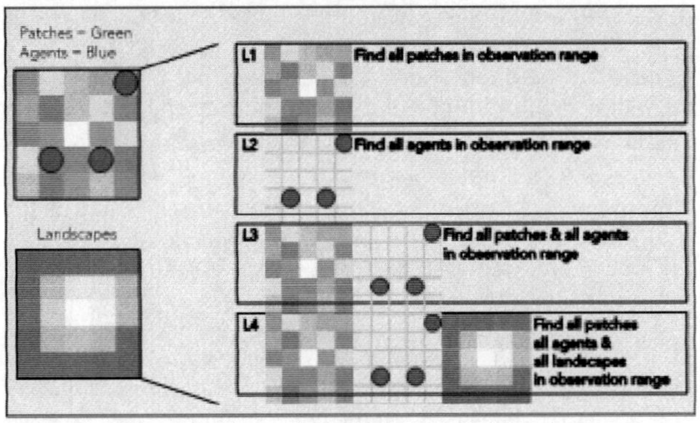

Figure 3. Observation Module Types and Level.

The Orient phase comprises two components: complexity and stochasticity, which together create a matrix of various mental model levels that determine how agents perceive their current situation. Agents' complexity value determines the equation into which observed values are input, ranging from a simple mental model of $Y_t = Y_{t-1}$ where the past experiences will be the same as future, to complex specifications where $Y_t = Y_{t-1} + X_{1t-1} + X_{2t-1} \ldots + X^{p}_{kt-n}$ to incorporate more complex past history and exogenous polynomial expressions. The stochasticity value influences the degree of random noise or interference added to each equation, reflecting the spectrum of uncertainty or misperceptions from deterministic (no impact) to entirely random (total impact). Figure 4 illustrates how various combinations of complexity and stochasticity influence the equations underlying the mental models.

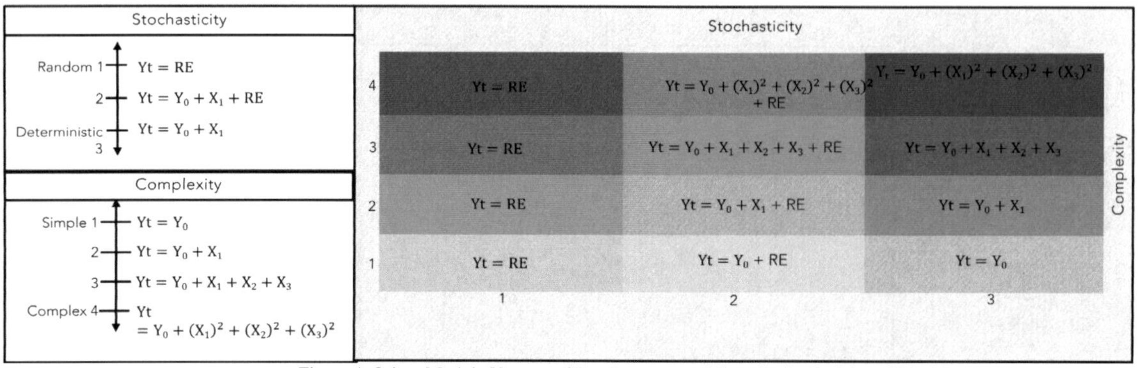

Figure 4. Orient Module Vectors of Randomness and Complexity for Mental Model.

The Decide phase presents agents with decision trees that vary in complexity from simple, single-level trees to more complex structures with three levels as shown in Figure 5. With each additional level, the decision tree expands, offering a broader set of choices for the agents to consider. At the simplest level, agents decide whether to move or not, with an associated move cost. Increasing cognitive decision capabilities, at the next level agents can decide to move towards desirable resource locations or move towards competitors. At the highest cognitive decision level, agents evaluate complex decisions: whether to stay put, move away from competition, approach resources, and whether their movement should be full or partial given costs and competitors.

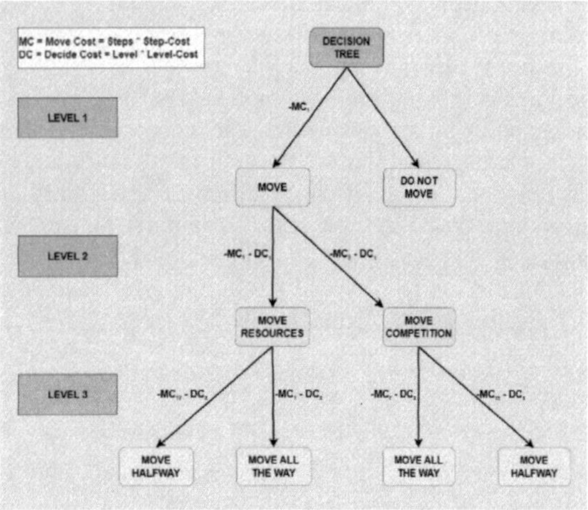

Figure 5. Decide Module Decision Tree Calculus and Depth.

The Act module enables agents to navigate their decision tree to identify optimal courses of action that maximize expected utility. Simpler agents process the decision tree, evaluating each potential decision's outcomes and costs before selecting the action that yields the greatest expected utility. If agents have additional capacity, they can anticipate the future landscape at time *t+1*, and act strategically by integrating foresight into their decision tree to refine their strategy before executing the course of action. This strategic foresight allows the agents to identify the competitive landscape of their destination patch and update the expected utility of the destination accordingly.

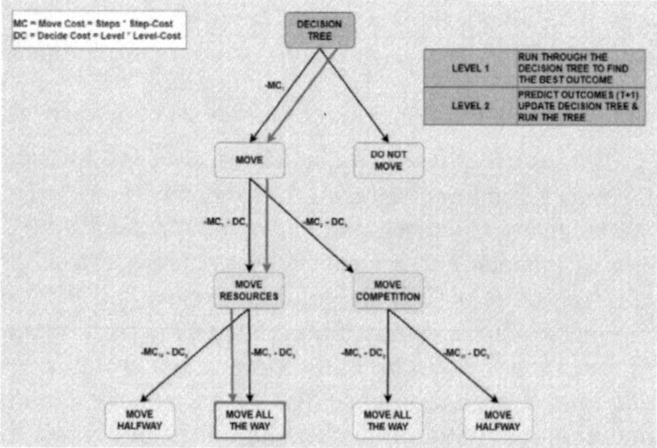

Figure 6. Act Module Decision Tree Calculus.

After progressing through the OODA loop, an agent executes its action: either moving or capturing resources. The discrepancy between an agent's expected and actual outcome dictates the feedback loop, influencing how agents update their mental models. Minimal or no discrepancies between agent outcomes and expectations, signify slight improvements or deteriorations in fitness, and result in the absence of single-loop learning. Significant discrepancies between expected and actual outcomes present single-loop learning opportunities, prompting agents to adjust the Orient phase to more closely align with reality.

For double-loop learning, the rate of change in outcomes dictates the frequency, strength, and type of feedback. Small changes in outcomes do not trigger feedback, whereas significant changes can lead to either positive or negative feedback learning opportunities. Positive feedback leads the agent to further enhance the capacity of the OODA step it last improved, provided it has not reached its maximum. Negative feedback prompts the agent to roll back any previous enhancements in capacity. Through the interplay of single-loop and double-loop learning capturing 'lessons learned' agents can adeptly navigate a dynamically evolving landscape, adjusting to changes in environmental resources and the co-evolution of competitors to optimize their fitness functions.

IV. RESULTS

A. *Baseline*

Here, we first establish a baseline to gauge typical performance of agents within our OODA simulation, setting the standard for comparison. This baseline involves generating normal distributions for the initial values of each individual OODA component. To ensure a realistic environment, we craft a landscape that maintains a balance between scarcity and abundance of resources.

We employ various scenarios that deviate from this baseline to examine how agents respond to shifts in agent capabilities and environmental factors. These scenarios are critical for evaluating the robustness and adaptability of the agents' decision-making processes. These scenarios are assessed using metrics that measure resource management, survival, and decision-making capability, offering insights into the effectiveness of cognitive strategies within the OODA loop. By comparing agent performance across these varied scenarios with the baseline, we draw nuanced conclusions about the efficacy of different strategies embedded in the OODA loop framework.

TABLE 1. BASELINE INITIAL CONDITIONS AND PARAMETER VALUES

Parameters	*Description*	*Base value*
Population	Total number of agents	25
Agent Resources	The initial number of resources for agents	75:25
Environment Resources	The initial number of resources for environment	75:25
Observation Range	How many steps the agents can see around them	4:1.25
Move Cost	The resource cost for agents to move one step.	1
Regrow Time	The number of ticks it takes for the environment to regrow their resources.	1
Energy Loss	An absolute attrition value in resources for agents each tick.	1
Observe Score	The Observe Step score of agents	2.5:0.75
Complexity Score	The Complexity Step score of agents	2:1
Stochasticity Score	The Stochasticity Step score of agents	1.5:0.75
Decide Score	The Decide Step score of agents	2:0.5
Act Score	The Act Step score of Agents	1.5:0.25

Figure 7 below depicts four separate simulation plots. The first one is the starting environment given initial conditions. Agents are yellow circles, with the color indicating their overall sum of their OODA scores, lighter colors indicate lower values, while darker hues signify higher values. The environment is characterized given resource density, with higher resource values in darker shades of blue. The second plot is a phase portrait of the populations' average summed OODA score by their average fitness score outcomes. The third times series plot details Simple, Moderate and Smart agents' average fitness outcomes over 1000 iterations. Finally, the last plot shows the resulting environment and competitive landscape at the end of the simulation.

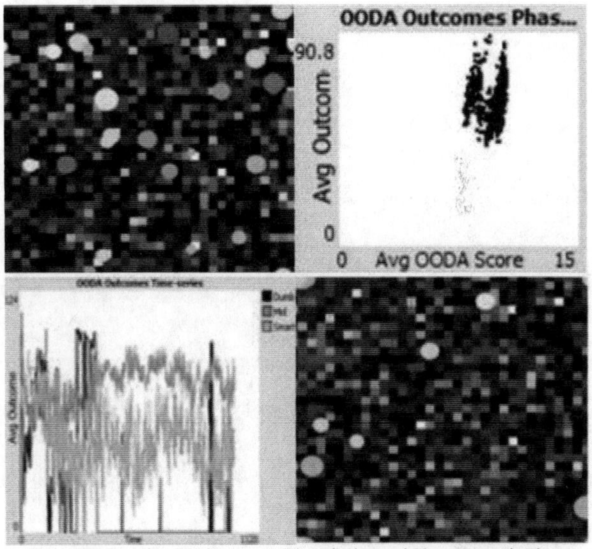

Figure 7. Baseline Environment, Time Series and Phase Portrait Plots.

In our baseline scenario, agents quickly reach equilibrium within the first two hundred iterations, with Simple agents perishing and Moderate and Smart agents achieving relatively stable, but oscillatory fitness outcomes. Moderate agents consistently emerge as the most successful agent type, having the highest average outcome on fitness scores. The phase portrait illustrates that agents quickly identified and adhered to a stable equilibrium, with the average OODA score hovering around 8, indicating little double loop learning. This suggests that the agents are capable but not maximally intelligent and stop learning early. The time series plot reveals a population bifurcation of OODA scores: a few extremely smart agents with the highest scores survive, alongside a larger group of agents with moderate intelligence. Diving into individual module score details, interestingly for Observe, Decide, and Act components, agents do not require the highest capacity scores to survive. This demonstrates that rather than having additional capacity to observe the landscape, decide among more options, or predict one step into the future, the most critical ability for agents is synthesizing observations using the highest capability mental model and is consistent with prior literature. Simply put, agents that lack sensemaking orientation of their environment, despite access to information, decision-making process and action execution, do not survive.

B. A Low Resource Landscape

We define the first scenario by modifying the baseline conditions to create an environment with scarce resources and increasing energy loss. Previously, the environment had resource ranges from 25 to 125 units; this has been adjusted to 0 to25. Additionally, we have doubled the energy loss of move costs from 1 to 2. This creates a harsher, more competitive environment as agents must now vie for a significantly reduced pool of resources.

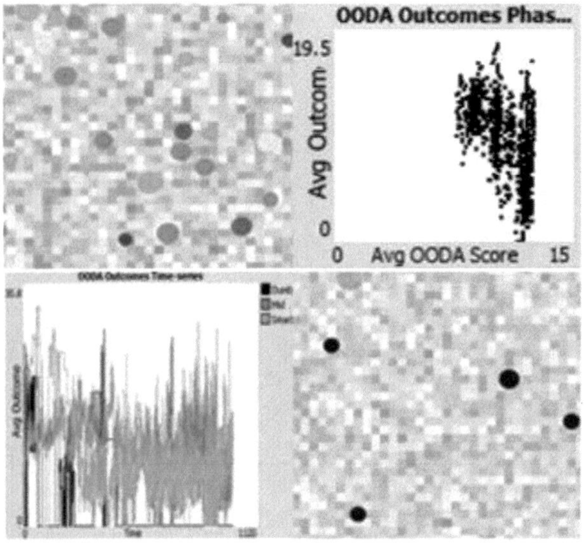

Figure 8. Scenario 1 Environment, Time Series and Phase Portrait Plots.

In this challenging scenario, only six agents survive: four are classified as Smart and two as Moderate in overall summed OODA score intelligence. In this harsh landscape, while Smart agents have a higher survival rate, Moderate agents achieve slightly better outcomes, though by a smaller margin than the baseline. Under this scenario, survival is exclusive to agents with the highest capacity for Orientation. The most complex equation and no noise are required to survived. Contrary to the baseline scenario, a premium is placed on the observational ability, as evidenced by most agents possessing the highest Observe scores. Decision and Act capacity remains low, as agents survive and thrive by being reactive quickly. Also, Smart agents remain stationary, exploiting resources from their immediate location given higher move costs in a resource poor environment. Conversely, Moderate agents actively seek out better resources while incurring higher costs.

C. Low Resource Landscape with Global Knowledge

In our second scenario, agents have the added advantage of perceiving a significantly wider environmental range while maintaining the same harsh environment as in the above scenario. Previously limited to a view range of 0 to 5, agents can now perceive an expanded range of 0 to 20. This dynamic aims to explore how balancing the challenging environment with the agents' enhanced global environmental Observe capabilities affects their mental models and leads to the evolution of agents optimized to maximize their fitness function. Such adaptations parallel the evolution technology to increase human situational awareness.

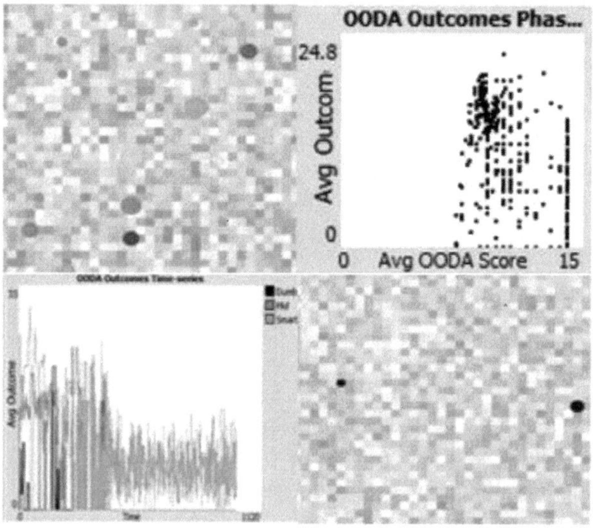

Figure 9. Scenario 2 Environment, Time Series and Phase Portrait Plots.

Here, we see Smart agents dominating the landscape, in contrast to Moderate and Simple agents who exhaust themselves in an attempt to capture all possible gains by expending excessive energy. Smart agents leverage their superior OODA summed capacity to accurately assess the landscape, recognizing the advantage of patient anticipation over frantic movement in this harsh, resource poor environment. Although they do not surpass Moderate agents' early gains during the simulation, they maintain consistency in fitness outcomes. This consistency may highlight additional benefits of Decision and Action phases, empowering agents with a considerably broader range of strategic courses of action.

D. Harsh World, Smart Agents

Given observed difficulties agents face in challenging environments, we now adjust the scenario to agent at high levels of summed OODA intelligence. Within their observation range, which remains extensive, each agent can now perceive all other actors, resources, and landscapes. Each agent also consistently employs the most sophisticated mental model available. Each agent can use the full decision tree to see which option is best. Finally, each agent can see the best outcome with the next tick in mind, inducing strategic behavior.

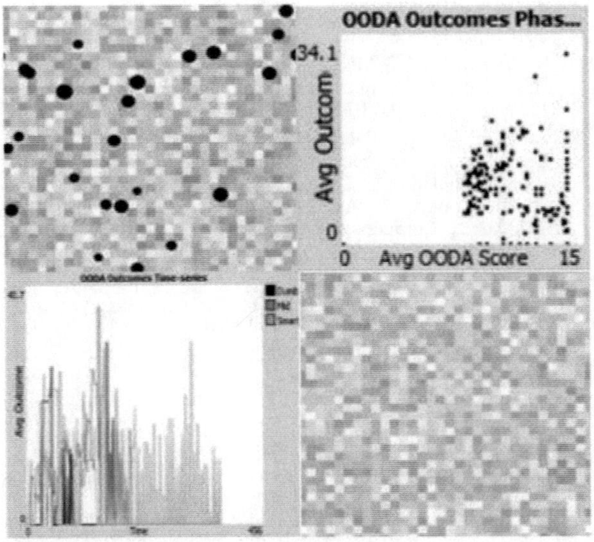

Figure 10. Scenario 3 Environment, Time Series and Phase Portrait Plots.

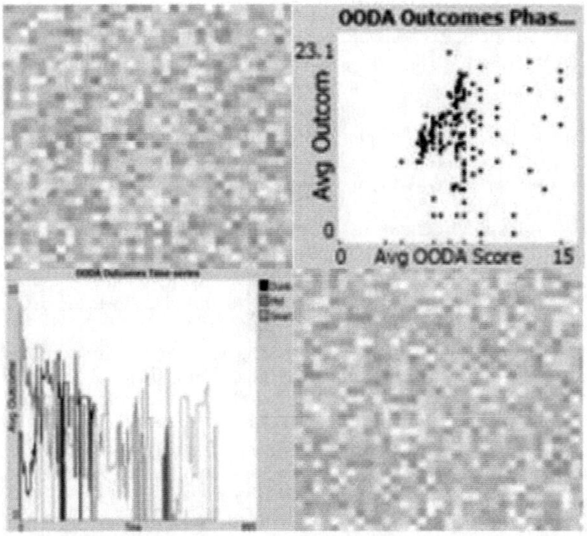

Figure 11. Scenario 4 Environment, Time Series and Phase Portrait Plots.

Even with the above cognitive advantages, this harsh environmental scenario proves too challenging for long term fitness achievement and survival. In a multitude of simulation runs, all agents inevitably perish within the first few hundred iterations. Agents consistently exhibit low average outcomes, demonstrating their inability to sufficiently adapt to the landscape. Actors with the highest OODA scores incur significant costs due to the increased complexity of their decision-making processes. This complexity makes each action more resource intensive as they navigate their decision trees. In a resource poor environment, the cost of strategic complexity is high.

E. Harsh World, Simple Agents

Building on the above, our final scenario assesses agent performance given with the lower OODA capacities in harsh, resource poor environments.

In the same extremely harsh environment, agents with low OODA scores demonstrate performance comparable to that of their more sophisticated counterparts. Whereas Smart agents employ complex models and strategize to endure difficult environments for future gains, agents with minimal OODA capacities react more spontaneously. However, given resource scarcity and competition costs, these produce almost equally ineffective outcomes on fitness scores.

V. CONCLUSION

In this paper, we set out to explore cognitive simulation capabilities, by agentizing Boyd's OODA loop in a dynamic, competitive environment. By specifying and controlling cognitive abilities in each OODA module, we focused on fitness outcomes based upon varying levels of capabilities at each step. Our findings demonstrate that this approach opens a myriad of simulation possibilities. Furthermore, we observed the interactive effects of increasing or decreasing cognitive capabilities.

Some of our next steps include extending scenarios to include adding varying degrees of agent competition across dynamic resource landscapes to further calibrate OODA modules and feedbacks. Once complete, we will perform quasi-global sensitivity testing to extract key model drivers and dependencies to make inferences on cognitive behavior across each OODA step. This also allows detailed exploration of both single and double loop learning mechanisms across different competitive environments.

We believe the development of OODA loops for human decision-making represents a significant advancement in understanding and improving decision-making processes. Building on Boyd's original framework, many other researchers have validated the foundations, provided empirical evidence, and outlined practical implications for incorporating OODA loops into multiple domains and contexts. By explicitly embracing the dynamic and iterative nature of human decision-making, hopefully both individuals and organizations can enhance their ability to navigate increasingly complex environments.

REFERENCES

[1] M. Abdollahian, "Surfing the Conflux: Technology, Information Environments and Great Power Competition Convergence," 2021, doi: 10.1007/978-3-030-64473-4_1.

[2] W. B. Arthur, “Inductive reasoning and bounded rationality”, American Economic Review, vol. 84, 1994, pp. 406–411.

[3] J. Boyd, "The Essence of Winning and Losing," 1987. Available online: https://warontherocks.com/2014/10/boyd-the-essence-of-winning-and-losing/.

[4] L. Brumley, C. Kopp, and K. B. Korb, “The Orientation step of the OODA loop and Information Warfare,” in Proceedings of the 7th Australian Information Warfare & Security Conference 2006, C. Vailli and A. Woodward, Eds., Perth, Australia: School of Computer and Information Science, Edith Cowan University, 2006, pp. 18–25.

[5] A. T. Denazau and D. C. North, “Shared Mental Models: Ideologies and Institutions,” Kyklos, vol. 47, 1994, pp. 3–31, doi: 10.1111/j.1467-6435.1994.tb02246.x.

[6] D. A. Deptula, “Effects-based operations: Change in the nature of warfare,” Aerospace Education Foundation, Defense and Airpower Series, 2001. Available online: https://secure.afa.org/Mitchell/reports/0901ebo.pdf.

[7] M. R. Endsley, “Toward a theory of situation awareness in dynamic systems,” Human Factors, vol. 37, no. 1, 1995, pp. 32–64, doi: 10.1518/001872095779049543.

[8] J. M. Epstein and R. Axtell, Growing Artificial Societies: Social Science from the Bottom Up, Washington, DC: Brookings/MIT Press, 1996.

[9] S. Fowler, A. Hansen, and S. Carpenter, "OODA Loops: A Foundation for Real-Time Decision Making in Agile Software Development," in Proceedings of the 48th Hawaii International Conference on System Sciences, 2015.

[10] S. Frost, K. Goebel, and J. Celaya, “A Briefing on Metrics and Risks for Autonomous Decision-making in Aerospace Applications,” AIAA Infotech at Aerospace Conference and Exhibit 2012, 2012, doi: 10.2514/6.2012-2402.

[11] C. González, J. F. Lerch, and C. Lebiere, "Understanding the Role of Time Pressure and Uncertainty in Decision-Making Strategies: An Experimental Study using the OODA Loop," Decision Support Systems, vol. 117, 2019, pp. 12-22.

[12] N. Hanaki, A. Peterhansl, P. S. Dodds, and D. J. Watts, “Cooperation in evolving social networks,” mimeo, 2004.

[13] G. Hofstede, Culture's Consequences: International Differences in Work-Related Values, Sage Publishing, 1980.

[14] J. G. Johnson and J. R. Busemeyer, “Decision making under risk and uncertainty,” WIREs Cognitive Science, vol. 1, 2010, pp. 736-749, doi: 10.1002/wcs.76.

[15] G. Klein, Sources of Power: How People Make Decisions, 20th ed., The MIT Press, 1998, doi: 10.2307/j.ctt1v2xt08.

[16] G. A. Klein, J. K. Phillips, E. L. Rall, and D. A. Peluso, "A Data-Frame Theory of Sensemaking," in Expertise Out of Context: Proceedings of the Sixth International Conference on Naturalistic Decision Making, Lawrence Erlbaum Associates, 2006, pp. 113-155.

[17] F. Osinga, Science, Strategy and War: The Strategic Theory of John Boyd, Eburon Academic Publishers, 2005.

[18] C. Richards, “Boyd’s OODA Loop,” Necesse, vol. 5, no. 1, 2020, pp. 142-165.

[19] T. C. Schelling, “Dynamic models of segregation,” The Journal of Mathematical Sociology, vol. 1, no. 2, 1971, pp. 143-186.

[20] M. W. Sellers, H. Sayama, and A. D. Pape, “Simulating systems thinking under bounded rationality,” Complexity, vol. 2020, 2020, Article ID 3469263, 12 pages.

[21] E. J. Teal and A. L. Leibovitch, "Applying OODA Loops to Increase Organizational Agility," Cutter Business Technology Journal, vol. 30, no. 3, 2017, pp. 35-40.

[22] M. W. Voss, A. F. Kramer, C. Basak, R. S. Prakash, and B. Roberts, "Are Expert Athletes ‘Expert’ in the Cognitive Laboratory? A Meta-Analytic Review of Cognition and Sport Expertise," Applied Cognitive Psychology, vol. 24, no. 6, 2010, pp. 812-826.

[23] N. Vriend, “ACE Models of Endogenous Interactions,” in Handbook of Computational Economics, vol. 2, 2006, pp. 1047-1079, doi: 10.1016/S1574-0021(05)02021-6.

[24] Z. Yang, M. Abdollahian, P. Neal, and J. Kaplan, “Human Development Dynamics: Network Emergence in an Agent-Based Simulation of Adaptive Heterogeneous Games and Social Systems,” in Agent-Based Approaches in Economic and Social Complex Systems VIII, 2015, pp. 3-14, doi: 10.1007/978-4-431-55236-9_1.

A Method for Estimating Blood Flow Condition from Skin Tone Information in Real Face Images

Miku Shimizu, Naoaki Itakura, Kazuyuki Mito, Kaito Hino, Kohei Okura, Tota Mizuno
The University of Electro-Communications
1-5-1, Chofugaoka, Chofu, Tokyo, Japan
e-mails: m.shimizu.0320@gmail.com itakura@uec.ac.jp k.mito@uec.ac.jp kai.vas.1023@gmail.com
xzjb2957@gmail.com mizuno@uec.ac.jp

***Abstract*—In this study, we investigate a method to obtain detailed blood flow changes from nasal images. We have previously estimated autonomic nervous activity as an indicator of stress by focusing on the R-B component values (Difference value between R and B component values, the three primary colors of color) of the nasal region in real face images. In fact, changes in R-B component values were found to correspond to large stress fluctuations. However, the effect of noise due to light reflection and shadows could not be taken into account. If the effects of light intensity can be removed, the accuracy of the assessment of autonomic nervous activity can be improved, which would greatly contribute to the development of emotion estimation methods. As a method for this purpose, we propose the introduction of the R+G+B value (Total value of the three primary colors of light: R-component value, G-component value, and B-component value) index, which is black when the R+G+B value is close to 0 and white when the R+G+B value is close to 765. This study will clarify the usefulness of this index by using a heat map that reflects the number of pixels present, with R+G+B values on the x-axis and R-B component values on the y-axis. When this method was applied to an experiment in which changes in blood flow were intentionally induced, characteristic changes in distribution were observed at locations where changes in blood flow occurred. This suggests that by focusing on the locations in the heat map where changes corresponding to changes in blood flow rate are observed, it will be possible to remove the effects of light intensity regardless of differences in people or environments. By applying the proposed method, it is possible to construct a stress estimation system that can be easily used by anyone and contribute to the development of the interface field.**

Keywords - Real face image; Blood flow; Heat map; Stress.

I. INTRODUCTION

In recent years, the need for emotion estimation has increased for humans to lead more comfortable lives, for example by measuring fatigue and concentration levels in the workplace and improving the workplace environment by introducing appropriate rest systems. Methods for emotion estimation using various biological information, such as heartbeat pulse waves, electroencephalography (EEG) and thermal images have been investigated. Unlike other methods, the method using thermal imaging does not cause stress to the subject. It does not restrict the subject's behavior, as it uses a non-contact infrared thermography camera. This makes it a useful method for emotion estimation. In addition to thermal images, methods using real images have also been studied in recent years as a more cost-effective and easy-to-use method of emotion estimation for everyone. We have been studying methods for estimating autonomic nervous activity, which is an indicator of stress, from real face images taken with a webcam. However, the effects of light exposure caused by differences in the shooting environment and by facial irregularities have reduced the accuracy of the evaluation. There have been no studies that have examined the effects of light intensity. However, considering that this stress estimation system is to be operated in a real environment, it is considered to be a problem that needs to be solved as soon as possible, since there are no restrictions on how the system is to be used to take pictures, and the pictures are not always taken under the same conditions. Therefore, this study attempts to solve this problem.

The rest of the paper is structured as follows. Section 2 introduces previous studies on stress estimation, Section 3 describes the proposed method, and Section 4 examines the results of the actual implementation of the proposed method and its effectiveness. Section 5 concludes our work.

II. PREVIOUS STUDY

Many emotion estimation methods have been studied using facial thermal images. Previous emotion estimation using facial thermal images has been based on the differential temperature between the nasal area, which is a sympathetic index of autonomic nervous activity, and the forehead area, which is less affected by autonomic nervous activity [1]. Skin temperature is the antagonistic temperature between the conducted heat of deep body temperature, changes in blood flow under the skin and environmental temperature. Therefore, the differential temperature between the nasal and forehead areas is an index that captures changes in peripheral blood flow under the skin in the nasal area due to the low influence of environmental temperature changes and deep body temperature [1]. Furthermore, a method that utilizes temperature changes not only in the nasal area but also in the entire face is also being considered. Since evaluation in combination with multiple facial regions is now possible, it is possible to estimate autonomic nervous activity with higher precision than with conventional methods [2]. However, these previous methods require the use of an infrared thermography camera, which is costly.

Therefore, as a solution to the cost problem, we have studied a method to evaluate autonomic nerve activity with the same accuracy as facial thermal images by acquiring changes in peripheral blood flow using real facial images, which can be easily acquired by anyone [3]. The real facial image captured by a visible light camera, such as a web camera, is the reflected light on the skin surface that is not absorbed by capillaries and subcutaneous tissues among the light transmitted into the skin. As shown in Figure 1, the R component has the deepest depth of transmission, followed by the G and B components, in that order. Based on these facts, we considered that the R-B component value, which is the difference between the R component with the deepest penetration depth into the subcutaneous region and the B component with the shallowest penetration depth, could be used to capture changes in the peripheral blood flow rate through the subcutaneous region. In our previous study, we obtained the variation of R-B component values in the nasal region during a 10-minute mental arithmetic task, suggesting the possibility of evaluating stress variation in response to switching events, such as the timing of calculation errors during a mental arithmetic task or at the end of a mental arithmetic task [3]. However, in the methods of previous studies [3], all pixels acquired as the nose were used for analysis. Therefore, the R-B component values are calculated including information that does not include changes in blood flow, such as blown-out highlights and blocked-up shadows caused by changes in light intensity and nostrils in the nasal area, which may reduce the accuracy of obtaining changes in blood flow. So, it is necessary to identify whether the pixels used represent the effect of light intensity or blood flow conditions.

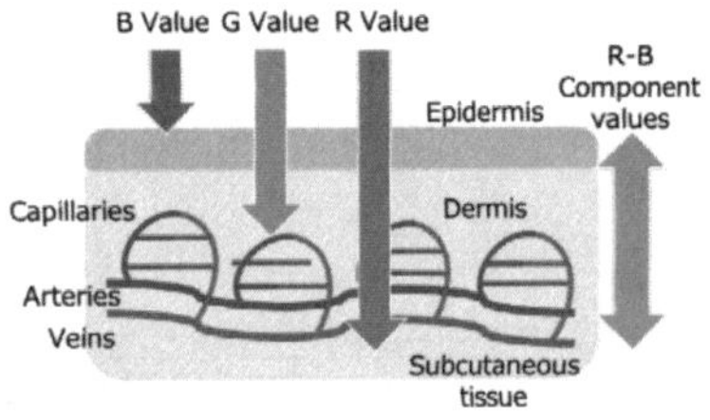

Figure 1. Transmission depth by wavelength of RGB light.

In this study, we propose to observe the distribution of color information of pixels corresponding to the nasal area in each frame by creating a heat map with R-B component values on the vertical axis and R+G+B values on the horizontal axis. Using the proposed method, we believe it is possible to observe how the characteristics of pixels that do not contain information on changes in blood flow, such as white highlights and blocked shadows due to changes in light intensity, differ from pixels that represent changes in blood flow. By clarifying this difference, it will be possible to remove the effect of light intensity from the nasal image and capture only changes in blood flow, using the nature of the data, thus enabling a more accurate estimation of autonomic nervous activity.

III. Proposed Method

The purpose of this study is to clarify the distribution and characteristics of pixels corresponding to the nose by creating heat maps, and to devise a method to quantitatively remove the effect of light intensity and acquire only blood flow changes. The heat map should be created as shown in Figure 2, with R-B component values on the vertical axis and R+G+B values on the horizontal axis. The reason for adopting R+G+B values on the horizontal axis is that R+G+B values close to 0 indicate black color and those close to 765 indicate white color, and we thought it would be possible to distinguish pixels that correspond to white skips or shadows by using R+G+B values to limit pixels of interest.

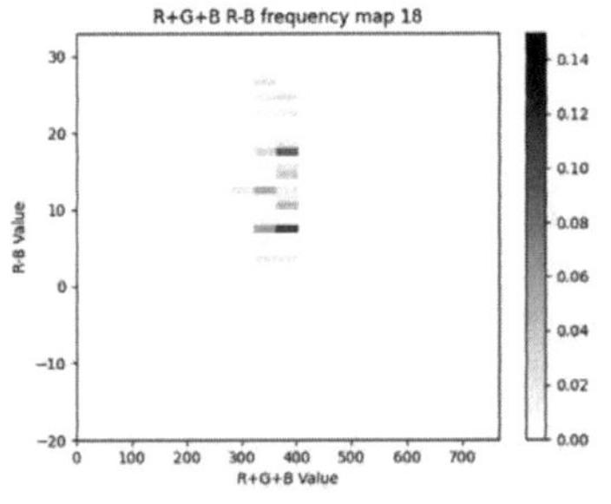

Figure 2. Heat Map Example.

The proposed method was implemented in a video of an upstream vascular compression experiment in which changes in blood flow can be intentionally induced. By creating this heat map for each frame, it is possible to reveal how the distribution changes when changes in blood flow occur, such as during vascular compression or release, and how the effect of light intensity is distributed over time.

IV. Results

Figure 3 shows the time-series data of R-B component values in the nasal area when the proposed method is applied to an experiment in which blood flow changes are intentionally induced, and Figure 4 shows the results of the heat map. Figure 4 (a) shows the heat map before the blood flow change at the 20-second point in Figure 3, (b) shows the after the blood flow change at the 30-second point in Figure 3, and (c) shows the 50-second point in Figure 3 when the blood flow change occurred again and the condition returned to the same as in (a).

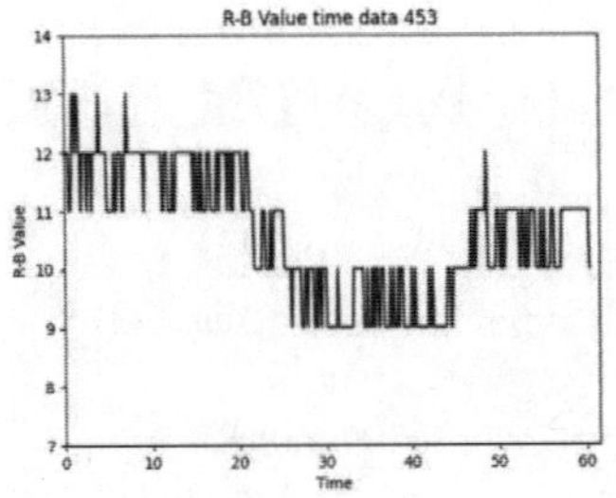

Figure 3. Time series data of R-B component values of the nasal area.

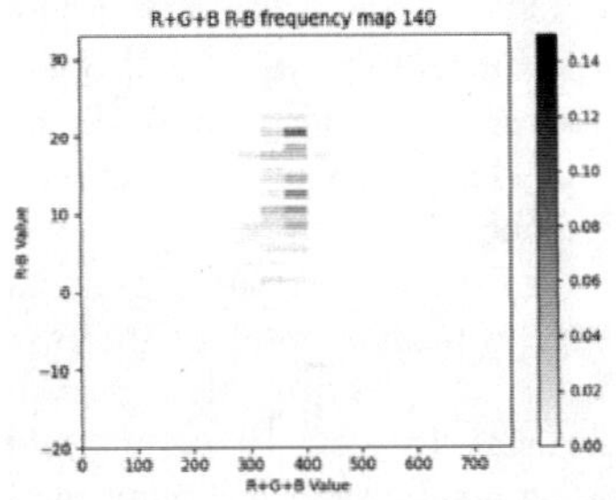

(a) Before the blood flow change at the 20-second point

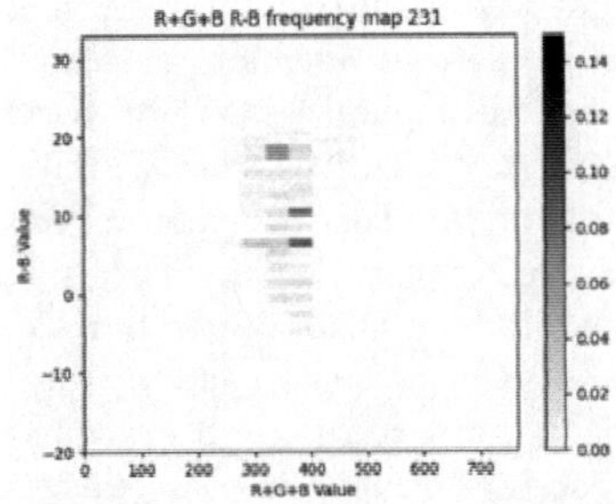

(b) After the blood flow change at the 30-second point

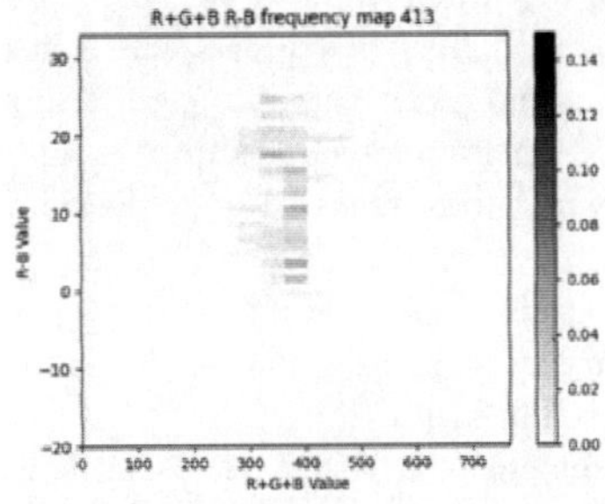

(c) the blood flow change occurred again and the condition returned to the same as in (a)

Figure 4. Heat map results.

As can be seen from the results of (a) and (b), when a blood flow change occurs and blood flow slows down, the distribution of pixels in the nasal area does not move horizontally, but tends to drop vertically overall. This is thought to be because the R component of arterial blood decreased and the B component of venous blood increased due to the slowing of blood flow, resulting in a decrease in only the R-B component value without much change in the total R+G+B value. When the blood flow improved and returned to the initial state again, there was an overall tendency for the distribution to be pulled up vertically, as in (b) to (c), with (c) returning to a distribution similar to that in (a). However, the shape of the distribution does not completely return to the same state, but is slightly elongated vertically, leaving remnants of the distribution in (b), suggesting that when blood flow is impaired, the effect appears instantaneously, but when blood flow is improved from a bad state, it does not return instantaneously but slowly.

V. CONCLUSION

The purpose of this study was to examine the relationship between changes in blood flow and changes in pixel distribution by creating a heat map with two axes: the R-B component values, which allow us to see changes in blood flow, and the R+G+B values, which are pixel coloration. The results showed that, using the proposed method, heat maps tend to show characteristic changes in the time at which changes in blood flow occur. In the present experiment, the characteristics of the heat maps were more pronounced because we used an experiment in which changes in blood flow were intentionally induced. However, in an actual environment in which a stress estimation system is used, changes in blood flow are not likely to occur as frequently as in this experiment. Therefore, there is a need to examine whether the proposed method is still useful under actual operational conditions.

In addition, changes in the features of the heat map were visually confirmed this time, which is not sufficient to reflect them in the system. Therefore, it is considered necessary to quantitatively discriminate between this change in blood flow rate and the corresponding heat map features. If quantification of discrimination becomes possible, it will be possible to obtain only the changes in blood flow rate from skin color information without regard to individual differences in skin color, such as suntan, or light intensity in the shooting environment, eliminating the effects of light intensity, and this will improve the development of this system.

REFERENCES

[1] H. Zenju, A. Nozawa, H. Tanaka, and H. Ide, "Estimation of Unpleasant and Pleasant States by Nasal Thermogram", Transactions on Electronics, Information and Systems, vol. 124, no. 1, pp. 213-214, 2004.

[2] S. Matsuno, T. Mizuno, H. Asano, K. Mito, and N. Itakura, "Estimating Autonomic Nerve Activity Using Variance of Thermal Face Images", Artificial Life and Robotics, vol. 23, no. 3, pp. 367-372, 2018.

[3] M. Shimizu, Y. Matsumoto, N. Itakura, K. Mito, and T. Mizuno, "Evaluation of Methods for Estimating Autonomic Nervous Activity Using a Web Camera", Artificial Life and Robotics, vol. 28, pp. 718-725, 2023.

Opportunities and Challenges in Implementing a Virtual Ward for Heart Failure Management

Sehrish Rafique*, Farshid Amirabdollahian*, Ganesh Arunachalam† and Patrick Holthaus*
*Robotics Research Group, University of Hertfordshire, Hatfield, United Kingdom
Email: {s.rafique, f.amirabdollahian2, p.holthaus}@herts.ac.uk
† The Princess Alexandra Hospital NHS Trust, Harlow, United Kingdom
Email: ganesh.arunachalam@nhs.net

***Abstract*—The management of heart failure and post-heart surgery has been a major interest in healthcare. The cardiac unit has improved over time, undergoing significant innovations to improve the quality of services and patient outcomes. Researchers play a significant role in progressing innovative solutions, from co-design and idea conception to conducting impact analyses. These often involve identifying correlations between interventions and outcomes to improve the quality of care. In the context of heart failure, there is an ever-increasing workload that is impacted by the lack of resources, and staff, and the increasing number of elderly population with heart conditions and associated co-morbidities. The COVID-19 pandemic has compounded these existing challenges. These challenges provide the impetus for seeking technological interventions. In the UK, The National Health Service encourages such initiatives where patients are looked after via digital technologies, under the *Virtual Ward* concept. This paper adopts a two-pronged approach, exploring the needs of the patients and clinicians and the potential of digital technologies to address those needs. By evaluating current challenges, the current state of the technology, and its limitations, this paper provides insights for future interventions that facilitate a *Virtual Ward* for the management of heart failure in the community.**

***Keywords*—Heart failure management; virtual ward; technological challenges**

I. INTRODUCTION

Heart failure is quite common amongst older people, with more than 10% of those over 70 years old experiencing it [1]. In heart failure patients, about 17% may pass away within a year from any cause, and up to 44% may need rehospitalisation within that same time frame. At the same time, the cost of inpatient care puts a considerable burden on the care system in England [2]. According to statistics from the British Heart Foundation [3], the costs related to heart and circulatory diseases are approximately £10 billion each year. In the UK, about 7.6 million people have heart and circulatory diseases and as people get older and the population grows, more people may develop these conditions. Currently, there are roughly 4 million men and 3.6 million women with heart and circulatory issues. It is predicted that more than half of people in the UK will experience a heart or circulatory problem during their lives [3]. Surprisingly, there are about twice as many people dealing with heart and circulatory diseases in the UK compared to those with cancer and Alzheimer's combined. Every year in the UK, approximately 49,000 individuals under 75 succumb to heart and circulatory diseases. In recent years, hospitals have encountered various challenges [4], including staff shortages, economic burden, increased population as well as an increase in chronic conditions and the impact of the COVID-19 pandemic [5].

Improving Heart Failure (HF) management has been a long-standing challenge in medical research [6] driven by the goal of enhancing healthcare quality, patient survival rates, and satisfaction with medical protocols. However, healthcare systems, specifically cardiac units, have been significantly impacted in recent years due to staff shortages and economic burdens [2]. These challenges have resulted in medication errors [7], food delivery mistakes, lack of attention and care, and in some cases, fatalities due to carelessness [7]. Moreover, the average length of hospital stay decreased from 8.2 days in 2000/01 to 4.5 days in 2018/19 [8]. This reduction reflects an emerging shift towards alternative care delivery models, including home care options. While hospitals strive to provide optimal care, they cannot substitute for home comfort. Research indicates that most patients strongly desire to expedite discharge and return home as soon as they regain consciousness [9], typically within three to four days. However, the transition from hospital to home-based care for managing HF and post-heart surgery presents complex challenges. Patients with a history of HF require continuous monitoring, proper medication management, regular checkups, maintaining a healthy diet, and rehabilitation sessions to support their recovery [10]. Despite patients who desire early discharge and prefer home-based care due to comfort preferences and economic issues, it is important to acknowledge the complexities and challenges associated with a community health setting.

The establishment of a virtual ward can benefit this group of patients. A virtual ward can be defined as a remote monitoring and healthcare management system that enables medical professionals to oversee and support patients in their own homes, and bridges this gap by delivering hospital-level care in a familiar environment.

This paper examines the current needs of patients with HF and the challenges they face in hospitals and homes. We then explore current state-of-the-art technological solutions for looking after patients at home and highlight their limitations and shortcomings. Specifically, we explore the technology from the perspective of the *Virtual Ward* concept and its potential to provide hospital-level care within the comfort of patients' homes. This paper aims to contribute to the ongoing discourse on enhancing patient care in cardiac healthcare settings by critically assessing existing approaches and their shortcomings with the idea of informing a new list of requirements for future innovations in this domain.

In Section II, we first outline the current needs and challenges in managing HF. Following this, we discuss current technological solutions designed to address these needs, and analyse their shortcomings in Section III to identify the gaps that require further exploration and resolution.

II. Needs and Challenges in HF Management

Healthcare systems today are facing several challenges. They deal with increasing numbers of patients, limited resources, and changing healthcare needs. This section discusses existing work in the healthcare domain and identifies those needs and challenges [2].

Existing literature highlights strain on the healthcare system in the UK and worldwide due to the increasing population [4], shortage of medical staff, gaps in monitoring patients [2], medication errors [7], and patients food delivery errors [11]. These issues often result in the potential impact on morbidity and mortality [7]. The aftermath of COVID-19 further added to these challenges [5] with an increased number of patients, shortage of staff, beds, ventilators, and Intensive Care Units (ICUs) [5]. HF is one of the critical health issues to manage that requires immediate attention and such issues cannot be escalated for later resolution due to high mortality rates [5]. This underscores the importance for researchers to explore different and better ways of taking care of patients to handle current and future crises at hospitals. In the following subsections, we have explored individual challenges in healthcare units that affect patients in general, with a focus on HF management and cardiac units.

A. Challenges in Medication Management

In a study [12], researchers investigated hospital prescribing errors by staff and nurses in Georgia and Colorado. The results revealed that approximately 19% of medications were administered wrong, either at the wrong time, in an incorrect dose, or unauthorised manner. This highlights the urgency for innovative approaches to avoid prescription errors. Moreover, insights from the Norwegian Incident Reporting System from 2016 to 2017 [7] have been shared. In this report, 3,557 medication errors were reported, and most of the errors occurred during medication administration (68%), followed by prescribing (24%) and preparation/dispensing stages (6%). The leading types of errors were dosing errors (38%), omissions (23%), and incorrect medication prescribing (15%). Alarmingly, over half of all errors were harmful (62%), with 5.2% causing severe harm, and 0.8% resulting in fatalities. Apart from medication errors during the hospital stay, such errors also occurred during the admission and discharge times. A study comprising 904 patients found that 29.4% of patients have experienced at least one unintended medication [13]. These unintended medication errors were serious or very serious in 36% of patients and potentially moderate in almost 40%. This risk later increased with proceeding treatments. The general practitioners or nurses were identified as the most effective sources of administering wrong medicines.

Another paper focused specifically on the National Health Service (NHS) in England [2] has revealed economic burden and medical errors within hospitals. According to the annual national estimate, there is a substantial number of medication errors with 237 million across the medication process, with primary care accounting for 38.4% of these. The economic burden associated with definitely avoidable adverse drug events is estimated at £98,462,582 per year, resulting in 181,626 bed-days consumed and causing or contributing to 1708 deaths. This led to hospital stays and the cost of hospital admission to £83.7 million; causing 627 deaths in primary care, while secondary care resulted in extended hospital stays counting to £14.8 million cost, and causing or contributing to 1081 deaths.

B. Diet Management Challenges

In addition to medication, diet management is also an important part of recovery for all patients and most importantly for heart failure patients. Studies identified that proper diet management helps control risk factors such as high blood pressure, high cholesterol levels, and obesity [14]. For many people, HF can stem from obesity, as there is a strong correlation between obesity and HF [15]. Therefore, diet management holds significance. Typically, during hospital stays, patients receive food as directed by doctors. However, many errors were seen in the past in the diet management of patients. A case study conducted in Thailand highlighted many complaints about wrong food delivery, making up 37.4% of all complaints in 2017 [11]. The primary reasons found for food delivery errors included wrong orders (not passing on the right information), catering the wrong food to patients, and errors made by doctors in prescriptions. Research also found instances of malnutrition in patients with chronic or severe illnesses, particularly in hospital settings. It has been revealed that malnutrition is often not recognised or underestimated, leading to increased morbidity, mortality, longer hospital stays, and higher treatment costs [16].

C. Monitoring Issues

Monitoring patients at hospitals has often been a challenge across various departments, specifically in those units where continuous monitoring is required, such as in cardiology wards or mental health wards [17]. These wards encounter difficulties in monitoring patients due to the limited manpower. The increasing number of patients places considerable strain on the existing resources. To overcome the issue of manual monitoring and shortage of staff, researchers have developed some monitoring tools, like remote physiologic monitoring devices, to monitor patients' vital signs, symptoms, and other health indicators remotely [18]. However, there are technical issues such as inconsistent data transmission, missing data points, or malfunctioning in these devices leading to unreliability of remote monitoring systems. Moreover, the patient's discomfort presents another challenge as many older adults or those with cognitive impairments may not be able to use and properly activate the monitoring devices. Thus, monitoring patients remains an open challenge in hospitals as well as in remote monitoring setups.

D. Challenges with Rehabilitation Programs

Physical rehabilitation plays a crucial role in HF management and post-heart surgery. Rehabilitation programs help patients regain their strength, enhance cardiovascular health, improve overall quality of life, and most importantly reduce the potential risk of future cardiac problems. Researchers have examined several challenges associated with rehabilitation programs including limited access to services due to high cost, geographic barriers, and issues with personalisation to individual needs and delivery [19]. Another challenge associated with rehabilitation programs is the lack of interdisciplinary collaboration among different practitioners including psychologists, surgeons, and therapists [19]. Additionally, studies identified a shortage of staff in cardiac rehabilitation centres, which poses a significant challenge since cardiac rehabilitation programs require specialised expertise to provide tailored rehabilitation based on individual patient needs [20]. Neglecting the need for rehabilitation programs leads to decreased quality of life, with increased disabilities, injuries, or chronic health conditions among cardiac patients. Therefore, it is important to address the problems faced in rehabilitation programs [19].

E. Struggles with Emotional Needs

Recognising the crucial link between physical and mental health is crucial [21]. People coping with heart disease, and congestive HF encounter beyond their physical challenges. They encompass an emotional battle of social isolation, fear, and uncertainties about other aspects of life since their everyday life is challenging. Despite the advancement in medical technology, the psychological aspect also needs attention, as patients often decline certain treatments because of fear, which poses a challenge for medical staff and effective management [21].

HF and chronic heart diseases not only affect older people, but also children. Children with heart problems and their families suffer through emotional stress, financial burdens, and physical exhaustion in this process [22]. Many individuals often turn to spiritual support for comfort, hope, and strength [17]. Therefore, medical practitioners must provide comprehensive and tailored support and acknowledge their emotional needs thereby enhancing the overall quality of life of patients and families impacted by heart failure.

F. Post-Open Heart Surgery Delirium

In addition to medicine errors, diet management problems, and emotional and physical therapy problems, HF patients often face delirium after open heart surgery [23]. Delirium is a state of mind where people get severe confusion and cognitive difficulties, and this can occur from a multitude of causes. Notable amongst them are side effects of medicines, stress and trauma, and sleep disturbance. To address this challenge, there is a need to train medical staff and patients to help support and perform daily activities during recovery, so that the risk of delirium is reduced.

III. Current Solutions and their Shortcomings

The field of HF management has witnessed significant innovations. In this section, we aim to highlight current research efforts and proposed solutions, with special attention on addressing the shortcomings of these proposed solutions, summarised in Table I, laying the groundwork for future improvements in research.

A. Cost Effective AI Applications to Address Staffing Gap and Monitoring

In the realm of Artificial Intelligence (AI) applications in healthcare, several studies show the promising potential [12]. Advancements in varied medical specialities such as anaesthesiology are significant [24] and indicate that most complex anaesthetic tasks will be performed by robots in the near future. Additionally, wearable devices show potential to enhance patient monitoring. A wearable system mHealth has been developed that replaced the physical follow-up with remote electronic visits, i.e. this device measures the blood pressure, temperature, electrocardiogram (ECG), and weight of patients [25]. The experiment was conducted on 730 adult patients and results showed that automatic measurements with mHealth device can enhance the Postoperative Atrial Fibrillation (POAF) after heart surgery within three months. Such systems showcase the importance of remote monitoring in improving patient outcomes. Several new remote care systems have been launched that are surpassing human capabilities [26], by offering real-time monitoring, analysis, reminders, and personalised rehabilitation programs and care. A study on patients who had undergone a heart procedure called Transcatheter Aortic Valve Replacement (TAVR) revealed that smartwatches have effectively detected cardiac issues such as irregular heart rhythms post-hospital discharge [27]. This highlights their potential as valuable tools for remote monitoring and follow-up care. Integration of smart systems addresses the problems in traditional systems [19]. However, advanced monitoring systems have some limitations, including the lack of electroencephalogram (EEG) monitoring, and insufficient focus on chronic disease or specific contexts such as HF. Additionally, these systems need more clinical validation to enhance their efficacy.

B. Smart Diet and Weight Management Applications

People with heart problems should maintain a healthy diet and weight [15]. Existing works such as Speak4Diet app [14] monitor dietary intake and identify deficiencies in nutrients. This AI-based app analyses and tracks the composition of the user's diet and provides personalised recommendations for improvement. While such apps demonstrate considerable potential, there is room for improvement including consistent

TABLE I
SUMMARY OF CHALLENGES, CURRENT SOLUTIONS, AND SHORTCOMINGS IN HEART FAILURE MANAGEMENT

Needs and Challenges	Current Solutions	Shortcomings and Problems
Medication Management	Automatic Medication Dispensing System [28] Smart Medication Error Reporting Tool [29]	Limited functionality of Automated System [28] Medication Errors [12], [7], [2], [13]
Dietary Management	Improved Food Delivery Systems [30] Mobile App for Tracking Dietary Intake [14]	Food Delivery Errors [11] Lack of Personalised Dietary Plans Malnutrition in Patients [16]
Cost and Space Management [2]	AI applications in Nursing [31]	Implementation Challenges [5] Health Inequalities [4] Shortage of Staff and Beds [8] Economic Feasibility Issues [8]
Patient Monitoring	Self Management App [32] Remote Monitoring [18]	Technical Issues With Remote Monitoring [18] Staff Shortage Leading to Health Inequalities [4]
Emotional Needs of Patients [21]	Emotional Wellness Sessions with Psychologists Socially Assisted Robot for Cardiac Rehabilitation [26] Comprehensive Support Programs [33]	Depression and Anxiety [21] Lack of Corporation by Patients in Treatment [9] Lack of Emotional Awareness [22]
Physical Rehabilitation Programs	Virtual and In-person Rehabilitation Programs [34] AI-based Exercise Prescription [35]	Lack of Personalisation for Heart Patients [20] Lack of Interdisciplinary Collaboration [34]
Post-open Heart Surgery Delirium [23]	Staff and Patient Training Programs	Lack of Delirium Awareness [36] Inadequate Support Systems [23]
Heartbeat Abnormality Detection	Heart Sound Abnormality Detection [37] Diagnosis of Heart Rhythm Abnormalities [38]	Limited Clinical Validation [37] Data Privacy Concerns [5]
Prediction of Heart Failure	Early Screening Programs [10] Data-driven Risk Prediction Models [39]	Limited Clinical Trials [10] Interpretation Challenges [40]

user adherence, minimising data entry errors, limitation to food database, refining portion size estimation, and enhancing the sophistication in tailoring advice to individual health goals, preferences, and dietary restrictions.

The sudden weight gain in heart failure patients can signal underlying cardiovascular issues and it is recommended that patients weigh themselves regularly [15]. A weight gain of three to five pounds in a week or two to three pounds in a day signals that the heart is not pumping blood properly. There are existing applications for weight management such as an explainable AI tool for predicting weight loss success for people who are trying to lose weight [41]. Similarly, another chatbot has been introduced to assist people in managing their weight loss journey and provides motivational and sentimental support [42]. Despite achieving a good accuracy such as above 80%, there are concerns regarding adoption and trust. Moreover, the weight monitoring applications for managing HF patients should be contextually aware of the purpose of identifying correct trends. Future research is required to address these concerns. Apart from monitoring heart patients, an application focused on HF management can also help address the issue of obesity.

C. Automatic Medication Management Systems

Effective medication management stands at the top of care for HF treatment and post-care. Researchers have introduced an automatic dispensing machine that handles medicines dispensation automatically [28]. This machine was developed to help people living in faraway places like tribal areas where getting medicine can be hard. The machine holds basic and emergency medicine and can also check vitals like blood pressure and temperature. When it is running low on medicine, it can be refilled based on remote information. A smart medication error reporting tool has also been introduced for enhancing the patients' safety [29]. Moreover, a systematic review has revealed the efficacy of mobile health apps in helping heart patients stick to their medications [43]. These apps generally demonstrated acceptable usability. However, ensuring the accuracy of medication administration and contributing to usability and effectiveness remains a significant challenge and further work is required in this domain to fully realise the potential of these systems.

D. Personalised Rehabilitation Programs

Irfan et. al [26] studied 43 patients to find the effectiveness and acceptability of socially assistive robots in personalised care at cardiac rehabilitation programs. The results derived from 26 patients(who finished the whole program), showed the effectiveness of robot assistance and personalising in the rehabilitation program, particularly during intense training. However, some failures in sensor data recognition were noticed, suggesting the need for future work to enhance sensor data recognition. Researchers have made significant efforts in therapy programs, such as AI-based personalised prescription by GPT-4 model [35]. Moreover, AI-based rehabilitation has been explored for patients with cerebrovascular accidents to reduce psychological stress [44]. Virtual reality-based therapy programs have been proposed to manage postural dizziness [45], and wearable robotic exoskeletons have been developed to enhance upper-limb rehabilitation [33]. Furthermore, researchers are utilising smartphones to study gait patterns to gain insights into an individual's personality [46]. Additionally, individual patient profiles are considered for tailored medical therapy [47].

Despite the potential of such effective therapy programs, these programs lack comprehensive clinical evaluations, encounter implementation challenges in real-world environments, and demonstrate a lack of precision. Therefore, more efforts are needed to enhance the usability and universality of these programs.

E. Early Diagnosis of Cardiac Complications and Abnormalities

The prediction of any health issue is critical in healthcare as it enables early identification and timely intervention for improved quality of life. Researchers have presented numerous works for the prediction of different diseases [32]. In another study [48], researchers proposed advanced methods for HF prediction using deep learning and a dataset of real healthcare records. This approach was effective for anomaly detection and risk factor refinement early intervention. Additionally, many similar researches open avenues for electronic health record data to explore HF, revealing significant variations in left ventricular ejection fraction [49]. Furthermore, [50] have proposed a motion-based analysis method for survival prediction of HF patients and their work highlights its potential for assisting clinical practitioners in personalised therapy planning for patients. Another study presents extensive insights on survivors of adolescent/adult Hodgkin lymphoma to develop prediction models for coronary heart disease and HF [40]. The model was accurate at predicting the risk of heart problems about two to three decades in advance. Such models can help doctors to screen and treat heart issues in Hodgkin lymphoma survivors at an early stage.

Despite significant progress in the research domain, clinical validation and real-world implementation represent crucial limitations in current solutions. Improvement in these areas will bridge the gap between technology and medicine, leading to better healthcare systems.

F. The initiative of Virtual Ward Care for HF Management

Addressing the issues in managing HF, including those encountered at hospitals in general and post-COVID-19 challenges, alongside meeting the patients' preferences, it is conceivable that the implementation of a *Virtual Ward* capable of managing complete HF care at home could be an effective solution. Despite the problems associated with different technological interventions highlighted earlier, with the rapid evolution of AI, robotics, and wearable technology, new solutions can be derived to overcome these limitations. Drawing inspiration from successful *Virtual Ward* models designed for acute respiratory infection and frailty, the NHS has also introduced the idea of a *Virtual Ward* care for people with HF [6]. The objective is to provide personalised care, monitoring, medication recommendations, personalised therapy, and individualised dietary prescriptions at patients' homes. This will also reduce the processes of admissions and re-admissions to the hospital, resulting in cost savings and supporting a near-real-time decision-making system. The focus lies in enhancing digital systems to remotely monitor patients, early identification as well as prediction of deterioration, timely intervention, and managed load.

Existing literature highlights challenges in current cardiac units and healthcare systems. Assistive technologies have a high potential to significantly improve HF management and promote home-based *Virtual Wards* [32]. Tasks such as early detection of declining cardiac function before they become clinically apparent, optimisation of remote monitoring systems and predictive analytics for hospital readmission risk assessment are more suitable for an AI-based system to excel. These functionalities hold significant promise if provided with clinical validations and personalisation.

IV. Conclusion and Future Work

In this paper, we have explored current challenges for HF patients from a UK perspective and presented some of the current technical solutions to provide home care for HF patients in the UK and worldwide. Managing HF is becoming more complex, with the current solution facing specific challenges if implemented in people's homes. While existing technologies facilitate the rapid transition of patients to their own homes, we have pointed out shortcomings and the potential for future improvement, highlighting the need for more advanced systems. Emerging technological solutions, such as the NHS *Virtual Ward* Care initiative, show the potential to improve patient care and better management. Future work in this domain can also contribute to the evolution of care pathways for HF, including the assessment of the effectiveness of such technological innovations.

References

[1] A. Eggerth, D. Hayn, and G. Schreier, "Medication management needs information and communications technology-based approaches, including telehealth and artificial intelligence," *British Journal of clinical pharmacology*, vol. 86, no. 10, pp. 2000–2007, 2020.

[2] R. A. Elliott, E. Camacho, D. Jankovic, M. J. Sculpher, and R. Faria, "Economic analysis of the prevalence and clinical and economic burden of medication error in England," *BMJ Quality & Safety*, vol. 30, no. 2, pp. 96–105, 2021.

[3] B. H. Foundation, "UK Factsheet," accessed: 2024-04-25. [Online]. Available: https://www.bhf.org.uk/-/media/files/for-professionals/research/heart-statistics/bhf-cvd-statistics-uk-factsheet.pdf

[4] G. B. Prato, *Health Inequalities and Ethics of Responsibility: A Comparative Ethnography*. Cham: Springer International Publishing, 2023, pp. 19–43.

[5] E. F. Kaplan *et al.*, "Cardiac Surgery Outcomes During the COVID-19 Pandemic Worsened Across All Socioeconomic Statuses," *The Annals of Thoracic Surgery*, vol. 115, no. 6, pp. 1511–1518, 2023.

[6] NHS, "Guidance note: virtual ward care for people with heart failure," accessed: 2024-04-25. [Online]. Available: https://www.england.nhs.uk/long-read/guidance-note-virtual-ward-care-for-people-with-heart-failure/

[7] A. Mulac, K. Taxis, E. Hagesaether, and A. G. Granas, "Severe and fatal medication errors in hospitals: findings from the Norwegian Incident Reporting System," *European Journal of Hospital Pharmacy*, vol. 28, no. e1, pp. e56–e61, 2021.

[8] L. Bosque-Mercader and L. Siciliani, "The association between bed occupancy rates and hospital quality in the English National Health Service," *The European Journal of Health Economics*, vol. 24, no. 2, pp. 209–236, 2023.

[9] G. N. Levine *et al.*, "Psychological Health, Well-Being, and the Mind-Heart-Body Connection: A Scientific Statement From the American Heart Association," *Circulation*, vol. 143, no. 10, pp. e763–e783, 2021.

[10] A. Ranjbar, J. Ravn, E. Ronningen, and O. Hanseth, "Enabling Clinical Trials of Artificial Intelligence: Infrastructure for Heart Failure Predictions," *Studies in health technology and informatics*, pp. 177–181, 2023.

[11] S. Tonjang and N. Thawesaengskulthai, "Patient Food Delivery Error in the Hospital: A Case Study in Thailand," in *Proceedings of the 2019 International Conference on Management Science and Industrial Engineering*, 2019, pp. 151–156.

[12] K. N. Barker, E. A. Flynn, G. A. Pepper, D. W. Bates, and R. L. Mikeal, "Medication Errors Observed in 36 Health Care Facilities," *Archives of Internal Medicine*, vol. 162, no. 16, pp. 1897–1903, 09 2002.

[13] C. Breuker *et al.*, "Medication Errors at Hospital Admission and Discharge: Risk Factors and Impact of Medication Reconciliation Process to Improve Healthcare," *Journal of Patient Safety*, vol. 17, no. 7, pp. e645–e652, 2021.

[14] C. K. Suryadevara, "Revolutionizing dietary monitoring: a comprehensive analysis of the innovative mobile app for tracking dietary composition," *International Journal of Innovations in Engineering Research and Technology*, vol. 10, no. 88, 2023.

[15] P. L. Alebna, A. Mehta, A. Yehya, A. da Silva-de Abreu, C. J. Lavie, and S. Carbone, "Update on obesity, the obesity paradox, and obesity management in heart failure," *Progress in Cardiovascular Diseases*, 2024.

[16] K. Norman, C. Pichard, H. Lochs, and M. Pirlich, "Prognostic impact of disease-related malnutrition," *Clinical nutrition*, vol. 27, no. 1, pp. 5–15, 2008.

[17] M. Mion *et al.*, "Follow-up care after out-of-hospital cardiac arrest: a pilot study of survivors and families' experiences and recommendations," *Resuscitation plus*, vol. 7, p. 100154, 2021.

[18] B. Greenwald *et al.*, "Feasibility of remote physiologic monitoring (rpm) in geriatric psychiatry clinic patients," *The American Journal of Geriatric Psychiatry*, vol. 32, no. 4, pp. S131–S132, 2024.

[19] O. Ljungqvist *et al.*, "Opportunities and Challenges for the Next Phase of Enhanced Recovery After Surgery," *JAMA surgery*, vol. 156, no. 8, pp. 775–784, 2021.

[20] L. A. Richardson *et al.*, "Clinician-leaders in cardiac rehabilitation: Clinical exercise physiologists," *Journal of Clinical Exercise Physiology*, vol. 13, no. s1, pp. 12–12, 2024.

[21] M. Lalic, "Help My Heart but Don't Forget My Mind: Facing Psychological Challenges of CHF Patients."

[22] N. D. Nayeri, Z. Roddehghan, F. Mahmoodi, and P. Mahmoodi, "Being parent of a child with congenital heart disease, what does it mean? a qualitative research," *bmc Psychology*, vol. 9, pp. 1–8, 2021.

[23] O. de la Varga-Martínez, R. Gutiérrez-Bustillo, M. F. Muñoz-Moreno, R. López-Herrero, E. Gómez-Sánchez, and E. Tamayo, "Postoperative delirium: An independent risk factor for poorer quality of life with long-term cognitive and functional decline after cardiac surgery," *Journal of Clinical Anesthesia*, vol. 85, p. 111030, 2023.

[24] M. Feinstein, D. Katz, S. Demaria, and I. S. Hofer, "Remote Monitoring and Artificial Intelligence: Outlook for 2050," *Anesthesia & Analgesia*, vol. 138, no. 2, 2024.

[25] T. E. Biersteker *et al.*, "Mobile health vs. standard care after cardiac surgery: results of The Box 2.0 study," *EP Europace*, vol. 25, no. 1, pp. 49–58, 08 2022.

[26] B. Irfan *et al.*, "Personalised socially assistive robot for cardiac rehabilitation: Critical reflections on long-term interactions in the real world," *User Modeling and User-Adapted Interaction*, vol. 33, no. 2, pp. 497–544, Apr 2023.

[27] X. Liu *et al.*, "Wearable Smartwatch Facilitated Remote Health Management for Patients Undergoing Transcatheter Aortic Valve Replacement," *Journal of the American Heart Association*, vol. 11, no. 7, p. e023219, 2022.

[28] M. Penna, D. V. Gowda, J. J. Jijesh, and Shivashankar, "Design and Implementation of Automatic Medicine Dispensing Machine," in *2017 2nd IEEE International Conference on Recent Trends in Electronics, Information & Communication Technology (RTEICT)*, 2017, pp. 1962–1966.

[29] R. Thabet, E. Lamine, M.-H. Cleostrate, M.-N. Cufi, and H. Pingaud, "Towards a novel spontaneous medication error reporting tool for enhancing patient safety," in *2022 IEEE/ACS 19th International Conference on Computer Systems and Applications (AICCSA)*. IEEE, 2022, pp. 1–6.

[30] S. Carino, J. Porter, S. Malekpour, and J. Collins, "Environmental Sustainability of Hospital Foodservices across the Food Supply Chain: A Systematic Review," *Journal of the Academy of Nutrition and Dietetics*, vol. 120, no. 5, pp. 825–873, 2020.

[31] L. Van Bulck, R. Couturier, and P. Moons, "Applications of artificial intelligence for nursing: has a new era arrived?" *European Journal of Cardiovascular Nursing*, vol. 22, no. 3, pp. e19–e20, 10 2022.

[32] E.-Y. Choi, J.-S. Park, D. Min, S. Ahn, and J.-A. Ahn, "Heart Failure-Smart Life: a randomized controlled trial of a mobile app for self-management in patients with heart failure," *BMC cardiovascular disorders*, vol. 23, no. 1, pp. 1–10, 2023.

[33] M. A. Vélez-Guerrero, M. Callejas-Cuervo, and S. Mazzoleni, "Artificial Intelligence-Based Wearable Robotic Exoskeletons for Upper Limb Rehabilitation: A Review," *Sensors*, vol. 21, no. 6, p. 2146, 2021.

[34] H. M. Dalal, P. Doherty, S. T. McDonagh, K. Paul, and R. S. Taylor, "Virtual and in-person cardiac rehabilitation," *BMJ*, vol. 373, 2021.

[35] I. Dergaa *et al.*, "Using artificial intelligence for exercise prescription in personalised health promotion: A critical evaluation of OpenAI's GPT-4 model," *Biology of Sport*, vol. 41, no. 2, pp. 221–241, 2023.

[36] B. Sadeghirad *et al.*, "Perioperative Factors Associated with Postoperative Delirium in Patients Undergoing Noncardiac Surgery: An Individual Patient Data Meta-Analysis," *JAMA network open*, vol. 6, no. 10, pp. e2 337 239–e2 337 239, 2023.

[37] Z. Wang, K. Qian, H. Liu, B. Hu, B. W. Schuller, and Y. Yamamoto, "Exploring interpretable representations for heart sound abnormality detection," *Biomedical Signal Processing and Control*, vol. 82, p. 104569, 2023.

[38] H. Zhu *et al.*, "Automatic multilabel electrocardiogram diagnosis of heart rhythm or conduction abnormalities with deep learning: a cohort study," *The Lancet Digital Health*, vol. 2, no. 7, pp. e348–e357, 2020.

[39] S. Nandy, M. Adhikari, V. Balasubramanian, V. G. Menon, X. Li, and M. Zakarya, "An intelligent heart disease prediction system based on swarm-artificial neural network," *Neural Computing and Applications*, vol. 35, no. 20, pp. 14 723–14 737, 2023.

[40] S. de Vries *et al.*, "Development and Validation of Risk Prediction Models for Coronary Heart Disease and Heart Failure After Treatment for Hodgkin Lymphoma," *Journal of Clinical Oncology*, vol. 41, no. 1, pp. 86–95, 2023.

[41] G. J. Fernandes *et al.*, "An Explainable Artificial Intelligence Software Tool for Weight Management Experts (PRIMO): Mixed Methods Study," *Journal of medical Internet research*, vol. 25, p. e42047, 2023.

[42] A. R. Rahmanti *et al.*, "SlimMe, a Chatbot With Artificial Empathy for Personal Weight Management: System Design and Finding," *Frontiers in Nutrition*, vol. 9, p. 870775, 2022.

[43] S. Al-Arkee *et al.*, "Mobile Apps to Improve Medication Adherence in Cardiovascular Disease: Systematic Review and Meta-analysis," *Journal of medical Internet research*, vol. 23, no. 5, p. e24190, 2021.

[44] R. Kamakshi, "To Determine the Effectiveness of Artificial Intelligence in Neurorehabilitation and in Poststroke Psychological Impact–A Pilot Study," *Indian Journal of Physical Medicine & Rehabilitation*, vol. 32, no. 1, pp. 14–16, 2022.

[45] E. Mempouo, K. Lau, F. Green, C. Bowes, and J. Ray, "Customised vestibular rehabilitation with the addition of virtual reality based therapy in the management of persistent postural-perceptual dizziness," *The Journal of Laryngology & Otology*, vol. 135, no. 10, pp. 887–891, 2021.

[46] S. Rafique, M. Ehatisham-ul Haq, K. Ibrar, A. Yasin, F. Murtaza, and M. A. Azam, "Assessment of Human Personality Traits Using Smartphone Sensing," in *Science and Information Conference*. Springer, 2023, pp. 613–622.

[47] G. M. Rosano *et al.*, "Patient profiling in heart failure for tailoring medical therapy. A consensus document of the Heart Failure Association of the European Society of Cardiology," *European journal of heart failure*, vol. 23, no. 6, pp. 872–881, 2021.

[48] C. Zhou *et al.*, "Risk factor refinement and ensemble deep learning methods on prediction of heart failure using real healthcare records," *Information Sciences*, vol. 637, p. 118932, 2023.

[49] P. Adekkanattu *et al.*, "Prediction of left ventricular ejection fraction changes in heart failure patients using machine learning and electronic health records: a multi-site study," *Scientific reports*, vol. 13, no. 1, p. 294, 2023.

[50] S. Guo *et al.*, "Survival prediction of heart failure patients using motion-based analysis method," *Computer Methods and Programs in Biomedicine*, vol. 236, p. 107547, 2023.

Analysis and Enrichment of Description in Restaurant Review through Follow-Up Interaction

Kaho Mizobata and Ryosuke Yamanishi
Graduate School of Informatics, Kansai University
Ryozenji 2-1-1, Takatsuki, 569-1095, Japan
Email: {k987336, ryama}@kansai-u.ac.jp

***Abstract*—This paper proposes a framework to enrich restaurant reviews by providing follow-up questions to reviewers about absent elements in their original reviews. Utilizing ChatGPT, we investigated enhancing the detail and organization of reviews by examining 26 participants' interactions across food, environment, and user experience. The results suggested that the follow-up interaction encouraged more informative reviews by highlighting omitted details. Especially, it effectively increases mentions of the restaurant's atmosphere and personal experiences alongside food descriptions. This approach offers insights into factors influencing review content, such as review writing experience and dining context. We believe that the findings will be helpful for customers as a guide to writing reviews and suggest the effectiveness of follow-up interaction in writing reviews.**

***Keywords*-Follow-up interaction; computational approach for food and eating activities; Large Language Model-supported system.**

I. Introduction

When selecting a restaurant from numerous options, customers frequently refer to restaurant reviews posted on websites. These reviews directly reflect the experiences and impressions of reviewers who have actually visited the restaurants. The review is a precious source of restaurant information for customers. Reviews significantly influence customers' impressions of restaurants before their visit, and the content of these reviews can greatly affect the restaurant's patronage [1]. Restaurants undertake various approaches to attract customers through reviews: offering the first drink, a plate of desserts, and optional services for free, such as writing a review or posting photos and videos with some specific tags.

Restaurants try to attract customers through some initiatives. Let us consider that the handled content differs between writing reviews and posting tagged photos and videos. Reviews primarily deal with text, while photos and videos mainly involve visuals and sounds. The text in reviews can detail various aspects of the experience in the restaurant. The reviews can tell not only the taste, smell, and texture of the food, but also the ambiance and environment of the restaurant, its location, and the attitude of the staff. Moreover, they sometimes provide the circumstances leading up to the reviewer's visit and individual events for each reviewer in the restaurant. These types of information are helpful for customers to select a restaurant. On the other hand, photos and videos may not offer as much detailed information as reviews. They can provide attractive and impressive visual information, e.g., the appealing appearance of food [2], customers' facial expressions after eating. To attract customers through visually appealing content, restaurants have been making various efforts to make their dishes look more appetizing.

Reviews are potentially able to provide much valuable information for customers, but most of them do not provide sufficient detail about the restaurant. Just one word like "good" or "bad" can not be a source to be referred to. Accordingly, so many customers focus on photos and videos, and then restaurants emphasize visual and sound content as an advertisement. It is not too much to say that this trend ignores something that can not be recorded in photos and videos. If the review can be improved as its potential, the customers can receive more information for aspects not shown in photos and videos, e.g., smells of coffee and the kindness of staff. We thus investigate the following research questions;

- RQ 1 What memory challenges do customers face when detailing a restaurant?
- RQ 2 What types of information can be missed in reviews?
- RQ 3 Does the follow-up interaction enrich the description in reviews?

In this paper, we ask reviewers to describe their dining experience twice. From the investigation, we study what they remember and easy to describe from different perspectives. When reviewing a dining experience, the memories the reviewer recalls are not text but sensory information from their senses: visual, auditory, olfactory, gustatory, and tactile inputs. For RQ 1, This study explores how reviewers verbalize and express these memories in text, what information is easier or harder to recall, and what information can be expressed in text but not in photos or videos, and vice versa. By clarifying these aspects, we aim to understand the trends in review writing and consider how to enrich the content of reviews based on these findings. To investigate RQ 2 and RQ 3, we prepare the follow-up system introducing ChatGPT. As a review is input, the system identifies aspects that exist and do not exist in the review. The system shows the follow-up question to encourage reviewers to detail the missed aspects in mind. The aspects in the original and revised reviews are comparatively analyzed. Then, we consider the effectiveness of follow-up interaction in enriching reviews.

II. Related Work

Restaurants can be classified into numerous segments, with criteria: the level and quality of service, customer participation in the dining experience, price, quality of food, and ambiance

[3]–[6]. Based on these criteria, restaurants can be categorized into fast food, casual dining, fine dining, and business food service, among others. There are many elements unique to each segment, while common elements (e.g., accessibility, menu diversity, and a certain level of cleanliness) across the segments exist. Existing papers discussed which restaurant segment can meet customer expectations and what elements enhance customer satisfaction [7]–[9]. These studies have shown that casual dining restaurants adequately meet customer expectations, and the quality of food and restaurant services significantly impacts customer expectations. It has also been confirmed that the price of food affects customer satisfaction, especially in fast food and casual dining restaurants [10], [11].

Let us focus on the unique elements of each restaurant segment. It is evident that aspects like food quality, restaurant service, and price are crucial elements for relatively low-priced dining options. These elements are related to the customers' dining experience and their overall experience in the restaurant. There are many studies that have used different aspects necessary for customer satisfaction in reviews, extracting various evaluations of restaurants from reviews [12]–[17]. These studies have enabled the automatic evaluation of restaurants based on reviews and feature extraction. They analyzed elements necessary for customer satisfaction in restaurants from various points of view.

However, these studies do not enrich the content of reviews to enhance the customer experience.

This research analyzes 1) what aspects are likely to be described in reviews, 2) in what order they are typically described, and 3) what content is recalled through follow-up interaction. It aims to identify points that satisfy customers and make them want to write reviews, contributing to enriching customer experiences and the management strategies of restaurants. Furthermore, by identifying the elements customers look for in restaurants from reviews. The proposed system introduces ChatGPT to point out missing elements in reviews. This paper investigates the effectiveness of follow-up interaction to enrich the content in reviews to be more comprehensive and informative.

This study introduces ChatGPT to identify missing elements in restaurant reviews. Through the experiments, we investigate the effectiveness of follow-up interactions in making reviews more comprehensive and informative. It is reasonable to say that the improved reviews are valuable for both customer experiences and restaurant management.

III. Proposed Method

Figure 1 shows the framework of the proposed system and its interaction. In Section III, we developed a system to detect existing/absent elements in reviews and to enrich reviews through follow-up interaction. The review elements are preset to ChatGPT with prompt engineering.

A. Elements in restaurant reviews

This paper defines the elements in restaurant reviews as encompassing all aspects related to dining; we consider that the experience of dining out includes before and after visiting the restaurant itself. To empirically extract these elements, the first author conducted a systematic survey of restaurant reviews on a popular dining website [18].

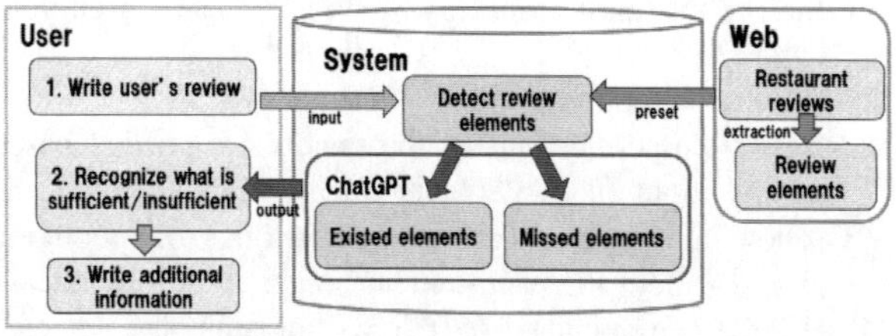

Figure 1. The framework of the proposed system and its interaction. A system introducing ChatGPT where review elements extracted from reviews are learned. The system give feedback the viewpoints missed in a review to users as a follow-up.

TABLE I
REVIEW ELEMENTS INCLUDED IN RESTAURANT REVIEWS. THERE ARE THREE POINTS OF VIEW IN REVIEW ELEMENTS: FOOD, RESTAURANT, AND REVIEWER (I.E., THE USER.) THE INDEX OF ELEMENTS IS ASSIGNED TO THE LEFT OF EACH ELEMENT.

ID	Food	ID	Restaurant	ID	Reviewer
1	taste	8	place	16	when
2	texture	9	budget/price	17	who
3	appearance	10	interior/decoration	18	why
4	smell	11	staff	19	feeling
5	ingredients	12	customer	20	event
6	volume	13	season	21	user age
7	food combination	14	history of store	22	hunger level
		15	limited event	23	satisfaction

This involved analyzing a diverse range of reviews to identify common themes and descriptors used by customers. The extracted elements reflect the holistic dining experience and are represented in Table I, which is preset in the proposed system. For analytical clarity, these elements were categorized into three perspectives: food, the restaurant's environment, and the reviewer's experience. This categorization was based on the frequency and significance of mentions in the reviews, allowing us to distill the most impactful aspects of the dining experience as perceived by customers.

Note, the elements were heuristically selected in this paper. It is not crucial to the goal of our study, which is to investigate the effectiveness of follow-up interaction in enriching reviews. Although, the data-driven approach to preparing the elements will be our future work.

B. Follow-up interaction with ChatGPT

The system introduces ChatGPT as a conversational model of Large Language Models: LLM.

We set the following prompts to ChatGPT;

[PROCEDURES]

Please assist in creating a restaurant review. Follow the steps outlined below to provide support in writing restaurant reviews.

1) Inform the participants by saying, "Please enter your review."
2) Have the participants input their review.
3) Detect which elements of the review are present based on the input of participants, identifying which of the following categories each element belongs to: {about the food}, {about the environment}, {about the reviewer}.
4) Briefly communicate to the participants the detected elements from their review.
5) Inform the participants of any missing elements, ensuring that there are at least three elements mentioned in the review under each category {about the food}, {about the environment}, {about the reviewer}.

The elements of restaurant reviews described in Section III-A are preset to ChatGPT. We conducted prompt engineering for ChatGPT to detect existing and absent elements from an input review. When participants input their dining experiences at a restaurant, the system identifies which elements exist in the review. The system represents all elements included in a review for each perspective. Also, the system represents more than three absent elements for each perspective if the review does not include all of the elements in Table I completely. After representing these, the system suggests reviewer add the absent elements to comprehensively enrich the review. Note, users may add any descriptions other than absent elements suggested by the system.

We observed how the system works through test cases in advance. Reviews randomly selected from a website were input into the proposed system. It was confirmed that the proposed system successfully identified some existing and absent elements in nine reviews out of ten reviews. One error case only represented existing elements but did not show absent elements as a suggestion. For such error cases, the proposed system could represent correct absent elements as the experimenter additionally prompted "detect the absent elements" as an problem solver. Therefore, we decided to constantly monitor the interaction in the experiment and appropriately prompt the problem solver if the system would unexpectedly work.

IV. Experimental Settings

In Section IV, using the proposed system described in Section III, we experimented with writing restaurant reviews. The reviews written by participants and their interaction with the proposed system were analyzed from various points of view.

A. Procedures

The experiment was conducted as three steps shown in Figure 1. The procedures of the experiment were as follows;

1) Each individual participant had a dining experience.
2) The participant wrote a review about his/her dining experience and took the feedback from the proposed system.
3) The participant wrote additional information to enrich the description in the review according to the system's suggestions.

We studied the reviews written by the participants for each element and perspective based on the profiles of the participants.

B. Participant Profiles

A profile survey was conducted on 26 participants before writing the review and interacting with ChatGPT. The survey included six items: the participant's age, gender, experience with writing reviews, the timing of the dining experience mentioned in the review, the amount paid at the restaurant, and the timezone of the dining experience. Table II shows the profile survey of participants.

In our experiment, the survey investigated the degree of familiarity with writing reviews in addition to basic information about the participants. We asked whether the participants have written reviews regularly, spontaneously, for some exogenous incentives (e.g., for a reward,) or never. This survey aimed to clarify whether differences in familiarity with writing reviews lead to differences in the review aspects focused on. The survey on the timing of the dining experience mentioned in the review was designed with four options: within one week, two weeks, three weeks, and four weeks. This questionnaire would clarify whether the elapsed time since the dining experience influenced the review aspects focused on. The survey on the amount paid at the restaurant was conducted with four options: below 2,000 JPY, between 2,001 and 4,000 JPY, between 4,001 and 6,000 JPY, and above 6,000 JPY. This questionnaire was prepared to study whether there was a relationship between the amount paid and the review aspects focused on. The survey on the timezone of the dining experience had three options: morning, noon, and evening. We used the result of this survey to clarify whether there was a relationship between the timezone and the review aspects focused on.

V. Results

Table III shows the results of the experiment. In the table, for each participant, originally described elements, originally absent elements suggested by the system, and added elements by follow-up interaction are listed as the index of review elements. In Section V, we study the overall review elements through the interactions. Moreover, we focus on the participants' profiles, the timing of the dining experience, and the amount paid to more deeply consider the interaction of writing reviews with follow-up interaction.

A. Discussions for review elements through follow-up interactions

This Section studies the overall results of the experiment. We focus on the trends in originally described elements, originally absent elements suggested by the system, and added elements by follow-up interaction. It was confirmed that food, restaurant, and reviewers were all described in the originally described and added elements in the reviews. Moreover, the

TABLE II

PARTICIPANT'S PROFILES. IT SHOWS THE PARTICIPANT ID, AGE, GENDER(M/F), EXPERIENCE IN WRITING RESTAURANT REVIEWS, WHEN THE EXPERIENCE WAS MENTIONED IN THE REVIEW, THE BUDGET(JPY) FOR THE DINING, AND THE TIMEZONE OF THE EXPERIENCE.

ID	Age	gender	Experience	When	Budget(JPY)	Timezone
1	21	M	Voluntary	1 week ago	1-2,000	Evening
2	21	M	No experienced	4 weeks ago	4,001-6,000	Evening
3	20	M	No experienced	1 week ago	1-2,000	Evening
4	22	F	Voluntary	4 weeks ago	2001-4,000	Evening
5	22	F	Exogenous	1 week ago	1-2,000	Daytime
6	20	M	No experienced	3 weeks ago	2001-4,000	Evening
7	20	M	No experienced	2 weeks ago	1-2,000	Evening
8	20	M	Exogenous	1 week ago	1-2,000	Daytime
9	20	M	No experienced	1 week ago	1-2,000	Evening
10	19	M	No experienced	1 week ago	1-2,000	Evening
11	20	M	No experienced	1 week ago	1-2,000	Evening
12	20	M	No experienced	1 week ago	1-2,000	Evening
13	20	M	No experienced	4 weeks ago	1-2,000	Evening
14	20	M	No experienced	1 week ago	2,001-4,000	Evening
15	24	F	No experienced	1 week ago	1-2,000	Evening
16	21	M	No experienced	1 week ago	1-2,000	Daytime
17	23	M	Exogenous	1 week ago	1-2,000	Evening
18	51	F	Exogenous	4 weeks ago	1-2,000	Evening
19	21	M	No experienced	3 weeks ago	1-2,000	Evening
20	22	M	No experienced	1 week ago	1-2,000	Daytime
21	22	M	No experienced	1 week ago	1-2,000	Daytime
22	23	M	No experienced	1 week ago	2,001-4,000	Evening
23	23	M	No experienced	1 week ago	2,001-4,000	Evening
24	22	M	Voluntary	1 week ago	6,001-	Evening
25	22	M	No experienced	1 week ago	1-2,000	Evening
26	24	F	Exogenous	2 weeks ago	2,001-4,000	Evening

users added not only the suggested elements but also other elements through follow-up interaction. From these results, the follow-up interaction by the proposed system helped reviewers to enrich their reviews as informative and comprehensive. These results follow RQ 1, RQ 2 and RQ 3.

Throughout both originally described and added elements, it was confirmed that there were highly co-occurred elements: taste and texture, taste and ingredients, and taste and food pairing. Co-occurrence of taste and texture happened in reviews listing the characteristics of the dish. For co-occurrences of taste and ingredients, Reviews explaining ingredients in the dish and what taste the ingredients had included the co-occurrence of taste and ingredients. Taste and food pairing co-occurred in reviews describing the combinations of ordered dishes on that day, including combinations of their tastes.

The total number of elements throughout interactions indicated that taste-related elements were most frequent in both originally described and added reviews. Almost all reviews mentioned the taste of the food. It thus suggested that the taste was the easiest element to describe in reviews rather than others. Many reviews started with a description of taste and went to others. From these results, there might be a common idea among reviewers that "restaurant reviews should have descriptions of taste."

Focusing on elements only in the original descriptions, reviews commonly included taste, and budget/price, i.e., elements related to foods. Such elements were easily described with reviewers' feelings before and after eating. The descriptions of reviews actually explained the taste and price in relation to reviewer's feeling. These results suggested that the taste and price were significant points to evaluate restaurants.

Let us focus on added elements after the proposed system suggested absent review elements in a review. The added reviews commonly include not only elements related to taste but also ones related to the restaurant's environment: place and budget/price. Although the system did not suggest, reviewers additionally mentioned elements related to taste through the follow-up interaction. This result also supported that reviewers emphasized taste-related elements in reviews. We confirmed that elements concerning place were not commonly mentioned in originally described reviews, which were added after follow-up interaction. Moreover, added reviews included more elements related to staff and interior/decoration. The results showed the elements concerning the restaurant were increased after follow-up interactions.

B. Discussions for profiles of participants

We focus on the reviewers' profiles shown in Table II. In the following discussion, we consider the experience of writing reviews, the timing of the experience, and the amount paid at the restaurant. Note that all the participants were in their twenties, their genders were unbalanced and not sufficiently evident for discussion, and most visited restaurants in the evening. The following discussions regarding the results in Table III are thus limited to these profiles.

1) Experience for writing reviews: It was found that there were no significant differences in originally described and added elements between voluntary and exogenous for those who experienced writing reviews. So, whether the experience

TABLE III
REVIEW ELEMENTS IDENTIFIED BY EXPERIMENT REVIEWERS. EACH COLOR-CODED NUMBER REPRESENTS A DIFFERENT PERSPECTIVE: BLUE FOR FOOD, RED FOR RESTAURANTS, AND ORANGE FOR REVIEWERS. THE ORDER OF NUMBERS IS THE SAME AS THE ORDER OF APPEARANCE IN A REVIEW.

Participant's ID	Originally described elements	Originally absent elements suggested by the system	Added elements by follow-up interaction
1	119 5 4	9 11 17	10 9 11 8 12 17 15
2	16 9 19 1	11 12 8	12 8
3	8 9 1 2 7 6 23 19	3 4 11 12 16 17 18	16 18 11
4	9 17 7 1	8 2 3 15 22	2 1
5	2 1 10 19	3 4 11 12 13 15 17 22 23	16 17 22 23 11
6	10 18 19 7	1 5 6 8 9	6 7 9 11 19
7	8 10 19 13 1 12	16 17 18 19 20	1 13 6 9 11 14 15 16 19 21
8	11 1 7 9	5 9 16 23	16 12 7 9
9	8 5 1	10 11 16 17	16 17 8 10 11
10	17 9 6 23 8 14 1 13 14 15	5 3 4 7 11	5 3 4
11	1 9 22 7	8 10 13 15	10 19
12	1 2 5 6 17 9 19	8 10	8 10
13	1	4 5 21 22 23	7 6 23
14	1	3 17 10 19	3 5 17 19
15	16 18	1 2 3 5 6 7 8 9 10	7 1 9 8 19 11
16	8 16 12 7 1 18 19	2 3 9 11 13 18 20 21	18 9
17	16 12 1 2 6 18 19	8 9 19 20	8 9
18	8 2 1 5 7 19 3 2 23	4 17 19	4 19 10 17 12
19	16 17 12 19 1	5 10 12 13 17	9 1 5 10 12 13
20	1 2 6	8 9 10 11 12 14 15 18 20 21	16 12 10 11 23
21	1 19	1 5 6 19	1 5 6 23
22	8 17 16 1 11 10	3 7 6 10 20 22 23	6 23 10
23	17 9 19 6 1	12 13 14 15	11 15 1
24	1 17 7 18 19	22 23 16	17 20 9 18 11 16
25	3 2 5 1 10 11 19	1 8 16	10 16 1
26	8 1 19	10 9 7	11 9

of writing a review itself had a more significant meaning than the desire to write one. Participants without review writing experience often described elements of their satisfaction in their reviews. In contrast, reviews from participants with writing experience less frequently mentioned their satisfaction; it seemed that satisfaction was not crucial for experienced reviewers.

Let us focus on the originally described elements. Participants with review writing experience included food-related elements, particularly mentioning taste after an introduction of the reviewer or context of dining. These participants mentioned multiple perspectives of dining (i.e., food, restaurant, and reviewer) in a review, though those with no experience in writing reviews mentioned a few elements. On the other hand, reviewers inexperienced in writing reviews tended to describe fewer elements. Their common perspective of their reviews was the "reviewer" him/herself. They described how they had felt the taste and the context of dining without any preambles. These findings suggested that experienced reviewers could provide objective and comprehensive assessments in a review; they would take into account the reader's experience while reading the review. In contrast, participants without prior experience in writing reviews tended to write more subjective reviews, focusing on their personal feelings.

For added elements after the follow-up interaction, experienced participants in writing reviews improved the review to include more elements about the restaurant, while elements for food were less. The review consisting of originally described and added elements covered all types of perspectives in restaurant reviews. The inexperienced reviewers also could improve their reviews by adding some elements absent in their original ones. It was suggested that the follow-up interaction could improve the reviews; it seems to be effective for even experienced reviewers.

2) Timing of dining experience: Originally described reviews differed between the dining experience and the timing of writing reviews. It was suggested that participants who had dined more than two weeks ago focused more on the restaurant and reviewer perspectives. In contrast, participants who had dined within a week focused more on "food." These results suggested that recent experiences led to more detailed memories of the food itself, while older memories brought more about the environment and context for dining.

3) Amount paid: We discuss the experimental results by focusing on the amount paid at the restaurants mentioned in the reviews. The tendencies of the reviews were different between amounts paid less than 2,000 JPY and paid more than 2,001 JPY.

The participants who had paid less than 2,000 JPY often mentioned elements for food in the original and added reviews. The participants who had dined economical foods did not focus on restaurant and user perspectives. It seems that the important aspect for experiences with economical foods were food itself. The participants who had paid more than 2,001 JPY mentioned all of perspectives food, restaurant and user; that is, their review is well organized. It seemed that they focused on not only foods but also environment and context of dining for the experience with expensive costs. These findings suggested that the payment should not be just for foods, but for the overall dining experience.

VI. Conclusion

This study has investigated writing reviews with follow-up interaction. In this paper, we have set the following research questions;

RQ 1 What memory challenges do customers face when detailing a restaurant?

RQ 2 What types of information can be missed in reviews?

RQ 3 Does the follow-up interaction enrich the description in reviews?

The answers to each research question have been as follows;

Ans. 1 Without differences of experience or not, it is hard for customers to detail all perspectives of a dining experience by him/herself.

Ans. 2 Perspectives for restaurants and users tend to be absent. Especially in restaurants with less amount paid, the customers focused more on taste.

Ans. 3 Follow-up interaction as pointing out the absent elements is effective to revise the reviews in the written reviews. Adding descriptions enriches reviews from multiple perspectives.

These answers follow the RQ 1, RQ 2 and RQ 3 that could not be followed in related works.

In the future outlook of this paper, we identify several challenges that need to be addressed to enhance the robustness and validity of our research findings;

1) Validation of the results across broader demographics and provide more generalizable insights.
   - Increasing participant numbers.
2) Eliminating any biases that could arise from uneven participant demographics and heuristically prepared review elements.
   - Balancing participant profiles.
   - Resolving empirical basis for review elements.
3) Detailed analysis of how participants engage with interaction prompts for a deeper comprehension of the effects of interaction models.
   - Observation of participant interaction: which prompts elicit the most informative responses and how participants navigate the review process.
4) Developing strategies to handle and accurately process unclear or suboptimal review inputs.

These steps will significantly contribute to the refinement of our experimental design. We believe that the AI-supported review system ultimately leads to more comprehensive and informative restaurant reviews that can better serve consumers and restaurant management.

References

[1] H. Li, F. Meng, M. Jeong, and Z. Zhang, "To follow others or be yourself? social influence in online restaurant reviews," *International Journal of Contemporary Hospitality Management*, vol. 32, no. 3, pp. 1067–1087, 2020.

[2] K. Takahashi, T. Hattori, K. Doman, Y. Kawanishi, T. Hirayama, I. Ide, et al. "Estimation of the attractiveness of food photography based on image features," *IEICE Transactions on Information and Systems*, vol. E102.D, no. 8, pp. 1590–1593, 2019.

[3] C. C. Muller and R. H. Woods, "An expanded restaurant typology," *The Cornell Hotel and Restaurant Administration Quarterly*, vol. 35, no. 3, pp. 27–37, 1994.

[4] R. Di Pietro and A. Milman, "Retention factors of tipped hourly employees in the casual dining restaurant segment: exploratory research in central florida," *International Journal of Hospitality & Tourism Administration*, vol. 9, no. 3, pp. 244–266, 2008.

[5] J. Ha and S. S. Jang, "Consumer dining value: Does it vary across different restaurant segments?" *Journal of Foodservice Business Research*, vol. 15, no. 2, pp. 123–142, 2012.

[6] J. Kivela, "Restaurant marketing: selection and segmentation in hong kong." *International Journal of Contemporary Hospitality Management*, vol. 9, pp. 116–123, 1997. [Online]. Available: https://api.semanticscholar.org/CorpusID:153757243

[7] J. Dziadkowiec and A. S. Rood, "Casual-dining restaurant preferences: A cross-cultural comparison," *Journal of Foodservice Business Research*, vol. 18, no. 1, pp. 73–91, 2015.

[8] R. B. DiPietro and C. G. Partlow, "Customer expectations of casual dining restaurants: the case of liberty tap room," *International Journal of Hospitality & Tourism Administration*, vol. 15, no. 4, pp. 376–393, 2014.

[9] C. Peng, A. Bilgihan, and J. Kandampully, "How do diners make decisions among casual dining restaurants? an exploratory study of college students," *International Journal of Hospitality & Tourism Administration*, vol. 16, no. 1, pp. 1–15, 2015.

[10] F. Ali, M. Amin, and K. Ryu, "The role of physical environment, price perceptions, and consumption emotions in developing customer satisfaction in chinese resort hotels," *Journal of Quality Assurance in Hospitality & Tourism*, vol. 17, no. 1, pp. 45–70, 2016.

[11] M. C. Ottenbacher and R. J. Harrington, "The product innovation process of quick-service restaurant chains," *International Journal of contemporary hospitality management*, vol. 21, no. 5, pp. 523–541, 2009.

[12] B. Ahiladas, P. Saravanaperumal, S. Balachandran, T. Sripalan, and S. Ranathunga, "Ruchi: Rating individual food items in restaurant reviews," in *Proc. the 12th International Conference on Natural Language Processing*, 2015, pp. 209–214.

[13] J. S. Kang, P. Kuznetsova, M. Luca, and Y. Choi, "Where not to eat? improving public policy by predicting hygiene inspections using online reviews," in *Proc. the 2013 Conference on Empirical Methods in Natural Language Processing*, 2013, pp. 1443–1448.

[14] R. Panchendrarajan, N. Ahamed, P. Sivakumar, B. Murugaiah, S. Ranathunga, and A. Pemasiri, "Eatery: a multi-aspect restaurant rating system," in *Proc. the 28th ACM Conference on Hypertext and Social Media*, 2017, pp. 225–234.

[15] D. Gräbner, M. Zanker, G. Fliedl, M. Fuchs *et al.*, "Classification of customer reviews based on sentiment analysis," in *Proc. Information and Communication Technologies in Tourism 2012*, 2012, pp. 460–470.

[16] B. Snyder and R. Barzilay, "Multiple aspect ranking using the good grief algorithm," in *Proc. Human Language Technologies 2007: The Conference of the North American Chapter of the Association for Computational Linguistics*, 2007, pp. 300–307.

[17] B. Lu, M. Ott, C. Cardie, and B. K. Tsou, "Multi-aspect sentiment analysis with topic models," in *Proc. 2011 IEEE 11th international conference on data mining workshops*, 2011, pp. 81–88.

[18] Tabelog: https://tabelog.com/ (retrieved: Apr. 25, 2024)

HD vs. 4K Driven Remote Tower Optical Systems

What is the better Optical Sensor?

Julia Schön, Jörn Jakobi, Sina Felten, Giulia Troyer, Andreas Nadobnik, Tim Rambau & Felix Timmermann
Institute of Flight Guidance, Department Human Factors
German Aerospace Center (DLR), Germany
e-mail: julia.schoen@dlr.de; e-mail: joern.jakobi@dlr.de; e-mail: sina.felten@dlr.de; e-mail: giulia.troyer@dlr.de; e-mail: andreas.nadobnik@dlr.de; e-mail: tim.rambau@dlr.de; e-mail: felix.timmermann@dlr.de

Abstract—**The purpose of this study was to investigate the rationale performance in between of 4K versus Full HD cameras in the context of a Remote Tower Optical System. Live videos from operational traffic at a German regional airport were recorded with both sensor types under different visibility condition. 23 air traffic controllers and aerodrome flight information officers compared and rated the different videos with respect to perceived video quality, detection and recognition range performance. Results show that, at least in this setting, in some situations, the 4K camera performs significantly better than the Full HD camera, but the effects are small and a clear decision without considering any other configuration parameters cannot be made unrestricted. The number of pixels of the sensor for instance is just one of many other parameters, which have to be considered in order to provide a well-tuned video stream, which supports an appropriate detection and recognition rate as well as a high-quality appearance.**

Keywords-HD; 4K; Camera; RemoteTower.

I. INTRODUCTION

A. *Characteristics of Full HD and 4K Cameras*

Remote Tower is a prospering concept to provide aerodrome Air Traffic Services (ATS) more efficiently. The out-of-the-window view from the Air Traffic Control (ATC) tower is captured via video cameras and relayed to a controller working position in a Remote Tower Center (RTC), which is located independent of the location of the actual airport. Out of such RTCs many airports can be operated, which creates synergies in terms of flexibility, efficiency and cost-effectiveness. In order to continue to handle the traffic safely and efficiently as from a conventional ATC tower, the quality of the video stream is of central importance. Particular attention is paid to the choice of the best camera sensor. 4K sensor cameras are increasingly entering the Remote Tower market, as the latest generations can compensate for the disadvantages compared to the currently used Full HD sensor cameras and thus, bring the 4K advantages into focus. But is the 4K really the better sensor for an Remote Tower Optical System (RTOS)?

Finally, all is about to find a well-tuned RTOS set-up, providing an optimal video performance to meet the operational needs as well as infrastructure and cost constraints. For that purpose and in accordance to [1], many "glass-to-glass" (from the sensor lens to the display) parameters have to be considered, including but not limited to:

- number of pixels (e.g., HD vs 4K),
- sensor size,
- Field of View (FoV) (set by focal length),
- angular resolution (pixel/degree),
- color depth,
- video compression in terms of maximum bitrate and bit per pixel
- CODEC implementation, e.g., H.264 or H.265,
- light sensitivity,
- contrast,
- video update rate (fps),
- network latency,
- jitter,
- noise,
- packet loss,
- display resolution,
- size of the display and
- distance of the display from operator.

The aim of outweighing these factors is to deliver best possible user experience and the required detection and recognition range performance by using today's video technology [1]. Increasing the performance of one parameter does not necessarily increase the overall performance of the entire RTOS. The ideal output is often achieved by wisely orchestrating multiple parameters. More specifically, it does not help to rely solely on high resolution (pixel per degree) to increase detection performance, when other parameters like light sensitivity or video compression rate do not promote the higher resolution. Typical parameters to be taken into consideration are described in the following sub chapters.

1) Sensor Size and Light Sensitivity

4K cameras have four times more pixels than HD cameras, but often still the same sensor size because the size of the sensor is limited by the housing size of the cameras. This results in the fact that a 4K pixel has only ¼ of the area of an HD pixel at the sensor (Figure 1). The detection capability of very small details is highly dependent on the number of photons of this detail, which are reaching the sensor (Figure 2).

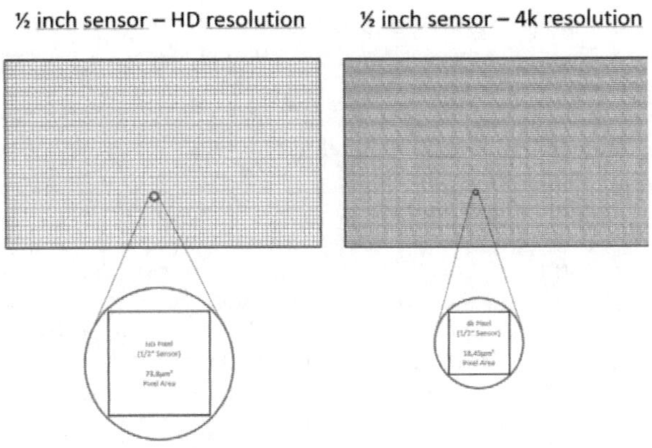

Figure 1. Pixel Sizes of HD vs. 4K Sensors.

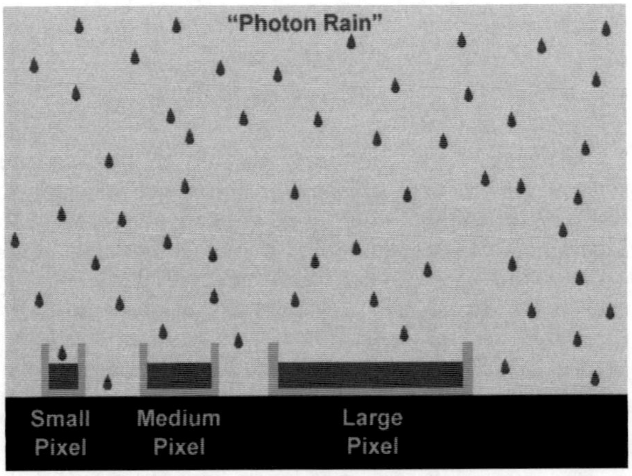

Figure 2. Photon Rain on different Pixel Sizes.

A larger pixel size guarantees a collection of a larger number of photons, which increases the visibility of the specific detail/object. Therefore, the following general rule to detect small details apply: The larger the pixel size, the higher the visibility/detection rate. However, technologies evolve over the time and from sensor generation to sensor generation the 4K sensor size increased from 1/2 to 4/3 inches and further the number of photons needed to detect an object/detail could be lowered.

This means that newer 4K sensor generations need fewer photons to detect an object than older sensor generation and so reaches similar light intensity as the current HD cameras, but with a four times higher resolution (by the same FoV).

2) Bandwidth and Processing Resources

Due to the circumstance that 4K resolution contains four times the amount of pixels HD resolution does, using 4K technology in an environment that requires video processing would result in the fourfold demand of processing power of the video processing infrastructure, and thus also in the fourfold amount of bandwidth required for transmitting the video data from the camera at the airport to the Remote Tower center. Today the power needed to process and encode large 4K video streams is provided on System-on-Chip (SoC) processors, which can cope with this large bitrate demand, but only up to a certain performance limit, to avoid the overheating of the processor inside the camera. Such powerful 4K-generation processors with an extended processing power are relative cheap nowadays, which results into the fact, that the same powerful processors are used in modern HD cameras too. Hence, in practice the same maximum processing performance is facilitated in HD and 4K cameras, resulting in a very similar performance referring to maximum bitrate and bandwidth consumption. But the 4K delivers four times more pixels, thus the bit per pixel rate of the 4K camera is usually lower. As a consequence, given the same pixel per degree resolution in between of 4K and HD videos (4K in contrast to HD with fourfold FoV), the quality of the 4K video is poorer than the quality of the HD video – it contains more artefacts, which makes it more difficult to detect specific objects (e.g., aircraft) in the 4K image compared to the HD image (see Figure 3).

However, in practice this effect will usually be compensated by adapting the FoV of the 4K camera to gain more pixel per degree (= higher angular resolution) to exploit the advantage of having the fourfold number of pixels.

3) High Dynamic Range

Current industry standards use High Dynamic Range (HDR) to improve the detection of moving objects, both in the sky and on the ground. HDR combines overexposed, ideally exposed, and underexposed images into one resulting image. While underexpose images are well suited to detect objects in the sky, overexposed images are better suited to detect objects on the ground. Combining these images into one provides an ideal basis for object detection. Until recently, HDR was a feature, which was only supported by HD cameras, but by today is also common standard for 4K cameras.

B. Performance Criteria

1) Detection and Recognition Range Performance

The operator using an RTOS typically is an Air Traffic Control Officer (ATCO) or an Aerodrome Flight Information Service Officer (AFISO) who provides ATS to the airspace and aerodrome user (usually pilots). ATCOs/AFISOs aim for preventing collisions, organizing and expediting the flow of air traffic either by granting instructions and clearances or only by traffic information. For that purpose, on their video screens they have to have the traffic in sight in terms of detection and recognition of aircraft arriving and departing from the airport, in order to monitor landings and take-offs, as these are the most safety critical flight phases. So, the required

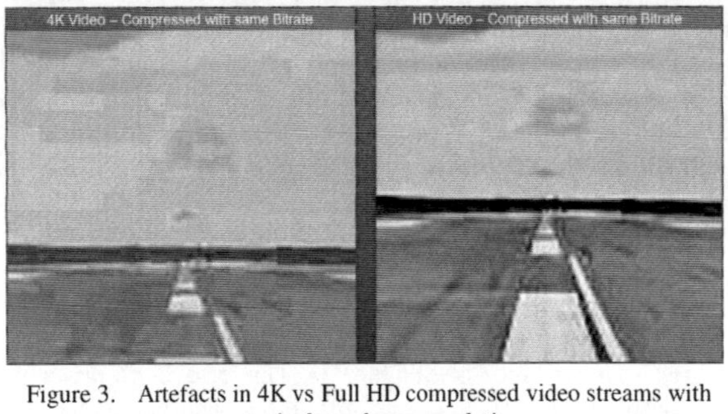

Figure 3. Artefacts in 4K vs Full HD compressed video streams with same pixel per degree resolution.

performance of the camera(s), which is the crucial part of the overall RTOS, is mainly driven by *what* (w.r.t. the object size) and *where* (w.r.t. the distance) the operator has to be able to "see" something to provide the required ATS [1]. Such operational requirements are aerodrome and use case specific and are further split into *detection* and *recognition* range performance requirements. The terms are seen in the sense of Johnson's definition [2], who distinguished in between of "an object is discernible by the operator" (detection) and "main features of the object can be determined, sufficient to discern its object class" (recognition). Both constructs are crucial elements of an RTOS and mainly drives its performance requirements.

Reuschling et al. [3] investigated detection and recognition range performances by comparing infrared and visual spectrum cameras in an RTOS context. Also Jakobi & Hagl [4] applied the EUROCAE [1] strategy to evaluate detection and recognition range performances in relation to different video update rates but so far, the detection and recognition range performances related to 4K sensors compared to HD sensors has not been investigated systematically in an RTOS context.

2) Quality of video streams

Another parameter to decide about the performance of an RTOS performance is the quality of the video stream. There are subjective and objective assessments methods, but it has been shown that objective quality assessments, such as Peak Signal-to-Noise Ratio (PSNR), correlate poorly with subjective ratings [5]. However, since a subjectively perceived quality of the video is the method of choice to get high operational acceptance and values from the operators, a subjective assessment seems to be more informative. If the operator is not convinced of the system quality, errors can emerge by expressed mistrust in the system. Confidence in a system plays a mediator role in the system reliability [6]. Particularly, flickering and low-resolution streams were barely accepted in past research [4] [7] [8]. Furthermore, video quality parameter like noise, color appearance, and sharp or blurry edges and textures play a role in perceived video quality.

C. Research Question and Hypothesis

The introduction showed which HD and 4K technologies can be found today, and what advantages, disadvantages, opportunities, risks and limitations exist. In a nutshell, today 4K sensor technologies almost equal levels of light intensity of the HD technology in the range of 0.05 for color images and 0.01 lux for black-and-white images with an aperture of 1.5. Furthermore, the latest 4K camera models also support HDR. 4K cameras delivers four times more pixels than a Full HD sensor, so the FoV of a 4K camera is four times larger with the same pixel/degree resolution or vice versa, with the same FoV the horizontal x vertical resolution is four times larger than a Full HD camera (or a combination of both parameters). However, standard 4K images are usually compressed heavier by the internal camera processing, in the sense of lower bit per pixel rates, which then in turn leads to poorer image quality (see Figure 3). This effect can probably be compensated by a higher pixel per degree resolution. Common RTOS 4K camera settings work with a combination of slightly higher FoV and a slightly higher pixel per degree resolution to compensate the poorer pixel quality of 4K compared to HD cameras to bring the detection range in 4K footage to a similar or (preferably) to a slightly higher level compared to the HD footage.

One can therefore postulate that with such typical configurations the same detection and recognition performance are to be gained and further, very similar operator assessments of the video quality are to be expected in between of 4K and HD technology. The substantive hypotheses are therefore formulated as follows:

$H_{0,1}$: There are no differences between HD and 4K cameras in terms of their detection range performance.

$H_{0,2}$: There are no differences between HD and 4K cameras in terms of their recognition range performance.

$H_{0,3}$: There are no differences between HD and 4K cameras in terms of their perceived video quality.

II. METHOD

A. Participants

Overall goal of this study was the comparison of HD versus 4K camera technology in the operational context of ATS provided by ATCOs or AFISOs using an RTOS. Since detection and recognition of traffic is not only a mere perception test but also highly affected by the operator's expertise and situation awareness, operator experts, being ATCOs and AFISOs, had to be selected as test subjects for the experiment. They were recruited directly from airports and air navigation service providers asking if anyone would be interested in taking part in such an experiment.

In total 23, two female and 14 male ATCOs between the ages of 22 and 60 years (M = 36.14, SD = 11.73) as well as 7 male AFISOs between 27 and 66 years (M = 46.67, SD = 15.03), all of German nationalities, participated in the experiment. 1 male ATCO was excluded from the data analysis, as the experiment failed mid-way by technical reasons, resulting in 22 valid participants in the end.

The ATCOs participated voluntarily and they were compensated for their travel and accommodation expenses and their working hours. The study was performed in accordance with the General Data Protection Regulation (EU) 2016/679.

B. Design and Material

1) Camera Specs

The different cameras should prove themselves in different operational areas of interest, different visibility conditions and with different aircraft (object) sizes. Three different network cameras were selected:

- AXIS Q1647-LE (called: "HD"),
- AXIS Q1798-LE (called: "4K-1")
- Sony SNC-VB770 (called: "4K-2")

The first two AXIS cameras are commercial off-the-shelf cameras and very representative, because they are used by the Remote Tower supplier industry for today's RTOS installations. Both are from the same manufacture (AXIS) and therefore will serve as well-suited candidates for this study.

The Sony 4K-2 is an older 4K type from the year 2016, which was chosen to see how much 4K camera technology has progressed over the past seven years. All cameras have been configured by engineers of the supplier industry in the best possible way as they would be used as one of several fixed composite cameras to gain a single panoramic image, usually 360°, in an operational implementation. Depending on the operationally required vertical FoV and the required pixel/degree resolution, the cameras are positioned vertical or horizontal ranging from usually 7 up to 16 cameras for a 360° panorama. Therefore, the camera types slightly vary in between with respect to the pixel/degree resolution and they also slightly vary with all other specification and configuration, since each camera type is tuned in a way to get a high-quality image and best detection and recognition performance out of it. TABLE I. shows the main technical specifications and settings of the three used cameras HD, 4K-1 and 4K-2.

2) *Camera Set up & Selection and Processing of Video Material*

The three cameras were set up at the research airport Braunschweig-Wolfsburg (EDVE) on the roof of a building at the German Aerospace Center (DLR) campus, very close to and in similar height like the operational Tower cabin (Figure 4). They were attached to an aluminum extruded profile for easy parallel alignment. The cameras were powered and networked using Power over Ethernet (PoE). The origin out-of-the-camera video streams were relayed to and recorded on a Linux-based file server.

TABLE I. TECHNICAL SPECIFICATIONS AND CONFIGURATIONS OF THE THREE CAMERAS "HD", "4K-1", AND "4K-2"

	HD	4K-1	4K-2
Lens	F1.4	F1.7	F1.4
HDR	yes	yes	yes
Image sensor size	1/2 inch (12,7 mm)	4/3 inches (33,9 mm)	$1\,^3/_8$ inches (35 mm full frame)
FoV [p]	1920 x 1080 Full HD	3840 x 2160 UHD	3840 x 2160 UHD
FoV [°]	43° x 24°	60° x 33°	54° x 32°
Resolution in pixel per degree [ppdeg]	45	65	68
Total number of pixels	2,073,600	8,294,400	8,294,401
Target frame rate (fps)	30	30	30
Total number of pixels per second (pps)	62,208,000	248,832,000	248,832,001
Video compression	H.264 High	H.264 High	H.264 High
Max bitrate [Mbit/s]	50	50	32
Average max bit per 1000 pix per camera	804	201	129

Figure 4. Camera mounting.

Two different viewing conditions (areas of interest) were decided for: one facing east to capture the Instrumental Flight Rules (IFR) traffic approaching and landing on runway (RWY) 26 via its Instrument Landing System (ILS) approach and the second one facing north to capture incoming Visual Flight Rule (VFR) traffic, entering the ATC control zone (CTR) via the mandatory reporting points NOVEMBER 1 and 2. To ensure consistency among the aircraft sizes, the same type of aircraft was chosen within each camera position. For the east facing position, a medium sized aircraft Dornier 328, and for the north view small sized aircraft like a Diamond Aircraft DA40 and a Piper PA-28 became the matter of choice. Seven different weather and visibility conditions for the camera facing east (see Figure 5 to Figure 11 (METAR of the selected time in brackets)) were decided for.

Figure 5. **Opposite Sun** (23th April 2023 METAR EDVE 110550Z 25009KT 9999 VCSH SCT024 OVC037 07/04 Q1008=).

Figure 6. **Rain** (20th April 2023 METAR EDVE 200550Z 08006KT 050V110 9999 -RA SCT008 BKN010 OVC034 05/04 Q1020=).

Figure 7. **Dusk** (28th April 2023 METAR EDVE 281850Z 12005KT 8000 BKN028 11/10 Q1010=).

Figure 8. **CAVOK with Clouds** (27th April 2023 METAR EDVE 271550Z VRB03KT CAVOK 12/M04 Q1020=).

Figure 9. **Significant Clouds** (2nd May 2023 METAR EDVE 020550Z 28008KT 9000 SCT010 OVC012 10/08 Q1018=).

Figure 10. **Low Visibility** (2nd May 2023 METAR EDVE 020620Z 30008KT 5000 -DZ BKN005 BKN007 OVC014 10/09 Q1019=).

Figure 11. **Blue Sky** (3rd May 2023 METAR EDVE 030550Z VRB01KT 9999 BKN035 04/02 Q1029=).

For the camera position facing North opposite sun is not relevant. Also, low visibility and dusk does not play a role because the incoming traffic being VFR traffic, which is exclusively flying under visual meteorological conditions (VMC), which excludes low visibility and dusk conditions. Therefore, only three different visibility conditions for the camera facing north were decided for (see Figure 12 to Figure 14 (METAR of the selected time in brackets)).

For both camera positions, recordings were gathered over a period of six weeks lasting from April until June 2023. Afterwards with the support of historical METAR data [9] the desired visibility conditions were scanned and watched for suitable traffic and selected when appropriate.

Figure 12. **Sun-yes_clouds-no** (13th May 2023 METAR EDVE 130950Z 11012KT CAVOK 19/05 Q1021=).

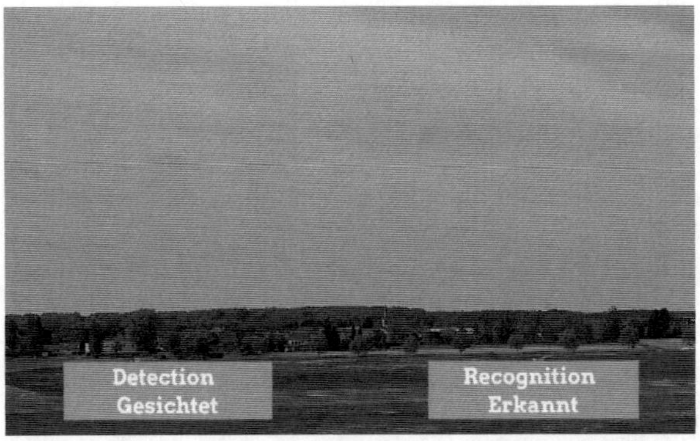

Figure 13. **Sun-yes_clouds-yes** (18th May 2023 METAR EDVE 181450Z 09003KT 020V180 CAVOK 15/02 Q1027=).

Figure 14. **Sun-no_clouds-yes** (22nd May 2023 METAR EDVE 221520Z 10008KT 070V130 CAVOK 25/13 Q1012=).

Multiplying the number of cameras with the number of visibility conditions for each camera position sums up to a total of 3 x 7 (east) + 3 x 3 (north) = 30 video streams. Each file was watched individually by the experimenter to capture the exact moment when the first pixel of the aircraft appeared in the video in order to set objectively the earliest time, when something can be detected phenomenologically. When assessed these time stamps, the distances from the camera to the aircraft's position at this time stamp was calculated. For this purpose, datasets from the OpenSky Network [10] for the medium sized aircraft and with surveillance data delivered by the DLR owned local ADS-B/MLAT/FLAM Jetvison surveillance system [11] in combination with Google Earth for the small sized aircraft were retrieved. For calculating the distances for aircraft, formulae like the Pythagorean theorem [12] were applied in which the very small effect of the curvature of the earth was neglected to keep it simple. Also, the altitude of the building (21m), where the cameras were located on, was discarded for the distance calculation for the small aircraft due to neglectable accuracy gains.

Besides the video material, corresponding audio files with ambient aerodrome sound and with all relevant pilot/ATCO radio communication were retrieved from the long-time recordings. Finally, the video files were cut and merged with the corresponding audio files.

As the used 4K camera settings had a greater FoV compared to the HD camera (see TABLE I. , the 4K FoV presentation would need a bigger screen, when using a pixel per pixel presentation. In order to present the 4K and HD video streams on the same screen in full screen mode, the 4K videos were cropped to align them to the same size as the HD videos, yet maintaining the quality and pixel per pixel presentation.

To process the video material, FFmpeg multimedia framework [13] was used to cut the videos and merge them with the corresponding audio files. Also, for cropping the merged 4K files, the FFmpeg bitstream filter was the matter of choice. Furthermore, Audacity [14] and the Python module MoviePy [15] were applied to cut and merge the audio files.

3) Experimental set up

The experiment was set up via PsychoPy [16] and split into two parts. Part one assessed the test subjects' detection and recognition range performance, part two assessed the perceived video quality. In total the test subjects watched 3 x 7 + 3 x 3 = 30 video streams, whereas the order was randomized. All videos and corresponding audio files are presented pixel-true (pixel-per-pixel) in landscape orientation with Full-HD resolution size of 1920 x 1080 pixels on a 27-inch display with Quad HD (QHD) resolution of 2560 × 1440 pixel (see Figure 15). Via headset the test person could hear the ambient sound and the radio communication between ATCO and pilot.

They were instructed to click the "detection" button via mouse, when the aircraft was spotted, and secondly, on the "recognition" button, when the object was recognized as a medium or small aircraft. When they clicked by mistake, they could click again because only the last click was considered for later analysis. In order to avoid learning effects for the test subjects, the video's starting point of the scene was slightly different in every video.

After having the aircraft detected and recognized, the test subject was requested to judge about the general perceived video quality on a Likert scale ranging from 1 to 5. At last, the test subjects should rate the legibility of a lettering sign situated in a distance of 240 m, again on a Likert scale ranging from 1 to 5. Afterwards, they could click "next" and move on to the next video stream.

With part two of the experiment, the test subject moved to a 43-inch display with a 3840 × 2160 (4K UHD) resolution. On this display video streams of all three cameras (HD, 4K-1 and 4K-2) were presented simultaneously and pixel-true, and the test subject was instructed to compare the videos against each other with respect to five different video quality parameters in the sense of:

- **Motion**: Movements smooth vs. flickering
- **Noise**: noise vs. noise-free
- **Color**: colors bleeding vs. natural
- **Edges**: blurring vs. sharp
- **Textures**: blurring vs. sharp.

Sliders from minimum to maximum without any value scaling were used. When all five parameters for each of the three cameras had been rated (5 x 3 = 15 in total), the test person could go on to the next three-way comparison out of a total of 7 + 3 = 10 aircraft approach scenarios (see Figure 16).

Figure 15. Test Subject conducting the detection and recognition task.

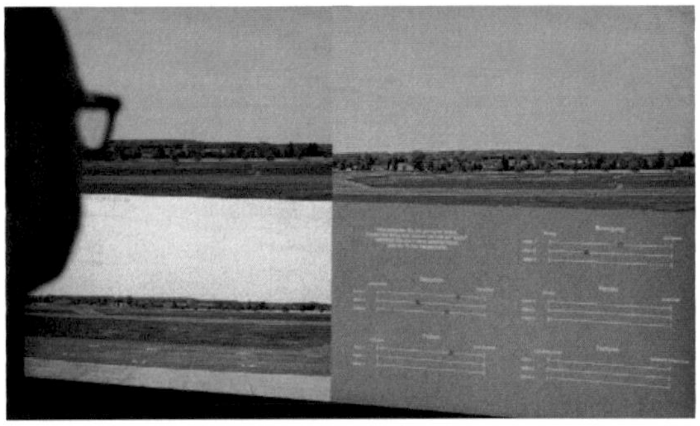

Figure 16. Test Subject conducting the perceived video quality evaluation task comparing three video streams out of the three cameras.

4) Planned Statistical Tests

As the test subjects should undergo all test conditions, a two-way repeated measures ANOVA were planned to conduct for both the detection and the recognition rate performance. Where sphericity is not met, the Greenhouse-Geisser adjustment will be performed. Following the recommendation of Bakeman [17], the effect size will be reported as the generalized eta squared (η^2_G) [18]. Post-tests were planned to determine the differences between the cameras, should they prove to be significant. For each video quality parameter, a pairwise comparison of the cameras was foreseen to conducted. This should be done via a paired-samples t-test. Should the data not meet the necessary assumptions for ANOVAs and t-tests, nonparametric solutions were intended to be used. Values are to be treated as outliers when they are above quartile Q2 + 1.5*IQR or below Q1 – 1.5*IQR.

III. Results

A. Detection Range Performance

For the RWY26 approaches (cameras facing east) the test subjects watched video streams from seven different weather/visibility conditions each with three different camera recordings, in total 21 in a randomized sequence, and decided about the detection time, when the DO328 aircraft was spotted. Figure 17 depicts the detection range performance distances in a graphical bar chart diagram. Distances are in

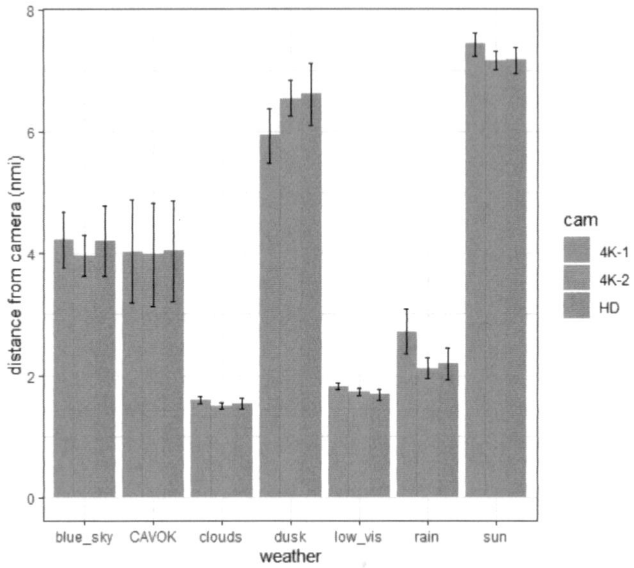

Figure 17. RWY26 Detection Range Performance - bar chart statistics for distances [nmi] via "Cam" and "Weather" condition.

nautical miles (nmi) from the sensor lens to the aircraft. Standard deviations are shown as error bars.

To prove for significant differences, a 3 x 7 two-way repeated measures ANOVA with the two Independent Variables (IV) "Cam" (3 cameras) and "Weather" (7 different visibility conditions) and the Dependent Variable (DV) "distance" revealed a significant result for IV "Weather" but not for IV "Cam" as it was postulated by hypothesis $H_{0,1}$. However, the main factor effects are hard to interpret since also the Cam*Weather interaction became significant (TABLE II.).

In average, over the different weather/visibility condition the cameras do not differ with respect to the detection range performance. However, there are significant differences between the cameras for each single weather/visibility condition. TABLE III. shows the post-hoc tests differences and their significance values: Within the IV "Weather" categories "Opposite-Sun", "Rain", "Dusk", "Significant Clouds" and "Low Visibility" the detection range performances differ significantly between the cameras. The 4K-1 is significantly worse in "Dusk" and significantly better in "Opposite-Sun", "Rain", "Significant Clouds" and "Low Visibility". Within "CAVOK with Clouds" and "Blue Sky" there are no significant differences.

TABLE II. 3 X 7 TWO-WAY REPEATED MEASURES ANOVA FOR DETECTION DISTANCES (DF = DEGREES OF FREEDOM, F = F-VALUE, P = ERROR PROBABILITY, *** HIGHLY SIGNIFICANT; D= DIFFERENCE; η^2_G = EFFECT SIZE ETA SQUARE)

	df n	df d	F	p		η^2_G
Cam	2.00	14.00	2.017	0.170		0.027
Weather	1.57	10.97	489.115	0.000	***	0.965
Cam*Weather	12.00	84.00	6.434	0.000	***	0.208

TABLE III. PAIRWISE T-TEST COMPARISON OF THE CAMERAS FOR DETECTION DISTANCES WITH BONFERRONI ADJUSTMENT (T = T-VALUE; *** EXTREMELY SIGNIFICANT; ** HIGHLY SIGNIFICANT; * SIGNIFICANT; D= DIFFERENCE (NMI); CI = CONFIDENCE INTERVALL)

Group 1	Group 2	n1	n2	t	df	p	p-adjusted		D	95% CI
Sun										
4K-2	HD	12	12	0.0389	11	0.970	1.000		0.002	[-0.102, 0.106]
4K-2	4K-1	12	12	-4.4417	11	0.001	0.003	**	-0.292	[-0.437, -0.147]
HD	4K-1	12	12	-4.7897	11	0.001	0.002	**	-0.294	[-0.429, -0.159]
Rain										
4K-2	HD	17	17	-1.1857	16	0.253	0.759		-0.073	[-0.204, 0.058]
4K-2	4K-1	17	17	-8.0395	16	0.000	0.000	***	-0.605	[-0.764, -0.445]
HD	4K-1	17	17	-6.8933	16	0.000	0.000	***	-0.532	[-0.695, -0.368]
Dusk										
4K-2	HD	15	15	0.0283	14	0.978	1.000		0.003	[-0.222, 0.228]
4K-2	4K-1	15	15	5.6031	14	0.000	0.000	***	0.642	[0.396, 0.888]
HD	4K-1	15	15	4.5887	14	0.000	0.001	**	0.639	[0.340, 0.938]
CAVOK										
4K-2	HD	16	16	-0.0650	15	0.949	1.000		-0.018	[-0.610, 0.574]
4K-2	4K-1	16	16	-0.0314	15	0.975	1.000		-0.008	[-0.562, 0.546]
HD	4K-1	16	16	0.0394	15	0.969	1.000		0.010	[-0.524, 0.544]
Clouds										
4K-2	HD	16	16	-2.0835	15	0.055	0.164		-0.040	[-0.080, 0.001]
4K-2	4K-1	16	16	-7.0150	15	0.000	0.000	***	-0.104	[-0.135, -0.072]
HD	4K-1	16	16	-3.1882	15	0.006	0.019	*	-0.064	[-0.107, -0.021]
Low Visibility										
4K-2	HD	17	17	2.5877	16	0.020	0.059		0.045	[0.008, 0.082]
4K-2	4K-1	17	17	-5.0577	16	0.000	0.000	***	-0.093	[-0.132, -0.054]
HD	4K-1	17	17	-7.2145	16	0.000	0.000	***	-0.138	[-0.179, -0.098]
Blue Sky										
4K-2	HD	13	13	-1.5676	12	0.143	0.429		-0.243	[-0.580, 0.095]
4K-2	4K-1	13	13	-2.1447	12	0.053	0.159		-0.290	[-0.585, 0.005]
HD	4K-1	13	13	-0.1946	12	0.849	1.000		-0.047	[-0.579, 0.484]

The small aircraft approaching via mandatory reporting point November 1 and 2 (camera facing north) were usually spotted in 2-3 nmi (TABLE IV.), but since the aircraft made a turn downwind at N2 flying west the distances increased again out of physical recognition range. Figure 18 shows the approach path of a small VFR aircraft incoming from the North (cyan line). The red line (from camera to the church of the village in the north of the airport) served as orientation line to match times in the video and Google Earth. Further, a calculated line in yellow, with respect to the first pixel appearance, is shown.

TABLE IV. shows the objectively measured detection distances, when the first pixel appeared. Differences are not significant, so do not vary over "Cam" or "Weather". TABLE V. shows a pie chart matrix for the subjective detection performance, in which grey symbolizes "detected", white symbolizes "not detected".

There are no main differences in between of the cameras, just the visibility conditions show severe differences. The small aircraft was hardly detected in blue sky (Sun-yes / Clouds-no) but therefore almost every time detected in cloudy conditions with shaded sun (Sun-no / Clouds-yes). For each of the three visibility conditions, a Cochran's Q test was conducted to detect possible camera differences within a certain visibility condition. Only the test for one of the three conditions (Sun-yes / Clouds-yes) revealed a significant camera difference, $Q(2) = 11.46$, $p = 0.003$. Descriptively, detection rates were highest for the 4K-2 camera.

B. Recognition Range Performance

Figure 19 depicts the recognition range performance distances in a graphical bar chart diagram for RWY26 approaches (cameras facing east). There are significant differences in between of the "cameras", in between of the "Weather" conditions, but also significant interaction effects, that is, main effects "Cam" and "Weather" cannot be interpreted unambiguously (see TABLE VI.).

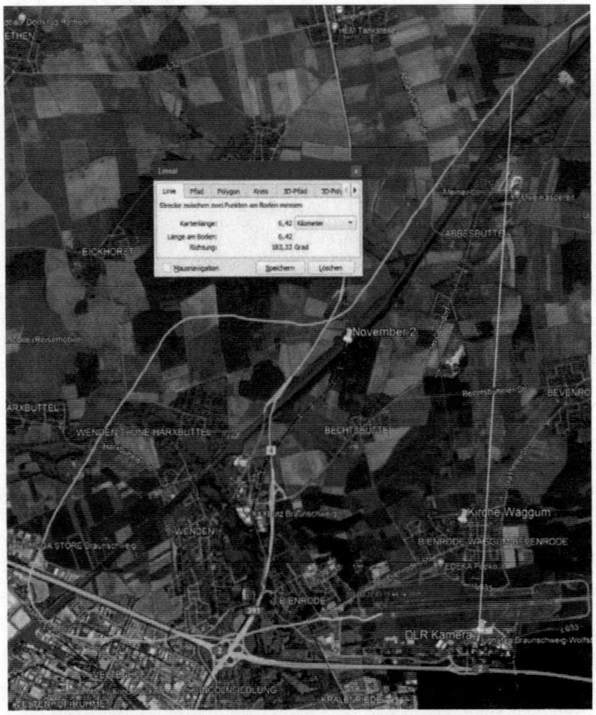

Figure 18. Approach path of small VFR aircraft from the North.

TABLE IV. DISTANCES FIRST PIXEL APPEARANCE FOR SMALL AIRCRAFT APPROACHING FROM THE NORTH

Weather	Cam	nmi
CAVOK Sun-yes_clouds-no	4K-1	2,74
	4K-2	2,18
	HD	1,97
CAVOK Sun-yes_clouds-yes	4K-1	3,33
	4K-2	3,18
	HD	3,66
CAVOK Sun-no_clouds-yes	4K-1	3,37
	4K-2	3,46
	HD	3,39

TABLE V. PIE CHART MATRIX FOR DETECTION PERFORMANCE FOR SMALL AIRCRAFT (GREY = "DETECTED", WHITE = "NOT DETECTED")

		Cameras		
		4K-1	4K-2	HD
Visibility	CAVOK Sun-yes Clouds-no	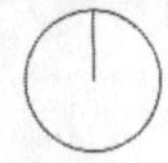		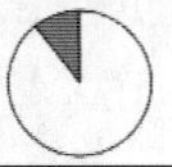
	CAVOK Sun-yes Clouds-yes	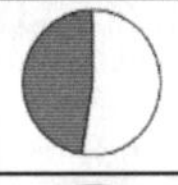	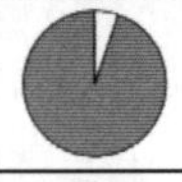	
	CAVOK Sun-no Clouds-yes	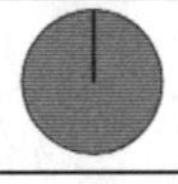		

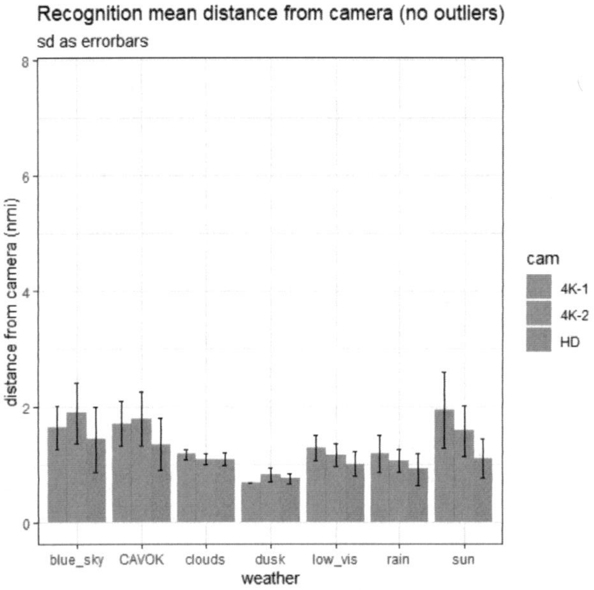

Figure 19. Descriptive bar chart statistics for RWY26 Recognition Range Performance via IV "Cam" and "Weather".

TABLE VI. 3 X 7 TWO-WAY REPEATED MEASURES ANOVA FOR RECOGNITION DISTANCES

	df_n	df_d	F	p		η^2_G
Cam	2	10	12.720	0.002	**	0.136
Weather	6	30	29.801	0.000	***	0.644
Cam*Weather	12	60	5.286	0.000	***	0.224

TABLE VII. shows the post-hoc tests differences and their significance values: Rather identically to the detection results, the 4K-1 is significantly worse in "Dusk", but significantly better in "Opposite-Sun", "Rain", "Significant Clouds" and "Low Visibility", and "CAVOK with Clouds". In "Blue Sky" conditions there are no significant camera differences.

TABLE VII. PAIRWISE T-TEST COMPARISON OF THE CAMERAS FOR RECOGNITION DISTANCES WITH BONFERRONI ADJUSTMENT (T = T-VALUE, D= DIFFERENCE; CI = CONFIDENCE INTERVALL).

	Group 1	Group 2	n1	n2	t	df	p	p-adjusted		D	95% CI
Sun											
	4K-2	HD	16	16	6.0218	15	0.000	0.000	***	0.436	[0.282, 0.580]
	4K-2	4K-1	16	16	-3.9825	15	0.001	0.004	**	-0.397	[-0.609, -0.184]
	HD	4K-1	16	16	-6.3142	15	0.000	0.000	***	-0.833	[-1.110, -0.552]
Rain											
	4K-2	HD	15	15	3.3314	14	0.005	0.015	*	0.211	[0.075, 0.348]
	4K-2	4K-1	15	15	-1.6355	14	0.124	0.372		-0.124	[-0.286, 0.039]
	HD	4K-1	15	15	-5.1496	14	0.000	0.000	***	-0.335	[-0.475, -0.195]
Dusk											
	4K-2	HD	15	15	0.0283	14	0.978	1.000		0.003	[-0.222, 0.228]
	4K-2	4K-1	15	15	5.6031	14	0.000	0.000	***	0.642	[0.396, 0.888]
	HD	4K-1	15	15	4.5887	14	0.000	0.001	**	0.639	[0.340, 0.938]
CAVOK											
	4K-2	HD	15	15	3.7923	14	0.002	0.006	**	0.410	[0.178, 0.643]
	4K-2	4K-1	15	15	0.5594	14	0.585	1.000		0.057	[-0.160, 0.274]
	HD	4K-1	15	15	-3.0866	14	0.008	0.024	*	-0.354	[-0.599, -0.108]
Clouds											
	4K-2	HD	13	13	0.6653	12	0.518	1.000		0.018	[-0.041, 0.077]
	4K-2	4K-1	13	13	-3.8178	12	0.002	0.007	**	-0.094	[-0.148, -0.040]
	HD	4K-1	13	13	-4.1448	12	0.001	0.004	**	-0.112	[-0.171, -0.053]
Low Visibility											
	4K-2	HD	17	17	4.7938	16	0.000	0.001	***	0.149	[0.083,0.215]
	4K-2	4K-1	17	17	-3.8858	16	0.001	0.004	**	-0.119	[-0.184, -0.054]
	HD	4K-1	17	17	-5.8124	16	0.000	0.000	***	-0.268	[-0.366, -0.170]
Blue Sky											
	4K-2	HD	16	16	3.9000	15	0.001	0.004	**	0.482	[0.218, 0.745]
	4K-2	4K-1	16	16	1.7166	15	0.107	0.321		0.194	[-0.047, 0.435]
	HD	4K-1	16	16	-2.3452	15	0.033	0.100		-0.288	[-0.549, -0.026]

The following boxplots descriptively depict all RWY26 detection and recognition distances, one boxplot diagram for each "Weather", seven in total (Figure 20). The dashed lines show the objective detection time, pre-assessed by the experimenter by replaying the video streams back and forth to objectively decide for, when the first pixel truly appeared. Within the boxplots, there are 50% of all values. The whiskers show the latest values which are still within 1.5 * interquartile range (IQR).

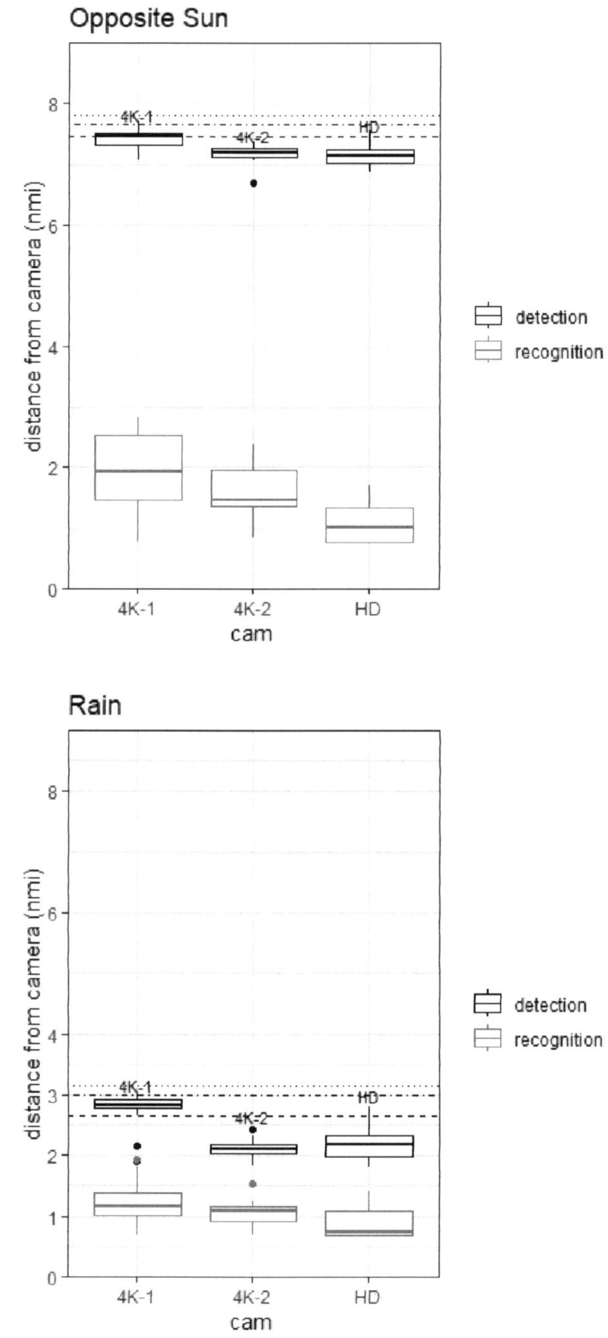

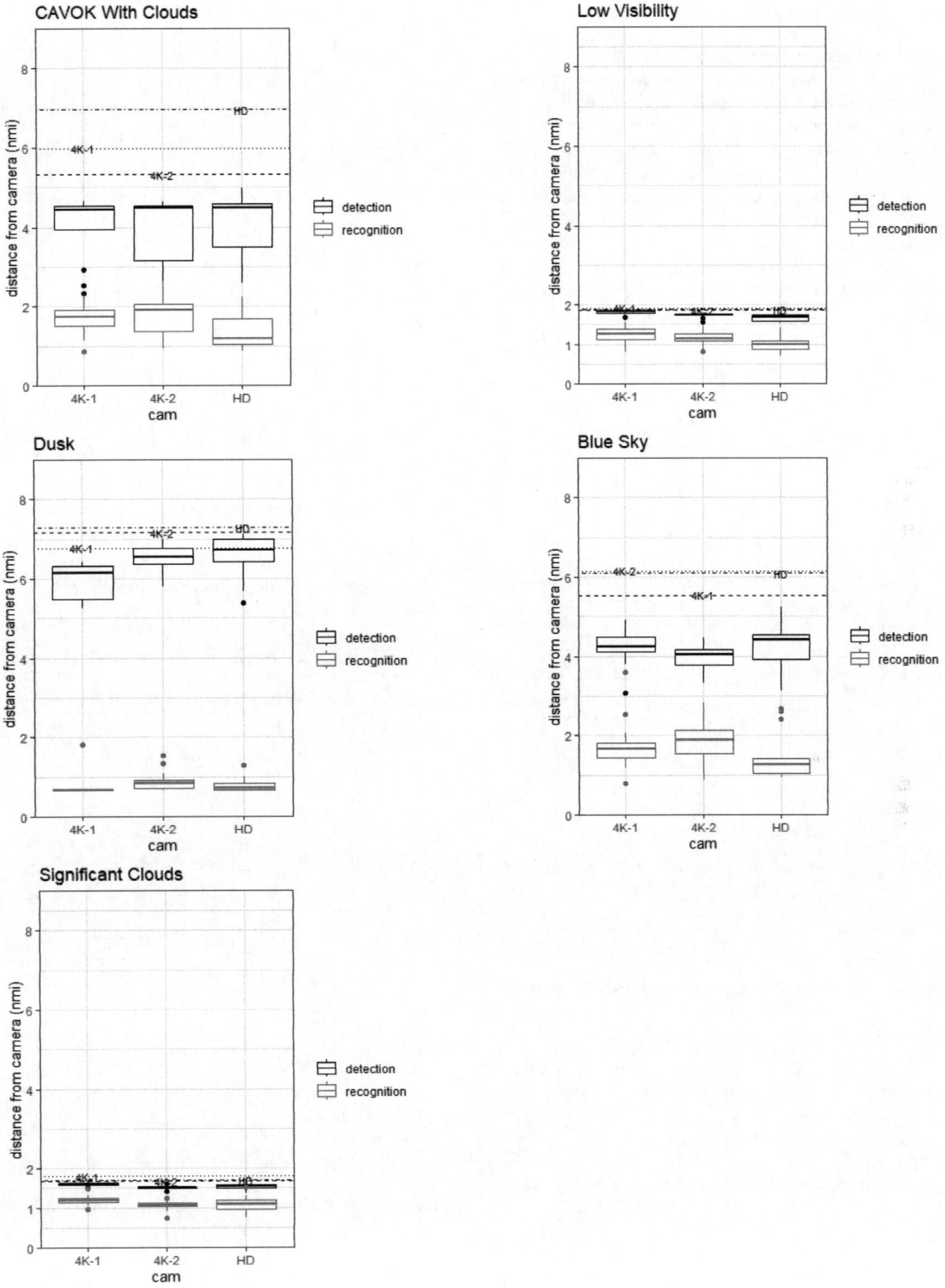

Figure 20. Seven Boxplot diagrams for each of seven different "Weather" conditions showing RWY26 approaches with distances for objective pixel appearance (dashed lines), Detection (black) and Recognition (red) Range Performances w.r.t. each of the three cameras (IV "Cam").

C. *Perceived Video Quality*

1) *Results for each Video Quality Category*

In part two of the experiment, the test subjects were asked to judge the perceived video quality in between of the three simultaneously presented camera video streams via all 10 different weather/visibility conditions (see Figure 16). Their answers were summed up over the "Weather" conditions and the cameras "Cam" compared against each other via the five different video quality categories: "Motion", "Noise", "Color", "Textures", "Edges".

The results are presented descriptively via median boxplots and by inferential static analysis pairwise t-tests. When significant differences were gained, it is marked by stars behind the p-value and in bold letters of the better performing camera (see Figure 21 to Figure 25 and TABLE VIII. to TABLE XIII.).

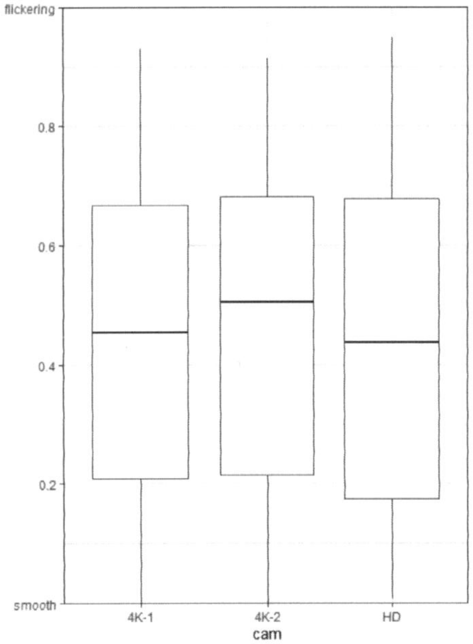

Figure 21. "Motion" - Boxplot diagrams with median and IQRs via three different cameras.

TABLE VIII. PAIRWISE T-TESTS FOR CATEGORY "MOTION"

Group 1	Group 2	n1	n2	t	df	p	p-adjusted		D	95% CI
4K-2	HD	200	200	1.85	199	0.066	0.199		0.025	[-0.002, 0.051]
4K-2	4K-1	200	200	1.44	199	0.152	0.456		0.017	[-0.006, 0.040]
HD	4K-1	200	200	-0.658	199	0.511	1.000		-0.008	[-0.032, 0.016]

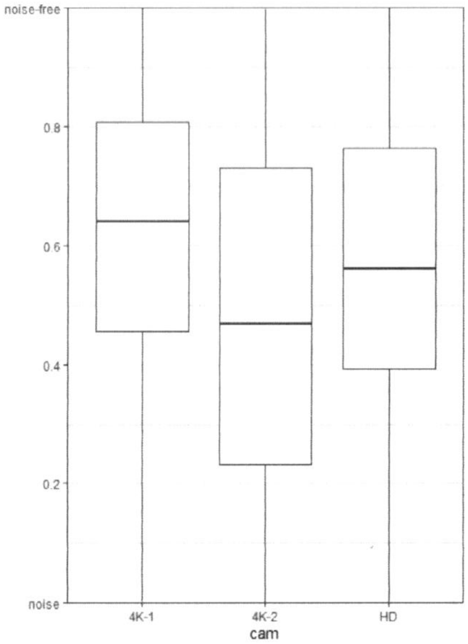

Figure 22. "Noise" - Boxplot diagrams with median and IQRs via three different cameras.

TABLE IX. PAIRWISE T-TESTS FOR CATEGORY "NOISE"

Group 1	Group 2	n1	n2	t	df	p	p-adjusted		D	95% CI
4K-2	**HD**	200	200	-3.03	199	0.003	0.008	**	-0.068	[-0.111, -0.024]
4K-2	**4K-1**	200	200	-5.80	199	0.000	0.000	***	-0.126	[-0.169, -0.083]
HD	**4K-1**	200	200	-2.62	199	0.010	0.028	*	-0.059	[-0.014, -0.103]

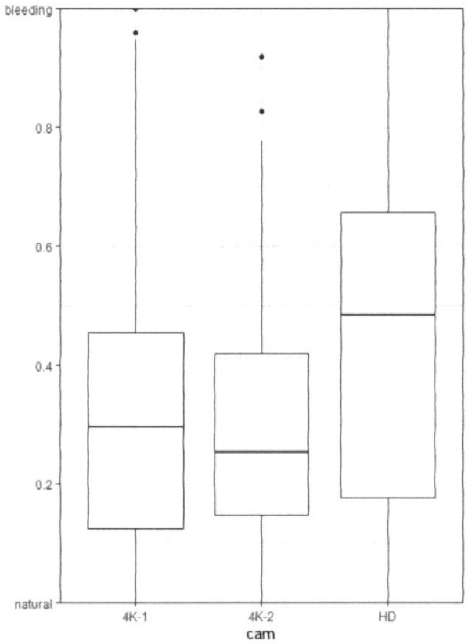

Figure 23. "Color" - Boxplot diagrams with median and IQRs via three different cameras.

TABLE X. PAIRWISE T-TESTS FOR CATEGORY "COLOR"

Group 1	Group 2	n1	n2	t	df	p	p-adjusted		D	95% CI
4K-2	HD	200	200	-6.77	199	0.000	0.000	***	-0.163	[-0.211, -0.116]
4K-2	4K-1	200	200	-1.19	199	0.237	0.711		-0.022	[-0.059, 0.015]
HD	**4K-1**	200	200	5.53	199	0.000	0.000	***	0.141	[0.192, 0.091]

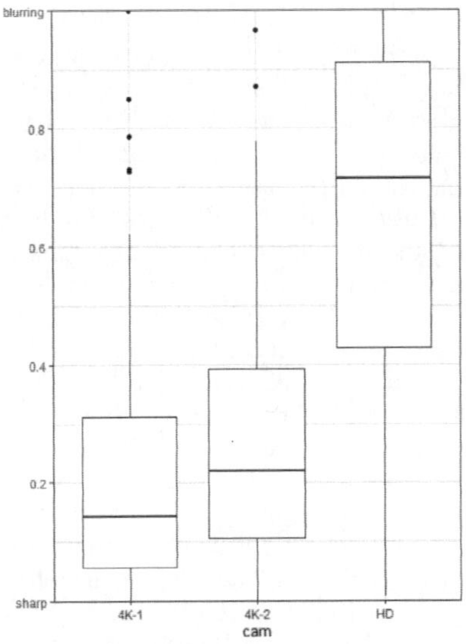

Figure 24. "Edges" - Boxplot diagrams with median and IQRs via three different cameras.

TABLE XI. PAIRWISE T-TESTS FOR CATEGORY "EDGES"

Group 1	Group 2	n1	n2	t	df	p	p-adjusted		D	95% CI
4K-2	HD	200	200	-15.00	199	0.000	0.000	***	-0.388	[-0.439, -0.337]
4K-2	**4K-1**	200	200	3.74	199	0.000	0.001	***	0.058	[0.028, 0.089]
HD	**4K-1**	200	200	16.40	199	0.000	0.000	***	0.446	[0.500, 0.393]

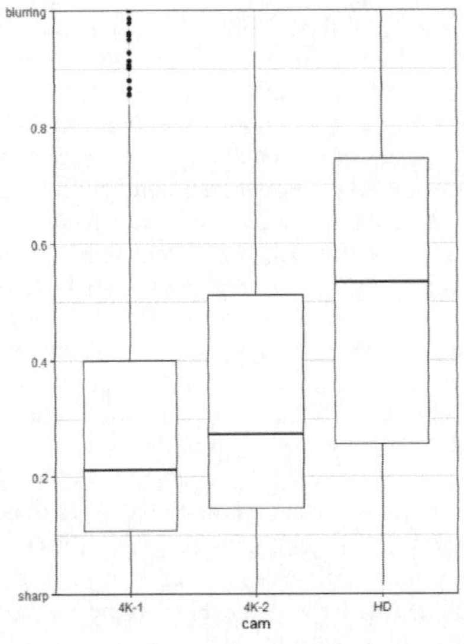

Figure 25. "Textures" - Boxplot diagrams with median and IQRs via three different cameras.

TABLE XII. PAIRWISE T-TESTS FOR CATEGORY "EDGES"

Group 1	Group 2	n1	n2	t	df	p	p-adjusted		D	95% CI
4K-2	HD	200	200	1.92	199	0.056	0.169		0.039	[-0.001, 0.080]
4K-2	**4K-1**	200	200	-6.83	199	0.000	0.000	***	-0.173	[-0.223, -0.123]
HD	**4K-1**	200	200	-7.81	199	0.000	0.000	***	-0.212	[-0.266, -0.159]

2) General Perceived Quality of Video

After watching the 21 videos for the RWY26 approaches, the test subjects were asked to rate their general perceived video quality on each single watched video, without the chance to compare it with simultaneously presented videos. TABLE XIII. shows the pairwise t-tests results and the respective descriptive boxplot diagram is seen in Figure 26 for the ratings on a Likert scale ranging from 1 to 5.

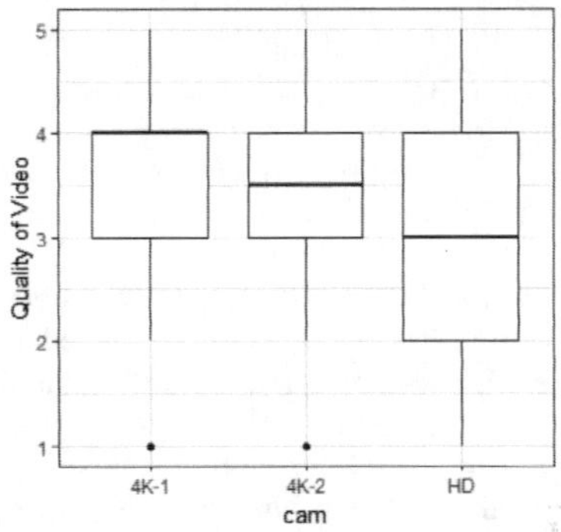

Figure 26. Video Quailty - Boxplot diagrams with median and IQRs showing the ratings for three different cameras via all 10 weather/visibility conditions and all video quality categories.

TABLE XIII. VIDEO QUALITY FOR THREE CAMERAS - PAIRWISE T-TESTS

Group 1	Group 2	n1	n2	t	df	p	p-adjusted		D	95% CI
4K-2	HD	126	126	3.33	125	0.001	0.003	**	0.294	[0.119, 0.468]
4K-2	4K-1	126	126	-2.15	125	0.033	0.100		-0.206	[-0.017, -0.396]
HD	**4K-1**	126	126	-5.10	125	0.000	0.000	***	-0.500	[-0.306, -0.694]

Two of the camera-pairwise comparison became significant, the 4K-1 and the 4K-2 are rated significantly higher than the HD camera.

3) Readability of the Lettering sign

With each of the 3 "Cam" x 7 "Weather" = 21 RWY26 approach videos, the test subjects were asked to judge the readability of sign lettering 240m away from the camera on a 5-point Likert scale. See TABLE XIV. and the respective descriptive boxplot diagram Figure 27.

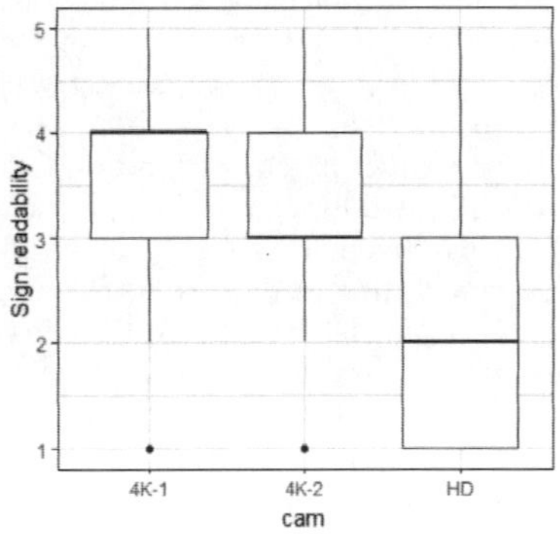

Figure 27. Lettering Sign Readability - Boxplot diagrams with median and IQRs via three different cameras for over all seven RWY26 weather/visibility conditions".

TABLE XIV. PAIRWISE T-TESTS FOR "SIGN READABILITY

Group 1	Group 2	n1	n2	t	df	p	p-adjusted		D	95% CI
4K-2	HD	126	126	18.6	125	0.000	0.000	***	1.440	[1.290, 1.600]
4K-2	4K-1	126	126	-0.36	125	0.723	1.000		-0.040	[0.182, -0.261]
HD	**4K-1**	126	126	-12.0	125	0.000	0.000	***	-1.480	[-1.240, -1.730]

Both 4K cameras are significantly better in readability than the HD camera.

IV. DISCUSSION OF THE RESULTS

The overall goal of the study was to compare the performance of 4K vs. Full HD cameras in an RTOS environment, focusing on detection and recognition range performances, and the subjectively perceived video quality.

With respect to "detection", results did not show a significant effect on the main factor "Cam", but only on the "Weather" factor and on the "Cam x Weather" interaction. Therefore, hypothesis $H_{0,1}$ will not be rejected, saying: "There are no differences between HD and 4K cameras in terms of their detection range performance". However, in dependence on the "Weather" conditions there are significant differences between the cameras, even when the effects are rather small.

For instance, in "Rain" and in "Low Visibility", the 4K-1 is better than the HD camera, but, on the other side, much worse in the "Dusk" condition. The older generation 4K-2 camera often performs in between of the 4K-1 and HD performance. The same result pattern occurred with the detection of small aircraft from the North: There are no significant differences in between of the cameras over all "Weather" conditions.

With respect to "recognition", there too is a significant main effect on "Weather" but also on "Cam" and its interaction, which makes the main effect "Cam" hard to interpret. Therefore, also $H_{0,2}$ cannot be rejected and will be retained, saying: "There are no differences between HD and 4K cameras in terms of their recognition range performance". Again, there are significant differences in between of the cameras under the different "Weather" condition, saying, quite often the 4K-1 shows the better performance but also the HD has its advantages (see TABLE VII.).

Finally, $H_{0,3}$ states that there are no differences between HD and 4K cameras in terms of their perceived video quality. Except for the *Motion* category, where no significant differences could be found, which would not have been expected, since all cameras operated with the same video update rate of 30fps, the 4K cameras always performed significantly better than the HD. The 4K cameras are perceived to be sharper in terms of *textures* and *edges*, with more *color fidelity* and lower *noise*. $H_{0,3}$ is therefore rejected and the alternative hypothesis is to be assumed stating: "4K cameras in this setting deliver a better perceived video quality". This decision is supported by the two further tests in which the test subjects were asked to generally assess the quality of the video, and also to assess the readability of a lettering sign 240m away. In both tests, the 4K cameras performed significantly better than the HD camera.

How can this result pattern be explained and what conclusions can be drawn for future implementations of an RTOS? As postulated in the three hypotheses, based on the technical performance and configurations of 4K and HD cameras used in this study, no tremendous performance differences were assessed, even if the 4K cameras were able to show significant advantages in some situations and with the perceived video quality. On the technical performance level, both (putting the old generation 4K-2 camera aside), the HD and 4K-1 camera, deliver at 50 Mbps max bitrate. By the chosen FoV, the 4K delivers 65 pix/°, the HD only 45 pix/°, saying, the 4K therefore has a higher angular resolution, but possibly loses this advantage again because the 4K has four times more pixels to deliver, which cannot be delivered with the same bit per pixel rate like the HD can do, because, in average, with a maximum bitrate of 50 Mbps, the 4K can process 1000 pixel with 200 bits, the HD instead up to 800 bits per 1000 pixel (see TABLE I.). These contrasting effects of a higher 'angular resolution' and lower 'bits/pix*10^3' rate probably compensate each other and detection and recognition rates are rather similar in between of 4K and HD, with slight advantages for the 4K in this experiment setting (TABLE I).

On the other hand, an RTOS typically delivers a 360° panoramic video stream with multiple cameras arranged in a circle and sums up the horizontal FoV of each camera into an overall 360° panorama. In our setting, with a 4K horizontal FoV of 60°, at least six (better seven cameras including some overlap needed when the streams get stitched to each other), and with the HD FoV of 43° at least nine cameras would be needed for a full 360° panorama video stream. With a maximum data stream of 50Mbps per camera, the nine HD cameras would consume 450Mbps, the 4K panorama just 7 x 50Mbps = 350Mbps. The bandwidth needs for HD panorama would be much higher, and thus the costs. However, both, 450, but also 350Mbps would be much too much and/or expensive for most prevailing infrastructures. The data streams have to be further compressed, down to a typically used maximum of 100Mbps (depending on the prevailing infrastructure and other constraints, often it is even less). To achieve this the HD panorama stream has to be compressed much more than the 4K panorama stream, factor 4.5 compared to 3.5. It cannot be stated directly what comes out of it because this panorama setting has not been tested but one would assume that the performance of the HD will continue to lose out compared to 4K panorama solutions. Furthermore, in this setting, the vertical FoV of the 4K is slightly higher, 33° for 4K and only 24° for the HD panorama, which would be another advantage for the 4K solution.

It is further to be noted that when transmitting more (up to four times more) pixels and if these pixels are to be presented pixel by pixel (pixel-true), more displays or higher resolution displays (typically 4K instead of HD) are needed. Since the pixels become smaller with more pixels presented on the same display size, the controller also has to move closer to the displays in order to resolve the presented pixels with the human eye resolution of approx. 60pix/°. With a 4K 27-inch display for instance, the eye distance from the display must not be greater than 53 cm, which becomes a challenging factor for the design of an RTOS working position.

The bottom line is that 4K is probably the better alternative. Even when the single sensor is slightly more expensive (by about 25%), energy-intensive with a smaller bit/pixel ration, the 4K offers on the positive side a better ratio of FoV and angular resolution, a slightly better detection and recognition performance, and a better perceived video quality. Further on, in a 360° panorama composition fewer cameras are needed, which compensates costs and energy consumption and improves the bit/pixel ratio compared to the HD solution.

V. CONCLUSION & OUTLOOK

In a nutshell, what is the better optical sensor for an RTOS, 4K or HD? Based on the current state of the art technology, there is no 100% clear answer. When comparing *individual* 4K and Full HD cameras, the measured performance differences in this setting were rather marginal. Although this study revealed slight advantages for the 4K camera, the advantages depend very much on the weather/visibility conditions and the camera settings chosen. The selected settings of the individual cameras in this comparison were chosen as they would be used in a 360° RTOS video panorama. In such a 360° composition of several individual cameras it is to be expected that the slight advantages of 4K technology would become even more apparent.

All cameras under investigation in this study facilitated the same codec H.264. More modern codecs like H.265 or AV1 allow higher max bitrates and thus could improve the overall quality of the video streams. On the other hand, the encoding principles of modern codecs tend to eliminate small details. This could even lead to a reduction of the detection performance compared to H.264. The influence of codec and bitrate needs to be investigated in a separate study.

REFERENCES

[1] EUROCAE: ED-240B - Minimum Aviation System Performance Standard for Remote Tower Optical Systems 2023. www.eurocae.net [retrieved: April, 2024].

[2] R. B. Johnson, "Analysis of image forming systems," Warfare Electrical Engineering Department, U.S. Army Research and Development Laboratories (ed.) Intensifier Symposium. AD 220160, pp. 244–273, Ft. Belvoir, Va. 1958.

[3] F. Reuschling, A. Papenfuss, J. Jakobi, T. Rambau, E. Michaelsen, and N. Scherer-Negenborn, "Designing and Evaluating a Fusion of Visible and Infrared Spectrum Video Streams for Remote Tower Operations," Fürstenau, N. (ed.) Virtual and Remote Control Tower. Research Topics in Aerospace, pp. 445–487. Springer International Publishing, Cham 2022.

[4] J. Jakobi and M. Hagl, "Which Minimum Video Frame Rate is Needed in a Remote Tower Optical System?," Fürstenau, N. (ed.) Virtual and Remote Control Tower. Research Topics in Aerospace, pp. 405–426. Springer International Publishing, Cham 2022.

[5] Q. Huynh-Thu and M. Ghanbari, "The accuracy of PSNR in predicting video quality for different video scenes and frame rates," Telecommun Syst 2012. https://doi.org/10.1007/s11235-010-9351-x

[6] J. D. Lee and K. A. See, "Trust in automation: designing for appropriate reliance," Human factors 2004. https://doi.org/10.1518/hfes.46.1.50_30392

[7] J. D. McCarthy, M. A. Sasse, and D. Miras, "Sharp or smooth?,"Dykstra-Erickson, E., Tscheligi, M. (eds.) Proceedings of the SIGCHI Conference on Human Factors in Computing Systems. CHI04: CHI 2004, Vienna Austria, 24 04 2004 29 04 2004, pp. 535–542. ACM, New York, NY, USA 2004. https://doi.org/10.1145/985692.985760

[8] K. T. Claypool and M. Claypool, "On frame rate and player performance in first person shooter games, " Multimedia Systems 2007. https://doi.org/10.1007/s00530-007-0081-1

[9] M. Pietras-Szewczyk and L. Szewczyk, "Streamlining of Obtaining and Processing Data from Ogimet Service Using Python Language Script." GaEE 2019. https://doi.org/10.7494/geom.2019.13.1.51

[10] M. Schafer, M. Strohmeier, V. Lenders, I. Martinovic, and M. Wilhelm, "Bringing up OpenSky: A large-scale ADS-B sensor network for research," IPSN-14 Proceedings of the 13th International Symposium on Information Processing in Sensor Networks. 2014 13th ACM/IEEE IPSN, Berlin, Germany, 15.04.2014 - 17.04.2014, pp. 83–94. IEEE 2014. https://doi.org/10.1109/IPSN.2014.6846743

[11] jetvision® is a brand of the Günter Köllner Embedded Development GmbH, 2010. https://jetvision.de

[12] R. P. Agarwal, "Pythagorean Triples before and after Pythagoras," Computation 2020. https://doi.org/10.3390/computation8030062

[13] FFMPEG: multimedia framework, 2023. https://ffmpeg.org/

[14] Muse Group & contributors: Audacity 2014. https://www.mu.se/audacity

[15] Zulko: MoviePy. Python 2017. https://pypi.org/project/moviepy/

[16] J. Peirce et al., "PsychoPy2: Experiments in behavior made easy," Behavior research methods 2019. https://doi.org/10.3758/s13428-018-01193-y

[17] R. Bakeman, "Recommended effect size statistics for repeated measures designs," Behavior research methods 2005. https://doi.org/10.3758/BF03192707

[18] S. Olejnik and J. Algina, "Generalized eta and omega squared statistics: measures of effect size for some common research designs," Psychological methods 2003. https://doi.org/10.1037/1082-989X.8.4.434

Human-Machine Interface for Real-Time Interaction Focused on LiDAR SLAM Feature Extraction

Natalia Prieto-Fernández
Department of Electric, Systems and Automatics Engineering
Universidad de León
León, Spain
email: nprif@unileon.es

Sergio Fernández-Blanco
Universidad de León
León, Spain
email: sfernb03@estudiantes.unileon.es

Álvaro Fernández-Blanco
Universidad Carlos III de Madrid
Madrid, Spain
email: 100505928@alumnos.uc3m.es

José Alberto Benítez-Andrades
Department of Electric, Systems and Automatics Engineering
Universidad de León
León, Spain
email: jbena@unileon.es

Francisco Carro-De-Lorenzo
TRESCA Ingeniería S.A.
León, Spain
email: fcarro@tresca.es

Carmen Benavides
Department of Electric, Systems and Automatics Engineering
Universidad de León
León, Spain
email: carmen.benavides@unileon.es

***Abstract*—The development of Human-Machine Interfaces (HMIs) capable of visualising real-time processed data from robotic systems is of essential importance today. These graphical user interfaces play a crucial role in the smooth and efficient interaction between humans and robots, resulting in a significant improvement in the productivity and safety of various industrial and scientific applications. In this context, the present work addresses the design and development of an innovative human-machine interface for real-time 2D Light Detection and Ranging (LiDAR) based Simultaneous Localization and Mapping (SLAM). Such interface has been implemented in MATLAB and establishes an effective communication with the Robot Operating System (ROS) environment. Its straightforward design, planned for real-time teleoperation, facilitates the acquisition and analysis of data from sensors and actuators of a robotic system. The real-time processing of the data supports computationally expensive tasks, such as those associated with SLAM processing. Indeed, feature extraction for environment mapping from 2D LiDAR data is one of its applications.**

Keywords-Human-Machine Interface (HMI); Light Detection and Ranging (LiDAR); Simultaneous Localization and Mapping (SLAM); teleoperation.

I. INTRODUCTION

The development of Human-Machine Interfaces (HMIs) capable of visualising real-time processed data from robotic systems represents a major milestone in the evolution of automation and robotics. Advances in these fields have led to the creation of autonomous robots capable of navigating complex environments, making their own sensor-based decisions and completing specific missions without the need for constant human supervision. The level of autonomy of a robot is intrinsically related to the level of human intervention [1]. Even robots with a high degree of autonomy may require human guidance in dangerous or unknown situations, where human criterion and expertise cannot yet be replaced. It is in the face of critical events [2][3][4], such as remote medical care, disaster response and inspection of hazardous infrastructure, where the development of graphical user interfaces for teleoperation becomes essential.

HMI allows human operators to interact with the robot in a seamless way, as well as to monitor and control the robotic system effectively [5]. Moreover, these interfaces can contribute to the early detection and resolution of problems or challenges that may arise during robotic operation, resulting in increased efficiency and safety levels [6]. Furthermore, they are particularly valuable in environments where rapid and accurate decision-making requires fast processing of large volumes of data. This environmental information stems from the sensors available to each robotic system. Most robotic platforms can be programmed in Robot Operating System (ROS) environment, which may be complex for users without prior experience in robotics. In this sense, the implementation of robotic systems that use technologies such as Light Detection and Ranging (LiDAR) based Simultaneous Localization and Mapping (SLAM) to capture data from the environment, or communication through ROS, has generated a growing demand for graphical user interfaces capable of managing and visualising this data in real time.

Our work focuses on the design and development of an HMI capable of controlling a LiDAR SLAM robotic system in real time while ensuring seamless communication between ROS and MATLAB. The graphical user interface we propose is simple and intuitive for the user compacting the visualisation of the raw data from sensors, the data processed in ROS as well as the data processed in MATLAB. It is accessible from any PC and, most importantly, enables the visualisation of signals in real time. This paper is organized as follows: Section II provides a review of related work. In Section III, the robotic system is described. SLAM methodology is defined in Section IV. Section V contains the details of our HMI. In Section VI, HMI experiments are presented. Finally, conclusions are to be found in Section VII.

II. Related Work

HMIs are more complex than mere control panels. They provide a virtual window through which operators can view and interact with the environment. These interfaces must be intuitive and efficient, as any delay or confusion in communication could result in major consequences.

The healthcare sector serves as an example of a highly demanding environment. Surgeons can teleoperate surgical robots as long as they have access to acceptable real-time image and data. Advances in HMI technology significantly improve the accuracy and safety of medical procedures [3][7][8].

The exploration of hostile environments is another area where the teleoperation of robotic systems simplifies human tasks. Many robots are used in search and rescue (SAR) missions [9][10]. In such situations, robots can perform tasks that are dangerous or inaccessible to human operators.

In the industrial domain [11][12], LiDAR or camera-equipped robot teleoperation for tasks such as mapping and inspection benefits greatly from data processing and analysis capabilities. This facilitates decision-making and monitoring of operations in real time, improving efficiency and safety in production environments.

The ability to process and visualise data in real time is key to the success of teleoperation. In this context, the integration between ROS and different programming environments, such as MATLAB, plays a crucial role. ROS provides a solid platform for robot control and perception, while MATLAB offers powerful signal processing and data analysis capabilities. The effectiveness of the combination of both systems has been demonstrated in several case studies [13][14][15]. Indeed, our HMI proposal integrates ROS and MATLAB. The objective of this work is the development of bidirectional communication between the robotic system and the human operator, featuring real-time processing of sensor data and movement commands. Unlike other graphical interfaces, the proposed HMI focuses on the visualisation of SLAM data, in particular the key points extracted from the 2D LiDAR sensor of the mapped environment. In addition, our HMI displays the data processed in different environments, here ROS and MATLAB, in real time.

III. Robotic System

The robotic system used in this work is responsible for performing SLAM tasks. It creates a two-dimensional map of the environment in which it operates, while simultaneously determining its precise position.

All experiments have been carried out with 4WD Rover Zero 3, developed by *Rover Robotics*. The robot is shown in Figure 1, along with the sensors used for the characterisation of the surrounding environment. For visualisation purposes, the camera *Intel® RealSense™ D435i* has been employed. An omnidirectional 2D LiDAR sensor has been used for mapping and positioning tasks in real time, namely *RPLiDAR S2* from *Slamtec*. The signals from the sensors are processed by the *Intel NUC10i* mini PC located on board. Obtained data is analysed in real time using the ROS framework. The robot is remotely controlled from a virtual joystick implemented in the designed HMI.

Figure 1. Teleoperated robotic system used in SLAM experiments.

Both the robotic platform and the external PC running the HMI are connected to the same network via WiFi. Information exchange between both systems, represented by dashed arrows in Figure 2, is thus allowed.

IV. SLAM Methodology

Our robot is designed to perform real-time mapping and positioning tasks using SLAM technology. This involves collecting data from sensors, camera and LiDAR, to build a map of the environment. At the same time, it uses this data to estimate the position and trajectory of the robot within the map. Since these tasks require large processing power, part of the computational load is delegated to MATLAB. This leads the HMI to play a key role in the acquisition and visualisation of sensor data, ROS data as well as MATLAB data allowing the robot to make informed decisions and navigate in a guided manner in real-time within its environment. The system architecture and the flow of information between the different system components is shown in Figure 2.

A. LiDAR SLAM

The map and the trajectory followed by the robot are obtained in real time by means of Google's *Cartographer* [16]. It runs on the ROS framework of the mini PC that is integrated in the robotic system. This algorithm works with submaps to facilitate information processing. As the robot moves, *Cartographer* gradually adds the LiDAR sensor readings to the last generated submap [17].

B. Feature extraction

Mapping any environment generates a large volume of information. The current trend in SLAM processing is to reduce this raw data to a set of characteristics that define the mapped profile [18]. In structured environments [19], it is very common to use extraction techniques that focus on identifying key features such as straight sections, curved sections and corners. These features are essential to understand and properly represent the geometry of the environment.

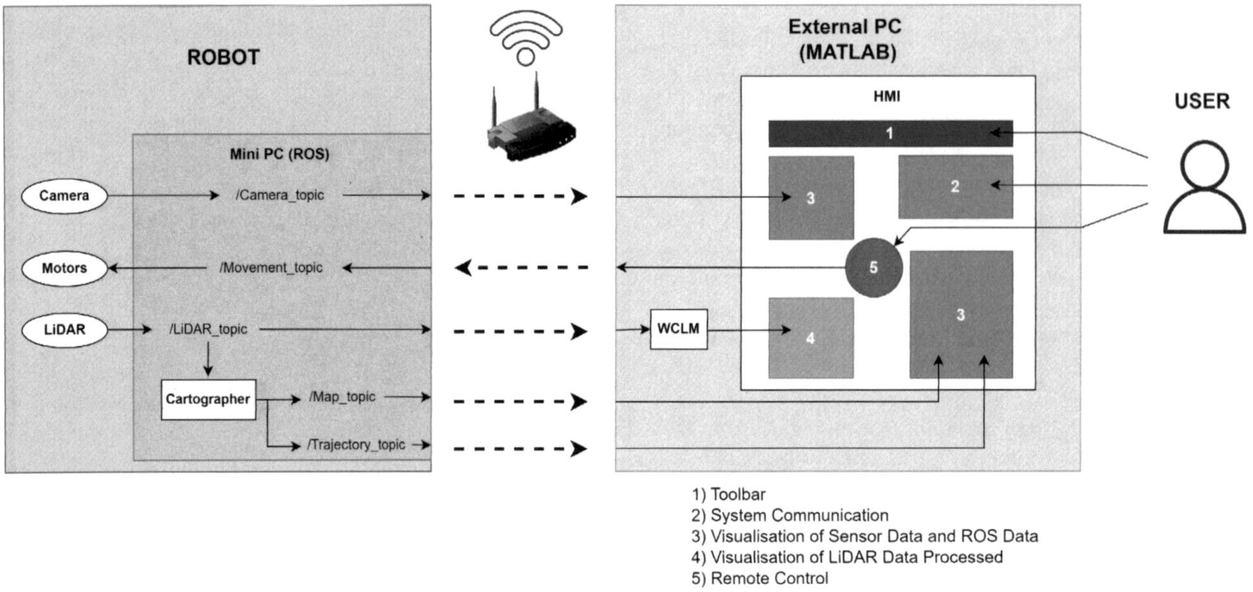

Figure 2. System Architecture Diagram.

The profile under study is structured. Therefore, we will extract its corners in real time from the current LiDAR scan. This part of the process is performed on MATLAB. We use Weighted Conformal LiDAR-Mapping (WCLM) [20] for this purpose. This methodology allows for the extraction of corners while determining their uncertainties, using the data provided by a 2D LiDAR sensor (distance ρ and angle θ).

From the readings x_i and y_i corresponding to each point of the mapped profile, the coordinates x_Q and y_Q defining each straight line in the inverse domain (1) can be extracted [20].

$$x_Q \cdot \mathbf{x_i} - y_Q \cdot \mathbf{y_i} = 1 \tag{1}$$

The expressions for x_Q and y_Q are (2) and (3), respectively.

$$\widehat{x_Q} = \frac{\left(\sum_i w_i x_i\right)\left(\sum_i w_i y_i^2\right) - \left(\sum_i w_i y_i\right)\left(\sum_i w_i x_i y_i\right)}{\left(\sum_i w_i x_i^2\right)\left(\sum_i w_i y_i^2\right) - \left(\sum_i w_i x_i y_i\right)^2} \tag{2}$$

$$\widehat{y_Q} = \frac{\left(\sum_i w_i x_i\right)\left(\sum_i w_i x_i y_i\right) - \left(\sum_i w_i y_i\right)\left(\sum_i w_i x_i^2\right)}{\left(\sum_i w_i x_i^2\right)\left(\sum_i w_i y_i^2\right) - \left(\sum_i w_i x_i y_i\right)^2} \tag{3}$$

Where the weighting factor is $\omega_i = \frac{1}{\sigma_\rho^2 (\rho\sigma_\theta)^2}$, while σ_ρ and σ_θ are the uncertainties in distance and angle of the laser rangefinder, respectively.

The covariance matrix C_Q can be obtained as follows [20].

$$C_Q = \begin{bmatrix} V_{\widehat{x_Q}} & C_{\widehat{x_Q}\widehat{y_Q}} \\ C_{\widehat{x_Q}\widehat{y_Q}} & V_{\widehat{y_Q}} \end{bmatrix} \tag{4}$$

Once the parameters x_Q and y_Q of the straight lines and their uncertainties are known, the corner coordinates of the mapped profile x_c and y_c can be extracted following equations (6) and (7), respectively.

$$x_{Q_i} \cdot x_c - y_{Q_i} \cdot y_c = 1 \tag{5}$$

$$x_c = \frac{y_{Q_{i+1}} - y_{Q_i}}{x_{Q_i} \cdot y_{Q_{i+1}} - y_{Q_i} \cdot x_{Q_{i+1}}} \tag{6}$$

$$y_c = \frac{x_{Q_{i+1}} - x_{Q_i}}{x_{Q_i} \cdot y_{Q_{i+1}} - y_{Q_i} \cdot x_{Q_{i+1}}} \tag{7}$$

The covariance matrix of the corners is defined by (8).

$$C_c = J_c \cdot \begin{bmatrix} V_{x_{Q_i}} & C_{xy_{Q_i}} & 0 & 0 \\ C_{xy_{Q_i}} & V_{y_{Q_i}} & 0 & 0 \\ 0 & 0 & V_{x_{Q_{i+1}}} & C_{xy_{Q_{i+1}}} \\ 0 & 0 & C_{xy_{Q_{i+1}}} & V_{y_{Q_{i+1}}} \end{bmatrix} \cdot J_c^T \tag{8}$$

Where J_c is the Jacobian matrix of corner parameters with respect to line parameters x_Q and y_Q.

V. HMI MODEL

The aim in the design and development of the HMI is to facilitate the control of a SLAM robotic system using 2D LiDAR technology. This interface is designed to perform this function in different indoor environments, whether in industrial, domestic or similar contexts. Its design should be intuitive and accessible to a wide variety of users, even those without previous experience in handling ROS based systems.

Real-time bidirectional communication between the human operator and the robotic system must be facilitated by this interface. This communication has to be smooth and efficient facilitating users' decision making. As all data from the sensors is processed in ROS, information must be transferred to the interface. In this way, it is available to the user without having to directly access ROS. For this purpose, we have chosen MATLAB R2023a as the programming environment for the design and development of both the interface and the processing of the signals from ROS.

A. HMI Design

The interface we propose has been entirely designed using MATLAB's *App Designer*. One of the main advantages of using this environment is the ability to generate standalone applications that can be run outside MATLAB. This allows the interface, once designed, to be exported as an independent application using *MATLAB Compiler*. The generated executable can be installed on any device and is compatible with a wide variety of operating systems, the main ones being Windows, Linux and macOS. This makes our HMI an accessible interface for any user.

The resulting graphical user interface is presented in Figure 3. This interface has been carefully designed to provide an intuitive and efficient user experience. Other designs such as [15] were tested but the proposal presented below extends the functionalities of the interface, provides more information by displaying features extracted from 2D LiDAR data in real time with a more compact visualisation. It is divided into five sections as each one defines a specific functionality of the application, see Figures 2 and 3.

1) Toolbar: This section provides quick access to the key functions of the application. These functions include the display of previously stored data, the possibility to perform delayed analysis and the ability to save processed data.

2) System Communication: In this section, users can configure the communication between ROS and MATLAB providing the robot's IP address.

3) Visualisation of Sensor Data and ROS Data: A significant part of the interface is dedicated to the visualisation of raw data as well as the data processed in ROS. This includes the real-time transmission of the camera information, as well as the Geographic Information System (GIS) representation of the map and the path followed by the robot, which are generated by the mapping algorithm *Cartographer*. These visual elements provide the user with a clear and complete representation of the robot's environment.

4) Visualisation of LiDAR Data Processed: Another essential function of the application is the LiDAR data analysis area where the WCLM algorithm detects the corners of the mapped environment. Here, the interface allows visualisation of the LiDAR data processed directly in MATLAB. This involves the extraction of the corners that make up the environment and the subsequent reconstruction of the profile using this information. This real-time LiDAR data analysis is a valuable feature that allows users to obtain detailed information about the surrounding environment.

5) Remote Control: A virtual joystick has been incorporated in the centre of the interface. This interactive component allows users to send movement commands to the robot in an intuitive and precise way.

Real-time updating of the user interface has been one of the challenges faced both in the design of the interface and in the work in general.

B. Signal Processing

One of the main milestones of this work is the ability to process data from the sensors and send instructions to the robot in real time. This is possible through MATLAB's *ROS Toolbox*. This tool allows communication and interaction between MATLAB and ROS. In this case, it allows for the implementation of the WCLM algorithm [20] in MATLAB with the LiDAR data from ROS.

The main objective is being able access to the available *topics* in ROS from the HMI. In this way, messages can be sent and received between both systems. Among the wide variety of options offered by the *ROS Toolbox*, we will focus on initiating communication with ROS, subscribing to the *topics* of the sensors and *Cartographer*, publishing in the *topics* related to the control of the actuators and closing the communication.

The first step is knowing the IP address of the robot in order to establish communication from the interface. Once the connection to the *ROS Master* has been initiated, the information from the camera, the LiDAR sensor and the map and trajectory data can be accessed by subscribing to the *topics* that host these messages. Movement commands to the robot are published in the *topic* designated for this purpose. Finally, when the exploration is completed or the HMI is closed, both systems are disconnected.

VI. Experimental Results

The 4WD Rover Zero 3 robot was employed in the experiments, which involved mapping the corridors on the ground floor of the Technological Building of the School of Industrial, Computer and Aerospace Engineering of the University of León. This research addressed several aspects. First and foremost, we sought the effective visualisation of the resulting map on GIS. In second place, we evaluated the effectiveness of the bidirectional communication between the robot and the Human Machine Interface used in the study. Third, a calculation process of the uncertainties associated to the measurements was launched.

The first step was to analyse the data processed in ROS from *Cartographer*. In Figure 4, the map can be seen in yellow, and the trajectory followed by the robot, in blue. This information is represented by MATLAB on a satellite image provided by Google. This *Cartographer*-generated map is built as the robot moves through the environment. Please note that the robot is teleoperated from the HMI, which sends instructions in real time. A human operator makes the movement decisions based on the data stream from the camera.

The fluent real-time communication between the two systems, i.e., the robot and the HMI, results in an efficient interaction between the operator and the robot. This constant flow

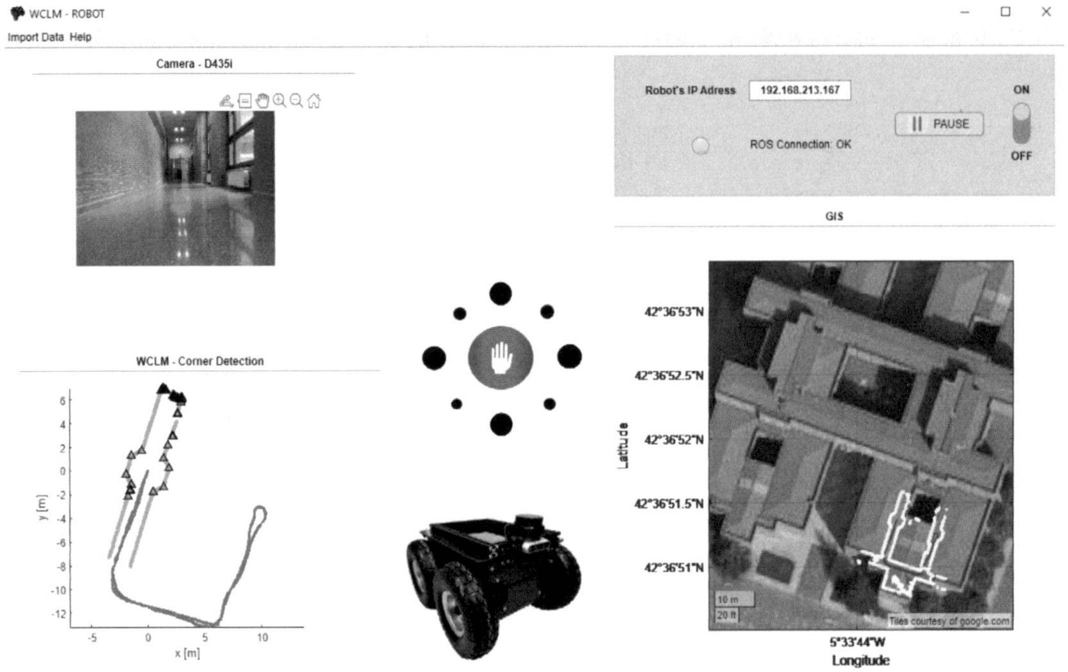

Figure 3. Human-Machine Interface for industrial robot teleoperation.

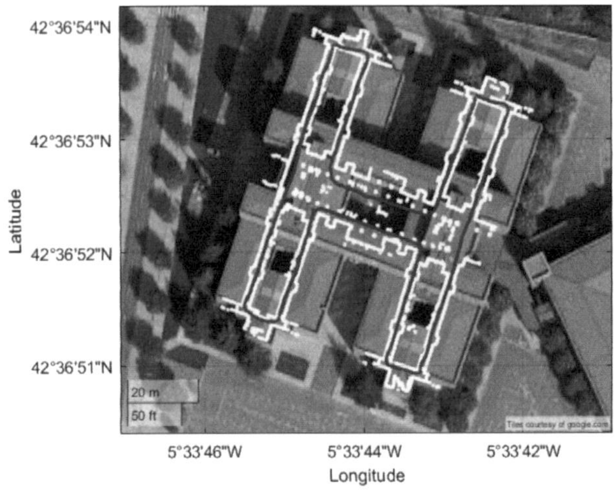

Figure 4. Map (yellow) and trajectory (blue) followed by the robot during the mapping of the Technological Building of the School of Industrial, Computer and Aerospace Engineering of the University of León.

of information benchmarks one of the fundamental aspects of this work: the efficiency of bidirectional communication. This has been noted by several users, who also indicated an intuitive interface.

Since *Cartographer* does not provide us with the uncertainty levels for each point on the map, we have extracted the features of the environment mapped by the LiDAR sensor. For this purpose, the WCLM method proposed by Prieto-Fernández et al. [20] is used. Following this methodology, it is enough to have the LiDAR measurements and to know the uncertainty of the sensor used to determine the coordinates of the corners and their uncertainties. According to the information provided by the manufacturer, its angular resolution is ($\sigma_\theta = 0.12/2^o$), and its depth accuracy ($\sigma_\rho = \pm 5\ cm$).

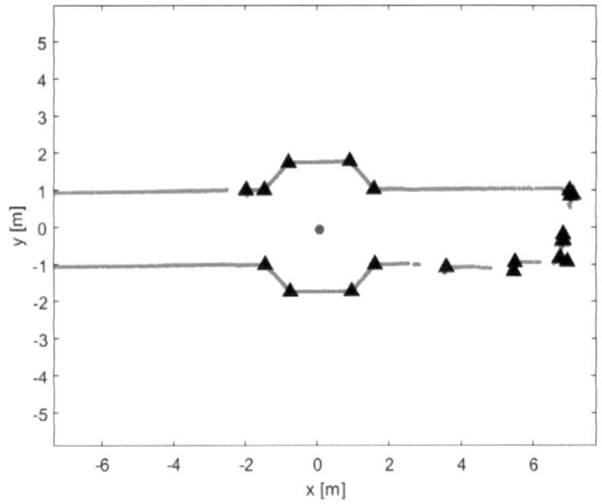

Figure 5. WCLM for corner extraction for position A. The LiDAR data is presented in pink, corners are highlighted in black and sensor position in blue.

Figures 5 and 6 show the same corridor of the Technology Building mapped from two different positions, which allows to observe how the uncertainty of the same corners varies

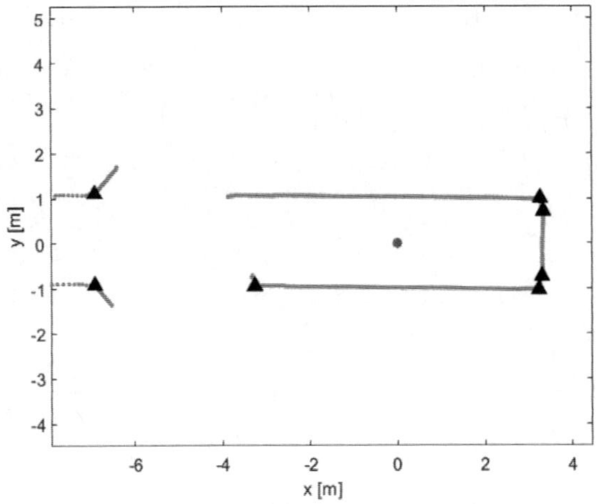

Figure 6. WCLM for corner extraction for position B. The LiDAR data is presented in pink, corners are highlighted in black and sensor position in blue.

according to the acquisition point. The measurements were taken from the point marked in blue, the mapped profile is represented in pink and the corners obtained by the WCLM method are highlighted in black.

TABLE I
WCLM CORNER DETECTION AT POSITION A

Corner	x_c [m]	y_c [m]	σ_{x_c} [mm]	σ_{y_c} [mm]
1	-1.500	-0.948	18.040	3.816
2	-0.808	-1.675	19.345	11.250
3	0.888	-1.664	19.455	11.350
4	1.549	-0.933	19.579	8.236
5	3.530	-1.018	28.563	4.473
6	5.384	-1.109	28.535	19.950
7	5.427	-0.874	29.045	5.182
8	6.896	-0.860	27.371	7.634
9	6.685	-0.752	21.567	16.372
10	6.745	-0.299	24.151	12.443
11	6.788	-0.286	30.484	15.737
12	6.771	-0.122	30.117	23.151
13	6.971	0.913	22.910	18.326
14	7.052	0.951	30.833	17.280
15	6.956	1.059	45.764	14.571
16	1.520	1.087	16.943	3.901
17	0.834	1.836	18.108	10.170
18	-0.861	1.795	20.021	11.556
19	-1.525	1.066	21.029	10.480
20	-2.038	1.063	27.201	9.364

TABLE II
WCLM CORNER DETECTION AT POSITION B

Corner	x_c [m]	y_c [m]	σ_{x_c} [mm]	σ_{y_c} [mm]
1	-6.921	-0.919	29.243	13.652
2	-3.261	-0.943	19.219	2.340
3	3.233	-1.027	23.780	2.168
4	3.304	-0.735	13.786	143.877
5	3.335	0.707	11.264	112.222
6	3.263	1.002	35.472	2.791
7	-6.921	1.109	26.825	12.249

The data presented in tables I and II includes the Cartesian coordinates of these corners as well as their uncertainties. Uncertainty levels are found to be intrinsically related to the number of points that delimit each corner. This relationship is explained by the fact that the corners are generated from the intersection of straight sections, and the number of points involved in the calculation of these straight sections significantly influences the uncertainty of the resulting corner. Matching corners on both maps are highlighted with the same colour in both tables. Please note that the same point may have different uncertainty levels in each map. This is due to the relative distance between corner and sensor in each scenario. In the case of red and green labelled corners, position A is characterised by the sensor being closer to these corners, which leads to higher data availability for position calculations, thus resulting in a lower uncertainty compared to position B. The case of the yellow corner is inverse: at position B, a larger amount of information is available compared to position A, resulting in a lower uncertainty.

These observations show the influence of the relative location of the sensor with respect to the objects of interest on the accuracy and uncertainty of the measurements. The reliability of the results is found to strongly depend on careful consideration of the position and layout of sensors.

VII. CONCLUSION

This work addresses one of the key challenges in signal processing within robotic systems focused on 2D LiDAR SLAM. The developed graphical user interface enables remote analysis and bidirectional communication in real time with the robot, thereby enhancing control and decision making capabilities and broadening application range into a variety of industrial and scientific contexts.

The main achievement of the HMI is its ability to control and monitor the robotic system both in real time and deferred scenarios while visualising the data processed in different environments, ROS and MATLAB. The latter endows the interface with multidisciplinary versatility, allowing users to generate their own data analysis code outside of the ROS environment. It facilitates the collection, visualisation and storage of such information for further processing, which is particularly valuable in research and development environments.

We can conclude that the resulting HMI meets the initial objectives. It is an intuitive and efficient interface, aimed at a wide range of users. Versatility is coupled with accesibility, since multiple platforms are supported and MATLAB is not required on the end device, turning the resulting product into a plug-and-play commodity for any user.

ACKNOWLEDGMENT

This research has been carried out thanks to TRESCA Ingeniería S.A. within the framework of the Research Project on *Survey Systems for Hostile Structured Environments using Simultaneous Localization And Mapping (SLAM) Systems with Lidar Technology*. The project has been co-financed by the ERDF, Thematic Objective 1, which seeks to promote technological development, innovation and quality research, and the

Regional Government of Castilla y León, through the institute for the Business Competitiveness of Castilla y León (ICE).

References

[1] J. J. Choi, Y. Kim, and S. S. Kwak, "The autonomy levels and the human intervention levels of robots: The impact of robot types in human-robot interaction," in *The 23rd IEEE International Symposium on Robot and Human Interactive Communication.* IEEE, 2014, pp. 1069–1074.

[2] J. P. Queralta *et al.*, "Collaborative multi-robot search and rescue: Planning, coordination, perception, and active vision," *IEEE Access*, vol. 8, pp. 191 617–191 643, 2020.

[3] B. S. Peters, P. R. Armijo, C. Krause, S. A. Choudhury, and D. Oleynikov, "Review of emerging surgical robotic technology," *Surgical endoscopy*, vol. 32, pp. 1636–1655, 2018.

[4] A. Wichmann, B. D. Okkalioglu, and T. Korkmaz, "The integration of mobile (tele) robotics and wireless sensor networks: A survey," *Computer Communications*, vol. 51, pp. 21–35, 2014.

[5] A. Steinfeld *et al.*, "Common metrics for human-robot interaction," in *Proceedings of the 1st ACM SIGCHI/SIGART conference on Human-robot interaction*, 2006, pp. 33–40.

[6] T. Fong and C. Thorpe, "Vehicle teleoperation interfaces," *Autonomous robots*, vol. 11, pp. 9–18, 2001.

[7] H. Su *et al.*, "State of the art and future opportunities in mri-guided robot-assisted surgery and interventions," *Proceedings of the IEEE*, vol. 110, no. 7, pp. 968–992, 2022.

[8] H. Lv *et al.*, "Gulim: A hybrid motion mapping technique for teleoperation of medical assistive robot in combating the covid-19 pandemic," *IEEE Transactions on Medical Robotics and Bionics*, vol. 4, no. 1, pp. 106–117, 2022.

[9] T. Klamt *et al.*, "Supervised autonomous locomotion and manipulation for disaster response with a centaur-like robot," in *2018 IEEE/RSJ International Conference on Intelligent Robots and Systems (IROS).* IEEE, 2018, pp. 1–8.

[10] A. F. Winfield *et al.*, "eurathlon 2015: A multi-domain multi-robot grand challenge for search and rescue robots," in *Towards Autonomous Robotic Systems: 17th Annual Conference, TAROS 2016, Sheffield, UK, June 26–July 1, 2016, Proceedings 17.* Springer, 2016, pp. 351–363.

[11] D. Aschenbrenner, M. Fritscher, F. Sittner, M. Krauß, and K. Schilling, "Teleoperation of an industrial robot in an active production line," *IFAC-PapersOnLine*, vol. 48, no. 10, pp. 159–164, 2015.

[12] M. M. Dalvand and S. Nahavandi, "Improvements in teleoperation of industrial robots without low-level access," in *2014 IEEE International Conference on Systems, Man, and Cybernetics (SMC).* IEEE, 2014, pp. 2170–2175.

[13] I. Cerulo, F. Ficuciello, V. Lippiello, and B. Siciliano, "Teleoperation of the schunk s5fh under-actuated anthropomorphic hand using human hand motion tracking," *Robotics and Autonomous Systems*, vol. 89, pp. 75–84, 2017.

[14] R. Su, K. Xu, L. Zhao, and P. Yu, "A heterogeneous master-slave teleoperation method for 7-dof manipulator," in *2021 China Automation Congress (CAC).* IEEE, 2021, pp. 1740–1744.

[15] N. Prieto Fernández, M. Bayón Gutiérrez, S. Fernández-Blanco, Á. Fernández-Blanco, F. Carro de Lorenzo, and J. A. Benítez-Andrades, "Desarrollo de un hmi en ros-matlab para la teleoperación de robots industriales," in *XLIV Jornadas de Automática.* Universidade da Coruña. Servizo de Publicacións, 2023, pp. 720–725.

[16] W. Hess, D. Kohler, H. Rapp, and D. Andor, "Real-time loop closure in 2d lidar slam," in *2016 IEEE international conference on robotics and automation (ICRA).* IEEE, 2016, pp. 1271–1278.

[17] R. Yagfarov, M. Ivanou, and I. Afanasyev, "Map comparison of lidar-based 2d slam algorithms using precise ground truth," in *2018 15th International Conference on Control, Automation, Robotics and Vision (ICARCV).* IEEE, 2018, pp. 1979–1983.

[18] V. Nguyen, S. Gächter, A. Martinelli, N. Tomatis, and R. Siegwart, "A comparison of line extraction algorithms using 2d range data for indoor mobile robotics," *Autonomous Robots*, vol. 23, pp. 97–111, 2007.

[19] P. Núñez, R. Vázquez-Martín, J. Del Toro, A. Bandera, and F. Sandoval, "Natural landmark extraction for mobile robot navigation based on an adaptive curvature estimation," *Robotics and Autonomous Systems*, vol. 56, no. 3, pp. 247–264, 2008.

[20] N. Prieto-Fernández, S. Fernández-Blanco, Á. Fernández-Blanco, J. A. Benítez-Andrades, F. Carro-De-Lorenzo, and C. Benavides, "Weighted conformal lidar-mapping for structured slam," *IEEE Transactions on Instrumentation and Measurement*, vol. 72, pp. 1–10, 2023.

Surface Skin Blood Flow Dynamics during Muscle Contraction Using Filtered Camera

Naoki Yamamoto, Tota Mizuno, Miku Shimizu, Kazuyuki Mito, and Naoaki Itakura
University of Electro-communications
1-5-1, Chofugaoka, Chofu, Tokyo, Japan
e-mail: y2330121@gl.cc.uec.ac.jp, mizuno@uec.ac.jp, m.shimizu.0320@gmail.com, k.mito@uec.ac.jp, itakura@uec.ac.jp

***Abstract*—The purpose of this study is to elucidate the surface skin blood flow dynamics during muscle contraction using real images with filters that pass near-infrared wavelengths. It has been shown that the depth of transmission differs depending on the RGB color components. In the previous study, it was suggested that the blood flow state obtained from the R-B component value, which is the difference between the deepest R component value and the shallowest B component value, may be used as one of the evaluation indices of muscle activity. However, the use of the near-infrared light component, which has a deeper penetration depth into the subcutaneous region than the RGB light component, has not yet been examined in this method. The near-infrared light component has a possibility to measure the blood flow state inside the subcutaneous tissue with high accuracy, because the light penetrates deeper into the subcutaneous tissue than the RGB light component. Therefore, in addition to the RGB light components used in the conventional method, a visible light camera equipped with a filter that transmits wavelengths above the near-infrared light component is used. In the experiment, a load equivalent to 40% of Maximum Voluntary Contraction (MVC) was applied to the subject's upper arm. The subjects were kept in a resting state, and then the load was applied to their arms and they were kept in a resting state again. As a result, the R component values with the filter showed a larger change than the R-B component values without the filter when the load was applied. This result indicates that the R-B component with filter can capture the changes in blood flow more easily than the conventional method.**

Keywords- Real image, muscle, Filter, Blood Flow.

I. INTRODUCTION

Assessment and estimation of autonomic nervous activity, which changes in response to situations such as fatigue and concentration, can help humans to lead a comfortable life. It has been shown that autonomic nervous system activity affects blood flow. The methods to measure changes in subcutaneous blood flow include evaluation using thermal images of the face using an infrared thermography camera and evaluation using real images using a visible light camera such as a web camera. In particular, the real image method can be used for various applications because it does not require any special equipment for measurement.

Various studies have been conducted on the method using real images, and it has been clarified that the depth of transmission of each color component of visible light (RGB) to the skin differs depending on the color. Using this property, it has been suggested that by focusing on the R-B component values, it may be possible to obtain the state of peripheral blood flow and evaluate autonomic nervous system activity [1]. It was also suggested that the blood flow state obtained from the R-B component values could be used as one of the evaluation indices of muscle activity that enables the estimation of muscle fatigue. However, these methods have not yet investigated the use of the near-infrared light component, which has a deeper penetration depth into the subcutaneous region than the RGB light component.

In this study, we will examine whether a visible light camera equipped with a filter that transmits wavelengths near the wavelengths of near-infrared light that can be acquired can be used to measure subcutaneous blood flow in the biceps brachii muscle with high accuracy and to evaluate muscle activity.

II. PROPOSED METHOD

The near-infrared light component penetrates deeper into the subcutaneous tissue than the RGB light component, and thus has the potential to measure the state of blood flow inside the subcutaneous tissue with high accuracy. For this reason, in addition to the RGB light component used in the conventional method, a new visible light camera equipped with a filter that transmits wavelengths above the near-infrared light component is used. We will evaluate the possibility of highly accurate measurement from the RGB light component and the RGB light component of the camera equipped with the filter.

III. EXPERIMENT SUMMARY

Before the experiment, green tape was applied to the subject's upper arm so that it formed a rectangle, and the analysis area was limited to the green tape. During the experiment, two smart phones were placed in a position where the rectangle formed by the green tape and the entire area from the subject's wrist to the shoulder were captured by an external camera.

In order to obtain data during muscle contractions that cause significant changes in epidermal blood flow, isometric contraction experiments were conducted to minimize the effects of noise generated by body movements. First, the subject's Maximum Voluntary Contraction (MVC) was measured to identify the location of the platform; MVC was measured three times for 10 s. MVC was calculated by measuring muscle forces at 2, 5, and 8 s and averaging them.

Next, using the calculated MVC, four different wavelength transmission filters (560 nm, 600 nm, 640 nm, and 660 nm) were attached to one smartphone in turn, and the following procedure was performed a total of four times.

First, the subject sat in a resting position for 60 seconds. Next, the elbow joint angle was maintained at 90° and the subject held a weight with 40% load by hand for 45 seconds, then the weight was removed and the subject again sat in a resting position for 60 seconds.

IV. RESULTS ANALYSIS AND CONCLUSION

A. Comparison of B-component values for each filter

Time series data of the wavelength of the B component acquired from cameras with filters on the entire upper arm were compared among four types of filters. The wavelength of the B component is generally between 460 and 500nm. There is a large difference in the B-component values between filters with wavelengths below 600 nm and above 640 nm, and a large change in the B-component values between filters with wavelengths of 640 nm and 660 nm. In natural environments, the sensitivity of the camera itself also changes due to changes in light intensity. When using such a filter, it is necessary to keep the light level constant. In this study, we used a filter that transmits light from wavelengths below 600 nm, which is sufficient for the filter to function even under fluorescent light, where the light intensity does not change to some extent. The higher the cutoff frequency of the filter, the lower the visible light component that can be acquired, and the lower the amount of light that can be acquired, the more the sensitivity of the camera is automatically increased. Therefore, the B-component values at 560nm to 640nm are higher than those at 640nm due to the increase in the sensitivity of the camera. On the other hand, the B-component values are lower at 660nm than at 640nm. It is considered that the pass-cut function of the filter works more strongly than the sensitivity adjustment to reduce the B-component values.

B. Comparison of data with and without filter

The time series data of the variation of the R-B component values obtained from the camera without the filter and the R component values obtained from the camera with the filter for the entire upper arm of subject 1 are shown in Figure 1 for the 560-nm filter and the 660-nm filter. Figure 1 shows that both component values decrease between 60 and 110 seconds when the camera is loaded by the weighted camera, regardless of the presence or absence of the filter.

In Figure 1-(a), during the period of 60-110 seconds, the R component with the filter shows a larger change than that of the R-B component without the filter. Therefore, the proposed method can capture changes in blood flow more easily than the conventional method. On the other hand, fluctuations are observed in the unfiltered R-B component values between 120 and 160 seconds, but not in the filtered R component values. Whether these fluctuations are noise or not is not clear, and is a subject for future study.

In Figure 1-(b), we can see that the R component with filter contains higher frequency fluctuations than the R-B component without filter in the period from 80 to 120 seconds. It is considered that the difference between the R- and B-component values cancels out the fluctuations caused by the subject's movements and other factors.

From the above, it can be concluded that this method can easily capture the amount of change and can be applied to the measurement of minute changes in blood flow, such as in medical applications. On the other hand, the R-B component value of the conventional method that takes the difference value may be utilized for general applications where the shooting environment changes.

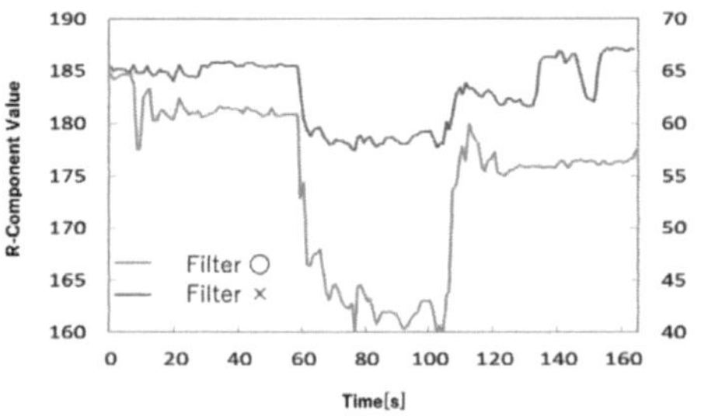

(a) 560 Filter

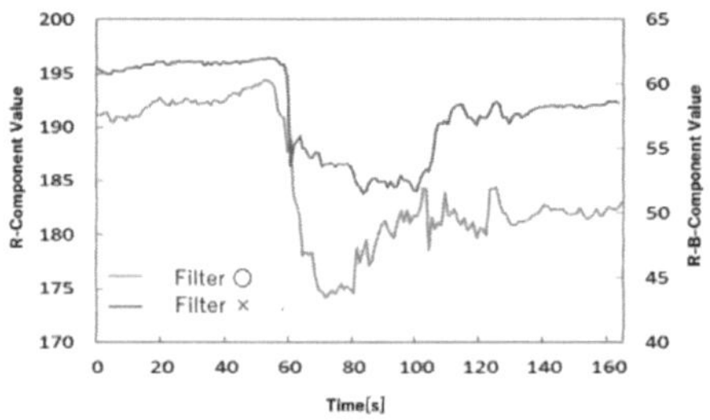

(b) 600 Filter

Figure 1. Change in R component value with filter and R-B component value without filter

REFERENCES

[1] M. Shimizu, Y. Matsumoto, N. Itakura, K. Mito, and T. Mizuno, "Evaluation of Methods for Estimating Autonomic Nervous Activity Using a Web Camera", 27th International Symposium on Artificial Life and Robotics (AROB), 2022.

Evaluating the Impact of a Personal Data Communication Policy in Human-Robot Interactions

Lewis Riches
Robotics Research Group
University of Hertfordshire
College Lane, UK
email: l.riches@herts.ac.uk

Kheng Lee Koay
Robotics Research Group
University of Hertfordshire
College Lane, UK
email: k.l.koay@herts.ac.uk

Patrick Holthaus
Robotics Research Group
University of Hertfordshire
College Lane, UK
email: p.holthaus@herts.ac.uk

Abstract—**Personal companion robots are increasingly integrated into households, offering tailored experiences through personalisation. However, using multiple communication pathways heightens the risk of inadvertent personal data exposure. This paper presents a novel communication policy designed to mitigate such risks by dynamically adjusting communication strategies based on the sensitivity of the shared data. We measure participant preferences for these adaptive communication methods through empirical assessment. Our findings indicate that the proposed policy effectively minimises personal data exposure, fostering increased trust in the robot's handling of sensitive information.**

Keywords-Personalisation; Personal Data Communication; Human-Robot Interaction; Perceptions Of Privacy

I. INTRODUCTION

Health care assistance [1], butler services [2], and educational tutors [3], the roles a companion robot could take within a person's home are starting to be explored in research. Leveraging techniques such as personalisation, social companion robots can learn from the user and adapt their behaviour to provide a unique and custom experience [4]. Regardless of their role within the home, these robots will need to communicate with the user. As such, research within this field has brought about a multitude of different communication pathways, including audible [5], visual [6] and sign language [7], to name but a few. Using these communication methods, social companion robots can personalise their communication method and topic of communication to the user. While multimodal communication pathways are vital, such methods increase the risk of personal data exposure, as identified by Calo [8].

With access to the private space of a home, along with personalisation techniques, social companion robots have easy access to sensitive and personal data about their user. A robot's ability to communicate personal data is akin to that of humans. Robots need to have social awareness, understand the relationship between people, what type of personal data they are communicating, and the impact of exposing such personal data within the context. Unlike Human-Computer Interaction (HCI), where a device needs to be unlocked [9] or have some form of user intervention to communicate personal data. However, to put manual intervention into social companion robots before they can communicate anything would impede the natural communication experience a robot would provide.

A simple solution to fix these communication issues would be to prevent the robot from entering private spaces within the home [8], control what personal data it can collect through sensors [10] and give it limited personal data. However, such techniques hamper the functions of personalisation. Butler et al. [11] and Klow et al. [12] show that people are willing to give up more sensitive personal data to gain benefits and functions. These tradeoffs mean people want to give a robot their personal data to get personalised features and tasks done in specific ways, even with the added risk of exposure through communication. For example, giving a robot your medical information to enable features such as medication reminders or the robot adapting its communication style if you have hearing loss. Withholding essential personal data required for personalisation features due to concerns about data exposure is similar to denying a chef access to a kitchen out of fear of hazards. Instead, we propose to put policies in place at the communication layer of the robot to protect personal data.

Within HRI, there are currently limited communication strategies for addressing this. An approach put forward by Marchang et al. [13] is to use a blockchain approach, where only authorised personnel can be present for the robot to communicate personal data. Such a technique is viable in HCI but requires manual intervention (Face ID), impeding natural communication. A common approach used within research studies is to use consent forms that do not require a communication policy and either use fake personal data for the participant or use only authorised personal data. For example, Di Napoli et al. [14] turn off video recording and skeletal tracking to ensure that only the desired personal data is collected. While ethically sound, both approaches lack consideration for how the robot would need to communicate in the real world.

In a real-world domestic setting, a robot needs to understand what it is saying to be able to assess if it is appropriate to say within a specific context. This means understanding the sensitivity of the personal data, the people within a given context, and the impact of sharing the personal data within that context. Findings from [15] [16] show that the sensitivity of different personal data items is different. Both works also show that personal differences can also influence these perceived sensitivities.

This work looks at how a communication policy could use

perceptions of personal data sensitivity to determine how to communicate personal data. In particular, this work takes the classification of personal data by Riches et al. [16] and applies a different communication style for low, medium and high-concern personal data. Within this work, we want to explore if such a policy provides appropriate and safe communication of personal data while building trust in the robot's ability to handle personal data. For this purpose, this work aims to answer the following research questions:(**RQ1**) Can a communication policy based on the concern of personal data exposure (personal data concern classification) positively influence people's views on a robot's communication of personal data (e.g. convenient, helpful and trustworthy)? (**RQ2**) How does such a communication policy influence people's trust towards the robot compared to no communication policy? (**RQ3**) Does such a policy provide a more appropriate way for a robot to communicate personal data to the user in different social contexts when a third party is present? Section II presents the design and implementation of a hybrid study, while the results are analysed in Section III. The implications of the findings for Human-Robot Interaction (HRI) are discussed in Section IV, followed by the conclusion in Section V.

II. Methodology

The study presented in this paper comes from an ethically approved hybrid study, which was conducted both online (aSPECS/PGR/UH/05388) and in person (aSPECS/PGR/UH/05389). These studies had a robot communicating three pre-determined personal data reminders created for the study to the participant in front of a third party. It was decided to do an online and in-person version of this study to see if there was a difference in participant perceptions when experiencing the interactions in person compared to seeing it online through a video. The reminders communicated by the robot were chosen to cover the three classifications of concern found by Riches et al. [16]: Low (Preferences), Medium (Political opinions) and High (Financial Records). The full wording of the reminders was:

- Preferences (Low Concern): "Your favourite TV program, the NFL, is on tomorrow, and you enjoy eating cookies and drinking coke while watching this. Would you like me to add this to your shopping list?"
- Political Opinions (Medium Concern): "You need to renew your membership for the Orange Political Party as it expires next week, and there are key votes happening in the coming months. Would you like me to renew this for you now?"
- Financial Records (High Concern): "Your phone bill is due today, totalling £60. You need to pay this as you have been late on this for the last few months. Would you like me to pay this for you now?"

The scenario narrative was that the participant was in their home, and a neighbour came around for a chat. The participant and neighbour were sitting at the dining room table having a drink when the robot came to the participant with a few personal data reminders. For this study, we had two scenarios: a trusted neighbour scenario and a new neighbour scenario. We defined a trusted neighbour as someone the participant had known for 5-plus years and looked after their house when the participant went on holiday. We defined a new neighbour as someone the participant had never met before and had only moved in a day ago. In each scenario, we had two conditions.

The **control condition** was where the robot used no communication policy, saying all three personal data reminders out loud. The **experimental condition** was where the robot used our classification policy to communicate all three reminders. Our classification policy communicated personal data based on the sensitivity of the personal data [16] within the reminder. Low-concern personal data was said out loud in full; for medium-concern personal data, the robot asked the user whether they wanted it said out loud or sent to their phone; for high-concern personal data, these were sent directly to the user's phone.

The robots used in the studies were different. The online study used the Humanoid Pepper [17] robot along with the Non-Humanoid Fetch [18] robot. We chose these two robots to see if their anthropomorphism influenced participants' perceptions of the robot handling and communicating their personal data. We only used Fetch for the in-person study as the Pepper robot could not navigate reliably. This is to avoid participant's responses being influenced by the robot's navigation abilities. For the in-person study, the University of Hertfordshire Robot House [19] was used to provide a realistic domestic setting to immerse participants in the story.

A. Procedure

For both studies, participants first completed a pre-trial questionnaire. This questionnaire collected participants' age, gender, smart assistant use, Ten Item Personality Index (TIPI) [20], Negative Attitudes Towards Robotics (NARS) [21], and experience with robotics. The final question of this section aimed to understand participants' perceptions of approval for a robot to know and store the thirteen items of personal data classified in [16]. The question provided a picture and description of the robot, then asked, "Please rank your approval of <Fetch or Pepper> collecting and storing the following personal data for generating and communicating tailored reminders." Participants rated this approval on a 5-point Likert scale from Strongly disapprove to Strongly approve. For the in-person study, only fetch was used, and participants also had the chance to interact with Fetch physically and see how it moves and communicates before answering this question. For the online study, the robot the participants experienced was between-subject and randomised which robot they experienced.

1) Online: The online study focuses on the preferred communication policy in the presence of a third party (not focusing on the relationship between the user and the third party) and whether the robot's appearance (pepper and fetch) influences the participant's preferences.

After the pre-trial questionnaire, participants watched two videos and answered the post-condition questionnaire after each video. Each video showed one of the two conditions (Communication policy used). The order in which these were shown was randomised and counterbalanced, so the order did not influence participants' perceptions. The videos were filmed in first person as if the participant was experiencing them, akin to the in-person study. For the scenario (neighbour type) of the videos, no details were given in the videos about who the third party was. This detail was asked in the post-condition questionnaire.

2) In-Person: The in-person study focuses on the third party present and their relationship to the user. It allows participants to imagine themselves in the role and act with the third party as if it were their neighbour (new or trusted).

After the pre-trial questionnaire, participants participated in one scenario (neighbour type) with two conditions (communication policy). This meant the participant acted twice, once with the robot using the control policy (no communication policy) and once with it using the experimental policy (classification communication policy), with both times being with the same neighbour (new or trusted). The scenario chosen for each participant was randomised and counterbalanced, and the order of the conditions was counterbalanced. After each interaction, participants would then complete a post-condition questionnaire.

The post-condition questionnaire consisted of four questions. Firstly, participants were asked, "Based on how it communicated your reminders in this interaction, would you trust the robot's ability to provide reminders while keeping your personal data secure?" choosing either yes or no and giving a qualitative reason. The second question asked, "Based solely on the interaction, please rank your approval of <Fetch or Pepper> collecting and storing the following personal data for generating and communicating tailored reminders as it did in the interaction." participants rated this on a 5-point Likert scale from Strongly disapprove to Strongly approve for all 13 personal data items identified previously from [16]. Question three was different between the two studies. The online study was split into two parts and asked about each neighbour: "Please rank your approval of how the robot communicated each reminder if the neighbour present was a <new or trusted> neighbour.". The in-person study asked, "Please rank your approval of how the robot communicated each reminder in front of your neighbour.". For both studies, participants rated these on a 5-point Likert scale from Strongly disapprove to Strongly approve for each of the three personal data reminders listed previously. The final question asks, "Please rank whether you agree or disagree with the following statements and explain your rankings" with participants rating their agreement on a 5-point Likert scale from Strongly disagree to Strongly Agree for three statements. The statements were, "I am happy with the way the robot communicated my personal data", "My personal data is safe when the robot communicates my reminders to me", and "The way the robot communicated my personal data was natural".

B. Participants

In total, we collected responses from 220 participants. Of the 182 participants in the online study, 89 self-identified as male and 93 self-identified as female, with a median age of 35 and a range of 18 - 84. Of the 38 participants in the in-person study, 20 self-identified as male and 18 as female, with a median age of 27 and a range of 19 - 51.

III. RESULTS

In this paper, we performed two studies, one online and one in-person. Using Mann-Whitney U tests, we found no statistical difference between the results from both studies. As such, the results in this paper will report the combination of both studies. While the online study used two different robots, whereas the in-person study only used one, there were also no statistical differences between these, meaning we were able to combine the results.

A. Effect of a communication policy on perceptions of trust

Participants were asked which communication protocol they would prefer to use in daily life. 84% of participants chose the experimental policy, with the remaining 16% choosing neither and no participants choosing the control policy. When asked, "Would you trust the robot's ability to provide reminders while keeping your personal data secure?" 85% of participants said no, and 15% said yes for the control policy, with 14% saying no and 86% of people saying yes for the experimental policy. This difference in trust rating was statistically significant ($Z = -13.92$, $p =< .001$). On giving reasons for their rating, the main themes for not trusting the control policy were feeling their personal data was unsecured, having no control over their personal data and feeling uncomfortable with their personal data being exposed (see examples below):

- Unsecured
  - "The robot's speech did not uphold the safety of my data."
  - "I didnt feel like my personal data is secure. So I couldn't trust the robot with my personal details"
- No Control
  - "The absence of control over my data was a glaring issue."
  - "I have no control over the reminders or what the robot says"
- Uncomfortable
  - "It just felt uncomfortable when the robot mentioned the orange party. Even if the political party I am a member of is known. I would not like this kind of information to be revealed to a new neighbour. Also, the phone not being paid can be embarrassing."

In the reasoning given for why participants trusted the experimental policy, the two main themes were the robot asking for consent and not saying highly sensitive information out loud (see examples below):

- Asking for Consent

- "Having different levels of security on different aspects of data felt reassuring. Especially being able to choose on some of the data."
- "The robot asked for consent first to say it out loud/sent as a text message. This part of interaction helped to build trust."
- "The robot waited for my consent before disclosing any personal information that's why I trust the robot's ability to keep my data secure."

- Not saying Sensitive information out loud
  - "Sending reminder to my phone is a really good idea comparing to saying them loudly"
  - "Using the notification based approach is perfect saving the sensitive data issue"

Participants were asked to rate their agreement with two statements for each of the communication policies:

- I am happy with the way the robot communicated my personal data
- My personal data is safe when the robot communicates my reminders to me

For the control policy, 81% of participants disagreed with being happy with the way the robot communicated their personal data, and 85% disagreed with their personal data feeling safe when the robot communicated it. For the experimental policy, 68% agreed with being happy with the way the robot communicated their personal data, and 78% agreed with their personal data feeling safe when the robot communicated their personal data. The central theme of why participants agreed or disagreed with these statements was the fact the robot did or did not say the personal data out loud (see examples below):

- Disagree
  - "It revealed potentially sensitive data to another person"
  - "I feel that fetch, although said what he wanted to remind me of, he went into too much detail in front of my new neighbour. "
  - "It could have omitted the sensitive information from the reminder rather than just saying it all out"
- Agree
  - "Sending financial reminders to my phone meant it felt safe and under my control. I was not worried it would reveal sensitive information."
  - "It has classified senstive data and only voiced out non-senstive data and it was able to send a notification for the sensitive data"
  - "I liked that it could use my phone to send me the reminder rather then just saying everything out loud"

Participants were asked, "Please rank your approval of <Fetch or Pepper> collecting and storing the following personal data for generating and communicating tailored reminders". This was done before experiencing any scenarios (pre) and after experiencing each communication policy with the same assigned robot (Fetch or Pepper). For all personal data items other than preferences, the approval for the robot

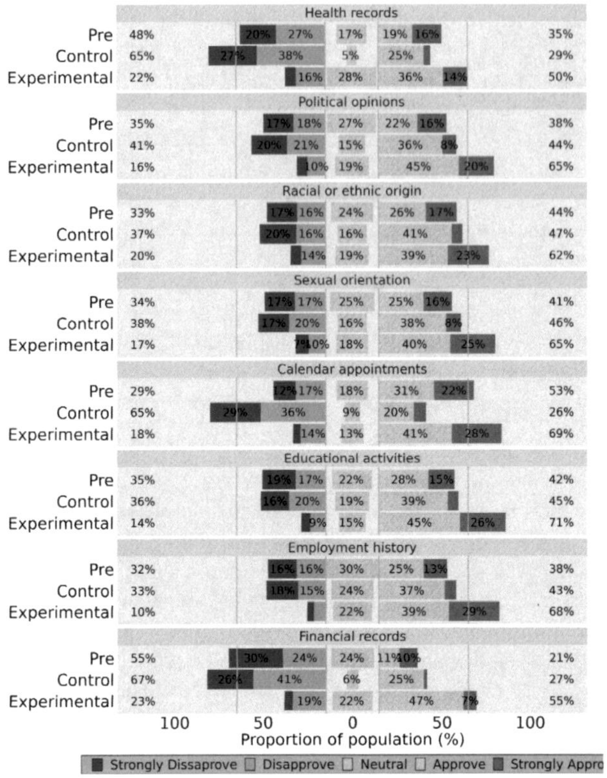

Figure 1. A bar graph showing the distribution of participants' ratings for a robot to know and store personal data items.

to know and store the personal data after demonstrating the experimental policy was higher than the control policy and initial perceptions. The results of this question are shown in figure 1.

Using Mann-Whitney U tests the difference between the pre-approval and approval for the experimental policy was statistically significant for Health records ($z = -4.17$, $p =< .001$), Political opinions ($z = -5$, $p =< .001$), Educational activities ($z = -6.15$, $p =< .001$), Sexual orientation ($z = -5$, $p =< .001$), Racial or ethnic origin ($z = -3.82$, $p =< .001$), Financial records ($z = -7.54$, $p =< .001$), Employment history ($z = -6.74$, $p =< .001$), and Calendar appointments ($z = -3.2$, $p = 0.001$). In all cases, approval increased for the experimental policy over the pre-approval ratings.

Using Mann-Whitney U tests, the difference between the approval for the control policy and the experimental policy was statistically significant for Health Records ($z = -7.9$, $p =< .001$), Political opinions ($z = -5.92$, $p =< .001$), Educational activities ($z = -7.09$, $p =< .001$), Sexual orientation ($z = -5.65$, $p =< .001$), Racial or ethnic origin ($z = -5.23$, $p =< .001$), Financial records ($z = -8.53$, $p =< .001$), Employment history ($z = -7.17$, $p =< .001$), and Calendar appointments ($z = -10.21$, $p =< .001$). In all cases, approval increased for the experimental policy compared to the control policy.

Using Mann-Whitney U tests, the difference between the pre-approval and the approval for the control policy was statistically significant for Health records ($z = 3.35$, $p = 0.001$) and Calendar appointments ($z = 7.15$, $p =< .001$). In both cases, approval decreased for the control policy compared to the pre-approval rating.

Comparing the change in approval between the control policy and experimental policy showed a split based on the sensitivity of the personal data. Approval change between control policy and experimental policy for medium concern personal data items (Political Opinions, Racial or Ethnic Origin, Sexual Orientation, Educational Activities, and Employment History) had a 21% to 25% decrease in disapproval ratings, while neutral ratings changed by -4% to 4%, and approval ratings increased by 21% to 26%. Approval change for High Concern personal data (Health Records, Calendar Appointments, and Financial Records) had a disapproval decrease of 41% to 47%, while neutral increased by 4% to 23%, and approval increased by 21% to 43%.

B. Perceptions of Personal Data Reminder Communication

Participants were asked to rate their approval of how the two communication policies communicated the three personal data reminders. These ratings are shown in figure 2. The figure shows that for all three reminders, approval for the experimental policy was higher than approval for the control policy.

Using Mann-Whitney U tests the approval rating for the two policies when a **new** neighbour is present was found to be statically significant for all three personal data reminders: Phone Bill ($z = -12.91$, $p =< .001$), Political Party ($z = -12.82$, $p =< .001$), and Preferences ($z = -4.08$, $p =< .001$). When a **trusted** neighbour was present, there were also statistically significant differences between the approval of both communication policies: Phone Bill ($z = -9.85$, $p =< .001$), Political Party ($z = -9.53$, $p =< .001$), and Preferences ($z = -2.28$, $p = 0.023$). In all cases, approval increased for the experimental policy compared to the control policy.

For the control policy, there was no statistical difference between participants' approval ratings by neighbour type for all three reminders. However, a slight trend is shown, with approval for the trusted neighbour being higher than for the new neighbour, showing some influence of the neighbour type on the approval rating. For the control communication policy, the approval for the Phone Bill reminder had majority disapproval for both neighbours, with 64% disapproval for the trusted neighbour and 72% for the new neighbour. The preferences reminder has majority approval for both neighbour types, with 82% approval for a trusted neighbour and 76% for a new neighbour. For political opinions, the approval ratings are split over approve, neutral and disapprove, showing participants' ambivalence for this reminder. Political opinions have 41% disapprove, 26% neutral, and 31% approve of a trusted neighbour, 47% disapprove, 29% neutral, and 22% approve of a new neighbour.

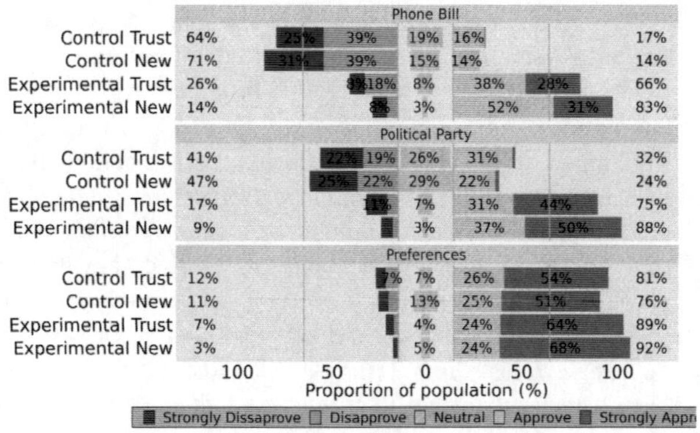

Figure 2. A bar graph showing the distribution of approval ratings for the different personal data reminders.

For the experimental policy, approval ratings for the neighbour types were found to be statistically different using Mann-Whitney U tests for Phone Bill ($Z = -2.31$, $p = .021$) and Political Party ($Z = -2.18$, $p = .029$) reminders. In both cases, approval ratings decreased for a trusted neighbour compared to a new neighbour. Approval drops by 17% for the phone bill reminder and 13% for the political party reminder. While approval drops, both neighbour types have a majority approval for the experimental policy. Phone bill has an overall approval rating of 66% for a trusted neighbour and 83% for a new neighbour, while Political Party has an approval rating of 75% for a trusted neighbour and 88% for a new neighbour.

In participants' qualitative responses, the common theme as to why approval was lower for a trusted neighbour was that they felt like they were hiding information from the neighbour. This is because when the robot notifies the user of a medium or high concern reminder, it still says the personal data item but does not go into detail. For example, political opinions are a medium concern personal data, so the robot would say, "I have a reminder about your political opinions would you like this saying out loud?". This caused participants to feel uncomfortable as the third party heard that they had a reminder on this but could not know what it was about. Participants gave feedback that instead of saying the personal data item in the reminder, the robot could instead say a generic statement such as "I have an important reminder for you".

IV. DISCUSSION

This work presents a hybrid study conducted online and in person. This work aimed to see how a communication policy based on the classification of personal data exposure sensitivity [16] is perceived when used to communicate personal data reminders in front of a neighbour. We manipulated the neighbour type, either being a new or trusted neighbour.

Our approach presented was to use a classification-based communication policy. This policy uses the sensitivity of the personal data being communicated to adapt how it communicates the reminder. **RQ1** wanted to see if such a policy positively influenced views on a robot communicating personal data. The results presented show that the majority of participants were very happy with the robot communicating using this classification policy while feeling their personal data was secure with the robot.

RQ2 aimed to understand if a communication policy could influence trust in the robot communicating personal data. Our findings suggest that trust is influenced by the communication policy. The majority of participants (86%) said they would trust our classification policy to provide reminders using personal data while keeping the personal data secure. When participants were asked if they trusted the control policy, 85% said they would not trust it to keep their personal data secure while communicating it. The results also show that after experiencing our communication policy, participants were more approving of a robot knowing and storing personal data items. Further, after experiencing the control policy, the disapproval rating increased for the robot to know and store personal data items. This means that through the display of the classification policy alone, trust is built between the user and the robot to handle personal data.

RQ3 looked at whether a classification communication policy could appropriately communicate personal data when a third party is present. For all three personal data reminders, the classification policy had a majority approval for communicating the personal data. However, when comparing this approval between neighbour types, approval decreased for a trusted neighbour compared to a new neighbour. Participants' reasons for this were that saying the topic of the communication made it seem like they were hiding something from their neighbour. Instead, a more generalised statement could be used while still notifying users of a reminder that needs their attention.

Our results found no influence of the robot's anthropomorphism (Humanoid or Non-Humanoid) on participants' approval ratings. These results agree with the findings from Rossi et al. [22], who found that a robot's appearance does not influence the trust of a robot to have personal data.

V. Conclusion

The classification policy presented in this work increased the participant's approval of the robot knowing and storing personal data for personalised communication. These results show that demonstrating secure communication of personal data improves users' trust in the robot having the personal data. For HRI, this means that instead of inhibiting personalisation by not allowing the robot access to personal data, the robot can demonstrate secure personal data communication. This approach would allow personalisation to be uninhibited, removing the need for users to make privacy trade-offs for personalisation gains [11] [12].

References

[1] H.-M. Gross *et al.*, "Robot companion for domestic health assistance: Implementation, test and case study under everyday conditions in private apartments," in *2015 IEEE/RSJ IROS*, 2015, pp. 5992–5999.

[2] M. M. A. de Graaf and S. Ben Allouch, "The evaluation of different roles for domestic social robots," in *2015 24th IEEE RO-MAN*, 2015, pp. 676–681.

[3] D. Leyzberg, S. Spaulding, and B. Scassellati, "Personalizing robot tutors to individuals' learning differences," in *Proceedings of the 2014 ACM/IEEE HRI.* ACM, 2014, pp. 423–430.

[4] W. Ho, K. Dautenhahn, M. Y. Lim, and K. Du Casse, "Modelling human memory in robotic companions for personalisation and long-term adaptation in hri." in *Frontiers in Artificial Intelligence and Applications*, vol. 221, 01 2010, pp. 64–71.

[5] M. Heckmann and A. Richter, "Assistance system and method for providing information to a user using speech output," Germanys Patent EP3 772 735, Feb. 10, 2021.

[6] K. L. Koay *et al.*, "Hey! there is someone at your door. a hearing robot using visual communication signals of hearing dogs to communicate intent," in *2013 IEEE ALife*, 2013, pp. 90–97.

[7] P. Uluer, N. Akalın, and H. Köse, "A new robotic platform for sign language tutoring," *International Journal of Social Robotics*, vol. 7, no. 5, pp. 571–585, Nov. 2015.

[8] R. M. Calo, "Robots and privacy," in *Machine Ethics and Robot Ethics*. Routledge, 2020, ch. 33, pp. 491–505.

[9] C. Bhagavatula *et al.*, "Biometric authentication on iphone and android: Usability, perceptions, and influences on adoption," *Proceedings 2015 Workshop on Usable Security*, pp. 1–10, 2015.

[10] J. Klow *et al.*, "Privacy, utility, and cognitive load in remote presence systems," in *11th ICSR*. Berlin, Heidelberg: Springer-Verlag, 2019, pp. 730–739.

[11] D. J. Butler, J. Huang, F. Roesner, and M. Cakmak, "The privacy-utility tradeoff for remotely teleoperated robots," in *2015 10th ACM/IEEE International Conference on Human-Robot Interaction (HRI)*, 2015, pp. 27–34.

[12] J. Klow *et al.*, "Privacy, utility, and cognitive load in remote presence systems," in *Proceedings of the Companion of the 2017 ACM/IEEE International Conference on Human-Robot Interaction*, ser. HRI '17. New York, NY, USA: Association for Computing Machinery, 2017, pp. 167–168.

[13] J. Marchang and A. Di Nuovo, "Assistive multimodal robotic system: Security and privacy issues, challenges, and possible solutions," *Applied Sciences*, vol. 12, p. 2174, 2022.

[14] C. Di Napoli, G. Ercolano, and S. Rossi, "Personalized home-care support for the elderly: a field experience with a social robot at home," *User Modeling and User-Adapted Interaction*, vol. 33, no. 2, pp. 405–440, Apr 2023.

[15] A. Rossi, G. Perugia, and S. Rossi, "Investigating customers' perceived sensitivity of information shared with a robot bartender," in *Social Robotics: 13th International Conference, ICSR 2021, Singapore, Singapore, November 10-13, 2021, Proceedings*. Berlin, Heidelberg: Springer-Verlag, 2021, pp. 119–129.

[16] L. Riches, K. L. Koay, and P. Holthaus, "Classification of personal data used by personalised robot companions based on concern of exposure," in *Social Robotics*. Cham: Springer Nature Switzerland, 2022, pp. 228–237.

[17] Aldebaran, "Pepper." [Online]. Available: https://www.aldebaran.com/en/pepper [retrieved: April, 2024]

[18] Zebra, "Autonomous mobile robots." [Online]. Available: https://www.zebra.com/us/en/products/autonomous-mobile-robots.html [retrieved: April, 2024]

[19] P. Holthaus, "Robot house." [Online]. Available: https://robothouse.herts.ac.uk/ [retrieved: April, 2024]

[20] S. D. Gosling, P. J. Rentfrow, and W. B. Swann, "A very brief measure of the big-five personality domains," *Research in Personality*, vol. 37, pp. 504–528, 2003.

[21] T. Nomura, T. Suzuki, T. Kanda, and K. Kato, "Measurement of negative attitudes toward robots," *Social Behaviour and Communication in Biological and Artificial Systems*, vol. 7, pp. 437–454, 2006.

[22] A. Rossi, K. L. Koay, and S. Rossi, "Evaluating people's perception of trust and privacy based on robot's appearance," in *2023 32nd IEEE International Conference on Robot and Human Interactive Communication (RO-MAN)*, 2023, pp. 1928–1933.

The Use of Artificial Intelligence for Personalized Learning: Teacher Perspective

Trym Simensen Nerem
Norwegian University of Science and Technology
Department of Design
Gjøvik, Norway
e-mail: trym.s.nerem@ntnu.no

Simen Frogner Hellesnes
Norwegian University of Science and Technology
Department of Design
Gjøvik, Norway
e-mail: simenhell@gmail.com

Yavuz Inal
Norwegian University of Science and Technology
Department of Design
Gjøvik, Norway
e-mail: yavuz.inal@ntnu.no

Carlos Vicient Monllaó
Norwegian University of Science and Technology
Department of Design
Gjøvik, Norway
e-mail: carlos.vicient@ntnu.no

***Abstract*— This study aimed to explore teachers' current practices around the personalization of education for students with reading comprehension challenges. We also delved into their experiences and opinions on using artificial intelligence in this regard. Interviews with teachers from various schools and varying degrees of experience were the primary data. Study results showed that insufficient time and resources were the most prominent challenges for teachers, followed by the number of different levels and needs they had to adapt to. Teachers were positive about using artificial intelligence and had used it before, but very few of them had tried integrating artificial intelligence to provide personalized education. The most prominent critique was a lack of trust in the accuracy of texts generated with artificial intelligence. Misuse of artificial intelligence by educators and students (e.g., cheating) was reported as a fear, prompting a discussion on the importance of educating everyone on the proper use of technology in the ecosystem. Overall, teachers see artificial intelligence as an opportunity to mitigate their ongoing challenges regarding personalized education and augment students' engagement by tailoring learning experiences to each student's needs, preferences, and learning styles.**

Keywords- Artificial Intelligence; Generative AI; Personalized Learning; Adapted Education; Reading Comprehension.

I. INTRODUCTION

The Norwegian educational system has faced two critical issues in recent years: the decrease in the number of new applicants for all teacher education programs [1] and the high amount (44%) of active teachers considering leaving their profession [2]. This is despite most teachers (86%) reporting that they enjoy being a teacher; however, as a possible explanation, teachers experience significant time pressure, with the majority (93%) reporting that various tasks are hindering them from doing their pedagogical work [2]. These tasks diminish teachers' available time for learning-related tasks, such as text adaptation, leaving them with insufficient time to create personalized learning materials for their students.

Personalized learning is a fundamental pedagogical principle and is important in helping students reach their potential [3][4]. It enables teachers to tailor their courses based on each student's needs, preferences, and learning styles and provide equal opportunities to all students instead of creating a learning environment based on a traditional one-size-fits-all approach. In Norway, all students have the right to receive personalized education by law [5]. Teachers are responsible for planning and holding the class and ensuring all students receive their entitled individual learning. In a typical class, there are significant differences in the level of students and learning difficulties, such as Attention Deficit/Hyperactivity Disorder (ADHD), reading and writing difficulties, and language difficulties. Teachers need enough time to support each student's development, which requires more effort. This leads to the process of providing personalized education being complex and challenging.

One possible avenue worth exploring is to mitigate this problem by using Artificial Intelligence (AI). AI-assisted solutions have the potential to provide a personalized learning environment and equalize education for everyone [6]. AI can enhance education quality in multiple ways, such as data recording, pattern detection, and adaptation [7]. With its ability to analyze large datasets, AI can generate texts of good quality for end users, making it a valid option when considering text processing. It has the capabilities to be used as an intelligent tutoring system [8] as well as generating alternative text for non-text content, auto-captioning for videos, word prediction, text simplification [9], and text adaptation for individuals with cognitive and learning challenges [10]. By using AI as a learning tool, teachers could save time adapting education, and students could gain more personalized learning materials.

Previous research has shown that AI-assisted solutions have been proven to be effective in personalized learning within the educational context by enhancing educational material, students' engagement, and learning outcomes [11][12]. Further, learners and instructors have positive attitudes toward AI integration for personalized education [6]. However, exploring the use of AI to personalize education around text adaptation for individual students' levels has been a low priority [12][13], highlighting the current study's novelty.

Taken together, this study's aims are twofold: first, it aims to understand the current practices of teachers from the primary to secondary level, the challenges they encounter, and their solutions to provide personalized education. Second, we explored teachers' opinions on using AI to personalize the learning process within the educational context and their experience with AI. We believe the study results contribute insights into the current issues regarding AI integration into personalized education and teachers' perspectives.

The remaining part of the paper proceeds as follows: Section 2 explains the study's methods and reasonings in detail. Section 3 presents the study's findings, focusing on two key themes: teachers' current practices of personalized education and their opinions on using AI for this purpose. Section 4 contains comparisons to earlier research and analysis of the results. The final section concludes the study and presents recommendations for future research.

II. Methods

We conducted an exploratory study to understand teachers' practices on personalized education for students with different reading comprehension levels and their perspectives on AI integration in educational settings. The interview was the primary data collection method, and it included teachers in various schools and all school levels with varying degrees of experience.

A. Participants

A total of 20 teachers participated in the study, representing 15 different Norwegian schools. Participants were selected based on their involvement in courses with a significant emphasis on text-related content. A deliberate effort was made to ensure representation from each level of the school system by including a minimum of five teachers from elementary school, eight from middle school, and five from high school. In addition, there were two teachers from a learning center, a school for adults providing special education or primary and lower secondary school education. The teachers' experience varied from two years up to 41 years, with the average being 17.4 years. The most common course taught was Norwegian (n=15, 75%), followed by social studies (n=9, 45%) and science (n=7, 35%). On average, the teacher's self-reported digital literacy was 3.7 out of 5, with the lowest result being 3 out of 5. All teachers use a PC or a tablet besides their mobile phones. They spend, on average, six to seven hours daily on digital devices.

B. Interview Guidelines

The interview guidelines comprised three sections. The first section focused on gathering teachers' demographic information, including age, years of experience, courses they teach, and their responsibilities in the school. We also asked at which school level they taught to better understand the focus on personalized education and how it was performed at the different school levels.

The second section delved into the teachers' work and thoughts around personalized education within reading comprehension. We investigated how teachers implement strategies for reading comprehension - examining the frequency and scope of these personalizations, the tools they utilize, and any challenges they face implementing them. Additionally, we aimed to understand the methods they consider most effective for personalized learning and whether there are strategies they would integrate more if afforded additional time. Another important topic in this section was how this personalized education was tailored towards different learning difficulties.

The final section focused on teachers' awareness and perspectives on using AI in education. The questions aimed to uncover their familiarity with the technology, instances of its utilization in teaching practices, perceived educational applications, and any associated concerns. Through these questions, we sought insights into the nuanced dynamics of teachers' relationships with AI regarding its practical integration and broader pedagogical considerations.

C. Procedure

The interviewees were acquired through a mix of personal networks, directly emailing random teachers at schools in the surrounding area and contacting school administrators. Given the interview's strong focus on reading comprehension, one of the prerequisites was that the teacher taught at least one text-based subject. We also aimed to limit the number of teachers to three per school, and in cases where there were multiple teachers from the same school, they had to belong to different sections. Physical interviews were used for the teachers in the local area. Otherwise, the interview was conducted via video call. Two researchers were present during the interviews to guide the process and take notes.

D. Data Analysis

Data from the interviews was sorted by entering all the interview responses into a spreadsheet. The answers were organized by having each question as a column and the interviewee number as rows. This gave us a good overview of the data, and we could sort by different data points to examine links and differences between subgroups of interviewees. The first analysis round was done by reviewing each question individually and writing down the main themes and findings. This helped create a baseline of data that we could then analyze further to find patterns and extract the relevant information. In the next step of the analysis, we used the established themes to do a thematic analysis of our data [14]; the main themes were current practices for personalized education and how teachers approach AI in education.

III. Results

The findings from the interviews are presented in two sections. The first section explores teachers' perspectives on personalized reading comprehension education, while the second section focuses on experiences and reflections regarding AI integration.

A. Personalized Education

Current Situation. Time availability was a significant concern among interviewed teachers. When asked about their ability to adjust teaching to meet student needs, most teachers (n=16, 80%) highlighted a deficiency in time. The remaining teachers (n=4, 20%) reported having sufficient time without encroaching upon their work hours. Two of the teachers who reported having sufficient time clarified that this was due to their class being about half the size of a normal-sized (around 15 rather than 30) class, with one saying, *"Yes, I have enough time since there are few students in my class, but it can still be difficult when many students are struggling."* The other two teachers who expressed having enough time were affiliated with high schools, indicating a notable discrepancy among K-13 level educators.

A contributing factor to most teachers' time constraints is the significant amount of time teachers use on personalized learning through text adaptations. Within any given class, there is a large variety of students' reading levels; one teacher noted that there are up to 10 different levels that must be adapted to. This makes it harder for teachers to adapt to each student as they first must find the correct level to adapt to and then do the actual adaptation, with one stating, *"Managing the capacity and resources for following up on the students is a problem, 3 out of 4 can follow the class, but the challenge is picking up the rest."* There were 11 (55%) teachers providing a direct number of students for whom they made extra adaptations regarding reading comprehension. The result showed that 91% (n=10) of those teachers were doing extra adaptation for 17% of their students or more, with the highest reported number being 42%. These adaptations, in combination with the adaptations done for the remaining students, resulted in a high amount of time spent adapting for reading comprehension. Of the teachers (n=16, 80%) who provided a clear amount of time spent providing these adaptations, 56% (n=9) reported spending 3.5 hours per week or more adapting texts.

Challenges. A significant number of teachers (n=10, 50%) emphasized that students had different prerequisites regarding reading skills. They mentioned the importance of parents focusing on their children starting to read early and the extent of this support. Another frequently mentioned cause (n=8, 40%) was the support students received through kindergarten and the school system. Here, the quality of educators and the economic conditions in kindergartens and schools were mentioned as important factors, with one saying, *"It matters a lot how the school is tailored to the students. With greater resources in the school, students will benefit more."* Further, some teachers (n=4, 20%) highlighted societal changes as a significant cause of what they perceived as a marked negative trend in reading abilities in recent years. It was explained that students generally read less, thus negatively affecting their overall reading level. One teacher pointed out that reading has faced competition from other digital devices, suggesting that this has had a detrimental effect on attention spans and reading endurance. Another teacher believed there had been a clear negative trend in reading skills in the Norwegian school system since the introduction of tablets/computers to all students, considering it to be a direct cause of this trend.

When teachers adapt texts for students, they make sure the difficulty level of the text fits the student, as well as differentiate how the text is adjusted based on which learning difficulties the students have. A teacher clarified this issue by saying, *"If two students in the class need a simplified text, I often think they need the same one when, in fact, they should each get one."* This is one of the reasons why adapting texts is time-consuming and demanding, as teachers often need to adapt texts in more ways than just having different difficulty levels. Interviewed teachers expressed how they adapted texts to students with ADHD, reading and writing, language, and cognitive difficulties. For students with ADHD, the teachers emphasized the need for short, concrete, interesting, and well-structured texts. This could involve creating useful summaries of the texts. For students with language difficulties, the focus was more on simplified language and especially on replacing difficult words. There was a high focus on oral solutions for students with reading and writing difficulties. This could either be through text-to-speech programs or by discussing topics orally. Teachers also emphasized the importance of repetition and practice time for these students. For students with cognitive difficulties, teachers mentioned the importance of connecting topics to their personal experiences. The texts should also be simplified, engaging, and provide concrete information.

Solutions. In practice, providing personalized education varies from teacher to teacher and is currently done by changing teachers' methods and tailoring the tasks and texts the students work with. Some teachers (n=9, 45%) adapt what methods they use, with one saying, *"I try to make good PowerPoints that both simplify what is written in the textbook, as well as drawing out the essence."* Another teacher uses a reading technique to ensure every student follows along; *"We always read and listen at the same time; for those with reading difficulties, it often helps to have the text read out loud."* On the other hand, some (n=4, 20%) adapt by offering different amounts and difficulty levels of tasks. This includes harder tasks and texts for the stronger students and simpler ones for those struggling. A teacher explained this strategy: "*I always have to make sure to have extra tasks for the quickest students. I spend a lot of time finding tasks in the book or online for the weaker students so they can also get a feeling of mastery.*" Adaption of texts was mentioned by many teachers (n=12, 60%), especially having texts of the right level, with one stating, *"We have access to* *texts divided into levels. This way, it is simpler for those who struggle with reading. We have a book divided into moon-texts that are simpler than sun-texts. I adapt tasks according to reading level so every student will accomplish something."* This includes content length, sentence length, ease of language, difficulty levels of terms, text structure, and how well the students can engage with the text.

Acquiring texts of the correct level falls on the teacher in most situations, with 65% (n=13) of the teachers mentioning that they adapt texts they have found. The advent of the digitalization of the school system has helped this. One of the teachers highlighted that *"In many ways, it's easier since the students got digital textbooks; it's easier to give them individual tasks. And I can choose the text amount and adjust it for the students."* Additionally, public tools are available for all teachers, such as support websites for the different curriculum books and tools available for students to assist in reading comprehension, like programs for reading out loud, books of a lower level, and digital books. Only two teachers (10%) took the next step into digitally assisted adapted education by using AI to write and adapt texts for them, with one stating, *"I use ChatGPT, it generates texts, and if there are two or more levels, I get it to make more texts."*

B. Artificial Intelligence in Educational Settings

Teachers' Opinions on AI. All teachers were somewhat familiar with artificial intelligence (mostly ChatGPT). Most teachers had used ChatGPT (n=14, 70%), and almost half had used it for an educational purpose (n=9, 45%) (e.g., as a writing partner, for research, to make illustrations, to create texts on certain words, and to introduce it to students). Overall, most (n=15, 75%) were positive towards AI integration. Only one teacher was negative to using AI: *"A lot of what you learn is new skills, not only knowledge. [...] The students must learn how to struggle with a hard task, this way they will feel a sense of mastery when they complete it".* Another teacher approached AI as a supplementary tool highlighting human control: *"I think it could be a positive thing, but it depends on how it is used. If you let it take over and don't think for yourselves, it would be inconvenient, and you would not get anything useful out of it. It could be useful if it is used as a tool to supplement but not take over."* Similarly, five teachers (25%) specifically underscored a fear that the wrong use of ChatGPT could take over too much and lead to the students not learning the process of learning and their texts losing the "human factor."

Opportunities and Negative Aspects of AI. The most frequently mentioned opportunities of AI were that it could be used for personalized education (n=8, 40%), with one saying, *"It could be used for level adapted reading. I could add multiple criteria, such as interests and sentence design to the AI and receive a text."* Another teacher mentioned that AI could be used as an assistant for substitutes and help with some students, mentioning, *"It can be used for writing or reading difficulties, and in cases where you have a substitute teacher, they can get some support from the AI."* Saving time was also stated by some participants (n=5, 25%), and one teacher mentioned it as the foremost reason for using AI: *"First and foremost, it is time-saving."* Using AI to make tasks was noted by 25% (n=5) of the teachers, and one of them talked about their idea for an AI-powered app: *"You could make an app with multiple choice questions that know the student and then spread out questions according to the level of the student."* A few teachers (n=3, 15%) shared a positive outlook on AI, albeit with the caveat that the current system may not support it, with one stating, *"I think it's good, I think it is underutilized in the school, and there are a lot of opportunities, but you have to rethink the educational system."*

The most prominent critique of AI was a lack of trust in the accuracy of AI's answers, especially when it comes to younger students using it. A teacher explained this concern: *"I think many students lack the basic general knowledge and source criticism not to trust ChatGPT. They may take its facts for granted and not read through and evaluate whether it's correct or wrong."* Additionally, some teachers (n=5, 25%) mentioned that students may use it to cheat and that it is difficult for teachers to notice or prove it. Another group of teachers (n=6, 30%) displayed a concern that implementing AI in school without providing a proper education on how to use it could have a negative effect on students' learning outcomes. One teacher raised their concerns by asking, *"Will they remember what they learned from ChatGPT? And will the students learn the process of acquiring information themselves?"*

AI Integration. Regarding the use of AI in education, seven teachers (35%) highlighted various ways AI could contribute to adapting teaching to students. Four (20%) suggested that AI could help strengthen weaker students. Two teachers suggested that AI could be used to generate individually tailored texts. Furthermore, one teacher explained that a student's specific challenges and interests could be incorporated into the text, creating an optimized reading practice for a particular student. Another suggestion mentioned by two teachers (10%) is to utilize the strengths of AI in an AI-based assessment tool: *"Assessment of students takes up much time. If an AI could continuously assess the students, it would have a better foundation for accurate evaluation."* One teacher also proposed how AI could be used for personalized education by leveraging the potential of an enhanced text-to-speech version.

A desire to focus on teaching students how to use AI and understand its possibilities and limitations was expressed by five teachers (25%). This group wanted to use different methods, such as using AI to teach students about source criticism, making effective prompts, searching for information, acquiring knowledge, and finding inspiration for topics they can write essays about.

IV. Discussion

Personalized education has been increasingly a standard in the Norwegian educational system. Teachers endeavor to provide personalized learning for students using various resources, such as printed materials, support websites, or electronic documents. However, it requires additional effort to properly meet each student's needs, preferences, and learning styles. This study explored current issues affecting personalized education and teachers' experiences and opinions on using AI for this purpose. With the advent of large language models like ChatGPT, Google Bard, and GitHub Copilot, coupled with their widespread proliferation, an exciting opportunity has arisen to use AI for text adaptation to individual students' levels of comprehension. However, teachers' opinions on AI and competence in its use are crucial for the prevalence of the technology to be integrated successfully into education.

In line with previous research [6], in our study, almost all teachers, regardless of age, years of experience, and geographical location, held a positive attitude toward using AI for educational purposes. We initially expected the younger generation to be more open to accepting AI. Still, the study shows a homogenous distribution of opinions, with no definitive separation based on the above-mentioned demographics. This could show that the teachers, in general, are open to using AI in the educational context. However, despite their positive outlook, very few teachers have experienced using AI for text adaptations to personalize their students' learning journey. This leads us to highlight the importance of education for prospective teachers in teacher education programs and active teachers to integrate, such emerging technologies effectively, as we observed that most teachers in the study had an abstract idea of how AI would be utilized in education. Most envisioned it as a chat solution, not a possible learning tool.

Teachers are at the center of personalized education; therefore, addressing their concerns about AI is important to understand how to support them with their work on AI-assisted learning. There are six main challenges under human-centered AI: human-AI interaction, human well-being, governance and independent oversight, responsible design of AI, privacy, and design and evaluation frameworks [15]. Similarly, through the interviews, we found teachers' most prominent concern to be where the AI gets its information and, generally, a worry about the truthfulness and accuracy of AI-generated content. Additionally, the teachers reported fear of misuse of the technology by educators and students during human-AI interaction. They believe teachers should use AI to support the learning practices of their students properly and be careful about providing clear guidelines on the ethical use of AI, as students may use it for cheating.

Therefore, in a similar vein, ethical issues in the use of AI [16] and its practical implementations should be integrated into the curriculum to help students familiarize themselves with the technology and gain more insight into its proper use. This integration is important for all levels of students, from primary to secondary schools to higher education, to prepare them for the future, as AI will likely continue to transform the world profoundly.

We found that a lack of time is one of the biggest challenges in providing personalized education. The teachers spent significant time tailoring texts for multiple students in the class. Even though personalized education has been a priority in Norwegian schools, teachers experience an increased time challenge due to escalated non-pedagogical tasks [2]. This, combined with the decrease in teacher education programs and a high number of inundated teachers [1], paints a picture of a future where the challenges regarding sufficient time could be even greater. A possible solution to mitigate the problem could be to automate parts of the personalization through AI technology.

Molenaar [17] describes a model of six levels of AI-automation regarding personalized learning ranging from no AI assistance through AI teacher assistance to full automation, where AI takes all controls and handles the tasks automatically without teacher involvement in the process. The model explains the roles and responsibilities from both educators' and learners' perspectives. Based on the results of our study, we observe that teachers are not ready for full automation, as they highlighted the importance of human judgment and control on AI-generated content and mostly see AI-assisted solutions as supplementary learning material that can help teachers deliver better teaching. Although there is a surge in the use of AI in almost every area, including education, both teachers and students need more time to digest the technology and thereby fully embrace it. When considered in the context of education, we suggest the role of AI in the integration should be appropriately clarified.

A key part of our study was investigating how teachers adapt the education for students with various learning difficulties. It is, however, important to remember that all students have equal right to personalized learning. With teachers' current time constraints, they may feel obligated to prioritize and focus on students struggling to follow the rest of the class. This could result in them not having sufficient time to properly adapt to their stronger students and therefore not reaching their potential learning outcome. By improving the teachers' efficiency when adapting to their weaker students, teachers can save time, which can then be used to adapt to their stronger students, resulting in a better learning outcome for all levels of students.

V. CONCLUSION AND FUTURE WORK

AI-assisted solutions can democratize education by scaffolding students' learning journeys based on their individual needs, preferences, and learning styles. As teachers play a central role in personalized education, their opinions on the use of AI within the educational context are crucial for the pervasiveness of the technology. Based on the results of our study, we conclude that a lack of time is a prominent challenge in providing a personalized learning environment. Teachers see AI as an opportunity to mitigate their ongoing challenges and enhance students' engagement. However, distrust in the accuracy of AI-generated texts and fear of misuse of the technology by both educators and students are common concerns. The teachers have little experience using AI in an educational setting, indicating a need for training to use the technology properly. This study focused on one aspect of personalized education (i.e., text adaptation for students with reading comprehension challenges), teachers' current practices, and opinions on AI. Students' learning styles and personal characteristics affect their learning preferences [18], suggesting that future research should focus on the "student" aspect of AI integration for personalized education. Additionally, with the widespread proliferation of generative AI, there is a need to explore the effective use of prompts to get maximum benefit from AI integration in education.

REFERENCES

[1] Samordna Opptak, "Pressemelding 24.04.23," 24 April 2023. [Online]. Available from: https://www.samordnaopptak.no/info/om/sokertall/pressemelding-240423-bm.pdf [retrieved: April, 2024]

[2] C. Pedersen, R. B. Reiling, F. F. Vennerød-Diesen, R. Alne and A. Skålholdt, "Evaluering av norm for lærertetthet: Sluttrapport" [Evaluation of the Norm for Teacher Density: Final Report], NIFU, 2022.

[3] M. L. Bernacki, M. J. Greene, and N. G. Lobczowski "A systematic review of research on personalized learning: Personalized by whom, to what, how, and for what purpose (s)?," Educational Psychology Review, April 2021, pp. 1675-1715, doi: 10.1007/s10648-021-09615-8.

[4] H. Dumont and D.D. Ready, "On the promise of personalized learning for educational equity," NPJ Science of Learning, Aug 2023, vol. 8, Art.no. 26, doi: 10.1038/s41539-023-00174-x

[5] Norway. Education Act, § 1-3 Adapted Education. Amended 2018.

[6] A. Al-Badi, A. Khan, and Eid-Alotaibi, "Perceptions of Learners and Instructors towards Artificial Intelligence in Personalized Learning," Procedia Computer Science, April 2022, vol. 201, pp. 445-451, doi:10.1016/j.procs.2022.03.058

[7] M. Ninaus and M. Sailer, "Closing the loop – The human role in artificial intelligence for education," Front. Psychol., Aug. 2022, vol. 13, doi:10.3389/fpsyg.2022.956798.

[8] H. P. Maffon et al. "Architecture of an intelligent tutoring system applied to the breast cancer based on ontology, artificial neural networks and expert systems," The Sixth International Conference on Advances in Computer-Human Interactions, *ACHI,* IARIA, Feb 2013, pp. 210-214, ISSN: 2308-4138, ISBN: 978-1-61208-250-9

[9] T. Makati, "Machine learning for accessible web navigation," Web for all conference, (W4A '22), April 2022, Art. no. 23, pp. 1-3, doi:10.1145/3493612.3520463.

[10] S. Abou-Zahra, J. Brewer, and M. Cooper, "Artificial Intelligence (AI) for Web Accessibility: Is Conformance Evaluation a Way Forward?" Web for all conference (W4A '18), April 2018, Article 20, pp. 1-4, doi:10.1145/3192714.3192834.

[11] Z. Rasheed, S. Ghwanmeh, and A. Z. Abualkishik, "Harnessing Artificial Intelligence for Personalized Learning: A Systematic Review," Data and Metadata, Dec 2023, vol. 2, pp. 146-146, doi: 10.56294/dm2023146

[12] A. Bhutoria, "Personalized education and Artificial Intelligence in the United States, China, and India: A systematic review using a Human-In-The-Loop model," Computers and Education. Artificial Intelligence, April 2022, vol. 3, doi:10.1016/j.caeai.2022.100068.

[13] K. C. Li and B. T.-M. Wong, "Artificial Intelligence in Personalised Learning: A Bibliometric Analysis," Interactive Technology and Smart Education, May 2023, vol. 20, pp. 422–445, doi:10.1108/ITSE-01-2023-0007.

[14] V. Braun and V. Clarke, "Using thematic analysis in psychology," Qualitative Research in Psychology, Jan 2006, vol. 3, no. 2, pp. 77-101, doi:10.1191/1478088706qp063oa

[15] O. Ozmen Garibay et al. "Six Human-Centered Artificial Intelligence Grand Challenges," International Journal of Human–Computer Interaction, April 2023, vol. 39, pp. 391-437, doi: 10.1080/10447318.2022.2153320.

[16] J. Borenstein and A. Howard, "Emerging challenges in AI and the need for AI ethics education," AI and Ethics, Oct 2021, vol. 1, pp. 61-65, doi:_10.1007/s43681-020-00002-7

[17] I. Molenaar, "Personalisation of learning: Towards hybrid human-AI learning technologies," in OECD Digital Education Outlook 2021: Pushing the Frontiers with Artificial Intelligence, Blockchain and Robots, OECD, Oct 2021, pp. 57-72, doi: 10.1787/589b283f-en.

[18] Y. Inal and H. Guner, "Ensuring success in a large scale software project: An examination of the learning styles and characteristics of the potential end users," Gazi University Journal of Science, vol. 28, pp. 535-540, 2015.

Design of Japanese Character Input Screen for Smartwatch

Kaito Hino, Tota Mizuno, Shingo Tanaka, Miku Shimizu, Kazuyuki Mito and Naoaki Itakura
Graduate School of Informatics and Engineering
The University of Electro-Communications
1-5-1 Chofugaoka, Chofu, Tokyo, Japan
e-mail: kai.vs.1023@gmail.com, mizuno@uec.ac.jp, cleaveil06@yahoo.co.jp, m.shimizu.0320@gmail.com,
k.mito@uec.ac.jp, itakura@uec.ac.jp

Abstract—**The demand for smartwatches has been growing in recent years, and opportunities to perform operations on smartwatches are increasing. However, the screen size of smartwatches is small, and complex input such as character input is often erroneous. Another problem is the high screen occupancy of software keyboards. Therefore, there is a need for a better input screen design for smartwatches. Since Japanese input has more characters than alphabetical input, it is necessary to provide many options. Therefore, we have proposed a new Japanese character input screen design for smartwatches. The user interface design should allow many selections to be made on a small screen with touch input. The proposed design has keys arranged in a circular pattern at the edge of the screen, allowing for a large key display while minimizing screen occupancy. The input operation is by touch and slide, and the slide allows multiple selections to be made from a single key. This design has resulted in superior input speed and accuracy, as well as screen occupancy, compared to the previous design. We investigate and evaluate user interface designs that allow users to input characters more comfortably.**

Keywords-smartwatch; character input; interface;

I. INTRODUCTION

In recent years, with the development of technology, various types of smart devices have become popular. According to the "Telecommunication Usage Trend Survey" by the Ministry of Internal Affairs and Communications, the ownership rate of mobile terminals will be as high as 97.3% by 2021 [1]. Among these, wristwatch-type smartwatches are attracting attention. According to a survey by MM Research Institute, the domestic sales volume in fiscal year 2020 is expected to increase by 19.9% compared to the previous year, indicating that the smartwatch market is expanding [2]. Therefore, the demand for smartwatches is expected to grow further in the future, and more user-friendly functions are required.

Recently, touch input and voice input are the most common input interfaces for smartwatches. Touch input is an intuitive input method because users can input data by touching the input target displayed on the screen. On the other hand, there are some problems with touch input. For devices with a small screen area, such as smartwatches, the size of the input target is so small that the input is misinterpreted as if a neighboring button is pressed during touch input. This is called the Fat Finger problem [3]. In addition, the conventional software keyboard on smartwatches has a very large screen occupancy ratio, and the area where the user can see the input characters is small. In addition, since the input target is not physically separated from the screen, it is necessary to check the input target while gazing at the screen while inputting. In the voice input method, the input is made by speaking the input to a microphone. Since this input method does not require the user to touch the screen of the device for input, it avoids the problems mentioned for touch input, such as pressing the wrong button. However, voice input is difficult to use in public places, such as libraries and hospitals where voices are not allowed, and in noisy places, such as crowded places and under elevated railway tracks, thus limiting the environment in which it can be used. It is also reported that many people are not comfortable with the actual voice input [4]. To solve these problems, various input interfaces have been studied.

Currently, touch input is the most common input method for smartphones. Therefore, touch input, which is familiar to many users, is also used in smartwatches. For Japanese input, Romaji input and Kana input are commonly used. In Romaji input, you enter Japanese sounds using the English alphabet, which are automatically converted to Hiragana. In Kana input, hiragana is entered directly using the Japanese keyboard layout. In previous research, touch input for smartwatches with small screens has been studied extensively. Various input methods have been proposed, such as character input by a combination of stroke gestures and taps [5], character input by slide-in [6], and a circular kana input interface [7]. However, none of these methods can solve the Fat Finger problem or the screen occupancy problem.

Therefore, we proposed a new screen design for touch input and conducted a character input experiment [8]. The proposed screen design consists of 12 keys on a circle at the edge of the screen, with consonants and vowels arranged in a clockwise direction. Character input is performed by touch and slide, and the screen vibrates when the selected character changes during input. The experimental results showed that the average character input speed per minute was 41.5 character par minute, and the error rate was 2.1%. These results are superior to those of conventional touch input methods for smartwatches and demonstrate the usefulness of the proposed method. It is considered that the clockwise arrangement of keys enables intuitive input, and the placement of keys at the edge of the screen maximizes key display size resulting in higher accuracy.

In this study, we will investigate screen designs with better usability. Character input experiments will be conducted to investigate how screen design affects the accuracy and speed of character input.

The rest of the paper is structured as follows. In Section II, we present our proposed method. Section III present the experiments and we conclude our work in Section IV.

II. PROPOSED METHOD

In this study, we propose a screen design and input behavior as a character input method for smartwatches.

A. Screen Design

A character input screen design for a circular smartwatch was created based on a previous study [8]. In addition, a half-circle shape design was created in consideration of the fact that the keys are hidden by the fingers while inputting. These screen designs are shown in Figures 1 and 2. Since the screen size of a smartwatch is very small, we used the edge of the screen as the input area to make the input area as large as possible. In the design of Figure 1, twelve keys are arranged in a circular pattern at the edge of the screen, and 144 choices can be made by setting the screen state to two levels. In the design shown in Figure 2, the seven keys are arranged in a half-circle shape at the edge of the screen, and the number of choices is sufficient for character input by changing the state of the screen. These proposed designs have only two adjacent keys, reducing the possibility of pressing the wrong key compared to conventional keyboard designs.

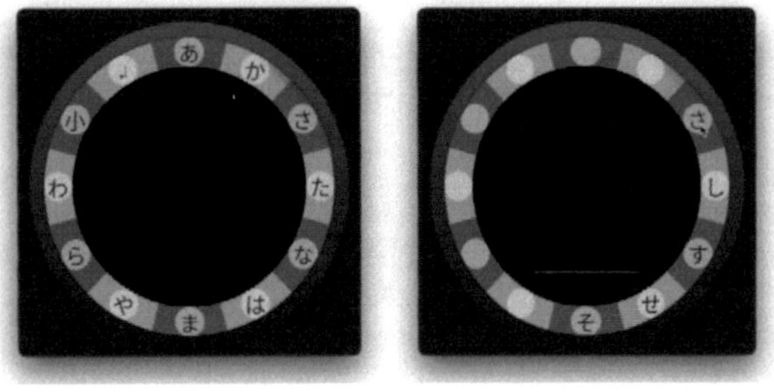

(a) Initial screen design (b) Design after screen transition

Figure 1. Proposal input screen design.

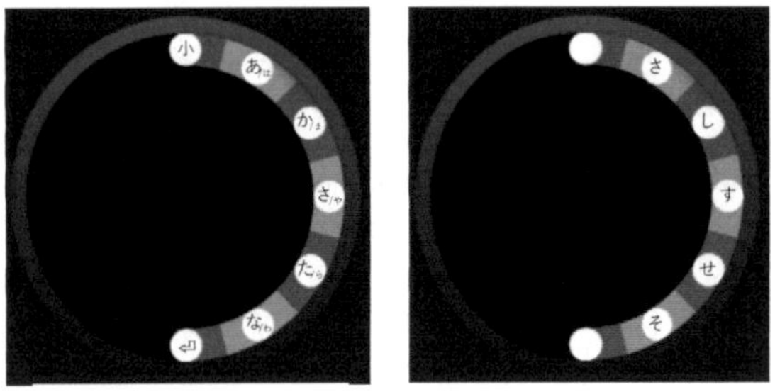

(a) Initial screen design (b) Design after screen transition

Figure 2. Proposal input screen design.

B. Input Action

Input operations are performed by touching or sliding within the colored input area of the proposed screen design. In this proposed method, touch means touching the screen with a finger, and slide means sliding a finger on the screen. When inputting with the design shown in Figure.1, after selecting a character by touch in Figure 1 (a), the display change second state such as Figure 1 (b). To select a character, slide your finger to the position of the character you wish to enter, and release your finger. These operations allow the characters to be entered. The input operation for the half-ring design (Figure 2) is the same as in Figure 1, where characters can be entered by touch and slide. In addition, two characters are contained in one key, so that selection is made with or without a flick toward the center of the screen.

III. EXPERIMENTAL METHOD

The device used for the experiment is a Google Pixel Watch 2 (diameter: 41mm, resolution: 320ppi) running Wear OS by Google. The experimental application is developed using Flutter. The application record touch logs and input characters in addition to the input functionality of the proposed method. The experiment is conducted in a seated position with the experimental terminal attached to the non-dominant arm, and the subjects input with their dominant hand. The subjects practice typing after the explanation of the input method to them before the experiment. The subjects input the Japanese words displayed on the experimental terminal 30 times. This task is performed with each of the proposed designs.

IV. CONCLUSION

In this study, we aimed to explore the design of input screens to make character input on smartwatches more comfortable. Specifically, we proposed two input screen designs: one with keys arranged in a circular layout and the other with keys arranged in a half-circular layout, and conducted character input experiments. The results indicated that the circular design had a higher input accuracy, while the half-circular design had a faster input speed. Additionally, when considering the overall input efficiency, which combines both accuracy and speed, the half-circular design was found to be superior. Furthermore, it was confirmed that the proposed designs showed better input efficiency compared to conventional methods.

The significance of this study lies in improving the comfort of character input on smartwatches, thereby providing users with a more user-friendly input screen.

For future research, it is necessary to consider screen designs not only for Japanese input but also for other languages. This will enable comfortable character input for global users of smartwatches.

REFERENCES

[1] Ministry of Internal Affairs and Communications, "Results of the 2021 Telecommunications Usage Trends Survey," Availab le from: https://www.soumu.go.jp/johotsusintokei/statistics/da ta/220527_1.pdf [retrieved: Apr., 2024].

[2] MM Research Institute, “Smartwatch Market Size Trends, Forecasts and Usage,” Available from: https://www.m2ri.jp/release/detail.html?id=508 [retrieved: Apr., 2024].

[3] K. A. Siek, Y. Rogers, and K. H. Connelly, “Fat finger worries: how older and younger users physically interact with PDAS,” Proc. the 2005 IFIP TC13 international conf. Human-Computer Interaction (INTERACT), pp. 267-280, 2005.

[4] KDDI, "Half of respondents find searching for information by text input 'troublesome' and over 70% find voice search in public 'embarrassing,'" 40% of respondents want to use voice control of home appliances "if no one is at home," Available: http://news.kddi.com/kddi/corporate/newsrelease/2017/10/05/besshi2726.html [retrieved: Apr., 2024].

[5] N. Ozaki, S. Honda, T. Tanaka, K. Akita, and Y. Sagawa, "A Character Input Method for a Rectangular Smartwatch by Combination of Stroke Gesture and Tap," IPSJ Journal, vol. 59, no. 8 pp. 1511-1519, 2018.

[6] K. Akita, T. Tanaka, and Y. Sagawa, “SliT: Character input method for smart watch with low screen occupancy,” Journal of Human Interface Society : human interface, vol. 21, no. 1 pp. 131-140, 2019.

[7] T. Tojo, Y. Honda, T. Kato, and S. Yamamoto, “BubbleSlide: Annular Layout Japanese Kana Text Entry Interface for Smartwatches,” IPSJ Journal, vol. 60, no. 11 pp. 2075-2084, 2019.

[8] K. Hino, T. Mizuno, Y. Matsumoto, K. Mito, and N. Itakura, "Study of Character Input Using Mounted Sensor in Smartwatch," 28th International Symposium on Artificial Life and Robotics (AROB), OS14-1, 2023.

Data Handling for PLC-based Research Facilities - How to Interact With Data?

Dennis Marschall*, Nicola Bergs*, Daniel Sept*, Michael Butzek*, Nikolaos Margaritis*, and Ghaleb Natour*†
*Engineering und Technologie (ZEA-1), Central Institute of Engineering, Electronics and Analytics (ZEA)
Forschungszentrum Jülich GmbH, 52425 Jülich, Germany
†Welding and Joining Institute, Faculty of Mechanical Engineering
RWTH Aachen University, 52062 Aachen, Germany
email: [d.marschall, n.bergs, d.sept, m.butzek, n.margaritis, g.natour]@fz-juelich.de

Abstract—**The simple access to and long-term storage of measurement data at research facilities play an important role and represents an essential basis for scientific work. There are various solutions for data acquisition, such as the Experimental Physics and Industrial Control System (EPICS) Archiver or the TANGO Framework, which are particularly suitable for use with large scientific devices. For small to medium-sized Programmable Logic Controller (PLC) controlled systems, it is often not worth the effort of such a framework, so that there is often still a lot of room for improvement. This paper describes the development of a database-based acquisition system that offers the researcher easy access to the measurement data, while ensuring good usability. In addition to data storage, the system has the ability to transfer data like parameters or test routines to the PLC for execution.**

Keywords-data acquisition, plc-controlled system, long-term storage.

I. Introduction

In research facilities, the data storage of small to medium-sized systems and test setups is often based on text files. The measurement data generated in the Programmable Logic Controller (PLC) can either be written directly to a Comma-Separated-Values (CSV) -file in the PLC [1] and stored on the file system, or it can be read out by third-party software products [2][3], such as LabView© or Matlab© and then stored as a file. The resulting text files are often transferred from the PLC to the data storage or analysing device using portable mass storage devices or File Transfer Protocol (FTP) communication. Past events, such as the best-known attack on PLC control systems with the Stuxnet worm, which was initiated via an USB stick [4], have shown that the use of portable mass storage devices on control systems and plant networks should be avoided. In various research facilities, the use of mobile data storage devices such as USB sticks is even generally prohibited. Also, the classic FTP exhibits security deficiencies owing to its age and intended use [5]. Although some of these issues have been addressed through extensions like Secured FTP (SFTP), it is advisable to check the protocol utilization within the plant network.

Large-scale facilities, such as particle accelerators or telescopes, can make good use of existing software frameworks such as Experimental Physics and Industrial Control System (EPICS) or TANGO [6]. In addition to the general functionalities of a Supervisory Control and Data Acquisition (SCADA) system, EPICS also offers the option of saving measurement data via the Archiver, exporting it or filtering it directly with own written analysis code [7]. These platforms are scalable to small systems, but the effort required to set up and maintain such a system is not negligible. In addition, such a system can only be used by researchers who have advanced knowledge of how to operate the system. Direct use by researchers who have not worked with the system before is therefore unlikely.
The following paper presents the implementation of a solution that is somewhere between the simplest file-based solution and the existing but too complex systems. In addition to safety and availability aspects, good usability by the researcher is a top priority in order to minimise the training period and avoid operating errors. The solution offers the opportunity to easily access the system's measurement data and also provides test routines in the form of parameter files which are then available in the control system.

In Sections II the basic idea and system concept is described. Section III then discusses the identified use context of the system, before the detailed technical implementation is described in Section IV.

II. System Concept

The fundamental idea of this concept is to combine the best aspects of the three components PLC, Human Machine Interface (HMI) and Databases in order to increase the scalability and adaptability for different scientific devices, while minimising the resulting issues. This is achieved by using a different approach once a component exhibits significant deficiencies in a specific area or is unsuitable for the task. While PLC and HMI Systems (in particular those produced by the same manufacturer) work well together when it's about high reliability and operation of scientific devices, they have limitations in complex user interactions and the provision of measurement data in different ways and formats. Especially when the data must be retained for an extended period and the queries to select the data are highly complex. In such cases, customised web-based systems with specialised Databases offer significant advantages. The system is designed to enable the initial contact with the researcher via a customised web application (web app). The researcher can upload the desired experiment, while being able to use convenient software such as Excel tables to describe the different stages. This is the used by the PLC and HMI System to execute its control mechanisms. Following completion of the experiment, the researcher can interact with the web app to specify which data in which format is required. A challenge was to find the right balance between the enhanced adaptability through the use of web app and database, while maintaining the integrity of the PLC control process.

III. Ease of Use

In order to achieve good usability with the system which was to be developed, the project was started with a context analysis in which the 22 Deutsche Akkreditierungsstelle (DAkkS) guiding questions [8] were used in a revised version to carry out a semi-structured interview with the researchers. A significant challenge was the wide range of applications for scientific devices and systems. In order to find a homogeneous user group, we focused on research facility that are usually operated and managed by just a few or even one person, as the use of large SCADA systems is often not possible for these types of systems. These facility were PLC controlled plants, laboratory setups or scientific devices operated at the Research Centre Jülich.

The analysis resulted a core task, shown in Figure 1 to upload a previously defined parameter file and to download the relating measurement data again in the same way after execution. These task can be divided into 4 interactive steps, which are described in the following.

A new experiment always starts with defining the test steps of the scientific device and documenting them, for example, in the form of an Excel table or a CSV file. This file is referred to below as the parameter file and contains general data and system parameters such as operating points, holding times, priorities and dependencies. Fields can be defined which are only filled in by the PLC during execution. These can be timers, counters, comment fields, or other variables available in the PLC.

The parameter file can then be uploaded in the second step inside the Data Management Portal (DMP) (Figure 3) using the upload parameter file function. During the upload, a plausibility check of the parameter file is carried out, which can be configured for the specific facility. This configuration can contain area exceedings of working points, missing working points, duplicate step numbers or incorrect priorities. In case of an error inside the file, the upload is denied by the DMP and the user receives an error list to revise their parameter file. If the parameter file does not contain any errors, it is saved to the database. This process generates an unique experiment ID, which is shared with the DMP user during the upload. If the researcher wants to make changes inside the uploaded parameter file before starting the file in the research facility, the file can be modified by upload it again via the DMP. The portal uses the general data from the file to check whether it is a new file or an existing one. If the file already exists, the database entry will be updated.

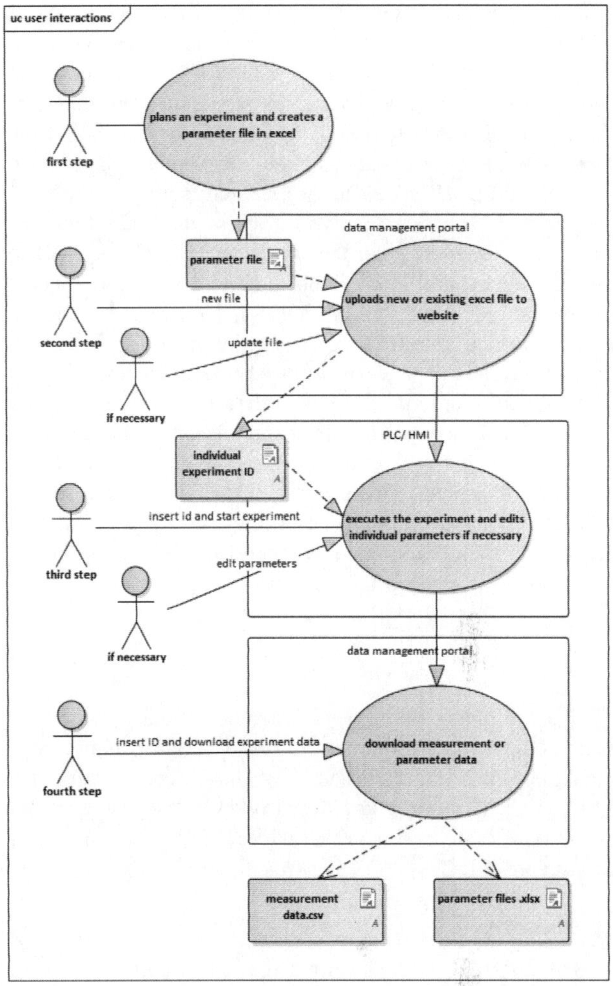

Fig. 1. User interactions.

The third step of the process describes the actual execution of the experiment. In contrast to the previous preparatory steps, this step must be carried out on the HMI of the facility. By entering the experiment ID in the HMI system, the PLC accesses the database and loads the parameter file into the temporary memory. The individual steps can be viewed in the HMI system and edited until they are executed by the PLC. During the experiment, the PLC creates a copy of the parameter file as a log file. In this log file, existing fields to be completed by the PLC are then filled in automatically. This can be, for example, the start time, end time or the hold time of an individual step. A comment function is included within the HMI system. If a comment is written, this is also recorded in the log file with a timestamp, so that the researcher can easily and safely document events during operation. After the test has been completed, the log file is automatically saved in the database. In addition to the log file, all measurement data are also saved cyclically in the database, whereby the cycle time can be selected and adapted to the measuring application.

If an active experiment is running, the cyclic data is tagged with the experiment ID to ensure better identification. If no active test is running, the cyclic data is logged with the tag "no active test" and a timestamp. Step four describes that the researcher wants to access the measurement data and log files, after the experiment has been completed. This is again done via the DMP, access to the research facility or the HMI system is no longer required. To access the dataset for the experiment, one can enter the experiment ID. Use this ID to directly access the data or apply filters to retrieve specific information, as illustrated in Figure 3. The selected data can be downloaded as a CSV file using the download button. A distinction can be made between the German and English CSV format in order to fit to the different evaluation software products. This means that the experiment can be analysed by the researcher independently of the research facility. The data remains stored in the database after downloading so that the data can be accessed again at any time via the DMP. In addition to the cyclical measurement data, the parameter log file can be downloaded the same way.

IV. IMPLEMENTATION

Figure 2 shows the general structure of the system. The main component is a database for all data and parameters as a Single Source Of Truth (SSOT). This is connected to the PLC, the HMI system and the developed data management portal (DMP) webserver, which is described in the following subsections.

A. *Database*

Due to the desired scalability and adaptability of the system to different scientific devices, the Not only Structured Query Language (NoSQL) database MongoDB is used, which is not restricted to a fixed data schema like Structured Query Language (SQL) Databases [9]. The used structure which resembles the often used JavaScript Object Notation (JSON) -format and the possibility to optimise collections for use with time series data strengthens this decision. Alternative databases which also have time series functionality would be for example InfluxDB.

The current hosting solution is realised using a local MongoDB [10] docker container on a QNAP Network Attached Storage (NAS) model TS-473A with 4*4TB Disks in a Raid10 Setup. This leads to a higher output-rate and could tolerate up to two disk failures in the best-case.

Due to the docker setup, it is possible to host this solution on every machine which is able to run a docker environment. Search speed for queries is improved using the time series functionality and indexes for certain fields. The NAS is currently doing daily snapshots of the necessary folders, which can be manually saved on an external drive for later restoration. The saved data can also be kept on the NAS-System, this is only limited due to the available amount of disk space and the lifespan of the disks.

An experiment simulating four machines producing the same dataset (about 150 values with integers, boolean values and floating point numbers) every second for about 12 years used about 26 GB of disk space for the entire MongoDB data folder.

B. *PLC based database connection*

1) Connection: To establish the functionalities for system communication, it is essential to utilise function blocks from Beckhoff Automation GmbH & Co. KG (Beckhoff) libraries within the PLC. Building upon these components, the engineering process involves crafting appropriate advancements, to expand the functionality of the building blocks to create a system with working communication between the PLC and the database. To enable access through the PLC, various settings are required. The chosen database must be initialised using the TF6420-Database Server [11] extension tool from Beckhoff and a connection must be established via the IP address in the required network. The created database contains an ID for target identification in later workflow stages. This number cannot be dynamically assigned by the user, instead, it is incremented numerically. A "Standard Connection String Format" is selected as the communication basis, meaning that data and queries from the PLC are sent and received in string format, structured into a JSON format within this string. In the realm of communication, the TwinCat 3 (TC3) Database Library [12] is employed for tasks such as inquiries or filter configurations. For the formatting of data into JSON strings or the conversion of these strings into structures, the TC3 JSON XML [13] is essential. For example, to retrieve data already present in the database, the following process is required. Using the Query-Builder Function block with the included functionality of QueryOptionDocumentDB [12], a search in the database is triggered via the PLC. A string must be generated containing the desired search information, to serve as filter for exploring the database. This serves as a filter and is passed to the Query Find function. To ensure a correct access to the desired data, the search location in the form of the Collection Name as a string must be passed to the block. To initiate a request, the ExecuteDataReturn [12] method of the QueryBuilder module can be employed to submit a query to the database. The ID of the desired database needs to be selected in addition to the filters and collection settings. Upon the successful execution of a request, signifying the retrieval of the intended data, the data can be formatted based on user preferences using methods from the fbNoSQLResult [12] module. This can be done either by converting it into a string (fbNoSQLResult.ReadAsString) [12] or, alternatively, directly into a predefined structure within the PLC (fbNoSQLResult.ReadAsStruct) [12]. The string is more flexible but also more complex, as desired individual data must be extracted and assigned to a PLC variable. With structure formatting, this happens automatically. In this context, it is essential to ensure an exact match in the structural configuration between the PLC and the database entry. The data must be absolutely identical in their structural format; otherwise, the transfer would going

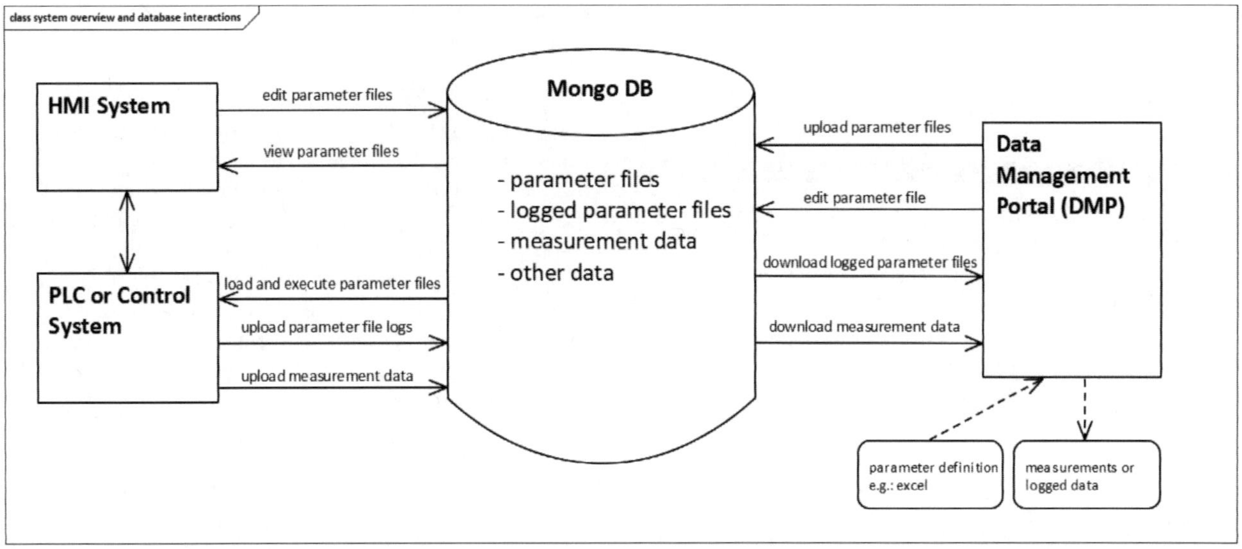

Fig. 2. System overview and database interactions.

to fail. The process for writing data and information utilised the same functionalities as the request process. Only the query function is switched to QueryOptionDocumentDB Update [12] or QueryOptionDocumentDB InsertOne [12], depending on the application's requirements.

*2) **Problems and Limitations**:* To establish a functional communication system, different challenges must be addressed. The definition of filters in a JSON format occurs at the user level and must precisely match to a pattern. Deviations lead to communication errors, making troubleshooting more difficult, especially for complex filters. Information written to the database must be in JSON format. Beckhoff provides a block "fbJsonDataType.AddJsonValueFromSymbol" [13] to automate this task and store the result into a string. The standard size of strings is 255 characters. However, this is often not sufficient, so this range must be declared manually larger. This leads to problems with greater data records. Changes, such as ISO date adjustments, in this string may render it unable to be graphically represented. Errors in conversion or subsequent edits may not be visually inspected, complicating the identification process. The mentioned example process occurs whenever timestamps are a factor. The PLC operates with its own date time type, which does not fit with the ISO date type. In cases where specific specifications are necessitated within the string, such as executing a unit conversion for the database, manual string manipulation becomes complex. Beckhoff offers a range of fundamental functions in its TC2 Utilities library [14], including find, insert, or delete functions. These functions serve to locate and modify essential positions, variables, or information elements. Nonetheless, it is worth noting that the procedure becomes notably time-consuming when dealing with larger volumes of data (length of the string). The temporary storage of information for preceding or future processing can occupy a significant amount of internal memory due to the string's size. This may negatively impact PLC task and cycle times. The communication between the PLC and the database does not operate at the cyclic speed of the PLC, leading to delays in processing data and issues with cyclic logging intervals. Due to the strict arrangements regarding variable declarations and structure setups, the flexibility provided by the database, with its NoSQL system, is limited via the PLC. It therefore does not exploit the full potential of the selected database type.

*C. **Data Management Portal***

The DMP, shown in Figure 3 is realised using a website with two structurally separated "Apps" to interact with the user, shown in Figure 3. One App is responsible for uploading and downloading parameter files, while the other is used for interacting with measurement data, including providing various CSV formats. A more detailed explanation of the different options can be found in Section III. The website is build using the Django Framework [15] which is python based and most designs are realised using the Django Template Language (DTL) and the Bootstrap Framework [16].

This subsection provides a more detailed explanation of the DMP. It outlines the processes involved in validation, the Database used and how the communication with the DMP works. Additionally, it identifies potential issues and limitations.

*1) **Validation**:* The validation is used every time a parameter file is uploaded. It is realised with the Frictionless Framework [17], which provides tools to validate, transform and enrich data. Structures called schemas are written inside a JSON Document to specify the requirements for the parameter files. It can specify constraints like minimum, maximum, field

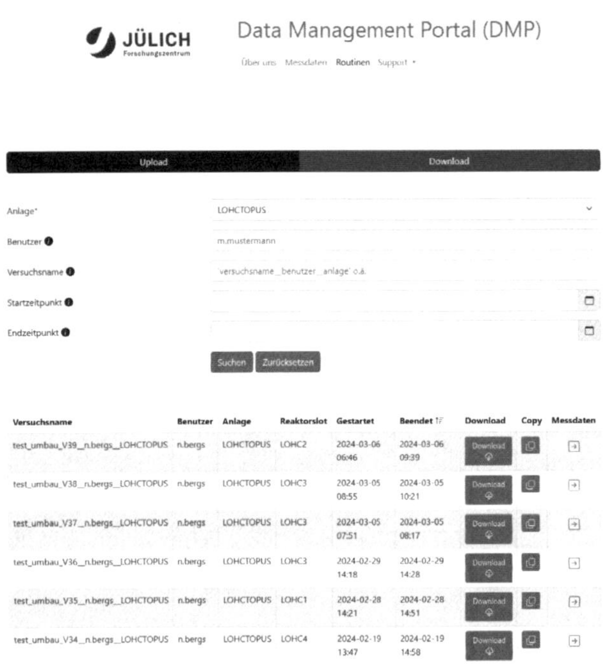

Fig. 3. DMP - upload and download app.

types and flags for requirement of fields. Later on, transformation pipelines can also be specified. Once the parameter file does not conform to the schema, the user will receive a comprehensive list of errors and violated constraints to rectify them.

*2) **Database**:* Django by itself doesn't support MongoDB. Its language (python), which is often used in the scientific community, and the amount of additional usable packages compensates for this fact. This leads to a faster adaptability of the software. In order to be able to use the Django Queries for simple models, we use the Djongo Mapper [18]. More complex and nested structures like the time series datasets are queried using the PyMongo Library [19].

*3) **Queries**:* Each page in the DMP has a form similar to Figure 3 where the user can restrict or expand the search results by specifying time, creator, experiment ID and other parameters. These search parameters are passed to the Django backend, where a query is dynamically generated. This query is then sent to MongoDB and the results are processed and returned to the user. In the default case, with no search parameters, the results are capped to reduce query time.

*4) **Problems and Limitations**:* By using the DTL and the main principles of Django, most of the website content is created in the backend and sent completely to the user. This approach can lead to longer waiting times if there is a high workload, like long computations or transformations. The concept also reaches its limits when a lot of interactivity is needed. This would need further use of JavaScript or a JavaScript Framework like Vue.js [20]. Although the DMP ensures that the parameter files are validated and correct, it is possible to corrupt the data via the PLC or HMI connections if used incorrectly.

D. *HMI based database connection*

In addition to the PLC, the HMI system can also access the database directly. This is done via a server extension written in C# on the HMI server. The extension uses the MongoDB Driver and the MongoDB Binary JSON (BSON) data type. A query of the database for all available object IDs with the corresponding experiment names can thus fill a list element or a combo box with the parameter files available in the database. The complete entry of the experiment ID can be simplified by selecting the corresponding list element from the query. The database connection can be used to load complete parameter files into the temporary memory of the HMI server so that they can then be edited using the graphical tools available in the HMI. To save the changes, the temporary data set can then be uploaded back into the database. HMI-side access to the database always makes sense, if the operation or visualization can take place independently of the PLC. In this way, the limitations of PLC-based database communication described in Section IV-B2 can be minimised.

V. CONCLUSION AND OUTLOOK

The developed concept for data handling in research facilities covers the interaction principles of the ISO 9241-110 [21] in many cases due to the user-centred approach. Suitability for the user's tasks is the focus of the entire concept in order to avoid unnecessary steps and ensure easy access to the measurement data.

MongoDB as central data storage offers great flexibility and controllability due to the large number of interfaces. In addition to the integration of the DMP, the PLC and the HMI included in the developed concept, various other software tools and hardware platforms can of course be connected to the system. The hardware requirements to connect the MongoDB database are very low, so that a communication-enabled ESP32 board can already be connected to the database to serve as a data logger.

The realised validation of uploaded parameter files, described in Section IV-C1, protects new system users from operating error and helps them to comply with system limits. Forms and task-related help files, stored in the DMP, guide new users through the use of the tool. An iterative development process with different prototypes, which was carried out through expert-based usability evaluations with researchers, has led to a user interface that meets user expectations.
Further tests are pending following the launch of the system. It is planned to carry out observational user tests with "Thinking Aloud" by new, inexperienced users. As the concept can be implemented in various systems with only minor adjustments, the total number of DMP users will add up in a long-term perspective so that usability can also be measured in future using tools such as the SUMI [22]. This was previously not possible due to the individual systems with only a few users and offers further potential for improvement.

The analysed user needs also result in further extensions for the future such as the DMP can only be used to store parameters, as well as measurement data and make them easily accessible. A graphical representation of the data, which has so far only been implemented inside the HMI system via its own data memory, would be a potential extension of the DMP. The integration of plot or dashboard environments or even the direct evaluation of measurement data using a Jupyter notebook [23], which is integrated in the DMP, can further increase the usability of a scientific device and lead to consistent evaluation results, especially with changing researchers. However, any extension must take into account the scalability of the system and its adaptability to different scientific facilities. Depending on future requirements, the individual components of the systems could be extended or improved. For example, a 3-2-1 Backup Strategy [24], use of the Django authentication system or adaptations to achieve high availability and redundancy could be implemented.

REFERENCES

[1] Beckhoff Automation GmbH and Co. KG, "TE1000 TwinCAT 3 PLC-Library: Tc3 System", December 2023.

[2] Beckhoff Automation GmbH and Co. KG, "TE1410 TwinCAT 3 — Interface for MATLAB®/Simulink®", September 2022.

[3] Beckhoff Automation GmbH and Co. KG, "TF3710 TwinCAT 3 — Interface for LabVIEW™", February 2024.

[4] M. Baezner and P. Robin, "CSS Cyber Defense Hotspot Analysis Stuxnet", Version 1 ETH Zürich, October 2017.

[5] D. Springall, Z. Durumeric and J. A. Halderman, "FTP: The Forgotten Cloud" 2016 46th Annual IEEE/IFIP International Conference on Dependable Systems and Networks (DSN), 2016.

[6] C. Böhme, C. Deliege, M. Simon, M. Thelen, V. Kamerdzhiev, R. Modic and Ž. Oven, "Challenges of the COSY Synchrotron Control System Upgrade to EPICS" 2024 19th Int. Conf. Accel. Large Exp. Phys. Control, Cape Town, South Africa, 2023.

[7] L. R. Dalesio, M. R. Kraimer and A. J. Kozubal, "EPICS Architecture", Argonne National Laboratory Argonne, New Mexico, January 1991.

[8] DAkks Deutsche Akkreditierungsstelle, "Leitfaden Usability Version 1.3 [Usability guide version 1.3]", 2010.

[9] R. Deari, X. Zenuni, J. Ajdari, F. Ismaili and B. Raufi, "Analysis And Comparision of Document-Based Databases with Relational Databases: MongoDB vs MySQL," 2018 International Conference on Information Technologies (InfoTech), Varna, Bulgaria, 2018.

[10] 'MongoDB', https://www.mongodb.com/ [Online], Accessed: 2024.03.06.

[11] Beckhoff Automation GmbH and Co. KG, "TF6420 TwinCAT 3 Database Server", December 2023.

[12] Beckhoff Automation GmbH and Co. KG, "TF6420 TwinCAT 3 PLC-Library: Tc3 Database", December 2023.

[13] Beckhoff Automation GmbH and Co. KG, "TE1000 TwinCAT 3 PLC-Library: Tc3 JsonXml", May 2022.

[14] Beckhoff Automation GmbH and Co. KG, "TE1000 TwinCAT 3 PLC-Library: Tc2 Utilities", November 2023.

[15] "Django Project", https://www.djangoproject.com/ [Online], Accessed: 2024.03.05.

[16] "Bootstrap Library", https://getbootstrap.com/ [Online], Accessed: 2024.03.05.

[17] "Frictionless Data", https://frictionlessdata.io/introduction/ [Online], Accessed: 2024.03.05.

[18] "Djongomapper", https://www.djongomapper.com/ [Online], Accessed: 2024.03.05.

[19] "PyMongo 4.6.2 documentation", https://pymongo.readthedocs.io/en/stable/ [Online], Accessed: 2024.03.05.

[20] "Vue.js", https://vuejs.org/ [Online], Accessed: 2024.03.05.

[21] DIN-Normenausschuss Ergonomie (NAErg) , "Ergonomics of human-system interaction - Part 110: Interaction principles (ISO 9241-110:2020); German version EN ISO 9241-110:2020".

[22] J. Kirakowski and M. Corbett, "SUMI: the Software Usability Measurement Inventory", British Journal of Educational Technology, 1993.

[23] "Project Jupyter Documentation", https://docs.jupyter.org/en/latest/ [Online], Accessed: 2024.03.06.

[24] "What is a 3-2-1 Backup Strategy?", https://www.seagate.com/de/de/blog/what-is-a-3-2-1-backup-strategy/ [Online], Accessed: 2024.03.05.

Investigating the Impact of Website Menu Presentation Style on User Performance

Knut Ole Kvilhaug Magnussen[1st], Kasper Iversen, and Georgios Marentakis
Faculty of Computer Science, Engineering and Economics
Høgskolen i Østfold
Halden, Norway
email: {komagnus, kasperi, georgios.marentakis}@hiof.no

***Abstract*—This paper investigates website navigation menu presentation styles. An experiment comparing three menu styles vertical, horizontal, and radial was conducted to determine their effect on user performance and preference. Although menu presentation style did not affect task completion time and error rate significantly, its effect on task completion time variance was significant and Radial menus were most inconsistent in terms of task completion time. Users preference was highest for horizontal menus.**

Keywords-Human-computer interaction; Human-Web Interaction; Interface Design; User Experience; Navigation User interface design.

I. INTRODUCTION

One aspect of website design is the implementation of navigation menus as they constitute the primary conduit through which users navigate and interact with a website's content.

Menu design has been a subject of significant discourse in Human Computer Interaction [1], however, few studies have focused on the web. This is important as menu design influences the user experience and performance. Novices unfamiliar with the menu content and command locations have to search for items visually and visual search dominates the overall selection time [2]. However, users quickly develop and rely on spatial knowledge for menu item locations (i.e., they become expert users) if the layout of the menu is stable [3], [4]. Consequently, visual search time decreases and the overall selection time then depends mainly on decision and pointing times [5], [6].

Even though physical appearance and colour play an important role on user experience, the same holds for menu layout and design features [7]. There have been different proposals for menu presentation styles in the literature which include horizontal, vertical, or radial menus. While several comparisons on menu organization have been made, fewer studies compare menu presentation styles to each other especially in the context of web navigation. We present here such an investigation. In the background section, we analyse existing research on the impact of menu presentation style and their application on user navigation patterns on websites. Subsequently, in the methods section we describe how we facilitated a controlled experiment three menu presentation styles vertical, horizontal and radial are compared. The objective is to determine if a given presentation style, among the tested variations, results in the most effective and efficient performance and enhances the hedonic user experience. In the results section we present our findings from the experiment, while in the discussion section we discuss what the results mean for our research question before we conclude the paper in the conclusion section.

II. BACKGROUND

Menus are a well-studied topic in Human Computer Interaction (HCI) and several studies have investigated the influence of menu design on user experience and performance. The main parameters that are varied in the experiments are menu width and depth, whereas menu design and placement have received less attention.

Kim, Jacko, and Salvendy present [1] a comprehensive summary of investigations with respect to menu structure (width and depth), ordering, but also menu type on computers and mobile phones discussing both two- and three-dimensional menus. Three-dimensional menus leverage the depth dimension to provide additional information and enhance usability, however, the challenges associated with 3D interaction have influenced their potential. For our study we focus on 2D menus.

A significant aspect in menu design is breadth versus depth, i.e., the number of options available in each menu level versus the number of levels a user encounters as they move through the menu to a target item. Early findings supported the conclusion that a broader menu was more effective than a deeper one [8]. Miller [8] investigated the impact of menu configurations on speed and accuracy in an interactive computer terminal environment. He observed in his study a U-shaped function in goal acquisition time, with an optimal configuration of two menu levels and eight choices per level. This is because increased depth involves additional visual search and associated uncertainty about the location of a target menu item. However, excessive breadth can also lead to a crowded display. Therefore breadth should also be used with moderation and a balance between breadth and depth needs to be achieved. Contrary to the Miller's two-level approach [8], Kingsburg and Andre's [9] study on three-level menus suggests positive effects when distributing menu levels on different planes. Their findings also revealed that placing the first menu level on the left side of the screen had a positive impact. Furthermore, when the second and third menu levels were grouped in the same plane opposite from the primary menu, it resulted in improved user performance. Their research also revealed that users preferred menus situated in the left or

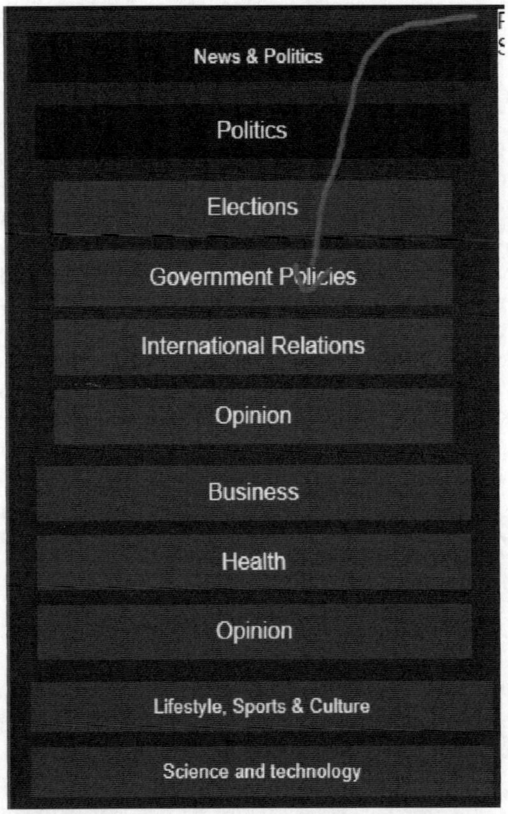

Figure 1: The vertical menu used in experiment.

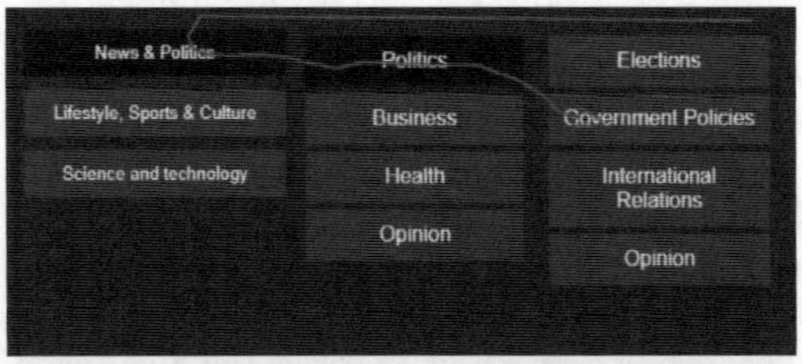

Figure 2: The horizontal menu used in experiment.

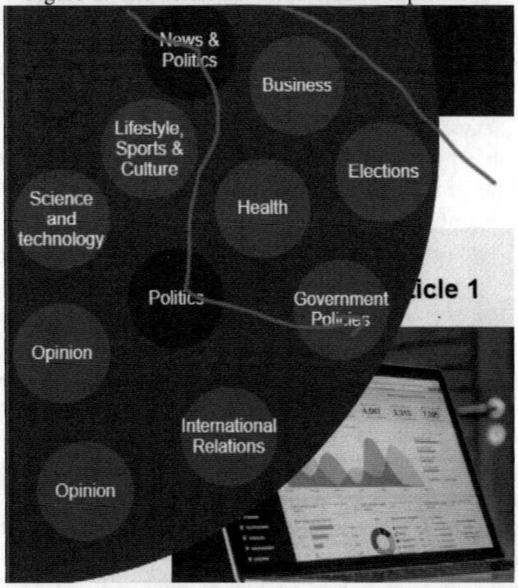

Figure 3: The radial menu used in experiment.

right planes. These findings are significant for the design of multi-level website menus and this experiment.

Moreno-Bote, Ramírez-Ruiz, Ramírez-Ruiz and Hayden [2] also investigated the breadth-depth dilemma in multi-alternative risky choices. Their study found that optimal strategy depends on capacity available. With limited capacity, favouring breadth is advantageous. However, when you have greater capacity a transition happens, emphasizing the importance of choosing the right balance between breadth and depth. When screen is small as in mobile devices, breadth must be limited due to practical considerations and narrow hierarchies perform better [10]. Filling the screen as much as possible without requiring scrolling while keeping a reasonable font size is the optimal solution when small screens are considered [11].

Another aspect of menu design is adaptation, i.e., whether a menu is static or the content is adjusted dynamically. Even though adaptation, can increase performance as frequent options appear first, it may increase learning time and slow down users until they become accustomed to this style [12]. A benefit for user design adaptable menus has been reported [13].

A third aspect discussed in the literature is menu ordering. Categorical menus are useful when categories can give a clue to target items, while alphabetical menus provide an advantage compared to random menus as users can guess the location of items in next levels [3], [14] [15]. This has been investigated for various tasks in experiments: (a) Search for a known item; (b) Search for the first suitable item with a known target characterization; (c) Search the most suitable item with a known target characterization; and (d) Browsing among the items. Categorical performs better in most cases an exact word is not required to be found.

A further parameter in relation to menu design is menu type. Several researchers compared hierarchical to fisheye menus. Hierarchical menus are also classified as categorical index menus (simply placing all items in a categorical index) as well as horizontal and vertical cascading menus (hierarchically cascade the menu items upon mouse-over). Fisheye menus magnify a menu region while elements in other regions are shown in gradually reduced sizes and can thus accommodate more items. Index menus have been found to lead to a more efficient interaction compared to hierarchical menus [10], perhaps due to a more tight layout on screen and visibility. Furthermore, users are faster and more accurate in finding known items with hierarchical compared to fisheye menus.

Another menu type arranges items on the circumference of a circle and is called radial [16], pie [6], or marking menu. Radial layouts were initially used to support small, single level menus. Support for hierarchies was first realized by a series of single level radial menus. Pie menus were compared to a linear menu in expert mode, using 8 item menus, yielding 15% faster selections [6]. Marking menus generalize to multiple hierarchies by presenting each level in the displayed menu as a separate pie menu [4], [17], [18] and also provide an expert selection mode, in which the user can issue a straight 'mark' in the direction of a desired item without the actual menu being displayed. Radial menus are generalized to multiple hierarchies by presenting the elements in the next level in overlapping or non-overlapping menus. The Wave Menu presents new levels at the centre of the menu circle, while *inverted* Wave Menus outside the initial circle. Wave menus typically perform better than overlapping pie menus in which only one hierarchy level is visible at each time. The efficiency of such menus is higher than this of vertical menus as long as the number of items is small and no additional hierarchy levels are used. In another approach, radial menus expand outwards, however, the elements are not distributed over the whole circle but rather placed next to each other along the circumference of the corresponding level [16].

Parush and Yuviler-Gavish [19] explored navigation structures, endorsing broader horizontally oriented menus for potentially faster task completion. Their emphasis on considering device-specific factors further underscores the need to assess user interactions across various devices.

Significant work has been directed in modelling menu performance. This involves visual search times and mouse movement in relation to the target width and distance to target [20]. Another relevant model is Drury's model (1971) [21] which has been reformulated as Steering Law in the context of HCI [22]. This model posits that movement time is linearly related to the ratio of path length (A) to path width (W), offering invaluable insights for designing interfaces in precision-critical applications.

Kořistová and Spiratos [23] observed a correlation between mega menus and heightened user experience, while conversely noting the detrimental effects of hamburger menus and neutral impact of horizontal menus.

Cuddihy and Spyridakis [24] shifted the focus towards user comprehension and navigation, emphasizing the importance of visually distinct navigation schemes. Their exploration introduced the intriguing concept of perceived knowledge gain. They suggest that user experience goes beyond mere comprehension; it involves how users subjectively interpret and assess their own learning experiences within the context of the provided navigation schemes. These insights led them to incorporate user feedback on perceived knowledge gain within experimental designs.

Yu, Roh and Han compared a simple selection menu as well as global (next level in the screen centre) and local (pull-down) navigation menus [25]. They found that participants performed better in searching with the pull-down menu but were faster in browsing with the global and local navigation aid menu. However, users' perception of the three menu designs was not significantly different.

Bodrunova and Yakunin's research [5] introduced the concept of menu complexity and its influence on navigational behavior. The distinctions between productive and non-productive search strategies offer a promising framework for evaluating various menu presentation styles efficiency.

A. Summary

Several studies have identified menu structure, type, adaptation, and ordering as factors influencing user performance. Looking more closely at our application domain, the web, menus tend to be placed either on the top or the side of the screen and expand along the horizontal or vertical dimension respectively. Horizontal menus are space-efficient and often have a familiar placement on top of websites. Vertical menus, often also called side menus, are a popular choice in web interfaces. Their visibility on the website makes them accessible without the need for additional interactions. The style is a valuable tool for designers seeking intuitive and accessible content organization. Radial menus are not as common. The literature indicates that radial menus can offer advantages in terms of seek time, error rates, and minimizing drift distance. However, the radial menu's appropriateness depends on other factors like the number of items on the menu, space on the website and user preferences. Based on the literature, it is not easy to make predictions with respect to user performance and preference in horizontal, vertical, and radial menus in the context of a web page. This is especially true if menus are balanced in terms of breadth and width. and no significant interaction problems appear. However, the visual style of the menus is considerably different, therefore it is quite interesting to investigate if this can lead any performance differences but also how user preference is affected. Web menus differ from mobile applications the option to hover thereby requiring its own study. To investigate this research question regarding user performance with the three menu types we designed an experiment in which users selected items with a horizontal, vertical, and radial menu.

III. Method

A. Experiment design

The independent variables were the menu type (vertical, horizontal, and radial) and trial (1-3). Both were repeated measures. The dependent variables were task completion time as measured by the time taken to complete the tasks and task completion accuracy as measured by the menu selection error rate. As Kingsburg and Andre's [9] study suggests, users prefer menus placed on the left or right planes of a website and we have used this preference to create menus that align with user expectations. The horizontal menu used in the experiment, along with an example mouse-path, is displayed in Figure 2. The vertical menu was also located on the left side of the website [26]. Figure 1 displays menu and an example mouse-path for a vertical style [26]. The radial menu with mouse-path used in the experiment is displayed in Figure 3 [27]. The various study's on breadth/depth led to the menus in this experiment being 3 levels with 4 options per level. Elements were ordered alphabetically in each level.

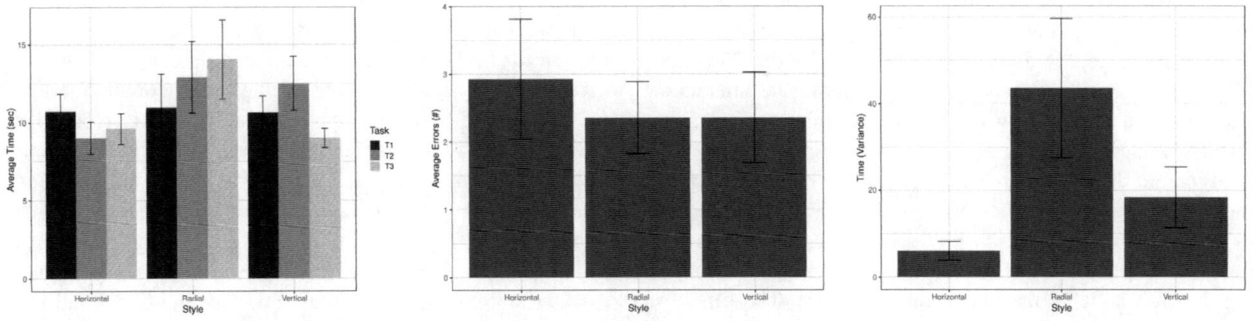

(a) (b) (c)

Figure 4: Graph showing (a) the average task completion time, (b) task completion errors, and (c) standard deviation of task completion time in the different conditions in the experiment. Error bars how standard error of the mean.

B. Apparatus & Materials

The experiment was created as an HyperText Markup Language (HTML) web site with a page using JavaScript code and Cascading Style Sheets (CSS) for design (Figure 1). The experiment website was created in a news-website manner due to its commonness.

C. Tasks

To mimic the typical web menu use cases from previous experiments, [3], [14], [15] each participant were required to navigate to a specific section of the website using only the navigation menu. Paths were randomly generated for each participant. An example of this is: *"Find the section for Music under the Lifestyle, Sports & Culture part of the page"*, meaning that they have to find the button labeled "music" in the navigation menu. Participants performed three trials with each menu type.

D. Procedure

Before engaging in the evaluation tasks, each participant were provided with a 90 seconds familiarization period for each of the three navigation styles. To maintain validity, a standardized A-Z categorization structure was established for each style, neutralizing its impact on performance evaluation. The same laptop was used by all participants to ensure the same form, size and interaction style.

Participants were presented with a starting screen containing a start-button and the text for where to navigate. When the start button was clicked, the test sequence which is explained in the section "Tasks" began. After the completion of the tasks, the following questions were asked: **Q1:** How would you rate your overall experience with the website navigation on a scale from 1-10, where 10 is the best? **Q2:** What made you not rate it higher/ lower? **Q3:** Were there any aspects of the navigation that you found particularly frustrating or confusing? **Q4:** What did you like about the menu navigation on the website? **Q5:** Were there any specific design elements or features that you felt made navigation more straightforward?

After the questionnaire for each presentation style, participants were introduced to the next style, and the entire process repeated. Once the participant had repeated the process for the 3 menu types, the following questions were asked: **OQ1:** Which menu presentation style did you find the easiest to use, and why? **OQ2:** Opposed to the others, were there any specific design elements or features that you felt made navigation more straightforward? The researchers took notes on the participants responses. This approach gathered insights into the hedonic user experience and performance in the various menu presentation styles.

E. Participants

A sample of 14 participants, all university college students, were recruited using a Google form. Some students studied computer science-related subjects at a bachelor level, while others studied unrelated subjects. All participants reported familiarity with computers and web-based navigation. Each participant was presented and signed a consent form, where they could read about the experiment and how their personal data would be processed, used, and eventually deleted.

F. Data analysis

The hypotheses were examined by testing for significant differences in the dependent variables among the three menu styles. Quantitative analysis involved two-way repeated measures analysis of variance (ANOVA) to examine the effects of style on completion time and error rate, while one-way ANOVA assessed variance in completion time among styles. Post-hoc t-tests with Holm correction were conducted to identify specific differences between styles. Qualitative text data, representing users experience, was analyzed systematically by categorizing responses and identifying common themes across different menu styles. The ratings (0-10) provided by the users in first round of questions were added together to get an average rating for each menu style.

IV. RESULTS

The data on task-completion time and error rate are displayed in Figure 4. Figure 4a shows average tasks completion time in the three trials and the menu presentation styles in the experiment. The variation between styles and trials is small.

The same was the case for error rate, shown in Figure 4b. Task completion time and error rate were analyzed using two-way (Trial $\times$ Type) repeated-measures ANOVAs. Neither the effect of trial nor the effect of style was significant. The interaction between trial and style was also not significant. The same results appeared for error rate.

Figure 4c shows the variance in task completion time for the three menu styles in the experiment. This was also analyzed using a one-way ANOVA with variance in task completion time per participant as the dependent variable and menu presentation style as the independent variable. The effect of menu presentation style was significant F(2.26) = 4.26, p = 0.025. The calculated effect size of the tests was $\eta^2 = 0.15$ with a Greenhouse-Geisser correction value of $\varepsilon = 0.67$. Post-hoc t-tests with Holm correction for pairwise comparisons shows that the horizontal style led to smaller variance in completion time among trials compared to the radial style (p = 0.03). However, all other pairwise comparisons were not significant. The difference in variance in completion time among trials was not significant when comparing vertical to radial or vertical to horizontal.

For vertical, Horizontal and Radial menu style the average rating was respectively 6.78, 8.92 and 7.92 (**Q1**). People preferred the width for overview, against length like offered in vertical presentation style (**Q2**). Nothing was frustrating other than area of focus in center for vertical presentation style (**Q3**). Every menu type gave good overview, but level-separation was clearest in horizontal and radial presentation style (**Q4**). The vertical presentation style had a natural mouse-path, while horizontal and radial presentation style had clear level separation (**Q5**).

Overall people preferred the horizontal menu presentation style, as it gave the best overview and was the most "common" (**OQ1**). The clear level separation of the horizontal menu made it easy to see where to click next, while the width gave good overview (**OQ2**).

V. Discussion

Our study set out to examine the influence of the menu presentation styles radial, vertical and horizontal on user navigation behaviors and task completion rates on a website. We examined the hypothesis that there would be a statistically significant difference in user performance as measured with task completion time and error rate among these three menu styles.

The result showed that the average task completion time and the average task completion errors were not affected by menu presentation style. Interestingly, trial number also did not consistently impact completion times across menu styles, as evidenced by the non-significant main effect for the trial. All menu styles were therefore used equally well. Contrary to our initial hypothesis, the style of menus did not have a statistically significant effect on task completion time and error rates which challenges the notion that differences in the examined menu styles play a significant role in minimizing user errors during navigation tasks.

However, the variance in task completion time varied significantly across menu styles and the main effect of presentation style on the variance of the average completion time for each participant was significant. On average, task completion time varied more when menu type was radial and less so when it was horizontal or vertical. However, only the difference between horizontal and radial menus was significant indicating that radial menus led to less consistent performance in the experiment.

Qualitative insights from participants align with the quantitative results, indicating a preference for the horizontal presentation style due to its clear level separation and overall familiarity. However, it is noteworthy that the horizontal style, while efficient in terms of completion times, exhibited on average the highest average error rate. These qualitative findings provide nuanced context, suggesting a correspondence between user preferences and observed quantitative outcomes.

The observed variance in completion times across menu styles indicates that designers should carefully consider the trade-offs between different menu types, particularly concerning efficiency in completing tasks. We cannot explicitly refer to the exact reason for this result. One possibility is that the variance in task completion times for the radial menu is due to the lack of familiarity with such menus. However, it is not possible to conclude without further experimentation.

It is essential to acknowledge certain limitations in our study. The selected tasks might not fully represent the complexity and diversity of real-world user interactions. Additionally, participant characteristics, such as affinity for technology and prior experience with certain menu styles, were not explicitly controlled and could have influenced the results. Future research should therefore explore these factors more comprehensively.

Considering the usability facets within the wider menu design context, while the examined styles may not significantly impact completion times or error rates, other usability dimensions such as learnability, efficiency, and satisfaction still play crucial roles in shaping the overall user experience. By acknowledging the nuances of user preferences, task efficiency, and accessibility considerations, designers can make informed decisions about menu design to create interfaces that are not only functional but also intuitive and user-friendly.

VI. Conclusion

In this study, we investigated the impact of menu type on navigation performance as measured by task completion time and task completion rates. Participants navigated a website using radial, vertical, and horizontal menus. The results showed that menu presentation style did not affect task completion time and error rate significantly. However, the variance in completion times was affected significantly by menu presentation style and radial menus showed the highest variance and less uniform performance. Users expressed a preference for the width in the overview.

REFERENCES

[1] K. Kim, J. Jacko, and G. Salvendy, "Menu design for computers and cell phones: Review and reappraisal," https://www.tandfonline.com/doi/full/10.1080/10447318.2011.540493, Feb. 2011, retrieved: April, 2024.

[2] R. Moreno-Bote, J. Ramírez-Ruiz, J. Drugowitsch, and Hayden, B. Y., "Heuristics and optimal solutions to the breadth-depth dilemma," *Proc Natl Acad Sci U S A*, vol. 117, no. 33, pp. 19 799–19 808, 2020.

[3] E. E. Schultz Jr and P. S. Curran, "Menu structure and ordering of menu selection: independent or interactive effects?" *ACM SIGCHI Bulletin*, vol. 18, no. 2, pp. 69–71, 1986.

[4] S. Zhao and R. Balakrishnan, "Simple vs. compound mark hierarchical marking menus," in *Proceedings of the 17th annual ACM symposium on User interface software and technology*, 2004, pp. 33–42.

[5] S. S. Bodrunova and A. Yakunin, "Impact of menu complexity upon user behavior and satisfaction in information search," https://link.springer.com/chapter/10.1007/978-3-319-92046-7_5, Jun. 2018, retrieved: April, 2024.

[6] J. Callahan, D. Hopkins, M. Weiser, and B. Shneiderman, "An empirical comparison of pie vs. linear menus," in *Proceedings of the SIGCHI conference on Human factors in computing systems*, 1988, pp. 95–100.

[7] C. Ling, W. Hwang, and G. Salvendy, "A survey of what customers want in a cell phone design," *Behaviour & Information Technology*, vol. 26, no. 2, pp. 149–163, 2007.

[8] D. P. Miller, "The depth/breadth tradeoff in hierarchical computer menus," *Proceedings of the Human Factors Society Annual Meeting*, vol. 25, no. 1, pp. 296–300, 1981, retrieved: April, 2024. [Online]. Available: https://doi.org/10.1177/107118138102500179

[9] J. R. Kingsburg and A. D. Andre, "A comparison of three-level web menu navigation structures," *Proceedings of the Human Factors and Ergonomics Society Annual Meeting*, vol. 48, no. 13, pp. 1513–1517, 2004, retrieved: April, 2024. [Online]. Available: https://scholarworks.sjsu.edu/cgi/viewcontent.cgi?article=3588&context=etd_theses

[10] M. Bernard and C. Hamblin, "Cascading versus indexed menu design," *Usability News*, vol. 5, no. 1, 2003.

[11] S.-C. Huang, I.-F. Chou, and R. G. Bias, "Empirical evaluation of a popular cellular phone's menu system: theory meets practice," *Journal of Usability Studies*, vol. 1, no. 2, pp. 91–108, 2006.

[12] J. Mitchell and B. Shneiderman, "Dynamic versus static menus: an exploratory comparison," *ACM SigCHI Bulletin*, vol. 20, no. 4, pp. 33–37, 1989.

[13] L. Findlater and J. McGrenere, "A comparison of static, adaptive, and adaptable menus," in *Proceedings of the SIGCHI conference on Human factors in computing systems*, 2004, pp. 89–96.

[14] J. Hollands and P. M. Merikle, "Menu organization and user expertise in information search tasks," *Human Factors*, vol. 29, no. 5, pp. 577–586, 1987.

[15] J. E. McDonald, J. D. Stone, and L. S. Liebelt, "Searching for items in menus: The effects of organization and type of target," in *Proceedings of the human factors society annual meeting*, vol. 27, no. 9. SAGE Publications Sage CA: Los Angeles, CA, 1983, pp. 834–837.

[16] K. Samp and S. Decker, "Supporting menu design with radial layouts," in *Proceedings of the International Conference on Advanced Visual Interfaces*, 2010, pp. 155–162.

[17] G. Kurtenbach and W. Buxton, "The limits of expert performance using hierarchic marking menus," in *Proceedings of the INTERACT'93 and CHI'93 conference on Human factors in computing systems*, 1993, pp. 482–487.

[18] ——, "User learning and performance with marking menus," in *Proceedings of the SIGCHI conference on Human factors in computing systems*, 1994, pp. 258–264.

[19] A. Parush and N. Yuviler-Gavish, "Web navigation structures in cellular phones: The depth/breadth trade-off issue," https://shorturl.at/DEL48, May 2004, retrieved: April, 2024.

[20] A. Cockburn, C. Gutwin, and S. Greenberg, "A predictive model of menu performance," in *Proceedings of the SIGCHI conference on Human factors in computing systems*, 2007, pp. 627–636.

[21] C. G. Drury, "Movements with lateral constraint," *Ergonomics*, vol. 14, no. 2, pp. 293–305, 1971, retrieved: April, 2024. [Online]. Available: https://doi.org/10.1080/00140137108931246

[22] J. Accot and S. Zhai, "Scale effects in steering law tasks," in *Proceedings of the SIGCHI conference on Human factors in computing systems*, 2001, pp. 1–8.

[23] M. Kořistová and C. Spiratos, "Navigation user interface design," https://www.diva-portal.org/smash/get/diva2:1566833/FULLTEXT01.pdf, May 2021.

[24] E. Cuddihy and J. H. Spyridakis, "The effect of visual design and placement of intra-article navigation schemes on reading comprehension and website user perceptions," https://shorturl.at/OTX46, Jul. 2022, retrieved: April, 2024.

[25] B. M. Yu, S.-Z. Roh, and S. Han, "The effect of different menu styles on the user's perception and performance on the www," in *3rd Annual Topics on Distance Learning*, 2001, retrieved: April, 2024.

[26] G. Hulle. (2019) Vertical or horizontal menus? and why? Retrieved: April, 2024. [Online]. Available: https://www.linkedin.com/pulse/vertical-horizontal-menus-why-ganesh-hulle/

[27] J. Callahan, D. Hopkins, Weiser, M., and B. Schneiderman. (1988) An empirical comparison of pie vs linear menus. [Online]. Available: https://dl.acm.org/doi/pdf/10.1145/57167.57182

Dark vs. Light Mode on Smartphones: Effects on Eye Fatigue

Fathima Jubina Pathari, Yvonne Nielsen, Liv Ingrid Andersen, and Georgios Marentakis
Department of Computer Science and Communication
Østfold University College
Halden, Norway
email:{fathima.j.pathari, yvonne.nielsen, liv.i.andersen, georgios.marentakis}@hiof.no

***Abstract*—Excessive smartphone use is quite common and can result in various health issues, such as migraines, eye strain, and cognitive fatigue. Dark mode, also called negative polarity, has gained popularity in recent years and several authors have suggested that it may help reduce eye strain. However, there is conflicting evidence with respect to the impact of display modes on eye strain, especially concerning smartphone use. To investigate this aspect closer, we present a study which explores the impact of smartphone display modes - specifically light and dark modes - on self-reported eye fatigue in two different ambient lighting conditions, dim and bright. We observed a significant reduction in eye fatigue with the use of dark mode in bright ambient conditions, while this effect was not significant in dim ambient lighting. Additionally, positive polarity did not significantly affect eye fatigue in either dim or bright lighting conditions. We discuss these findings in relation to existing literature.**

Keywords-eye fatigue; display mode; ambient light; dark mode; light mode.

I. INTRODUCTION

Nowadays, most people have access to a smartphone [1]. There are currently over one billion smartphone users worldwide and the majority are heavily reliant and attached to their phones. Studies indicate that individuals spend more time with their smartphones than with their family and friends [2]. Statistics show that the average mobile user spends more than 5 hours staring at the device per day [1].

Extended staring at a smartphone screen can cause certain health problems, such as migraines, dark circles under the eyes, weakening of the eyesight, head and neck pain, and it can also result in physical, mental, and cognitive fatigue [2]. Another drawback is the development of Computer Vision Syndrome (CVS). CVS is a range of eye and vision problems that are associated with the use of digital screens [3]. The terms "CVS" and "Digital Eye Strain" (DES) are used interchangeably [4]. Symptoms include tired and irritated eyes, trouble focusing, etc. It can be caused by activities that require intense eye use, like looking at a digital screen or looking at very bright lights [5]. CVS affects nearly 60 million people globally, with one million new cases each year [4].

The blue light technology used in smart screens is one of the main causes of eye fatigue, primarily due to its high energy and shorter wavelength, typically ranging from 380 to 500 nanometers [2]. Frequent smartphone use exposes people to a large amount of blue light. If blue light falls on the retina for extended periods, it can lead to the gradual destruction of photoreceptor cells, potentially causing eye cancer [2].

The dark mode is designed to reduce the amount of light emitted by device screens while ensuring the minimum color contrast ratios necessary for readability [6]. The widespread adoption of dark mode by major platforms signifies a pivotal moment in the evolution of this feature, indicating more than just a passing trend; it represents a fundamental shift in mobile app design trends. However, despite its popularity, there is little evidence as to the effectiveness of dark mode [7]. This aspect is further complicated by the fact that mobile phones are used in different times of the day and in different environments with variations in lighting conditions. The effect of ambient lighting conditions is also not entirely understood. Importantly, most studies target larger screens and smartphones are not evaluated as often [7].

Given the widespread use of light and dark modes on smartphones, this study aims to investigate the impact of smartphone display polarity, in particular dark and light modes, on users' experiences of eye fatigue in different ambient lighting conditions, specifically bright and dim ambient light conditions. The paper is structured as follows. Section II provides relevant background on the study, while Section III details the methodology employed, including the experiment design, hypotheses, apparatus and materials, tasks and instructions, and participant information. Section IV presents a detailed analysis of the results of the quantitative study. Finally, Section V discusses the findings, and Section VI concludes the paper.

II. BACKGROUND

Zayed and co-authors [4] analyzed data from a demographic and ergonomic factors and a CVS Questionnaire (CVS-Q) designed to assess DES using a sample of 108 IT professionals. They found that 82% of participants reported some form of DES. Further to subjective assessment through questionnaires Bhanu Priya & Subramaniyam [2] discuss various other methods for assessing visual fatigue and eye strain, such as eye trackers or biomedical instrumentation.

Light and dark modes are essentially different display polarities. Light mode (positive polarity) is the oldest and most commonly used, but dark mode (negative polarity) has been gaining more popularity over the last two years, as evidenced by the increasing number of applications and operating systems that support this setting [6], [8]. The use of dark themes predates the implementation of dark mode in smartphones. Dark themes have been used in user interfaces for video and photo editing software, including applications like Sublime,

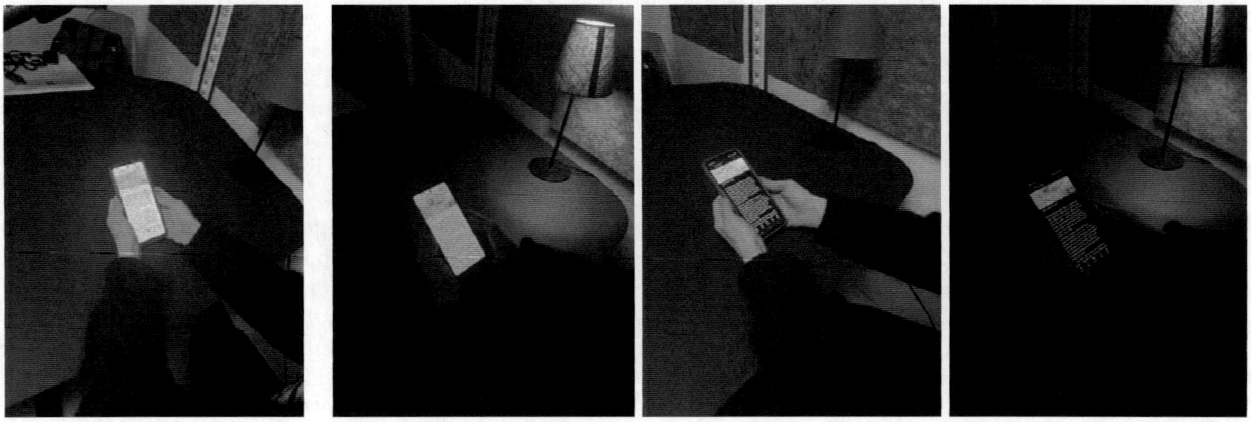

(a) (b) (c) (d)

Figure 1. Illustration of a participant exposed (a) to bright ambient light and positive display polarity, (b) low ambient light and negative display polarity (c) bright ambient light and positive display polarity (d) low ambient light and negative display polarity.

Atom, Visual Studio, and various others since several years [9].

Dark mode user interfaces use light-colored text (typically white or light grey) on a dark or black screen to reduce the amount of light that is emitted by device screens [10]. They are supported by Android and Apple phones and dark mode is often recommended for those with sensitive eyes. In certain cases, dark mode gives the impression of a more natural lighting environment, making it feel more comfortable to use [9] and can help save power and enhance the interface aesthetics [8].

Display polarity may impact visual acuity and a positive polarity is generally recommended if visual acuity is important [11]. A positive polarity results in higher overall brightness, which leads to a smaller pupil size that is good for attending to visual detail [11], [12]. For example, proofreading is done more effectively with a positive polarity [12]. Furthermore, there is evidence for a higher text comprehension using positive polarity displays [13] and black-on-white text was found to be significantly more legible than white-on-black text in dim environments [14].

However, the results on the effect of display polarity on eye fatigue are mixed. This could be because the advantage in visual acuity due to a positive polarity may possibly come at the expense of higher visual fatigue [15], [16]. Xie et al. [17] found reduced visual fatigue due to using negative polarity in a dark environment using a 27-inch display. However, the light mode was the preferred mode among the participants at high luminance contrast ratios. Ericson et al. present a similar finding in that the dark mode reduced visual fatigue more in a dark environment [18], [19]. Rempel et al. [18] report shorter response times using negative polarity. Wang et al. [20] found no effect on visual fatigue when comparing positive and negative polarity. When studying visual fatigue in Virtual Reality head-mounted displays, it was found that dark mode (negative polarity) increased visual acuity in dim virtual environments, while light mode increased acuity in bright virtual environments. Dark mode was preferred among the participants and was shown to reduce visual fatigue in both low light and day light environments [19], [21].

While light mode remains the traditional and widely used option, the increasing popularity of dark mode is evident in the growing number of applications adopting this setting. However, evaluation results on exploring whether one mode is more beneficial for eye health based on scientific and statistical evidence or if it is simply a matter of personal preference. Importantly, there is a lack of research using mobile phone screens as most studies are done using larger displays (14-27 inches CRT or LCD displays) [7]. We address this gap by specifically comparing the impacts of light and dark modes in different ambient light settings.

III. METHOD

We designed an experiment to explore the relationship between the smartphone display mode and ambient lighting condition on eye fatigue when using a smartphone.

A. Experiment Design

Independent variable smartphone display polarity had two levels (negative and positive polarity corresponding to dark mode and light mode) as did variable ambient lighting condition (bright and dim ambient lighting). The experiment used a mixed-model design with ambient lighting as between-subjects and display light mode as within-subjects variable.

A CVS questionnaire combining questions and Likert scale items was used to measure the eye fatigue of the participants. This questionnaire was adapted from a previous study on eye fatigue [17], [22] based on the Visual Fatigue Scale (VFS) developed by Heuer and Hollendiek. The questionnaire begins with demographic questions, followed by questions about eye health (such as prescriptions, allergies, and dry eyes), and the average screen time during a day. Participants then use six Likert scale to respond to questions that assess various aspects of visual discomfort on a scale from 1 to 10: (1) It is hard for me to see the screen clearly, (2) I have a strange feeling in my eyes, (3) I have sore eyes such as acerbity, tingling, or swelling, (4) The brightness of the screen numbs my eyes, (5) Looking at the screen, I feel dizzy or fuzzy, (6) I feel a headache. Eye fatigue is then calculated as the average of these ratings.

B. Hypotheses

Given supporting evidence in the literature, we hypothesized that the use of dark mode on smartphones will lead to significantly less eye fatigue in users compared to the use of light mode, especially in dim ambient lighting conditions.

C. Apparatus & Materials

The smartphone used in the experiment was a Samsung Galaxy A53 with an Android operating system and built-in light and dark mode display options. Its screen size, measured diagonally, is 6.5 inches in the full rectangle and 6.3 inches accounting for the rounded corners. The experiment was conducted in a dark laboratory room without a window. The room lights and a small lamp were used to simulate the high and low ambient lighting. Figures 1a and 1b depict the experiment performed with light mode on the smartphone under bright and dim ambient lighting, respectively. Meanwhile, Figures 1c and 1d illustrate the experiment conducted with dark mode on the smartphone under bright and dim ambient lighting, respectively.

To perform the experimental tasks, a number of applications were used. These were Microsoft Start: news and more, text messaging app, Quora, and Reddit. These are all well-known apps used for day-to-day tasks and are made to be used in both dark and light modes. The luminance level was measured to be 460 Lux in bright ambient light mode and 33 Lux in dim ambient light mode. Smartphone screen luminance was 1300 Lux (positive polarity) and 450 Lux (negative polarity) when ambient light was high and 140 Lux (positive polarity) and 9.3 Lux (negative polarity) when ambient light was low. Smartphone luminance varied in accordance with the automated screen brightness adaptation of the smartphone.

D. Tasks and Instructions

During the experiment, participants performed a number of tasks in each display polarity mode. Tasks were designed to be of the same type but had different characteristics. The first task was to read the article "6 common sleep myths debunked", which had a reading length of 7 minutes, on the Microsoft Start app. The article was opened on the phone when they started. The second task was then to find the phone's text message app and write a short text of three sentences summarizing the article without sending it. For the third task, they were asked to locate the Reddit app on the phone, open it, search for posts using the phrase "tips for better sleep", find three different pieces of advice and create a new post mentioning them. The tasks in the second part in which the alternative light mode was used were identical to the first, except that the participants read the article "The psychological immune system: four ways to bolster yours", used the Quora app for the last task instead of Reddit, and searched for posts using the phrase "tips for a better immune system". Following each task group, participants were asked to fill out the aforementioned questionnaire to assess symptoms of eye fatigue.

E. Procedure

Prior to the experiment starting, each participant received a briefing regarding the experiment's objectives, the expected duration, the procedure, the right to withdraw, which data would be collected, and provided consent for participation.

Counterbalancing was used to mitigate potential biases and order effects. Participants were divided into two groups, each experiencing one of the two different ambient lighting conditions. Within each group, the participants were randomly allocated to two subgroups, where the first started out with negative polarity (dark mode) and switched to positive polarity (light mode), and vice versa. Participants completed the eye fatigue questionnaire after finishing each display polarity tasks. During this time, the phone's display polarity was switched by the experiment conductors. The experiments were conducted within working hours between 9 am and 4 pm. It took about 15 minutes to complete each task group.

A pilot test was executed in advance to assess the timing of the experiment tasks, the flow between them, the switching between display modes, and participant instructions.

F. Participants

Participants were invited via email. A total of 18 IT students participated in the experiments, aged between 20 and 50 years, with eleven males and seven females, with nine participants assigned to each ambient lighting group. The average duration of mobile phone usage of the participants is 7.94 hours per day. IT students were targeted due to easy access, due to sharing a common foundation for experiencing eye fatigue from regular screen exposure due to participation in a computer-based study program, and good technological abilities and familiarity with smartphone usage.

IV. RESULTS

Figure 2c shows the average value of eye fatigue in the different conditions in the experiment. It can be seen that during bright ambient light, eye fatigue is on average lower for the negative compared to the positive display polarity, while during dim ambient light, eye fatigue for positive display polarity is lower when compared to negative. Figures 2a and 2b show eye fatigue for each participant. We see that the tendency for a lower eye fatigue when display polarity is negative compared to when it is positive mentioned above is observed for all participants. The inverse tendency for lower eye fatigue when display polarity is positive compared to when it was negative in dim lighting conditions appears in five out of the nine participants tested here.

A two-way mixed model Ambient Lighting x Display Polarity ANOVA was conducted on the results. The main effect of Ambient lighting and of Display Polarity was not

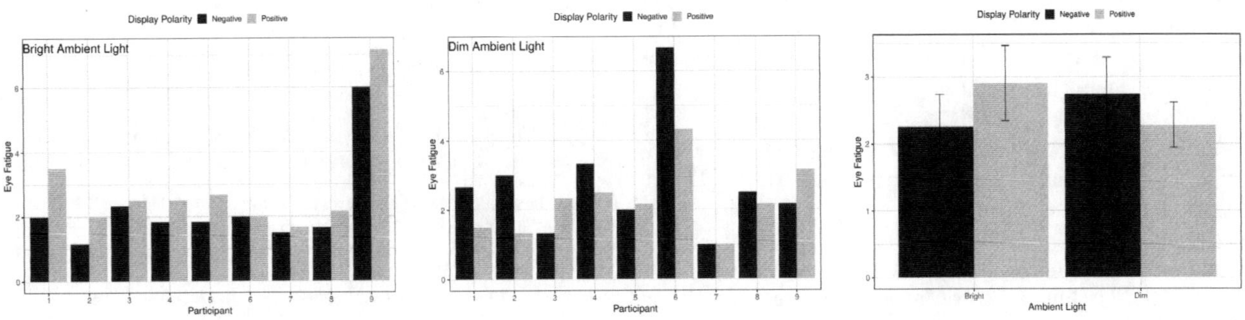

(a) (b) (c)

Figure 2. Eye fatigue versus display polarity for (a) bright and (b) dim ambient light for each participant and (c) eye fatigue versus ambient light and display polarity. Error bars show the standard deviation of the mean.

significant. The Ambient Light x Display Polarity interaction was significant F(1, 14) = 7.13, p = 0.016, η^2=0.039. Pair-wise comparisons were conducted using t-tests, as appropriate for the within and between-subject comparisons. The Holm adjustment method was applied to control family-wise error rates. When ambient light was bright, negative polarity (dark mode) led to significantly lower eye fatigue compared to positive polarity (light mode) (p = 0.004). This difference was not significant when ambient lighting was dim. Furthermore, according to the t-tests, eye fatigue did not vary significantly when comparing bright and dim ambient lighting conditions with the positive polarity display mode.

V. Discussion

Our investigation was motivated by the desire to investigate *how the use of positive and negative display polarities (dark and light modes) in bright and dim ambient light conditions affects eye fatigue among smartphone users*. We designed and performed an experiment which compared different display modes in two ambient lighting conditions. Data were collected using the average value of the Likert scales from a related computer vision questionnaire, similar to the methodology employed in other studies [10]. In addition, we evaluated internal consistency to ensure the reliability of the questionnaire used to measure eye fatigue. The Cronbach's alpha coefficient found a value of 0.865, indicating good reliability and internal consistency among the items [23].

According to our analysis, the effects of Display Polarity and Ambient Lighting were not significant. However, the interaction between ambient lighting and display polarity was significant. This suggests that the effect of ambient lighting could depend on display polarity, and vice versa. Indeed, post-hoc tests showed that during bright ambient light conditions, participants exhibited significantly lower levels of eye fatigue when using negative polarity (dark mode) compared to positive polarity (light mode). This occurred, however, only in bright ambient light conditions, as the effect of display polarity on eye fatigue was not significant in dim lighting. The result of lower eye fatigue in a bright environment when using a negative display polarity on a smartphone screen is novel as this question has not been addressed before in the context of interaction with a smartphone screen as the one used here.

Pedersen et al. [8] found no effect of display polarity in the daytime in terms of productivity and quantity of errors. Sethi [7] reports higher mental demand when using positive compared to negative polarity in a bright environment and that younger adults showed higher cognitive load using when using negative polarity in a dim environment. Wang et al. [20] found no significant effect of display polarity on eye fatigue. On the other hand, Erickson et al. [21] found a higher preference and better overall usability, hedonic quality, and pragmatic quality for a negative display polarity in dim lighting conditions when using a see-through display. However, they did not measure eye fatigue. Xie et al. [17] on the other hand find that negative polarity reduces eye fatigue in dim lighting conditions. We found a similar finding but not in dim but in bright ambient lighting conditions. [17] did not test bright lighting conditions. So while our result is consistent with some of the studies in the literature, there are studies that report an advantage due to negative polarity in dim lighting conditions or even an advantage due to positive display polarity in bright ambient light conditions.

The inconsistency may be related to differences in the screen size but also individual differences. As mentioned earlier, we used a 6.5 inches screen which is much smaller than the 27 inches screen used in [17]. Furthermore, in contrast to the bright ambient conditions in which all participants reported lower eye fatigue when using the display in the negative polarity (dark mode), the eye fatigue ratings were not as consistent across participants when ambient lighting was dim. Five out of nine reported lower fatigue with positive polarity, three out of nine with negative polarity, while one out of nine reported no difference. In our study, luminance levels were 460 Lux in bright ambient light mode and 33 Lux in dim ambient light mode (less dim than 3 lux for ambient light in [17]) while the brightness of the smartphone screen changed automatically to yield 1300 Lux (positive polarity) and 450 Lux (negative polarity) when ambient light was bright and 140 Lux (positive polarity) and 9.3 Lux (negative polarity) when ambient light was dim. Screen luminance was higher than ambient by 840 Lux (positive polarity) and 107 Lux (negative polarity) in the case of bright ambient luminance levels and lower by 10 Lux (positive polarity) and 23.7 Lux for dim ambient lighting conditions. Perhaps, the large difference in the bright ambient conditions could also have influenced the results. This is a hypothesis we would like to investigate further in future research. Additionally, while our study provides valuable insights, we acknowledge the limitations associated with our relatively small sample size. To mitigate this limitation, we intend to enlarge our subject pool in the future study.

VI. CONCLUSION

Our study aimed to explore the impact of display polarity under varying ambient lighting conditions on eye fatigue. The experiment involved performing a number of specific tasks using smartphones. The analysis revealed no main effect of either ambient light or display mode. However, the interaction between ambient light and display mode was significant and pairwise comparisons using t-tests showed that negative display polarity led to a significant decrease in eye fatigue in bright ambient lighting while the effect was not significant in dim ambient lighting. Larger-scale studies may provide more insight into the relationship between display modes and eye fatigue for smartphones.

REFERENCES

[1] "Digital 2023: Global overview report," Jan. 2023, publication Title: DataReportal – Global Digital Insights. [Online]. Available: https://datareportal.com/reports/digital-2023-global-overview-report

[2] D. B. Priya and M. Subramaniyam, "A systematic review on visual fatigue induced by tiny screens (smartphones)," in *IOP Conference Series: Materials Science and Engineering*, vol. 912. IOP Publishing, 2020, p. 062009.

[3] M. Rosenfield, "Computer vision syndrome (aka digital eye strain)." *Optometry in practice*, vol. 17, pp. 1–10, 2016.

[4] H. A. M. Zayed, S. M. Saied, E. A. Younis, and S. A. Atlam, "Digital eye strain: Prevalence and associated factors among information technology professionals in Egypt," *Environmental Science and Pollution Research*, vol. 28, pp. 25 187–25 195, 2021, publisher: Springer.

[5] R. Ansorge, "Eye fatigue: Causes, symptoms, and treatment," Feb. 2023, publication Title: WebMD. [Online]. Available: https://www.webmd.com/eye-health/eye-fatigue-causes-symptoms-treatment

[6] J. Ferrer, "Why is dark mode so captivating?" Feb. 2024. [Online]. Available: https://uxdesign.cc/why-is-dark-mode-so-captivating-92f2ed4e0dc5

[7] T. Sethi and M. Ziat, "Dark mode vogue: Do light-on-dark displays have measurable benefits to users?" *Ergonomics*, vol. 66, no. 12, pp. 1814–1828, Dec. 2023.

[8] L. A. Pedersen, S. S. Einarsson, F. A. Rikheim, and F. E. Sandnes, "User interfaces in dark mode during daytime – Improved productivity or just cool-looking?" in *Universal Access in Human-Computer Interaction. Design Approaches and Supporting Technologies*, M. Antona and C. Stephanidis, Eds. Cham: Springer International Publishing, 2020, vol. 12188, pp. 178–187.

[9] H. Eisfeld and F. Kristallovich, "The rise of dark mode: A qualitative study of an emerging user interface design trend," Sep. 2020, backup Publisher: Jönköping University.

[10] S. Popelka, A. Vondrakova, and R. Skulnikova (Filicka), "The effect of day and night mode on the perception of map navigation device," in *2022 Symposium on Eye Tracking Research and Applications*. Seattle WA USA: ACM, Jun. 2022, pp. 1–6.

[11] C. Piepenbrock, S. Mayr, I. Mund, and A. Buchner, "Positive display polarity is advantageous for both younger and older adults," *Ergonomics*, vol. 56, no. 7, pp. 1116–1124, Jul. 2013.

[12] C. Piepenbrock, S. Mayr, and A. Buchner, "Smaller pupil size and better proofreading performance with positive than with negative polarity displays," *Ergonomics*, vol. 57, no. 11, pp. 1670–1677, Nov. 2014.

[13] A.-H. Wang, J.-J. Fang, and C.-H. Chen, "Effects of VDT leading-display design on visual performance of users in handling static and dynamic display information dual-tasks," *International Journal of Industrial Ergonomics*, vol. 32, no. 2, pp. 93–104, Feb. 2003. [Online]. Available: https://www.sciencedirect.com/science/article/pii/S0169814103000416

[14] J. Dobres et al., "Utilising psychophysical techniques to investigate the effects of age, typeface design, size and display polarity on glance legibility," *Ergonomics*, vol. 59, no. 10, pp. 1377–1391, 2016.

[15] A. Buchner and N. Baumgartner, "Text – Background polarity affects performance irrespective of ambient illumination and colour contrast," *Ergonomics*, vol. 50, no. 7, pp. 1036–1063, Jul. 2007.

[16] A. Buchner, S. Mayr, and M. Brandt, "The advantage of positive text-background polarity is due to high display luminance," *Ergonomics*, vol. 52, no. 7, pp. 882–886, Jul. 2009.

[17] X. Xie, F. Song, Y. Liu, S. Wang, and D. Yu, "Study on the effects of display color mode and luminance contrast on visual fatigue," *IEEE Access*, vol. 9, pp. 35 915–35 923, 2021, publisher: IEEE.

[18] A. G. Rempel, R. Mantiuk, and W. Heidrich, "Display considerations for improved night vision performance," *cic*, vol. 19, no. 1, pp. 191–194, Jan. 2011. [Online]. Available: https://library.imaging.org/cic/articles/19/1/art00039

[19] A. Erickson, K. Kim, G. Bruder, and G. F. Welch, "Effects of dark mode graphics on visual acuity and fatigue with virtual reality head-mounted displays," in *2020 IEEE Conference on Virtual Reality and 3D User Interfaces (VR)*. IEEE, 2020, pp. 434–442.

[20] A.-H. Wang and M.-T. Chen, "Effects of polarity and luminance contrast on visual performance and VDT display quality," *International Journal of Industrial Ergonomics*, vol. 25, no. 4, pp. 415–421, 2000, publisher: Elsevier.

[21] A. Erickson et al., "An extended analysis on the benefits of dark mode user interfaces in optical see-through head-mounted displays," *ACM Transactions on Applied Perception*, vol. 18, no. 3, pp. 1–22, Jul. 2021.

[22] P. Tian et al., "Effects of paradigm color and screen brightness on visual fatigue in light environment of night based on eye tracker and EEG acquisition equipment," *Sensors (Basel)*, vol. 22, no. 11, p. 4082, May 2022.

[23] B. Sharma, "A focus on reliability in developmental research through Cronbach's alpha among medical, dental, and paramedical professionals," *Asian Pacific Journal of Health Science, APJHS*, vol. 3, no. 4, pp. 271–278, Dec. 2016.

Comparative Assessment of 2D and Mixed Reality Interfaces for Improving Situational Awareness

Nazım Yiğit Kavasoğlu
Dept. of Computer Engineering
Istanbul Technical University
Aselsan
Ankara, Turkey
e-mail: nykavasoglu@aselsan.com.tr

Gökhan İnce
Dept. of Computer Engineering
Istanbul Technical University
Istanbul, Turkey
e-mail: gokhan.ince@itu.edu.tr

***Abstract*—Environmental factors, such as fog and darkness, significantly limit the visibility of security personnel. In addition, limited field knowledge and inexperience can lead to misinterpretation of events, which may endanger both the task and human lives. Our study compares the situational awareness of participants and the effectiveness of purpose-built mobile applications and Mixed Reality (MR) glasses in security-related scenarios for navigation involving capturing a moving hostile target in a forested environment. Results of the experiments in terms of task completion time, navigation accuracy and questionnaire responses show that the utilization of MR technology improves situational awareness and user engagement compared to the 2D map-based mobile applications.**

Keywords*—*mixed reality; situational awareness; head mounted displays.

I. INTRODUCTION

Situational Awareness (SA) is a theoretical framework that involves comprehending various events within a confined time and spatial context to gain a better understanding of the surroundings [1]. Military operations or national security frequently unfold in unfamiliar and unmapped territories. Consequently, knowing the environment becomes beneficial.

Mixed Reality is a powerful tool for security personnel in military camps, providing a comprehensive and effective approach to protect personnel, equipment, and sensitive information [2]. Mobile technologies, such as Head Mounted Displays (HMD) and MR applications, can enhance their vision by providing relevant data and minimizing distractions [3]. The effectiveness in challenging settings depends on the utilization of Command, Control, Communications, Computers, Information, and Intelligence (C4I2) tools. C4I2 tools are optimal performance that can be effective in increasing the SA of security personnel [4]. Applications of MR have proven to be valuable for security personnel, as they enhances SA and facilitate the attainment of mission objectives with greater efficiency [5]. These applications can help security personnel in foggy places obtain information in invisible places.

In this study, a radar simulation application was created using a surveillance radar as a sensor, and two purpose-built applications, which are a mobile map-based application and an MR application, were developed. This study aims to investigate potential differences in usability level between these two purpose-built applications through experiments. In experiments, participants delve into two different groups for simulating a security-related scenario. One group used the mobile application while the other group used the MR application. When the task was finished, participants were asked to fill out questionnaires. Also, task completion times and deflection errors were calculated. This analysis will provide valuable insights into the applications' efficacy and help draw meaningful conclusions about their respective performances based on the data collected from participants.

The rest of the paper is organized as follows. Section II provides and overview of the relevant studies that have contributed insights to the present study. Section III explains problem definitions and proposed applications. Section IV gives information about the experiments conducted on participants. Section V includes results. Section VI contains a discussion of potential ways for future research related to the subject matter of the study. Lastly in Section VII, results of the conducted experiments is given.

II. LITERATURE REVIEW

Augmented Reality (AR) and MR changed how we navigate our environment by mixing virtual and real worlds. The impact of civil navigation through various applications, advancements, and research findings was examined to evaluate how AR and MR were employed.. Jin et al. compare the effectiveness of Natural User Interface (NUI) using HMD with AR and Graphical User Interface (GUI) in storytelling [6]. The results show that NUI is more effective in terms of user engagement, immersion and enjoyment. When using NUI, participants feel more present in the story world. The GUI, on the other hand, is perceived as less immersive and interesting.

Dong et al.'s research compares the external and visual behaviors of users using AR and 2D maps for pedestrian way-finding [7]. AR offers a more intuitive and immersive experience, allowing users to see their surroundings, receive directional prompts, and adapt to their location and orientation. 2D maps are found to be less engaging and difficult to interpret.

Rocha et al. propose a mobile application that integrates AR and accessibility features [8]. The system combines AR with audio instructions and haptic feedback, providing real-time information about the user's surroundings. The findings indicate that the system displayed an enhancement in navigating unfamiliar environments.

Chimielewski et al. report on an AR system using mobile devices and sensors to aid decision-making and SA in military combat scenarios [9]. The developed system uses accelerometers and gyroscopes to provide orientation and position. The case study shows that the AR system improved soldiers' understanding of situations, assessed threats, and made informed decisions. The paper highlights the potential of AR technology to improve safety and effectiveness on the battlefield.

You et al.'s study reviews the use of AR in urban warfare scenarios, highlighting potential benefits such as enhanced SA, improved decision-making, and increased safety for soldiers [10]. The proposed system overlays real-time data onto soldiers' fields of view, providing a comprehensive picture of their surroundings and the battlefield.

Commercial products utilizing AR/MR exist, and the literature review delves into how AR and MR have shaped diverse business sectors. Eyekon is a wearable computer that uses a support system based on intelligent agents [11]. It aims to provide a comprehensive representation of real weapons to maximize SA in a battlefield environment, using smart icons. It also uses brightness for detecting depth and arrow guidance to direct attention to specific targets. Juhnke et al. accomplish their objective by constructing a framework known as the Intelligent Augmented Reality Model (iARM) [12]. iARM's objective is to establish an AR interface that bridges the gap between the physical environment and the user through the use of a smart screen. Microsoft partnered with the US Army to develop a customized version of the HoloLens called the Integrated Visual Augmentation System (IVAS) for military use [13]. The IVAS has several characteristics such as digital overlays, night vision capabilities, ballistic protection, and hearing protection which are highly suitable for military operations.

The purpose of this study is to show how MR user interfaces surpass mobile map-based applications in the context of military use, as well as to provide empirical evidence to support the hypothesis that MR user interfaces improve performance and effectiveness for security applications. This study aims to improve academic knowledge and practical use of MR user interfaces in security scenarios by carrying out an analysis.

III. Proposed Physical Security Applications

A. Problem Definition and Design Issues

The maintenance of border security holds significant importance for all countries. Since not all borders contain physical barriers, this matter poses a challenge for border security. Cameras and radars are widely utilized gadgets for safeguarding borders between countries. The utilization of radar is typically entrusted to an operator. If any atypical activity is identified on the radar display, the operator will proceed to examine the reliability of the stated activity. If the activity does not qualify as an emergency, the operator shall proceed with examining the radar screen. If it qualifies as an emergency, the operator will initiate contact and provide the required information. Security personnel will proceed to the target location to evaluate the situation. These personnel are often equipped with body armor and weaponry. They lack access to radar screens, and their sole method of obtaining information is through walkie-talkie. The issue in this particular scenario relates to communication. Enhancing the efficiency of communication could provide benefits for security personnel.

The mobile and MR applications proposed in this paper are developed to address the issue described above. Security personnel need a tool for obtaining information about the target. Having access to this information in real time can allow them to anticipate potential dangers.

B. Overview of the Proposed System

The general structure of the proposed system is shown in Figure 1. The system is composed of four fundamental components. It includes a radar, a server, a mobile device, and an HMD. Due to privacy and security issues, a simulator is used for mimicking the radar outputs in experiments.

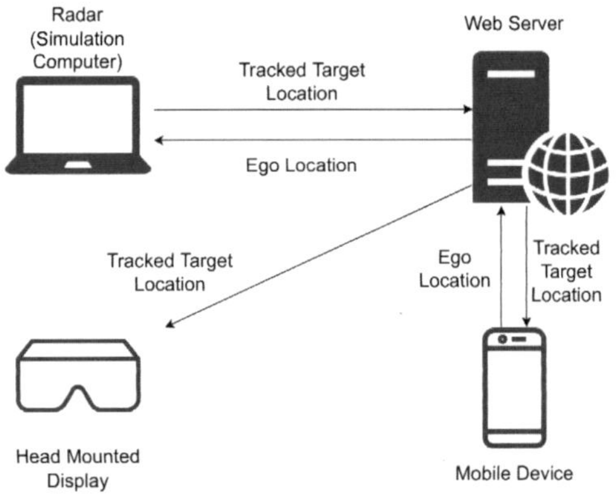

Figure 1. General structure of the proposed system.

The MR application works on an HMD while the mobile application operates on a mobile device. The web server uses a database and a server. Meanwhile, the simulation application runs on a computer.

C. Radar and Web Server

The radar produces a signal characterized by a particular frequency and subsequently examines the received signals in order to identify and classify the detected objects. The detections possess data regarding the coordinate system and processed signal outcomes. The detection algorithm receives these pieces of information as input to the algorithm which can determine whether the detected signal is a target or a false alarm. If the output of the algorithm corresponds to a specific target, additional information such as geolocation and identification (e.g., human, animal, vehicle) is computed. The utilization of a simulation is employed during the target and tracked target location creation process, followed by uploading these locations to the web server in a sequence. The generated tracked target locations correctly represent the location of the target.

The tracked location is uploaded on the web server via HTTP requests by the radar simulation. JSON is used as the data format. An example tracked target location data is presented such as {"trackId":1, "latitude":39.71, "longitude":32.15, "horizontal":43.7, "vertical":28.2}.

To determine horizontal and vertical distances, origin and tracked target location are used. The origin location is the geolocation where security personnel begin using the HMD. It is also the location where the radar is positioned. The haversine formula is used for calculating distances between two points on a spherical surface using the coordinates of the two locations. The formula to calculate the distance between the location information of the security personnel and the shortest route involves calculating the distance of the point perpendicular to the line.

Communication between simulation and mobile/MR applications is provided by the web server application. The application serves three functions: responding to requests related to the geographical origin location, responding to the geographical location of the ego (in our experiment the ego location is the participant location) and responding to requests about the tracked target location. The web server receives HTTP requests from the simulation and the mobile application and stores them in its database. When the mobile or MR application requests an update of the tracked target location, the web server responds to these requests as in Figure 1.

D. Mobile Application

A mobile application has been designed with a 2D map-based user interface to function as a physical security application. The mobile application user interface is shown in Figure 2.

Figure 2. Mobile application user interface (when held horizontally).

Satellite images, ego and tracked target locations are visualized on the map. The ego location is acquired through the GPS and the tracked target location is retrieved from the web server.

E. MR Application

An MR application is developed and deployed on the HMD for the purpose of visualizing the tracked target location, which is aimed to serve as a security personnel HMD. The tracked target location in the web server is requested from the application and the target object can be displayed on the screen. A screenshot taken from the MR interface is shown in Figure 3.

Figure 3. MR application user interface.

Since the MR engine uses object display by the coordinate system consisting of three axes (x,y,z) and sensory location in real-world uses geo-location, merging them on the same plane is needed. This merging is made possible through a conversion of origin location to x,y,z axes. For HMD's accurate object visualization, its display needs to be aligned with the north direction. This mapping can be seen in Figure 4 (N represents North for the real-word coordinate system).

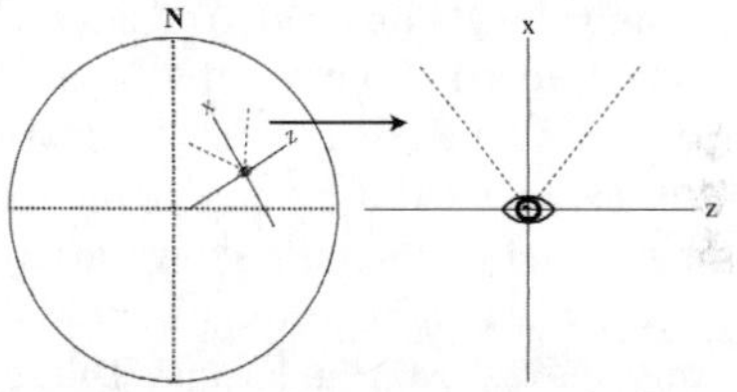

Figure 4. MR Engine (left panel) and Real-world (right panel) coordinate systems.

HoloLens 2, which was used as the main HMD in our study, has a maximum draw distance for displaying objects. A displayed virtual object is constrained to be visible up to 50 meters. An object which has a distance beyond 50 meters can not be rendered on HMD. As seen in Figure 5, the target location on the MR plane is projected on a 30 meters radius from the HMD. This will create a virtual target location so that the virtual location will always be visible regardless of how far the target is located. Calculations are made with the tracked target and ego locations and the object's virtual position is displayed on the HMD.

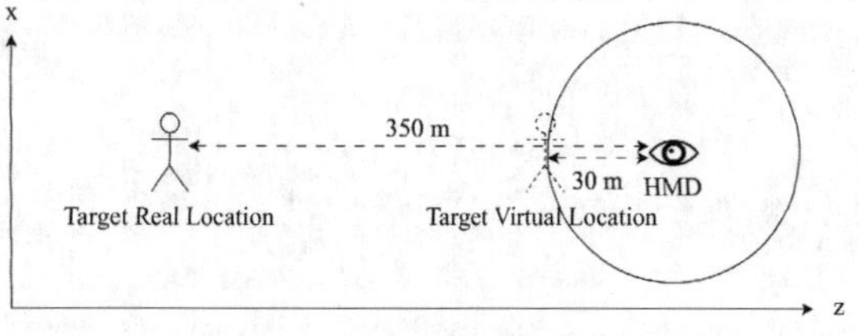

Figure 5. HMD draw distance.

The visibility of objects is significantly compromised when HMDs are used in outdoor environments. In order to enhance the visibility of the target object, a red color layer is added.

IV. Experiments

A. Hardware and Software

The web server application was developed using Firebase. To establish communication with the radar simulation, the mobile device, and the MR applications, Firebase functions were used. Meanwhile, the radar simulation application was developed for console application with Java 17 spring boot.

During the development process of the mobile application, Kotlin version 1.6 was used. Samsung S20FE smartphone was used for the deployment using Android Studio. The mobile application made use of Mapbox as its map service provider. The Microsoft HoloLens 2 was selected as the preferred HMD for the MR application. The MR application was created using the Unity platform and compiled specifically for the Advanced Reduced Instruction Set Computer (RISC) Machine (ARM) 64-bit architecture. This compilation was provided by the Mixed Reality Toolkit (MRKT).

B. Experimental Scenario

The experimental scenario was carried out in an environment with a moderate presence of trees, pathways, a pond, a bridge, man-made objects, etc. as shown in Figure 6, because the real-life surveillance, monitoring and tracking activities take place in similar environments. An average person is capable of walking the outer perimeter of this particular region in a time frame of six minutes, covering a total distance of 400 meters. Also, the best and the worst possible routes from the origin to the targeted location are shown in Figure 6. Red dots show target movement in the experiment. The movement stops shortly after the experiment begins. This ensures that participants are confident that they have reached the targeted location. The shortest path is around 170 meters while the longest path is around 250 meters.

Figure 6. Experiment area (Upper panel: top view, lower panels: photos taken at the given locations).

In this experiment, participants start by positioning themselves at the origin location and proceed to use the mobile device or put on the HMD. Before starting, a hand weight is provided to the participant to simulate the security personnel's hands being occupied and physically hindered with additional weight. After the virtual data (for the 2D map or the MR content) are displayed on the application, the timer is initiated, prompting the participant to take action in locating and tracking the target. Since the simulation of the target is moving, the locations change continuously. Simultaneously with the start of the participant walking, the mobile application sends the ego location to the web server. Once the participant arrives at the tracked target location, the timer stops and the elapsed time is computed. Each participant tracked the target location once using only one application. The target location followed the same route for both applications. The experiment comes with limitations, such as the requirement to carry weight at all times and the restriction of the participant to not leave the designated area.

C. Participants

Two groups of participants were randomly selected, with each group consisting of 15 individuals, resulting in a total of 30 participants. The first group (Group 1) used the mobile application, whereas the second group (Group 2) used the MR application. All individuals within Group 1 had prior experience using a mobile navigation application of some kind. Conversely, 53 percent of the participants in Group 2 had prior experience using AR/MR applications.

D. Evaluation metrics

This study uses four evaluation methods. Objective measurements, such as task completion time and navigation accuracy measurements, are obtained through impartial methods. It was aimed to compare both mobile and MR applications in terms of guidance accuracy by calculating the deviation from the ideal shortest route toward the target. An example of deviation is shown in Figure 7. From each geographical coordinate in the participant's walking route, the perpendicular deviation from the shortest path is retrieved.

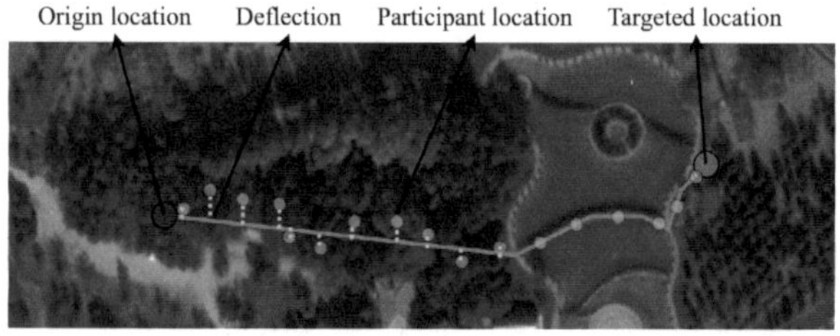

Figure 7. Illustration of the calculation of deflection error.

Subjective measurement surveys, such as NASA Task Load Index (TLX) and Post Study System Usability Questionnaire (PSSUQ), rely on subjective assessments [14] [15]. The Appendix lists the questions of the questionnaire.

V. RESULTS

A. Task Completion Performance

Table I shows the time taken by the participants to complete the experiment. Based on the results, participants who used the MR application (Group 2) arrived quicker to the target compared to participants who used the mobile application (Group 1).

Based on the comments made by participants using the mobile application, they experienced a loss when using the application while holding the weight in their hands. They also

TABLE I
AVERAGE TASK COMPLETION TIME RESULTS

Group	Time (min.)
Group 1	3:37 ±1:01
Group 2	2:54 ±0:28

stated that they initially allocated some time to determine the optimal route to reach the targeted location on the map.

Participants in Group 2 commented that they perceived it as straightforward to determine which way to proceed initially, because they were able to see the terrain, path and environmental objects clearly while walking. However, they reported that, when faced with the obstacle of crossing the pond, it took some time to decide on the right path.

B. Navigation accuracy

The findings related to the navigation accuracy errors can be seen in Table II. Based on the results, it was observed that individuals using MR applications showed a higher degree of proximity to the shortest path in comparison to those using the mobile application.

TABLE II
AVERAGE DEFLECTION ERROR

Group	Error (meters)
Group 1	6.60 ±2.10
Group 2	3.17 ±1.34

During the experiment, the participants encountered deviations from the shortest path because of the decisions they made while navigating toward the targeted location. As a result, mobile application users exhibited both a delay and a higher degree of deviation. The participants who used the mobile application indicated that they had difficulty initially determining where they would go.

C. Results of NASA TLX Questionnaire

The findings from the NASA TLX Questionnaire are displayed in Figure 8. According to the results, the metric with the lower score is considered preferable over the others in each of the six metrics. The scale for each metric ranges from 1 (the best outcome) to 21 (the worst outcome). These scores are computed by averaging all participants' scores using the two applications.

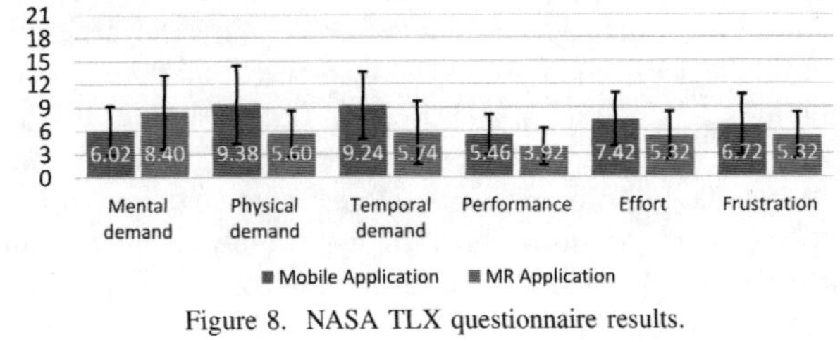

Figure 8. NASA TLX questionnaire results.

The mental demand is seen as the sole outcome in favor of the mobile application. The mental demand score is 6.02 for the mobile application and 8.4 for the MR application. Based on the t-test result, p=.118 shows that there is no important statistical difference between the results. According to the participants, the mobile application makes use of a user interface that is more recognizable. However, participants faced difficulties when trying to simultaneously participate in both the physical environment and the virtual representation using the MR application.

In all other performance categories except the mental demand, the MR application outperformed the mobile application. It is shown that physical demand has the highest difference between the mobile (9.38) and MR (5.6) applications (p=.019). The participants expressed that the physical weight they had in their hands posed challenges while using the mobile application. The temporal demand score of the mobile application (9.24) is statistically significantly higher than the MR application (5.74) (p=.031). The outcome can be related to the temporal inefficiency encountered by individuals using the mobile application. The performance of the MR application (3.92) is observed to be better than that of the mobile application (5.46) (p=.101). The participants were provided with information about task completion times and the accuracy of reaching the targeted location. Based on the findings, it was observed that the users of the MR application perceived themselves to have achieved higher levels of success. The mobile application's effort score (7.42) is higher than the MR application's (5.32) (p=.089). According to the feedback provided by participants using the mobile application, it was occasionally necessary for them to disrupt their use of the application. Due to comparable factors, it is stated that the frustration score is greater on the mobile application (6.72) in contrast to the MR application (5.32) (p=.278).

D. Results of PSSUQ

The PSSUQ enables participants to share their thoughts and recommendations regarding the interfaces they tested. PSSUQ consists of nineteen questions that assess the general system usefulness, information quality and interface quality of the applications. The scale for each metric ranges from 1 (the best outcome) to 7 (the worst outcome). These scores are computed by averaging all participants' scores using the two applications. The results of PSSUQ are presented in Figure 9. Based on the results, the overall score indicates that the MR application (2.22) showed improved usability compared to the mobile application (3.15).

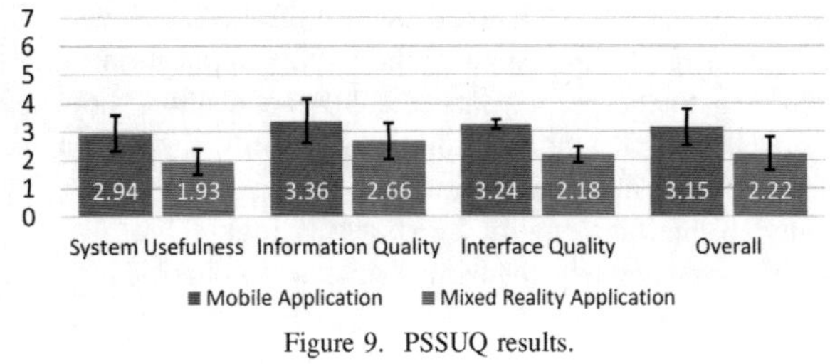

Figure 9. PSSUQ results.

System usefulness scores show that the MR application (1.93) provided better satisfaction than the mobile application (2.94). Participants reported that the MR application was easier and more comfortable for object tracking. The individual results of the system usefulness section are shown in Figure 10.

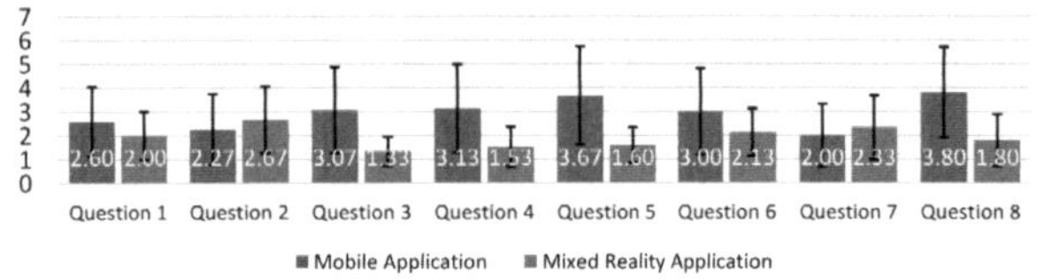

Figure 10. PSSUQ system usefulness results.

T-test two-tailed values of Q3 (p=.002), Q4 (p=.006), Q5 (p=.002) and Q8 (p=.002) show that there is a significant statistical difference in favor of the MR application. The results given by participants who used the MR application (1.33, 1.53, 1.60) in Q3, Q4, and Q5 were comparatively lower than those given by participants who used the mobile application (3.07, 3.13, 3.67). The reason for this outcome is that the participants in Group 2 said that they were able to finish the experiment with greater effectiveness, speed, and efficiency. These findings align with the outcomes of the analyses carried out on task completion time and navigation accuracy. Based on the finding of Q8, it was observed that participants had the belief that they could achieve higher levels of productivity more quickly when using the MR application (1.80) as opposed to the mobile application (3.80). The reason for this can be because of the hand weights.

The information quality shows a similar pattern. The MR application (2.66) gives higher quality information than the mobile application (3.36). The participants who used the MR application reported that they got back to the route easily when they got off the route due to obstacles in the surroundings. The results can be seen in Figure 11.

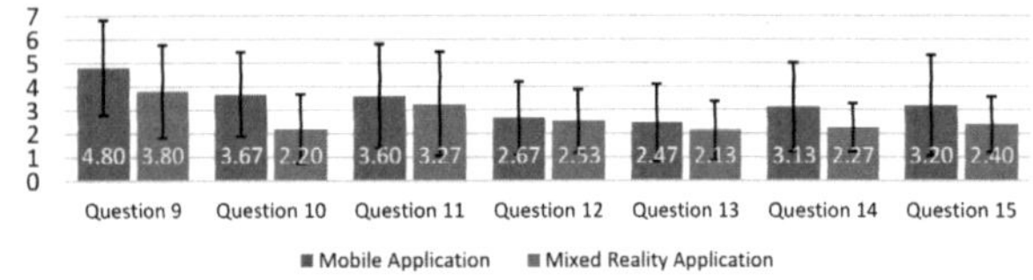

Figure 11. PSSUQ information quality results.

According to the responses to Q10, it was observed that participants who used the MR application (2.20) were able to recover more easily when they made a mistake than those who used the mobile application (3.67) (p=.021).

Interface quality difference is also in favor of the MR application (2.18) compared to the mobile application (3.24). According to the participants, the MR application shows an improved interface quality due to its ability to present the tracked object in three dimensions within a real plane. The results on interface quality are shown in Figure 12.

Both applications provided a sufficient amount of information to the participants. However, based on the responses to Q17, it was observed that the participants think the mobile application (3.07) has a lower number of required features compared to the MR application (1.87) (p=.050). This is believed to be caused by the disparity in the presentation of identical information between the two applications.

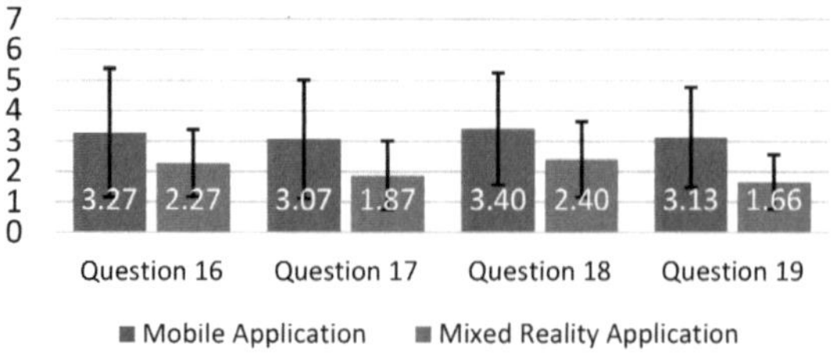

Figure 12. PSSUQ interface quality and overall satisfaction results.

Based on the findings of Q19, which is directly related to the overall system satisfaction, it can be concluded that participants expressed a higher level of satisfaction with the MR application (1.66) compared to the mobile application (3.13) (p=.006). There is no statistically significant difference observed for the remaining questions.

VI. Discussion

This study intends to contribute to the academic understanding and practical implementation of MR user interfaces in military settings. Based on the findings, it can be inferred that the utilization of mixed reality technology has the potential to provide an enhancement to the situational awareness of security personnel.

Several methods have been discussed for a more effective use of the study that has been conducted. In the beginning, to track the target more accurately, navigation arrows can be used to navigate to the tracked location.

In addition, in mixed/augmented reality systems, calibration is crucial to ensure the accurate display of information, particularly in physical security contexts. To enhance the geolocation system, it is suggested that the north calibration method could be improved by using the position of the sun and moon or by placing the surface on an elevation map.

In the future, elevation maps can be used to improve the object placement on the MR plane. Also, experimenting with different and more comprehensive security scenarios and assigning different tasks will enrich the qualitative and quantitative measurements regarding both interfaces.

VII. Conclusion

This study focused on the comparison of the mobile and MR applications, utilizing a user interface for physical security. The mobile application used a 2D map-based interface, incorporating satellite images, and user and tracked locations. The MR application used MR to visualize the targeted location. Based on the tests conducted in a forested environment, it has been observed that using the MR application resulted in an enhanced SA. We found that participants who used the MR application were more efficient than those who used the mobile application in terms of task completion times and deflections from the ideal route. According to the results of NASA TLX and PSSUQ, the mobile application is easier to learn than the MR application. Meanwhile, the MR application users believe they could become productive faster using this system.

VIII. Appendix

NASA Task Load Index questions are listed below.

- **Mental Demand:** How mentally demanding was the task?
- **Physical Demand:** How physically demanding was the task?
- **Temporal Demand:** How hurried or rushed was the pace of the task?
- **Performance:** How successful were you in accomplishing what you were asked to do?
- **Effort:** How hard did you have to work to accomplish your level of performance?
- **Frustration:** How insecure, discouraged, irritated, stressed, and annoyed were you?

The questions of Post Study System Usability Questionnaire are listed below.

- **Q1:** Overall, I am satisfied with how easy it is to use this system.
- **Q2:** It was simple to use this system.
- **Q3:** I could effectively complete the tasks and scenarios using this system.
- **Q4:** I was able to complete the tasks and scenarios quickly using this system.
- **Q5:** I was able to efficiently complete the tasks and scenarios using this system.
- **Q6:** I felt comfortable using this system.
- **Q7:** It was easy to learn to use this system.
- **Q8:** I believe I could become productive quickly using this system.
- **Q9:** The system gave error messages that clearly told me how to fix problems.
- **Q10:** Whenever I made a mistake using the system, I could recover easily and quickly.
- **Q11:** The information (such as online help, on-screen messages and other documentation) provided with this system was clear.
- **Q12:** It was easy to find the information I needed.
- **Q13:** The information provided for the system was easy to understand.
- **Q14:** The information was effective in helping me complete the tasks and scenarios.
- **Q15:** The organization of information on the system screens was clear.
- **Q16:** The interface of this system was pleasant.
- **Q17:** I liked using the interface of this system.
- **Q18:** This system has all the functions and capabilities I expect it to have.
- **Q19:** Overall, I am satisfied with this system.

References

[1] J. Woodward and J. Ruiz, "Analytic Review of Using Augmented Reality for Situational Awareness," in IEEE Transactions on Visualization and Computer Graphics, vol. 29, no. 4, pp. 2166-2183, 2023.

[2] Å. Fasth Fast-Berglund, L. Gong, and D. Li, 'Testing and validating Extended Reality (xR) technologies in manufacturing', Procedia Manufacturing, vol. 25, pp. 31-38, 2018.

[3] Z. Pan, A. D. Cheok, H. Yang, J. Zhu, and J. Shi, 'Virtual reality and mixed reality for virtual learning environments', Computers & Graphics, vol. 30, no. 1, pp. 20-28, 2006.

[4] T. Saarelainen and J. Jormakka, 'C4I2-Tools for the Future Battlefield Warriors', Fifth International Conference on Digital Telecommunications, pp. 38-43, 2010.

[5] A. Mitaritonna and M. J. A. Guerrero, 'Improving Situational Awareness in Military Operations using Augmented Reality', in International Conference in Central Europe on Computer Graphics and Visualization, pp. 53-58, 2015.

[6] Y. Jin, M. Ma, and Y. Zhu, 'A comparison of natural user interface and graphical user interface for narrative in HMD-based augmented reality', Multimedia Tools and Applications, vol. 81, no. 4, pp. 5795-5826, 2022.

[7] W. Dong et al., 'What is the difference between augmented reality and 2D navigation electronic maps in pedestrian wayfinding?', Cartography and Geographic Information Science, vol. 48, pp. 1-16, 2021.

[8] S. Rocha and A. Lopes, 'Navigation Based Application with Augmented Reality and Accessibility', Conference on Human Factors in Computing Systems, pp. 1-9, 2020.

[9] M. Chmielewski, K. Sapiejewski, and M. Sobolewski, 'Application of Augmented Reality, Mobile Devices, and Sensors for a Combat Entity Quantitative Assessment Supporting Decisions and Situational Awareness Development', Applied Sciences, vol. 9, p. 4577, 2019.

[10] X. You, W. Zhang, M. Ma, C. Deng, and J. Yang, 'Survey on Urban Warfare Augmented Reality', ISPRS International Journal of Geo-Information, vol. 7, no. 2, p. 46, 2018.

[11] J. D. Hicks, R. A. Flanagan, P. Petrov, and A. D. Stoyen, 'Eyekon: augmented reality for battlefield soldiers', 27th Annual NASA Goddard Software Engineering Workshop, pp. 156-163, 2003.

[12] J. Juhnke, D. Delaney, T. Wheeler, B. R. Johnson, and J. Cohn, 'Aiding Complex Decision Making Through Augmented Reality', Proceedings of the Human Factors and Ergonomics Society Annual Meeting, vol. 54, no. 19, pp. 1717-1721, 2010.

[13] J. Luckenbaugh, 'Integrated Visual Augmentation System', National Defense, vol. 108, no. 839, pp. 37-38, 2023.

[14] S. G. Hart, 'Nasa-Task Load Index (NASA-TLX); 20 Years Later', Proceedings of the Human Factors and Ergonomics Society Annual Meeting, vol. 50, no. 9, pp. 904-908, 2006.

[15] J. Lewis, 'Psychometric evaluation of the post-study system usability questionnaire: The PSSUQ',Proceedings of the Human Factors and Ergonomics Society Annual Meeting, vol. 2, pp. 1259-1263, 1992.

Preliminary Results from Functional and Usability Assessment of the WiGlove - a Home-based Robotic Orthosis for Hand and Wrist Therapy after Stroke

Vignesh Velmurugan
Robotics Research Group
University of Hertfordshire
Hatfield, United Kingdom
email: v.velmurugan@herts.ac.uk

Luke Jai Wood
Robotics Research Group
University of Hertfordshire
Hatfield, United Kingdom
email: l.wood@herts.ac.uk

Farshid Amirabdollahian
Robotics Research Group
University of Hertfordshire
Hatfield, United Kingdom
email: f.amirabdollahian2@herts.ac.uk

***Abstract*—Robotic orthoses have emerged as a promising tool to provide an opportunity for supporting therapy at home for post-stroke hand and wrist rehabilitation. Despite their benefits, usability issues have hampered the acceptance of such devices. To overcome this, the WiGlove was designed following a user-centred approach that involved user evaluations to validate the prototype in an iterative process. This article presents the methodology and early findings of the WiGlove's first co-design iteration involving functional and usability evaluation by two-stroke survivors. The findings offer initial evidence for meeting the user requirements while identifying areas for improvement to enhance its usability and acceptance. Additionally, the article highlights the challenges encountered in conducting such long-term usability evaluations conducted at stroke survivors' homes.**

***Keywords*—Stroke rehabilitation; Robot-aided rehabilitation; Home-based therapy; Hand-wrist orthosis; user-centred design.**

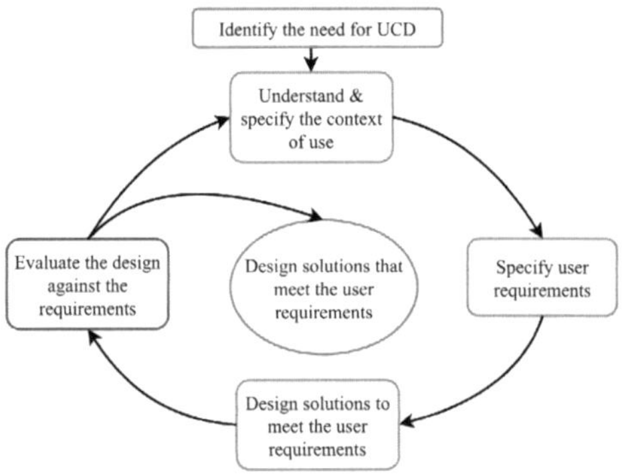

Figure 1. Iterative User-Centred design (ISO 9241-210:2019) [8].

I. Introduction

Hand impairments in stroke survivors significantly impact their ability to perform the Activities of Daily Life (ADL). With the prevalence of stroke increasing [1], traditional one-to-one therapy lacks scalability and creates excessive demand on the healthcare systems, which can be further exacerbated in periods of extreme pressure as seen during the COVID-19 pandemic. Therefore, home-based rehabilitation approaches with a remote monitoring opportunity by therapists have gained interest in recent years. Robotic devices that allow the user to train at home without any external assistance have the potential to act as valuable instruments to support additional doses of therapy in the comfort of patients' homes. Patients are free to train for as long as needed, whenever they want. Integrating computer games in therapy has the potential to further enhance motivation and adherence to training independently at home [2]. Current solutions for the distal arm segment that provides the aforementioned benefits are typically designed to train either the wrist or fingers separately but not together, disregarding the synergy between these two segments. Given the significance of coordinated use of both segments for several functional tasks such as drinking from a cup or picking up objects, this approach could hinder functional recovery. While there are devices available (Table I) that allow training of both segments simultaneously, usability issues often limit their suitability for independent use in a home environment.

To address this, the following objectives were set for our work:

1) Facilitate safe home-based therapy.
2) Provide the ability to interact with games to improve engagement and motivation.
3) Allow the fingers and wrist to be trained together, accounting for their synergy.
4) Provide support in performing ADL activities using the orthosis's ability to counter abnormal synergies.

Fulfilling some of the above (points 1-3), the state-of-the-art SCRIPT Passive Orthosis (SPO) [6] is a wired device, which uses elastic cords to passively assist with flexion/extension exercises of the wrist and fingers. Its sensors allow interaction with therapeutic games on a computer and remote monitoring by therapists. Although it demonstrated the feasibility of such a system, it suffered from various functional and

TABLE I. ORTHOTIC DEVICES USED FOR THE REHABILITATION OF THE WRIST AND FINGERS TOGETHER

Device Name	Mode of Operation	Assisted DoF	Suitable for home-based	Wireless/ Wired	Interaction with games
Hand Mentor [3]	Active	2 (1 for fingers + 1 for wrist)	The peripherals of the actuation mechanism makes it unsuitable	Wired	No
HWARD [4]	Active	3 (1 for fingers, 1 for thumb, 1 for wrist)	The peripherals of the actuation mechanism makes it unsuitable	Wired	No
SCRIPT Active Orthosis [5]	Passive	6 (1 per finger + 1 for wrist)	Study showed that the bulky size, unsafe and complicated appearance prompted the user's to deem it less suitable [5]	Wired	Yes
SCRIPT Passive Orthosis [6]	Passive	6 (1 per finger + 1 for wrist)	Studies showed that it was suitable home environment [6]	Wired	Yes
[7]	Active	18 (3 per finger + 4 for thumb + 2 for wrist)	Active actuation with multiple motors could lead to potential risk factors and therefore require supervision, complicated and unsafe appearance	Wired	Yes (VR)

usability issues such as time decay of sensors, difficulty with donning/doffing, and tethers that prevent stroke survivors from training while performing ADL [9]. Using the learning from the SPO, the WiGlove advances this state-of-the-art through a User-Centred Design (UCD) approach.

This approach is characterised by an iterative design process (Figure 1) with user evaluation at various stages of development and has been shown to result in enhanced usability and user acceptance [10],[11]. Furthermore, identification of the user requirements and ensuring their fulfilment forms the core of the UCD of medical devices [12]. This paper discusses a similar approach to how the WiGlove's design addresses the user requirements and their validation through functional and usability evaluation with stroke survivors. WiGlove is a wearable, wireless, passive dynamic, robotic orthosis, which allows hemiparetic stroke survivors to train their wrist and fingers independently at their homes.

Beginning with a detailed discussion of the user requirements for an ideal home-based hand rehabilitation device and the different features of the first prototype of WiGlove designed to address them in Section II, this paper presents the evaluation methodology (Section III) and its initial findings (Section IV). It also discusses the challenges involved in conducting an unsupervised, long-term, user evaluation in the homes of participants experiencing motor impairments (Section VI).

II. USER-CENTRED DEVELOPMENT OF WIGLOVE

Firstly, a review of the literature that also included the findings of SCRIPT's focus groups and in-depth interviews[13] were used to compile a list of user requirements (**RQs**) that are broadly classified into functional and usability elements.

A. Functional requirements

RQ1: **Adjustable functional assistance.**
Hand impairments in stroke survivors often manifest in the form of hyperflexion that results in a clenched fist and a fully flexed wrist. Shortening and elongation of the flexor and extensor muscles of the hand respectively, which affects the wrist and finger flexion has been

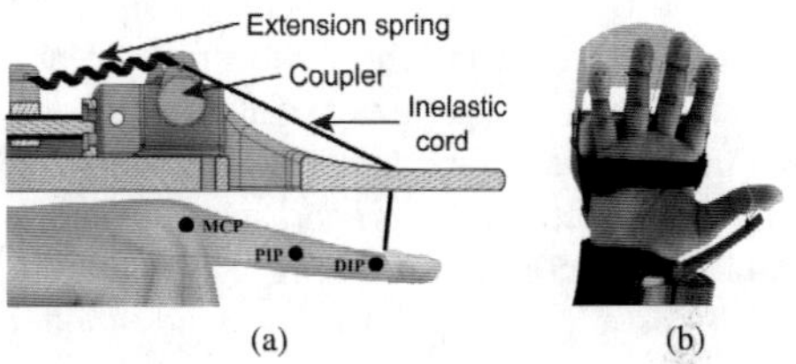

Figure 2. Images showing the extension assistance mechanism and the open palm design of the WiGlove.

observed after long periods of hyperflexion. To offset this the WiGlove (Figure 3) provides assistance with extension using extension springs that passively open the hand allowing them to actively perform flexion exercises against the springs' resistive forces (Figure 2a). Active initiation and movement have been shown to enhance functional recovery [14]. The therapists can choose from a range of springs with different stiffness to ensure optimal assistance and challenge while training. Throughout its operation, the device remains passive, relying on a motorised adjustment mechanism only to allow easy adjustment of the tension controlled with a tablet interface.

RQ2: **Does not hinder any of the natural Range of Motions (RoM) of the joints.**
Although only the joint extension is assisted, it is designed to ensure that it does not hinder any of the natural RoM required to perform ADL. The use of inelastic cords to transmit the torque and flexible interconnection between the forearm and hand modules ensures that ab/adduction of the fingers and the wrist is unrestricted.

RQ3: **Self-aligning centre of rotation (CoR).**
The use of a base-to-distal mechanism where the only point of interaction with the fingers is at the fingertips using inelastic cords eliminates the concern of injury and discomfort due to the misalignment between the device and finger joint axes prevalent in exoskeletal devices.

RQ4: **Measurement of finger and wrist motion.**

The WiGlove measures the flexion angles of the fingers and the wrist to allow the therapists to monitor the progress of training. This is achieved using a potentiometer for each finger and the wrist. Since the mechanism only generates a single flexion value per finger, accurate and direct measurement of the intra-digit angles (metacarpophalangeal (MCP), proximal interphalangeal (PIP) and distal interphalangeal (DIP)) is challenging and therefore are estimated. The analogue output is interpreted using a microcontroller that transmits them via Bluetooth. It also permits playing therapeutic computer games to enhance motivation while capturing performance metrics.

RQ5: **Accommodate different hand dimensions.**
To guarantee comfort, the WiGlove is customised according to the user's hand dimensions by adjusting the length of the inelastic cord, choosing the appropriate guide slot on the finger extension structure and custom printing the forearm module based on the wrist's width using a parametric design approach.

RQ6: **Visual and tactile transparency.**
The WiGlove's open-palm design and silicone fingercaps preserve the user's haptic experience by ensuring that tactile perception is maintained while grasping objects. The finger mechanism's extension structure, which directs the inelastic cord to the fingertips, is constructed of transparent material, providing visual feedback during training. This visual and tactile transparency adds to this sensory stimulation and neural modulation potential.

B. *Usability requirements*

RQ7: **Ease of donning/doffing.**
SPO's user trials reported that stroke survivors found it difficult to slide their hand through the forearm shell and to pass the velcro straps through loops of the finger caps while donning. To avoid that, elastic straps with hooks are used to don/doff the forearm and hand module of the WiGlove. The inherent elasticity of the silicone fingercaps helps them cling to the fingertips eliminating the need for velcros. This allows users with one unimpaired arm to independently use the device at home with ease.

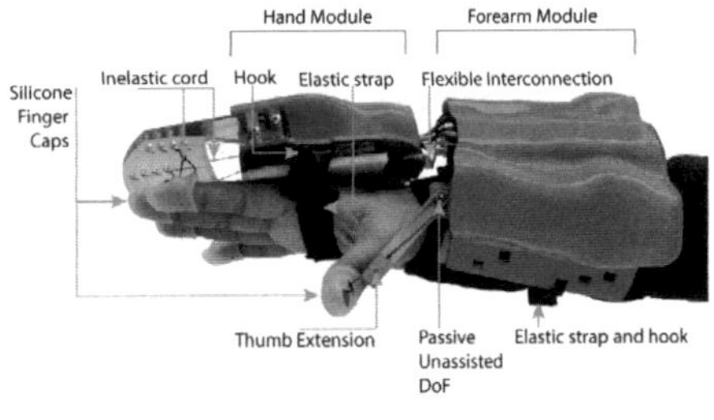

Figure 3. WiGlove.

RQ8: **Safe to use at home.**
Given the absence of a clinician's supervision, the WiGlove's passive operation and design eliminates excessive forces, or any potential pinch points and lack of sharp edges ensuring the safety of the user and the family members. Bluetooth communication and the built-in power supply eradicate any tripping hazard due to wires and tethers.

RQ9: **Smaller space requirement and increased mobility.**
The WiGlove-tablet system's compact size and wireless operation provide stroke survivors with the flexibility to train in different areas of their homes without being tethered to a computer or power supply. This location flexibility can help provide access on demand, allowing duration and repetition flexibility.

RQ10: **Require relatively less technical proficiency to operate.** The WiGlove has a simple control interface involving two push-button switches one for turning the glove on/off and one for adjusting the tension. Apart from this, it does not require the users to perform any maintenance tasks making it easy to learn and use.

III. Evaluation Methodology

The resulting prototype was subjected to the following technical and usability evaluations to ensure the fulfilment of the above-mentioned user requirements.

A. *Evaluation of the functional requirements*

The previous section discusses how **RQ1, RQ3, RQ5** and **RQ6** were addressed by virtue of specific design features. The following experiments were performed to evaluate if the WiGlove satisfied the remainder of the functional requirements.

1) Joint angle sensors: To evaluate the repeatability of the joint angle sensing mechanism, a method akin to the one employed in SCRIPT [9] is used. Repetitions of flexing the fingers to a closed fist followed by an extension to a flat position were performed for 5 seconds each. The corresponding digital sensor output is logged to analyse the repeatability. Similar experiments were also performed while grasping 3D printed cylinders of varying diameters (Large = $84\mathrm{mm}\phi$, Medium = $60\mathrm{mm}\phi$, Small = $50\mathrm{mm}\phi$), inline with the dimensions utilised in SCRIPT.

2) Range of Motion: The joints' achievable natural range of motion differs from person to person and depends on the individual's physical characteristics [9]. Since this is further reduced in stroke survivors with impaired hands, to validate this requirement, the measurements are performed on a healthy individual using a clinical goniometer.

B. *Evaluation of the usability requirements*

The user-centred methodology strives to ensure this is designed into the system through usability evaluations with the end-users in the formative stages [11]. Accordingly, evaluation with physiotherapists with experience in stroke rehabilitation was used to iteratively improve WiGlove's usability [15].

TABLE II. PARTICIPANT CHARACTERISTICS

Characteristics	Participant A	Participant B
Gender	Male	Male
Age (years)	78	43
Time post-stroke (months)	15	27
Impaired hand	Left (Non-dominant)	Left (Non-dominant)
Baseline BBT (no. of blocks/60 secs)	0*	6
Baseline NHPT	0 pegs in 300 seconds	3 pegs in 300 seconds

* Modified version only counting the number of blocks picked and dropped.

Subsequently, this section presents a preliminary usability evaluation conducted to validate **RQ8-RQ10** as a part of UCD involving stroke survivors.

Custom-fit WiGloves were provided to two hemiparetic stroke survivors who experienced hand impairments to train at home without the assistance of the therapist. They were also provided a touchscreen tablet that can be used with the WiGlove to play therapeutic games. that Box and Block Test (BBT)[16] and Nine Hole Peg Test (NHPT)[17] were administered at the beginning of the study to record their baseline fine and gross manual dexterity. As evident from the performance in these tests, **participant A** suffered from significant impairments in the arm resulting in a fully flexed wrist and fingers without any voluntary RoM in extension (Table II). Before the participation, his hand therapy was restricted to three five-minute sessions per week with a therapist. On the other hand, the impairments of **participant B** were moderate with a significantly reduced tone allowing him to perform relatively better in the baseline assessments. Although previous therapy involving functional electric stimulation resulted in a reduction in the hand's spasticity, he still suffers from a reduced voluntary RoM in finger and wrist extension. Henceforth, participants A and B are referred to as **pA** and **pB** respectively.

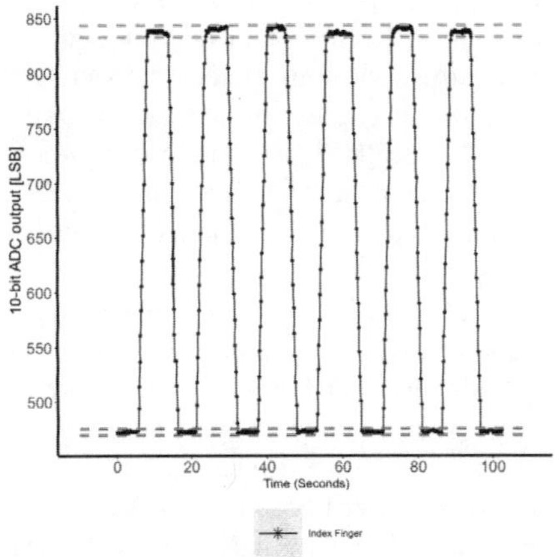

Figure 4. Repeatability of the index finger's joint angle measurements during repetitions of finger flexions (green region) to a closed fist followed by an extension to a flat position (red region).

The various aspects involved in using the device were demonstrated to the participants. They were encouraged to use the glove for exercises, play games on the tablet, or wear the glove while performing ADL. During the first week, both participants required support in the form of specific doubts about the donning method and adjustments of the assistance mechanism beyond which they trained on their own. They were not prescribed an exercise schedule; rather, they were encouraged to train at their convenience. The study was aimed at a duration of 6 weeks with an intermediate assessment at 3 weeks. In line with literature that demonstrated the efficacy of using qualitative assessments to evaluate the usability of orthoses [11], this study used a semi-structured interview with open-ended questions to record the participants' feedback in separate 25-minute sessions evaluating if **RQ8-RQ10** are met. The audio responses during this interview were recorded, transcribed using Microsoft Word's built-in transcription tool and analysed. Additionally, QUEST 2.0 questionnaire [18] and System Usability Scale (SUS) [19], were used to qualitatively evaluate satisfaction with the device. This study serves to demonstrate WiGlove's initial proof-of-concept, paving the way for subsequent large-scale feasibility assessments. Having undertaken measures to ensure participants' safety and privacy, this study was approved by the University's Ethics Committee (Ethics protocol number: aSPECS/ PGR/ UH/ 05084(1)).

IV. RESULTS

A. Technical evaluation

Since the sensing mechanism employed is the same across all fingers, the readings from the index finger's sensor expressed in Lease Significant Bit (LSB) are presented here to demonstrate its repeatability (Figure 4). The standard deviation of the readings at fully flexed and fully extended positions were 1[LSB] and 2[LSB] respectively. Similarly, the results of other repeatability experiments corresponding to the grasping tasks are presented in Table III. With respect to **RQ2**, the measured maximum achievable joint angles with and without the WiGlove are presented in Table IV. The labels "Flex", "Ext", "Abd", "Add" and "P Abd" correspond to Flexion, extension, abduction, adduction and palmar abduction, respectively.

TABLE III. MEAN AND STANDARD DEVIATIONS OF THE ADC OUTPUT AT DIFFERENT CONDITIONS EXPRESSED IN LEAST SIGNIFICANT BIT (LSB).

		Closed fist	Large grasp	Medium grasp	Small grasp
Flexion	Mean	839	783	745	657
	SD	1	1	1	1
Extension	Mean	473	473	473	473
	SD	1	1	1	1

B. Usability evaluation

The results discussed in this manuscript correspond to the data gathered at the end of the first 3 weeks of a 6-week study. **pA** and **pB** offered a SUS rating of 75 and 70 out of 100 respectively and the same QUEST 2.0 score of 3.75 out of 5. These scores reflect a level of satisfaction ranging from "more or less satisfied" to "quite satisfied" on the former scale, and a rating of "OK" to "good" on the SUS scale. Furthermore, Table V presents a summary of the participants' remarks and specific quotes pertaining to the usability requirements from the interview.

TABLE IV. RANGE OF MOTION MEASUREMENTS

			Natural RoM	With SPO	With WiGlove	ADL
WRIST		Flex	76°	40°	74°	70°
		Ext	-58°	-20°	-52°	-60°
		Abd	28°	0°	25°	20°
		Add	31°	0°	31°	30°
THUMB	MCP	Flex	100°	60°	100°	100°
		Ext	0°	0°	0°	0°
		P Abd	50°	50°	50°	50°
	PIP	Flex	80°	15°	80°	80°
		Ext	40°	0°	0°	10°
FINGERS	MCP	Flex	90°	60°	90°	90°
		Ext	10°	0°	0°	10°
		Abd	25°	25°	25°	25°
		Add	0°	0°	0°	0°
	PIP	Flex	100°	80°	100°	100°
		Ext	0°	0°	0°	10°
	DIP	Flex	80°	15°	80°	80°
		Ext	0°	0°	0°	0°

V. DISCUSSION

Beginning with the functional requirements, excellent repeatability was observed in the sensor readings without any time decay, presenting marked improvements compared to SPO[9]. However, examining the individual flexion and extension instances reveals a higher intra-individual variability during flexion. This can be attributed to the tremors in the fingers that occur when held at maximum flexion, where the resistive forces of the spring are at their highest. The results of the grasping tasks serve to corroborate further the remarkable repeatability of the sensing mechanism, as well as its capacity to differentiate between various grasp sizes. Despite not measuring the intra-digit angles as mentioned earlier, the excellent repeatability of these sensors would be adequate to enable the therapists to keep track of changes in the overall range of motion of each finger and for interacting with the games thereby satisfying **RQ4**.

Similarly, Table IV shows that while wearing the WiGlove, the healthy individual was able to perform most of the natural RoM without any restrictions. Even in cases where the natural RoM is slightly restricted, it is still above that required to perform ADL. However, the 10° extension of MCP, PIP and DIP required to perform ADL is blocked by WiGlove's finger extension structure. Since it is used without any supervision, this is essential to mitigate the risk of over-extension. These results support that the WiGlove's design satisfies **RQ2**.

The participant's feedback during the interview confirms the safety (**RQ8**) and the general ease of use (**RQ10**) of the WiGlove. They did not encounter any safety issues for the user or the other members of the family in the 3 weeks of use. Furthermore, apart from **pA** requiring a change of size for one of the finger caps in the first week, both participants did not require any technical assistance with its operation.

pB demonstrated the WiGlove's ease of independently donning and doffing. Despite this not being the case with the first participant who experienced severe impairments in the arm, this shows a promising sign towards supporting **RQ7** for moderately impaired hemiparetic stroke survivors. Given that the major obstacle for **pA** was the weakness in the shoulders, in the next stage, we aim to explore the use of arm supports (such as SaeboMAS used with SPO) while doffing for stroke survivors with severe impairments in the proximal joints of the arm. **pB** reported occasional challenges in coordinating the two modules during donning due to the flexible interconnections. He proposed that incorporating a stiffer connecting element would enhance usability. Given the significance of maintaining wrist ab/adduction freedom, further investigation is necessary to strike an optimal balance.

The advantages of the WiGlove's wireless operation were evident as it provided the flexibility of training location, which also extended to the workplace in the case of **pB**. Along with their remarks on its ease of storage, both participants validated **RQ9**. Unlike **pA**, whose mobility was restricted, we anticipated that the WiGlove's location flexibility would allow **pB** to train while performing ADL. Despite it allowing him to grasp different everyday objects such as a cup, TV remote, key, etc., **pB** was restricted by the limited RoM with forearm pronation. Furthermore, we identified that the extension structure was a hindrance while picking small objects from a flat surface. This will be addressed in future design iteration through custom length extension that does not come in the way.

VI. CHALLENGES

Considering the advantages of user evaluations in the User-Centred Design (UCD) process, this study's long-term duration and home-based nature present unique challenges. Compounded by the participants' motor function impairments, this section discusses the challenges encountered in conducting this study.

It was observed that the unsupervised nature of the training resulted in the participants developing distinct practices based on individual comfort levels concerning donning and doffing methods, training duration, and other factors. While this can be seen as a positive feature, such inter-individual variability precludes straightforward comparisons of behaviour between participants. Similar variability in users' behaviours prompted the researchers to not follow specific task completion protocols in a user evaluation of a tele-manipulated echo device in a clinical setting [10] which supports our study's similar approach.

In the case of **pB**, he was also undergoing functional electrical stimulation therapy concurrent to participating in this study. While this precludes a direct evaluation of the efficacy of the intervention utilising the device, withholding secondary therapy poses an ethical dilemma by potentially depriving the participant of beneficial treatment. Additionally, prior exposure to different devices and techniques could introduce a unique bias in their feedback (**pB**) compared to other participants. Therefore, the variability introduced by such factors necessitates the analysis of each participant's feedback and performance as individual case studies.

Given that the study is being conducted within the homes of stroke survivors, the influence of other family members cannot be disregarded. Our observations indicate that, in both cases, spousal encouragement was reported to significantly

TABLE V. SUMMARY OF THE PARTICIPANTS' FEEDBACK ON THE WIGLOVE'S USABILITY

Requirement	Participant A	Participant B
RQ7	Unable to independently don and required assistance due to excessive tone in the shoulders. But was able to doff. "**Ease to remove finger caps and fore arm**"	Was able to independently don/doff. "**it takes in a few sessions for me to wear it, So now like I'm doing it by myself, I don't need anyone's help.**"
RQ8	Did not perceive any safety issues	Did not perceive any safety issues "**there is no safety issues and it has small battery in the glove which is charged. There are no safety concerns.**"
RQ9	Found it easy to store and train at different parts of the house. "**When kids are coming, its not a problem hiding it**"	Very portable. Trained at different parts of home and also took it to the office to train. "**You know storage is easy because that comes in two parts. You can always fold it**", ""
RQ10	Perceived it to be straightforward and easy to use.	Had some difficulty with donning the hand module in the beginning but otherwise found it easy to use

enhance participant adherence to training as demonstrated by the quote below. Therefore, it is crucial to consider this aspect and its impact on the intervention while assessing participant engagement at the end of the study's duration.

pB - "*Had it not been (my wife), I wouldn't have used the glove more often the way I have used it over the last few weeks. So she has always encouraged me to wear the glove and help me initially to wear the glove*"

VII. CONCLUSION AND FUTURE WORK

This paper presents the design methodology for WiGlove as a home-based passive dynamic orthosis used for post-stroke rehabilitation of the hand and wrist. Part of a user-centred design approach, this study performed a combination of laboratory-based technical evaluation and a 6-week home-based usability evaluation involving two hemiparetic stroke survivors. The early findings provide promising evidence towards the fulfilment of the user requirements and helped to identify potential areas of improvement to be addressed in the next iteration of this UCD process. Although promising, these findings should be interpreted with caution as these correspond to the first 3 weeks of a 6-week study and only involved two stroke patients. The results from the complete duration of the study will be used to further improve its design and provide evidence to support further user evaluation involving a larger number of participants with varying levels of impairments. Furthermore, this paper also reports on the unique challenges posed by the unsupervised and long-term nature of the study for the consideration and discussion of the greater research community.

REFERENCES

[1] R. Colombo *et al.*, "Design strategies to improve patient motivation during robot-aided rehabilitation," *Journal of neuroengineering and rehabilitation*, vol. 4, pp. 1–12, 2007.

[2] Y. Chen K. T. Abel J. T. Janecek Y. Chen K. Zheng and S. C. Cramer, "Home-based technologies for stroke rehabilitation: a systematic review," *International journal of medical informatics*, vol. 123, pp. 11–22, 2019.

[3] N. G. Kutner R. Zhang A. J. Butler S. L. Wolf and J. L. Alberts, "Quality-of-life change associated with robotic-assisted therapy to improve hand motor function in patients with subacute stroke: a randomized clinical trial," *Physical therapy*, vol. 90, no. 4, pp. 493–504, 2010.

[4] C. D. Takahashi L. Der-Yeghiaian V. Le and S. C. Cramer, "A robotic device for hand motor therapy after stroke," in *9th International Conference on Rehabilitation Robotics, 2005. ICORR 2005.* IEEE, 2005, pp. 17–20.

[5] S. Ates I. Mora-Moreno M. Wessels and A. H. Stienen, "Combined active wrist and hand orthosis for home use: Lessons learned," in *2015 IEEE International Conference on Rehabilitation Robotics (ICORR)*. IEEE, 2015, pp. 398–403.

[6] F. Amirabdollahian *et al.*, "Design, development and deployment of a hand/wrist exoskeleton for home-based rehabilitation after stroke-script project," *Robotica*, vol. 32, no. 8, pp. 1331–1346, 2014.

[7] S. Ito H. Kawasaki Y. Ishigure M. Natsume T. Mouri and Y. Nishimoto, "A design of fine motion assist equipment for disabled hand in robotic rehabilitation system," *Journal of the Franklin Institute*, vol. 348, no. 1, pp. 79–89, 2011.

[8] "ISO 9241-210:2019(en): Ergonomics of human-system interaction — Part 210: Human-centred design for interactive systems," International Organization for Standardization," Standard, 2019.

[9] S. Ates *et al.*, "Technical evaluation of and clinical experiences with the script passive wrist and hand orthosis," in *2014 7th International Conference on Human System Interactions (HSI)*. IEEE, 2014, pp. 188–193.

[10] M. Giuliani *et al.*, "User-centred design and evaluation of a tele-operated echocardiography robot," *Health and Technology*, vol. 10, pp. 649–665, 2020.

[11] J. T. Meyer S. O. Schrade O. Lambercy and R. Gassert, "User-centered design and evaluation of physical interfaces for an exoskeleton for paraplegic users," in *2019 IEEE 16th International Conference on Rehabilitation Robotics (ICORR)*. IEEE, 2019, pp. 1159–1166.

[12] J. L. Martin E. Murphy J. A. Crowe and B. J. Norris, "Capturing user requirements in medical device development: the role of ergonomics," *Physiological measurement*, vol. 27, no. 8, p. R49, 2006.

[13] N. Nasr *et al.*, "The experience of living with stroke and using technology: opportunities to engage and co-design with end users," *Disability and Rehabilitation: Assistive Technology*, vol. 11, no. 8, pp. 653–660, 2016.

[14] A. Basteris S. M. Nijenhuis A. H. Stienen J. H. Buurke G. B. Prange and F. Amirabdollahian, "Training modalities in robot-mediated upper limb rehabilitation in stroke: a framework for classification based on a systematic review," *Journal of neuroengineering and rehabilitation*, vol. 11, no. 1, p. 111, 2014.

[15] V. Velmurugan L. Wood and F. Amirabdollahian, "A user-centred design and feasibility analysis of the wiglove - a home-based rehabilitation device for hand and wrist therapy after stroke," in *The Sixteenth International Conference on Advances in Computer-Human Interactions, IARIA 2023*, pp. 134–139.

[16] A. Yurkewich S. Ortega J. Sanchez R. H. Wang and E. Burdet, "Integrating hand exoskeletons into goal-oriented clinic and home stroke and spinal cord injury rehabilitation," *Journal of Rehabilitation and Assistive Technologies Engineering*, vol. 9, p. 20556683221130970, 2022.

[17] D. T. Wade, "Measurement in neurological rehabilitation," *Current Opinion in Neurology*, vol. 5, no. 5, pp. 682–686, 1992.

[18] L. Demers R. Weiss-Lambrou and B. Ska, "The quebec user evaluation of satisfaction with assistive technology (quest 2.0): an overview and recent progress," *Technology and Disability*, vol. 14, no. 3, pp. 101–105, 2002.

[19] J. Brooke *et al.*, "Sus-a quick and dirty usability scale," *Usability evaluation in industry*, vol. 189, no. 194, pp. 4–7, 1996.

Co-Design of an Adaptive User Interface for the Visually Impaired People

Audrey Ambles, Dominique Leclet-Groux, Alexis Potelle
Laboratory MIS
University of Picardie Jules Verne
Amiens, France
audrey.ambles@u-picardie.fr, dominique.groux@u-picardie.fr, alex.potelle@u-picardie.fr

Abstract—**This article presents an adaptable 2D interface for visually impaired people. Its goal is to enable them to recognize 3D objects on a simple computer screen. This alternative to 3D or immersive glasses, which are difficult for visually impaired individuals to use, offers 2D renderings of 3D objects enhanced by image processing. It leverages the richness of information inherent in 3D objects without relying on segmentation and voice transcription. It also allows for customization of the 2D interface and personalization based on the visual impairment condition. The article discusses the co-design with visually impaired of the 2D interface and the evaluation of its usability.**

Keywords—Adaptive user interfaces; Design methods; Interface design for people with disabilities; Usability testing and evaluation.

I. INTRODUCTION

This article presents the co-design process with the visually impaired of an Adaptive 2D Visualization Interface. The visual impairment is defined by the World Health Organization when visual acuity is less than 3/10 after optical correction and/or when the visual field is less than 10°. This population is inherently heterogeneous. Each person has her specificities and perceives things uniquely. They use their residual vision in their daily activities when possible [22].

This work aims to use the residual vision of the visually impaired to improve 3D object recognition.

To explore and recognize 3D objects, various solutions exist, such as the use of 3D glasses or VR headsets, but these devices are difficult to use for the visually impaired [18].

We propose an alternative device adapted to visually impaired people, based on the use of an ordinary 2D screen without semantic segmentation and voice transcription.

To make the recognition of 3D objects possible on 2D screens, the renderings of 3D objects are augmented by image processing and a suitable interface. The interface then offers visually impaired, visualization aids (outlines, zoom, lighting effects, etc.) and settings functions (menu choice, font, background, etc.).

Section II describes the general co-design process, considerations for the visually impaired, and provides a state of the art of existing visualization interfaces adapted for this audience. Section III details our interface co-design with our visual impaired and the tools used by us. Section IV describes our 2D visualization interface and Section V presents its evaluation. We conclude with our research perspectives.

II. RESEARCH CONTEXT

A. Co-design

Co-design is a method that involves the end user in the product design and development process. This design is multidisciplinary, collective and collaborative [5]. Co-design stems from user-centered design. It aims to gather user input and convert it into design choices. The co-design cycle is divided into four phases [25].

1. The analysis phase identifies user's needs. The tools used are document studies, questionnaires, interviews and observation methods.
2. The ideation phase allows collaboration, contribution and creativity. The tools used are brainstorming, brainwriting and focus groups.
3. The design phase defines the appropriate functionalities to be developed. This phase results in the proposal of a high-fidelity prototype with interface specifications and the features. The tools used include paper or digital mock-ups. The development is then carried out following a spiral development cycle [6] incorporating design testing to validate both features and the interface.
4. The evaluation phase values the final application and measures the user's satisfaction (usability and usefulness criteria). The user-centered, heuristic, and analytical evaluations can be employed [4][11].

When the co-design is dedicated to the design of products for a specific disability is named inclusive co-design [19] and the tools used in four phases are not suitable.

B. Considerations for co-design with the visually impaired

For a sighted person, the field of view is very wide [10]. The processing of information perceived by sight is parallel. This is much more challenging, or even impossible, for visually impaired who compensate their deficiency through the sense of touch and/or hearing.

The problem is that the tactile perceptual field is less efficient than sight for Braille reading tasks, as it made up of successive and discontinuous elements [28]. For example, when a visually impaired person reads a document, he or she has to rely mainly on memory and exert significant effort to memorize. This is due to the fact that they do not have a global vision of the text's structure [9].

In contrast to the persistent nature of sight, auditory perception operates through a mode of analysis that is considered fleeting. Auditory memory in the visually impaired therefore entails a high cognitive load, as it is sequential in nature [12].

The co-design tools available for visually impaired must consider their sensory perception. Reference [1] recommend observation and oral interviews, specifying that anything involving paper must be excluded. Reference [7] emphasize the careful use of brainstorming to avoid fatiguing visually impaired. Reference [26] recommend the use of high-fidelity software prototypes.

C. *Visualization Interfaces for the Visually Impaired*

2D interfaces now offer numerous accessibility features [3][23]. Windows users have, for example, access to features such as screen reading, improved contrast, and magnification.

3D interfaces by using augmented or virtual reality can assist visually impaired allow visual experiences of the real world. In augmented reality, "ForeSee" prototype allows users of virtual reality headsets to zoom in, enhance and invert contrasts in real-time [30]. This device lacks an interface for activating these features; users must verbally request them. Other visual augmentation systems in augmented reality, such as the one proposed by [14] involving Google Glass to enhance contrast perception through edge detection.

Similarly, the device by Hicks et al. aims to improve depth perception for obstacle avoidance [13]. Google Glass has a minimal interface for setting edge detection and displaying edge type. System in [13] has no interface, as its sole purpose is to enhance the depth of objects between them.

In virtual reality, [31] have developed "SeeingVR", a framework of 14 features to enrich the visual experience in virtual reality video games with assistive functions such as magnification, edge detection, contrast enhancement, voice description of annotated objects or text to speech. Similar to "ForeSee", the selection and adjustment of treatments are done through a voice input system, without an interface, which can lead to a poor gaming experience.

The utilization of virtual reality headsets can pose challenges for individuals with visual impairments. System latency, stemming from computational processes, along with inaccurate distance perception, contributes to difficulties in headset usage [17].

We offer an alternative to immersive visualization systems for viewing 3D objects on a simple computer screen. This 2D interface offers a range of accessibility features to meet the specific needs of the visually impaired. Our ambition is to provide an enhanced visual experience while avoiding the drawbacks associated with existing immersive systems. Our interface also takes advantage of the wealth of information inherent in 3D objects without the need for semantic segmentation and voice transcription.

III. Co-Designing the Interface

A. *Selection of tools for Visually Impaired participants*

As highlighted in section I-B, to design the interface 2D, we selected co-design tools suitable for visually impaired. We chose tools that depend on hearing but do not involve too much cognitive load, as recommended by [1].

Interviews encourage interaction and discussion. They can be directive (based closed questions), semi-directive (open questions), or free (the interviewee chooses the themes).

Direct observation is a mediation tool to collect verbal and behavioral data (video capture and field diary).

Brainstorming aims to generate ideas orally, and relies on spontaneous creativity.

Software prototype (digital mock-up). For the development phase, we adopted an iterative development approach using successive cycles (spirals), based from the spiral model [6]. In each iteration, the prototype is evaluated through design tests. Evaluators check if the objectives are achieved and decide on new objectives if necessary. This process allows for continuous risk assessment, ensures quality, and limits the number of spirals.

User-centered evaluations focus on the utility and difficulty level (assessed through questionnaires, interviews, and electronic monitoring) and also assessing the understanding of terminology.

Nielsen's and Bastien & Scapin's heuristic evaluations use evaluation grids to inspect usability (ergonomics, standards, controls, etc.) [4][21].

B. *Analysis phase*

First, we studied pathologies and various forms of visual impairment. We used "OpenViSim" [15] to simulate their vision and better understand the visual perception of partially sighted. We focused on the main pathologies: retinitis pigmentosa (impaired peripheral vision), retinopathy (vision obstructed by spots), age-related macular degeneration (impaired central vision), cataracts (severe myopia).

Then, we conducted semi-structured interviews with 10 visually impaired to gather their needs and expectations. The interviews consisting of questions divided into 3 themes: visual perception, expectations, needs in terms of viewing 3D objects. They lasted on average one hour. The analysis of these interviews highlighted that all participants use tools to assist them in daily tasks (mobility, object identification, reading content, etc.). They use, when they can their residual vision. Additionally, when using digital tools, they express dissatisfaction with the lack of adaptation and personalization, admitting that in some cases, it does not really help them.

C. *Ideation phase*

The ideation phase continued with brainstorming sessions. During these sessions, we ensured that our participants were not cognitively overloaded: limited duration to a maximum of one and a half hours, in the morning, with regular breaks, in small groups, allowing time for speaking, reformulating, writing down ideas, and repeating them orally.

These sessions led to a list of the 2D interface specifications: interface setting *(customize fonts, object background and menus)* and visualization functions *(zoom, appearance, outlines, static and dynamic lightning, and texture substitution)*.

Only five fonts have been selected: Arial, Liberation, Luciol, Tiresias and OpenDys, to limit an overloaded selection menu (demand of visually impairs) and to align with the minimalism criterion [21]. Arial and Liberation are frequently used fonts in the daily lives of visually impaired individuals. Luciole and Tiresias are recommended for all pathologies [20]. OpenDys is a font for dyslexic persons but used also by visually impaired. This font improve readability by making letters more distinct and less likely to blend together. This font, like all sans-serif fonts is recommended for the visually impaired as it improves readability by making letters more distinct and less likely to blend [24].

Four highly contrasted colour themes have been chosen for the menus: white *(white background and elements, black fonts and outlines)*, light gray *(light gray background, white elements, black fonts and outlines)*, dark gray *(dark gray background, black elements, white fonts and outlines)* and black *(black background and elements, white fonts and outlines)*. They are important for retinopathy and cataracts because they improve readability and distinction between interface elements. Adjustments to the thickness of menu and button borders have been chosen to improve item detection.

We've also added the ability to customize the background scene contrast, the menu which can be placed on the left or on the right side of the screen. Regarding the interface elements, the use of buttons, sliders, dropdowns are possible adhering to standards for visually impaired accessibility [29].

The visualization functions selected to help recognize 3D objects compensated for loss of detail, contrast or sharpness, color alteration and distorted depth perception. The digital treatments use the geometric data of 3D objects or the luminosity information obtained after 2D rendering. Seven functions requiring minimal parameterization on the part of the visually impaired have been selected: digital zoom, navigation around the object and automatic framing, sharpness and contrast, brightness and saturation, outlines, texture, play of lights.

D. Design phase

We developed a software prototype, with Unity, following a spiral cycle. We wanted people to interact with the prototype without going through digital simulation, where interactions are predefined. Unity is a cross-platform game engine used in virtual/augmented reality [27]. Its native features include the ability to create 2D/3D renderings, design user interfaces and customize them. The visual rendering quality and performance of applications can be optimized using shaders. Shaders enable the implementation of special effects such as post-processing without compromising performance.

Three design test cycles were carried out to produce the 2D visual interface presented in next section. The second cycle approved the interface setting. The third cycle validated the visualization functions.

During these tests, interviews based on semi-structured questions were conducted. The duration was approximately one hour, always in the morning with regular breaks. A free-form interview concluded the session to gather verbal suggestions. Direct observation (with video) was also used.

IV. 2D Interface Description

A. Visualization functions

Among the available visualization functions, object navigation enhances the perception of 3D dimensions. Combined with digital zoom, it allows for enlarging a specific part of the object, thereby providing a detailed view.

The appearance adjustment functions (sharpness, saturation, brightness, contrast) help minimize visual injury. They enhance details, adjust brightness differences between light and dark areas, and limit glare.

The outlines functions enhance important structural elements such as the silhouette, pronounced color variations, or changes in the curvature of the object's surface. They facilitate the understanding of the object's characteristic features without relying on vocal cues.

Lighting effects utilize cast shadows to enhance the perception of spatial dimension. They can be either static or dynamic to reduce navigation operations.

Texture substitution alters an object's visual appearance, aiding comprehension by eliminating reflections and enhancing spatial dimension perception.

All features can be combined according to preferences and needs. A detailed presentation of these treatments can be found in [2].

Figure 1 shows a treatment applied to a 3D object: a cactus. The screenshot on the left shows the 3D object without pathology. The middle screenshot shows the object as seen by a visually impaired person suffering from myopia and tunnel vision. The screenshot on the right shows the 3D object with edge computed from colour gradient to delineate and identify the other small cactus.

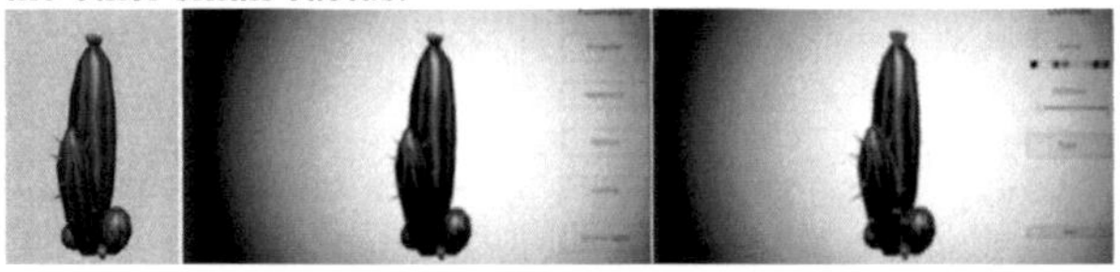

Figure 1. Screenshot, the cactus plant without processing (on the left) and with treatments (on the right): edge computed from colour gradient.

B. 2D interface settings

Interface settings allows the visually impaired to modify fonts, menus, and object background. Figure 3 shows examples of interface configurations: menu position, background color and font choice.

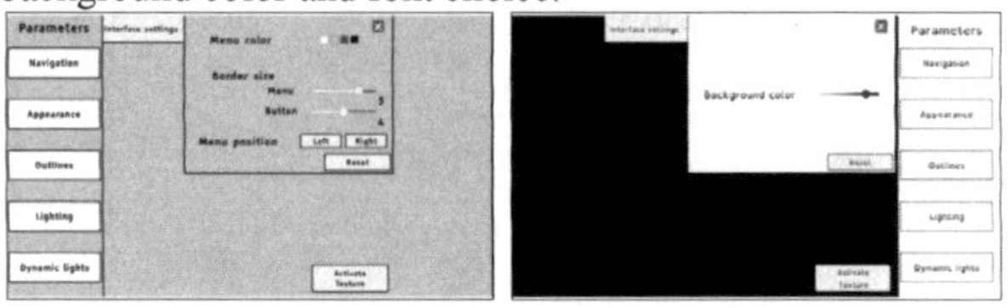

Figure 2. On the left, the menu is on the left, the background is grey, the menu theme is light grey and the font is Luciole. On the right, the menu is on the right, with a black background, white theme and OpenDys font.

V. 2D INTERFACE EVALUATION

A. *Evaluation criteria*

The evaluation of the interface focused on usability and utility criteria [11]. Usability ensures interface clarity, customization simplicity and easy navigation. Structured menus, clear instructions and minimal elements enhance usability by improving accessibility and functions memorization. Utility evaluates how visual enhancement functions contribute to improving users' perception of 3D models. The results of the utility evaluation are detailed in [2].

To assess the usability of the interface, we utilize the ergonomic evaluation grids by Bastien and Scapin (ergonomic criteria) and Nielsen (heuristic), which we combine [16] to extract criteria that we evaluate based on end-user satisfaction [8]. This allows participants to indicate whether they are satisfied with the interface and find it accessible. We have compiled these criteria in a table entitled "Criteria Composition" [32]. The criteria we have selected for usability evaluation are ease of use (is the interface easy to manipulate?), interface minimalism (do the presented information not cause visual overload?), reactivity (does the interface provide immediate feedback?), adherence to standards and clear designation, and finally flexibility (does the interface adapt to visual preferences and technological habits?).

B. *Final evaluator*

Four visually impaired as end users have been involved in the evaluation phase, whose visual conditions are in Table I. These persons did not participate in the co-design of the tool. The participants have different visual conditions, but some similarities can still be observed: P2 and P3 have retinitis pigmentosa, P3 and P4 have only half of their visual field).

TABLE I. PARTICIPANT INFORMATION IN THE FINAL EVALUATION.

Participants	**P1**	**P2**	**P3**	**P4**
Pathologies	Nystagmus	Pigmentary retinopathy	Pigmentary retinopathy Scotoma	Meningioma Optic nerve atrophy
Visual acuity	Left: 1/10 Right: 1/10	Left: 1/20 Right: 4/10	Left: blind Right: 1/10	Left: blind Right: 1/20
Visual field	Total	Tunnel vision	Tunnel vision, blind spot effect	Cannot see out of right part in the right eye
Light sensitivity	Yes	Yes	Yes	Yes
Color vision	Good	Need contrasts	Need contrasts	Need contrasts

C. *Protocol and evaluation*

The evaluation sessions lasted on average 1 hour and 30 minutes and were recorded. They were structured as follows: collection of visual conditions (as found in Table I), presentation of interface customization and visual enhancement functions, followed by a task to test interface usage, which involved exploring 7 3D models (unannotated) representing everyday objects.

To present the interface customization and visual enhancement functions, we asked the participants to navigate autonomously within the interface and activate these functions. We began by configuring the interface, asking them to adjust the fonts, then the menus, and finally the object background. Next, we asked them to activate and adjust the visual enhancement functions to explore them.

We used evaluation grids (in the form of semi-structured interviews) to assess the interface [33]. Participants could respond "Yes", "No", or "Not really", and were encouraged to share their feelings and comments throughout the session. We also considered user preferences by observing their interface usage while adjusting the interface rendering. Additionally, we gathered participants' feelings through open-ended questions at the end of the evaluation.

D. *Results and analysis*

We evaluated 80 questions regarding the usability of the interface. The criterion "Ease of Use" (includes 20 questions) concerns the use of interface elements. "Interface Minimalism" (21 questions) concerns visual information overload. "Reactivity" (3 questions) concerns real-time feedback. "Adherence to Standards and Clear Designation" (8 questions) concerns the understanding of the interface through standards and labels. Finally, "Flexibility" (18 questions) concerns the adaptation of the interface to users, both in terms of visual and usage preferences.

To assess participant satisfaction based on our criteria, we calculated the average of responses categories to the questions for each criterion. Figure 4 summarizes the participants' responses, in percentages, for these criteria. These results confirm that the usability is highly satisfactory ("yes" responses are above 75% for all criteria).

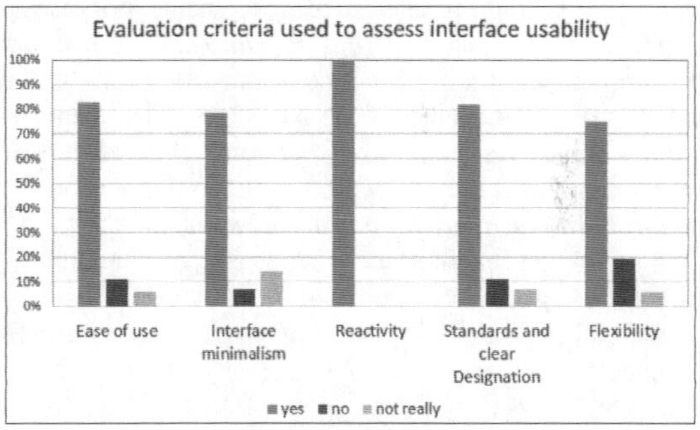

Figure 3. The response rate of participants per evaluation criterion.

Additionally, we analyzed the reasons behind the "no" and "not really" responses for each question to extract qualitative information. We won't delve into the analysis of the 5 criteria here. Instead, we focus of the following 3 criteria: "Ease of Use", "Interface Minimalism", and "Flexibility".

Participants found the interface "easy to use" (83% according to Figure 4). The difficulties encountered are specific to participant's visual condition. Participants with reduced vision indicated that they did not appreciate using sliders. In response to the question "*Is selecting a choice via slider suitable?*", P3 answered "no", stating that "*I need some adaptation time because the elements are too small*", and P4 answered "not really", specifying that the sliders are "*disruptive*". They do not perceive the changes well when moving the slider cursor due to a lack of perception of visual changes (difficulty in distinguishing variations) and precision (coordination or depth perception issues). Participants with retinitis pigmentosa do not appreciate the use of the dropdown menu. They both answered "no" to the question "*Is selecting a choice via dropdown menu suitable?*", stating that the font size is too small and the scroll bar is not sufficiently contrasted.

It is also noteworthy that the checkbox is the most difficult element to use for 3 participants, regardless of their visual conditions. One participant answered "no" to the question "*Is selecting a choice via checkbox suitable?*" and the other 2 answered "not really". This element is too small, and the difference between selecting and deselecting is not significant. Additionally, all participants expressed a desire to be able to adjust the size and contrast of the mouse cursor to facilitate interaction with the interface.

We weren't surprised by feedback on the choice of elements. Visually impaired users prefer buttons to checkboxes, which are more difficult to use because they are smaller and less customizable. Adjustment of the mouse cursor was also planned and will be integrated into a future version of the interface.

Regarding the "minimalism of the interface", participants found that the interface is not visually overloaded (77% according to Figure 4). Visual information overload also corresponds to participants' visual conditions.

When participants have reduced vision, they experience reduced visual acuity (which can lead to blurred vision), limited spatial perception, and low-contrast perception. They find that interface elements are small and have difficulty positioning the mouse pointer on these elements. For example, in response to the question "*Does visualization via dropdown menu suit and not overload?*", they both answered "no" and specified that it is because of the font size. Participants with retinitis pigmentosa prefer the harmonization of interface elements or menus: they answered "yes" to the question "*Do you want harmonization of interface elements?*".

We found that the interface settings are correlated with the pathology categories of the visually impaired. The visual impaired those with similar pathologies have common preferences.

For the "flexibility", participants find that the interface adapts to their visual and technological preferences (75% according to Figure 4). All participants found the font size too small, even when increased to the maximum. We also collected the interface settings for each participant. After presenting the interface and its functions, they can adjust the interface as they wished. The settings for each participant are summarized in Table II below.

The interface settings for these four participants are all different. The uniqueness of these settings illustrates the link between the participants' visual conditions and their needs and preferences for interface rendering. Participants suffering from retinal pigmentary disorders (participants P2 and P3 in Tables I and II) preferred the interface in a "dark" theme, with a dark background for the 3D objects. Participants with reduced vision (P3 and P4 in the Tables) preferred bold text because reading is difficult for them.

The interface rendering parameter choices highlight the importance of customizing interfaces to meet the individual needs of visually impaired with similar characteristics. Integrating visually impaired user profiles would allow pre-setting the interface and avoiding visual injury when launching the interface.

TABLE II. INTERFACE SETTINGS CHOSEN BY EACH PARTICIPANT[a]

Elements		P1	P2	P3	P4
Font	Type	Luciole	Luciole	Luciole	Luciole
	Size	4	10 (max)	10 (max)	10 (max)
	Bold	No	No	Yes	Yes
Menu	Theme	White	Black	Black	White
	Menu borders	5 (max)	2	5 (max)	5 (max)
	Button borders	5 (max)	1 (min)	5 (max)	5 (max)
	Menu position	Left	Left	Left	Right
3D model background		White	Dark gray	Black	White

a. All participants customized the interface to suit their individual needs. Similarities in the choice of settings were observed, especially among participants with similar visual conditions.

All participants answered "yes" to "*Is the application accessible to you?*". Furthermore, they were all able to perform the task of exploring the 3D models without help, thanks to the interface customized to their needs.

VI. CONCLUSION AND FUTURE WORK

This article presents a visualization interface for 3D objects designed for visually impaired individuals, using a standard 2D screen. This interface offers configuration functions and visualization aids to best utilize the residual vision of visually impaired individuals. It was evaluated by four end users with various visual impairments.

The results show that the usability is satisfactory for more than 75% for the five selected criteria. Future developments of the interface will involve adjusting the font size, using buttons instead of checkboxes, and supporting navigation both with the mouse and keyboard to ensure maximum accessibility. We propose to take into account in the user's profile the characteristics that enable parameters to be initialized according to the main pathologies.

Future perspectives will focus on visualization aid functionalities aimed at highlighting the symmetry properties of 3D objects (important in the natural object recognition process by humans).

REFERENCES

[1] J. Albouys-Perrois, J. Laviole, C. Briant, and A. M. Brock, "Towards a multisensory augmented reality map for blind and low vision people: A participatory design approach", in *Proceedings of the Conference on human factors in computing systems - CHI '18*, Montreal, QC, Canada: ACM, Apr. 2018, pp. 1-14. doi: https://doi.org/10.1145/3173574.3174203. Retrieved: April 10, 2024.

[2] A. Ambles, D. Leclet-Groux, A. Potelle, and E. M. Mouaddib, "Computer vision serving visually impaired people" in *International Symposium on Signal, Image, Video, and Communications - ISICV*, in press.

[3] R. Ani, E. Maria, J. J. Joyce, V. Sakkaravarthy and M. A. Raja, "Smart Specs: Voice assisted text reading system for visually impaired persons using TTS method" in *Proceedings of the International Conference on Innovations in Green Energy and Healthcare Technologies – ICIGEHT '17*, Coimbatore, India, IEEE, Mar. 2017, pp. 1-6. Retrieved: April 10, 2024.

[4] C. Bastien and D. Scapin, "Ergonomic criteria for the evaluation of human-computer interfaces", Doctoral dissertation, Inria, RT-0156, INRIA. 1993, pp. 79.

[5] S. Bφdker, K. Grφnbæk, and M. Kyng, "Cooperative design: techniques and experiences from the Scandinavian scene" in *Readings in human-computer interaction*, Morgan Kaufmann Publishers, pp. 215-224, 1995. doi: https://doi.org/10.1016/B978-0-08-051574-8.50025-X. Retrieved: April 10, 2024.

[6] B. W. Boehm, "A spiral model of software development and enhancement", *Computer*, IEEE, vol. 21, no. 5, pp. 61-72, May 1988. doi: 10.1109/2.59. Retrieved: April 10, 2024.

[7] A. Brock et al., "Methods and tools for participatory design with blind users" in *Proceedings of the 22nd Conference on Human-Computer Interaction – IHM '10*, Luxembourg, Luxembourg: ACM, Sept. 2010, pp. 65-72. doi: https://doi.org/10.1145/1941007.1941017. Retrieved: April 10, 2024 (in French).

[8] C. Deephouse, D. Goldenson, M. Kellner, and T. Mukhopadhyay, "The effects of software processes on meeting targets and quality" in *Proceedings of the Twenty-Eighth Hawaii International Conference on System Sciences - HICSS*, IEEE, vol. 4, pp. 710-719, Jan. 1995. doi: 10.1109/HICSS.1995.375677. Retrieved: April 10, 2024.

[9] A. Dufresne, O. Martial, and C. Ramstein, "Multimodal user interface system for blind and "visually occupied" users: Ergonomic evaluation of the haptic and auditive dimensions" in Proceeding of Human-Computer Interaction - Inteact'95, Lillehammer, Norway, 1995, pp. 163-168.

[10] J. J. Gibson, "The ecological approach to visual perception: classic edition", *Psychology Press*, First edition, 2014. ISBN : 978-0898599596.

[11] M. Grislin, and C. Kolski, "Evaluation of human-machine interfaces during interactive system development ", *Journal of Information Sciences and Technologies - TSI Series: Computer Techniques and Science*, vol. 15, no. 3, pp. 265-296, 1996. (in French).

[12] Y. Hatwell, "Images and non-visual spatial representations in the blind", in *Colloquium French National Institute of Health and Medical Research - INSERM*, John Libbey Eurotext Ltd, vol. 228, pp. 13-35, 1993.

[13] S. L. Hicks et al., "A depth-dased head-mounted visual display to aid navigation in partially sighted individuals", *PLoS ONE*, vol. 8, no. 7, pp. 1-8, Jul. 2013. doi: https://doi.org/10.1371/journal.pone.0067695. Retrieved: April 10, 2024.

[14] A. D. Hwang and E. Peli, "An augmented-reality edge enhancement application for google glass" *Optometry and Vision Science*, vol. 91, issue 8, pp. 1021-1030, Aug. 2014. doi: 10.1097/OPX.0000000000000326. Retrieved: April 10, 2024.

[15] P. R. Jones and G. Ometto, "Degraded reality: using VR/AR to simulate visual impairments," in *Proceedings IEEE Workshop on Augmented and Virtual Realities for Good - VAR4Good*, Reutlingen, Germany, IEEE, Mar. 2018, pp. 1-4. Retrieved: April 10, 2024.

[16] M. Maguire, "Methods to support human-centred design", *International journal of human-computer studies*, vol. 55, no. 4, pp. 587-634, 2001.

[17] M. Morel, B. Bideau, J. Lardy, and R. Kulpa, "Advantages and limitations of virtual reality for balance assessment and rehabilitation", *Clinical Neurophysiology*, vol. 45, issues 4–5, pp. 315-326, 2015. ISSN 0987-7053. Retrieved: April 10, 2024.

[18] M. Mott et al., "Accessible by design: an opportunity for virtual reality" in *2019 IEEE International Symposium On Mixed And Augmented Reality Adjunct - ISMAR-Adjunct,* Beijing, China, IEEE, Oct. 2019, pp. 541-545. doi:10.1109/ismar-adjunct.2019.00122. Retrieved: April 10, 2024.

[19] B. Nanchen et al., "Designing with and for people with disabilities: towards an integrated and transdisciplinary approach to inclusive design" in *Vulnerabilities and emerging risks: thinking and acting together for sustainable transformation: Proceedings of the 56th SELF Congress*, Genève, Suisse, Jul. 2022, pp. 371-377.

[20] F. Navamuel, "Three fonts designed for the visually impaired", in *ICT Tools*, Apr. 2023. Retrieved: April 10, 2024. [Online]. Available from: https://outilstice.com/2020/02/3-polices-de-caracteres-concues-pour-les-malvoyants/. (in French).

[21] J. Nielsen, "Heuristic evaluation", in J. Nielsen et R.L. Mack (Eds.), *Usability inspection methods*, New York, John Wiley & Sons, ACM, Chapter 2, pp. 25-62, 1994.

[22] R. M. A. van Nispen et al., "Low vision rehabilitation for better quality of life in visually impaired adults", in *Cochrane Database of Systematic Reviews 2020*, issue 1, no. CD006543 Jan. 2020. doi: https://doi.org/10.1002/14651858.CD006543.pub2. Retrieved: April 10, 2024.

[23] N. Parikh, I. Shah, and S. Vahora, "Android smartphone based visual object recognition for visually impaired using deep learning" in *2018 international conference on communication and signal processing – ICCSP*, Chennai, India, IEEE, Apr. 2018, pp. 420-425. doi: 10.1109/ICCSP.2018.8524493. Retrieved: April 10, 2024.

[24] E. Russell-Minda et al., "The legibility of typefaces for readers with low vision: A research review" in *Journal of Visual Impairment & Blindness*, vol. 101, issue 7, pp. 402-415, Jul. 2007. doi: https://doi.org/10.1177/0145482X0710100703. Retrieved: April 10, 2024.

[25] D. Schuler and A. Namioka, "Participatory design: principles and practices," in *CRC Press*, 1993.

[26] R. Sefelin, M. Tscheligi, and V. Giller, "Paper prototyping-what is it good for? A comparison of paper-and computer-based low-fidelity prototyping", in *Proceedings of CHI'03 extended abstracts on Human factors in computing systems - CHI '03*, Lauderdale, Florida, USA, ACM, Apr. 2003, pp. 778-779. doi: https://doi.org/10.1145/765891.765986. Retrieved: April 10, 2024.

[27] Unity. Retrieved: April 10, 2024. [Online]. Available from: https://unity.com/fr

[28] I. Verjat, "The functional cerebral asymmetry in manual tactilo-kinesthetic modality", *The Psychological Year*, vol. 88, no. 1, pp. 83-109, 1988. (in French).

[29] W3C Web Accessibility Initiative (WAI), 2024. Retrieved: April 10, 2024. [Online]. Available from: https://www.w3.org/WAI/ARIA/apg/patterns/

[30] Y. Zhao, S. Szpiro, and S. Azenkot, "Foresee: a customizable head-mounted vision enhancement system for people with low vision", in Proceedings of the 17th international ACM SIGACCESS Conference on Computers & Accessibility – ASSETS '15, ACM, Oct. 2015, pp. 239-249. doi: https://doi.org/10.1145/2700648.2809865. Retrieved: April 10, 2024.

[31] Y. Zhao et al., "SeeingVR: a set of tools to make virtual reality more accessible to people with low vision", in *Proceedings of the 2019 CHI Conference on Human Factors in Computing Systems – CHI '19*, ACM, May 2019, pp. 1-14. doi: https://doi.org/10.1145/3290605.3300341. Retrieved: April 10, 2024.

[32] The table of the "Criteria Composition". Created: March 2024. [Online]. Available from: https://extra.u-picardie.fr/nextcloud/index.php/s/AyrQzfsMgrDtJ7y

[33] The interface evaluation grids. Created: March 2024. [Online]. Available from: https://extra.u-picardie.fr/nextcloud/index.php/s/AyrQzfsMgrDtJ7

One-Handed Signs: Standardization for Vehicle Interfaces and Groundwork for Automated Sign Language Recognition

Akihisa Shitara[†*], Taiga Kasama[*], Fumio Yoneyama[*] and Yuhki Shiraishi[*]
[†]Graduate School of Library, Information, and Media Studies, University of Tsukuba, Japan
Email: theta-akihisa@digitalnature.slis.tsukuba.ac.jp
[*]Faculty of Industrial Technology, Tsukuba University of Technology, Japan
Email: {yonefumi, yuhkis}@a.tsukuba-tech.ac.jp

***Abstract*—In scenes where d/Deaf and hard of hearing (d/Dhh) individuals drive vehicles, they may face issues reliant on not only environmental sounds but also auditory information through communication. Therefore, we investigated the needs in scenarios where drivers drive in a car and proposed an in-car sign recognition standard using one-handed signs to improve communication issues d/Dhh drivers face. Specifically, we focused on one-handed signs in sign language conversations among d/Dhh individuals and selected sign language expressions based on one-handed signs assuming sign language recognition. We selected one-handed signs used in assumed context scenarios driving car situations where the one-handed sign was likely to occur. Additionally, we conducted surveys with d/Dhh individuals involved to assess whether they found these signs natural and acceptable. We also discussed the annotation rules for annotation labels in datasets intended for sign language recognition.**

Keywords–Deaf and hard of hearing; Sign language; Camera; Sensor glove; Recognition.

I. INTRODUCTION

In recent years, the Act for Eliminating Discrimination against Persons with Disabilities and the disqualification provisions stipulated in Article 88 of the Road Traffic Act in Japan have made it possible for d/Deaf and hard of hearing (d/Dhh) individuals to obtain a driver's license. In daily life, d/Dhh individuals can drive vehicles under certain conditions, such as wearing hearing aids or cochlear implants, or using magnifying glasses and displaying hearing impairment markers when not wearing assistive devices.

However, issues remain regarding environmental sounds related to emergency information from emergency vehicles and communication issues. Regarding environmental sounds related to emergency information from emergency vehicles, specific examples include the siren sounds of ambulances, fire trucks, and police cars. Hearing individuals are required to promptly clear the way or stop driving when they hear a siren sound. However, if d/Dhh individuals fail to notice the siren sound, they may unknowingly become involved in issues such as delaying rescue time for ambulances and fire trucks or violating stop orders by police cars.

Furthermore, communication problems arise when d/Dhh individuals engage in sign language conversations while driving. They may look away from the road to the passenger seat or be distracted by the rear seat, increasing the risk of accidents. Additionally, when hearing individuals who do not understand sign language are present, they may have to drive without being able to comprehend any information due to the lack of audio cues.

Therefore, we propose an in-vehicle sign language recognition standard focusing on two aspects: the installation location of drive recorders and the one-handed sign that occurs during sign language conversations between d/Dhh individuals. Moreover, with the practical application of speech recognition, voice user interfaces are also being put into practical use. Research on virtual assistants installed in smart homes and smartphones is particularly notable. However, accessibility issues remain for d/Dhh individuals who have difficulty using voice commands. Nevertheless, sign language recognition has been gaining momentum in recent years, and research on sign language interfaces as an application of sign language recognition is also progressing [1] [2]. Accordingly, as we elevate from our previous work on continuous fingerspelling recognition [3] to sign language recognition, we have established the following research topics:

1 Proposing limited sign language by selecting one-handed signs,

2 Evaluation of the one-handed signs by the parties concerned.

Regarding research topic 1, sign language recognition requires collecting information on the hand shapes, movements, positions of both hands, and facial information. However, for ASL, only short sentences have been studied. Similarly, for Japanese Sign Language (JSL), only short sentences in Signed Japanese (SJ), rather than true JSL, have been researched. Therefore, we focused on one-handed signs, which is also observed in sign language conversations between deaf individuals, and decided to use one-handed signs as a step in the process of elevating from continuous fingerspelling to sign language recognition. As it is difficult to assume situations where one-handed signs are likely to occur in daily life, we specifically focused on the scenario of driving a car, which is relatively easy to envision.

Regarding research topic 2, in most cases of data collection for sign language recognition, the parties concerned are asked to express predetermined sign language words or short sentences. However, to the best of our knowledge, there is no mention of whether this is acceptable and natural for the parties concerned. Therefore, all the authors, including three d/Dhh individuals, selected the content, sign language words, and short sentences spoken in the scenario of driving a car. Additionally, after data collection was completed, the parties concerned were asked to evaluate whether it felt natural and acceptable.

II. Related Work

Previous research on fingerspelling or sign language recognition has proposed two types of sensors for recognizing a series of operations in fingerspelling: contact-type sensor gloves and non-contact-type cameras.

1) Image recognition: Several methods have been proposed for recognizing hand shapes based on processing images of fingerspelling as captured by cameras. Mukai et al. [4] reported that a fingerspelling recognition method targeting 41 immobile characters in JSL resulted in an average recognition accuracy of 86%. They used a classification tree and machine learning based on a support vector machine to classify individual images. Hosoe et al. [5] used deep learning for recognition and achieved a recognition rate of 93%, but only for static fingerspelling. Jalal et al. [6] reported a recognition rate of 99% for American Sign Language (ASL) images based on a deep learning algorithm for static fingerspelling (i.e., excluding "J" and "Z"). However, the recognition accuracy could not be considered as sufficient for practical recognition in JF. Additionally, relatively few recognition results have been reported for dynamic fingerspelling (i.e., fingers moving when expressing a character). In a study of dynamic fingerspelling in JSL [7], the identification of hand shapes was performed using a kernel orthogonal mutual subspace method from images of hand regions obtained from distance images, and the classification of movements was performed using decision trees based on center-of-gravity coordinates. These results yielded a 93.8% identification rate. However, the recognition accuracy was insufficient for the practical recognition required for JF.

2) Sensor glove recognition: Several methods have been proposed for recognizing hand shapes based on measurement data acquired by contact-type sensor gloves. These methods can measure finger flexion, hand positions, and directional data. The measurement data are then sent to a personal computer, and a classification algorithm is used to recognize hand shapes. Cabrera et al. [8] paired the Data Glove 5 Ultra [9] sensor glove with an acceleration sensor to acquire information regarding the degree of flexion of each finger and wrist direction. They conducted test classification using 24 static fingerspelling characters in ASL, excluding "J" and "Z." Their neural network was trained using 5 300 patterns and achieved a recognition rate of 94.07% for 1 200 test patterns. Mummadi et al. [10] prototyped a sensor glove with multiple embedded inertial sensors. They collected French sign language fingerspelling data from 57 people and achieved an average recognition rate of 92% with an F1-score of 91%. Kakoty et al. [11] reported on a dataset of one-handed Indian sign language alphabets (C, I, J, L, O, U, Y, W), ASL alphabets (A to Z), and signed numbers (0 to 9), using a radial basis function with 10-fold cross-validation Using a kernel-supported vector machine, they achieved an average recognition rate of 96.7% and reported that the data were converted to speech. Chong et al. [12] placed six Inertial Measurement Units (IMUs) on the back of the palm and on each fingertip to capture their motion and orientations. Ultimately, 28 proposed word-based sentences in ASL were collected, and 156 features were extracted from the collected data for classification. Using the Long Short-Term Memory (LSTM) algorithm, the system achieved an accuracy of up to 99.89%. Notably, 12 people cooperated with us in the data collection experiment, but whether they were deaf or hearing people was unclear. Yu et al. [13] reported on the architecture of a data glove system comprising a stnm32MCU, flex4.5 bending sensor, mpu6050 six axis sensor, Bluetooth transmission module, and cellphone voice application. The system was developed and connected to a Java-based processing software. They reported that their system recognized sign language movements and could output the words to be said using the intelligent voice system. However, the glove does not feature global movement and rotation tracking. Glauser et al. [14] demonstrated a glove's performance in a series of ablation experiments while exploring various models and calibration methods. However, the glove does not come with a global translation and rotation tracking. Realizing a sign language recognition system requires hand orientations and motions. Among the various methods for performing JF recognition, the conductive fiber braid method [15] uses gloves woven with conductive fibers instead of flexion sensors. These gloves can recognize hand shapes and movements as they are directional gyro sensors incorporated into them. However, the recognition rate for JF ("a," "i," "u," "e," "o") based on Euclidean distance has been reported as only 60%.

3) Data collection: Regarding image recognition, several large-scale Continuous Sign Language Recognition (CSLR) benchmarks have been published [16]. For example, we introduced three large-scale CSLR benchmarks: PHOENIX-2014, Chinese Sign Language (CSL), and PHOENIX-2014-T. PHOENIX-2014 is a publicly available German Sign Language dataset and the most famous CSLR benchmark. This corpus is taken from broadcast news regarding the weather. The CSL dataset consists of 100 sign language sentences and 178 words related to everyday life. Fifty signers performed each sentence, resulting in 5,000 videos in total. A matched isolated CSL database containing 500 words is also provided for pre-learning. Each word was performed 10 times by 50 signers. PHOENIX-2014-T annotates the new videos with two annotations: the sign language terms for the CSLR task, and the German translation for the a Sign Language Translation (SLT) task. The vocabulary consists of 1,115 terms for sign language and 3,000 for German. This dataset is available in [17]. However, the data of these three large-scale CSLR benchmarks are insufficient to realize a highly accurate sign language recognition system using deep learning. Further research is being conducted to increase the amount of available data.

Extensive data for image recognition can be obtained from online sources. For example, the Shi et al. [18] dataset contains clips of fingerspelling sequences cut from sign language "in the wild" videos obtained from online sources such as YouTube and dafvideo.tv [19]. The datasets contain 5,455 training sequences from 87 signers of "ChicagoFSWild," 981 development (validation) sequences from 37 signers, and 868 test sequences from 36 signers, without overlapping signers among the three sets. Another dataset, "ChicagoFSWild+," contains 50,402 training sequences from 216 signers, 3115 development sequences from 22 signers, and 1,715 test sequences from 22 signers. Compared to ChicagoFSwild, the crowdsourcing setup of ChicagoFSWild+ enables the collection of considerably more training data while significantly reducing the efforts of experts and researchers.

Danielle et al. [20] expressed privacy concerns regarding contributing to a filtered sign language corpus, using very

TABLE I. QUESTIONNAIRE OF NEEDS SURVEY

ID	question
1	When conveying information such as navigation to a deaf or hard-of-hearing driver, what do you mainly use?
2	While driving, what content do you want to convey immediately to a deaf or hard-of-hearing driver?
3	While driving, how do you call out to a deaf or hard-of-hearing driver?
4	Have you ever felt anxious when talking to a deaf or hard-of-hearing driver while driving?
5	Have you ever felt difficulty when talking to a deaf or hard-of-hearing driver while driving?
6	How do you communicate with a hearing driver when you want to convey something while driving?
7	How do you communicate with a deaf or hard-of-hearing driver when you want to convey something while driving?
8	Have you ever wanted to use sign language to communicate with a hearing driver while driving?
9	Have you ever felt danger when using sign language communication while driving?
10	How do you call out to a deaf or hard-of-hearing person sitting in the passenger seat or back seat while driving?
11	How do you call out to a hearing person sitting in the passenger seat or back seat while driving?
12	Is there any content you want to communicate with the person in the passenger seat or back seat while driving?
13	Have you ever had difficulties communicating with a person who can use sign language sitting in the passenger seat or back seat while driving?
14	Have you ever had difficulties communicating with a person who cannot use sign language sitting in the passenger seat or back seat while driving?
15	What sign language (including pointing, gestures, classifiers, etc.) do you want to use for operating the car navigation system?
16	Apart from the car navigation system, are there any other occasions where you want to use sign language (including pointing, gestures, classifiers, etc.) to operate the car?

expressive avatars and blurred faces, which may affect the willingness to participate. Training on filtered data may improve the recognition accuracy. In the case of camera recognition, the look of the face is also captured; thus, privacy must also be considered. In contrast, sensor glove recognition does not require pictures of the face; thus privacy concerns are reduced and the data can be more simply collected.

III. NEEDS SURVEY

To understand the needs of d/Dhh individuals when driving a car, we collected data using a web-based questionnaire on Google Forms. The study has been approved by the ethics committee. The total number of respondents was 143, consisting of 88 males, 53 females, and 2 unspecified (mean age: 32.01, standard deviation: 13.87). Among the respondents, 121 individuals possess a driver's license. Regarding their identity, 68 people identified as Deaf, 20 as deaf, 35 as hard of hearing, 4 as hearing, 11 as having never thought about it or unsure, 3 as others, and 2 responses were invalid.

A. *Questionnaire and Results*

The questions of needs survey are listed in Table I. The results showed that regardless of the d/Dhh individual's identity, more than half of the respondents felt anxiety or difficulty when calling out to a d/Dhh driver while driving. Moreover, when asked about the information they want to convey immediately, over 80% of the respondents mentioned highly urgent information. This suggests that it is problematic to have difficulty conveying information that needs to be communicated immediately, such as danger, caution, or the presence of emergency vehicles.

Compared to Deaf individuals, hard of hearing individuals are more likely to use their voice when calling out to the driver while driving (with a significant difference). This suggests that Deaf individuals require a means of communication that does not rely on voice. Additionally, it was found that more than 75% of d/Dhh individuals wanted to use sign language to communicate with the driver while the vehicle is in motion. Over 75% of the respondents also reported having difficulties communicating with a person who can use sign language while sitting in the passenger seat. Furthermore, some respondents mentioned in the free-response section that they had experienced a sense of danger. However, more than 75% of the respondents indicated that they want to communicate with the person sitting in the passenger seat while driving.

IV. PROPOSAL OF VEHICLE INTERFACES STANDARD

The in-vehicle sign language recognition standard is as follows: Since the driver must always face forward, it is assumed that sign language data will be collected using a camera placed near the location where the drive recorder is installed or by using the drive recorder itself as a camera. The driver may also wear gloves while gripping the steering wheel. Moreover, since the driver needs to grip the steering wheel with at least one hand at a minimum, the sign language is limited to one-handed signs.

A. *One-Handed Signs*

We selected one-handed sign words and short sentences to be evaluated for sign language recognition, under the rule of not using grammar that employs facial expressions and other elements. Specifically, all authors, consisting of two deaf individuals, one d/Deaf individual, and one hearing individual, discussed and made the selections. It is worth noting that all authors possess a driver's license and have driving experience. The number of words chosen was 58, and the number of short sentences was 40 (Table II). The reason for the selection was based on the needs survey, which included three highly urgent pieces of information: "danger," "watch out," and "emergency vehicle," as well as some directions and small talk.

B. *Evaluation*

After completing the data collection experiment (refer to Section V-A), we immediately conducted the necessity of in-vehicle sign language recognition and the use of one-handed signs inside the vehicle. The evaluation was conducted with the cooperation of 22 participants, with an average sign language experience of 11.3 years (standard deviation of 7.1 years).

The results regarding the perceived necessity of in-vehicle sign language recognition and the use of one-handed signs inside the vehicle are shown in Figure 1. For the question "Did you feel the need for in-vehicle sign language recognition?", the options were categorized as follows: "Strongly Disagree," "Somewhat Disagree," and "Neither Agree nor Disagree" as negative, and "Strongly Agree" and "Somewhat Agree" as positive. The null hypothesis was set as "Negative and positive options are chosen at a ratio of 0.5 each." A binomial test was conducted, and the results showed that the null hypothesis was rejected at a two-sided significance level of 0.05 with p=0.017, confirming a significant difference. Similarly, for the question "Did you feel the need to use one-handed signs inside the vehicle?", the options were categorized as follows: "Strongly

TABLE II. LIST OF EXAMPLE SENTENCES: ORIGINAL (JAPANESE) AND ENGLISH TRANSLATION

ID	sentence	word1	word2	word3	word4	word5
s1	行きたい [I want to go.]	トイレ(w1) [toilet]	行く(w47) [go]	希望(w33) [want]		
s2	トイレや休憩大丈夫？ [Are restrooms and breaks okay?]	トイレ(w1) [toilet]	休憩(w2) [rest]	希望(w33) [want]		
s3	危険，落ち着いて見て [Danger, watch calmly]	危険(w3) [danger]	落ち着く(w4) [calm]	見る(w13) [look]		
s4	コンビニ，行きますか？ [Are we going to the convenience store?]	コンビニ(w6) [convenience]	行く(w47) [go]	か？(w37) [question]		
s5	あそこで止まってください [Please stop over there]	向こう(w25) [over there]	止まる(w44) [stop]	お願い(w48) [please]		
s6	赤信号だよ [It's a red light]	向こう(w25) [over there]	赤(w8) [red]	信号(w10) [traffic light]		
s7	おーい，青信号だよ [Hey, it's a green light]	手を振る(w11) [call]	青(w9) [blue]	信号(w10) [traffic light]		
s8	右見て [Look right]	右(w14) [right]	見る(w13) [look]			
s9	次の信号で右折 [Turn right at the next signal]	次(w16) [next]	信号(w10) [traffic light]	右(w14) [right]		
s10	速くしてもいいよ [You can speed up]	スピード(w43) [speed]	構わない(w38) [may]			
s11	ゆっくりで [Take it slow]	ゆっくり(w21) [slow]				
s12	次はどこ行く？ [Where are we going next?]	次(w16) [next]	行く(w47) [go]	場所(w17) [place]	何(18) [what]	
s13	次に左折するのはどこ？ [Where do we turn left next?]	次(w16) [next]	左(w15) [left]	場所(w17) [place]	何(w18) [what]	
s14	ここは直進 [Go straight here]	そこ(w34) [there]	直進(w19) [straight]			
s15	高速行くか？ [Shall we take the highway?]	高速(w19) [highway]	行く(w47) [go]	か？(w37) [question]		
s16	ガソリン（残量）大丈夫？ [Is the gas (level) okay?]	ガソリン(w24) [gazoline]	大丈夫(w23) [safe]	か？(w37) [question]		
s17	ガソリンスタンドどこ？ [Where is the gas station?]	ガソリン(w24) [gazoline]	場所(w17) [place]	何(w18) [what]		
s18	別の道があるか調べて [Check if there is another route]	別(w27) [another]	道(w22) [way]	調べる(w26) [search]	お願い(w48) [please]	
s19	ヘッドライトつけて [Turn on the headlights]	ヘッドライト(w30) [headlight]				
s20	ルームライト消して [Turn off the room light]	ルームライト(w31) [roomlight]	消す(w56) [turn off]			
s21	緊急車両が来るから右寄せて [Pull over to the right because an emergency vehicle is coming]	サイレン(w5) [siren]	来る(w32) [come]	右寄せ(w29) [right-aligned]		
s22	コンビニ行きたい [I want to go to the convenience store]	コンビニ(w6) [convenience]	希望(w33) [want]			
s23	コンビニは無い [There is no convenience store.]	コンビニ(w6) [convenience]	無い(w36) [none]			
s24	ガソリンスタンドはない [There is no gas station]	ガソリン(w24) [gazoline]	場所(w17) [place]	無い(w36) [none]		
s25	向こうで事故かも [There might be an accident over there]	向こう(w25) [over there]	事故(w7) [accident]	らしい(w49) [seem]		
s26	おーい，緊急車両，来ている [Hey, an emergency vehicle is coming]	手を振る(w11) [call]	サイレン(w5) [siren]	来る(w32) [come]		
s27	左に止めても構わない [You can stop on the left.]	左(w15) [left]	駐車(w57) [parking]	構わない(w38) [may]		
s28	それは難しい [That's difficult.]	難しい(w39) [hard]				
s29	ちょっと待って [Wait a moment.]	少し(w40) [little]	待つ(w41) [wait]			
s30	速くないか？ [Isn't that fast?]	スピード(w43) [speed]	過ぎ(w35) [over]	違う(w55) [different]		
s31	任せるよ [I'll leave it up to you.]	任せる(w42) [defer]				
s32	おーい，ウィンカー消して [Hey, turn off the turn signal.]	手を振る(w11) [call]	ウィンカー(w45) [blinker]	消す(w56) [turn off]		
s33	そこの前に停めて [Stop in front of that.]	そこ(w34) [there]	前(w12) [front]	駐車(w57) [parking]		
s34	次の交差点で左折だから，左寄せして [It's a left turn at the next intersection, so stay to the left.]	次(w16) [next]	交差点(w58) [intersection]	左(w15) [left]	左寄せ(w28) [left-aligned]	
s35	1つ目の信号で右折 [Turn right at the first traffic light.]	1つ(w51) [one]	目(w50) [eyed]	信号(w10) [traffic light]	左(w15) [left]	
s36	2つ目の交差点で左折 [Turn left at the second intersection.]	2つ(w52) [two]	目(w50) [eyed]	交差点(w58) [intersection]	左(w15) [left]	
s37	3つ目の交差点で右折だから，右寄せして [It's a right turn at the third intersection, so stay to the right.]	3つ(w53) [three]	目(w50) [eyed]	交差点(w58) [intersection]	右(w14) [right]	右寄せ(w29) [right-aligned]
s38	食べるところ調べて [Look for a place to eat.]	食べる(w54) [eat]	場所(w17) [place]	調べる(w26) [search]	お願い(w48) [please]	
s39	ご飯どうする [What shall we do for food?]	食べる(w54) [eat]	何(w18) [what]			
s40	ハザードランプ消して [Turn off the hazard lights.]	ハザードランプ(w46) [hazard lamp]	消す(w56) [turn off]	お願い(w48) [please]		

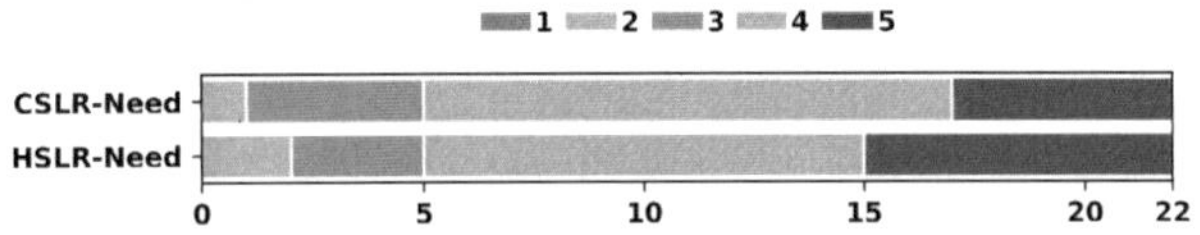

Figure 1. CSLR-Need represents the responses to the question "Did you feel the need for in-vehicle sign language recognition?"
HSLR-Need represents the responses to the question "Did you feel the need to use one-handed signs inside the vehicle?"
1: Strongly Disagree, 2: Somewhat Disagree, 3: Neither Agree nor Disagree, 4: Somewhat Agree, 5: Strongly Agree.

Disagree," "Somewhat Disagree," and "Neither Agree nor Disagree" as negative, and "Strongly Agree" and "Somewhat Agree" as positive. The null hypothesis was set as "Negative and positive options are chosen at a ratio of 0.5 each." A binomial test was conducted, and the results showed that the null hypothesis was rejected at a two-sided significance level of 0.05 with p=0.017, confirming a significant difference.

Additionally, we immediately conducted an evaluation of the one-handed sign words and short sentences that we had selected through discussion. The response data used was from the group that participated in when using the camera on data collection experiment (refer to Section V-A). The number of participants was 10, with an average sign language experience of 11.6 years (standard deviation of 5.76 years). However, we could only evaluate 57 out of the 58 one-handed sign words. Because, due to our oversight, we failed to include the evaluation item related to the one-handed sign word w58 ("交差点 [intersection]").

The responses to the question "Did you feel any unnaturalness in the one-handed sign expression for each word?" are shown in Figure 2. The options were categorized as follows: "1: Strongly Disagree," "2: Somewhat Disagree," and "3: Neither Agree nor Disagree" as positive, and "4: Somewhat Agree" and "5: Strongly Agree" as negative. The null hypothesis was set as "Positive and negative options are chosen at a ratio of 0.5 each." Using a binomial test, words were selected where the null hypothesis was not rejected at a two-sided significance level of 0.05, and no significant difference was confirmed (p=0.344) when the number of negative responses was 3 or more. The selected words were w2, w4, w6, w7, w10, w16, w22, and w27, totaling 7 words. Subsequently, we proceeded to verify their acceptability.

The responses to the question "Can you accept the one-handed sign expression for each word?" are shown in Figure 3. The options were categorized as follows: "1: Completely Unacceptable" and "2: Somewhat Unacceptable" as negative, and "3: Neither Acceptable nor Unacceptable", "4: Somewhat Acceptable," and "5: Acceptable" as positive. The null hypothesis was set as "Negative and positive options are chosen at a ratio of 0.5 each." For each short sentence, a binomial test was conducted. The results showed that at a two-sided significance level of 0.05, the null hypothesis was not rejected, and no significant difference was confirmed (In all cases, the number of negative responses was 1 or less).

The responses to the question "Did you feel any unnaturalness in the one-handed sign expression for each short

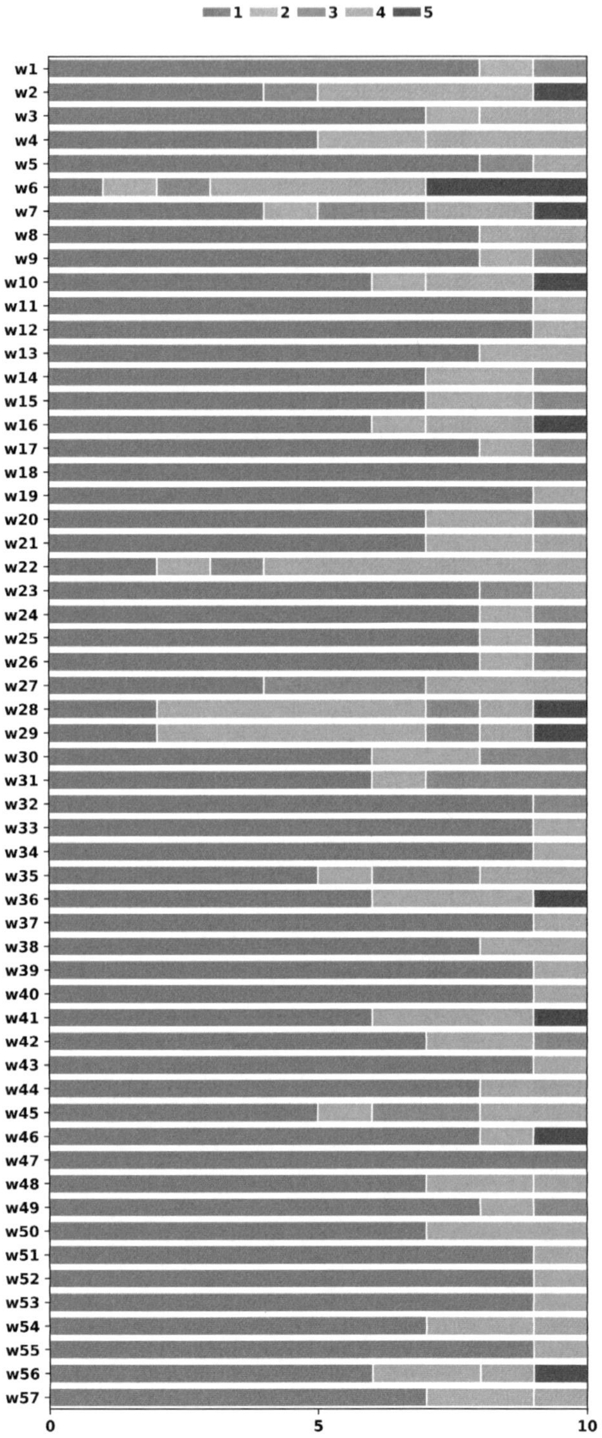

Figure 2. The responses for the question "Do you feel any unnaturalness in the one-handed sign expression?" for each word.
1: Strongly Disagree, 2: Somewhat Disagree, 3: Neither Agree nor Disagree, 4: Somewhat Agree, 5: Strongly Agree.

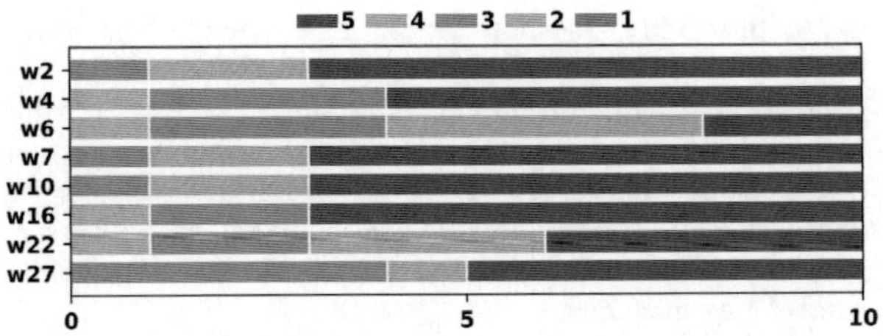

Figure 3. The responses for the question "Can you accept the one-handed sign expression for each word?"
1: Completely Unacceptable, 2: Somewhat Unacceptable, 3: Neither Acceptable nor Unacceptable, 4: Somewhat Acceptable, 5: Acceptable.

sentence?" are shown in Figure 4. The options were categorized as follows: "1: Strongly Disagree" and "2: Somewhat Disagree" as negative, "3: Neither Agree nor Disagree", and "4: Somewhat Agree" and "5: Strongly Agree" as positive. The null hypothesis was set as "Positive and negative options are chosen at a ratio of 0.5 each." Using a binomial test with a two-sided significance level of 0.05, we selected short sentences where the null hypothesis was not rejected, and no significant difference was confirmed (p=0.344) when the number of negative responses was 3 or more. We then proceeded to verify the acceptability of these sentences. The selected short sentences were s3, s4, s9, s12, s13, s18, s21, s24, s27, s32, s34, and s37, totaling 12 sentences.

Subsequently, we proceeded to verify their acceptability. The responses to the question "Can you accept the one-handed sign expression for each short sentence?" are shown in Figure 5. The options were categorized as follows: "1: Completely Unacceptable" and "2: Somewhat Unacceptable" as negative, "3: Neither Acceptable nor Unacceptable," and "4: Somewhat Acceptable," and "5: Acceptable" as positive. The null hypothesis was set as "Negative and positive options are chosen at a ratio of 0.5 each." For each short sentence, a binomial test was conducted. The results showed that at a two-sided significance level of 0.05, the null hypothesis was not rejected, and no significant difference was confirmed. (In all cases, the number of negative responses was 1 or less.)

V. Data Collection and Annotation Rules

To select the one-handed sign data for sign language recognition, we collected data from collaborators and asked them to evaluate the expression of the words. The data used in this data collection experiment is the same as the data evaluated through the questionnaire (refer to Section IV-A).

A. Data Collection Experiment

To simulate the in-vehicle environment, a webcam was placed below the mirror, and the positions of the driver seat and passenger seat were defined in Figure 6. Additionally, assuming that the driver is always facing forward while driving, a whiteboard was used, and the participants were asked to look at the whiteboard. A monitor was placed below the webcam to display the words and short sentences. For each short sentence, data was collected four times, and the process was conducted for both the driver seat and the passenger seat. In

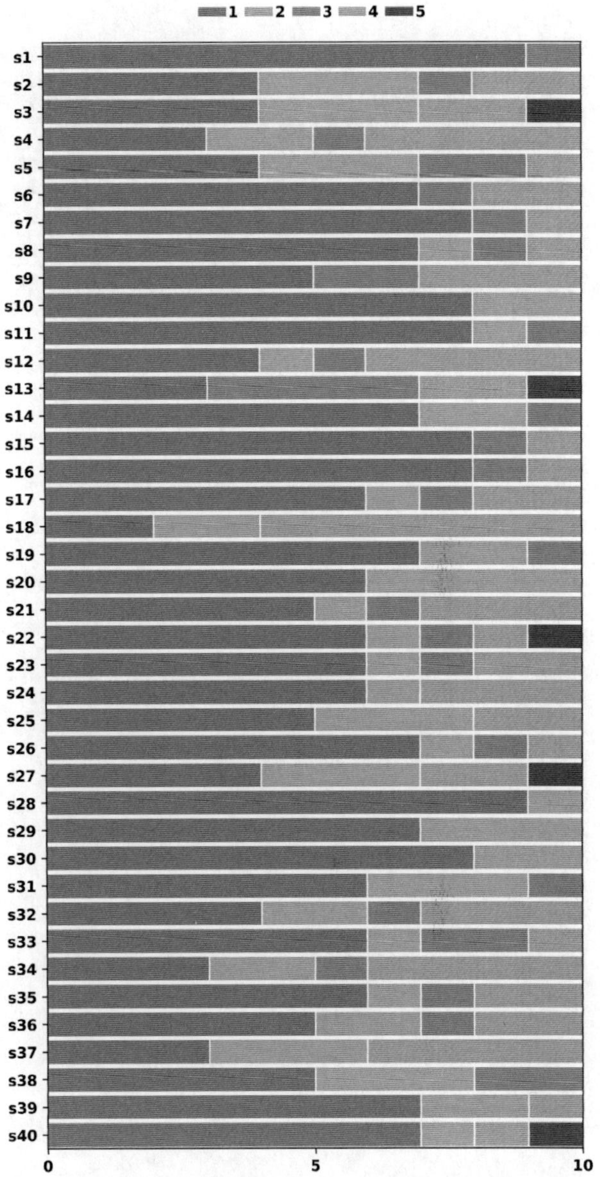

Figure 4. The responses for the question "Do you feel any unnaturalness in the one-handed sign expression?" for each short sentence.
1: Strongly Disagree, 2: Somewhat Disagree, 3: Neither Agree nor Disagree, 4: Somewhat Agree, 5: Strongly Agree.

this experiment, data was collected from 10 participants using a camera and 12 participants using gloves. When using the camera, participants were asked to continuously express each short sentence four times. However, when using gloves, each short sentence was collected once. The order of expression followed the order of the short sentences. It is worth noting that when using gloves, video data was also recorded for annotation purposes.

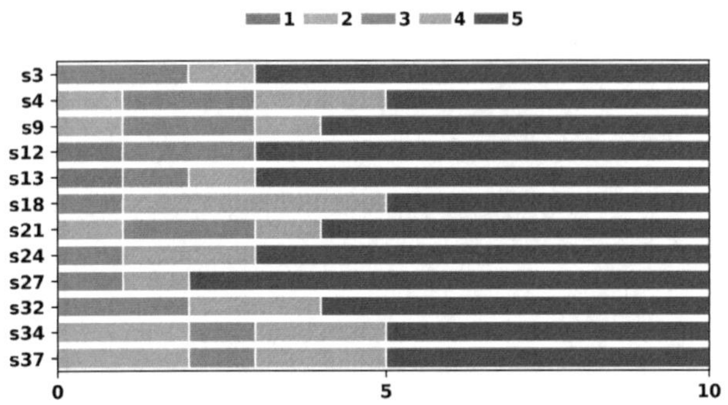

Figure 5. The responses for the question "Can you accept the one-handed sign expression for each short sentence?"
1: Completely Unacceptable, 2: Somewhat Unacceptable, 3: Neither Acceptable nor Unacceptable, 4: Somewhat Acceptable, 5: Acceptable.

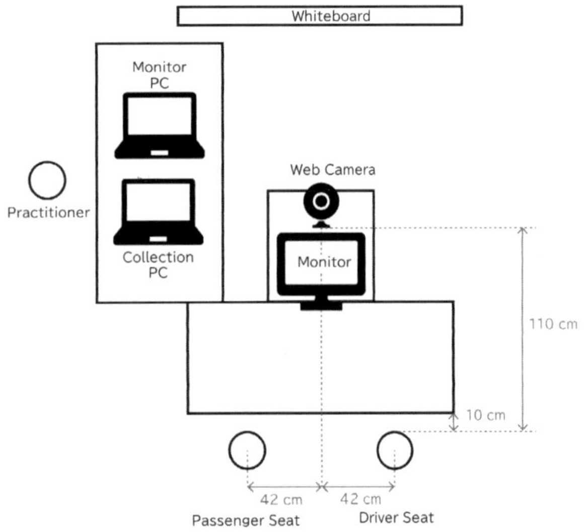

Figure 6. Data acquisition experiment.

B. Annotation Rules

The annotation labels are generally divided into "word" and "transition." The definition of a "word" is as follows:

For dynamic sign language expressions Start point: The moment when the handshape is determined and reaches the starting position. Even if the handshape is already determined, it is not considered the start point until it reaches the starting position. End point: The moment when either the handshape collapses or the hand moves away from the ending position.

For static sign language expressions Start point: The moment just before reaching the fixed position. (Ideally, the moment of reaching the fixed position is desirable, but it is difficult to judge.) End point: The moment when the hand moves away from the fixed position. (Ideally, the moment of reaching the fixed position is desirable, but it is difficult to judge.)

VI. Discussion

A. Validity of One-Handed Sign Expressions

In this study, as soon as the data collection experiment using cameras was completed, we verified the validity of the expressions by d/Dhh individuals through two questionnaires. However, it is necessary to increase the number of participants and consider participant attributes, such as sign language experience, JSL or SJ, identity, and involvement in deaf school communities to improve the validity and refine the word and sentence expressions.

B. Annotation Rules

"Here" and "There" Initially, we used "there" consistently, but in the short sentences, "there" and "here" were confused, and the expressions were different, so we decided to distinguish them. "Here": The handshape is "number 1," and the expression points to one's own feet. "There": The handshape is "number 1," but since it is a high-context expression in Japanese, it depends on which place is being pointed to. In this case, since the same place is being pointed to, we unified everything into a single "there" (having only one variation).

"Why" and "Go" Although we did not include "why" this time, we are concerned that the one-handed "why" expression may overlap with the "go" expression. For future reference, we will describe the differences. "Why/Reason (one-handed)": While making the handshape "number 1," twist the wrist downward from one's chest to the front (aiming for 45 to 90 degrees) twice. "Go": While making the handshape "number 1," twist the wrist downward from one's chest to the front (aiming for more than 80 degrees) once.

"(Number)th" Initially, we tried to distinguish between "(number)" and "th" in "(number)th". However, this arose from the concern that "(number)th" might be more commonly used in everyday life. Upon checking the videos, we found that "number" and "th" were expressed separately, so we decided to unify each "th" as a single "th".

C. Differences between Camera and Gloves

In this study, we focused specifically on in-vehicle sign language recognition as one of the one-handed sign interfaces. However, the differences between cameras and gloves, as well as which one is more suitable, have not yet been examined. As a future remaining tasks, it is necessary to evaluate the accuracy of sign language recognition using models trained separately on camera and glove data. Additionally, user studies should be conducted to determine which input interface is preferable for scenarios driving a car.

D. Limitation

In this study, the annotation process has not yet been completed, and the evaluation experiments using recognition have not been conducted. Moreover, as evident from the questionnaire results, it cannot be said with certainty that the validity of the expressions has been ensured by d/Dhh people. Moreover, since facial expressions and other grammatical elements are not targeted, it is assumed to be difficult to recognize JSL (refer to Section IV-A). In addition, the annotation labels are specific to the context of scenarios driving a car; the validity of the annotation labels is not considered high when generalized as everyday context.

VII. Conclusion and Future Works

This study investigated the issues faced by d/Dhh individuals in scenarios driving a car and proposed a solution using one-handed signs to improve communication. The research focused on selecting appropriate one-handed signs based on sign language conversations among d/Dhh individuals and evaluating their validity through surveys with the individuals concerned. The study also conducted a fundamental analysis of one-handed signs in sign language recognition, exploring the potential of using one-handed signs to facilitate the transition from recognizing continuous finger spelling to sign language recognition. The results suggest that introducing one-handed signs, as seen among d/Dhh individuals, could be a viable approach to address communication issues in scenarios driving a car.

Future works are as follows:

1) Expand the dataset: Collect a larger dataset of one-handed signs used in scenarios driving a car to improve the robustness and generalizability of the sign language recognition system.
2) Develop real-time recognition: Implement a real-time one-handed sign recognition system that can be integrated into vehicles to assist d/Dhh drivers in communication and navigation.
3) Conduct user studies: Perform extensive user studies with d/Dhh individuals to evaluate the effectiveness and usability of the proposed one-handed sign recognition system in real-world scenarios driving a car.
4) Refine annotation rules: Further refine the annotation rules for one-handed signs based on feedback from the d/Dhh community and research findings to establish a standardized approach for sign language recognition in scenarios driving a car.
5) Investigate multimodal approaches: Explore the integration of other modalities, such as facial expression or eye-tracking, to enhance the overall communication experience for d/Dhh drivers.

Addressing these future works will advance the assistive technologies for d/Dhh individuals in scenarios driving a car, ultimately improving their communication, safety, and overall driving experience.

Acknowledgment

This work was supported by Woven by Toyota, Inc., JSPS KAKENHI Grant Number #19K11411 and the Promotional Projects for Advanced Education and Research in NTUT.

References

[1] A. Glasser, V. Mande, and M. Huenerfauth, "Accessibility for deaf and hard of hearing users: Sign language conversational user interfaces," in Proceedings of the 2nd Conference on Conversational User Interfaces, ser. CUI '20. New York, NY, USA: Association for Computing Machinery, 2020, pp. 1–3. [Online]. Available: https://doi.org/10.1145/3405755.3406158

[2] T. Kato, A. Shitara, N. Kato, and Y. Shiraishi, "Notification, wake-up, and feedback of conversational natural user interface for the deaf and hard of hearing," International Journal on Advances in Software, vol. 15, 2022, pp. 54–64.

[3] Y. Shiraishi, A. Shitara, F. Yoneyama, and N. Kato, "Sensor glove approach for continuous recognition of japanese fingerspelling in daily life," International Journal on Advances in Life Sciences, vol. 14, 2022, pp. 53–70.

[4] N. Mukai, N. Harada, and Y. Chang, "Japanese fingerspelling recognition based on classification tree and machine learning," in 2017 Nicograph International (NicoInt). New York, NY, USA: IEEE (Institute of Electrical and Electronics Engineers), June 2017, pp. 19–24.

[5] H. Hosoe, S. Sako, and B. Kwolek, "Recognition of jsl finger spelling using convolutional neural networks," in 2017 Fifteenth IAPR International Conference on Machine Vision Applications (MVA), May 2017, pp. 85–88.

[6] M. A. Jalal, R. Chen, R. K. Moore, and L. Mihaylova, "American sign language posture understanding with deep neural networks," in 2018 21st International Conference on Information Fusion (FUSION). New York, NY, USA: IEEE (Institute of Electrical and Electronics Engineers), July 2018, pp. 573–579.

[7] M. Kondo, N. Kato, K. Fukui, and A. Okazaki, "Development and evaluation of an interactive training system for both static and dynamic fingerspelling using depth image," IEICE technical report, vol. 114, no. 512, 2015, pp. 23–28, (in Japanese).

[8] M. E. Cabrera, J. M. Bogado, L. Fermin, R. Acuna, and D. Ralev, "Glove-based gesture recognition system," in Adaptive Mobile Robotics. World Scientific, 2012, pp. 747–753.

[9] "5DT Data Glove 5 Ultra," 2019, URL: https://5dt.com/5dt-data-glove-ultra/ [retrieved: April, 2024].

[10] C. K. Mummadi, F. P. P. Leo, K. D. Verma, S. Kasireddy, P. M. Scholl, and K. Van Laerhoven, "Real-time embedded recognition of sign language alphabet fingerspelling in an imu-based glove," in Proceedings of the 4th International Workshop on Sensor-Based Activity Recognition and Interaction, ser. iWOAR ' 17. New York, NY, USA: Association for Computing Machinery, 2017, pp. 1–6. [Online]. Available: https://doi.org/10.1145/3134230.3134236

[11] N. M. Kakoty and M. D. Sharma, "Recognition of sign language alphabets and numbers based on hand kinematics using a data glove," Procedia Computer Science, vol. 133, 2018, pp. 55–62.

[12] T.-W. Chong and B.-J. Kim, "American sign language recognition system using wearable sensors with deep learning approach," The Journal of the Korea Institute of Electronic Communication Sciences, vol. 15, no. 2, 2020, pp. 291–298.

[13] X. Yu, S. Liu, W. Fang, and Y. Zhang, "Research and discovery of smart dumb gloves," in Journal of Physics: Conference Series, vol. 1865, no. 4. IOP Publishing, 2021, p. 042054.

[14] O. Glauser, S. Wu, D. Panozzo, O. Hilliges, and O. Sorkine-Hornung, "Interactive hand pose estimation using a stretch-sensing soft glove," ACM Transactions on Graphics (TOG), vol. 38, no. 4, 2019, pp. 1–15.

[15] R. Takada, J. Kadomoto, and B. Shizuki, "A sensing technique for data glove using conductive fiber," in Extended Abstracts of the 2019 CHI Conference on Human Factors in Computing Systems, ser. CHI EA ' 19. New York, NY, USA: Association for Computing Machinery, 2019, pp. 1–4. [Online]. Available: https://doi.org/10.1145/3290607.3313260

[16] H. Zhou, W. Zhou, Y. Zhou, and H. Li, "Spatial-temporal multi-cue network for continuous sign language recognition," in Proceedings of the AAAI Conference on Artificial Intelligence, vol. 34, no. 07, 2020, pp. 13 009–13 016.

[17] "PWTH-PHOENIX-Weather 2014-T)," 2019, URL: https://www-i6.informatik.rwth-aachen.de/~koller/RWTH-PHOENIX-2014-T/ [retrieved: April, 2024].

[18] B. Shi and et al., "Fingerspelling recognition in the wild with iterative visual attention," in 2019 IEEE/CVF International Conference on Computer Vision (ICCV), 2019, pp. 5399–5408.

[19] "Chicago Fingerspelling in the Wild Data Sets (ChicagoFSWild, ChicagoFSWild+)," 2019, URL: https://home.ttic.edu/~klivescu/ChicagoFSWild [retrieved: April, 2024].

[20] D. Bragg, O. Koller, N. Caselli, and W. Thies, "Exploring collection of sign language datasets: Privacy, participation, and model performance," in The 22nd International ACM SIGACCESS Conference on Computers and Accessibility, ser. ASSETS '20. New York, NY, USA: Association for Computing Machinery, 2020. [Online]. Available: https://doi.org/10.1145/3373625.3417024

A Facility Management System with Complaint Processing Using AR and BIM Integration

Muhammet Derviş Kopuz
Department of Computer Engineering
Istanbul Technical University
Istanbul, Turkey
email: kopuz17@itu.edu.tr

Gökhan İnce
Department of Computer Engineering
Istanbul Technical University
Istanbul, Turkey
email: gokhan.ince@itu.edu.tr

***Abstract*—Effective management of a facility is arguably one of the most pressing maintenance challenges leading to unpleasant experience and squandered resources worldwide. General issues, complaints, or feedback reported by occupants often lack a common structure and are devoid of the spatial data and digital records necessary for effective analysis and solution provision. In this study, we propose the use of Building Information Models (BIM) integrated with Augmented Reality (AR) for both occupants and Facility Management (FM) personnel to visualize their environment and access component information in order to improve complaint processing capabilities. The developed system enables users to create informed complaints directly linked with the elements in Building Information Models, all while maintaining a digital record of the process. Usability assessments demonstrate the effectiveness of this approach, showing enhanced information exchange, spatial awareness, and efficiency compared to traditional complaint processing techniques.**

Keywords- Facility Management; Building Information Models; Augmented Reality; Occupant Feedback.

I. INTRODUCTION

Facility Management (FM) is the collection of services and processes which plays a vital role in enhancing the quality of life, productivity and efficiency within a facility. The term "facility" is used for many diverse building types, such as homes, schools, hospitals, factories, etc.

Effective FM requires skilled professionals who oversee various aspects, including maintenance, repairs, inspections, and service provisions. With proper and efficient FM, systems facilities can save considerable monetary costs. Integrating smart technologies into FM systems can improve efficiency, save time while doing regular tasks, accelerate new worker training, and enhance work force distribution.

As indicated by Lewis et al. [1], it is estimated that 85% of a facility's lifecycle costs are incurred after the completion of the construction phase. One strategy to significantly mitigate the unnecessary expenditures is the implementation of Building Information Models (BIM) throughout the lifecycle of a facility. Frontczak et al. claim that occupant feedback can be a more reliable source of information than physical measurements, such as data from sensors, other mechanical sources, or default standards for assessing a building's performance [2]. Therefore, accurate evaluation and consideration of occupant feedback can enable a facility to operate with greater efficiency and create a more comfortable environment for its occupants.

Occupant feedback can serve as a diagnostic tool to aid facility managers in making more informed decisions regarding the planning, programming, and management of the facility. However, current FM systems often fall short in collecting this high-quality information in conjunction with contextual information. This includes details related to the specific building elements causing inconvenience, or spatial data related to the complaint.

Augmented Reality (AR) can be employed to visualize BIM within a real-world context, thereby enhancing spatial comprehension for both facility occupants and management personnel. This technology has the potential to improve the accuracy of on-site decision-making by decreasing the reliance on two-dimensional plans, thereby fostering a more interactive and immersive understanding of the facility's spatial layout and operational needs.

In our research, we advocate for the integration of existing BIM with AR frameworks, specifically designed for mobile devices, to ensure optimal user accessibility. By scanning real-world markers, users can visualize their environment in AR using the facility's BIM. This allows them to access all available information on the BIM, offering an interactive experience with BIM elements. This system lays the foundation for incorporating a digital history log into FM operations. Utilizing this system, occupants can report complaints or provide feedback directly linked to the relevant BIM elements, accompanied by precise spatial data. This enables FM personnel to conduct a prompt and assured analysis of the complaint, leveraging system capabilities, such as accurate AR visualizations and access to technical component information directly sourced from the BIM. Finally, this study evaluates the system's usability through three distinct usability test scenarios performed on the developed version of the system, in comparison to a traditional form-based 2D system.

This paper is structured as follows: Section II provides a literature review, Section III outlines the design of the proposed system, Section IV presents conducted experiments, Section V discusses results, and Section VI concludes with final remarks and future work.

II. LITERATURE REVIEW

El Ammari et al. propose a remote collaboration tool that utilizes a BIM based approach, enhanced with Mixed

Reality (MR) technologies, to automate specific aspects of a construction project [3]. Initially, they underscore similar potential advantages, such as increased efficiency and decreased analysis time, that can be achieved through the use of a similar application. Raimbaud et al. posit that AR communication methods can be effectively implemented within a supervisory context [4]. Given that each new employee's tasks should be supervised, either throughout or at the end of the process, by a more experienced colleague, transitioning this process to a remote and digital format can result in significant time savings for experienced workers. In their paper, Chalhoub et al. focus on the use of MR methods to enhance the assembly of electrical elements in construction [5]. To evaluate the effectiveness of this approach, they utilized a usability questionnaire. Similarly, Irizarry et al. [6] created MR test environments using AR and Virtual Reality (VR). They tasked participants with locating elements within the environment and accessing attached information, such as the latest inspection date. Following the tests, they measured the time taken by the participants to complete the tasks and conducted a questionnaire to gather quantifiable data.

Occupant feedback has various collection methods, such as calls, messages, emails, or surveys. Pritoni et al. [7] explored the use of a mobile application for collecting occupant feedback, while Barrios et al. [8] emphasized the use of wearable devices equipped with sensors. However, both these studies primarily focus on a single aspect, such as thermal comfort. In contrast, real-world feedback is typically more multifaceted and complex, necessitating extensive filtering and manual processing by FM teams, which can be labor-intensive and time-consuming, confirmed by Shalabi et al. [9].

Post-Occupancy Evaluation (POE) surveys enable facility managers to continuously implement improvements in their facilities by accurately identifying both short-term and long-term inconveniences and problems. However, given that most POE tools are not designed to record problems, they often fail to gather crucial details, such as the contextual information necessary for problem-solving. This limitation was reaffirmed by Li et al. [10], with particular emphasis on the inability to provide contextual information continuously in real-time.

Furthermore, as seen in Ilter et al. [11], most POE tools lack an extensive inquiry about the degree of occupant satisfaction. While POE tools do measure occupant satisfaction for certain parameters, they often fail to identify the reasons behind low satisfaction rates or the root causes of the complaints. Another significant limitation of POE tools is their failure to collect necessary location information related to an occupant's complaint or feedback. Despite evidence suggesting that linking feedback data with location information can increase system efficiency, confirmed by Hua et al. [12], many POE systems still do not collect location information. This lack of spatial context can hinder the effective resolution of complaints and the overall management of the facility.

Our research proposes the integration of BIM with AR, emphasizing the user experience and practicality for complaint processing operations for occupants. This integration allows the FM team to collect structured feedback enriched with precise spatial data. The enhanced access to information through our system enables swift complaint analysis and the simultaneous creation of digital records for the process, thus offering a practical and efficient solution for day-to-day FM operations.

III. Methodology

A. Problem Definition and Design Issues

According to the research of Ilter et al. [13], current POE tools are lacking in functionality in terms of gathering comprehensive information about occupant satisfaction rates within a facility. Our system plans to address this issue by offering an intuitive interface where occupants can provide detailed textual feedback about various aspects of a facility. By facilitating easy reporting options and providing users with a way to effortlessly track the status of their feedback, our systems aims to enhance communication between the occupants and the facility managers.

Current Post-Occupancy Evaluation (POE) tools exhibit lack of spatial occupant feedback. This issue can be addressed by integrating BIM with AR. AR enables occupants to identify their location and incorporate this spatial information into their feedback. This enhanced feedback, complete with spatial information, aids in identifying specific building elements related to the feedback.

As confirmed by Hua et al. [12], linking occupant location to evaluation data has been proven to enhance process efficiency. This integration of spatial data not only enriches the feedback but also aids facility managers in swiftly identifying and addressing issues, thereby improving overall FM operations. By visualizing occupant feedback within the BIM model with the aid of AR visualization, our proposed system aims to provide a refined and easily consumable information report to decision-makers. This visual representation of data can facilitate a more intuitive understanding of the feedback, thereby enabling more informed and effective decision-making in FM.

B. Proposed Complaint Processing System with the Integration of AR and BIM

The application consists of two interfaces, one tailored for the facility occupants and the other designed for the FM team. The former interface enables facility occupants to utilize the system for delivering feedback or lodging complaints, leveraging the visualizations offered by the system. Conversely, the latter interface allows the FM team to scrutinize and analyze the issues reported by the occupants. The ensuing discussion will commence with a description of the application from the perspective of the facility occupants.

1) Occupant Interface: Upon initial engagement with the application, the occupant is prompted to scan a pre-established marker image in the physical environment. This marker image serves as an anchor to precisely overlay the BIM within the AR framework. These markers are assumed to be placed in predefined static locations in the real world. Following the accurate positioning of the AR visualization over the real-world environment, participants are at liberty to navigate and interact with the BIM elements. Selection of a component within the BIM presents the information panel, which furnishes comprehensive details about the component, sourced directly from the BIM. Figure 1 illustrates the selection of a "Glass Door" component by tapping on its corresponding BIM image superimposed onto the camera view of the physical glass door. It is noteworthy to mention that a mock BIM is used due to the difficulty of acquiring a BIM of a real building.

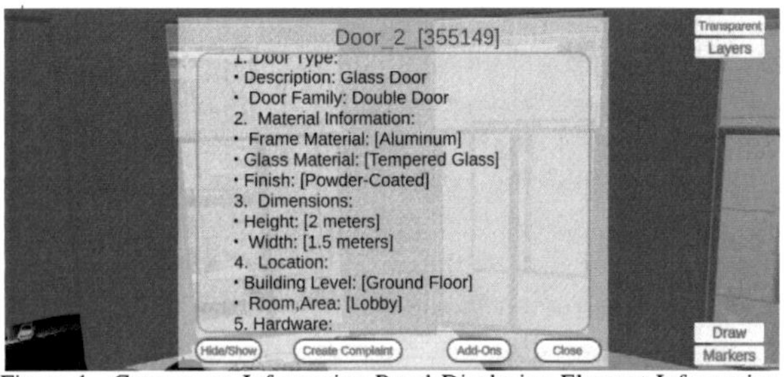

Figure 1. Component Information Panel Displaying Element Information.

By employing the "Hide/Show" button, users have the ability to activate or deactivate the rendering of the selected element. The "Create Complaint" button facilitates occupants in formulating informed complaints or delivering feedback, capitalizing on the information of the presented BIM element and directly associating them with the element in the BIM. This provides precise spatial data for the complaint and highlights the implicated element. All component and complaint correlations are established utilizing the component's unique ID sourced from Revit, a commercial BIM software, which guarantees precise tracking and identification of each component. The "Add-Ons" button is planned to be used for third-party API integration for applicable elements, such as sensor data, user manuals, etc. Using the "Close" button, users can close the open panels. Occupants also have the option to utilize the "Transparent" feature, which renders the BIM model transparent, thereby permitting them to see through the elements. The "Layers" button enables occupants to alternate between the rendering of various component groups, such as walls, doors, plumbing, etc., thereby offering a more lucid view of the BIM. This feature also allows occupants to view and interact with BIM elements that would typically be invisible. The "Draw" function allows occupants to sketch anchored shapes within the AR view, as depicted in Figure 2. Furthermore, the "Markers" function enables the placement of markers of varying colors and shapes. Both the "Draw" and "Markers" features empower users to articulate their thoughts within the 3D space, adding further detail to their complaints or feedback and facilitating more efficient communication of their concerns. If the occupant's issue is not directly associated with a BIM element, but rather pertains to a specific area, these features can be employed to mark an arbitrary area and attach their complaint to the markers. These features are designed to augment the occupant's interaction with the BIM model, fostering a more interactive and personalized view of the facility's components.

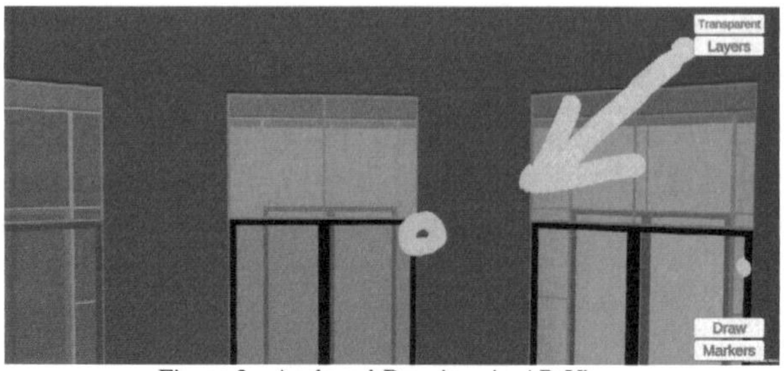

Figure 2. Anchored Drawings in AR View.

2) FM Personnel Interface: In addition to having access to all of the aforementioned functionalities, the FM team is provided with a few additional features intended to facilitate their tasks. The FM personnel can utilize "Filters" feature to filter the highlights of BIM elements associated with complaints, as in Figure 2. This functionality can be used to filter high-priority complaints and prioritize them accordingly. The "My Tasks" button allows FM team members to view a list of issues or complaints assigned to them, which have been submitted by facility occupants. Selecting an individual task reveals the details of that specific complaint and highlights the corresponding element within the BIM model so that FM personnel can initiate their analysis.

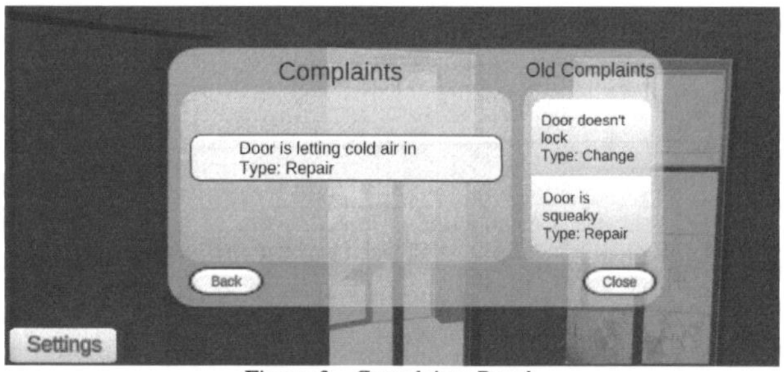

Figure 3. Complaints Panel.

If a FM worker selects a highlighted BIM element in the AR view, they can also access the complaints linked to the element using the "Complaints" button, as in Figure 3. This action opens the "Complaints" panel for the selected element. Within this section, FM workers can view both current and past complaints pertaining to the selected component, as illustrated in Figure 3. Selecting a specific complaint opens a detailed complaint panel with comprehensive data, including the individual who lodged the complaint, the time of creation, problem details, classification, etc. For past complaints, FM workers can view details about any inspection measures that were implemented as a result of the complaints, thereby providing a comprehensive history of each component's issues and the measures taken to resolve them.

In Figure 4, we can see an FM worker using the "Transparent" and "Filters" functionality to view BIM elements associated with complaints. Facility management workers can conduct inspections on the complaints using the "Inspection" button. The "Inspection" button is reachable by clicking on a

Figure 4. "Transparent" and "Filters" features used highlight elements in a mock BIM.

complaint and opening its details panel. This action opens the inspection panel for the workers, facilitating the inspection of the complaint related to the component. During the inspection, the worker can provide details about the analysis of the complaint, such as the root cause, desired action, required action, priority, status, performed action, assignee, required materials, additional information, etc. They have the option to resolve the complaint immediately if feasible, or reject the complaint if it is deemed irrelevant. If a complaint is beyond the worker's capacity to resolve, they can add their findings to the complaint details and assign the complaint to another facility management worker. For instance, an electrical complaint would necessitate the involvement of an electrical engineer.

IV. Experiments

A. Hardware and Software

The experiments were conducted using a Samsung Galaxy A70 mobile device. It is equipped with a Qualcomm Snapdragon 675 processor and 6GB of RAM. This device ensures that the application's performance and functionality can be evaluated on a rather low-cost device.

The application was developed using Unity game engine due to its cross-platform support for iOS and Android from a single codebase. Unity's AR Foundation framework was selected because of its superior tracking accuracy and performance against similar AR frameworks. The application launches with importing BIM, developed and sustained in Revit. The BIM model and its associated properties were exported independently, with a connection established through specific Revit IDs. To ensure the accurate rendering of materials, a customized pipeline in Blender was utilized.

In order to assess the performance of the proposed framework of AR and BIM integration, a conventional form-based 2D mobile application was developed that enables occupants to lodge complaints or offer feedback regarding their environment. This 2D application without AR also facilitates the scanning of markers and provides corresponding 2D floor layouts, allowing users to incorporate spatial data into their feedback by placing markers on the layout plan.

B. Participants

The study was conducted involving a total of 11 participants (10 males, 1 female), with an average age of 27 ± 2.69. The selection of participants was predicated on a composite metric encompassing their familiarity with AR frameworks, BIM, mobile device usage, and their respective professions. The intention was to engage participants possessing prior knowledge in the pertinent domains, thereby mitigating the learning curve. Participants' previous encounters with AR frameworks were primarily through gaming and simulation platforms as well as mobile applications. Six participants had previous exposure to BIM, attributable to their academic pursuits or professional engagements. The participants boasted diverse academic backgrounds and professional affiliations, spanning civil, manufacturing, computer, and support engineering. The entirety of the participant pool comprised prospective or current professionals in the respective fields.

C. Experimental Framework

Participants were assigned tasks in a step-by-step manner, which not only delineated the primary objective but also allowed a degree of flexibility for participants to explore their own approaches to task completion. Initially, the participants performed the first three tasks in the role of a facility occupant submitting a complaint or providing feedback, and the next three tasks in the role of an FM personnel member. For each task, participants first performed the task on the 2D application, then on the AR application.

Task 1: Participants were assigned the task of reporting a complaint regarding a window in an office space infiltrating cold air even when closed. They were expected to utilize the AR application, scan a marker to visualize the BIM model and select the problematic window element by clicking within the AR view. Participants were given the freedom to place markers, for instance, to indicate where the cold air was seeping in. Subsequently, they completed the remaining complaint details, such as type, additional information, etc., and finalized the complaint submission. In contrast, within the 2D application, the scanned marker presented the 2D floor layout plan, and participants were required to place a marker on the floor plan to incorporate spatial information. They then filled out the identical complaint details, with the addition of extra location information to accurately identify the problematic window among all windows in the space, thereby concluding the scenario.

Task 2: Participants were instructed to report an unpleasant odor in the workspace. Identifying the source of such odors can be complex due to the potential for various origins and sporadic occurrences. Therefore, providing detailed location information and the time of occurrence is crucial. Participants proceeded to fill out the complaint details and provide spatial information using the features of both applications.

Task 3: Participants were tasked with reporting a faulty light fixture in a conference space where all light fixtures are identical. Identifying the correct fixture can be challenging, often necessitating manual filtering and detailed descriptions in the absence of spatial data.

For **Task 4, Task 5** and **Task 6**, participants assumed the role of an FM employee. They were given three preconstructed scenes mimicking the complaints similar to the ones in **Tasks 1-3**. For example, **Task 4**'s scene already had the complaint created about the problematic window described in **Task 1**. Participants utilized the application to locate the source of the complaint, identify related BIM elements, view attached complaints, and analyze the issue.

Upon completion of all six tasks, participants were asked to complete the System Usability Scale (SUS) and a Post Evaluation Questionnaire (PEQ). SUS is a commonly used usability questionnaire developed by Brooke et al. [13] which consist of questions designed for responses on a 1 to 5 scale, ranging from "Strongly Disagree" to "Strongly Agree" summing to 100. The PEQ drew upon previous research conducted in this field by Yilmaz et al. [14], with additional customized questions and current and future design recommendations for the application regarding User Interface design and elements, evaluation of possible feature implementations and push notifications for gathering feedback. Based on the outcomes of these tests and the observations made throughout the experiments, the ensuing findings have been formulated.

V. RESULTS

A. Average Task Time Results

The results of **Tasks 1-3** can be seen in Table 1. The examination of the table reveals a marginal disparity in the time required to accomplish tasks between the AR application and the 2D counterpart. Nonetheless, participants attested that the AR application, featuring direct integration of BIM data, significantly heightened their spatial awareness. Consequently, this enhancement facilitated a more confident articulation of complaints and related elements. Users engaging with the 2D application faced challenges in locating some elements, necessitating a reliance on detailed verbal descriptions. In contrast, the AR application, leveraging BIM, enabled participants to effortlessly identify these elements, empowering them with a visual reference.

TABLE I
AVERAGE TASK COMPLETION TIME

Evaluation Metric	Tasks		
	Task 1	*Task 2*	*Task 3*
AR Application Avg. Task Completion Time (sec.)	72.10 ($\pm$14.46)	89.91 ($\pm$24.93)	67.82 ($\pm$16.97)
2D Application Avg. Task Completion Time (sec.)	88.73 ($\pm$18.71)	86.12 ($\pm$33.39)	75.46 ($\pm$22.82)

Being able to see technical information about the components allowed users to create more informed complaints with confidence indicated by participant's comments. How these informed complaints effect the process for FM personnel is much harder to measure. The genuine impact of complaints enriched with component information through the utilization of BIM for FM personnel proves challenging to discern within these basic artificial test scenarios. The true ramifications can be evaluated when the application is deployed in real-world settings, addressing authentic issues routinely encountered by FM personnel.

B. System Usability Survey Results

The AR application for the Occupant Interface garnered an average score of 71.9 ± 8.7 on the SUS scale. For the FM Personnel Interface, the AR application achieved a score of 73.2 ± 6.8. The average results for the AR application marginally fall into the "Good" category.

C. Post Evaluation Questionnaire Results

The following results are derived from participants evaluating the AR application using the PEQ. Participants indicated that the suggested AR application adequately met their daily needs, with a score of 4.46 ± 0.7. Although participants deemed the existing filtering method to be satisfactory in the AR application, with an average score of 4.2 ± 0.6, they suggested to incorporate a more detailed and customizable search system within the application. Notably, participants with experience in facility operations highlighted that a customizable search would allow management teams to create and save queries related to their responsibilities, thereby facilitating easy tracking of their work status.

Regarding the utilization of occupant feedback, participants stated that they could make more effective use of the feedback, with a score of 4.27 ± 0.5. From the perspective of a facility worker, participants suggested that this application would expedite the analysis of complaints/feedback, with an average score of 4.09 ± 0.7. Participants stated that they would find this application useful in their workspace from both a user's perspective and a facility worker's perspective, with a score of 4.64 ± 0.5. Participants expressed that they would utilize the application for the purpose of lodging complaints or offering feedback within their workplace or professional environment, with an average score of 4.36 ± 0.5. The overall satisfaction rate among users was determined to be 4.2 ± 0.6.

D. User Comments

From the FM personnel perspective, participants found being able to access history of past operations performed on a component useful, commenting that it can help save considerable time. Participants were asked how they feel about sharing their location information for the analysis of location tracking. With the exception of 3 participants, all participants indicated discomfort with sharing their location with third party applications. When queried about the use of hand gestures for navigating the application, 5 participants stated that utilizing hand gestures through camera gesture recognition could be advantageous. 8 participants posited that the incorporation of voice commands would be advantageous. Given the escalating ubiquity of AI companions, the utilization of voice commands to facilitate interaction may improve the efficiency of the system.

Finally, participants were asked whether the application can be used as a regular way of gathering occupant feedback by utilizing the push notification feature of mobile applications. Only 4 participants indicated they would opt to receive push notifications, whereas 5 participants were uncertain about this preference. Small incentives, such as rewards or points, could potentially motivate the remaining percentage of occupants to participate in these push notification programs, thereby assisting in the evaluation of subjective metrics within the facility. 3 participants deemed receiving daily push notification questions to be acceptable, with the general consensus favoring a once-a-week frequency. In this context, the push notifications could be structured more like a brief survey rather than a simple yes-or-no question to gather generic feedback. A brief survey could enable users to provide more detailed information over the period of a week. When participants were asked about, the types of subjects they would like to receive push notifications about safety and security and air quality were the most important factors for the participants, respectively, achieving a rate of 9 and 7 positive answers, as it can be seen in Table II.

TABLE II
ACCEPTANCE RATE FOR PUSH NOTIFICATION

Environmental Factor	Acceptance Rate
Safety and security	9/11
Air quality	7/11
Smell and odors	6/11
Accessibility	6/11
Humidity levels	5/11
Lighting conditions	5/11
Sensory stimuli	5/11
Temperature	4/11
Noise level	4/11

E. Discussion

Participants proposed a zoom in/pan to functionality, whereby the camera would transition from the user's current location to the location of the related BIM element associated with a complaint before slowly panning back to the user's original location. Participants also requested the implementation of a cross-section slider. The cross-section view functionality is frequently employed during construction stages, and participants indicated that it is occasionally utilized in addressing day-to-day management issues.

Participants also articulated a need for a more management-centric user interface for use in monthly or quarterly reports. They proposed the inclusion of a section for graphical analytics that encapsulates all feedback and complaints logged by the application. Participants believed that such metrics would be beneficial for frequent use in their reports and for evaluating site equipment. Furthermore, they mentioned that having easier access to the history of all these actions would provide a comprehensive overview, enabling managers to gain a better understanding of the overall condition of the facility.

Participants further proposed the inclusion of a tutorial or an onboarding guide to assist first-time users in comprehending and adapting to the application. By employing a simulated environment and tasks, the functionalities of the application could be effectively demonstrated to the users.

The incorporation of third-party communication platforms, such as chat and video applications, into the software represents a considerable stride towards fostering collaboration. This integration would facilitate communication with external parties who may not have direct access to the application, utilizing widely recognized tools. By capitalizing on these interactive meeting tools, users could articulate their concerns or issues to third parties with enhanced efficacy.

VI. Conclusion and Future Work

This paper proposed AR-BIM integration for FM operations. This integration has shown to offer a more interactive, user-friendly, and efficient approach to managing building data and collecting occupant feedback. The application's ability to collect spatial data with feedback provides comprehensive understanding of the user's experience, which is a significant advancement over existing feedback collection methodologies.

Future work could focus on refining the system and increasing ease of use based on the insights gathered during the usability tests, such as, a task history panel for FM personnel, improved search functionalities, etc. Moreover, conducting real-world trials to assess the application's efficacy within authentic FM operational scenarios could provide valuable insights into its effectiveness in terms of complaint comprehension and resolution time. Another promising avenue for future work could be investigating how this system could be used to facilitate other aspects of FM, such as predictive maintenance, resource management and space utilization.

References

[1] A. Lewis, D. R. Riley and A. Elmualim, "Defining High Performance Buildings for Operations and Maintenance," International Journal of Facility Management vol.1, 2010.

[2] M. Frontczak, S. Schiavon, J. Goins, E. Arens, H. Zhang and P. Wargocki, "Quantitative relationships between occupant satisfaction and satisfaction aspects of indoor environmental quality and building design," Indoor air, vol. 22(2), pp. 119–131, 2012.

[3] K. El Ammari and A. Hammad, "Remote interactive collaboration in facilities management using BIM-based mixed reality," Automation in Construction, vol. 107, 2019.

[4] P. Raimbaud, R. Lou, F. Merienne, F. Danglade, P. Figueroa and J. T. Hernandez, "BIM-based Mixed Reality Application for Supervision of Construction," IEEE Conference on Virtual Reality and 3D User Interfaces, 2019.

[5] J. Chalhoub, S. Ayer and S. Ariaratnam, "Augmented reality for enabling un- and under-trained individuals to complete specialty construction tasks," Journal of Information Technology in Construction, vol. 26, 2021.

[6] J. Irizarry, E. Karan and F. Jalaei, "Integrating BIM and GIS to improve the visual monitoring of construction supply chain management," Automation in Construction. vol. 31, pp. 241–254, 2013.

[7] M. Pritoni, K. Salmon, A. Sanguinetti, J. Morejohn and M. Modera, "Occupant Thermal Feedback for Improved Efficiency in University Buildings," Energy and Buildings. vol. 144, pp. 241-250, 2017.

[8] L. Barrios and W. Kleiminger, "The comfstat-automatically sensing thermal comfort for smart thermostats," IEEE International Conference on Pervasive Computing and Communications, pp. 257-266, 2017.

[9] F. Shalabi and Y. Turkan, "IFC BIM-based facility management approach to optimize data collection for corrective maintenance," Journal of performance of constructed facilities, vol. 31, 2017.

[10] P. Li, T. M. Froese and G. Brager, "Post-occupancy evaluation: state-of-the-art analysis and state-of-the-practice review," Building and Environment, vol. 133, pp. 187–202, 2018.

[11] D. Ilter, E. Ergen, D. Dönmez and I. Tekce, "A Critical Review of Post-Occupancy Evaluation (POE) Tools," 5th international Project and Construction Management Conference (IPCMC2018), 2018.

[12] Y. Hua, Ö. Göçer and K. Göçer, "Spatial mapping of occupant satisfaction and indoor environment quality in a LEED platinum campus building," Building and Environment, vol. 79, pp. 124-137, 2014.

[13] J. Brooke, "SUS: A quick and dirty usability scale," Usability Eval. Ind., vol. 189, 1995.

[14] N. Yılmaz, E. Ergen and D. Ilter, "A usability test protocol for evaluating mixed reality environments," European Conference on Computing in Construction, pp. 423-430, 2021.

Sign Language Writing System: Focus on the Representation of Sign Language-Specific Features

Nobuko Kato, Yuito Nameta, Yuhki Shiraishi
Faculty of Industrial Technology
Tsukuba University of Technology
Tsukuba, Japan
e-mail: {nobuko, yuhkis}@a.tsukuba-tech.ac.jp

Akihisa Shitara
Graduate School of Library, Information and Media Studies
University of Tsukuba
Tsukuba, Japan
e-mail: theta-akihisa@digitalnature.slis.tsukuba.ac.jp

***Abstract*—Achieving universal access in professional settings necessitates the development of computer-assisted input/output systems tailored to sign language, considering the perceptual characteristics of the deaf and hard of hearing individuals. This study examines sign language-specific features to elucidate the requirements for a sign language writing support system. Analysis of news sentences expressed in sign language reveals the prevalence of distinct expressions like topicalized and wh-cleft sentences. We explore a writing system that incorporates these features and conduct experiments involving transcribing sign language movies. The paper delineates the crucial features of sign language sentences for effective writing and outlines the requisite functions of the system based on actual writing experiments.**

Keywords-deaf and hard of hearing; sign language; visual language; sign writing; communication support.

I. Introduction

The enrollment of individuals with disabilities in higher education institutions and the emphasis on lifelong learning are increasing, necessitating expanded learning opportunities tailored to individual disabilities. In specialized educational settings like higher education, it is necessary to ensure effective information and communication methods aligned with the unique characteristics of each disability.

Various services are employed to facilitate communication for individuals who are Deaf and Hard of Hearing (DHH) in higher education institutions, including real-time captioning by transcriptionists, Automatic Speech Recognition (ASR), sign language interpretation, and notetaking. ASR technology is increasingly explored to automatically generate caption text for DHH users [1]. However, it is crucial to recognize that DHH individuals are bicultural and have the right to be educated in their native sign language [2]. Quality education delivered in national sign languages and national written languages is one of the key factors for fulfilling the education of deaf children and adult learners [3].

Some countries use sign language a method of expressing sign language words in the word order of spoken language, but it can be difficult for deaf people to understand [4]. Research on sign language interpreting in universities has indicated that it is important for deaf students to receive information using the correct sign language structure [5]. Also, written languages is pivotal for the academic success of deaf children and adult learners [3]. While some countries utilize sign language with word orders mirroring spoken language, it can pose comprehension challenges for deaf individuals [4]. Studies on sign language interpreting in universities highlight the significance of instructors' clear use of sign language, as perceived by deaf students [6]. Consequently, there is an anticipated rise in opportunities for specialized content learning facilitated by interpreters or direct sign language instruction in various countries.

Writing presents a significant challenge in sign language learning. Existing writing systems for spoken language (Figure 1d), are ill-suited for sign language, which constitutes a distinct language. Unlike hearing individuals who can write while listening (Figure 1a), deaf individuals must write while simultaneously watching sign language (Figure 1b).

Therefore, the development of a computer-based support system for writing sign language is essential to streamline the writing process and allocate more time for the comprehension of specialized content. To achieve this, it is imperative to delineate the functions such a system should encompass based on sign language characteristics.

This study aims to address the following research questions:

RQ1: What are the sign language-specific features crucial for writing specialized sign language content?
RQ2: How can sign language sentences be written while preserving sign language-specific expressions?

The remainder of this paper is structured as follows: Section II provides insights into sign languages and relevant prior research. Section III outlines the characteristics of signed sentences and presents the proposed method based on these characteristics. Section IV elaborates on the experimental methodology and results, while Section V discusses the findings based on the experimental results. Finally, Section VI presents a summary of the study.

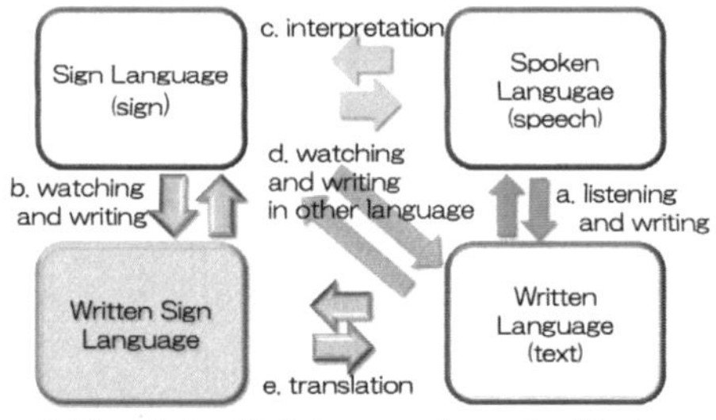

Figure 1. The relationship between spoken and written language.

II. Sign Language Notation Methods

A. Sign Language

Sign Language serves as a visual language used by the deaf community, where linguistic information is communicated not only through hand shapes and movements but also through non-manual markers such as facial expressions, gaze, and head movements [4].

Unlike spoken languages like Japanese, which are linear and rely on speech, sign languages are intricate, employing hand gestures, facial expressions, body movements, and spatial elements [4]. Thus, devising a writing system for sign languages demands innovative approaches distinct from those used for spoken languages.

B. Related Works

Efforts to transcribe sign languages into writing have taken two main approaches: iconographic and alphabetic (using letters from existing spoken languages) [7].

Iconographic methods entail symbolizing hand actions and describing words and sentences, offering the advantage of representing novel words and actions but often result in a high number of descriptions per word, primarily suited for analysis [8][9]. Notational systems like Si5S and ASLwrite prioritize writing but use specialized fonts for sign language, which makes it difficult for learners to correlate these systems with existing spoken language texts.

ASL-Gloss, another method, employs characters from existing spoken languages, using English words as labels to describe American Sign Language (ASL). This system follows ASL's word order and grammatical rules, with glosses used for teaching sign language and grammar [10]. Few studies have examined the use of ASL-gloss in actual educational settings, and examples that have examined the use of ASL-gloss as a potential method for improving reading and comprehension skills in people with severe hearing loss have not supported ASL-gloss as an effective method for improving comprehension [11].

An example of using Japanese as a label is when it is used as an intermediate language for machine translation between Japanese and Japanese Sign Language [12] .

In university settings, where comprehension hinges on understanding key spoken words, it is crucial for deaf students to receive information in semantically and syntactically correct sign language structure [5].

Therefore, our study adopts existing characters to describe terms and explores a method for diagrammatically representing the structure of sign language, aiming to address these challenges.

III. Sign Language Features and Proposed Method

A. Analysis of News Texts

To address RQ1, an analysis was conducted to explore sign language-specific expressions in texts containing specialized content. Owing to limited material of signed sentences expressing specialized content, sign language news was chosen for analysis. News sentences typically employ topic-specific vocabulary and present factual information in a logical manner.

We analyzed 44 sentences from Sign Language News, presented by four deaf news anchors at the Japan Broadcasting Corporation.

Table 1 showcases examples of non-manual markers observed during the analysis. Topicalized sentences introduce the topic at the outset, while Wh-cleft sentences feature a question word in the middle.

B. Results of the Analysis of Signed Language Sentences

The analysis of signed sentences in Sign Language News yielded the following insights:

- Complex sentences were prevalent in sign language news texts (32 out of 44 sentences).
- Presenting the topic at the beginning of the sentence was frequently used (34 out of 44 sentences).
- Topicisation, wh-cleft sentences, and reason-for sentences were used to introduce the topic.

Although Japanese sentences lacked topics, sign language sentences frequently presented topics using sign language-specific expressions, such as topicalisation/wh-cleft sentences or reason-for sentences explicitly stating the reason at the sentence's onset.

Thus, presenting the topic at the beginning of a sentence emerges as a sign language-specific feature crucial for facilitating comprehension by DHH individuals.

C. Proposed Method

To address RQ2, we propose a new writing system that incorporates the identified sign language-specific features.

Previously, we proposed a method to represent the spatial structure of sign language on a two-dimensional plane using symbols, such as spatial representation of subject and object [13]. This time, we focus on the macroscopic structure of sign sentences, aiming to highlight and visualize the topic in a manner conducive to DHH comprehension.

Furthermore, in specialized contexts, it is essential to accurately understand technical terminology in the spoken language. Hence, spoken language text is used as labels for sign words. Figure 2(a) illustrates an example of a topicalized sentence using Proposal A.

The sentence is enclosed in an outer-frame rectangle, with squares and circles representing subjects, objects, and predicates. The rectangle in the top left-hand corner denotes the topic (Figure 2(a)).

TABLE I. NON-MANUAL MARKERS OF SIGNS USED IN THE ANALYSIS

Sentence type	Non-manual markers
Topicalization	Eyebrows raised and eyes widened in the topic area at the beginning of the sentence
Wh-cleft sentence	Squinting and slightly shaking the head in the middle of a sentence
Causal relationship	Eyebrow raised and head forward and fixed in the part of the condition
Complex sentence	Nodding motion before and after the clause

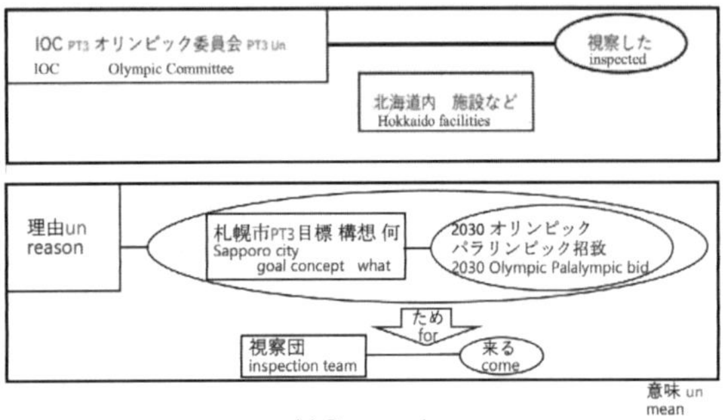

(a) Proposa A

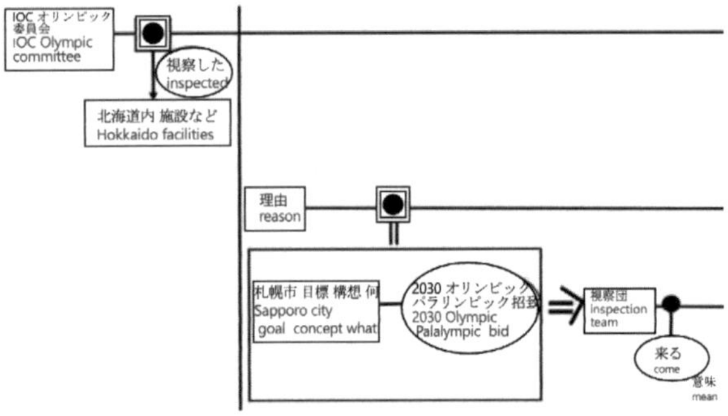

(b) Proposal B

Translation in English: The IOC Olympic member inspected facilities in Hokkaido. Because Sapporo City is aiming to bid for the 2030 Olympic and Paralympic Games.

Figure 2. Examples of a topicalization sentence and example of a reason sentence (Blue letters indicate translated English).

In Proposal B, which employs a single line to preserve the word's position in sign space across consecutive sentences, the branching point is surrounded by a double square to signify that the subject is the topic (Figure 2(b)).

IV. EXPERIMENT

A. Experimental Method

We conducted an experiment to test the efficacy of the proposed sign language writing methods, specifically based on Proposals A and B.

The participants comprised 12 university students who were either deaf or hard of hearing. Initially, the participants were briefed on the rules of the writing systems and engaged in practice sessions to familiarized themselves with reading written signs using the proposed methods.

During the experiment, participants were presented with a choice between Proposal A and Proposal B, based on their preference for ease of understanding. They were then shown a video featuring a sign language news program, where the first and second sentences were accompanied by a ticker displaying only the main points. The third sentence was presented solely in sign language, without any ticker. Participants were instructed to transcribe the third sentence using their chosen writing method.

This setup aimed to simulate scenarios commonly encountered in academic settings, where signs are often displayed alongside textual materials, such as slides, allowing students to simultaneously view both sign language and written or spoken language, such as English or Japanese.

Ethical approval for this study was obtained from the Research Ethics Review of Tsukuba University of Technology, where the experiment was conducted.

B. Experimental Results

In the sign language news watching and writing experiment, 10 out of 12 participants opted for Proposal A, while two participants preferred Proposal B.

In response to the topicalized sentence, 7 out of 10 participants who chose Proposal A accurately reflected the topic using the proposed method.

Although there were multiple possible labels for a single sign word, 11 out of 12 participants opted for a technical term as their label choice. However, errors in symbol selection and placement were observed, presumably owing to misinterpretation of sign language or the influence of the preceding context.

Figure 3 illustrates examples of the participants' writing. In Figure 3(a), "the sinking trigger" is correctly selected as the topic, with the proposed symbol correctly employed. Conversely, Figure 3(b) depicts correct topic selection but errors in placement of symbols were observed. It is inferred that the participant placed the topic in the subject position, possibly owing to its placement at the beginning of the sentence.

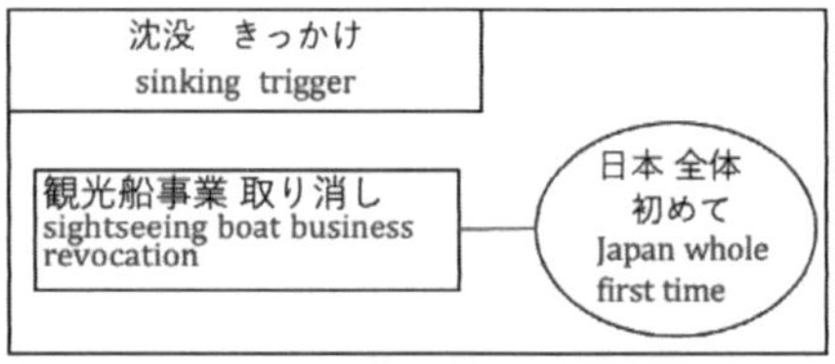

(a) Example 1 using Proposal A.

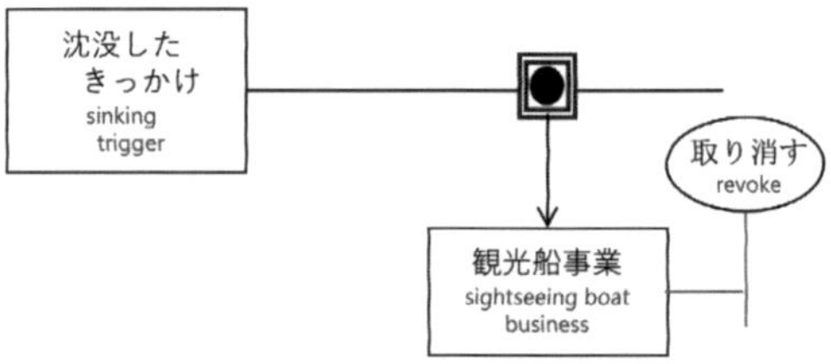

(b) Example 2 using Proposal B.

Translation in English: This is the first time in the nation that a tourist boat business license has been revoked as a result of an accident.
A list of sign labels: {sinking} {trigger} PT3 {sightseeing} {boat} {business} {revocation} PT3 {Japan} {whole} {first time}

Figure 3. Examples of participants writing from a sign language video using the proposed method (Reproduced from handwritten experimental results. Blue letters indicate translated English.).

V. Discussion

A. RQ1: Sign Language-Specific Features

Comparison between Japanese and signed news sentences revealed the following features:

- Complex sentences were often used, with over 70% exhibiting complexity, contrary to the common belief of sign sentences being short and simple. and many sentences presented a topic at the beginning of the sentence.
- The structuring of complex sentences in sign language often involves presenting the topic at the sentence's outset.

Sign language employs specific expressions like topicalization and wh-cleft to introduce and emphasize topics. For instance, in sentences indicating reasons, sign language presents the word "reason" at the beginning, followed by the logical marker "for," and conclude with a phrase expressing the result, a structure not mirrored in Japanese (Figure 2(a)).

These specific expressions are considered to serve as aids in conveying technical concepts in a digestible manner for DHH individuals.

B. RQ2：Writing Sign Language Sentences

Developing a writing system for sign language necessitates considering the characteristics of DHH individual's perceptual characteristics and information processing. Therefore, such a system must incorporate spatial representation, time-series depiction, and visualization of grammatical and logical structures.

We propose a method that projects spatial and time-series representations onto a 2D plane and uses symbols to represent grammatical and logical structures. In addition to the basic spatio-temporal representation, our approach focuses on the macroscopic structure of sentences, represented by Non-Manual Markers (NMMs) and other visual cues.

The experimental preference for Proposal A by 10 out of 12 participants underscores that the method of emphasizing the topic at the beginning is effective. Topic sentences are represented by NMMs such as raised eyebrows (Table 1). While NMMs are said to be challenging for learners to master, written signed sentences could aid in comprehending these expressions.

Regarding sign labels, 11 out of 12 participants used technical terms in real-time sign writing. In order to use technical terms as a label, we need to consider how the sign language and slides are presented.

In this experiment, the participants did not necessarily consider the structure of the whole sentence before writing the sentence but tended to record the sign labels in the order of time series. Although the basic word order in Japanese Sign Language is typically SOV (Subject-Object-Verb), word order can be changed to present a topic, and the first position in a sentence does not always indicate the subject. Moreover, in Japanese Sign Language, there are homonyms between nouns and verbs, making it difficult to distinguish between similar signs (for example, 'revoke' as a verb versus 'revocation' as a noun). The experiment revealed difficulties in selecting and positioning symbols (i.e., Figure 3(b)), highlighting the need for computer support, such as automatic placement and insertion of symbols.

C. Limitation

This study's limitations include the small number of participants in the experiment, variability in sign language proficiency, and the limited number of signed sentences. Further research with a large number of expressions and sentence patterns is needed to design a system that is useful for improving the learning performance of DHH people.

VI. Conclusion

This study aimed to develop a computer-assisted writing system tailored to the perceptual characteristics of DHH individuals, considering the visual and spatial nature of sign language and the unique characteristics of signed text. By analyzing news sentences expressed in sign language, we confirmed that numerous expressions specific to sign language are used, such as topicalized and wh-cleft sentences. To establish a new way of expression that is intuitive and understandable for the deaf, we proposed a writing system that reflects these features and conducted an experiment in which participants wrote a sign language video.

The results of the experiment demonstrate that by using the proposed method, participants could actually write signed sentences with sign language-specific features.

In the future, we intend to expand our research by conducting a broader survey involving a larger sample of sentences. This will enable us to further refine our proposed writing system and provide support for communication and learning for the DHH people.

Acknowledgment

This study was supported by JSPS KAKENHI (Grant number 22K02999, 19K11411). We would like to thank Editage for editing and reviewing this manuscript for English language.

References

[1] L. Berke, S. Kafle, and M. Huenerfauth, "Methods for evaluation of imperfect captioning tools by deaf or hard-of-hearing users at different reading literacy levels," Proceedings of the 2018 CHI Conference on Human Factors in Computing Systems, ACM, Apr. 2018, pp. 1–12. doi: 10.1145/3173574.3173665.

[2] K. R. Miller, "American Sign Language: Acceptance at the university level," Language, Culture and Curriculum, vol. 21, no. 3, pp. 226–234, Nov. 2008, doi: 10.1080/07908310802385899.

[3] WFD, "7 September 2016: WFD Position Paper on the Language Rights of Deaf Children," [Online]. Available from: http://wfdeaf.org/news/resources/wfd-position-paper-on-the-language-rights-of-deaf-children-7-september-2016/ [retrieved: 4, 2024]

[4] M. Huenerfauth and V. Hanson, "Sign language in the interface: access for deaf signers," in The Universal Access Handbook, CRC Press, pp. 1–18, 2009. doi: 10.1201/9781420064995-c38.

[5] J. Napier, "University Interpreting: Linguistic Issues for Consideration," Journal of Deaf Studies and Deaf Education,

vol. 7, no. 4, pp. 281–301, Oct. 2002, doi: 10.1093/deafed/7.4.281.

[6] H. G. Lang et.al., "A study of technical signs in science: implications for lexical database development," Journal of Deaf Studies and Deaf Education, vol. 12, no. 1, pp. 65–79, Aug. 2006, doi: 10.1093/deafed/enl018.

[7] D. A. Grushkin, "Writing Signed Languages: What For? What Form?," American Annals of the Deaf, vol. 161, no. 5, pp. 509–527, 2017, doi: 10.1353/aad.2017.0001.

[8] T. Hanke, "HamNoSys – Representing sign language data in language resources and language processing contexts," Proceedings of the 1st Workshop on the Representation and Processing of Sign Language, 2004, pp. 1-6.

[9] H. Van Der Hulst and R. Channon, "Notation systems," in Sign Languages, 1st ed., D. Brentari, Ed., Cambridge University Press, pp. 151–172, 2010, doi: 10.1017/CBO9780511712203.009.

[10] C. Valli and C. Lucas, Linguistics of American Sign Language: an introduction, 3rd ed. Washington, D.C: Gallaudet University Press, 2000.

[11] E. Rathkey, "Can ASL-gloss be used as an instructional tool to teach written English to the deaf?," Open Access Dissertations, paper 835, Jan. 2019, doi: 10.23860/diss-rathkey-emma-2019.

[12] K. Yano and A. Utsumi, "Pipeline signed Japanese translation using PBSMT and transformer in a low-resource setting," Journal of Natural Language Processing, vol. 30, no. 1, pp. 30–62, 2023, doi: 10.5715/jnlp.30.30.

[13] N. Kato, Y. Hotta, A. Shitara, and Y. Shiraishi, "Visually-structured written notation based on sign language for the deaf and hard-of-hearing," Proceedings of the 15th International Conference on Computer Supported Education - Volume 2: CSEDU, INSTICC. SciTePress, 2023, pp. 543–549. doi: 10.5220/0011988700003470.

Virtual Multiuser Environment for Adapted Physical Activity and Rehabilitation for Older Adults: Usability and Acceptance Evaluation

Malak Qbilat, André Thiago Netto and Hugo Paredes
INESC TEC and UTAD,
Porto – Portugal
e-mail: malak.m.irshed@inesctec.pt, andre.netto@inesctec.pt, hugo.paredes@inesctec.pt

Telma Mota and Fausto de Carvalho
Altice Labs
Portugal
e-mail: telma@alticelabs.com, cfausto@alticelabs.com

Vânia Mota
Ordem São Francisco,
Porto – Portugal
e-mail:
vaniamota@ordemsaofrancisco.pt

Dennis Beck
University of Arkansas,
United States
e-mail:
debeck@uark.edu

Abstract **Physical activity and socialisation are vital keys in enhancing health and well-being of older adults. This paper presents a usability, accessibility, and user acceptance evaluation study of a virtual multiuser environment that allowed users to train and socialise with other older adults under the supervision of a physical trainer. Researchers used an open-ended questionnaire to interview six participants who resided at nursing home. The identified issues will be considered in the next refinement phase of the system. These issues included the instability of avatars´ movements, and the need to provide the environment with a mechanism for reachable human support and integrate gamification approaches to enhance users´ commitment. They also involved the need to align the avatars´ location and size with the expected roles in the training sessions, and the importance of finding an alternative solution to detect users´ soft voices and transmit them to the environment. Screen´s size, height, and distance with the users are three correlated factors that should be standardised and optimised according to users´ needs and systems´ calibration demands.**

Keywords-Active Ageing; Virtual Reality; Adapted Physical Activity; Rehabilitation; Usability.

I. INTRODUCTION

The global proportion of older adults (over the age of 60) is expected to double between 2017 and 2050 [1]. Aging is often linked with deteriorating health and physical abilities; However, it can be a positive experience, and is commonly referred to as "active ageing" or "successful ageing.". Promoting active aging in the community is crucial in this regard. Regular Physical Activity (PA) positively affects the main determinants of active ageing: good physical and mental health, opportunities for social interaction, the ability to cope with disease symptoms and functional limitations [2][3].

Many scholars and designers recognize the potential of Virtual Reality (VR) technology to enhance older adults´ wellbeing, quality of care, and socialisation while also supporting their independence [4]. For instance, VR games interfaces such as the Wii [5], Kinect-based systems [6]-[8], Rehaboo [9], and REHABILITY [10] have been utilised in improving physical function, balance, and fall prevention of older adults. Additionally, XRHealth [11], Eodyne [12], and Clynx [13] offer personalised VR-based rehabilitation sessions for older adults, each tailored to individual cases and remotely supervised by professionals. Other VR based solutions adapt the multiuser feature to enhance user engagement and motivate the olders adults to exercise, such as the Social Bike [14], and the social collaborative VR-based exergame for rehabilitation [15] and Maestro Game VR [16] for physical and cognitive treatment.

Incorporating older users early in the design process through participatory (PD) and co-design methods will enhance the usability and acceptability of digital products or systems. The active involvement of older adults enables designers and developers to create solutions, which meet the users' requirements and preferences as well as understand the context in which they will use the solution. VR2Care [17] is a digital ecosystem developed using participatory and co-design methods to promote the physical activity and socialisation of older adults through the use of interactive technologies. Four partners, bringing their existing products [10] [18]-[20], are engaged in an integration process aimed at providing older adults with virtual environments for playing exergames or exercising individually or in groups with a trainer across various virtual settings. Additionally, VR2Care offers clinicians, physiotherapists, physical trainers, and caregivers a telemonitoring and onboarding tool for crafting training and rehabilitation plans, whether for single or group sessions in a Multi-User Environment (MUE). This tool enables the monitoring of participants' performance and includes a companion application for session management, along with safety sensors to detect falls or obstacles. VR2Care follows a co-design approach by actively involving future end-users in the requirements development [21], testing, and evaluation phases.

This study presents a preliminary usability, accessibility, and user acceptance evaluation of one of the VR2Care components, the Multi-User Environment. The results of this study will be used to refine the MUE to meet users 'needs and expectations. The structure of this paper is as follows. Section II provides an overview of the VR2Care ecosystem. Section III outlines the methods employed in this study. Section IV presents the results and a discussion of the study. Finally, Section V addresses the study´s conclusions and future work.

II. VR2CARE

VR2Care aims to create age-friendly virtual environments fostering the use of interactive technologies for the promotion of physical activity and social interaction. The practice of physical activity and training is performed in a realistic multiuser virtual reality environment, where users are represented with real human forms (avatars), with animations synchronised with natural movements (embodiment) and multimodal interactions combining voice, gestures, and body movement. The environment allows professionals to monitor and guide physical activity based on the specific requirements of each intervention. It accommodates a variety of activities, ranging from functional training to rehabilitation. Therefore, the VR2Care platform offers a unique setting for physical activity, training, and rehabilitation. It features intelligent interfaces within both single and multiuser environments, blending VR technologies for supervised exercise with natural interaction techniques. Additionally, it fosters socialization through physical activity within a metaverse context. The VR2Care concept surfaced from a need identified by the home care market in which state-of-the-art technology could be applied. The project aims to leverage VR multiuser technology from the lab to the market, piloting the prototypes with the involvement of professionals and primary end-users. The core of the VR2Care digital ecosystem is developed by technological partners with their own products, which are being adapted and integrated to meet the identified requirements for pilot scenarios. This vision leverages for a system-of-systems approach [22] a set of independent, useful systems integrated into larger systems that deliver unique capabilities [23] where individual components are regarded as systems with independent operationality, complemented by additional properties and features from the assemblage of components [24]. Figure 1 represents VR2Care architecture.

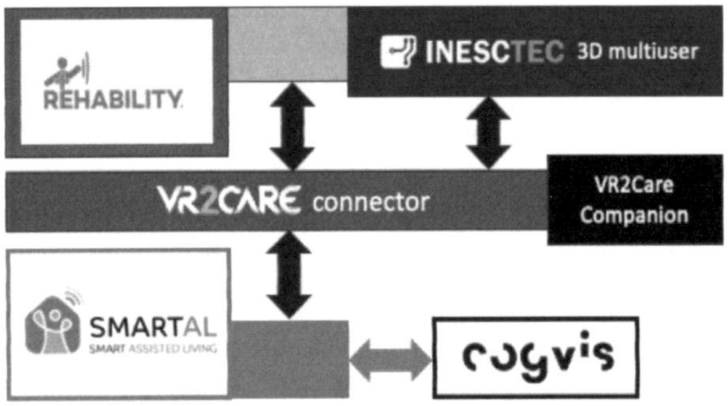

Figure 1. VR2Care architecture

VR2Care high-level functional architecture is composed by the following main modules:

1. Telemonitoring (SmartAL) [18], that allows caregivers and patients to define, manage and execute daily monitoring plans and gather gaming information to be processed in the gamification add-on.
2. The AI Motion Capture and Metrics (Cogvis) [20], that is able to detect poses, motion and falls while keeping the privacy of the patient.
3. The VR Environment, which is responsible for the natural interaction and multiuser embodiment, common to both the REHABILITY (single end-user) [10] and 3D Multiuser services (MUE) [19].

III. METHODS

This research will focus on evaluating the usability, accessibility, and user acceptance of the VR2Care MUE. Six older adults reside at nursing home care called Venerável Ordemde Terceira de Sao Francisco do Porto (OSF) in Portugal involved in the evaluation. Each older adult had a training session (10-15 minutes) using MUE under the supervision of the physical trainer in the nursing home. After each session, the researchers asked the participants to respond to an open-ended questionnaire, which was developed following Nielsen's model [25] to assess usability based on the five attributes: learnability, efficiency, memorability, error recovery, and satisfaction. Accessibility questions were included in the questionnaire to assess three factors: perceivability, operability, and understandability following the World Wide Web Consortium (W3C) [26] principles. The developed questionnaire also takes into account the Technology Acceptance Model (TAM) [27] to evaluate user acceptance, specifically focusing on Perceived Usefulness and Perceived Ease-of-Use aspects. Additionally, researchers made some notes from the field.

A. Participants

The participants were recruited from a nursing home (OSF), which was one of four pilot sites of VR2Care project. Table 1 shows the characteristics of the participants.

TABLE I. PARTICIPANTS´ CHARACTERISTICS

Characteristics	Number of participants
Weekly exercise	Once (*N*=2)
	Three times (*N*=1)
	None (*N*=3)
Experience in using electronic devices	Television and remote control (*N*=6)
	Smartphones (*N*=5)
	Laptop (*N*=3)
Education	Higher education (*N*=3)
	Primary education (*N*=3)
Profession	Farmer (*N*=1)
	Educational assistance (*N*=2)
	Architect (*N*=1)
	School teacher (*N*=2)
Type of disabilities (if any)	Vision: neutral with glasses (*N*=6)
	Hearing: difficult (*N*=1), neutral (*N*=2), easy (*N*=3)
	Motor: difficult (*N*=4), easy (N=2)
	Memory: very difficult (*N*=2), difficult (*N* =2), neutral (*N*=1), easy (*N*=1)

Older adults with severe cognitive or physical impairments were excluded from the study, in order to not burden vulnerable older adults and to ensure active participation. One caregiver and physical trainer from OSF participated in organizing the evaluation. The study involved a sample size of six participants. We opted for a small sample of participants because this study is a preliminary usability and acceptance study of the MUE. With this sample size, we obtained deeper qualitative insights that will be considered in the iterative design journey we followed in the VR2Care project. A subsequent evaluation study will involve a larger sample size of 60 participants for validation.

The six participants of this study (N=4 female, N=2 male), were with an average age of 84.17 (SD=5.78) years. Three of them did not exercise in a gym at all, but they walked 2-4 kilometres outside every day. The other three participants performed their exercises at the nursing home gym with a trainer. Participants reported different reasons for the difficulty of committing to regular exercises in the gym: previous injuries such as pelvic, spine injuries, and knee (N=2), social anxiety and shyness about training in front of people at the gym (N=1). Two of the participants had never heard of or used VR technology, while the other four participants heard about VR technology from TV. A few (N=2) thought that VR was something related to Artificial Intelligence (AI), and two others (N=2) had tried VR exergames.

B. Ethics

Ethics approval was obtained from the INESC TEC ethics committee. The researchers sought advice from the committee before conducting the evaluation with older adult participants. Moreover, each participant was requested to carefully read and sign the consent form to participate in the study. The form provided clear information to patients, emphasizing that their involvement in the research was entirely voluntary. It assured them that they could withdraw from the process at any point without facing consequences or needing to provide a reason. Patients would not be penalised or have their motives questioned; they simply needed to contact the researchers to withdraw.

C. Evaluation Setup

The VR2Care hardware package allowed end users to access the VR Environment (REHABILITY and MUE). It consists of a processing and communication unit (homekit) connected to a depth camera and a TV display, which enable the user to experience VR without requiring a specialised immersion device such as VR glasses. This approach ensured that the use of VR is not restricted by the audience or the cost of additional equipment. The VR environment was not displayed on a VR headset, but rather on a standard TV screen. This provided enough dimensions for user immersion. Users (the older adults and the trainer) interact with the environment through body movements, gestures, and voice, which simulates natural human interactions. Figure 2 shows an example of the VR2Care MUE setup that was deployed in the TV room at the nursing home.

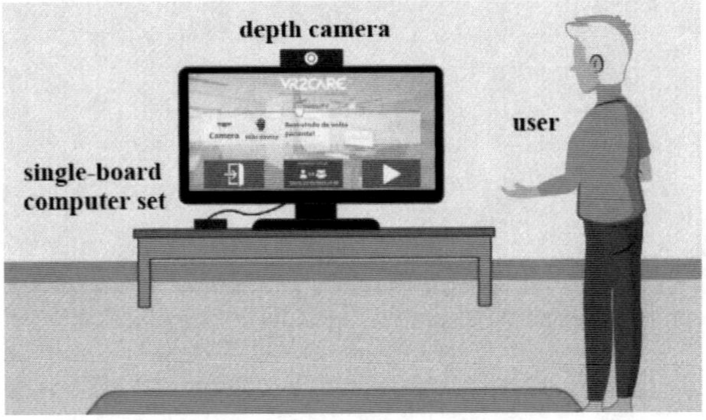

Figure 2. VR2Care MUE setup in the TV room at the nursing home.

The setup included a depth camera that is connected to a single-board computer, which was connected to the television. Utilising this computer, the VR2Care system enabled users to intuitively engage with the VR2Care MUE. Once the patient/trainer initiates the system, a calibration screen will be displayed (Figure 3). The camera then scans the user's body to align it to the avatar to represent their movements in the MUE. The user will need to use their hands and body to interact with the system to complete the calibration process and login to the MUE.

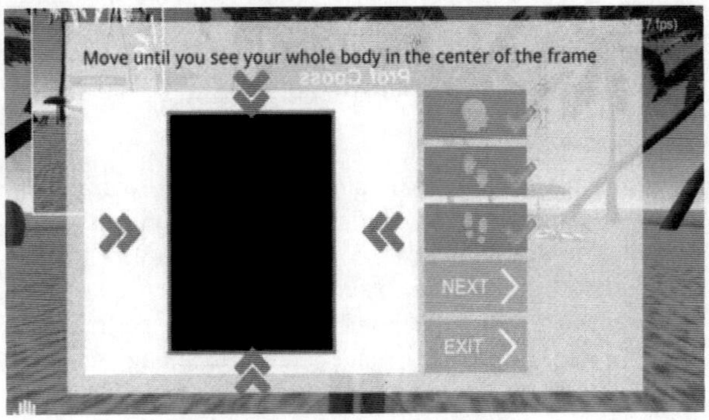

Figure 3. MUE – Calibration screen.

After completing the calibration process, the user will encounter the welcome screen and proceed to choose the MUE (Ambiente virtual in Figure 4). If patients join the training session earlier than the trainer, their avatars will be placed into a virtual waiting room, where they can communicate with each other using the voice channel. Once the trainer joins, patients will see their avatars in addition to the trainer's avatar (positioned in the upper left corner of the screen in Figure 5) in a training environment. The trainer will guide them to exercise. Patients and trainer can talk to each other during the session. But the trainer can talk to a specific patient using private voice channel.

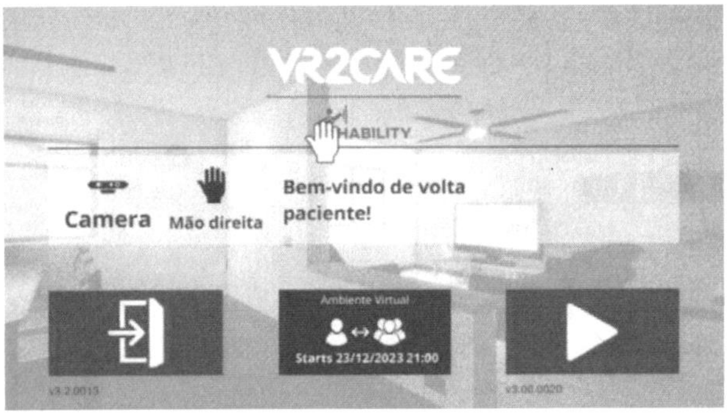

Figure 4. MUE – Welcome Screen. Translation "Portuguese"–English: "Camera"–camera; "Mão direita"–Right hand; "Bem-vindo de volta paciente"–Welcome back patient; "Ambiente Virtual"–Virtual Environment".

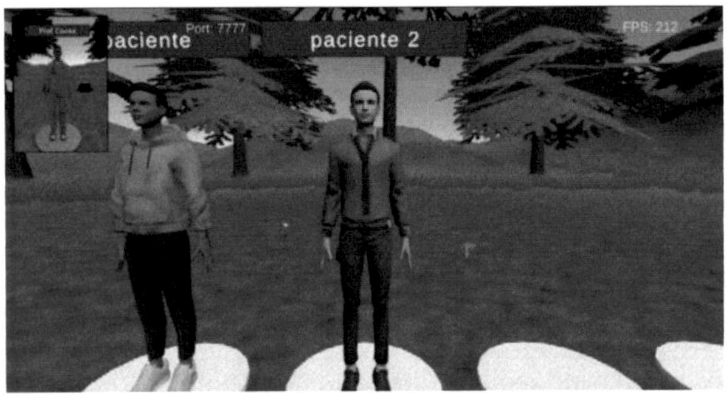

Figure 5. MUE – trainer (upper left corner) and patients.

Training session is terminated by the trainer once the planned exercises are completed.

D. Protocol

The same protocol was applied with each participant, where an introduction about VR2Care project were presented to the participant, followed by a request to read and sign the consent form. Then, two researchers conducted the pre-evaluation interview to gather participant´s demographic information and data pertaining to their physical activity and overall experience with electronic devices and VR technology. After that, a caregiver accompanied the participant to the TV room where the MUE setup was deployed. When needed, researchers assisted the participant during the calibration process to login to the training session. A third researcher joined the training session in the role of a patient (third avatar) to receive the training alongside the participant and to interact by voice with the patient in the MUE. Finally, the trainer initiated a 10-minute training session by performing three different upper-limb exercises: 1) shoulder flexion, 2) elbow flexion, and 3) stretching out. Following the sessions, each participant was interviewed by two researchers to answer the open-ended questionnaire.

IV. Results and Discussion

A. Semi-structured Interviews

The questionnaire focused on evaluating the MUE regarding three aspects: usability, accessibility, and user acceptance. Participants' responses to the open-ended questions were analysed using thematic analysis [28]. This section includes sentences quoted from the transcribed participant interviews.

1) ***Usability:*** five factors were measured to evaluate the usability of the MUE:

a) Efficiency: 5/6 participants found it easy to use the MUE to accomplish the exercises. Only one participant reported a little difficulty in using the MUE, due to the latency between the synchronisation of the user's actual body movements and his presented virtual avatar´s movements [*"P1: A bit difficult because I could not do the exercise exactly, the avatar was not showing my movements immediately"*].

b) Satisfaction: 4/6 participants were satisfied exercising using the MUE and think that it could help them to regularly exercise and socialise with other older adults during their stay at the nursing home. One participant was satisfied using the MUE for regular exercising if it is pre scheduled, but she did not think the MUE could help her to socialise with the others, because she liked to interact with people in reality ["*P4: Yes I am satisfied, but I prefer to exercise only if the session is previously scheduled, because I like to finish my daily tasks and go for walks in the city, I do not think this technology can help me talk to people because I prefer to talk to people in reality!*"]. Another participant was not satisfied, nor sure if the MUE could help him to regularly exercise and socialise with others because he experienced a latency in synchronising his body´s movements and his avatar´s movements in MUE, and also because he lacked understanding of how this technology works [*"P1: I am not satisfied because the avatar was not moving with me during the exercise, so I am not sure if this technology can help me to regularly exercise or interact with new people! I don't know much about this technology or how it works!"*].

c) Learnability: all participants easily learned how to interact with the MUE to exercise.

d) Memorability: one participant (P2) said they could use the MUE for the second time by themselves without any help. Another three participants think they could use the system but preferred to have someone to help just in case they needed it. Two of them (P3 and P5) have motor and memory difficulties. The other two participants insisted that they needed help to use the MUE for the next time ["*P1: it is not easy for me, I still need help!*"]. It is important to mention that this participant (P1) had short-term memory difficulties. ["*P4: I think I need someone to help me with it"*]. This participant (P4) had little experience with electronic devices, limited to TV and remote-control use.

e) Errors: 4/6 participants reported that they didn´t expierence any situation during the training session, which made them confused. On the other hand, one participant (P3) experienced confusion only at the beginning of the session during the system calibration process. The system did not provide any voice or text feedback after each calibration attempt, where users depended on the researcher to guide them every time a calibration failed [*"P3: I felt confused at the beginning of the session. It is a new thing! but later everything became clear for me*"]. The last participant (P1) indicated the latency in synchronising his body´s movements with his avatar´s movements as the only situation where he felt confused during the training session.

2) ***Accessibility:*** the following aspects were considered in the questionnaire to evaluate the accessibility of the MUE:

a) Perceivability: all participants could easily recognize all three avatars in the MUE (trainer´s avatar, older adult´s avatar, researcher´s avatar), and only one participant (P6) could not remember the researcher´s avatar, although she has no memory difficulty. It was noticed that during the training, this participant was distracted for a while because she was following her avatar, thinking that it was the trainer's avatar; hence, she repeated the same exercises over and over until one of the researchers in the TV room guided her to follow the trainer´s avatar movements. In addition, all the participants were able to easily recognize the "Enter" and "Exit" buttons on calibration screen.

For the environment´s design, 2/6 participants did not pay attention to the environment´s background or design, because they were focusing on the avatars to do the exercises. [*"P1: I did not pay attention to the environment´s design, because I was focusing on the trainer´s avatar and my avatar to do the exercises*"], [*"P4: I was focusing on the avatars, not on the environment!*"]. 3/6 participants stated that the environment´s background and design were good, but they preferred to see different environments in the future, like beach or forest background. One participant liked the environment´s background and design and would not change anything.

b) Operability: all participants indicated that using their hands and body motions to interact with the MUE was easy. Similarly, they agreed that it was easy to hear the trainer´s and the researcher´s voices and talk to them.

c) Understandability: 4/6 participants stated that they did not pay attention to the texts in the MUE (users´/avatars´ names), but focused on avatars while exercising. Two participants found the texts in the MUE easy to read. 5/6 participants reported that the navigation between the three screens (calibration screen, welcome screen, and the MUE environment) was logical and simple and they understood what they had to do on each screen. One participant (P1) thought that having the calibration screen in Portuguese would help him navigate to the next step of the interaction more effectively.

When asked if they could compare group training at a real gym to group training at the MUE, both of which were supervised by a physical trainer, all participants demonstrated an understanding of the differences between the two options. 4/6 of them preferred to have training in both the real gym and the MUE. ["P2: *both! I can train at home using this technology in private and go to a real gym to interact with people naturally*"], [*"P5: I can do both, but I'd like to have someone to help me when I need it*"]. Two participants (P4, P1) stated that they still preferred to exercise in a real gym. P4 was the lady with little experience in using electronic devices, and she liked to go daily on a walk in the city to interact with people. P1 thought that he could not use the MUE properly for exercising because the avatar was not showing his real body movements immediately. The participant was referring to the latency in synchronising his body´s movements with his avatar´s movements.

d) User acceptance: in terms of percived usefullness and ease-of-use, 5/6 participants found the MUE easy to use, and they would not change anything about the environment, except P6, who would like to see more players (trainees) in the MUE in the future, to talk and exercise with them. P2 expressed her concerns about the possibility of using AI to supervise her training session in the MUE. P3 explained that training attendance and commitment depended on his emotional state at the time right before the training, and not just on the technology itself.

One participant (P1) was not sure about the percieved usefulness and ease-of-use of the MUE, due to the latency in synchronising his body´s movements with his avatar´s movements, in addition to the Portuguese language issue on the calibration screen.

B. *Researchers observations/ Field notes*

Researchers made written observations during the evaluation. First, avatar´s size and location on the screen was vital in guiding the attention of the participant to recognize the different avatars in the MUE. Participants tended to think that the biggest avatar in the centre of the screen was the trainer until the researcher intervened and assisted them to locate the real trainer avatar, which was in the upper left corner of the MUE screen. Second, it was noticed that the researcher who joined the training session virtually could not hear the voices of 4/6 participants during the training session because their voices were soft and weak due to the voice agism of some participants. Third, the proper size of the screen was important for the vision for the participants. Researchers noticed one of the participants was trying to bend his body forward to get a better view of the screen, while another participant asked for help to get closer to the screen to see better. Fourth, the proper height of the screen helps users perform the exercises with correct postures. The screen was a too high for the participants causing them to raise their heads higher that what was required to complete the exercises. In addition to the standard distance between the participant and the screen to reach at successful calibration, which is noticed in this study to be 2 meters. Screen´s size, height, and distance from the users are three factors that should be standardised and adjusted at the training time to optimise participants' vision and posture, and a successful calibration. Table 2 summarises the identified usability, accessibility, and user acceptance issues, which will be considered in the next refinement process.

TABLE II. THE IDENTIFIED USABILITY, ACCESSIBILITY, AND USER ACCEPTANCE ISSUES

Category	Sub-category	Identified issues (*N*[a])
Usability	Efficiency	• The latency between the synchronisation of the user's actual body movements and *his* presented virtual avatar´s movements (*N=1*)
	Memorability	• The absence of a mechanism for a reachable human support when needed (*N=5*)
	Errors	• Calibration process may take the user many attempts to be successful. The system did not provide voice or text feedback after each calibration attempt by user (*N=1*)
Accessibility	Perceivability	• Trainer´s avatar was the smallest one located on the upper left corner of the screen, whereas participants tended to follow the centered and biggest avatar on the screen thinking that is trainer´s avatar (*N=1*) • The absence of a mechanism allowing users to select the MUE background according to their preference (beach, forest, etc., (*N=3*) • Screen size (55 inches) caused some difficulty in recognising the environment presented on the screen (*N=1*)
	Operability	• Participants voices were too soft and low to be detected by the built-in microphone in the depth camera. Other users (trainer and researcher) in the MUE were not able to hear the participants. • Screen height caused participants to raise their heads during the exercises, which affected their required postures. • Screen height, size and distance of interaction were not standardised, which caused some difficulties in interaction with the MUE.
	Understandability	• Calibration screen was in English, while participants spoke Portuguese only (*N=1*)
User acceptance	Perceived usefulness	• Fear of the potential of using AI to supervise the virtual training session. Fear to replace the natural interaction with virtual one (N=2) • The absence of gamification approaches in the MUE, as it could enhance users´ motivation and commitment to exercise, especially who suffer from depression or experience low feelings (*N=1*)

[a]Number of participants who reported or experienced the issue.

The results of this study showed that the majority of participants were satisfied with the MUE. They perceived it as an efficient technological tool to exercise and socialise with other people. Moreover, the majority could easily learn how to interact with the MUE, however, they agreed that they still preferred in-person, human support during the training. The MUE was accessible for most of the participants, as they could easily recognize the avatars and buttons in the environment. Additionally, they were satisfied with the design of the environment and could easily use their body motions and voice to interact. Also, they could easily read the texts in the MUE and understand the concept of training in a group virtually. Most participants agreed on the perceived usefulness and ease of use of the MUE.

Although the majority of participants thought that the MUE could help them to socialise with other older adults, they had a strong preference for in-person social interactions. They also appeared to have significant reservations about how they could use the MUE to socialise with other older adults, pointing to a need for better exemplars and scaffolding of these behaviours.

V. CONCLUSIONS AND FUTURE WORK

In summary, this study offered valuable insights of the usability, accessibility, and user experience of the VR2Care MUE as a multiuser environment to promote older adults' physical activity and socialisation. Six participants from a nursing home in Portugal were recruited for the evaluation. The detected issues were derived from a survey data of the older adult participants, as well as the researchers´ observations in the field. The main detected issues were:

1. The instability of avatars´ movement during the training sessions.
2. The need to provide a mechanism within the MUE to allow participants to contact in-person support.
3. Voice/text feedback for a multilingual calibration screen to keep users aware about the progress of the system calibration.
4. Avatars´ location and size must be aligned with the expected roles in the training sessions.
5. Users were not able to choose the environment background according to their preferences.
6. The MUE lacked gamification approaches to enhance users´ motivation and commitment.
7. Voice agism affected most of participants voice strength so that other MUE users could not hear them.
8. Raising awareness among older adults and educating them about the benefits of new technologies, could help in reducing the fear of using AI and VR in training sessions, besides the continuous involvement of them in the co-creation process.
9. Screen´s size, height, and distance from the users should be standardised and optimised according to users´ needs and systems´ calibration demands.

The identified usability, accessibility, and user acceptance issues will be considered in the coming refinement process of the MUE. Also, another usability and user acceptance evaluation study with a larger sample size of 60 participants will be conducted in four pilot sites from three EU member states, Portugal, The Netherlands, and Italy to allow longer usage of the MUE and by a more diverse user group.

ACKNOWLEDGMENT

The VR2CARE project has received funding from the European Union's Horizon 2020 research and innovation programme under Grant Agreement No. 951978.

REFERENCES

[1] G. Elizabeth and L. Smith, "Active Ageing in The Community. Exploring the Role of Community Activity Groups for Older Adults for Physical Activity, Health and Wellbeing," Ph.D. dissertation, Victoria, 2019.

[2] World Health Organisation, "World report on ageing and health," World Health Organisation, 2015.

[3] World Health Organisation, "The Role of Physical Activity in Healthy Ageing," World Health Organisation, 1998.

[4] L. N. Lee, M. J. Kim, and W. J. Hwang, "Potential of augmented reality and virtual reality technologies to promote wellbeing in older adults," *Applied Sciences*, vol. 9, no. 17, Sep. 2019, doi: 10.3390/app9173556.

[5] Nintendo, "Home - Nintendo," Nintendo. Available: https://www.nintendo.com/us/. Accessed: February 29, 2024.

[6] C. M. Yang, J. S. C. Hsieh, Y. C. Chen, S. Y. Yang, and H. C. K. Lin, "Effects of Kinect exergames on balance training among community older adults: A randomized controlled trial," *Medicine*, vol. 99, no. 28, pp. e21228, 2020, doi: 10.1097/MD.0000000000021228.

[7] M. C. Shih, R. Y. Wang, S. J. Cheng, and Y. R. Yang, "Effects of a balance-based exergaming intervention using the Kinect sensor on posture stability in individuals with Parkinson's disease: A single-blinded randomized controlled trial," *Journal of neuroengineering and rehabilitation*, vol. 13, no. 1, pp. 1-9, Aug. 2016, doi: 10.1186/s12984-016-0185-y.

[8] Y. Y. Liao, I. H. Chen, and R. Y. Wang, "Effects of Kinect-based exergaming on frailty status and physical performance in prefrail and frail elderly: A randomized controlled trial," *Scientific Reports*, vol. 9, no. 1, p. 9353, Dec. 2019, doi: 10.1038/s41598-019-45767-y.

[9] Rehaboo. "Rehaboo: Personalised Stroke Rehabilitation Program." Available: https://rehaboo.com/. Accessed: March 01, 2024.

[10] "i-Maginary". i-Maginary. Available: https://www.i-maginary.it/index-en.html?n=1#gallery. Accessed: March 01, 2024.

[11] "XRHealth Virtual Clinic: At-Home Virtual Reality Therapy." Available: https://www.xr.health/. Accessed: March 01, 2024.

[12] "Home - Eodyne." Available: https://www.eodyne.com/. Accessed: Mar 01, 2024. [Online].

[13] "Clynx." Available: https://www.clynx.io/index.html#Motiphy+. Accessed: May 10, 2023.

[14] S. Arlati *et al.*, "A social virtual reality-based application for the physical and cognitive training of the elderly at home," *Sensors*, vol. 19, no. 2, pp. 261, Jan. 2019, doi: 10.3390/s19020261.

[15] S. H. H. Shah, A. S. T. Karlsen, M. Solberg, and I. A. Hameed, "A social VR-based collaborative exergame for rehabilitation: codesign, development and user study," *Virtual Reality*, vol. 27, no. 4, pp. 3403–3420, Dec. 2023, doi: 10.1007/s10055-022-00721-8.

[16] L. Kruse, S. Karaosmanoglu, S. Rings, B. Ellinger, and F. Steinicke, "Enabling immersive exercise activities for older adults: A comparison of virtual reality exergames and traditional video exercises," *Societies*, vol. 11, no. 4, p. 134, Dec. 2021, doi: 10.3390/soc11040134.

[17] M. Qbilat *et al.*, "VR2CARE: An Age-Friendly Ecosystem for Physical Activity, Rehabilitation, and Social Interaction," in *2023 International Conference on Intelligent Metaverse Technologies & Applications (iMETA)*, IEEE, Sep. 2023, pp. 1-5, doi: 10.1109/iMETA59369.2023.10294571.

[18] "eHealth Smart Assisted Living – Altice Labs." Available: https://www.alticelabs.com/products/ehealth-smart-assisted-living/. Accessed: Feb. 08, 2024.

[19] F. Cassola, L. Morgado, F. de Carvalho, H. Paredes, B. Fonseca, and P. Martins, "Online-Gym: A 3D Virtual Gymnasium Using Kinect Interaction," *Procedia Technology*, vol. 13, pp. 130–138, 2014, doi: 10.1016/j.protcy.2014.02.017.

[20] "Cogvis Startseite - cogvis." Available: https://cogvis.ai/. Accessed: Feb. 08, 2024.

[21] M. Qbilat *et al.*, "Co-designing Interactive Technologies for Community Aware Physical Training and Rehabilitation in the VR2Care Digital Ecosystem," *Workgroup on Interactive Systems in Healthcare (WISH) at CHI 2023, ACM. Apr. 2023.*

[22] E. Y. Nakagawa, Marcelo Gonçalves, Milena Guessi, Lucas B. R. Oliveira, and Flavio Oquendo, "The state of the art and future perspectives in systems of systems software architectures," in *The First International Workshop on Software Engineering for Systems-of-Systems*, 2013, pp. 13–20.

[23] S. P. Welby, "Department of Defense: Systems Engineering," FY 2012 Annual Report." [Online]. Available: www.acq.osd.mil/se.

[24] J. Klein and V. V. Hans, "A systematic review of system-of-systems architecture research.," in *the 9th International ACM Sigsoft Conference on Quality of Software Architectures*, 2013, pp. 13–22.

[25] J. Nielsen, Usability engineering. Morgan Kaufmann, Amsterdam, 1994.

[26] "Accessibility Principles | Web Accessibility Initiative (WAI) | W3C." Available: https://www.w3.org/WAI/fundamentals/accessibility-principles/. Accessed: March 03, 2024.

[27] F. D. Davis, "Perceived usefulness, perceived ease of use and user acceptance of information technology," MIS Quarterly, pp. 319-340, 1989.

[28] V. Braun and V. Clarke, "Reflecting on reflexive thematic analysis," *Qualitative Research in Sport, Exercise and Health*, vol. 11, no. 4, pp. 589–597, 2019, doi: 10.1080/2159676X.2019.1628806.

LIME-Aided Automated Usability Issue Detection from User Reviews: Leveraging LLMs for Enhanced User Experience Analysis

Bassam Alsanousi
Computer Science and Engineering
University of North Texas
Denton, USA
email: bassamalsanousi@my.unt.edu

Stephanie Ludi
Computer Science and Engineering
University of North Texas
Denton, USA
email: stephanie.ludi@unt.edu

Hyunsook Do
Computer Science and Engineering
University of North Texas
Denton, USA
email: hyunsook.do@unt.edu

***Abstract*—Mobile applications have become essential in today's digital landscape so optimizing their User eXperiences (UX) is essential. Our study explored the application of Large Language Models (LLMs), including some Bidirectional Encoder Representations from Transformers (BERT) family architectures and advanced pre-trained models like Generative Pre-trained Transformer (GPT) by OpenAI GPT-3.5, GPT-4, and Llama 2 by Meta (zero and few-shot), for detecting usability issues in user reviews. The methodology encompassed data preprocessing, sentiment analysis, fine-tuning LLMs, and interpretability techniques, notably Local Interpretable Model-Agnostic Explanations (LIME). The findings indicated that the fine-tuned LLMs, particularly, Robustly Optimized BERT Approach (RoBERTa), XLNet, and DistilBERT were relatively successful in identifying the usability issues, achieving an accuracy rate of 96%. The study also assessed advanced pre-trained models Llama 2, GPT-3.5, and GPT-4, which generally fell short of the performance achieved by fine-tuned models. Finally, we also discovered the use of LIME that helped in understanding the decision-making processes of the fine-tuned models.**

Keywords-Human-Computer Interaction (HCI); Artificial Intelligence (AI); Usability; Large Language Models (LLMs); Local Interpretable Model-Agnostic Explanations (LIME).

I. INTRODUCTION

The rapid advancement of mobile technology over the past decade has revolutionized software creation and usage. According to [1], an average individual spends approximately 4.2 hours on apps daily. This interest has resulted in the expansion of mobile app stores such as Google Play and the Apple App Store. For instance, the Apple App Store has an impressive collection of close to two million apps [2]. These mobile app platforms allow users to provide feedback through ratings and reviews to provide invaluable insights into app updates and user preferences. Analyzing this feedback has become a significant and ongoing research area [3]. User reviews, while concise, offer insights into UX, bug reports, and suggested improvements [4].

Properly interpreting these user reviews for optimizing UX can assist developers in enhancing app quality [5] [6]. However, for popular apps that receive numerous reviews daily, manual analysis can become challenging [4]. A semantically-aware automated approach can effectively identify and categorize usability concerns while analyzing user reviews for usability issues. This approach can potentially reduce analysis time and provide developers with clear feedback to improve product usability. As we encountered in our previous research [7], handling numerous reviews was challenging without such a fully automated approach.

Recent advances in Natural Language Processing (NLP), specifically the development of LLMs, present promising opportunities for automated text analysis. These models have demonstrated remarkable proficiency in understanding and classifying textual data across various domains or tasks [8]–[11].

Chang et al. [8] provided an overview evaluation for LLMs in different domains and NLP tasks, including but not limited to sentiment analysis, text classification, question-answering, and summarization in medical, educational, social sciences, and other areas. [9] investigated the effectiveness of traditional app review classification models compared to LLMs models such as, BERT, XLNet, RoBERTa, and ALBERT. Their finding showed that these LLMs significantly outperformed conventional models, emphasizing the promise of domain-specific LLMs in app review classification. Another work [10] proposed an approach to classify multi-label user reviews into four Non-Functional Requirements (NFRs). Lastly, the authors in [11] introduced a BERT-based model that was fine-tuned to classify issues such as bugs, enhancements, or questions. Their proposed approach demonstrated noteworthy capabilities, particularly excelling in the classification of questions.

Despite their widespread application, the specific efficacy of LLMs in detecting usability issues in user reviews remains ripe for exploration. Our research focuses on this area, investigating the capability of LLMs to accurately identify usability concerns in user reviews. By doing this, we aim to illustrate how LLMs can be effectively used to improve the usability of mobile apps through enhancing UX analysis.

One of the most recognized and commonly referenced definitions of usability comes from ISO 9241, which states, "the extent to which specified users can use a system, product or service to achieve specified goals with effectiveness, efficiency, and satisfaction in a specified context of use " [12]. Our study aims to categorize user reviews into positive and negative through sentiment analysis. We employ sentiment analysis as a strategic tool to guide our focus toward reviews that are more likely to offer actionable insights for usability enhancements. This classification is an initial step in identifying the usability issues mentioned in the reviews. Previous research suggests that negative reviews are more informative about potential problems [4]. By concentrating on these negative reviews, we aim to pinpoint specific usability aspects related to effectiveness, efficiency, and satisfaction that need improvement.

Several studies [7] [13]–[15] have analyzed user reviews of mobile apps to pinpoint usability challenges and improve software quality through manual or semi-automated approaches. These efforts underscore the growing need for more semantically-aware techniques, aiding developers in refining the quality of these apps [15]. As technology continuously reshapes how users interact and engage, a vast volume of user reviews needs to be analyzed automatically and semantically-aware to improve the usability of mobile apps.

In this context, we contribute by developing an automatic, semantically-aware technique leveraging LLMs to analyze user reviews. This approach will provide developers with a more efficient method to improve the usability of mobile applications and enhance the overall UX With these objectives in mind, our research desires to answer the following questions (RQs):

RQ1: How effectively can LLMs semantically detect usability issues related to effectiveness, efficiency, and satisfaction from user reviews?

RQ2: Which fine-tuned LLMs have the most accurate results in classifying usability issues from user reviews?

RQ3: How do the classifications from pre-trained models via APIs, such as GPT-3.5, GPT-4, and Llama 2, compare to fine-tuned LLMs?

RQ4: How does applying explanation techniques such as LIME enhance understanding model predictions for detecting usability issues?

This paper is structured as follows: Section II looks at recent work related to this study. Section III details the methodology. Section IV highlights the results, and Section V discusses the findings. Section VI addresses potential factors affecting the study's validity. In closing, Section VII concludes the paper and proposes suggestions for future work.

II. Related Work

This section presents some background by examining past approaches to usability evaluation, the recent rise of leveraging LLMs for text classifications, and the importance of LIME in evaluating the model's performance. Earlier studies have introduced historical approaches and recent advances, and we seek to link them to contribute to the amelioration of usability evaluation.

A. Previous Usability Evaluation Approaches

Over the years, researchers have explored different ways to understand users' experiences with software. A notable advancement in this field is the work of El-Halees [13]. This author proposed an innovative approach using opinion-mining techniques to evaluate the subjective usability of software systems. Their experiments showcased the potential of such methods. Drawing inspiration from this, our research delves into the automated analysis of user reviews, especially using LLMs for richer insights.

In a related study, Alhejji et al. [14] looked at problems in mobile banking apps by analyzing user reviews. Their manual analysis sheds light on the strengths and weaknesses of usability for these applications. The focus on sentiment analysis evoked the power of user feedback in improving app usability. Their results indicate that the possibilities of automated techniques imply the coming of an age with an enormous amount of feedback that can be efficiently analyzed to obtain usability insights.

Another study by Alsanousi et al. [7] discussed usability problems in AI-enabled mobile learning apps by analyzing user reviews. Their semi-automated methodology of user review analysis using sentiment analysis and keyword-based approaches gave insights into AI-related challenges that impacted the usability attributes related to user satisfaction, effectiveness, and efficiency. The research strained us toward considering an automatic method to refine usability and UX analysis.

Finally, Diniz et al. [15] looked at how user reviews might indicate specific usability issues. They found that many reviews mentioned common usability problems. However, they also found challenges in manually sorting these reviews. Diniz et al.'s work highlighted the potential benefit of automated tools, especially those that can understand the context and sentiment of user comments.

B. Leveraging LLMs for Text Classification

In recent developments, expanding LLMs have started a new period in text classification, bringing many new opportunities. Hadi and Fard [9] explored the effectiveness of traditional app review classification models compared to LLM models such as BERT, XLNet, RoBERTa, and ALBERT. They developed LLMs by including more domain-specific app reviews in the pre-training process. Their results showed that these LLMs significantly outperformed conventional models, emphasizing the promise of domain-specific LLMs in app review classification without requiring extensively labeled datasets.

Building on the theme of using BERT-based models, Kaur and Kaur [10] introduced MNoR-BERT model. This model was specifically fine-tuned to classify NFRs derived from mobile app user reviews. Their goal was ambitious: to refine the categorization of reviews into distinct NFR types such as, dependability and performance, shifting away from previous keyword-driven and machine-learning methodologies. MNoR-BERT marked a significant evolution in parsing NFRs from user reviews, pushing the boundaries beyond traditional approaches.

Similarly, Siddiq and Santos [11] introduced a BERT-based model, fine-tuned to classify issues such as, bugs, enhancements, or questions. This model was optimized using a vast

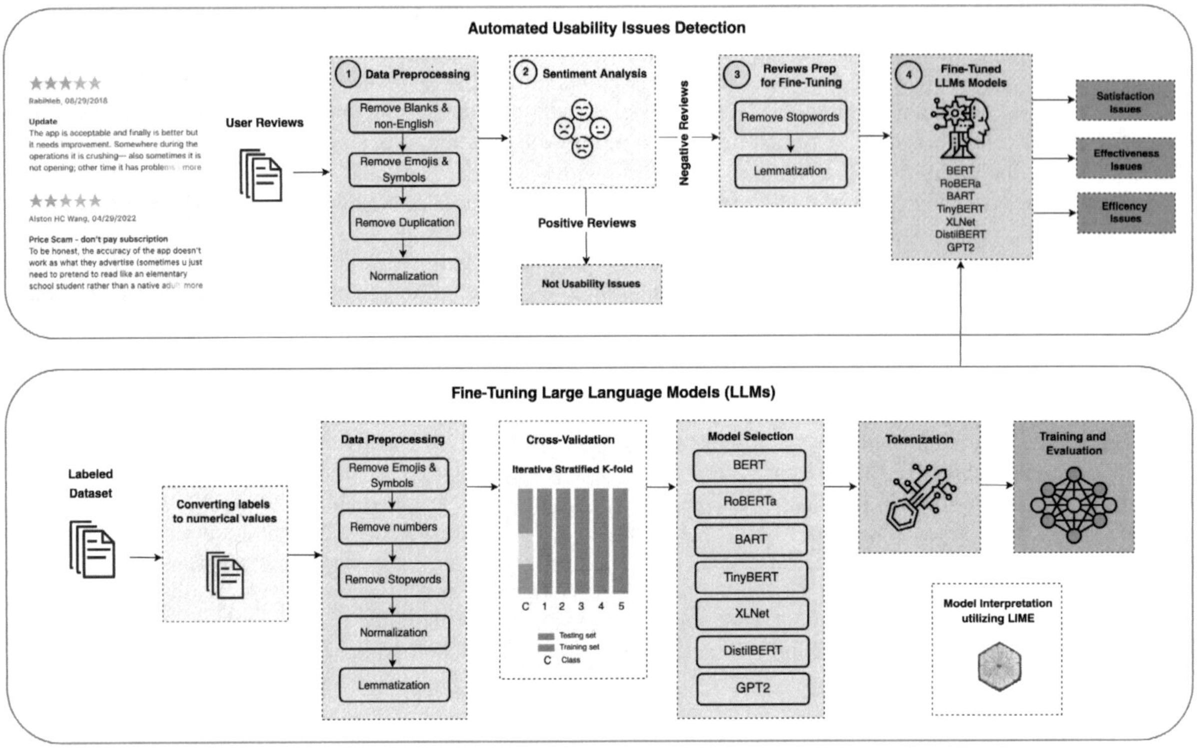

Figure 1. Proposed approach.

dataset from real GitHub projects, encompassing over 800,000 labeled issues. Remarkably, their model demonstrated noteworthy capabilities, particularly excelling in the classification of questions. Our research draws inspiration from their work as we leverage LLMs to explore the detection of usability issues, aiming to enhance the quality of mobile apps and UX.

Finally, BERT has also been used by Algamdi et al. [16] to classify mobile app reviews into five usability categories. They found that BERT was superior to Support Vector Machine (SVM) in multi-class classification. The specified usability factors achieved effective classification of app review issues. In contrast, our approach emphasizes different usability attributes and leverages various LLMs.

C. Model Understandability Through Utilizing LIME

Recent work by Rabby and Berka [17] utilized LIME for multi-class classification interpretation. Their study emphasized the importance of LIME in understanding complex models in classification, offering guidance for practitioners. Similarly, another work by Alharbi et al. [18] demonstrated the usefulness of LIME for evaluating fake news detection models. They established LIME's utility for providing localized interpretability to elucidate predictions and limitations of fake news detectors, improving model trustworthiness. In line with these studies, our research aims to investigate how the application of LIME aids in evaluating the performance of LLMs to detect usability issues from user reviews.

Our research builds on prior studies, acknowledging the importance of advanced technology in analyzing user reviews. These earlier studies mark significant milestones in the evolution of usability analysis and utilizing LLMs for various software engineering tasks. Our contribution lies in applying a semantically-aware sentiment analysis approach using LLMs to detect usability issues related to satisfaction, effectiveness, and efficiency to improve mobile app usability and UX. Additionally, we incorporate LIME to enhance model interpretability, ensuring transparency and trustworthiness in our usability evaluation process.

III. METHODOLOGY

In this study, we aim to develop an automated tool utilizing LLMs to detect usability issues from user reviews. As illustrated in Figure 1, our methodology consists of four key steps. This includes initially identifying usability issues in an automated manner, as indicated in the upper box of the figure. Further, the lower box in the figure illustrates the processes for fine-tuning various LLMs and applying LIME to detect and interpret multi-class usability issues.

A. Model Selection Rationale

In our study, we selected seven different LLMs, namely BERT [19], RoBERTa [20], Bidirectional and Auto-Regressive Transformer (BART) [21], the smallest open source pre-trained BERT model (TinyBERT) [22], XLNet [23], DistilBERT [24], and GPT2 [25], for detecting and classifying user reviews into satisfaction, effectiveness, or efficiency usability issues. Each model has unique specifications, as detailed in Table III [26].

BERT and RoBERTa are based on words in context to improve text understanding, but they are computationally heavy [19] [23]. RoBERTa is an improved version of BERT transformer by longer training and more data, which leads to better performance [20]. Similarly, BART combines BERT and GPT and may therefore be used to generate new text and understand its contents at the same time. BART is trained by corrupting the input text using various techniques. The main limitations of BART are that it needs careful tuning for certain applications [21].

TinyBERT is an attempt to make BERT's capabilities available on a system with limited processing power and energy resources [22]. Likewise, DistilBERT is a small, fast, and cheap training version of BERT. It is the distilled version of BERT, designed in a way that most of its performance has been kept, but it is lighter and faster [24].

GPT-2 is an autoregressive LLM developed by OpenAI to generate coherent and contextually relevant text one word at a time within a sentence [25]. Meanwhile, XLNet utilizes the best from BERT and autoregressive models such as GPT by providing better long-range dependencies capturing multiple benchmarks. XLNet is also computationally heavy [23].

We also selected advanced pre-trained models that can be accessed via Application Programming Interfaces (APIs), that is, GPT-3.5 and GPT-4 by OpenAI and Llama 2 (llama-2-13b-chat) by Meta. GPT-3.5 and GPT-4 have much larger training corpora and model sizes. They generate human-like text, understand context much better, and can even do some specific tasks without additional fine-tuning. Despite their power, GPT-3.5 and GPT-4 are not fully trustworthy in some tasks due to hallucinations that make errors [8] [27], and computationally costly specifically, GPT-4 [28]. On the other hand, Llama 2 by Meta differs mainly in universal robustness across various tasks, including complex reasoning tasks, and low computational costs [8]. However, Llama 2 might give unpredictable, harmful, or biased content because it was trained on publicly available online datasets [29].

B. Usability Factors

Our research aims to identify usability issues within user reviews, considering factors related to satisfaction, effectiveness, and efficiency, aligning with the ISO 9241-11 standard, as outlined in Table I [13]. To identify usability issues, we employed a methodology similar to previous studies [7] [13] [14], focusing on these quality factors found within user reviews. These factors formed the basis of our approach's categories. Table II presents examples of each class and corresponding user reviews marked as usability issues.

C. Data Collection

The proposed approach was trained and evaluated using a manually labeled dataset from mobile banking apps [14]. This dataset included **8,376** reviews—which were categorized as

TABLE I
USABILITY FACTORS.

Usability Factors	Definition
Effectiveness	Assesses the users' ability to achieve their goals accurately and completely. Focuses on the extent to which users can accomplish their objectives.
Efficiency	Evaluates the level of effectiveness relative to the resources expended. Helps determine how efficiently users can attain their goals.
Satisfaction	Measures users' overall comfort and attitudes toward the product's usage. Reflects how users find the product's usage enjoyable and satisfactory.

positive, negative, or neutral—from both iOS and Android platforms. However, our objective was to detect usability issues, so we selected only the negative reviews **3,609** highlighting usability issues related to satisfaction, effectiveness, and efficiency. To boost the model's proficiency in differentiating between positive and negative feedback, essential for accurately identifying reviews related to usability issues, we added a randomly selected subset of **232** positive and neutral reviews. Consequently, the final dataset, as shown in Figure 2, comprised a total of **3,841** reviews.

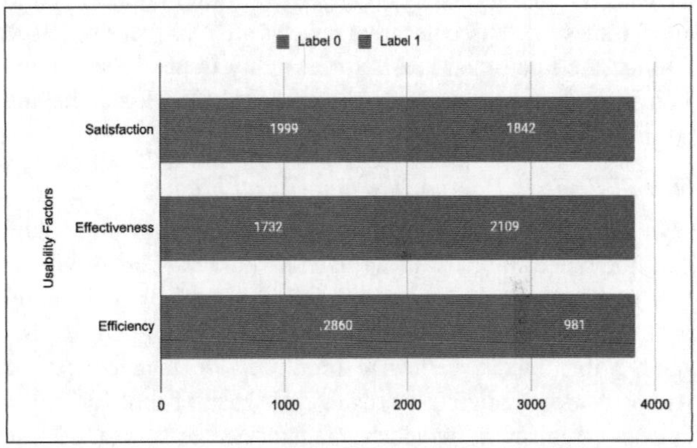

Figure 2. Dataset.

D. Automated Usability Issues Detection

This subsection details the four steps employed in our approach to automatically detect usability issues from user reviews, as illustrated in the upper box of Figure 1. Each step is designed to progressively analyze and extract relevant information from the reviews, ultimately identifying specific usability concerns.

Step 1: *Data preprocessing*

We employed the Natural Language Toolkit (NLTK) [30], a set of libraries for NLP, to enhance the accuracy of our approach by filtering out irrelevant and noisy data. The initial step in preparing our data involved the removal of empty reviews, which did not have enough significant information. Subsequently, we excluded non-English reviews to maintain a focus on a single language. We then eliminated emojis

TABLE II
EXAMPLES OF MULTI-CLASS CLASSIFICATION AND CORRESPONDING USER REVIEWS AS USABILITY ISSUES.

Multi Classes	User Reviews Examples
Effectiveness, Efficiency, and Satisfaction	"The new update is bad and the app is slow and sometimes gives errors"
Satisfaction	"The worst banking app in the world."
Efficiency	"The application is slow and takes a long time to open and navigation between menus is slow"
Effectiveness	"The application needs new maintenance and a new update. The amount does not appear in the account."
Satisfaction and Effectiveness	"The app keeps crashing. It's very frustrating."

and symbols such as, '([/.() [— @],]', which can muddle the data. Additionally, we removed numbers, as they often do not contribute meaningfully to our text analysis. Another crucial step was the removal of duplicate entries to ensure the uniqueness and relevance of our data. Finally, we normalized the text, converting everything to a uniform style [31].

Step 2: *Sentiment Analysis*

In this phase, we utilized a fine-tuned DistilBERT model for sentiment analysis. Our choice of this model was influenced by its accuracy of 91.3%, as illustrated in Hugging Face [32]. This model categorizes textual data as positive or negative, assigning a confidence score ranging from 0 to 1 [33]. Our analysis focused primarily on negative reviews often linked to apps' issues [4]. These negative reviews were further processed through the fine-tuned LLMs for usability issue classification. Conversely, positive reviews were generally labeled as having no usability issues.

Step 3: *Reviews Prep for the Fine-Tuned Model*

In this step, we again prepared the reviews to align with the fine-tuned models using NLTK library. This involved two fundamental processes: removing stopwords and applying lemmatization. Stopwords commonly used, such as "is," "and," "the," and "are," were removed. We then performed lemmatization, reducing words to their base or root form. For example, "crashing" would be transformed to "crash." These steps helped enhancing the training approach used for the fine-tuned models [34].

Step 4: *Using the Best Fine-tuned LLMs*

During this phase, we used the best fine-tuned model among the seven selected LLMs, namely BERT, RoBERTa, BART, TinyBERT , XLNet, DistilBERT, and GPT2, in detecting and classifying usability issues into satisfaction, effectiveness or efficiency.

E. Fine-tuning LLMs

The lower box in Figure 1 in the proposed approach represents the methods for fine-tuning the seven picked LLMs to detect and classify usability issues from user reviews. First of all, all experiments were executed on an NVIDIA Tesla T4 GPU with 16GB of GDDR6 memory and FP32 CUDA cores. We then configured the batch size to 16 for this fine-tuning process and adjusted Adam's optimizer learning rate to 2e-5, conducting the training over four epochs. This process begins with data preparation, which involves loading user reviews and their associated labels (satisfaction, effectiveness, efficiency) from a CSV file. Then, we prepared our dataset by converting labels into numerical values. This step is essential for managing the encoded data effectively, particularly given the multi-labeled nature of our dataset. Following this, we utilized NLTK and implemented several steps to refine our data to achieve higher precision in subsequent stages. Our first step in this process was the removal of emojis and symbols. We then removed numbers and discarded stopwords, as these elements often introduce noise and do not add significant information [35]. Eventually, we normalized the text, converting all to the same style.

Thereafter, we used a cross-validation technique employing Iterative Stratification, which was especially appropriate for our unbalanced multilabel dataset to guarantee a balanced distribution of labels across training and test sets and reduce the risk of overfitting [36]. This technique provided a strong foundation for model validation and was more thorough than splitting a single dataset [9]. In particular, we carried out the k-fold iterative stratification cross-validation on the dataset five times. After this, we chose one of the seven models, and then we applied the suitable tokenization based on the selected model. Then, we started training and evaluating the chosen model. Next, the same thing has been done for all seven selected models. The training time and validation loss were computed, where every fold involved a specific training and evaluation cycle. We carefully monitored these important performance metrics for each model.

F. Using pre-trained models such as GPT-3.5, GPT-4 and Llama 2

In our comparative analysis, we additionally explored the performance of pre-trained models accessed via APIs using Python scripts. These models include GPT-3.5 and GPT-4 by OpenAI and Llama-2 by Meta (Llama-2-13b-chat few-shot and zero-shot). This was undertaken to assess how these models, without fine-tuning, fare against the fine-tuned LLMs in the previous steps. We utilized the same dataset and evaluation technique for this phase. Each pre-trained model was then applied to perform prediction tasks on this dataset.

G. Evaluation metrics

We employed several crucial metrics to evaluate the proposed approach's effectiveness: overall accuracy, precision,

TABLE III
DETAILS ABOUT THE FINE-TUNED LLMS EMPLOYED IN OUR RESEARCH

Model	Architecture	Parameters	Layers
BERT	bert-base-cased	110M	12
RoBERTa	roberta-base	125M	12
BART	bart-base	140M	6
TinyBERT	General 4L 312D	14M	4
XLNet	xlnet-base-cased	110M	12
DistilBERT	distilbert-base-cased	65M	6
GPT2	gpt2	117M	12

recall, and the F1-score. The concept of 'overall accuracy' pertains to the percentage of cases that have been correctly identified. Precision assesses the percentage of relevant cases determined among those retrieved, whereas Recall measures the percentage of relevant cases accurately retrieved from the entire pool of relevant cases.

For classification evaluations, accuracy evaluates the proportion of correct predictions (true positives and negatives) out of all predictions, as shown in **(1)**. Precision is determined by the percentage of accurately identified instances in a specific category out of all instances categorized into that category, as per **(2)**. Recall, in contrast, is calculated by the proportion of accurately identified instances in a specific category compared to the total number of actual instances in that category, as indicated in **(3)**. 'TP' (True Positive) in these formulas stands for the count of instances correctly classified into a particular category, 'FP' (False Positive) represents the count of cases wrongly classified into that category (thus TP + FP is the total number classified into that category), and 'FN' (False Negative) denotes the count of instances not classified into that category (therefore TP + FN is the total number of cases actually belonging to that category). The F1-score is an evaluative measure that integrates precision and recall by applying a harmonic mean, as outlined in **(4)**.

The formula to compute the **Accuracy** is:

$$\text{Accuracy} = \frac{\text{TP}+\text{TN}}{\text{TP}+\text{TN}+\text{FP}+\text{FN}} \quad (1)$$

The formula to compute the **Precision** is:

$$\text{Precision} = \frac{\text{TP}}{\text{TP}+\text{FP}} \quad (2)$$

The formula to compute the **Recall** is:

$$\text{Recall} = \frac{\text{TP}}{\text{TP}+\text{FN}} \quad (3)$$

The formula to compute the **F1-score** is:

$$F1 = 2 \cdot \frac{P \cdot R}{P+R} \quad (4)$$

H. LIME Interpretation

Within our methodology, we integrated LIME to interpret the predictions made by LLMs to detect usability issues related to satisfaction, effectiveness, and efficiency and evaluate their performance. LIME allowed us to generate localized explanations for the predictions, shedding light on how LLMs arrived at their decisions.

IV. RESULTS

In this results section, we answer four research questions focused on the capabilities of LLMs in detecting usability issues from user reviews. LLMs were assessed on their classification of usability problems related to satisfaction, effectiveness, and efficiency, considering various performance measures concerning their ability in semantic detection (RQ1), as well as identifying the most accurate models (RQ2). Next, we examined the effectiveness of using pre-trained models available via APIs such as, GPT-3.5 and GPT-4 and llama-2-13b-chat few-shot and zero-shot in contrast to fine-tuned LLMs (RQ3). Lastly, we focus on the use of LIME for the interpretation of model predictions (RQ4).

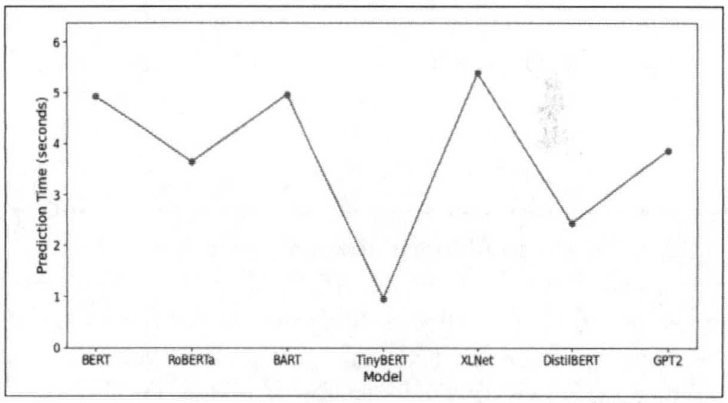

Figure 3. Prediction times of each model.

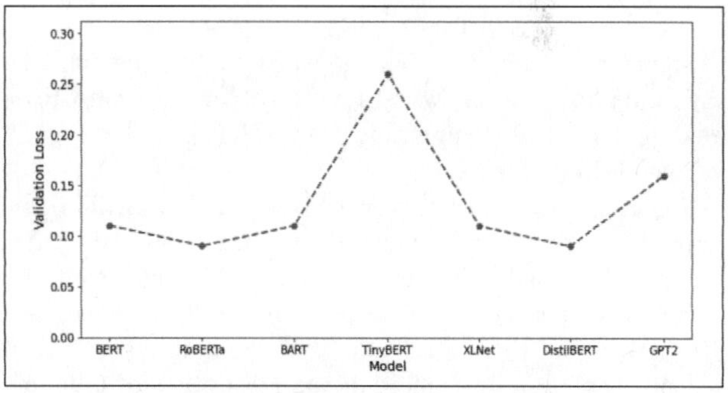

Figure 4. Validation loss of each model.

RQ1: How effectively can LLMs semantically detect usability issues related to effectiveness, efficiency, and satisfaction from user reviews?

LLMs have proven highly effective in semantically detecting usability issues. The performance data, including high accuracy as illustrated in Table IV, indicate that models such as RoBERTa, XLNet, and DistilBERT can accurately discern and categorize nuances in user reviews about effectiveness, efficiency, and satisfaction. The semantic detection is further validated by the LIME results, as shown in Figures 5,6, and 7

TABLE IV
PERFORMANCE RESULTS OF EACH LLM MODEL.

Model	Accuracy	Precision	Recall	F1-score	Training Time (s)
BERT	0.95	0.96	0.94	0.95	1645
RoBERTa	**0.96**	0.96	0.97	0.96	1336
BART	0.95	0.94	0.95	0.95	1619
TinyBERT	0.90	0.89	0.90	0.89	**173**
XLNet	**0.96**	0.95	0.96	0.95	1616
DistilBERT	**0.96**	0.96	0.96	0.96	**806**
GPT2	0.93	0.92	0.93	0.92	1526
Llama 2 - Zero-shot	0.41	0.86	0.71	0.74	-
Llama 2 - Few-shot	0.73	0.88	0.97	0.90	-
GPT-3.5	0.64	0.89	0.89	0.86	-
GPT-4	0.74	0.88	0.97	0.91	-

LIME plots for predicting classes, indicating that the models focused on key terms strongly associated with the users' expressions of usability concerns.

Summary for RQ1: RoBERTa, XLNet, and DistilBERT effectively identified usability issues in user reviews, as shown by their high accuracy and LIME analysis focusing on relevant key terms.

RQ2: Which LLMs have the most accurate results?

Our comprehensive evaluation of LLMs in detecting usability issues from user reviews involved an assessment based on accuracy, precision, recall, F1-score, validation loss, and training time, with detailed results in Table IV. Figure 3 highlights the prediction times of each model, showing notable variation. TinyBERT was the most efficient model, with a prediction time of 0.59 seconds, while XLNet was the least efficient at 5.38 seconds.

Figure 4 presents the validation loss of each model. The validation loss was the lowest for RoBERTa and DistilBERT, totaling 0.09. By comparison, TinyBERT had the highest validation loss of 0.26.

Regarding overall performance, BERT and RoBERTa performed better with an accuracy of 0.95 and 0.96 and an F1-score of 0.95 and 0.96, respectively. BERT's precision and recall were 0.96 and 0.94, respectively, after 1645 seconds of training. RoBERTa reached a lower training time of 1336 seconds after attaining precision and recall rates of 0.96 and 0.97 respectively.

BART and XLNet were also remarkable: 0.95 and 0.96 in accuracy. BART had 0.94 and 0.95 in precision and recall after 1619 seconds of training with an F1 score of 0.95. Similarly, after 1616 seconds of training, XLNet had precision and recall of 0.95 and 0.96 resulting in an F1 score 0.95.

Using the TinyBert architecture, the model's performance showed an accuracy of 0.90, with precision and recall of 0.89 and 0.90, resulting in an F1 score of 0.89 in just 173 seconds of training. GPT2, with training for 1526 seconds, achieved an accuracy of 0.93 and an F1 of 0.92, backed by precision and recall of 0.92 and 0.93.

Meanwhile, DistilBERT balanced high performance and reasonable training time, with an accuracy of 0.96, precision and recall of 0.96, and an F1-score of 0.96, all within 806 seconds of training.

Summary for RQ2: In our LLMs assessment for usability issue detection, RoBERTa, XLNet, and DistilBERT topped accuracy at 0.96 for each, with DistilBERT also excelling in training efficiency. TinyBERT, less accurate at 0.90, had the shortest prediction time of 0.59 seconds, highlighting its operational efficiency, whereas XLNet showed the longest prediction time of 5.38 seconds.

RQ3: How do the classifications from pre-trained models via APIs such as GPT-3.5, GPT-4, and Llama 2, compare to fine-tuned LLMs?

The analysis of advanced pre-trained models accessed via APIs such as Llama 2 and GPT versions, revealed mixed results. Llama 2, in a zero-shot, achieved modest results, notching a scoring accuracy of 0.41, paired with precision and recall scores of 0.86 and 0.71, culminating in an overall F1-score of 0.74. Meanwhile, Llama 2 in few shot demonstrated enhanced metrics, securing an accuracy score of 0.73 and precision and recall scores of 0.88 and 0.97, which gave rise to an F1-score of 0.90.

GPT-3.5 demonstrated moderate metrics, recording an accuracy score of 0.64 and matching precision and recall scores of 0.89, ultimately resulting in an F1-score of 0.86. Progressing further, GPT-4 exceeded anticipated benchmarks with an accuracy score of 0.74 and a precision score of 0.88 while securing an impressive recall of 0.97, collectively contributing to a final F1-score of 0.91.

While advanced pre-trained models like GPT-4 and Llama 2 few-shot demonstrated impressive abilities, it is evident that fine-tuned LLMs such as RoBERTa, XLNet, and DistilBERT still maintain an edge in performance. Their effectiveness in specific applications underscores their continued superiority over general-purpose, advanced pre-trained models.

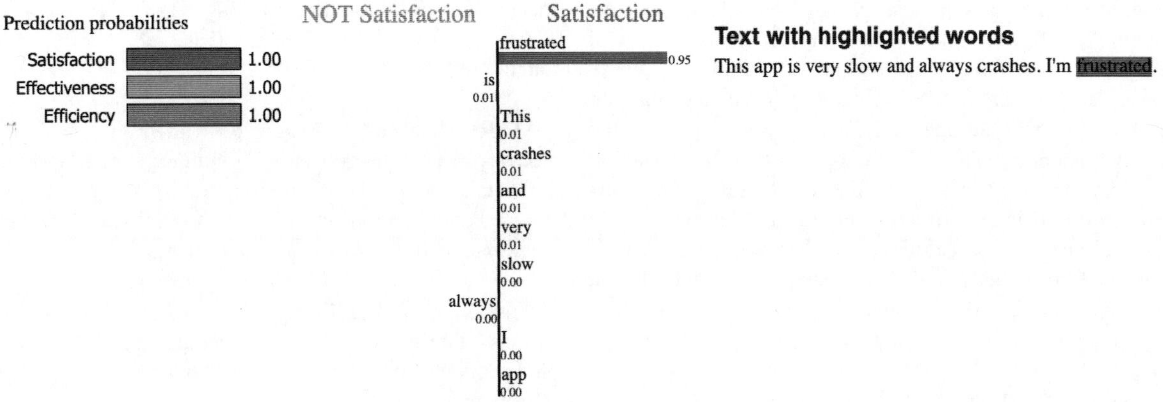

Figure 5. LIME plot for predicting satisfaction class.

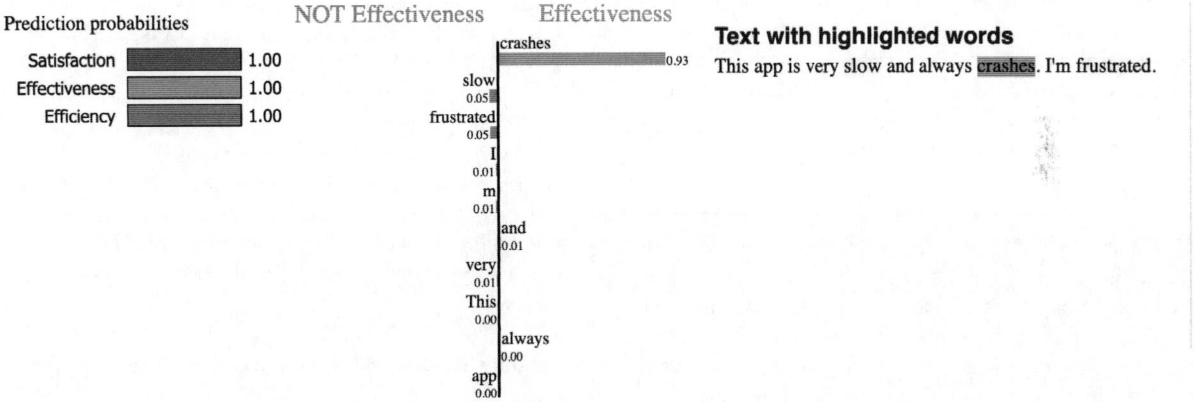

Figure 6. LIME plot for predicting effectiveness class.

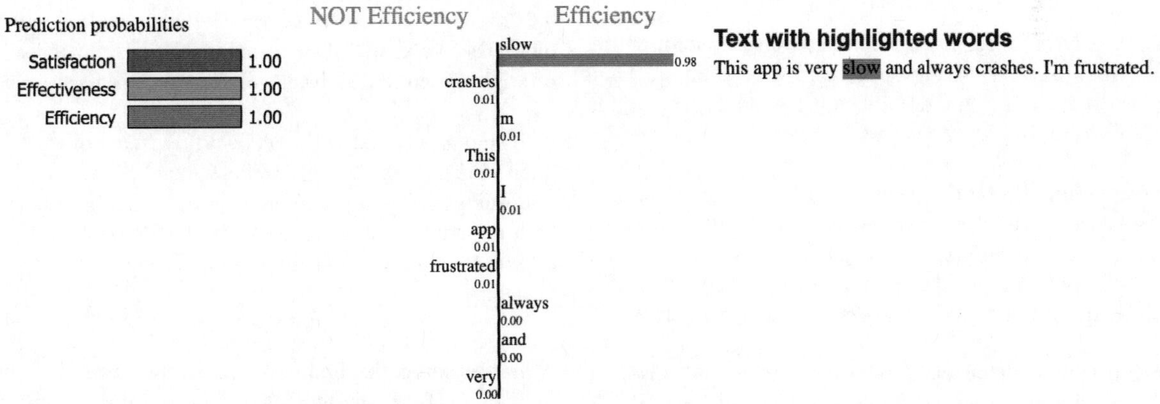

Figure 7. LIME plot for predicting efficiency class.

Summary for RQ3: Advanced pre-trained models accessed via APIs such as Llama 2 and GPT versions, showed mixed results compared to fine-tuned LLMs. Llama 2 had modest accuracy (0.41), GPT-3.5 improved (0.64 accuracy), and GPT-4 further excelled (0.74 accuracy). However, fine-tuned LLMs like RoBERTa, XLNet and DistilBERT still outperformed

RQ4: How does applying explanation techniques such as LIME enhance understanding model predictions for detecting usability issues?

The LIME interpretations have offered significant insights into the decision-making mechanisms of our models, as shown in Figures 5,6, and 7, which present the LIME plot for predicting satisfaction, effectiveness, and efficiency classes in a user review example "This app is very slow and always crashes. I'm frustrated." LIME plots were generated for each class, visually representing how different features influence the predictive outcomes. The bar's length indicated the prediction probability of each class, with associated class color, blue satisfaction, orange effectiveness and green efficiency.

For instance, the satisfaction, as illustrated in Figure 5, the word "frustrated" in the user review example has a significant impact, with the model associating it with a lack of satisfaction. In the effectiveness category, as shown in Figure 6, the term "crashes" in orange color is a strong predictor for detecting effectiveness issues. The LIME plot explicated that when users mention crashes, it highly indicated an effectiveness concern. Similarly, for efficiency in Figure 7, the words "slow" in green color is also significant feature for efficiency issues. The uniformity of prediction probabilities across all classes, with scores of 1.00, underlined the model's confidence in its predictions. The high prediction probabilities, coupled with the model's emphasis on specific keywords, corroborated the relevance of these terms in the context of usability issues.

Summary for RQ4: LIME effectively clarified model predictions for usability issues, highlighting how specific words like "frustrated," "crashes," and "slow" impact predictions in areas of satisfaction, effectiveness, and efficiency. High prediction probabilities emphasized the model's confidence and the relevance of these terms in usability analysis.

V. RESULTS DISCUSSION

This study revealed that LLMs effectively extract usability issues from user reviews. These findings were interpreted and inferred as follows in the discussion below. Our investigation yielded several important insights:

Efficacy in Semantic Analysis: LLMs showed a high performance in the semantic analysis of user reviews. It succeeded in identifying language features that indicate usability problems, thus demonstrating the potential of LLMs to automate and perfect the process of user review analysis.

Accuracy of Models: Among the above models, our findings showed that RoBERTa XLNet and DistilBERT are the best models for detecting usability problems in user reviews regarding their accuracy. This ability plays a significant role in product development and the customer satisfaction process, as an accurate understanding of the UX can result in significant improvements in mobile app analysis.

Enhancement of Model Interpretability: By introducing LIME to the models, the decision-making process has been improved to high levels of interpretability. It explained why specific reviews are flagged as highlighting usability issues, which is a true find for analysis that seeks clarity on model functioning and results.

Model Training Efficiency: DistilBERT and TinyBER models differed significantly in training time, which made them stand out due to the high speed. This implied that there is a tactical situation when frequent retraining is required or where speed of deployment is important.

Predictive Reliability: Validation loss metrics among various fine-tuned models demonstrated a satisfactory predictive ability, with lower loss scores implying greater reliability.

Performance of Advanced Pre-trained Models: The research also measured the performance of advanced pre-trained models accessible through APIs, including Llama 2, GPT-3.5, and GPT-4. Although Llama 2 zero shot and GPT-3.5 had lower accuracy, they continuously exhibited high precision, recall and F1-score. The GPT-4 and Llama 2 few shot variants showed promising performance with increased accuracy and F1 scores. These models could be useful for implementations in situations that do not require further fine-tuning. However, they may not be suitable for some tasks due to expensive computational costs and potential output errors.

Some Real-world Applications of These Models: Fine-tuned LLMs such as RoBERTa, XLNet, and DistilBERT can provide a more profound analysis of user feedback than commercial platforms, such as Appfigures [37], AppFollow [38], or Appbot [39], which might not offer AI capabilities. Additionally, fine-tuned LLMs are open source and many times less expensive than commercial tools, so these LLMs offer significant cost advantages for developers.

In summary, LLMs offer a powerful arsenal of methods for improving the UX through intelligent analysis of user reviews. The study highlights the broad scope of the capacities of both fine-tuned and advanced pre-trained models that provide different abilities for usability issue detection.

VI. THREATS TO VALIDITY

In presenting the findings of our study, we acknowledge several threats to validity that may influence the interpretation and generalization of our results:

Internal Validity:

Model Overfitting: While efforts were made to prevent overfitting through validation techniques, the possibility that models may have overfitted to particularities in the training data cannot be entirely ruled out. *Parameter Tuning:* The hyperparameters chosen for each LLM were based on a combination of best practices and iterative testing, but different configurations may yield varied results.

External Validity:

Dataset Specificity: The dataset used was specific to user reviews of mobile banking apps. The findings may not directly apply to other domains or types of textual data. *Language and Cultural Bias:* The study focused on English-language reviews. The models' performance in other languages or cultural contexts remains untested.

VII. Conclusion

Our study highlights the effectiveness of fine-tuned LLMs like BERT, RoBERTa, BART, TinyBERT, XLNet, and DistilBERT as well as advanced pre-trained models, namely, GPT-3.5 and GPT-4 by OpenAI and Llama 2 by Meta in detecting and classifying usability issues from user reviews. RoBERTa, XLNet, and DistilBERT outperformed other models based on the accuracy in evaluating user reviews, advanced pre-trained models also demonstrated promise, despite the significant divergence in accuracy levels. The use of interpretability methods, particularly LIME, played a significant role in improving the transparency and trustworthiness of fine-tuned models. In the next stage, we aim to apply our approach in a specific domain to deeply investigate usability and UX of mobile apps.

References

[1] "App annie," https://www.data.ai, retrieved: April, 2024.

[2] "Apple store," https://www.apple.com/app-store/, retrieved: April, 2024.

[3] M. Tushev, F. Ebrahimi, and A. Mahmoud, "Domain-specific analysis of mobile app reviews using keyword-assisted topic models," in *Proceedings of the 44th International Conference on Software Engineering*, 2022, pp. 762–773.

[4] Y. Wang *et al.*, "Where is your app frustrating users?" in *Proceedings of the 44th International Conference on Software Engineering*, 2022, pp. 2427–2439.

[5] N. Chen, J. Lin, S. C. Hoi, X. Xiao, and B. Zhang, "Ar-miner: mining informative reviews for developers from mobile app marketplace," in *Proceedings of the 36th international conference on software engineering*, 2014, pp. 767–778.

[6] J. Sauro and P. Zarolia, "Supr-qm: a questionnaire to measure the mobile app user experience," *Journal of Usability Studies*, vol. 13, no. 1, pp. 17–37, 2017.

[7] B. Alsanousi, A. S. Albesher, H. Do, and S. Ludi, "Investigating the user experience and evaluating usability issues in ai-enabled learning mobile apps: An analysis of user reviews," *International Journal of Advanced Computer Science and Applications*, vol. 14, no. 6, 2023.

[8] Y. Chang *et al.*, "A survey on evaluation of large language models," *ACM Transactions on Intelligent Systems and Technology*, vol. 15, no. 3, pp. 1–45, 2024.

[9] M. A. Hadi and F. H. Fard, "Evaluating pre-trained models for user feedback analysis in software engineering: A study on classification of app-reviews," *Empirical Software Engineering*, vol. 28, no. 4, p. 88, 2023.

[10] K. Kaur and P. Kaur, "Mnor-bert: multi-label classification of non-functional requirements using bert," *Neural Computing and Applications*, pp. 1–23, 2023.

[11] M. L. Siddiq and J. C. Santos, "Bert-based github issue report classification," in *Proceedings of the 1st International Workshop on Natural Language-based Software Engineering*, 2022, pp. 33–36.

[12] C. Rusu, V. Rusu, S. Roncagliolo, and C. González, "Usability and user experience: What should we care about?" *International Journal of Information Technologies and Systems Approach (IJITSA)*, vol. 8, no. 2, pp. 1–12, 2015.

[13] A. M. El-Halees, "Software usability evaluation using opinion mining." *J. Softw.*, vol. 9, no. 2, pp. 343–349, 2014.

[14] S. Alhejji, A. Albesher, H. Wahsheh, and A. Albarrak, "Evaluating and comparing the usability of mobile banking applications in saudi arabia," *Information*, vol. 13, no. 12, p. 559, 2022.

[15] L. d. N. Diniz, J. C. de Souza Filho, and R. M. Carvalho, "Can user reviews indicate usability heuristic issues?" in *CHI Conference on Human Factors in Computing Systems Extended Abstracts*, 2022, pp. 1–6.

[16] S. Algamdi, A. Albanyan, and S. Ludi, "Investigating the usability issues in mobile applications reviews using a deep learning model," in *2023 IEEE 13th Annual Computing and Communication Workshop and Conference (CCWC)*, 2023, pp. 0108–0113.

[17] G. Rabby and P. Berka, "Multi-class classification of covid-19 documents using machine learning algorithms," *Journal of Intelligent Information Systems*, vol. 60, no. 2, pp. 571–591, 2023.

[18] R. Alharbi, M. N. Vu, and M. T. Thai, "Evaluating fake news detection models from explainable machine learning perspectives," in *ICC 2021-IEEE International Conference on Communications*. IEEE, 2021, pp. 1–6.

[19] J. Devlin, M.-W. Chang, K. Lee, and K. Toutanova, "Bert: Pre-training of deep bidirectional transformers for language understanding," *arXiv preprint arXiv:1810.04805*, 2018.

[20] Y. Liu *et al.*, "Roberta: A robustly optimized bert pretraining approach," *arXiv preprint arXiv:1907.11692*, 2019.

[21] M. Lewis *et al.*, "Bart: Denoising sequence-to-sequence pre-training for natural language generation, translation, and comprehension," *arXiv preprint arXiv:1910.13461*, 2019.

[22] X. Jiao *et al.*, "Tinybert: Distilling bert for natural language understanding," *arXiv preprint arXiv:1909.10351*, 2019.

[23] Z. Yang *et al.*, "Xlnet: Generalized autoregressive pretraining for language understanding," *Advances in neural information processing systems*, vol. 32, 2019.

[24] V. Sanh, L. Debut, J. Chaumond, and T. Wolf, "Distilbert, a distilled version of bert: Smaller, faster, cheaper and lighter. arxiv 2019," *arXiv preprint arXiv:1910.01108*, 2019.

[25] OpenAI Community, "GPT2," https://huggingface.co/openai-community/gpt2, retrieved: April, 2024.

[26] Hugging Face, "Transformers Documentation (v4.39.3)," https://huggingface.co/docs/transformers/v4.39.3/en/index, retrieved: April, 2024.

[27] OpenAI, "GPT-4," https://openai.com/research/gpt-4, retrieved: April, 2024.

[28] S. Bubeck *et al.*, "Sparks of artificial general intelligence: Early experiments with gpt-4. arxiv," *arXiv preprint arXiv:2303.12712*, 2023.

[29] H. Touvron *et al.*, "Llama 2: Open foundation and fine-tuned chat models," *arXiv preprint arXiv:2307.09288*, 2023.

[30] "Nltk: Natural language toolkit," https://www.nltk.org/, retrieved: April, 2024.

[31] C. P. Chai, "Comparison of text preprocessing methods," *Natural Language Engineering*, vol. 29, no. 3, pp. 509–553, 2023.

[32] "Distilbert base uncased finetuned sst-2 english," https://huggingface.co/distilbert-base-uncased-finetuned-sst-2-english, retrieved: April, 2024.

[33] E. Chen, "Which factors predict the chat experience of a natural language generation dialogue service?" in *Extended Abstracts of the 2023 CHI Conference on Human Factors in Computing Systems*, 2023, pp. 1–6.

[34] U. Naseem, I. Razzak, and P. W. Eklund, "A survey of pre-processing techniques to improve short-text quality: a case study on hate speech detection on twitter," *Multimedia Tools and Applications*, vol. 80, pp. 35 239–35 266, 2021.

[35] H. Kour and M. K. Gupta, "An hybrid deep learning approach for depression prediction from user tweets using feature-rich cnn and bi-directional lstm," *Multimedia Tools and Applications*, vol. 81, no. 17, pp. 23 649–23 685, 2022.

[36] K. Sechidis, G. Tsoumakas, and I. Vlahavas, "On the stratification of multi-label data," in *Machine Learning and Knowledge Discovery in Databases: European Conference, ECML PKDD 2011, Athens, Greece, September 5-9, 2011, Proceedings, Part III 22*. Springer, 2011, pp. 145–158.

[37] Appfigures, "Overview of App Analytics and Market Data," https://appfigures.com/reports/overview, 2024, retrieved: April, 2024.

[38] AppFollow, "AppFollow: App Monitoring and Optimization," https://appfollow.io, retrieved: April, 2024.

[39] Appbot, "Appbot: Automated App Reviews and Ratings Analysis," https://appbot.co, retrieved: April, 2024.

Assessment of Differences in Human Depth Understanding in Cube Displays Using Light-Field Displays

Raymond Swannack, Oky Dicky Ardiansyah Prima
Graduate School of Software and Information Science
Iwate Prefectural University
152-52 Takizawa, Iwate, Japan
e-mail: g231s501@s.iwate-pu.ac.jp, prima@iwate-pu.ac.jp

Abstract—**Three-dimensional (3D) digital content continues to be a favored field of study both for academics, as well as businesses around the world. Virtual and augmented realities have received much consideration. The Light-Field Display (LFD), which allows users to view stereoscopic images from multiple viewpoints at the same time, provides a novel 3D experience. LFDs are complicated to set up, but this display has been made available for personal use. This study aims to evaluate the differences in task accomplishment between stereo versus motion-parallax cues for users performing 3D interactions on a multi-screen display. Our task scenario involves user tests for 3D depth understanding and questionnaires about the experience during the test. For each task, 3D contents are presented using stereo and motion parallax cues, using four LFD "Lume Pad" developed by Leia Inc. Results showed that depth understanding is aided by stereo cues. The Questionnaire showed that depth understanding was aided by the stereo cues from the LFD. Future work will include tests designed to further understand how beneficial stereoscopic cues are in a 3D display.**

Keywords-3D; Light-Field Display; Fish Tank VR; 3D human perception; stereoscopic vision.

I. INTRODUCTION

The human ability to view and understand three dimensions allows us to interact with the world in detail. Translating this to the digital field has not been an easy task. A Two-Dimensional (2D) screen is flat and as such does not have true depth, so the human eye does not interact with objects on a screen the same as it would with an object in the real world [1]. Steps have been taken to advance the perceived depth shown on these screens.

In recent years, the popularity of Virtual Reality (VR) and Augmented Reality (AR) headsets has greatly increased. Meta's Oculus and Apple's Apple Vision Pro have allowed people to immerse themselves in digital 3D worlds in ways that were only dreams a decade ago and the productivity advancements of such devices are only now being realized. AR specifically is being studied heavily for this purpose.

Advancements are also being made with hand-held displays, such as smartphones and tablets. While most of these advancements are being made with applications, some devices are being designed to be dedicated AR displays. One such device is an LFD. LFDs use curved lenses, known as lenticular lenses, to bend the light coming from the screen so that each of the user's eyes is shown a different image. This is similar to how a head-mounted display functions, but without the need to wear a headset. Another benefit is that multiple users can use a singular device to experience the stereoscopic visual cues.

Another form of virtual reality display is known as a Fish Tank VR display. These displays are 2D screens put together to form a 3D shape. The displays use their shape to introduce real depth to enhance the illusion of 3D depth shown on the 2D screens. While cubes and spheres are common, any shape could in theory be constructed using displays.

This study aims to measure a user's understanding of perceived depth with the use of a 3D display. Proposing Dice, a Fish Tank VR constructed with LFDs. Four LFDs are positioned to create the sides of the cube with an open top and bottom. By using LFDs, stereoscopic depth cues can be added to a cube display and their contribution to perceived depth can be measured.

The rest of the paper is structured as follows. In Section II, we present the details of the LFD hardware used in the experiment. Section III details the experiment methodology, such as the design concept, as well as the software and hardware used. The results of the experiment and the questionnaire are given in Section IV. Finally, we conclude our work in Section V, with our conclusion, discussion, and future work.

II. RELATED WORK

Kato and Prima [1] studied gaze characteristics in Mixed-Reality Environments. In this study, the researchers observed the gaze position of subjects when looking at an approaching target in a virtual space. Their research was conducted in two different types of rooms, one that had depth cues and one without. They showed that these rooms did not cause a significant difference in gaze accuracy. In their research, a head-mounted display was used to create stereoscopy. Dice does not use a head-mounted display but by creating stereoscopy with an LFD, similar results can hopefully be achieved.

One of the first cube displays is known as pCubee [2]. This display was constructed from five displays, one for each side of the cube and one to form the top of the display. It uses a gyroscope to measure users manipulating the display as well as head tracking to inform the display what orientation

Figure 1. Dice.

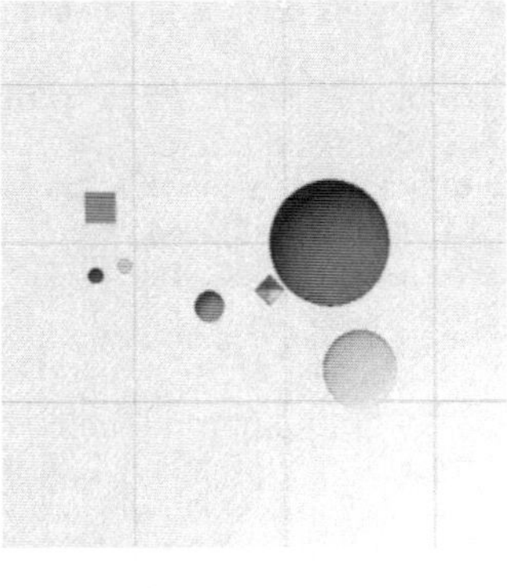

Figure 2. Layout of scene 1.

each screen should show. This allows for many forms of interaction with the display. It was shown that pCubee helped their users to perform tasks faster and with fewer errors than when using a standard computer with a 2D screen.

A key drawback of many VR and AR devices is that they only allow for a single user to have access to each device. CoGlobe [3] overcomes this by using active shutter glasses and user tracking. This display is designed to appear to be a 3D sphere, giving the illusion of depth without the edges and seams found in a cube display. Projectors generate images for each user while the active shutter glasses allow the user to only see the images that are intended for them.

III. Our Proposed Cube Display: Dice

Dice is designed with four tablets, as seen in Figure 1, with each screen representing a side of the cube. The top is open. A magnetic encoder was used to determine the rotation of the cube and to send that data to the computer. The Lume Pad uses vertical lenticular lenses, so users were asked to only rotate the cube and not to change its pitch or yaw. If the user could alter the pitch and yaw the Lume Pad's displays would struggle to create realistic stereoscopic images.

The tablets used in this research were the Lume Pad, an LFD tablet made by Leia Inc. This allows users to see the illusion of depth inside of a 2D screen by showing each eye a different image, creating stereopsis. The tablet boasts a 10.1-inch screen with a resolution of 2560x1600 pixels. To create the light field effect, the tablet displays four views at a time and uses its lenticular lenses to allow users to see two of these images at a time. This gives the user the stereoscopic images of an HMD-typed VR setup as well as the portability and ease of use of a tablet-typed AR device. The Lume Pad has a forty-degree viewing window, measured from the center of the display, producing what looks like a real 3D image to multiple users at one time.

To generate the different views, the Lume Pad generates four views in 2x2 grids. Each image has a resolution of 640x400 pixels but is displayed in such a way as to be perceived as having a higher resolution [4].

The device dissects the images and displays them under lenticular lenses so that the user sees different images with each eye. This achieves stereoscopy and gives the user the perception of depth within the 2D screen.

When Dice is rotated, a computer receives the rotation data and then informs each tablet display how to alter its display. To lessen the processing needed for each tablet the frame rate was reduced to twenty-four frames per second from the sixty frames per second that the tablets use natively. Also, when the LFD is turned on the resolution is reduced as four images are displayed on one screen. To reduce the impact of the graphics being diminished when the LFD is turned on, the graphics are set to 640x400 pixels when the LFD is turned off.

To assess the subject's understanding of the simulated depth within the screen, a 3D scene was created to be interacted with. The scenes include objects of differing sizes, shapes, and colors. In each scene there was one green pyramid and one green cylinder. The subjects were asked to pick which objects they believed were closest to the two green objects. The layout for scene 1, used for the first two tests, can be seen in Figure 2, while Figure 1 shows the same scene displayed on Dice. For each scene, the objects were moved and the sizes of some of the objects were changed. The scenes were designed in such a way as to emphasize different visual cues to find the correct answer.

This experiment was designed with Unity, using the Leia Unity Software Development Kit (SDK) [5]. Unity allows for easy setup of the scenes and the SDK facilitates the use of the Lume Pad's lenticular camera. This camera is complicated as one camera creates all four of the views for the LFD. Moreover, the stereoscopic display could be turned on and off as the experiments demanded.

IV. Assessment of Human Depth Understanding

The experiment was carried out as follows. First, the user sat at a table, positioned between 45 – 50 cm from Dice. This is the distance that Leia Inc. states is the best viewing distance for the Lume Pad tablet. Then the subject was shown a sample scene and asked to rotate the cube to understand how rotating the cube would change the display. At that time, the tablets were not displaying stereoscopic images. Then the subjects were shown their first scene and asked to determine which objects they thought were closest to the green objects. This was repeated five times before the stereoscopic display was turned on and five more scenes were shown to the user. In total each user performed twenty tests so a total of sixty tests were conducted. At the end, a short questionnaire was given to the user to gauge how they felt each style of display aided or hindered them.

Three volunteers participated in this experiment. Their ages ranged from 21 to 25 with a mean age of 23. All had normal or corrected-to-normal vision. Each layout had two answers, one for each of the target green objects, so a total of sixty answers were collected.

V. Results

At the conclusion of the experiment, subjects were given a questionnaire to ascertain how well they believed they had understood the test as well as how the test made them feel. The questions were as follows:

a. With the LFD turned off, how well do you feel that you understood the scene? Did you know where everything was?
b. With the LFD turned on, how well do you feel that you understood the scene? Did you know where everything was?
c. How confident were you in your understanding?
d. How much discomfort did you feel? Did your eyes hurt? Did you feel sick?

Subjects stated that they felt the scenes were difficult to understand in both settings. The LFD helped them to feel more confident in their understanding of the scenes, but they were still often uncertain about which objects were closest to the green objects. Most said that this came from needing to look far into the perceived depth of the display. No subjects stated any ill effects from the experiment. If the subject made any errors, these errors were discussed with the subjects to try to understand why the subjects made their decisions.

Despite the small sample size, an interesting trend can be observed. The number of errors using the LFD display cube was smaller than with the standard display cube. Five errors were recorded for the standard display cube while only two were recorded for the LFD display cube. The respective error rates are 17% for the standard display cube and 7% for the LFD display cube.

Out of the sixty tests performed, only test four was failed 100% of the time. In this test, stereoscopic cues were not shown and the user was asked to find the object closest to the green pyramid at the center of the scene. A yellow cylinder was placed 1.5 units from the pyramid while an orange sphere was positioned 2.25 units from the pyramid. Every user chose the orange sphere as the closer object. The reasoning for this was that other objects obstructed the view of the pyramid from many angles. The best angle to view the distance between these objects places the yellow sphere further from the camera than the other objects, making the perceived depth difficult to feel confident about. A similar test layout was presented later when the LFD was turned on and none of the subjects made an error on this test. It cannot be said with certainty that the stereoscopic cues from the LFD made this situation easier to understand.

VI. Conclusion And Future Work

In this study, we examined the users understanding of a 3D scene, given some constraints, with and without stereoscopic depth cues. While the subjects were more accurate with the stereo attempts, it is not conclusive that the human brain understands distance in the light field display more so than on a motion parallax display. These findings are preliminary and require further study.

In our next experiment, we will work to improve our tests. Firstly, more care must be taken to design tests that fit the constraints of Dice. In this experiment, the size of the screen was not originally considered as a limiting factor for depth perception, but subjects stated that the screen size made objects feel farther away than they would like.

Designing new tests that can emphasize the difference between an LFD and a standard display is also a priority. Firstly, it was shown that the LFD may help users perceive depth when other depth cues are removed. To this end, we wish to remove depth cues so that more focus is be placed on stereoscopy. This should give clearer data on the benefits of an LFD cube over a standard display cube. Improvements to the cameras can also be achieved. A better balance between the perceived depth of the scene and the convergence distance of the Lume Pad camera will make objects in the scene more in focus when not at the center of the scene.

More ways to interact with the scene will also be researched. There are multiple ways to interact with other cube displays, such as pCubee. Not all these forms of interaction can be utilized with our cube, but inspiration can be drawn from their concepts. Measuring the speed at which tasks are performed would also be noteworthy.

A point to be weary of is how much this technology relies on stereoscopic vision. There is an overabundance of depth cues that can confuse the human brain [7]. It is unclear if this affected the subjects in this test.

Finally, we wish to expand both the types of interactions as well as explore how multiple users can make use of our display. These are key features that similar displays make use of. With our preliminary findings being promising we believe that these can be implemented into our display as well. The use of an LFD instead of the standard 2D screen should facilitate interesting options without the need for user tracking of any kind.

References

[1] K. Kato and O. D. A. Prima, "3D Gaze Characteristics in Mixed-Reality Environment," eTELEMED 2021 : The Thirteenth International Conference on EHealth, Telemedicine, and Social Medicine, IARIA, pp.11-15, 2021.

[2] I. Stavness, B. Lam, and S. Fels, "pCubee: A Perspective-Corrected Handheld Cubic Display," Proceedings of the SIGCHI Conference on Human Factors in Computing Systems, pp. 1381-1390, 2010.

[3] Q. Zhou et al., "CoGlobe - A Co-located Multi-Person FTVR Experience," ACM SIGGRAPH 2018 Emerging Technologies. https://doi.org/10.1145/3214907.3214914.

[4] 3D Lightfield Experience Platform, https://www.leiainc.com/ [Retrieved March 2024]

[5] SDK and Developer Resources, www.leiainc.com/sdk. [Retrieved March 2024]

[6] J. E. Cutting and P. M. Vishton, "Perceiving Layout and Knowing Distances: The Integration, Relative Potecney, and Contextual Use of Different Information about Depth," Percept. Sp. Motion, 22(5), pp. 69-117, 1995.

[7] T. S. Murdison, G. Leclercq, P. Lefèvre, and G. Blohm, "Misperception of Motion in Depth Originates from an Incomplete Transformation of Retinal Signals," Journal of Vision, 19.12, pp. 21-21, 2019.